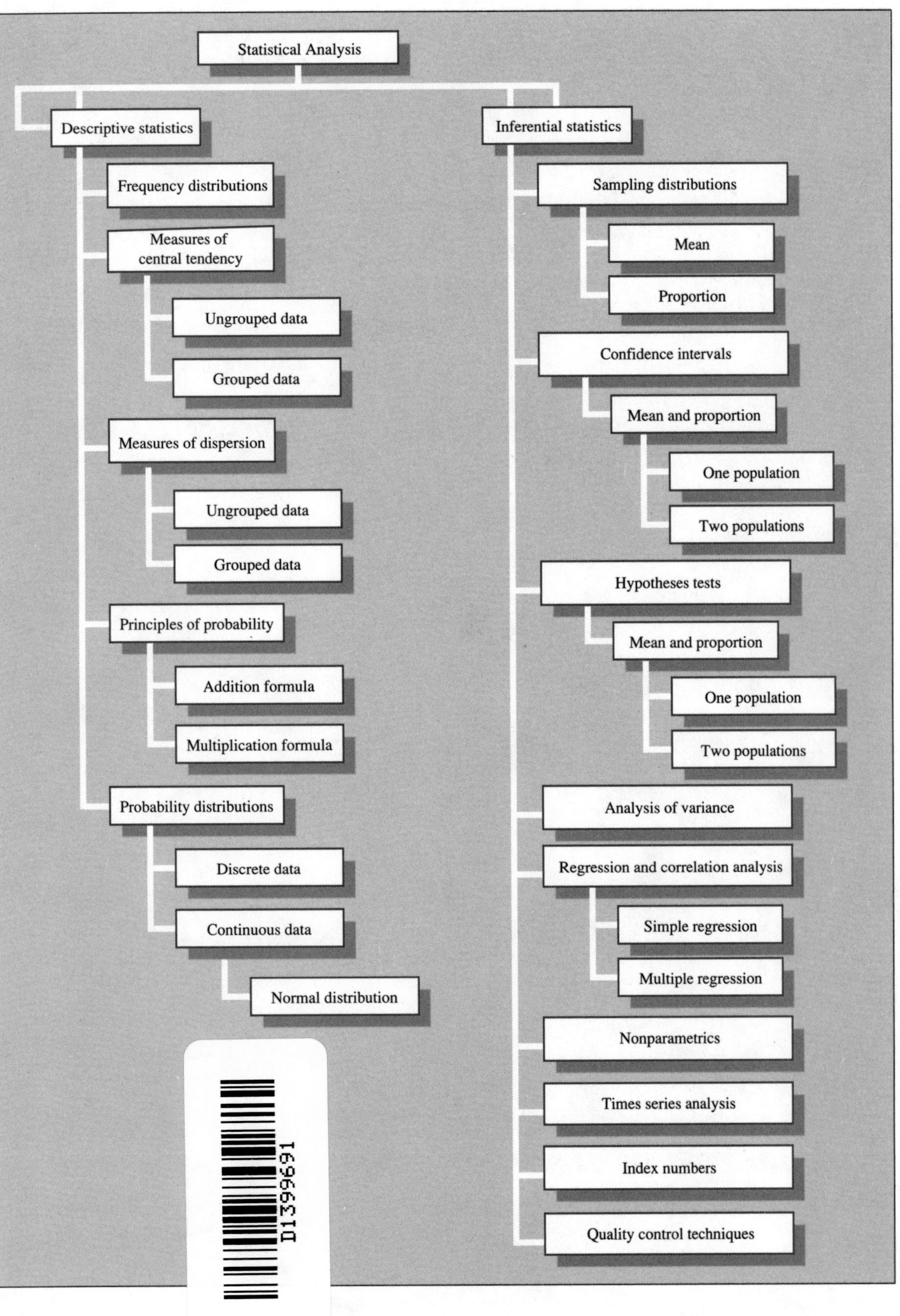
Statistical Analysis
Descriptive statistics
Frequency distributions
Measures of central tendency
Ungrouped data
Grouped data
Measures of dispersion
Ungrouped data
Grouped data
Principles of probability
Addition formula
Multiplication formula
Probability distributions
Discrete data
Continuous data
Normal distribution
Inferential statistics
Sampling distributions
Mean
Proportion
Confidence intervals
Mean and proportion
One population
Two populations
Hypotheses tests
Mean and proportion
One population
Two populations
Analysis of variance
Regression and correlation analysis
Simple regression
Multiple regression
Nonparametrics
Times series analysis
Index numbers
Quality control techniques

Applied Statistics for Business and Economics: An Essentials Version

Applied Statistics for Business and Economics: An Essentials Version

Third Edition

Allen L. Webster
Bradley University

Boston Burr Ridge, IL Dubuque, IA Madison, WI New York San Francisco St. Louis
Bangkok Bogotá Caracas Lisbon London Madrid
Mexico City Milan New Delhi Seoul Singapore Sydney Taipei Toronto

Irwin/McGraw-Hill

A Division of The ***McGraw-Hill*** *Companies*

APPLIED STATISTICS FOR BUSINESS AND ECONOMICS: AN ESSENTIALS VERSION, 3/E

This book is printed on acid-free paper.

1 2 3 4 5 6 7 8 9 0 DOW/DOW9 0 9 8 7

ISBN 0-256-22554-0

Vice president and editorial director: *Michael W. Junior*
Publisher: *Jeffrey J. Shelstad*
Senior sponsoring editor: *Scott Isenberg*
Senior developmental editor: *Gail Korosa*
Senior marketing manager: *Nelson W. Black*
Project manager: *Jean Lou Hess*
Senior production supervisor: *Madelyn S. Underwood*
Design manager: *Kiera Cunningham*
Interior and cover design: *Z Graphics*
Compositor: *Interactive Composition Corporation*
Typeface: *10/12 Times Roman*
Printer: *R. R. Donnelley & Sons Company*

Library of Congress Cataloging-in Publication Data

Webster, Allen.
Applied statistics for business and economics: an essentials version / Allen L. Webster.—3rd ed.
p. cm.—(The Irwin/McGraw-Hill series in operations and decision sciences)
Includes index.
ISBN 0-256-22554-0
1. Commercial statistics. 2. Economics-Statistical methods.
I. Title. II. Series.
HF 1017.W43 1998
519.5'02433—dc21 97-42444

http://www.mhhe.com

THE IRWIN/MCGRAW-HILL SERIES
Operations and Decision Sciences

OPERATIONS MANAGEMENT

Aquilano, Chase, and Davis
Fundamentals of Operations Management
Second Edition

Chase, Aquilano, and Jacobs
Production and Operations Management: *Manufacturing and Services*
Eighth Edition

Chu, Hottenstein, and Greenlaw
PROSIM for Windows
Third Edition

Cohen and Apte
Manufacturing Automation
First Edition

Dilworth
Operations Management
Second Edition

Flaherty
Global Operations Management
First Edition

Fitzsimmons and Fitzsimmons
Service Management: *Operations, Strategy, Information Technology*
Second Edition

Hill
Manufacturing Strategy: *Text & Cases*
Second Edition

Hopp and Spearman
Factory Physics
First Edition

Lambert and Stock
Strategic Logistics Management
Third Edition

Leenders and Fearon
Purchasing and Materials Management
Eleventh Edition

Lotfi and Pegels
Decision Support Systems for Operations & Management Science
Third Edition

Melnyk and Denzler
Operations Management: *A Value-Driven Approach*
First Edition

Moses and Seshadri
HOM Operations Management Software for Windows
First Edition

Nahmias
Production and Operations Analysis
Third Edition

Nicholas
Competitive Manufacturing Management
First Edition

Niebel
Motion and Time Study
Ninth Edition

Noori and Radford
Production and Operations Management
First Edition

Sanderson and Uzumeri
Managing Product Families
First Edition

Schroeder
Operations Management: *Decision Making in the Operations Function*
Fourth Edition

Schonberger and Knod
Operations Management: *Customer-Focused Principles*
Sixth Edition

Stevenson
Production/Operations Management
Fifth Edition

Vollmann, Berry, and Whybark
Manufacturing Planning & Control Systems
Fourth Edition

Zipkin
Foundations of Inventory Management
First Edition

BUSINESS STATISTICS

Aczel
Complete Business Statistics
Third Edition

Bowerman and O'Connell
Applied Statistics: *Improving Business Processes*
First Edition

Bryant and Smith
Practical Data Analysis: *Case Studies in Business Statistics*
Volumes I and II
First Edition

Cooper and Schindler
Business Research Methods
Sixth Edition

Delurgio
Forecasting Principles and Applications
First Edition

Doane, Mathieson, and Tracy
Visual Statistics
First Edition

Duncan
Quality Control & Industrial Statistics
Fifth Edition

Gitlow, Oppenheim, and Oppenheim
Quality Management: *Tools and Methods for Improvement*
Second Edition

Hall
Computerized Business Statistics
Fourth Edition

Hanke and Reitsch
Understanding Business Statistics
Second Edition

Lind and Mason
Basic Statistics for Business and Economics
Second Edition

Mason and Lind
Statistical Techniques in Business and Economics
Ninth Edition

Merchant, Goffinet, Koehler
Basic Statistics Using Excel
First Edition

Neter, Kutner, Nachtsheim, and Wasserman
Applied Linear Statistical Models
Fourth Edition

Neter, Kutner, Nachtsheim, and Wasserman
Applied Linear Regression Models
Third Edition

Shin
The Irwin Statistical Software Series: *Minitab, SAS, SPSS Guides*
Second Editions
Statgraphics
First Edition

Siegel
Practical Business Statistics
Third Edition

Webster
Applied Statistics for Business and Economics: *An Essentials Version*
Third Edition

Wilson and Keating
Business Forecasting
Third Edition

THE IRWIN/MCGRAW-HILL SERIES
Operations and Decision Sciences

QUANTITATIVE METHODS AND MANAGEMENT SCIENCE

Bodily, Carraway, Frey, Pfeifer
Quantitative Business Analysis: *Casebook*
First Edition

Bodily, Carraway, Frey, Pfeifer
Quantitative Business Analysis: *Text and Cases*
First Edition

Bonini, Hausman, and Bierman
Quantitative Analysis for Business Decisions
Ninth Edition

Hesse
Managerial Spreadsheet Modeling and Analysis
First Edition

Lotfi and Pegels
Decision Support Systems for Operations and Management Science
Third Edition

Stevenson
Introduction to Management Science
Second Edition

Turban and Meredith
Fundamentals of Management Science
Sixth Edition

To my loving wife Barbara: For all the promises that life holds.

Preface

As with the earlier editions of this text, this third edition continues to stress the importance of applying statistical analysis to the solution of common business problems. Every opportunity is used to demonstrate the manner in which statistics can effectively facilitate the many decisions that business managers face on an almost daily basis. Further, the presentation has been condensed to present the material in a more concise and compliant form. Several pedagogical characteristics described below have also been added to enhance the instructional advantages presented in the text.

This third edition of *Applied Statistics for Business and Economics: An Essentials Version* can be used effectively in either a one-semester or two-semester statistics course. While the material has been compressed to permit a streamlined discussion typical of a one-semester course, topical coverage remains sufficient to challenge even those students who complete their initial exposure to statistical analysis in a two-semester sequence.

Below is a brief description of pedagogical features contained in this edition.

Features Retained from Previous Edition

- ### Chapter Blueprint

  Each chapter opens with a flowchart showing the main topics to be covered and the manner in which they are interrelated. This allows the students the opportunity to organize the process they can use to master the material in that chapter.

- ### Three-Part Examples

  Every example of the statistical tools available to business decision-makers presents a realistic situation requiring a solution they typically face in managing a business. These examples consist of three parts. The first is the *Problem Statement* that describes the dilemma that must be resolved. The second part provides a complete and coherent *Solution* to that problem. Perhaps most important to the students, and what is absent in many other statistics texts, is the *Interpretation* of that solution. It does no good for students to solve a problem if they do not understand what that solution means.

- ### A Procedure for Business Report Writing

  Communication in business is inarguably essential. In order for a business to function as a unit, the individuals within that business must be able to communicate their ideas and thoughts. Appendix I describes and illustrates the manner in which a business report must be prepared in order to communicate essential proposals and recommendations to others who are interested in the results. Without this important skill, decision-makers are grossly disadvantaged in their efforts to manage a business.

- ### Solved Problems

  Each chapter also concludes with problems and elaborate solutions that reinforce the statistical tools presented in that chapter. This feature provides a convenient and helpful summary of the crucial tools students are expected to master.

- ### List of Formulas

  A handy list of all formulas presented in the chapter and a brief description of their use is also provided at the close of all chapters.

- ### Computer Applications

  Instructions are provided to show how the statistical tools can be performed on the computer. Computer printouts with emphasis on Minitab and Excel are presented along with a discussion of their important features.

- ### Computer Exercises

  The text comes with data disk containing several data files that can be accessed in Minitab, Excel, and ASCII formats. Each chapter provides the students with a problem they must solve based on the data in one of those files with the aid of the statistical tools discussed in that chapter. This provides the students with a realistic situation requiring the applications of the statistical techniques to the computer-based data set.

- ### Chapter Problems

  At the end of each chapter there is an ample supply of problems with a varying degree of difficulty that allow the students the opportunity to sharpen and refine their statistical skills. Again, these problems are of an applied nature that clearly demonstrate how statistics can aid in the business decision-making process.

New Features Added in the Third Edition

- ### Section Exercises

  Following each section within each chapter are several exercises the students must solve that reinforce their understanding of the material to which they have been exposed. This provides immediate feedback as to whether the students sufficiently comprehend the material in that section before proceeding on to the next.

- ### Setting the Stage

  Each chapter opens with a short narrative called *Setting the Stage* that presents a realistic case that can best be addressed using the statistical tools contained in the chapter. The nature of the problem that must be resolved is described and thus provides the students with a foundation upon which to base their readings and examination of the chapter material.

- ### Curtain Call

  A short section at the close of each chapter entitled *Curtain Call* refers the students back to *Setting the Stage*. Additional data and information are provided instructing the students to resolve the situation proposed in *Setting the Stage* by using the knowledge they have acquired in the chapter. This exercise combines the entire chapter into a single "package" that enhances students' overall comprehension of the material and effectively ties up all loose ends.

- ## From Stage to Real Life

The final segment in each chapter provides Web sites on the Internet that students can access to find additional data and information that can be used for further statistical study. These Web sites are specially selected to relate to the issues and concerns raised in *Setting the Stage* and *Curtain Call.*

Allen L. Webster

Contents in Brief

CHAPTER 1 The Role of Statistics, 2

CHAPTER 2 Describing Data Sets, 18

CHAPTER 3 Measures of Central Tendency and Dispersion, 38

CHAPTER 4 Principles of Probability, 74

CHAPTER 5 Probability Distributions, 100

CHAPTER 6 Sampling Distributions, 140

CHAPTER 7 Estimating with Confidence Intervals, 166

CHAPTER 8 Hypothesis Testing, 192

CHAPTER 9 Two Population Tests, 224

CHAPTER 10 Analysis of Variance, 264

CHAPTER 11 Simple Regression and Correlation, 314

CHAPTER 12 Multiple Regression and Correlation, 362

CHAPTER 13 Time Series and Index Numbers, 396

CHAPTER 14 Chi-Square and Other Nonparametric Tests, 444

CHAPTER 15 Quality Control Techniques, 496

APPENDIX I Business Report Writing, 535

APPENDIX II Answers to Selected Even-Numbered Problems, 541

APPENDIX III Statistical Tables, 551

INDEX 598

Contents

CHAPTER 1

The Role of Statistics, 2

1.1 Introduction, 5
1.2 The Importance of Statistics, 5
1.3 Career Opportunities in Statistics, 6
A. The Universal Application of Statistics, 6
B. Total Quality Management, 7
C. You Will Have a Need for Statistical Literacy, 8
1.4 Some Basic Definitions, 8
A. Populations and Parameters, 8
B. Samples and Statistics, 9
C. Variables, 9
1.5 The Importance of Sampling, 10
1.6 The Functions of Statistics, 11
1.7 Levels of Measurement, 12

CHAPTER 2

Describing Data Sets, 18

2.1 Introduction, 20
2.2 Methods of Organizing Data, 21
A. Frequency Distributions, 21
B. Contingency Tables, 24
2.3 Pictorial Displays, 27
Solved Problems, 30
List of Formulas, 33

CHAPTER 3

Measures of Central Tendency and Dispersion, 38

3.1 Introduction, 40
3.2 Measures of Central Tendency for Ungrouped Data, 41
A. The Mean, 41
B. The Median, 42
C. The Mode, 42
D. The Weighted Mean, 43
E. The Geometric Mean, 44
3.3 Comparing the Mean, the Median, and the Mode, 46
3.4 Measures of Dispersion, 47
A. The Range, 48
B. The Variance and the Standard Deviation of a Population, 48
C. Variance and Standard Deviation for a Sample, 50
3.5 Measures of Central Tendency and Dispersion for Grouped Data, 53
A. The Mean, 53
B. The Median, 54
C. The Mode, 54
D. Variance and Standard Deviation, 55
3.6 Other Measures of Dispersion, 57
3.7 Common Uses for the Standard Deviation, 59
A. Chebyshev's Theorem, 59
B. The Normal Distribution and the Empirical Rule, 59
C. Skewness, 62
D. Coefficient of Variation, 63
Solved Problems, 64
List of Formulas, 66

CHAPTER 4

Principles of Probability, 74

4.1 Introduction, 76
4.2 Experiments, Outcomes, and Sets, 42
4.3 Approaches to Probability, 77
4.4 Unions, Intersections, and the Relationships between Events, 80
4.5 Contingency Tables and Probability Tables, 82
4.6 Conditional Probability, 84

4.7 The Two Rules of Probability, 85
A. The Multiplication Rule, 85
B. The Addition Rule, 87
4.8 Bayes' Theorem, 89
4.9 Counting Techniques, 92
Solved Problems, 95
List of Formulas, 96

CHAPTER 5

Probability Distributions, 100

5.1 Introduction, 102
5.2 The Mean and the Variance of Discrete Distributions, 104
5.3 The Binomial Distribution—A Discrete Probability Distribution, 106
A. The Mean and Variance of a Binomial Distribution, 108
B. Cumulative Binomial Distributions, 109
C. Using the Computer, 110
5.4 The Hypergeometric Distribution, 111
A. Using the Computer, 113
5.5 The Poisson Distribution, 113
A. Using the Computer, 115
5.6 The Exponential Distribution, 116
A. Using the Computer, 117
5.7 The Uniform Distribution, 118
A. Using the Computer, 120
5.8 The Normal Distribution, 121
A A Comparison of Normal Distributions, 122
B. The Normal Deviate, 123
C. Calculating Probabilities with the Normal Deviate, 124
D. Calculating an X-Value from a Known Probability, 128
E. Normal Approximation to the Binomial Distribution, 130
Solved Problems, 132
List of Formulas, 135

CHAPTER 6

Sampling Distributions, 140

6.1 Introduction, 142
6.2 Sampling Distributions, 143
A. The Mean of the Sample Means, 144
B. The Variance and the Standard Error of the Sampling Distribution, 145
C. The Impact of Sample Size on the Standard Error, 147
6.3 The Central Limit Theorem, 148
6.4 Using the Sampling Distribution, 150
6.5 The Sampling Distribution for Proportions, 155
6.6 Sampling Methods, 158
A. Simple Random Sampling, 158
B. Systematic Sampling, 159
C. Stratified Sampling, 159
D. Cluster Sampling, 160
Solved Problems, 160
List of Formulas, 161

CHAPTER 7

Estimating with Confidence Intervals, 166

7.1 Introduction, 168
A. The Principle of a Confidence Interval, 169
7.2 Confidence Interval of Population Mean—Large Sample, 170
A. Interpretation of the Confidence Interval, 171
B. Confidence Intervals When μ Is Unknown, 172

7.3 Small Sample Intervals for the Mean–The t-Distribution, 174

7.4 Confidence Intervals for Population Proportions, 177

7.5 Controlling the Interval Width, 179

A. Decreasing the Level of Confidence, 179

B. Increasing the Sample Size, 180

7.6 Determining the Proper Sample Size, 180

A. Sample Size for μ, 181

B. Sample Size for π, 182

7.7 Properties of Good Estimators, 183

A. An Unbiased Estimator, 184

B. An Efficient Estimator, 185

C. A Consistent Estimator, 185

D. A Sufficient Estimator, 185

Solved Problems, 186

List of Formulas, 187

CHAPTER 8

Hypothesis Testing, 192

8.1 Introduction, 194

8.2 The Concept of Hypothesis Testing, 195

A. Critical Z-Values and the Rejection Regions, 196

B. The Level of Significance and the Probability of Error, 197

8.3 A Two-Tailed Test for μ, 198

8.4 One-Tailed Tests for μ, 201

8.5 p-Values: Their Interpretation and Use, 206

A. p-Value for Two-Tailed Tests, 207

8.6 Small-Sample Tests for μ, 209

8.7 Tests for π, 212

Solved Problems, 215

List of Formulas, 218

CHAPTER 9

Two Population Tests, 224

9.1 Introduction, 226

9.2 Interval Estimates with Independent Sampling, 227

A. Large Sample Estimation, 227

B. Small Sample Estimation: The t-Distribution, 230

9.3 Interval Estimates with Paired Sampling, 234

9.4 Confidence Intervals for the Difference between Two Proportions, 238

9.5 Selecting the Proper Sample Size, 240

A. Sample Size for $\mu_1 - \mu_2$, 240

B. Sample Size for $\pi_1 - \pi_2$, 241

9.6 Tests of Hypotheses about Two Means with Independent Sampling, 241

A. Large Sample Tests, 241

B. Small Sample Tests: The t-Distribution, 244

9.7 Hypotheses Tests with Paired Data, 245

9.8 A Test for the Difference between Two Proportions, 247

9.9 Comparing the Variance of Two Normal Populations, 248

Solved Problems, 250

List of Formulas, 254

CHAPTER 10

Analysis of Variance, 264

10.1 Introduction, 266

10.2 One-Way ANOVA: Completely Randomized Design, 268

A. The Principle behind ANOVA, 269

B. The Sum of Squares, 270

C. The Mean Sums of Squares, 272

D. An ANOVA Table, 274

10.3 Tests for Differences between Individual Pairs, 277
A. Test for Balanced Designs, 277
B. Tests for Unbalanced Designs, 280
10.4 Two-Way ANOVA: The Randomized Block Design, 283
10.5 Factorial Analysis, 292
10.6 Latin Square Design, 296
Solved Problems, 299
List of Formulas, 304

CHAPTER 11

Simple Regression and Correlation, 314

11.1 Introduction, 316
11.2 Determining the Simply Linear Regression Model, 318
11.3 Ordinary Least Squares: The Line of Best Fit, 320
11.4 An Example Using OLS, 323
11.5 Assumptions of the Linear Regression Model, 328
11.6 The Standard Error of the Estimate: A Measure of Goodness-of-Fit, 332
11.7 Correlation Analysis, 336
11.8 Limitations of Regression Analysis, 339
11.9 Tests for the Population Parameters, 340
A. Tests for β_1, 340
B. Tests for the Population Correlation Coefficient ρ, 342
11.10 Interval Estimation in Regression Analysis, 343
A. The Conditional Mean for Y, 343
B. The Predictive Interval for a Single Value of Y, 345
C. Factors Influencing the Width of the Interval, 347
11.11 Analysis of Variance Revisited, 348
Solved Problems, 349
List of Formulas, 356

CHAPTER 12

Multiple Regression and Correlation, 362

12.1 Introduction, 364
12.2 The Multiple Regression Model for Hop Scotch Airlines, 365
12.3 Evaluating the Model, 367
A. The Standard Error of the Estimate, 367
B. Coefficient of Multiple Determination, 369
C. The Adjusted Coefficient of Determination, 370
D. Evaluating the Model as a Whole, 371
E. Testing Individual Partial Regression Coefficients, 372
12.4 The Presence of Multicollinearity, 377
A. The Problems of Multicollinearity, 377
B. Detecting Multicollinearity, 378
C. Treating Multicollinearity, 380
12.5 Comparing Regression Coefficients, 381
12.6 Stepwise Regression, 383
A. Backward Elimination, 383
B. Forward Selection, 383
12.7 Dummy Variables, 383
12.8 The Curvilinear Case, 388
List of Formulas, 391

CHAPTER 13

Time Series and Index Numbers, 396

13.1 Introduction, 398
13.2 Time Series and Their Components, 399

A. Secular Trend, 400
B. The Seasonal Component, 400
C. Cyclical Variations, 401
D. Irregular Fluctuations, 401
13.3 Time-Series Models, 402
13.4 Smoothing Techniques, 402
A. Moving Averages, 403
B. Exponential Smoothing, 406
13.5 Trend Analysis, 410
13.6 Time-Series Decomposition, 413
A. Isolating the Seasonal Component, 413
B. Isolating the Cyclical Variation, 419
C. Irregular Variation, 420
13.7 The Use of Index Numbers, 421
A. A Simple Price Index, 421
B. Composite Price Indexes, 423
C. Weighted Composite Price Indexes, 424
13.8 Specific Indexes, 429
A. Consumer Price Index, 429
B. Other Indexes, 430
13.9 Uses for the CPI, 430
Solved Problems, 432
List of Formulas, 436

CHAPTER 14

Chi-Square and Other Nonparametric Tests, 444

14.1 Introduction, 446
14.2 Chi-Square Distribution (χ^2), 447
A. Goodness-of-Fit Tests, 447
B. Contingency Tables—A Test for Independence, 454
14.3 Sign Test, 459
14.4 Runs Test, 463
14.5 Mann-Whitney *U* Test, 467
A. Two-Tailed Test, 470
B. One-Tailed Test, 470
14.6 Spearman Rank Correlation, 472
14.7 Kruskal-Wallis Test, 476
Solved Problems, 481
List of Formulas, 485

CHAPTER 15

Quality Control Techniques, 496

15.1 Introduction, 499
15.2 A Brief History of the World Development of Quality Control, 499
15.3 Control Charts for Variables, 501
15.4 Control Charts for the Mean and Dispersion, 504
A. The $\overline{X}$-Chart, 504
B. The *R*-Chart, 507
15.5 Control Charts for Attributes, 511
A. *p*-Charts, 511
B. *c*-Charts, 515
15.6 Interpreting Control Charts, 518
15.7 Acceptance Sampling, 520
A. Different Sampling Plans, 522
B. Operating Characteristic Curves, 522
Solved Problems, 523
List of Formulas, 527

APPENDIX I

Business Report Writing, 535

A.1 Introduction, 535
A.2 The Need to Communicate, 535
A.3 The Characteristics of the Reader, 535
A.4 The Purpose of Statistical Reports, 536

A. The Executive Summary, 536
B. Introduction, 536
C. Methodology, 536
D. Findings, 536
E. Discussion and Interpretation, 536
F. Conclusions and Recommendations, 537
A.5 Illustrations and Examples, 537
A. The Executive Summary, 537
B. Introduction, 538
C. Methodology, 538
D. Findings, 538
E. Discussion and Interpretation, 539
F. Conclusions and Recommendations, 540

APPENDIX II

Answers to Selected Even-Numbered Problems, 541

APPENDIX III

Statistical Tables, 551

INDEX, 598

Applied Statistics for Business and Economics: An Essentials Version

CHAPTER 1

The Role of Statistics

Chapter Blueprint

This chapter introduces the concept of statistics as an organized study. You will be exposed to the general purpose of statistical analysis and the many ways in which statistics can help you find solutions to problems in your professional life.

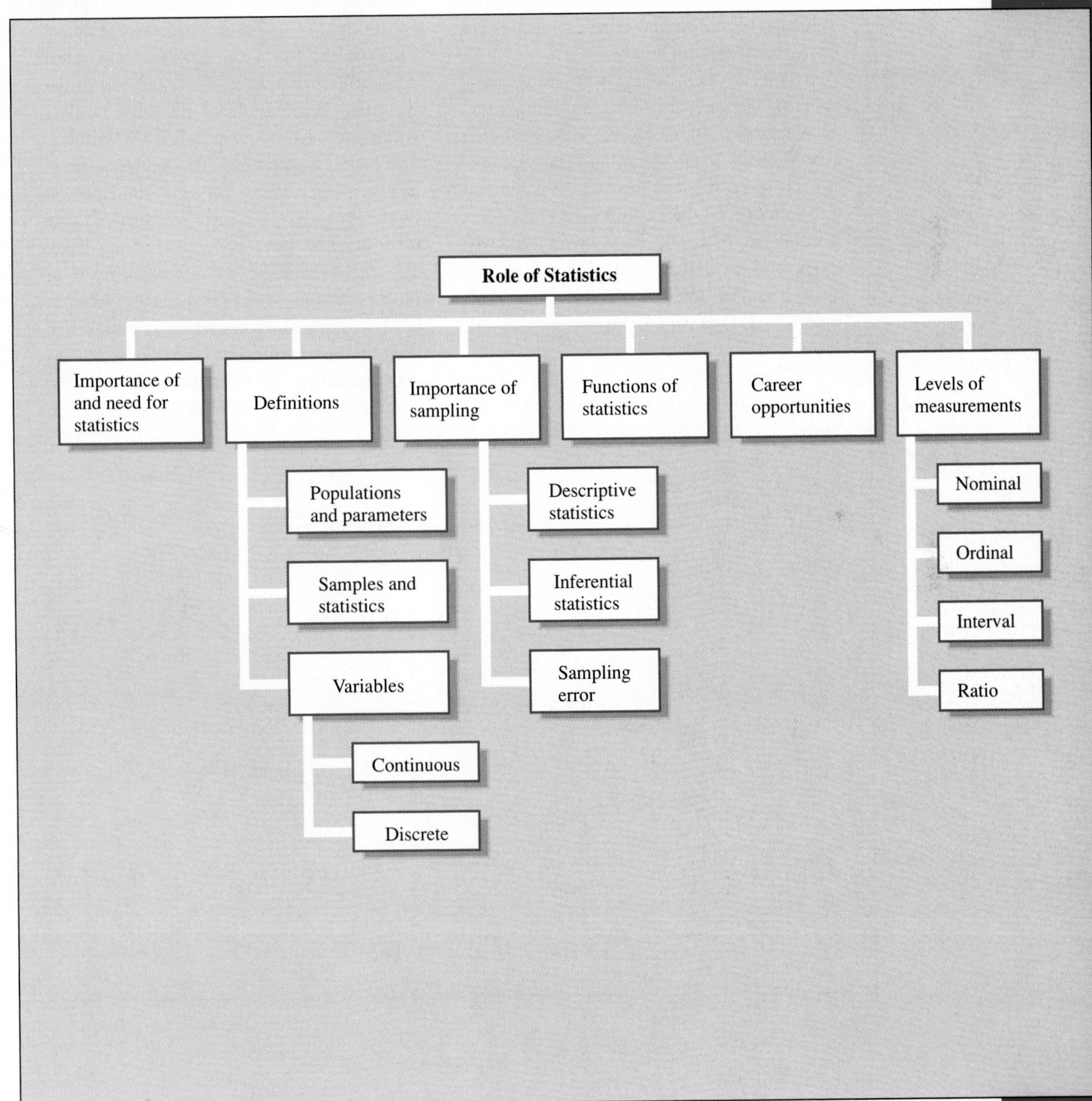

SETTING THE STAGE

Fortune (December 9, 1996) reports that a hiring frenzy has created a "sellers' labor market for nerds." The race for talent in the info-technology sector has generated such intense competition for "quant jocks and computer nerds" that job seekers with even minimum quantitative skills are besieged with offers. Talent is so scarce and demand is so high that companies are hiring able high schoolers and other companies are trying to steal them away.

Pete Davis, a senior systems and networking engineer for TIAC, an Internet service provider in Bedford, Massachusetts, has received at least 15 job offers since taking his present position—which isn't bad for someone who's all of 18 years old. Recruiters call or E-mail Davis with attractive stock options and lucrative pay raises. Although Davis' position is not entirely typical, the battle is on for employees who are trained in data analysis.

The strategy seems to paying off for businesses that aggressively seek out young talent capable of analyzing and understanding quantitative information. As the chart here shows, the profits of these firms have responded favorably, rising much faster than the profits of companies that are dragging their heels when it comes to entering the information age. The Education Industry Report, of St. Cloud, Minnesota, prepared an index of the profits of 15 firms that aggressively seek employees who can manage data and apply basic statistical and analytical thought to common business problems. This index, the Data Management Alert Assessment (DMAA) was compared to the National Association of Security Dealers Automated Quotations (NASDAQ) index. The results are obvious. The returns to firms hiring people who possess fundamental knowledge of statistics far outstrip those of firms that have not yet seen the light. The recognition by a growing number of businesses that effective managers need at least a rudimentary knowledge of statistical thought has precipitated, in the words of *Fortune*, a race for talent that resembles the agrarian frenzy of the Great Oklahoma Land Grab.

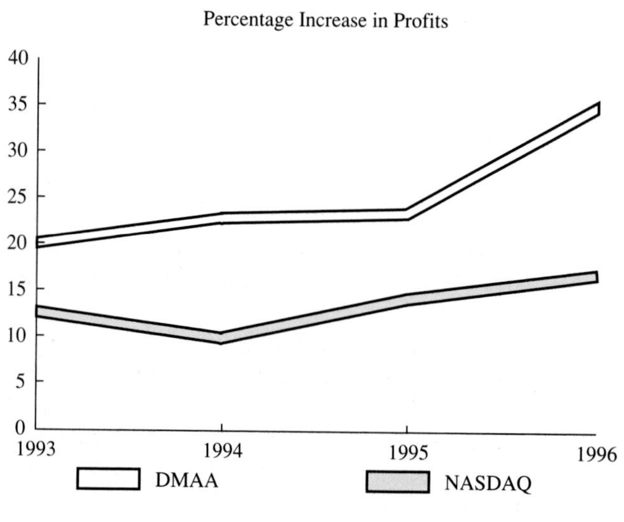

1.1 Introduction

As our world grows in complexity, it becomes increasingly difficult to make informed and intelligent decisions. Often these decisions must be made with less than perfect knowledge and in the presence of considerable uncertainty. Yet solutions to these problems are essential to our well-being and even our ultimate survival. We are continually pressured by distressing economic problems such as raging inflation, a cumbersome tax system, and excessive swings in the business cycle. Our entire social and economic fabric is threatened by environmental pollution, a burdensome public debt, an ever-increasing crime rate, and unpredictable interest rates.

If these conditions seem characteristic of today's lifestyle, you should be reminded that problems of this nature contributed more to the downfall of ancient Rome than did the invasion of barbarian hordes from the North. Our relatively short period of success on this planet is no guarantee of future survival. Unless viable solutions to these pressing problems can be found, we may, like the ancient Romans, follow the dinosaur and the dodo bird into oblivion.

This chapter will provide a general impression of what statistics is and how it can be useful to you. This overview of the nature of statistics and the benefits it can contribute will be accomplished by examining:

- Basic definitions of statistical tools.
- How sampling can be used to perform statistical analyses.
- The functions that statistics performs.
- How statistics can help you in your career.

We begin with a brief discussion of the meaningful role statistics plays in the important process of making delicate decisions.

1.2 The Importance of Statistics

Virtually every area of serious scientific inquiry can benefit from statistical analysis. For the economic policymaker who must advise the president and other public officials on proper economic procedure, statistics has proved to be an invaluable tool. Decisions regarding tax rates, social programs, defense spending, and many other issues can be made intelligently only with the aid of statistical analysis. Businessmen and businesswomen, in their eternal quest for profit, find statistics essential in the decision-making process. Efforts at quality control, cost minimization, product and inventory mix, and a host of other business matters can be effectively managed by using proven statistical procedures.

For those in marketing research, statistics is of invaluable assistance in determining whether a new product is likely to prove successful. Statistics is also quite useful in the evaluation of investment opportunities by financial consultants. Accountants, personnel managers, and manufacturers all find unlimited opportunities to utilize statistical analysis. Even the medical researcher, concerned about the effectiveness of a new drug, finds statistics a helpful ally.

Such applications and many others are repeatedly illustrated in this text. You will be shown how to use statistics to improve your job performance and many aspects of your daily life.

1.3 Career Opportunities in Statistics

In a few short years, you will leave the relative safety of your academic environment and be thrust headlong into the competitive world of corporate America. From a practical standpoint, you may be interested in how you can use your statistical background after graduation. There is no doubt that an academic experience heavily laced with a strong quantitative foundation will greatly enhance your chances of finding meaningful employment and, subsequently, demonstrating job competence.

When you find that dream job on the fast track of professional success, your employer will expect you to do two things:

1. Make decisions.
2. Solve problems.

These duties can be accomplished through the application of statistical procedures.

A. The Universal Application of Statistics

By becoming able to solve problems and make decisions, you will place yourself in high demand in the job market. If you can make incisive decisions while solving someone's problems, he or she will certainly be willing to reward you handsomely. The world often pays more to people who can ask the right questions to achieve fundamental objectives than to those charged with the responsibility of carrying them out. The answers are often quite obvious once the right questions have been asked. Statistical analysis will prove to be a great benefit in the proper formulation of these essential questions.

Employers recognize that the complex problems faced in today's world require quantitative solutions. An inability to apply statistics and other quantitative methods to the many common problems you encounter will place you at a stark disadvantage in the job market.

Almost all areas of study require statistical thought. Courses of study that depend heavily upon statistical analysis include, but are not limited to, marketing, finance, economics, and operations research. The principles learned in accounting and management also rely on statistical preparation.

Financial and economic analysts must often rely on their quantitative skills to devise effective solutions for difficult problems. An understanding of economic and financial principles permits you to apply statistical techniques to reach viable solutions and make decisions. Those of you aspiring to management or accounting positions, to be self-employed, or to obtain other careers in the industrial sector will find that a basic understanding of statistics not only improves your chances of obtaining a position but also enhances the likelihood of promotion by enriching your job performance.

Those persons employed in quantitative areas working with statistical procedures often enjoy higher salaries and avoid the dreadful dead-end jobs. Furthermore, early in their careers they usually find themselves in closer contact with high-level management. The proximity to the executive elite occurs because upper management needs the information and assistance which statistically trained people can provide. In the current labor market, employers simply do not want to hire or retain the statistically illiterate.

Whether your career aspirations tend toward private industry, public service with the government, or some other source of gainful livelihood, you will be much better served by your academic experience if you acquire a solid background in the fundamentals of statistical analysis.

B. Total Quality Management

As world competition intensifies, there arises an increased effort on the part of businesses to promote product quality. This effort, broadly referred to as *total quality management* (TQM), has as its central purpose the promotion of those product qualities considered important by the consumer. These attributes range from the absence of defects to rapid service and swift response to customer complaints. Today, most large businesses (as well as many smaller ones) have quality control (QC) departments whose function it is to gather performance data and resolve quality problems. Thus, TQM represents a growing area of opportunity to those with a statistical background.

TQM involves the use of integrated management teams consisting of engineers, marketing experts, design specialists, statisticians, and other professionals who can contribute to consumer satisfaction. The formulation of these teams, termed *quality function deployment* (QFD), is designed to recognize and promote customer concerns. Working jointly, the specialists interact to encourage product quality and effectively meet consumer needs and preferences.

Another common method of promoting product quality is the use of *quality control circles.* QC circles consist of a small group of employees (usually between 5 and 12) who meet regularly to solve work-related problems. Often consisting of both line workers and representatives of management, the members of these QC circles are all from the same work area, and all receive formal training in statistical quality control and group planning. Through open discussion and statistical analysis, QC circles can achieve significant improvement in various areas ranging from quality improvement, product design, productivity, and production methods, to cost reduction and safety. It is estimated that over 90 percent of Fortune 500 companies effectively use QC circles.

One of the most important elements of TQM is a body of statistical tools and methods used to promote statistical quality control (SQC). These tools help to organize and analyze data for the purpose of problem solving. One of these tools is the *Pareto chart.* Named after the Italian economist Vilfredo Pareto, this diagram identifies the quality problems that occur most often or that prove to be the most costly. Figure 1.1 shows a Pareto chart of the defects affecting the production of microwave ovens marketed by JC Penney.

Pareto charts often express the 80/20 rule: 80 percent of all problems are due to 20 percent of the causes. As Figure 1.1 shows, approximately 75 percent of all the problems are caused by the auto defrost feature and the temperature hold feature of the oven.

Figure 1.1
Pareto Chart

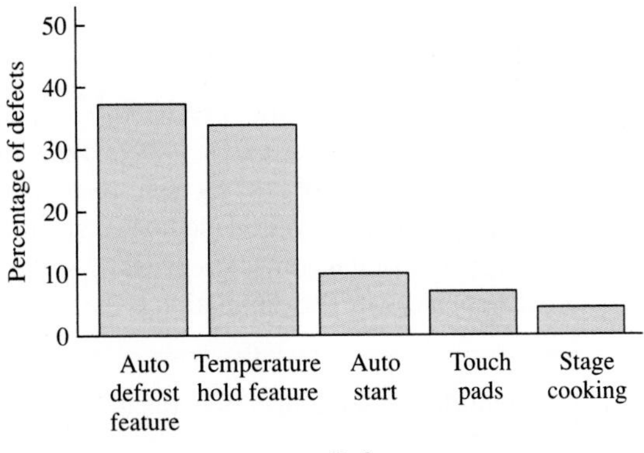

Source: *QC Circle,* JC Penney, 1993.

Broadly speaking, SQC is designed to assure that products meet minimum production standards and specifications. This objective is often furthered through the use of *acceptance sampling,* which is an integral part of SQC. Acceptance sampling involves testing a random sample of existing goods to determine whether the entire shipment, or lot, should be accepted. This decision is based in part on an *acceptable quality level* (AQL), which is the maximum number or rate of defects that a firm is willing to tolerate.

There is a growing realization among businesses that product quality must be maintained. If a firm is to compete successfully, it must take every precaution to ensure that its products meet certain basic standards. The importance of TQM can therefore not be overemphasized. The principles inherent in TQM are growing in popularity; they represent the future direction of applied statistical analysis in the business world. We will examine TQM in depth in Chapter 15.

C. You Will Have a Need for Statistical Literacy

You may believe that the type of work you intend to pursue will not require statistical analysis. Or you may argue that the staff of statisticians employed by your company will perform the necessary statistical work, and there is no need for you to master the details of statistical analysis.

Such is not the case. Even if the professional statisticians in your organization perform the necessary statistical work for you, it is still essential that you possess a certain level of statistical literacy. To determine how the statistical staff can assist you in your job performance, you must know what statistics is, what statisticians do, and how they go about doing it. When problems arise you must be able to determine how statistics can be of help. To do so, you must understand statistical procedures and be able to communicate with statisticians in a joint effort to design adequate solutions and render optimal decisions. Once you have acquired this solid familiarity with statistical analysis, you will marvel at the limitless ways statistics can assist you in solving problems that often arise in a business setting.

1.4 Some Basic Definitions

Every branch of scientific inquiry has its unique vocabulary. Statistics is no exception. This section examines some common terms used in statistical analysis. These definitions and expressions are essential to any comprehension of how statistical tests are carried out.

A. Populations and Parameters

In any statistical study, the researcher is interested in a certain collection or set of observations called the **population** (or universe). If the incomes of all 121 million wage earners in the United States are of interest to an economist assisting Congress in formulating a national tax plan, then all 121 million incomes constitute the population. If a tax plan is being considered only for those incomes in excess of, say, \$100,000, then those incomes above \$100,000 are the population. The population is the entire collection of all observations of interest.

> **Population** A population is the entire collection of all observations of interest to the researcher.

If the chief executive officer (CEO) for a large manufacturing firm wishes to study the output of all the plants owned by the firm, then the output of all plants is the population.

A **parameter** is any descriptive measure of a population. Examples are the average income of all those wage earners in the United States, or the total output of all the manufacturing plants. The point to remember is that a parameter describes a population.

> **Parameter** A parameter is a descriptive measure of the entire population of all observations of interest to the researcher.

B. Samples and Statistics

Although statisticians are generally interested in some aspect of the entire population, they generally find that populations are too big to study in their entirety. Calculating the average income of all the 121 million wage earners would be an overwhelming task. Therefore, we must usually be content to study only a small portion of that population. This smaller and more manageable portion is called a **sample**. A sample is a scientifically selected subset of the population.

> **Sample** A sample is a representative portion of the population which is selected for study because the population is too large to examine in its entirety.

Each month the U.S. Department of Labor calculates the average income of a sample of only several thousand wage earners selected from the entire population of all 121 million workers. The average from this sample is then used as an estimate of the average income for the entire population. Samples are necessary because studying entire populations is too time-consuming and costly.

A **statistic** is any descriptive measure of a sample. The average income of those several thousand workers computed by the Department of Labor is a statistic. The statistic is to the sample what the parameter is to the population. Of importance, the statistic serves as an estimate of the parameter. Although we are really interested in the value of the parameter of the population, we most often must be resigned to only estimating it with a statistic from the sample we have selected.

> **Statistic** A statistic describes a sample and serves as an estimate of the corresponding population parameter.

C. Variables

A **variable** is the characteristic of the sample or the population being observed. If the statistical advisor for the mayor of San Francisco is interested in the distance commuters must drive each morning, the variable is *miles driven*. In a study concerning the income of wage earners in the United States, the variable is *income*.

> **Variable** A variable is the characteristic of the population that is being examined in the statistical study.

A variable can be (1) quantitative or (2) qualitative. If the observations can be expressed numerically, it is a **quantitative** variable. The incomes of all the wage earners is an example of a quantitative population. Other examples include the heights of all people we might be interested in, scores students receive on a final examination in statistics, and the number of miles those commuters in San Francisco must drive each morning. In each case, the observations are measured numerically.

A **qualitative** variable is measured nonnumerically. The marital status of credit applicants, the sex of students in your statistics class, and the race, hair color, and religious preference of those San Francisco commuters are examples of qualitative variables. In every case, the observations are measured nonnumerically.

In addition, variables can be (1) continuous or (2) discrete. A **continuous** variable is one that can take on any value within a given range. No matter how close two observations may be, if the instrument of measurement is precise enough, a third observation can be found which will fall between the first two. A continuous variable generally results from measurement.

A **discrete** variable is restricted to certain values, usually whole numbers. They are often the result of enumeration or counting. The number of students in your class and the number of cars sold by General Motors are examples. In neither case will you observe fractional values.

Throughout your study of statistics you will repeatedly refer to these concepts and terms. You must be aware of the role each plays in the process of statistical analysis. It is particularly important that you be able to distinguish between a population and its parameters, and a sample and its statistics.

1.5 The Importance of Sampling

As noted, much of a statistician's work is done with samples. Samples are necessary because populations are often too big to study in their entirety. It is too time-consuming and costly to examine the entire population, and we must select a sample from the population, calculate the sample statistic, and use it to estimate the corresponding population parameter.

This discussion of samples leads to a distinction between the two main branches of statistical analysis: (1) descriptive statistics and (2) inferential statistics. **Descriptive statistics** is the process of collecting, organizing, and presenting data in some manner that quickly and easily describes these data. Chapters 2 and 3 examine descriptive statistics and illustrate the various methods and tools that can be used to present and summarize large data sets.

Inferential statistics involves the use of a sample to draw some inference, or conclusion, about the population from which that sample was taken. When the Department of Labor uses the average income of a sample of several thousand workers to estimate the average income of all 121 million workers, it is using a simple form of inferential statistics.

The accuracy of any estimate is of extreme importance. This accuracy depends in large part on the manner in which your sample was taken, and how careful you are to ensure that the sample provides a reliable image of the population. However, all too often, the sample proves not to be fully representative of the population, and **sampling error** will result. Sampling error is the difference between the sample statistic used to estimate the population parameter and the actual but unknown value of the parameter.

> **Sampling Error** Sampling error is the difference between the unknown population parameter and the sample statistic used to estimate the parameter.

There are at least two possible causes of sampling error. The first source of sampling error is mere chance in the sampling process. Due to the luck of the draw in selecting the sample elements, it is possible to unknowingly choose atypical elements that misrepresent the population. In the effort to estimate the population mean, for example, it is possible to select elements in the sample that are abnormally large, thereby resulting in an overestimation of the population mean. On the other hand, the luck of the draw may produce a large number of sample elements that are unusually small, causing an underestimation of the parameter. In either case, sampling error has occurred.

A more serious form of sampling error is **sampling bias.** Sampling bias occurs when there is some tendency in the sampling process to select certain sample elements over others. If the sampling procedure is incorrectly designed and tends to promote the selection of too many units with a particular characteristic at the expense of units without that characteristic, the sample is said to be biased. For example, the sampling process may inherently favor the selection of males to the exclusion of females, or married persons to the exclusion of singles.

> **Sampling Bias** Sampling bias is the tendency to favor the selection of certain sample elements over others.

A more thorough treatment of sampling bias is presented in a later chapter. Although sampling error can never be measured, since the parameter remains unknown, we must be aware that it is likely to occur.

1.6 The Functions of Statistics

We have repeatedly emphasized the usefulness of statistics and the wide variety of problems that it can solve. In order to more fully illustrate this wide applicability, let us examine the various functions of statistics. **Statistics** is the science concerned with the (1) collection, (2) organization, (3) presentation, (4) analysis, and (5) interpretation of data.

Although the first step in any statistical study is the collection of the data, it is common practice in a beginning statistics course to assume that the data have already been collected for us and now lie at our disposal. Therefore, our work begins with the effort to organize and present these data in some meaningful and descriptive manner. The data must be put into some logical order that tends to quickly and readily reveal the message they contain. This procedure constitutes the process of descriptive statistics, as defined, and is discussed in the next few chapters. After the data have been organized and presented for examination, the statistician must analyze and interpret them. These procedures rely on inferential statistics and constitute a major benefit of statistical analysis by aiding in the decision-making and problem-solving process.

You will find that through the application of precise statistical procedures, it is possible to actually predict the future with some degree of accuracy. Any business firm faced with competitive pressures can benefit considerably from the ability to anticipate business conditions before they occur. If a firm knows what its sales are going to be at some time in the near future, management can devise more accurate and more effective plans regarding current operations. If future sales are estimated with a reliable degree of accuracy, management can easily make important decisions regarding inventory levels, raw material orders, employment requirements, and virtually every other aspect of business operations.

1.7 Levels of Measurement

Variables can be classified on the basis of their level of measurement. The way we classify variables greatly affects how we can use them in our analysis. Variables can be (1) nominal, (2) ordinal, (3) interval, or (4) ratio.

A **nominal** measurement is created when names are used to establish categories into which variables can be exclusively recorded. For example, sex can be classified as "male" or "female." You could also code it with a "1" or a "2," but the numbers would serve only to indicate the categories and would carry no numerical significance; mathematical calculations using these codes would be meaningless. Soft drinks may be classified as Coke, Pepsi, 7-Up, or Ale 8. Each drink could be recorded in one of these categories to the exclusion of the others.

> **Nominal Measurements** Names or classifications are used to divide data into separate and distinct categories.

Table 1.1 illustrates the manner in which *Money* magazine classified different investment funds. Notice that each fund is placed in a particular category based on its financial behavior.

Table 1.1
Nominal Measures of Investment Funds

Category/Fund Name	
Aggressive Growth	**Money Market Funds**
Twenty Century Growth	Alger Portfolio
Janus	Mariner Government
Total Return	**Tax-Exempt**
Scudder	Kemper Municipals
Vanguard Star	
PaxWorld	
USAA Cornerstone	
Bonds	
Strong Short-Term	
Scudder Short-Term	

Source: *Money*, July 1992.

It is important to remember that a nominal measurement carries no indication of order of preference, but merely establishes a categorical arrangement into which each observation can be placed.

Unlike a nominal measurement, an **ordinal** scale produces a distinct ordering or arrangement of the data. That is, the observations are ranked on the basis of some criterion. Sears Roebuck, one of the nation's largest retailers, ranks many of its products as "good," "better," and "best." Opinion polls often use an ordinal scale such as "strongly agree," "agree," "no opinion," "disagree," and "strongly disagree."

As with nominal data, numbers can be used to order the rankings. Like nominal data, the magnitude of the numbers is not important; the ranking depends only on the *order* of the values. Sears could have used the rankings of "1," "2," and "3," or "1," "3," and "12," for that matter. The arithmetic differences between the values are meaningless. A product ranked "2" is not twice as good as one with a ranking of "1."

> **Ordinal Measurements** Measurements that rank observations into categories with a meaningful order.

The same issue of *Money* magazine mentioned above presented the rankings for investments based on risk levels shown in Table 1.2. Notice that the rankings of "Very High" risk, "High" risk, and "Low" risk could have been based on values of "1," "2," and "3," or "A," "B," and "C." But the actual differences in the levels of risk cannot be measured meaningfully. We only know that an investment ranked "High" carries greater risk than does one with a "Low" ranking.

Variables on an **interval** scale are measured numerically, and, like ordinal data, carry an inherent ranking or ordering. However, unlike the ordinal rankings, the differences between the values is important. Thus, the arithmetic operations of addition and subtraction are meaningful. The Fahrenheit scale for temperatures is an example of an interval scale. Not only is 70 degrees hotter than 60 degrees, but the same difference of 10 degrees exists as between 90 and 100 degrees Fahrenheit.

The value of zero is arbitrarily chosen in an interval scale. There is nothing sacrosanct about the temperature of zero, it is merely an arbitrary reference point. The Fahrenheit scale could have been created so that zero was set at a much warmer (or colder) temperature. No specific meaning is attached to zero other than to say it is 10 degrees colder than 10 degrees Fahrenheit. Thus, 80 degrees is not twice as hot as 40 degrees and the ratio 80/40 has no meaning.

> **Interval Measurements** Measurements on a numerical scale in which the value of zero is arbitrary but the difference between values is important.

Table 1.2
An Ordinal Ranking of Investment Risk

Investment	Risk Factor
Gold	Very high
Small-growth companies	Very high
Maximum capital gains	High
International	High
Option income	Low
Balanced	Low

Of all four levels of measurement, only the ratio scale is based on a numbering system in which zero is meaningful. Therefore, the arithmetic operations of multiplication and division also take on a rational interpretation. A ratio scale is used to measure many types of data found in business analysis. Variables such as costs, profits, and inventory levels are expressed as ratio measures. The value of zero dollars to measure revenues, for example, can be logically interpreted to mean that no sales have occurred. Furthermore, a firm with a 40 percent market share has twice as much of the market as a firm with a 20 percent market share. Measurements such as weight, time, and distance are also measured on a ratio scale since zero is meaningful, and an item that weighs 100 pounds is one-half as heavy as an item weighing 200 pounds.

Ratio Measurements Numerical measurements in which zero is a meaningful value and the difference between values is important.

You may notice that the four levels of measurement increase in sophistication, progressing from the crude nominal scale to the more refined ratio scale. Each measurement offers more information about the variable than did the previous one. This distinction among the various degrees of refinement is important, since different statistical techniques require different levels of measurements. While most statistical tests require interval or ratio measurements, other tests, called nonparametric tests (which will be examined later in this text), are designed to use nominal or ordinal data.

Chapter Exercises

1. The production director for the Ford Motor Company plant in Cleveland must report to her superior on the average number of days the employees at the plant are absent from work. However, the plant employs well over 2,000 workers, and the production director does not have time to examine the personnel records of all the employees. As her assistant, you must decide how she can obtain the necessary information. What advice do you offer?
2. Describe in your own words how statistics can be used to solve problems in various disciplines and occupations.
3. What specific occupation do you plan to pursue after graduation? If you are uncertain, choose the area in which you are most interested. Discuss in some detail, using specific examples, the types of problems that may arise, and the decisions you will have to make where statistical analysis may prove helpful.
4. In what manner will you use the services of the professional statistician in your organization once you find employment? Why is it unlikely that you will escape the need for a basic understanding of statistics?
5. Describe in your own words the difference between a population and a sample; between a parameter and a statistic.
6. What is the difference between a quantitative variable and a qualitative variable? Give examples.
7. Distinguish between a continuous variable and a discrete variable. Give examples of each.
8. A recent report in *Fortune* magazine revealed that the Japanese may soon control as much as 35 percent of auto sales in the United States. This compares with 28 percent in the late 1980s, and is up from only 8 percent in 1970. Does this information contain descriptive statistics, inferential statistics, or both? Explain.

9. What is the difference between descriptive statistics and inferential statistics? Which do you feel constitutes a higher form of statistical analysis, and why?

10. To what uses or functions can statistics be put? How do you think each might be used to solve real-world business problems? Give examples of specific problems that might arise and explain how statistics could be used to develop solutions and answers.

11. Select any population that interests you. Identify quantitative and qualitative variables of that population that could be selected for study.

12. If statisticians are actually interested in populations, why do they generally work with samples?

13. Are the following variables discrete or continuous?

   a. Number of courses students at your school are taking this semester. – d
   b. Number of passes caught by Tim Brown, wide receiver for the LA Raiders. – d
   c. The weights of Tim Brown's teammates. – c
   d. Weight of the contents of cereal boxes. – c
   e. Number of books you read last year. – d

14. Define sampling error and explain what causes it.

15. *Forbes* magazine (February 1997) reported data on lifestyles and conditions in several U.S. cities. Some of these data are reproduced here.

City	Population in Millions	Median Household Income	Best Business Hotel	Most Visited Attraction	Crime Rate per 100,000
Atlanta	3.5	$43,249	Ritz-Carlton Buckhead	Stone Mountain Park	846.2
Baltimore	2.5	43,291	Harbor Court	Harborplace	1,296.5
St. Louis	2.5	39,079	Hyatt Regency	Gateway Arch	263.4
Philadelphia	5.0	43,576	Bellevue	Liberty Bell	693.1
Raleigh-Durham	1.0	40,990	Radisson Plaza	State Fair	634.9

   a. Identify the *qualitative* and the *quantitative* variables.
   b. Which variables are discrete and which are continuous?
   c. Identify each variable as either nominal, ordinal, interval, or ratio.
   d. Which are descriptive and which are inferential?

16. The president of a fraternity on campus wishes to take a sample of the opinions of the 112 members regarding desired rush activities for the fall term.

   a. What is the population?
   b. How might a sample best be taken?

17. Viewers of the long-running TV daytime drama *All My Children* are to be sampled by the show's producer to learn their feeling about plans to kill off a popular character. What problems might arise in this effort? What would you recommend and why?

18. General Mills is concerned about the weight of the net contents of the boxes of Cheerios coming off the production line in its Detroit plant. The box advertises 36 ounces, and if less is actually contained in the box, General Mills could be charged with false advertising. As a newly hired member of the General Mills management team, you suggest that a sample of the boxes be opened and their contents weighed. The vice president of the quality control division asks what kind of sample should be taken. How do you respond?

19. Since production is down at the General Mills plant, it is possible to actually open up all the boxes produced during the most recent production period. Such a process would avoid

sampling error and produce more accurate results. Since the population of all boxes is not too large, is sampling necessary?

20. What level of measurement would you use in each of the following cases? Explain your answer.

  a. A system to measure customers' preferences for vehicles based on body style (such as convertible, van, truck, sedan, etc.).
  b. A system to evaluate employees based on the number of days they miss work.
  c. A system to identify cities of birth of customers.
  d. A system to record the population of the cities in which customers live.

21. In which level of measurement can each of these variables be expressed? Explain your answer.

  a. Students rate their statistics professor on a scale of "Terrible," "Not-So-Great," "Good," "Terrific," and "Greek God."
  b. Students at a university are classed by major, such as marketing, management, and accounting.
  c. Students are classed by major, using the values 1, 2, 3, 4, and 5.
  d. Grouping liquid measurements as pint, quart, and gallon.
  e. Ages of customers.

22. Cite several examples of radio or television commercials that use statistics to sell their products. Are they descriptive or inferential statistics? Which level of measurement do they use?

CURTAIN CALL

The *Occupational Outlook Handbook* (1996–1997 edition), published by the U.S. Department of Labor, is available in most libraries. It contains extensive career information on jobs in about 250 occupational categories covering almost 90% of the jobs in the U.S. economy. The handbook provides detailed descriptions of job responsibilities, work conditions, compensation, training, and job growth projections for the 1995–2005 time period.

Job openings for computer scientists and systems analysts are projected to be in the tens of thousands in the coming years, just for replacement positions. Job growth is expected to be the highest through the year 2005. Management analysts and consultants are another job group requiring strong quantitative skills. In this group job growth is projected to be greater than average. The same is true for economists and market research analysts.

In the *Occupational Outlook Handbook* at your university or local library, look up jobs in your areas of interest. What are the quantitative skill requirements for it? What are the job growth projections?

From the Stage to Real Life

There is a plentitude of career and job information available on the Internet. The two leading job listings sites are the Monster Board (*www.monster.com*) and America's Job Bank (*www.ajb.dni.us*). Using keyword searches, test out your occupational interests in the job seeker areas at these two sites. (Keywords can be obtained from the *Occupational Outlook Handbook* at the library.) On a national, or "all states" basis, how many current job openings are there in your field of interest? How are these jobs distributed geographically? What information on salaries is given in the job postings?

Explore the "Employment" and "Jobs" categories provided by the major search engines like Yahoo! to acquaint yourself with other career services available on the Internet. In particular, look at the resources for career planning, resumes, and salary information.

CHAPTER 2

Describing Data Sets

Chapter Blueprint

This chapter illustrates the many ways in which a large data set can be organized and managed to provide a quick visual interpretation of the information the data contain. These statistical tools allow us to describe a set of raw data in a concise and easy-to-read manner.

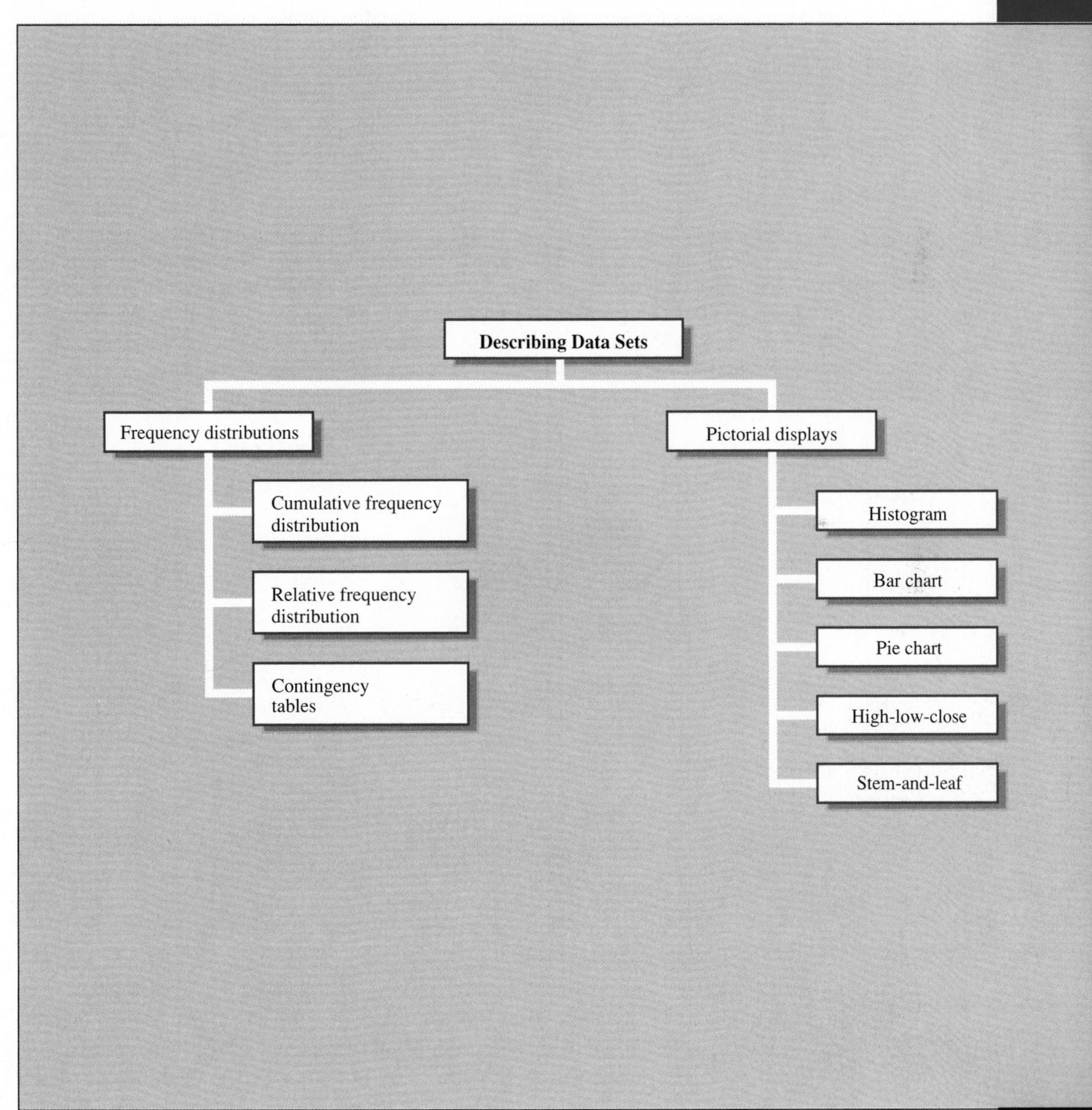

SETTING THE STAGE

College students looking forward to spring break this year face higher rates for car rentals than ever before (*Newsweek,* February 1997). A survey by *Business Travel News* revealed that in 1996 rates jumped 11.8 percent, and the increase in 1997 is anticipated to top that. The escalations in labor costs, insurance, and parking fees are cited as the major causes for these uncommon increases in travel expenses.

Most alarming to students eager to escape the rigors of academe is the fact that the largest rate increases are expected in those cities most likely to be favorite vacation retreats, including Miami, Houston, Phoenix, cities in Southern California, and other warm weather spots. As the pie chart shows, these popular areas already exceed the national average by a substantial amount. While, across the nation, travelers are paying an average of about $33 per day, rates in these more preferred areas approach $80.

To make matters worse for the vacationing hordes this summer, availability may be a problem. Rental companies are strongly urging those with travel plans to reserve early. Woe be to the student who, with dreams of skimming around Miami in a sporty convertible, must settle for a four-door sedan!

However, many car rental companies intend to penalize no-shows, those who reserve a car but fail to pick it up at the agreed time, with a healthy addition to their credit card accounts.

In preparation for your own long-awaited and well-deserved spring fling, you contact various rental companies and collect information on rates and selection. To help make the important decision regarding which car to rent, you then must prepare a summary of these vital details to your traveling buddies complete with all the pictorial displays and other means of describing data sets examined in this chapter.

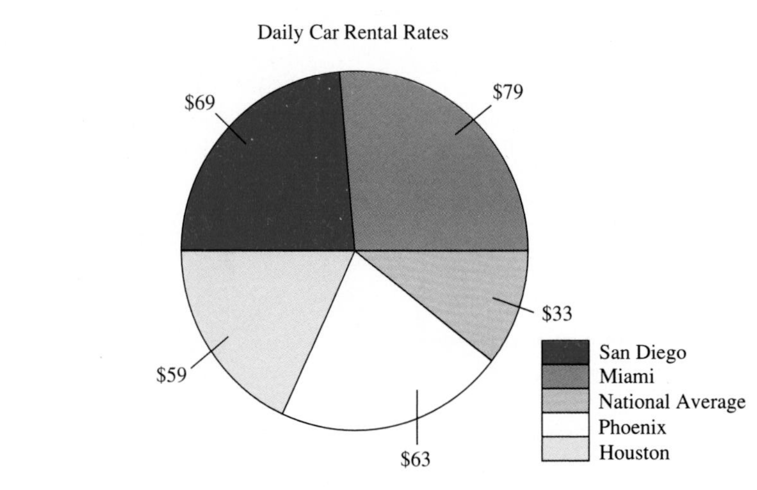

2.1 Introduction

Almost every statistical effort begins with the process of collecting the necessary data to be used in the study. For general purposes, we will adopt the convenient assumption that this often rather tedious task has already been completed for us and the data lie at our disposal.

This collection of raw data in itself reveals very little. It is extremely difficult to determine the true meaning of a bunch of numbers that have simply been recorded on a piece of paper. It remains for us to organize and describe these data in a concise, meaningful manner. In order to determine their significance, we must organize the data into some form so that, at a mere glance, we can get an idea of what the data can tell us.

Statistical tools that are particularly useful for organizing data include:

- Frequency tables, which place all the data in specific classes.
- Various pictorial displays that can provide a handy visual representation of the data.
- Contingency tables and stem-and-leaf designs, which also allow presentation of a large data set in a concise, discernible form.

2.2 Methods of Organizing Data

Several basic tools can be used to describe and summarize a large data set. The simplest, and perhaps least useful, is an **ordered array.** Assume that the IQ scores of five valedictorians from Podunk University are 75, 73, 91, 83, and 80. An ordered array merely lists these observations in ascending or descending order. The five values might appear as 73, 75, 80, 83, 91. The ordered array provides some organization to the data set; for example, it can now readily be seen that the two extreme values are 73 and 91. However, the usefulness of an ordered array is limited. Better techniques are needed to describe our data set. The rest of this section examines some common methods of organizing a large collection of data, thereby making it easier to more fully comprehend the information it contains.

A. Frequency Distributions

As the resident statistician for Pigs and People (P&P) Airlines, you are asked by the director of the Statistical Analysis Division to collect and organize data on the number of passengers who have chosen to fly on P&P. These data are displayed in Table 2.1 for the past 50 days. However, in this raw form it is unlikely that the director could gain any valuable information regarding flight operations. It is difficult to arrive at any meaningful conclusion by merely examining a bunch of numbers that have been jotted down. The data must be organized and presented in some concise and revealing manner so that the information they offer can be readily discerned. We will first examine how a frequency distribution can be used in your effort.

70–80

Table 2.1
Raw Data on the Number of Passengers for P&P Airlines

68	71	77	83	79
72	74	57	67	69
50	60	70	66	76
70	84	59	75	94
65	72	85	79	71
83	84	74	82	97
77	73	78	93	95
78	81	79	90	83
80	84	91	101	86
93	92	102	80	69

A **frequency distribution** (or frequency table) simply divides the data into classes and records the number of observations in each class, as shown in Table 2.2. It can now be

Table 2.2 Frequency Distribution for Passengers

Class (passengers)	Tally	Frequency (days)	Midpoint (M)
50 to 59	|||	3	54.5
60 to 69	||||| ||	7	64.5
70 to 79	||||| ||||| ||||| |||	**18**	74.5
80 to 89	||||| ||||| ||	12	84.5
90 to 99	||||| |||	8	94.5
100 to 109	||	2	104.5
		50	

readily seen, for example, that on 18 of the 50 days, between 70 and 79 passengers flew on P&P. At no time did the daily passenger list exceed 109. The airline rarely carried fewer than 60 passengers. The director can now detect trends and patterns that are not apparent from an examination of the raw data in Table 2.1. With information like this it becomes easier to make more intelligent and well-informed decisions regarding flight operations.

Notice that each class has a **lower bound** and an **upper bound.** The exact limits of these bounds are quite important. If the data in a frequency table are continuous, it is necessary to allow for fractional values. Our class boundaries would have to appear as:

50 and under 60
60 and under 70
70 and under 80
⋮

Of course, P&P cannot fly a fraction of a passenger, so the discrete nature of our present data set permits the use of the boundaries seen in Table 2.2. The **number of classes** in a frequency table is somewhat arbitrary. In general, your table should have between 5 and 20 classes. Too few classes would not reveal any details about the data; too many would prove as confusing as the list of raw data itself.

A simple rule you can follow to approximate the number of classes, c, is:

Determines the number of classes

$$2^c \geq n \qquad [2.1]$$

where n is the number of observations. The number of classes is the lowest power to which 2 is raised so that the result is equal to or greater than the number of observations. In our example for P&P, we have $n = 50$ observations. Thus,

$$2^c \geq 50$$

Solving for c, which can easily be done on a hand calculator, we find $2^6 = 64$. This rule suggests that there should be six classes in the frequency table. For convenience, more or fewer classes may be used.

The **class midpoint,** M, is calculated as the average of the upper and lower boundaries of that class. The midpoint for the first class in Table 2.2 is $50 + 59/2 = 54.5$.

The **class interval** is the range of values found within a class. It is determined by subtracting the lower (or upper) boundary of one class from the lower (or upper) boundary of the next class. The interval for the first class in Table 2.2 is $(60 - 50) = 10$. It is desirable to make all class intervals of equal size, since this facilitates statistical interpretations in subsequent uses. However, it may be convenient to use **open-ended** intervals that do not cite a lower boundary for the first class or an upper boundary for the last class. The last class in Table 2.2 might read "100 and up."

In the original construction of a frequency table, the class interval can be determined as:

Class interval for a frequency table

$$CI = \frac{\text{Largest value} - \text{Smallest value}}{\text{The number of desired classes}} \quad [2.2]$$

Since you decided on six classes for your frequency table, the class interval becomes:

$$CI = \frac{102 - 50}{6} = 8.7$$

Since 8.7 is an awkward number, the interval can be slightly adjusted up or down. For convenience, the interval of 10 was selected in forming Table 2.2.

We often want to determine the number of observations that are more than or less than some amount. This can be accomplished with a **more-than cumulative frequency distribution** or a **less-than cumulative frequency distribution.** A more-than cumulative frequency distribution is formed by subtracting the frequencies of previous classes as seen in Table 2.3. On all 50 days, at least 50 passengers boarded P&P Airlines. Thus, the cumulative frequency for the first class of Table 2.3 is 50. On three of those days, fewer than 60 passengers bought tickets. The cumulative frequency of the second class is therefore 47 (50 − 3). Since the number of passengers was less than 70 on 10 days, the cumulative frequency for the third class is 40 (50 − 10). The cumulative frequencies for the remaining classes are determined similarly.

Table 2.3
More-Than Cumulative Frequency Distribution for the Number of Passengers

Class (passengers)	Frequency (days)	Cumulative Frequency (days)
50 or more	3	50
60 or more	7	47
70 or more	18	40
80 or more	12	22
90 or more	8	10
100 or more	2	2
110 or more	0	0

A less-than cumulative frequency distribution is constructed by adding the frequencies of each class. Table 2.4 shows that at no time did fewer than 50 passengers fly P&P. The cumulative frequency of the first class is therefore zero. On three days fewer than 60 passengers boarded flights. The cumulative frequency of the second class is three. Since there were 10 days on which fewer than 70 passengers flew, Table 2.4 shows that the cumulative frequency of the third class is 3 + 7 = 10. Again, the cumulative frequencies of the remaining classes are determined in similar fashion.

Finally, a **relative frequency distribution** expresses the frequency within a class as a percentage of the total number of observations. In our present case, the relative frequency of a class is determined as the frequency of that class divided by 50. Table 2.5 shows, for example, that the relative frequency of the third class is $18/50 = 36\%$. This allows us to draw conclusions regarding the number of observations in a class relative to the entire sample.

Table 2.4
Less-Than Cumulative Frequency Distribution for Number of Passengers

Class (passengers)	Cumulative Frequency (days)	Frequency (days)
Less than 50	0	0
Less than 60	3	3
Less than 70	7	10
Less than 80	18	28
Less than 90	12	40
Less than 100	8	48
Less than 110	2	50

Table 2.5
Relative Frequency Distribution for Passengers

Class (passengers)	Frequency (days)	Relative Frequency
50–59	3	3 ÷ 50 = 6%
60–69	7	7 ÷ 50 = 14%
70–79	18	18 ÷ 50 = **36%**
80–89	12	12 ÷ 50 = 24%
90–99	8	8 ÷ 50 = 16%
100–109	2	2 ÷ 50 = 4%
	50	100%

Display 2.1
Frequency Table For P&P's Passenger Data

BIN	FREQUENCY	CUMULATIVE %
59	3	6.00%
69	7	20.00%
79	18	56.00%
89	12	80.00%
99	8	96.00%
109	2	100.00%

Almost all the statistical work we encounter can be done easily and quickly with the aid of modern computers. Display 2.1 contains the frequency table for P&P's passenger data, created with Microsoft Excel. You can specify a bin number corresponding to the upper bound of each class. The observations are then placed in the corresponding classes. Most computer packages will create similar output.

B. Contingency Tables

Frequency tables can organize data on only one variable at a time. If you wish to examine or compare two variables, a **contingency table** proves quite useful.

Table 2.6
Contingency Table for P&P Airlines

Age	Number of Flights per Year			
	1–2	3–5	Over 5	Total
Less than 25	1 (0.02)	1 (0.02)	2 (0.04)	**4 (0.08)**
25–40	2 (0.04)	8 (0.16)	10 (0.20)	20 (0.40)
40–65	1 (0.02)	6 (0.12)	**15 (0.30)**	22 (0.44)
65 and over	1 (0.02)	2 (0.04)	1 (0.02)	**4 (0.08)**
Total	5 (0.10)	17 (0.34)	**28 (0.56)**	50 (1.00)

Suppose that, in addition to collecting information on the number of passengers at P&P, you also obtained data on the passengers' ages and the number of flights they typically booked each year. Both variables can be detailed by a contingency table which lists number of flights across the top and ages down the side, as seen in Table 2.6. By dividing age into four categories and flights into three categories, you have created 12 *cells* in your table. You can now determine whether these two characteristics are related. You can see in the last column, for example, that the greatest number of passengers, 15 (or 30 percent), are in the 40–65 age category and fly more than five times a year. The fewest number of flyers, only 4, are less than 25 years old or 65 or older. A majority, 28, typically take more than five flights each year.

You could also display the information in each cell on the basis of gender. Of the 15 people in the 40–65 age level who fly over five times, eight may be men and seven may be women. The entry in that cell could then appear as 8,7 (0.30). All other relevant characteristics of the passengers could also be incorporated into the table. It is easy to imagine that such a descriptive profile could be very useful in identifying the typical passenger and establishing effective marketing policies.

Section Exercises

1. A data set contains 100 observations; the largest is 315 and the smallest is 56.

a. How many classes should the frequency table have?
b. What is the class interval?
c. What are the bounds and midpoints of each class?

2. In a recent study of 500 business graduates, the highest starting salary reported was $27,500 and the lowest was $19,900. You wish to create frequency table to analyze and compare these data to the job offers you have received.

a. How many classes will you put in your frequency table?
b. What is the class interval?
c. What are the bounds and midpoints of each class?

3. The following data are the incomes of 60 marketing executives for U.S. corporations. The data are in thousands of dollars.

58	76	89	45	67	34
64	76	34	65	45	39
79	74	56	71	85	87
74	38	69	79	61	71
69	62	56	38	69	79
71	54	31	69	62	39
65	79	47	46	77	66
55	75	62	57	77	36
73	72	64	69	51	50
40	50	74	61	69	73

a. Construct a frequency table for the data. Exercise care in selecting your class intervals. Show the cumulative and relative frequencies for each class. What conclusions can you draw from the table?

b. Present and discuss a more-than and a less-than cumulative frequency distribution.

4. From the data presented below, prepare a contingency table to evaluate 45 employees regarding their education level in years and the management level they currently hold. Divide education into three groups: group 1 for 10 to 12 years of education, group 2 for 13 to 15 years, and group 3 for 16 years and above. What patterns, if any, do you observe and what conclusions can you reach?

Management Level	Years of Education	Management Level	Years of Education
1	14	4	16
2	13	4	18
3	16	4	14
2	16	2	15
1	12	3	17
4	16	2	12
1	12	1	12
2	12	2	15
3	14	3	16
3	14	1	10
1	13	2	14
2	12	4	16
3	20	2	14
4	17	4	16
2	14	1	10
1	13	1	12
3	16	4	13
2	11	1	10
4	16	2	13
4	16	4	17
2	10	2	15
3	11	3	14
1	14		

5. A production process for construction materials is designed to generate containers of three weights: 10 pounds, 11 pounds, and 12 pounds. An examination of 40 of the containers records their actual weights and their intended weights. A container is considered "defective" if its actual weight differs by more than 0.5 pounds from its intended weight. Create a contingency table with these data that indicates how many of the containers in each of the three weight groups are within the allowable difference. Record the observations as "1" if defective and "2" if not defective. Can you detect any patterns? Does it appear that one weight group suffers a larger proportion of defects?

Actual Weight	Intended Weight	Actual Weight	Intended Weight
9.5	10	12.3	11
9.6	10	10.4	12
12.1	11	12.1	10
11.2	12	10.0	11
11.6	11	11.2	10
12.3	12	9.9	12

(Continued)

Actual Weight	Intended Weight	Actual Weight	Intended Weight
9.6	10	9.6	11
10.6	12	12.4	10
11.0	11	11.2	12
11.2	10	11.6	11
9.8	11	12.3	10
10.5	10	9.6	12
11.9	12	10.6	12
11.0	10	11.2	11
9.8	10	10.5	12
11.9	10	12.3	10
10.4	12	12.1	11
10.0	12	11.2	10
9.9	12	9.6	11
11.5	10	9.5	12

2.3 Pictorial Displays

Pictorial displays are also useful methods of describing data sets. A **histogram** places the classes of a frequency distribution on the horizontal axis and the frequencies on the vertical axis. Figure 2.1 shows the histogram for the frequency distribution in Table 2.2. It reveals details and patterns not readily discernible from the original raw data. The absolute as well as the relative frequencies of each class are clearly illustrated.

Figure 2.1
Histograms for P&P's Passengers

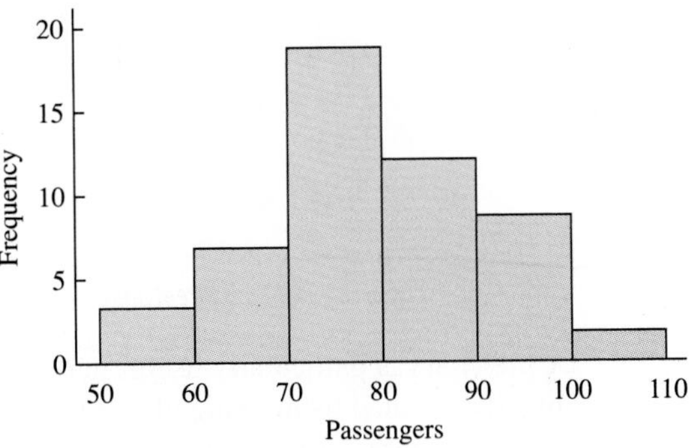

Figure 2.2
P&P Performance

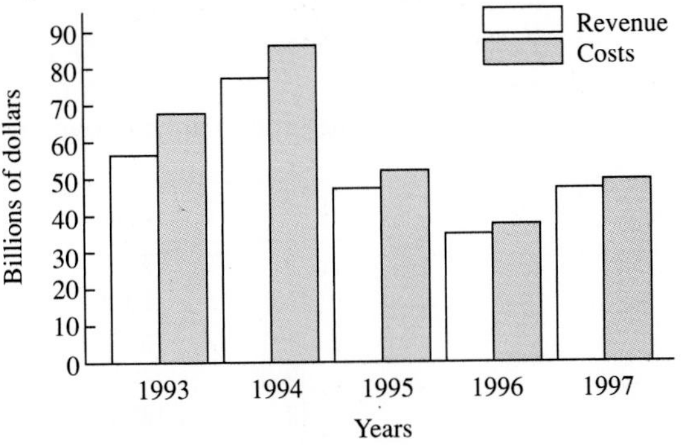

Similar to a histogram, a **bar chart** can show absolute amounts or percentages for two or more values on the vertical axis. Figure 2.2 demonstrates the costs and revenues for P&P Airlines.

Figure 2.3
Pie Chart

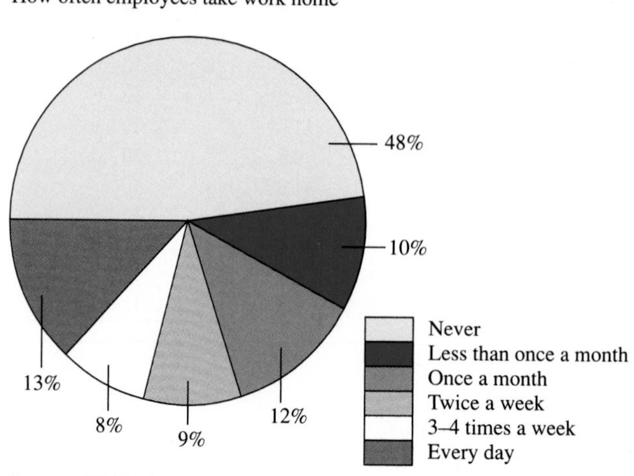

Source: *USA Today.*

Figure 2.4
High-Low-Close Chart for 15 Utilities

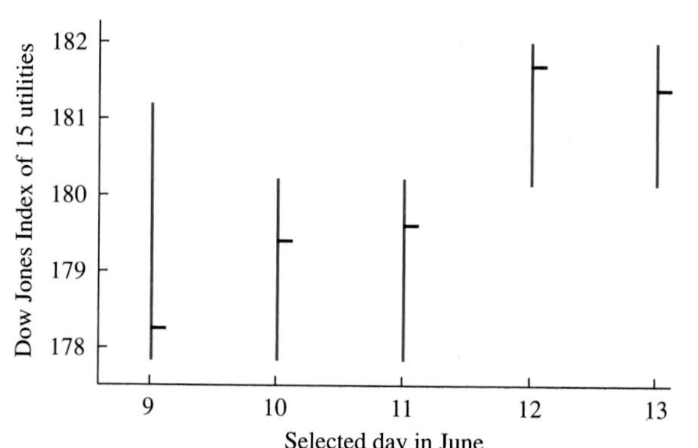

Source: *The Wall Street Journal.*

A **pie chart** is particularly useful in displaying relative (percentage) proportions of a variable. It is created by marking off a portion of the pie corresponding to each category of the variable. Figure 2.3 shows in percentages how often employees take work home from the office.

Financial data are often contained in a **high-low-close chart.** As the name suggests, it displays the highest value, the lowest value, and the closing value for financial instruments such as stocks. Figure 2.4 is such a display based on data taken from *The Wall Street Journal* for the Dow-Jones Index for 15 utilities over a five-day period based on the following data:

	High	Low	Close
June 9	181.07	178.17	178.88
10	180.65	178.28	179.11
11	180.24	178.17	179.35
12	182.79	179.82	181.37
13	182.14	179.53	181.31

Sometimes called *ticks and tabs,* the upper end of the vertical line, or tick, marks off the highest value that the index reached on that day; the lower end of the tick indicates the lowest value of the day. The closing value is shown by the little tab in between. Similar presentations could be made for commodities and currencies traded on the world's organized exchanges.

John Tukey, a noted statistician, devised the **stem-and-leaf design** as an alternative to the histogram to provide a quick visual impression of the number of observations in each class. Each observation is divided into two parts: a stem and a leaf separated by a vertical line. The precise design can be adjusted to fit any data set by identifying a convenient point where the observations might be separated forming a stem and a leaf. Fractional values such as 34.5, 34.6, 45.7, 45.8, and 56.2 might be divided at the decimal point producing a stem-and-leaf, such as:

Stem	Leaf
34	5, 6
45	7, 8
56	2

Notice that the stem and the leaf are placed in ordered arrays.

If a single stem contains a large number of observations in its leaf, it is common to divide it into two stems separated at the half-way point. Display 2.2 is the stem-and-leaf for our passenger data, provided by Minitab. The display contains three columns. The second and third show the stem and the leaf, respectively. There are three observations in the fifties: 50, 57, and 59. The first column displays the *depths,* indicating the sum total of observations from the top of the distribution for values less than the median (to be discussed later in this chapter) or to the bottom of the distributions for values greater than the median. The depth in parentheses, (9), shows the number of observations in the stem containing the median. For example, there are 19 observations from 50 up to 74 and 22 observations from 80 up to the maximum observation of 102. Notice that there are two stems for the seventies separating the observations at the midpoint between 74 and 75.

Display 2.2
Stem-and-Leaf for P&P

```
Character Stem-and-Leaf Display
Stem-and-leaf of pass  N = 50
Leaf Unit = 1.0
 1   5 : 0
 3   5 : 79
 4   6 : 0
10   6 : 567899
19   7 : 001122344
(9)  7 : 567788999
22   8 : 0012333444
12   8 : 56
10   9 : 012334
 4   9 : 57
 2  10 : 12
```

The *leaf unit* tells us where to put the decimal point. With leaf unit = 1.0, the first observation is 50. Leaf unit = 0.1 would mean the first observation is 5.0 and leaf unit = 10 would mean the first observation is 500.

Section Exercises

6. Construct a stem-and-leaf design from the following unemployment rates in 15 industrialized countries: 5.4 percent, 4.2 percent, 4.7 percent, 5.5 percent, 3.2 percent, 4.6 percent, 5.5 percent, 6.9 percent, 6.7 percent, 3.7 percent, 4.7 percent, 6.8 percent, 6.2 percent, 3.6 percent, and 4.8 percent.
7. Develop and interpret a histogram from the frequency table you constructed for Exercise 3.
8. *Investors' Report* (July 1996) stated that last month people had invested, in millions of dollars, the following amounts in types of mutual funds: 16.7 in growth funds, 12.5 in income funds, 28.2 in international funds, 15.9 in money market, and 13.9 in "other." Construct a pie chart depicting these data, complete with the corresponding percentages.
9. The changes from the previous month for investments in each of the funds in the previous problem were, respectively, 2.3, 1.5, −3.6, 4.5, and 2.9. Construct a bar chart reflecting these changes.

Solved Problems

1. A student organization is to review the amount students spend on textbooks each semester. Fifty students report the following amounts, rounded to the nearest dollar.

$125	$157	$113	$127	$201
165	145	119	148	158
148	168	117	105	136
136	125	148	108	178
179	191	225	204	104
205	197	119	209	157
209	205	221	178	247
235	217	222	224	187
265	148	165	228	239
245	152	148	115	150

a. Since $2^c \geq 50$ produces six classes, the interval for the frequency distribution is found as (highest − lowest)/6 = 265 − 104/6 = 26.8. An interval of 25 is used for convenience. This actually results in seven classes rather than the proposed six. No problem. If you set the lower boundary for the first class at 100 (again, for convenience you could use 104), the table becomes:

Class Interval	Frequency	M	Cumulative Frequency	Relative Frequency
100–124	8	112	8	0.16
125–149	11	137	19	0.22
150–174	8	162	27	0.16
175–199	6	187	33	0.12
200–224	10	212	43	0.20
225–249	6	237	49	0.12
250–274	1	262	50	0.02

b. The histogram and stem-and-leaf display provided by Minitab are:

```
Histogram of C1    N = 50

Midpoint   Count
   112.0       8   ********
   137.0      11   ***********
   162.0       8   ********
   187.0       6   ******
   212.0      10   **********
   237.0       6   ******
   262.0       1   *
```

```
Stem-and-leaf of C1          N = 50
Leaf Unit = 1.0

   3     10    458
   8     11    35799
  11     12    557
  13     13    66
  19     14    588888
  24     15    02778
  (3)    16    558
  23     17    889
  20     18    7
  19     19    17
  17     20    145599
  11     21    7
  10     22    12458
   5     23    59
   3     24    57
   1     25
   1     26    5
```

The three lowest amounts are \$104, \$105, and \$108. There are eight students who paid between \$104 and \$119. This corresponds to the frequency of the first class in the table above. The next highest is \$125. The median is in the stem for \$160.

2. On a scale of 1 to 4, with 4 being best, a consumer group rates the "social consciousness" of 50 organizations classified as public (indicated by a "1" in the data below), private (indicated by a "2"), or government controlled (indicated by a "3").

Type	Rating	Type	Rating
1	1	2	2
2	2	3	3
2	3	1	1
3	2	2	4
1	4	3	4
2	2	1	2
3	3	2	3
2	2	3	2
1	1	1	1
2	2	3	4
3	3	2	2
1	4	1	3

(Continued)

Type	Rating	Type	Rating
1	2	3	1
2	3	2	4
3	1	3	2
3	2	1	1
2	3	2	3
1	2	3	2
2	1	1	1
3	4	2	4
2	4	1	1
3	1	2	2
1	2	3	3
3	4	1	2
2	1	2	1

a. Prepare a contingency table complete with column and row totals and percentages. What conclusions might you draw? Minitab produces the table seen here. Notice that only two, or 4 percent, of the 15 public organizations received a rating of "4." Exactly twice that percentage of private and government organizations earned the highest rating. Of the 50 organizations, 14 percent of those receiving a "1" were public units. Of those receiving a "1," 53.85 percent were public. Many other facts are evident from an examination of the table.

```
ROWS: Type                          COLUMNS: Rating

                      1          2          3          4        ALL

  (Public) 1          7          5          1          2         15
                  46.67      33.33       6.67      13.33     100.00
                  53.85      29.41      10.00      20.00      30.00
                  14.00      10.00       2.00       4.00      30.00

 (Private) 2          3          7          5          4         19
                  15.79      36.84      26.32      21.05     100.00
                  23.08      41.18      50.00      40.00      38.00
                   6.00      14.00      10.00       8.00      38.00

(Government) 3        3          5          4          4         16
                  18.75      31.25      25.00      25.00     100.00
                  23.08      29.41      40.00      40.00      32.00
                   6.00      10.00       8.00       8.00      32.00

        ALL          13         17         10         10         50
                  26.00      34.00      20.00      20.00     100.00
                 100.00     100.00     100.00     100.00     100.00
                  26.00      34.00      20.00      20.00     100.00

CELL CONTENTS --
                COUNT
                % OF ROW
                % OF COL
                % OF TBL
```

List of Formulas

[2.1] $$2^c \geq n$$ Determines the number of classes in a frequency table

[2.2] $$CI = \frac{\text{Largest value} - \text{Smallest value}}{\text{The number of desired classes}}$$ Class interval for a frequency table

Chapter Exercises

10. Bill Bissey, vice president of Bank One in Indianapolis, has control over the approval of loans for local business development. Over the past five years the largest loan was $1.2 million, and the smallest was $10,000. He wishes to construct a frequency table with 10 classes. What would the boundaries of the classes be? What would the class interval be?

11. Mr. Bissey also maintains records on personal savings accounts. Of the 40 new accounts opened last month, the current balances are:

$ 179.80	$ 890.00	$ 712.10	$ 415.00
112.17	1,200.00	293.00	602.02
1,150.00	1,482.00	579.00	1,312.52
100.00	695.15	287.00	1,175.00
1,009.10	952.51	1,112.52	783.00
1,212.43	510.52	1,394.05	1,390.00
470.53	783.00	1,101.00	666.66
780.00	793.10	501.01	1,555.10
352.00	937.01	711.11	1,422.03
1,595.10	217.00	1,202.00	1,273.01

Construct a frequency table with seven classes. Are you working with continuous data or discrete data? Explain.

12. Using the data from Exercise 11, construct and interpret a relative frequency table and a cumulative frequency table.

13. Using the data from Exercise 11, construct a histogram.

14. Using the data from Exercise 11, construct a bar chart showing the percentages in each class.

15. Profits and losses for the 50 largest firms (by sales) on the Fortune 500 list for 1992 are given below in millions of dollars. The lowest value is a loss of $4,453 million (−4453), and the highest is a gain of $5,600 million. Construct a frequency table with the appropriate number of classes.

$-4,453	$-795	$ 423	$ 184	$ 97
5,600	1,567	454	258	939
-2,258	1,773	709	535	460
-2,827	1,484	-578	1,461	-387
2,636	20	368	601	-404
1,920	-1,021	755	-273	63
3,006	1,080	-732	1,681	308
1,403	17	-617	-142	73
1,294	311	1,154	454	97
1,293	942	-1,086	2,056	505

16. As a private economic consultant, you find it necessary to faithfully read *The Wall Street Journal* to remain current in your professional field. A recent report in *The Wall Street Journal* showed the following data for percentages of executives in 42 top U.S. corporations suffering from drug abuse problems.

5.9	8.8	14.3	8.3	9.1	5.1	15.3
17.5	17.3	15.0	9.3	9.9	7.0	16.7
10.3	11.5	17.0	8.5	7.2	13.7	16.3
12.7	8.7	6.5	6.8	13.4	5.5	15.2
8.4	9.8	7.3	10.0	11.0	13.2	16.3
9.1	12.3	8.5	16.0	10.2	11.7	14.2

a. Construct a stem-and-leaf design.
b. Construct the corresponding histogram.
c. Construct the frequency distribution and find the class midpoints.
d. Construct the relative frequency distribution.

17. The following data regarding where Americans spend their vacations were recently published in *Travel and Leisure:* city 31 percent; ocean 26 percent; lake 5 percent; mountains 10 percent; state and national parks 6 percent; small rural town 22 percent. As director of the tourism board for your state, it is your job to present these data in a pie chart.

18. Big Al, the local loan shark, currently has 120 outstanding accounts payable. Big Al's accountant informs him that of the 25 accounts in the $0 to $4,999 range, 10 are due, 5 are overdue, and the rest are delinquent, placing the debtor in danger of being visited by Big Al's enforcer. Of the 37 in the $5,000 to $9,999 range, 15 are due, 10 are overdue and the rest are delinquent. There are 39 in the $10,000 to $14,999 that show 11 are due, 10 are overdue, and the rest are delinquent. Of the remaining accounts, in the $15,000 and up range, 5 are due, 7 are overdue, and the rest are delinquent. Big Al wants to see a contingency table for these accounts. Interpret their significance by citing a few of the statistics you feel are most important and revealing.

19. The Dow Jones averages for 30 industrial stocks reported the following values in June of 1997. Construct a high-low-close chart based on these data.

	High	Low	Close
June 2	6119.31	6081.79	6093.35
3	6123.58	6084.82	6101.71
4	6144.15	6084.64	6099.40
5	6148.12	6111.13	6124.47

20. *Newsweek* (August 26, 1996) reported percentages of various drugs preferred by those eighth graders who had used drugs, and the percentage change since 1991 in the use of those drugs. Use the data on the 1996 rates of usage to create a pie chart and those on percentage changes to form a bar chart. Comment on the results.

Drug of Choice	1996 Usage Rate	Percentage Change Since 1991
Crack	2.7%	108%
Heroin	2.3	92
Marijuana	19.5	95
Cocaine	4.2	83
Cigarettes	46.0	5
Alcohol	25.3	−5

21. As a class project, a junior marketing student surveyed 20 local businesses in Peoria, Illinois, concerning their preference for a new product. Their responses were recorded as a "1" if they liked the product, a "2" if they disliked it, and a "3" if they had no opinion. Annual sales levels for the stores were also recorded as a

1	if sales were less than $50,000
2	if sales were $50,000 but less than $100,000
3	if sales were $100,000 but less than $200,000
4	if $200,000 or more

Construct a contingency table based on the data shown here. What conclusions can you reach?

Opinion	Sales	Opinion	Sales
1.00	4.00	3.00	1.00
1.00	4.00	2.00	1.00
3.00	3.00	3.00	2.00
1.00	4.00	3.00	4.00
3.00	1.00	1.00	4.00
3.00	1.00	1.00	4.00
3.00	1.00	1.00	4.00
1.00	2.00	3.00	4.00
2.00	3.00	2.00	4.00
1.00	4.00	3.00	1.00

Computer Exercise

Elizabeth Dunham is executive director of personnel operations for Minor Maturity Fashions, a clothing manufacturer that targets young women. She has collected data on weekly sales in hundreds of dollars over the past 100 weeks as well as payroll costs in thousands of dollars over the same period. However, Ms. Dunham is somewhat overwhelmed by the sheer volume of numbers she has at her disposal and is in need of assistance in organizing these data in some meaningful manner. She must gain some impression as to the nature of sales and payroll costs so that important information may be obtained for the forthcoming meeting of the board of directors. She also needs some advice regarding what features of these important variables are most meaningful.

Access the file MINOR and provide Ms. Dunham with all relevant frequency distributions and pictorial displays your software might generate. You may have to create some of these descriptive tools by hand if your software is not sufficiently flexible. Prepare a statistical report as detailed in Appendix I. Include all important parts of the statistical report including the executive summary and your conclusions and recommendations.

CURTAIN CALL

In the opening case you were to describe and characterize the data you have collected on car rental rates for your long-awaited spring break. Based on these data for daily rental charges from several companies in each city, prepare a detailed report describing your findings. Include as many of the tools discussed in this chapter as possible. Provide pictorial displays showing the average costs for each city as a percentage of the average cost of all cities.

Construct a contingency table showing each of the cities in the columns. Divide the data on rates into 3 to 5 groupings for the rows. Include column and row percentages and totals much as you did in Solved Problem 2.

City	Rate	City	Rate	City	Rate
Miami	85	Houston	58	San Diego	89
Houston	68	Phoenix	65	New Orleans	79
New Orleans	65	Houston	63	Miami	62
Miami	50	Phoenix	52	New Orleans	96
Miami	102	Houston	87	Miami	98
New Orleans	84	Houston	69	New Orleans	87
Miami	110	Miami	85	Houston	69
Phoenix	85	Phoenix	64	New Orleans	81
Houston	95	New Orleans	97	Houston	62
Phoenix	58	Phoenix	69	Phoenix	59
Houston	59	New Orleans	74	Houston	63
Phoenix	51	Phoenix	87	New Orleans	62
New Orleans	76	Houston	67	New Orleans	52

From the Stage to Real Life

On the Internet you can visit several national car rental companies and "Shopper's Guides" to compare car rental prices and make reservations. A selection of these sites is the following:

Shopping services:

Breeze Net's Guide to Airport Rental Cars *www.bnm.com*

Car Rental Shopper's guide *www.rent-cars.com*

National car rental companies:

Alamo *www.goalamo.com*

Avis *www.avis.com*

Budget *www.budgetrentacar.com*

Hertz *www.hertz.com*

Thrifty *www.thrifty.com*

Using actual price information obtained from these Internet sites, redo the contingency table you constructed in the *Curtain Call* exercise. Which of the cities of Miami, Houston, Phoenix, or New Orleans does the largest number of rental car companies service? Which offers the widest range of prices?

CHAPTER 3

Measures of Central Tendency and Dispersion

Chapter Blueprint

This chapter illustrates how an entire data set can be described with only a few numbers. You will see how useful measures of central tendency and measures of dispersion can be in statistical analysis.

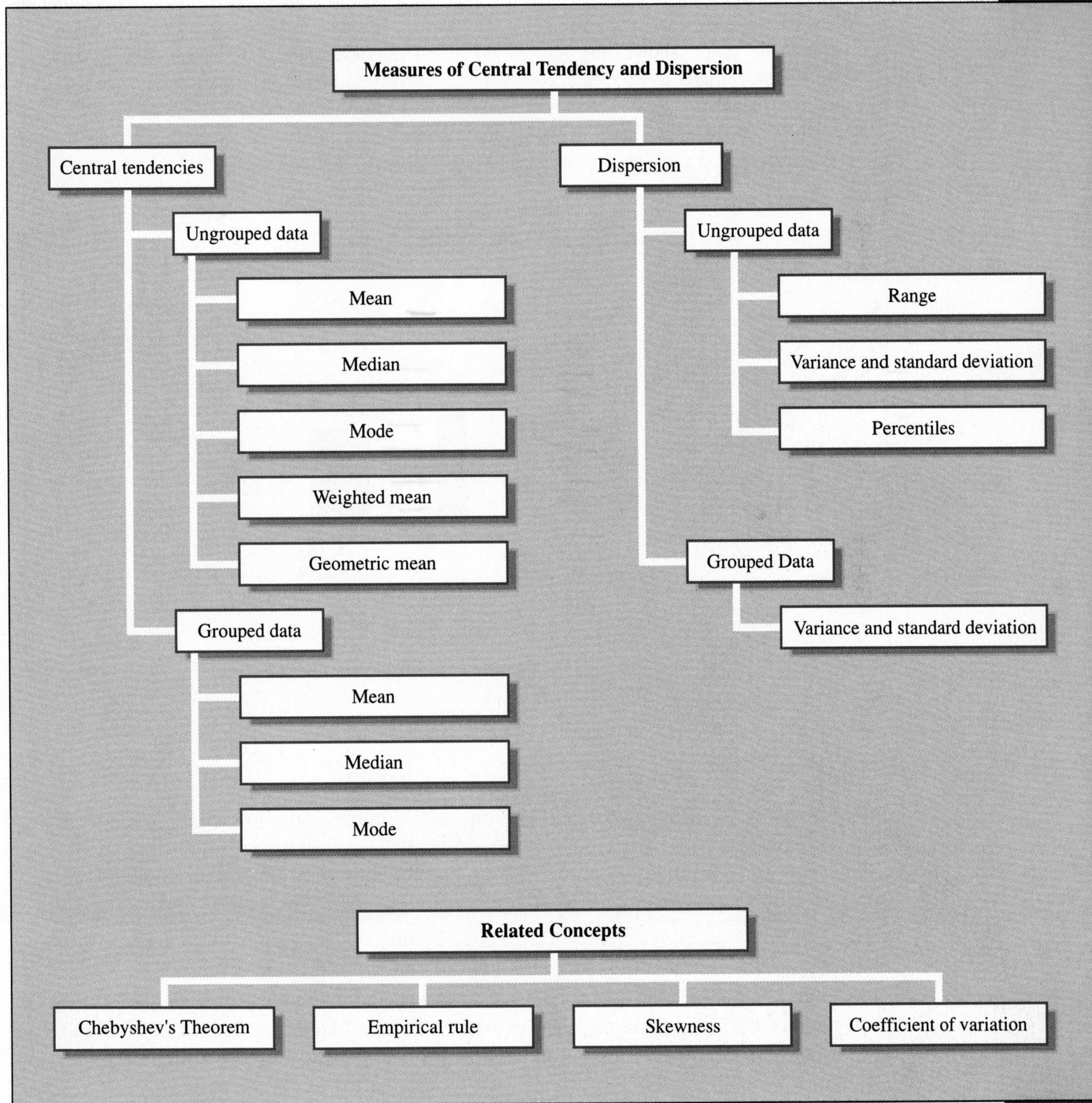

SETTING THE STAGE

Fortune (February 17, 1997) reported the average annual returns for three equity funds (Venture, Equity, and Growth) offered by Janus Funds, a large mutual fund company. As an investment analyst you are assigned the task of analyzing Janus's operations. To complete this job assignment you must prepare a descriptive account of the performance of the three funds shown in the chart.

As the graph shows, the returns on each of these funds have varied considerably over the years. There are many considerations that you must make in your analysis, and your immediate supervisor has stressed the importance of a thorough and precise presentation.

Many questions arise as to just how you might proceed. As this chapter reveals, there are many descriptive tools of statistical analysis that you can use to develop your analysis. Each tool plays an important role in providing valuable information. Descriptive statistics such as average returns and measures of dispersion will be very useful.

In this chapter we will examine many of the descriptive tools commonly used to convey valuable information in a concise and informative manner. Such practices reduce uncertainty and greatly facilitate the decision-making process.

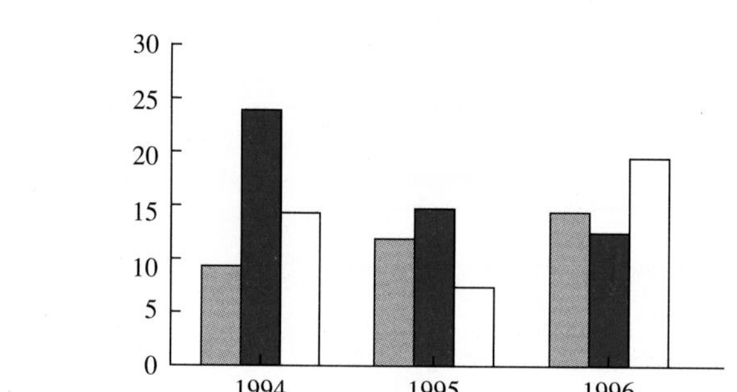

3.1 Introduction

Data, like students, often congregate around their favorite gathering spots. Students seem to flock to places such as football games; frat houses; popular bars and other watering holes; and, on rare occasions, even the library. Similarly, numbers seem to enjoy each other's company and are prone to collect around some central point referred to as the **measure of central tendency** or, more commonly, as simply the *average*. A measure of central tendency locates and identifies the point around which the data are centered.

A large data set can be quickly described in a succinct manner with a single number. If your professor tells you that the class average on the last statistics test was a 95, that tells you something. If you are told that the average was a 35, that tells you something entirely different.

In addition, **measures of dispersion** indicate the extent to which the individual observations are spread out around their center point. They measure the dispersion or variability of the data and reflect the tendency of the individual observations to deviate from that center point.

3.2 Measures of Central Tendency for Ungrouped Data

There are three common methods of identifying the center of a data set: the **mean,** the **median,** and the **mode.** Their calculation and interpretation will depend on the definition of "center." In each case they locate the point around which the data are clustered.

A. The Mean

The mean, or arithmetic mean, is the measure of central tendency commonly thought of as the average. To compute the mean of your last 10 statistics tests you simply add them up and divide by 10.

> **Arithmetic Mean** The measure of central tendency normally thought of as the average.

The mean of a population is the parameter μ (pronounced mu). If there are N observations in the population data set, the mean is calculated as:

Population mean
$$\mu = \frac{X_1 + X_2 + X_3 + \cdots + X_N}{N} = \frac{\sum_{i=1}^{N} X_i}{N} \qquad [3.1]$$

The Greek capital letter Σ is the summation sign telling you to add all the observations from 1 to N. The X_i denotes the individual observations. For simplicity's sake, the subscript and superscript will hereafter be dropped and the summation sign will appear by itself as simply Σ.

The mean of a sample is a statistic $\overline{X}$ (read X-bar). With n observations in the sample data set, the mean is determined as:

Sample mean
$$\overline{X} = \frac{X_1 + X_2 + X_3 + \cdots + X_n}{n} = \frac{\sum_{i=1}^{n} X_i}{n} \qquad [3.2]$$

Presume that a sample of monthly sales revenues in thousands of dollars for five months is found to be 56, 67, 52, 45, and 67. The mean is calculated as

$$\overline{X} = \frac{56 + 67 + 52 + 45 + 67}{5} = 57.4$$

B. The Median

The median is sometimes referred to as the *positional average,* because it lies exactly in the middle of the data set after the observations have placed into an ordered array. One-half of the observations will be above the median, and one-half will be *below* the median.

> **Median** The middle observation after the data have been put into an ordered array.

If the data set has an odd number of observations, the median *position* is found as

$$\text{Median position} = \frac{n+1}{2} \qquad [3.3]$$

Given our sample of sales revenues above, we must first place the data in an ordered array:

45, 52, 56, 67, 67

The position of the median value becomes

$$\text{Median position} = \frac{5+1}{2} = 3$$

or the third position. From the ordered array above it can be seen that this value is 56.

With a data set containing a even number of observations, it is necessary to average the middle two values. If revenues for a sixth month of 35 is added to our data set the ordered array becomes 35, 45, 52, 56, 67, 67. The median position is

$$\text{Median position} = \frac{6+1}{2} = 3.5$$

or the third and one-half position. The two values in the third and fourth positions are then averaged to yield a median of $52 + 56 = 54$. This means that, in one-half of the months, sales were below \$54,000, and, in one-half of the months, revenues exceeded that amount.

C. The Mode

The modal observation is that observation that occurs with the greatest frequency. Using our six observations above of 35, 45, 52, 56, 67, 67, the mode is 67. If a seventh observation of 56 were added, the data set would be *bimodal,* with modes of 56 and 67.

Example 3.1 **Measures of Central Tendency**

The February 17, 1997, issue of *Fortune* reported the 1996 profits of several Fortune 500 companies in millions of dollars, including:

Exxon	\$7,510	General Electric	\$7,280
Philip Morris	6,246	IBM	5,429
Intel	5,157	General Motors	4,289

Calculate the three measures of central tendency.

Solution: Mean: Treating the data as a sample, we have

$$\bar{X} = \frac{7{,}510 + 7{,}280 + 6{,}246 + 5{,}429 + 5{,}157 + 4{,}289}{6} = 5{,}985$$

Median: The data must first be put in an ordered array. If the data are not ordered, the position found using Formula 3.3 is meaningless.

4,289, 5,157, 5,429, 6,246, 7,280, 7,510

The median position is $(n + 1)/2 = 3.5$. The median is the average of the third and fourth values: $5{,}429 + 6{,}246 = 5{,}837.5$.

Mode: This data set has no mode since all the observations occurred with *equal* frequency.

Interpretation: The mean and median identify the center of the data set around which the observations are located.

D. The Weighted Mean

In our discussion of the mean, we assumed that each observation was equally important. However, in certain cases you may want to give some observations greater weight. For example, if your statistics professor threatens to count the final exam twice as much as the other tests when determining your final grade, then the score you get on the final must be given twice as much weight. That is, it must be counted twice in figuring your grade. This is exactly what the weighted mean does using Formula 3.4.

$$\bar{X}_W = \frac{\Sigma XW}{\Sigma W} \qquad [3.4]$$

where $\bar{X}_W$ is the weighted mean
X is the individual observations
W is the weight assigned to each observation

Assume you scored 89, 92, and 79 on the hour exams, and 94 on the final exam. These scores and their respective weights are reflected in Table 3.1. Formula (3.4) yields

$$\bar{X}_W = \frac{\Sigma XW}{\Sigma W} = \frac{448}{5} = 89.6$$

Table 3.1
Calculation of the Weighted Mean

Grade (X)	Weight (W)	XW
89	1	89
92	1	92
79	1	79
94	2	188
	5	448

This approach is the same as adding the score on the final exam twice in computing the average:

$$\bar{X}_W = \frac{89 + 92 + 79 + 94 + 94}{5} = 89.6$$

Weighted Mean The weighted mean takes into consideration the relative importance of the observations.

Example 3.2 Calculation of the Weighted Mean

Paul the Plumber sells five types of drain cleaner. Each type, along with the profit per can and the number of cans sold, is shown in the table.

Cleaner	Profit per Can (X)	Sales Volume in Cans (W)	XW
Glunk Out	$ 2.00	3	$ 6.00
Bubble Up	3.50	7	24.50
Dream Drain	5.00	15	75.00
Clear More	7.50	12	90.00
Main Drain	6.00	15	90.00
	$24.00	52	$285.50

You can calculate the simple arithmetic mean of Paul's profit as $24/5 = $4.80 per can.

Solution: However, this is probably not a good estimate of Paul's average profit, since he sells more of some types than he does of others. In order to get a financial statement more representative of his true business performance, Paul must give more weight to the more popular types of cleaner. The proper calculation would therefore be the weighted mean. The proper measure of weight would be the amounts sold. The weighted mean is then

$$\bar{X}_W = \frac{\Sigma XW}{\Sigma W} = \frac{\$285.50}{52} = \$5.49 \text{ per can}$$

Interpretation: The weighted mean is higher than the simple arithmetic mean because Paul sells more of those types of cleaner with a higher profit margin.

E. The Geometric Mean

The geometric mean can be used to show percentage changes in a series of positive numbers. As such, it has wide application in business and economics, since we are often interested in determining the percentage change in sales, gross national product, or any other economic series.

Geometric Mean The geometric mean provides an accurate measure of the average percentage change in a series of numbers.

The geometric mean (GM) is found by taking the nth root of the product of n numbers. Thus,

$$GM = \sqrt[n]{X_1X_2X_3\cdots X_n} \quad [3.5]$$

Most handheld calculators can compute the nth root of any number.

The geometric mean is most often used to calculate the average percentage growth rate over time of some given series. To illustrate its application in a business setting, consider the revenue figures in Example 3.3 for White-Knuckle Airlines, P&P's main competitor, over the past five years.

Example 3.3 **The Geometric Mean**

The CEO for White-Knuckle Airlines wishes to determine the average growth rate in revenue based on the figures in the table. If the average growth rate is less than the industry average of 10 percent, a new advertising campaign will be undertaken.

Revenues for White-Knuckle Airlines

Year	Revenue	Percentage of Previous Year
1992	$50,000	— —
1993	55,000	55/50 = 1.10
1994	66,000	66/55 = 1.20
1995	60,000	60/66 = 0.91
1996	78,000	78/60 = 1.30

Solution: It is first necessary to determine what percentage each year's revenue is of the previous year. In other words, the revenue in 1993 is what percentage of the revenue in 1992? This is found by dividing revenues in 1993 by those in 1992. The result, 1.10, reveals that 1993 revenues are 110 percent of revenues in 1992. Percentages for the three remaining years are also calculated. Taking the geometric mean of these percentages gives

$$\text{GM} = \sqrt[4]{(1.10)(1.2)(0.91)(1.3)} = 1.1179$$

Subtracting 1 in order to convert to an average annual increase yields 0.1179, or an 11.79 percent average increase over the five-year-period.

The simple arithmetic average, on the other hand, is

$$\overline{X} = \frac{1.1 + 1.2 + 0.91 + 1.3}{4} = \frac{4.51}{4} = 1.1275$$

or a 12.75 percent average change. We divide by 4, since there were four changes over the five-year period.

However, if an average increase of 12.75 percent based on the simple arithmetic average is applied to the series starting with $50,000, the results are

$$\$50{,}000 \times 1.1275 = \$56{,}375$$
$$\$56{,}375 \times 1.1275 = \$63{,}563$$
$$\$63{,}563 \times 1.1275 = \$71{,}667$$
$$\$71{,}667 \times 1.1275 = \$80{,}805$$

Since \$80,805 exceeds the \$78,000 White-Knuckle Airlines actually earned, the 12.75 percent increase is obviously too high. If the geometric mean growth rate of 11.79 percent is used, we get

$$\$50{,}000 \times 1.1179 = \$55{,}895$$
$$\$55{,}895 \times 1.1179 = \$62{,}485$$
$$\$62{,}485 \times 1.1179 = \$69{,}852$$
$$\$69{,}852 \times 1.1179 = \$78{,}088 \approx \$78{,}000$$

This gives us a value of \$78,088, which is much closer to the actual revenue of \$78,000.

Interpretation: The geometric mean represents the average change over time. Since the growth rate exceeds the industry average of 10%, the new advertising campaign will not be undertaken.

The geometric mean will always be less than the arithmetic mean except in the rare case when all the percentage increases are the same. Then the two means are equal.

3.3 Comparing the Mean, the Median, and the Mode

The mean is the most common measure of central tendency. It lends itself handily to further algebraic manipulation and interpretation. Unfortunately, the mean is affected by extreme values, or *outliers,* and, unlike the median, can be drastically biased by observations which lie significantly above or below it.

For example, for the data 4, 5, 6, 6, 7, 8, the mean and the median are both 6 and represent an excellent measure of the data's center point. If the last observation were 80 instead of 8, the mean would become 18, but the median is still be 6. Since the median is not affected by this extreme value, it better represents the six observations.

The mode is also less affected by a few atypical observations and remains 6 even if the last value was 80. However, if there is no mode, or if the data set is bimodal, its use can be confusing.

This does not imply that one measure is necessarily better than the others. The measure you choose might depend on the nature of the data or the manner in which the data are used. For example, Land's End, a popular retailer of camping equipment, would benefit little from the knowledge that the average size of the hiking boots it sold was 7.3492. More useful in future business decisions would be knowledge of the *modal* size—recognizing that it sold more boots of size 8 than any other.

However, assume that Land's End wishes to market a new camping tent. The dimensions of the tent would depend, among other things, on the average height of adults. Experience has shown that the mean serves quite well as a measure of central tendency when dealing with products that are built to conform to people's height. The size of doorways, countertops in homes and retail businesses, and much of the furniture that is manufactured is based on mean heights.

Section Exercises

1. Your firm is introducing a new computer chip that is advertised to perform statistical calculations much faster than those currently marketed. Twenty different calculations are made, producing the times in seconds seen below. Although you cannot misrepresent your product, you

wish to present the results in the manner most favorable to your firm. Determine the mean, the median, and the mode. Comment on the relative benefits of using each statistic.

3.2	4.1	6.3	1.9	0.6
5.4	5.2	3.2	4.9	6.2
1.8	1.7	3.6	1.5	2.6
4.3	6.1	2.4	2.2	3.3

2. As sales manager for Acme, Inc., you wish to calculate the measures of central tendency for your firm's profits levels over the last 12 months, given the following monthly profits in thousands of dollars:

$12.3	$14.3	$ 25.7
21.6	21.6	−12.8
22.3	18.0	23.1
−3.4	17.9	22.3

3. The plant director for Intel wants you to compare the mean wage rates for his plant in Palo Alto to that of a competitor's in nearby San Jose. Of the 6,012 employees he supervises, 1,212 earn $12.30 an hour, 650 are paid $15.50, 3,098 get $23.50, and the rest are paid $17.12. Of the 5,634 employees in the other plant, 1,654 earn $12.75, 815 receive $17.80, and the others are paid $20.10. Write a brief report for the director detailing the information he wants.

4. A large firm selling sports equipment is testing the effect of two advertising plans on sales over the last four months. Given the sales seen here, which advertising program seems to be producing the highest mean growth in monthly sales?

1998/1657 1.2
2267/1998 1-3
3432/2265 1.5.

Month	Plan 1	Plan 2
January	$1,657	$4,735
February	1,998	5,012
March	2,267	5,479
April	3,432	5,589

3.4 Measures of Dispersion

In our efforts to describe a set of numbers, we have seen that it is useful to locate the center of that data set. But identifying a measure of central tendency is seldom sufficient. A more complete description of the data set can be obtained if we measure how much the data are dispersed around that center point. This is precisely what measures of dispersion do. They indicate how much the observations deviate around their mean.

> **Measures of Dispersion** Measure the extent to which the individual observations are spread out around their mean.

Take for example the three small data sets seen here.

Data Set 1	Data Set 2	Data Set 3
0,5,10	4,5,6	5,5,5

All three have a mean of five. Are we therefore to conclude that the data sets are similar? Of course not. However, if we were told only their means, without seeing the observations, we might conclude a similarity. A more accurate impression of the data sets would result if we compared the degree to which the individual observations in each data set were dispersed or spread out around the mean of five. The observations in the first data set are quite scattered out above and below the mean, whereas those in the second data set are comparatively close to the mean. The first data set has a higher measure of dispersion than does the second. The third data set has no dispersion—all the observations are equal to the mean. Knowing this, we would be unlikely to mistakenly assume any similarity in the data sets merely on the basis of their mean. Measures of dispersion in this sense are quite useful and informative.

A. The Range

The simplest (and least useful) measure of dispersion is the range. The **range** is simply the difference between the highest and the lowest observations. Its advantage is that it is easy to calculate. Its disadvantage is that it considers only two of the perhaps hundreds of observations in the data set. The rest of the observations are ignored. The ranges of the three data sets above are 10, 2, and 0 respectively.

B. The Variance and the Standard Deviation of a Population

The variance and its square root, the standard deviation, are much more useful measures of dispersion. They provide a more meaningful measure of the extent to which the individual observations are spread out around their mean.

The **variance** is the "mean of the squared deviation from the mean." What does that mean in English? It means that you (1) find the amount by which each observation deviates from the mean, (2) square those deviations, and (3) find the average of those squared deviations. You then have the mean of the squared deviations from the mean.

Variance The mean of the squared deviations of the observations from their mean.

The variance for a population, σ^2 (read sigma squared) is

Population variance

$$\sigma^2 = \frac{(X_1 - \mu)^2 + (X_2 - \mu)^2 + (X_3 - \mu)^2 + \cdots + (X_N - \mu)^2}{N} = \frac{\Sigma(X_i - \mu)^2}{N} \quad [3.6]$$

where $X_1, X_2, X_3, \ldots, X_N$ are the individual observations
μ is the population mean
N is the number of observations

The standard deviation σ is

Population standard deviation

$$\sigma = \sqrt{\sigma^2} \quad [3.7]$$

Notice that since we are working with a population, the mean is μ, not $\overline{X}$ as it is for a sample, and the number of observations is N, not n as it is for a sample.

Standard Deviation The square root of the variance. It is an important measure of the dispersion of the data.

To illustrate, Chuckie Chambers sells five different insurance policies out of the trunk of his 1973 Plymouth. Their respective monthly premiums are \$110, \$145, \$125, \$95, and \$150. The average premium is

$$\mu = \frac{110 + 145 + 125 + 95 + 150}{5} = \$125$$

The variance is found by: (1) subtracting the mean of \$125 from each of the observations, (2) squaring these deviations, and (3) finding the average of these squared deviations. Following these three steps yields

$$\sigma^2 = \frac{(110 - 125)^2 + (145 - 125)^2 + (125 - 125)^2 + (95 - 125)^2 + (150 - 125)^2}{5}$$

$$= 430$$

Despite the common use of the variance, it presents two problems. It is a rather large number relative to the observation. As you can see, it is several times greater than even the largest observation. Due to its sheer size, the variance often becomes difficult to work with.

An even more distressing problem results from the fact that since the deviations are squared, the variance is always expressed in terms of the original data squared. In Chuckie's case, since he squared the deviations from the mean, it becomes 430 dollars squared—a unit of measure that makes no sense. In most instances, the variance is expressed in terms that have no logical meaning or interpretation.

However, both complications can be solved in a flash. Just find the standard deviation σ by taking the square root of the variance:

$$\sigma = \sqrt{430} = \$20.74$$

As easily as that, both problems are solved. You now have a much smaller number which is easier to work with, and, more important, it is now expressed in dollars since you took the square root of dollars squared.

The concept of the standard deviation is quite important in business and economics. For example, in finance the standard deviation is used as a measure of the risk associated with various investment opportunities. By using the standard deviation to measure the variability in rates of return offered by different investments, the financial analyst can gauge the level of risk carried by each financial asset. Generally, the higher the standard deviation of the rate of return of a particular investment, the greater the degree of risk. Consider the following example.

Example 3.4 **Variance and Standard Deviation of a Population**

Markus Boggs is manager of Nest Egg Investments. Recently, Markus was interested in the rates of return over the past five years of two different mutual funds. Megabucks, Inc. showed rates of return over the five-year period of 12, 10, 13, 9, and 11 percent, while Dynamics Corporation yielded 13, 12, 14, 10, and 6 percent. A client approached Boggs and expressed an interest in one of these mutual funds. Which one should Boggs choose for his client?

Solution: Notice that both funds offer an average return of 11 percent. Since both offer the same return on the average, the safer investment is the one with the smaller degree of risk as measured by the standard deviation. For Megabucks, Boggs finds

$$\sigma^2 = \frac{(12 - 11)^2 + (10 - 11)^2 + (13 - 11)^2 + (9 - 11)^2 + (11 - 11)^2}{5} = 2$$

The standard deviation is

$$\sigma = \sqrt{2} = 1.41\%$$

For Dynamics,

$$\sigma^2 = \frac{(13 - 11)^2 + (12 - 11)^2 + (14 - 11)^2 + (10 - 11)^2 + (6 - 11)^2}{5} = 8$$

The standard deviation is therefore

$$\sigma = \sqrt{8} = 2.83\%$$

Interpretation: Since Megabucks exhibits less variability in its returns and offers the same rate of return on the average as does Dynamics, Megabucks represents the safer of the two investments and is therefore the preferred investment opportunity.

C. Variance and Standard Deviation for a Sample

Make note: The previous examples relate to the variance and standard deviation for a *population.* The symbols σ^2 and σ are Greek letters typical of parameters.

Seldom do we calculate parameters. In most cases, we will instead estimate them by taking a sample and computing the corresponding statistics. With that in mind, this section examines the way in which we can calculate these important measures of dispersion as they relate to samples.

The variance and standard deviation for a sample represent measures of dispersion around the mean. They are calculated quite similarly to those for a population. The sample variance s^2 is

Sample variance $$s^2 = \frac{\Sigma(X_i - \bar{X})^2}{n - 1} \qquad [3.8]$$

and the sample standard deviation is

Sample standard deviation $$s = \sqrt{s^2} \qquad [3.9]$$

Notice that the mean in Formula (3.8) is expressed as $\overline{X}$, and not μ, since we are working with samples. Furthermore, you divide by $n - 1$ rather than N because you have $n - 1$ *degrees of freedom*, $df = n - 1$. The number of degrees of freedom in any statistical operation is equal to the number of observations minus any constraints placed on those observations. A constraint is any value that must be computed from the observations.

For example, assume you are to choose $n = 4$ numbers which must average $\overline{X} = 10$. Under these conditions, you are free to pick any three numbers you want—say your hat size, your age, and your IQ. Once those first three numbers are chosen, however, the fourth is predetermined if they are to average $\overline{X} = 10$. As Formula (3.8) illustrates, the variance uses the value for $\overline{X}$ which functions as a constraint and thereby reduces the degrees of freedom by 1. Hence, we divide by the number of observations, n, minus 1.

Another reason we divide by $n - 1$ is that a sample is generally a little less dispersed than the population from which it was taken. There is therefore a tendency for the sample standard deviation s to be a little less than the population standard deviation σ. This is unfortunate. Remember, we are trying to use the value of s as an estimation of σ. However, s will consistently underestimate σ. We must offset this condition by artificially inflating s by dividing by a slightly smaller number, $n - 1$, rather than n.

To illustrate the technique of determining these measures of dispersion for a sample, consider another problem Boggs has in the effort to help his clients make investment decisions.

Example 3.5 **Variance and Standard Deviation for a sample**

Mr. Boggs wishes to determine the stability of the price of a particular stock. He decides to base his judgment regarding stability on the standard deviation of the stock's daily closing price. Checking the financial pages, Boggs learns that the stock has been traded on the exchange for quite some time and there are many closing prices dating back several months. Rather than using all these prices, Boggs decides to simplify his arithmetic and select a random sample of $n = 7$ days. (Although 7 is probably too small a sample, it will serve our purposes for the moment.) He notes the closing prices of

$87, $120, $54, $92, $73, $80, and $63

Solution: Then, $\overline{X} = \$81.29$ and

$$s^2 = \frac{\Sigma(X_i - \overline{X})^2}{n - 1}$$

$$= \frac{(87 - 81.29)^2 + (120 - 81.29)^2 + \ldots + (63 - 81.29)^2}{7 - 1}$$

$$s^2 = 465.9 \text{ dollars squared}$$

$$s = \sqrt{465.9} = \$21.58$$

Interpretation: Boggs has estimated the mean closing price of the stock to be $81.29, with a tendency to vary above and below that price by $21.58. A further explanation of the use and interpretation of the standard deviation is offered later in this chapter. However, keep in mind that

Boggs can always interpret the standard deviation of $21.58 as a measure of the tendency of the closing prices to fluctuate around their mean of $81.29.

All these important statistics can be obtained from computer runs using various computer packages. Display 3.1 shows the Excell printout for our P&P data. Notice that the measures of central tendency and dispersion are given along with other statistics we will discuss later.

Display 3.1
Descriptive Statistics for P&P

Mean	78.36
Standard Error	1.599938774
Median	78.5
Mode	83
Standard Deviation	11.31327557
Sample Variance	127.9902041
Kurtosis	-0.036918787
Skewness	-0.05225955
Range	52
Minimum	50
Maximum	102
Sum	3918
Count	50

Section Exercises

5. Two processes are used to produce computer disks. Problems have arisen regarding variations in the sizes of these disks. Based on the sample data seen here for eight disk sizes in inches for each process, explain which process you would advise if your objective is to minimize the deviation in size around the mean.

Process 1		Process 2	
3.41	3.22	3.81	3.26
3.74	3.06	3.26	3.79
3.89	3.65	3.07	3.14
3.65	3.33	3.35	3.51

6. Explain in your own words what the variance and standard deviation measure. Why is their calculation slightly different for populations and samples?

7. An investment analyst suggests that you invest in Boomer Securities instead of Reliable Stocks. Given the annual rates of return shown below for a sample of each investment, what do you tell the analyst if you want to minimize your risk exposure?

Boomer		Reliable	
15.5%	3.6%	4.5%	6.2%
21.7	27.2	5.5	7.2
−7.8	2.2	3.5	4.2
−5.0	12.2	4.1	

8. Curly, Moe, and Larry sell life insurance for the Shemp Insurance Company. Mr. Shemp will promote one of his salesmen to a management position based on sales performance. His decision rests on which member of his sales force has (1) the highest average sales and (2) the most consistent sales record. Given the following weekly sample data for sales, which salesman gets the promotion?

Curly		Moe		Larry	
$ 986	$1,265	$645	$893	$534	$534
1,337	734	645	230	534	534
2,745	245	734	415	534	534
2,645	5,344	822	723	534	534
3,658	4,867				

3.5 Measures of Central Tendency and Dispersion for Grouped Data

In working with data that have been grouped into a frequency distribution, we do not know what the individual observations are. In the frequency table for P&P's passengers, Table 2.2, we know only that, on three days, somewhere between 50 and 59 passengers boarded an airplane. We do not have the exact counts on those three days. Without the specific values, the procedures shown above for calculating descriptive measures do not apply. Alternative approaches must be found. It should be kept in mind that computations made using grouped data are only approximations. Therefore, the ungrouped individual observations should be used when possible.

A. The Mean

In calculating the mean from grouped data, the assumption is made that the observations in each class are equal to the class midpoint. Although this may be a rather heroic assumption, it probably all balances out, since it is likely that some of the observations exceed the midpoint while others fall below it. Given this assumption, we must take into consideration the frequency and midpoints of each class when computing the mean using grouped data. Formula 3.10 does just that.

Grouped mean
$$\overline{X}_g = \frac{\Sigma fM}{n} = \frac{\Sigma fM}{\Sigma f} \qquad [3.10]$$

where f is the frequency or number of observations in each class
M is the midpoint of each class
n is the sample size and equals the combined frequencies in all classes.

The frequency table for Pigs & People Airlines developed in Chapter 2 is repeated in Table 3.2 for your convenience, along with the midpoints for each class, which, as you remember, are determined by averaging the upper and lower boundaries.

Using Formula (3.10), we can see that P&P flew a daily average of 78.7 passengers.

$$\overline{X}_g = \frac{\Sigma fM}{n} = \frac{3935}{50} = 78.7 \text{ passengers}$$

Table 3.2
Frequency Distribution for Passengers

Class (passengers)	Frequency (*f*) (days)	*M*	*fM*
50–59	3	54.5	163.5
60–69	7	64.5	451.5
70–79	18	74.5	1341.0
80–89	12	84.5	1014.0
90–99	8	94.5	756.0
100–109	2	104.5	209.0
	50		3935.0

Table 3.3
Frequency Distribution for Passengers

Class	*f*	Cumulative Frequency
50–59	3	3
60–69	7	10
70–79	18	28
80–89	12	40
90–99	8	48
100–109	2	50

B. The Median

If the data have been recorded in a frequency table, they cannot be placed in an ordered array to calculate the median. As an illustration, the frequency table for P&P Airlines is given in Table 3.3.

We must first find the median class of the frequency distribution. The **median class** is that class whose cumulative frequency is greater than or equal to $n/2$.

Since n is 50, we need to locate the first class with a cumulative frequency of 25 or more. The third class has a cumulative frequency of 28. The median can then be determined as

Median for grouped data

$$\text{Median} = L_{md} + \left[\frac{n/2 - F}{f_{md}}\right](C) \qquad [3.11]$$

where L_{md} is the lower boundary of median class (70)
F is the cumulative frequency of the class *preceding* the median class (10)
f_{md} is the frequency of the median class (18)
C is the class interval of the median class (10)

Using Formula (3.11), we obtain the median:

$$\text{Median} = 70 + \left[\frac{50/2 - 10}{18}\right]10 = 78.33 \text{ passengers}$$

We can then conclude that on 25 days—one-half of the 50 days surveyed—fewer than 78.33 passengers flew on P&P Airlines, and on the other 25 days, more than 78.33 passengers flew the friendly skies of P&P.

C. The Mode

Since by definition the mode is the observation that occurs most often, it will be found in the class with the highest frequency, called the **modal class**. To estimate the mode in the case of grouped data, we use Formula (3.12).

Mode for grouped data	$$\text{Mode} = L_{mo} + \left[\frac{D_a}{D_b + D_a}\right](C)$$	[3.12]

where L_{mo} is the lower boundary of the modal class
D_a is the difference between the frequency of the modal class and the class preceding it
D_b is the difference between the frequency of the modal class and the class after it
C is the class interval of the modal class

From Table 3.3, the mode is

$$\text{Mode} = 70 + \left[\frac{18 - 7}{(18 - 12) + (18 - 7)}\right](10) = 76.47 \text{ passengers}$$

D. Variance and Standard Deviation

If data are grouped into a frequency table, the variance and the standard deviation can be calculated as

Sample variance of grouped data	$$s^2 = \frac{\Sigma fM^2 - n\overline{X}^2}{n - 1}$$	[3.13]

and

Sample standard deviation of grouped data	$$s = \sqrt{s^2}$$	[3.14]

The passenger data for P&P Airlines will be used to illustrate.

Example 3.6 **Measures of Dispersion with Grouped Data**

The flight director for P&P requires information regarding the dispersion of the numbers of passengers. Decisions regarding scheduling and the most efficient size of planes to use depend on the fluctuation in the passenger load. If this variation in number of passengers is large, bigger planes may be needed to avoid overcrowding on those days when the passenger load is extensive. The frequency table for P&P is as follows:

Class (passengers)	f (days)	M	fM	M^2	fM^2
50–59	3	54.5	163.5	2,970.25	8,910.75
60–69	7	64.5	451.5	4160.25	29,121.75
70–79	18	74.5	1,341.0	5,550.25	99,904.50
80–89	12	84.5	1,014.0	7,140.25	85,683.00
90–99	8	94.5	756.0	8,930.25	71,442.00
100–109	2	104.5	209.0	10,920.25	21,840.50
	$n = 50$		$\Sigma fM = 3{,}935.0$		$\Sigma fM^2 = 316{,}902.50$

Solution: We calculated $\overline{X}_g$ in an earlier example as

$$\overline{X}_g = \frac{\Sigma fM}{n} = \frac{3935}{50} = 78.7$$

Therefore, Formula (3.13) gives us

$$s^2 = \frac{\Sigma fM^2 - n\overline{X}^2}{n-1}$$

$$s^2 = \frac{316{,}902.50 - 50(78.7)^2}{49} = 147.31 \text{ passengers squared}$$

$$s = \sqrt{147.31} = 12.14 \text{ passengers}$$

Interpretation: The flight director can now decide whether the planes currently in use can accommodate fluctuations in passenger levels as measured by a standard deviation of 12.14. If not, perhaps larger planes will be used to accommodate any overflow that might otherwise occur on those days with heavy traffic.

Section Exercises

9. Daily absenteeism at your office seems to be increasing. Last year an average of 47.8 employees were absent each day, with a standard deviation of 14.7 employees. A sample of data was gathered for the current year and placed in the frequency table shown below. Calculate the mean, the median, the mode, and the standard deviation for these data and compare them to those for the previous year. What conclusions do you reach?

Number of Employees Absent	Days That Number Was Absent
20–29	5
30–39	9
40–49	8
50–59	10
60–69	12
70–79	11
80–89	8
90–99	3

10. In the past, completion time for a certain job task in the offices at Harmon Electronics have shown the following statistics in hours: a mean of 12.2, a median of 13.2, and a mode of 14.5. The variance was 8.21. More recent data are reflected in the frequency table below. Mr. Harmon hires you as an outside consultant to evaluate changes in employee efficiency. Calculate the corresponding statistics based on these data, and prepare a brief report. What conclusions do you offer?

Hours to Completion	Number of Times the Task Took This Long
5 and under 7	4
7 and under 9	8
9 and under 11	12
11 and under 13	8
13 and under 15	5
15 and under 17	2

3.6 Other Measures of Dispersion

Although the variance and the standard deviation are the most useful measures of dispersion in statistical analysis, there are other ways the dispersion of a data set might be measured. These additional measures of dispersion are **quartiles, deciles,** and **percentiles.**

Every data set has three quartiles that divide it into four equal parts. The first quartile is that value below which 25 percent of the observations fall, and above which the remaining 75 percent can be found. The second quartile is right in the middle. One-half the observations are below it and one-half the observations are above it; in this sense, it is the same as the median. The third quartile is that value below which 75 percent of the observations are located, and above which the remaining 25 percent can be found.

The determination of quartiles is often useful. Many graduate schools, for example, will admit only those students in the top 25 percent (third quartile) of their applicants. Corporations often wish to single out those plants whose poor production records place them below the bottom quartile. With only a little imagination, it is possible to envision numerous instances in which the determination of quartiles might prove beneficial.

Deciles separate a data set into 10 equal subsets, and percentiles produce 100 parts. The first decile is that observation below which 10 percent of the observations are found, while the remaining 90 percent are located above it. The first percentile is that value below which 1 percent of the observations are located, and the rest are above it. A similar interpretation can be applied to the rest of the deciles and percentiles. Each data set has 9 deciles and 99 percentiles.

A percentile and its location in an ordered array are identified by means of subscripts. For example, the 15th percentile is indicated as P_{15}, and its location in the ordered array is L_{15}.

To illustrate the calculation of percentiles, assume that we have observations for the number of shares for 50 stocks traded on the New York Stock Exchange, as shown in Table 3.4. Notice that the data have been placed in an ordered array. The location of the Pth percentile is found as

Location of a percentile
$$Lp = (n + 1)\frac{P}{100} \qquad [3.15]$$

where Lp is the location in the ordered array of the desired percentile
n is the number of observations
P is the desired percentile

Assume that we wish to calculate the 25th percentile, P_{25}, for the stocks in Table 3.4. We must first find its location in the ordered array.

$$L_{25} = (50 + 1)\frac{25}{100}$$
$$= 12.75$$

Table 3.4
Numbers of Shares Traded on the NYSE (in 100's)

3	10	19	27	34	38	48	56	67	74
4	12	**20**	29	34	39	48	59	67	74
7	14	**21**	31	36	43	52	62	69	76
9	15	25	31	37	45	53	63	72	79
10	17	27	34	38	47	56	64	73	80

The resulting value of 12.75 tells us that the 25th percentile is located 75 percent of the way between the 12th observation of 20 and the 13th observation of 21, or $P_{25} = 20 + 0.75 (21 - 20) = 20.75$.

If we wish to calculate the 35th percentile, we find

$$L_{35} = (50 + 1)\frac{35}{100}$$

$$= 17.85$$

The 35th percentile is 85 percent of the way between the 17th observation of 29 and the 18th observation of 31, or $P_{35} = 29 + (0.85)(31 - 29) = 30.7$. Thus, 35 percent of the observations are below 30.7, and the remaining 65 percent are above 30.7.

Returning to deciles and quartiles for a moment, note that the first decile is equal to P_{10}, that the second decile is equal to P_{20}, and so on. Additionally, the first quartile is the same as P_{25}, the second quartile equals P_{50}, and P_{75} locates the third quartile. With that in mind, the calculation of deciles and quartiles becomes simply a matter of determining the appropriate percentiles according to the rules that we have just established.

A unique measure of dispersion is the **interquartile range** (IQR). The IQR is the difference between the first quartile and the third quartile. That is, $P_{75} - P_{25}$. One-half of the observations lie within this range. It consists of the middle 50 percent of the observations in that it cuts off the lower 25 percent and the upper 25 percent of the data points. As a result, the IQR provides a measure of dispersion that is not heavily influenced by a few extreme observations. The interquartile range is illustrated in Figure 3.1.

Figure 3.1
The Interquartile Range

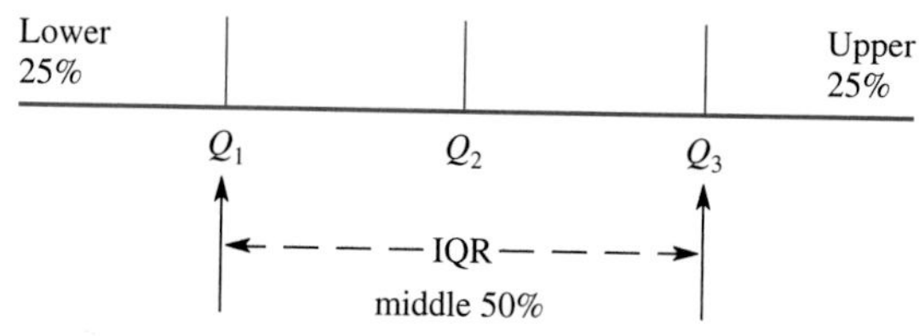

Section Exercises

11. Define in your own words:

a. The 80th percentile.
b. The fourth decile.
c. The third quartile.

12. Using the data from Table 3.4, calculate and interpret:

a. The interquartile range.
b. The median.
c. The 50th percentile.
d. The 70th percentile.
e. The third decile.

3.7 Common Uses for the Standard Deviation

As we have emphasized, the standard deviation is useful for describing a data set by measuring the extent to which the individual observations are spread out around their mean. There are at least two additional applications for the standard deviation: (1) Chebyshev's Theorem and (2) the Empirical Rule.

A. Chebyshev's Theorem

Chebyshev's Theorem (sometimes spelled Tchebysheff's Theorem) was formulated by the Russian mathematician P. L. Chebyshev (1821–1894). It states that for *any* data set, at least $1 - 1/K^2$ percent of the observations lie within K standard deviations of the mean, where K is any number greater than 1. Chebyshev's Theorem is expressed as

Chebyshev's Theorem
$$1 - \left[\frac{1}{K^2}\right] \qquad [3.16]$$

Thus, for example, if we form an interval from K = three standard deviations above the mean to three standard deviations below the mean, then at least

$$1 - \frac{1}{3^2} = 88.89\%$$

of all the observations will be within that interval.

Example 3.7 **Chebyshev's Theorem Applied to Pigs and People Airline**
Our earlier work in this chapter with the grouped data for P&P Airlines revealed a mean of 78.7 passengers per day, with a standard deviation of 12.14. In order to schedule times for a new route P&P opened, management wants to know how often the number of passengers is within K = two standard deviations of the mean, and what that interval is.

Solution: If we move two standard deviations $(2 \times 12.14) = 24.28$ passengers above and below the mean of 78.7, we will have an interval of $(78.7 - 24.28) = 54.42$ to $(78.7 + 24.28) = 102.98$ passengers. We can then be certain that at least

$$1 - \frac{1}{2^2} = 75\%$$

of the time, the number of daily passengers was between 54 and 103.

Interpretation: On at least 75 percent of the days (that is, 75 percent of 50 equals 37 days), the number of passengers was between 54 and 103. This provides the management of P&P with valuable information regarding how many passengers to prepare for in terms of in-flight operations.

B. The Normal Distribution and the Empirical Rule

More important, the standard deviation can be used to draw certain conclusions if the data set in question is *normally distributed.* The concept of a normal distribution is commonly encountered in statistical analysis and is of considerable importance. A thorough discussion of the normal distribution is presented in later chapters. However, an early introduction to this all-important concept will allow us to demonstrate a practical use for the standard deviation, and will set the basis for the more thorough investigation to come. A **normal distribution** is a distribution of continuous (not discrete) data that produces a bell-shaped, symmetrical curve like that shown in Figure 3.2.

Figure 3.2
A Normal Distribution

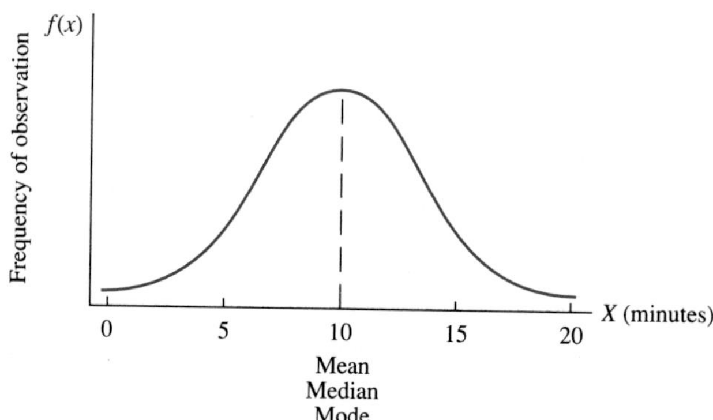

Assume that we have a large number of observations for the time, in minutes, that it takes skiers to complete a particular run. If the data are normally distributed, a graph of the frequency with which each observation occurs will take the shape of Figure 3.2. The observations at each extreme will occur relatively infrequently, but those observations closer to the middle will occur with increasing frequency, thereby producing the bell-shaped symmetrical curve. The modal observation, 10 in our case, is the one occurring with the greatest frequency and is therefore at the peak of the distribution. In a normal distribution, the mean, median, and the mode are all equal.

Of importance, one-half of the observations are above the mean and one-half are below it. This means that one-half of the area under the curve is to the left of the mean, and one-half of the area under the curve is to the right of the mean.

To illustrate how the standard deviation applies to the normal distribution, assume 1,000 skiers slalom down the bunny slope at Vail. The times for all skiers happen to be normally distributed, with a mean of $\mu = 10$ minutes and a standard deviation of $\sigma = -$ 2 minutes. The **Empirical Rule** tells us that if we include all observations within one standard deviation of the mean (one standard deviation above the mean and one standard deviation below the mean) we will encompass 68.3 percent of all the observations. That is, no matter what the mean is and no matter what the standard deviation is, we can be certain that 68.3 percent of the observations lie within one standard deviation of the mean if the observations are normally distributed.

Since the skiers averaged 10 minutes to complete the run, moving one standard deviation (that is, 2 minutes) above and below this mean of 10 produces a range of 8 to 12 minutes. Thus, according to the Empirical Rule, 683 (68.3 percent of the 1,000) skiers took between 8 and 12 minutes to get down the mountain.

Of course, if we move more than one standard deviation above and below the mean, we will encompass a larger percentage of the observations. The Empirical Rule specifies that

68.3 percent of the observations lie within plus or minus one standard deviation of the mean.

95.5 percent of the observations lie within plus or minus two standard deviations of the mean.

99.7 percent of the observations lie within plus or minus three standard deviations of the mean.

Given the skiers' times, one standard deviation (2 minutes) above and below the mean of 10 yields a range of 8 to 12 minutes. Two standard deviations (4 minutes) above and below the mean of 10 yields a range of 6 to 14 minutes. Three standard deviations (6 minutes) yields a range of 4 to 16 minutes. This is shown in Figure 3.3.

Figure 3.3
Normally Distributed Times of 1,000 Skiers

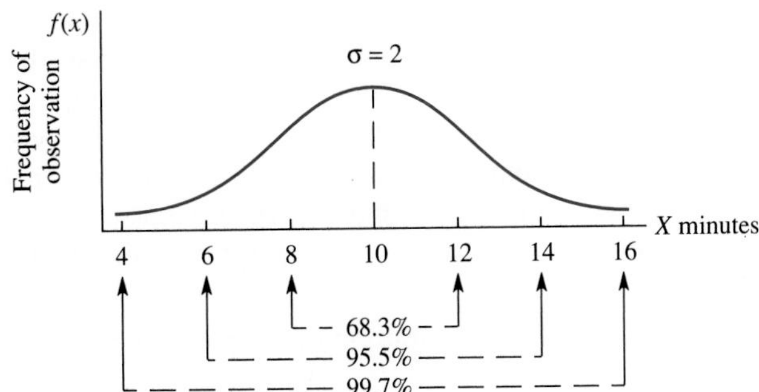

According to the Empirical Rule, 997 of the 1,000 skiers took between 4 minutes and 16 minutes to complete the run. Thus, only 3 of the 1,000 skiers were either very good skiers and took less than 4 minutes or were lousy skiers and took more than 16 minutes. An observation more than three standard deviations from the mean (above or below it) is a rarity and happens less than 1 percent of the time if the data are normally distributed.

It is also important to remember that the Empirical Rule describes the total area under the normal curve that is found within a given range. Not only did 68.3 percent of all the skiers take between 8 and 12 minutes to get safely down the mountain, but, in addition, 68.3 percent of all the area under the normal curve lies within the same 8- to 12-minute range.

If the observations are highly dispersed, the bell-shaped curve will be flattened and spread out. Assume a second group of skiers also averaged 10 minutes slushing over the moguls, but had a standard deviation of 4 minutes. The times of the second group are more dispersed than those of the first. The faster ski times were farther below 10, and the slower ski times were farther above 10 than the first group. This greater dispersion would be reflected in a normal distribution curve that is more spread out, as shown in Figure 3.4.

Figure 3.4
Two Normal Distributions with Equal Means but Different Standard Deviations

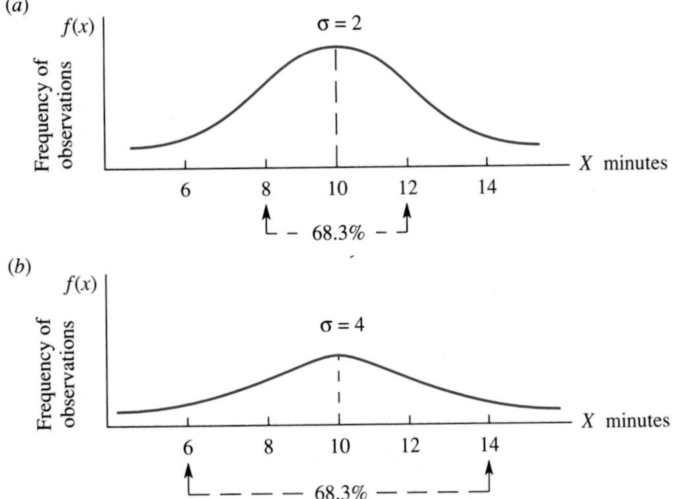

Both distributions are centered at the mean of $\mu = 10$ minutes, but the one with the greater distribution of $\sigma = 4$ minutes is more spread out than the set of observations with less dispersion. To encompass 68.3 percent of the observations in this more dispersed group, it is necessary to include all those within the interval from 6 to 14.

C. Skewness

Not all distributions are normal. Some are **skewed** left or right. In Figure 3.5, we find distribution curves for people's weights. In Figure 3.5(*a*), the distribution is said to be skewed right. It would seem that a few of the heavier people at the upper end of the weight scale (perhaps some larger males) pulled the tail of the distribution to the right. In a second distribution of weights shown in Figure 3.5(*b*), a few diminutive females pull the distribution toward the lower end, causing it to be skewed left.

Figure 3.5 Skewed Distribution of People's Weights

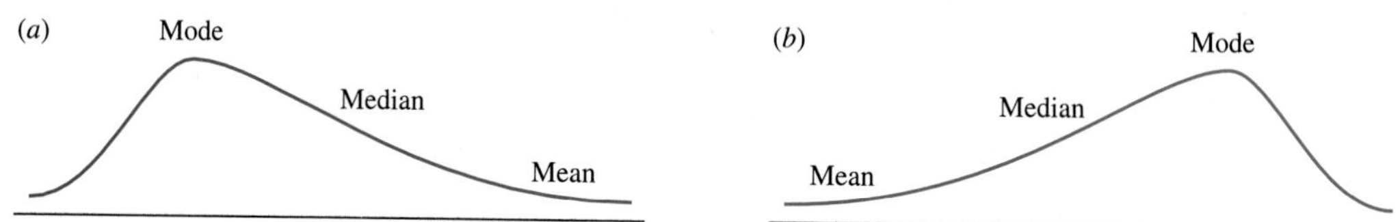

In both cases, the mode is, by definition, that observation occurring with the greatest frequency. It is therefore at the peak of the distribution. However, as we noted earlier, by its very nature, the mean is most affected by extreme observations. Therefore, it is pulled in the direction of the skewness more than is the median, which takes up residence somewhere between the mean and the mode.

Skewness can be measured by the **Pearsonian coefficient of skewness.**

Coefficient of skewness $$P = \frac{3(\overline{X} - \text{median})}{s} \qquad [3.17]$$

If $P < 0$, the data are skewed left, if $P > 0$, they are skewed right; if $P = 0$, they are normally distributed.

Example 3.8 **Skewness for P&P Passengers**

Using the grouped data from P&P's passenger list, we calculated $\overline{X} = 78.7$, $s = 12.14$, and the median $= 78.33$. Given this information, the CEO for P&P can plainly see that the data are skewed right, since the mean exceeds the median. In addition, he also wants a measure of the extent or degree of skewness.

Solution: We have

$$P = \frac{3(78.7 - 78.33)}{12.14} = 0.03$$

Interpretation: Since $P > 0$, the data for P&P are, as presumed, skewed right. The extent to which they are skewed is reflected in the value of the Pearsonian coefficient. If we were to graph the data, they would appear as in Figure 3.5(*a*).

D. Coefficient of Variation

As we have emphasized, an important use of the standard deviation is to serve as a measure of dispersion. However, certain limitations apply. When considering two or more distributions that have significantly different means, or that are measured in different units, it is dangerous to draw conclusions regarding dispersion merely on the basis of the standard deviation. It is like violating the old adage about comparing apples and oranges.

We must therefore often turn to the **coefficient of variation** (CV), which serves as a *relative* measure of dispersion. The coefficient of variation assesses the degree of dispersion of a data set relative to its mean. It is computed by dividing the standard deviation of a distribution by its mean, and multiplying by 100.

Coefficient of variation

$$CV = \frac{s}{\bar{X}}(100) \qquad [3.18]$$

The grouped data for P&P reported a mean of 78.7 passengers per day, with a standard deviation of 12.14 passengers. Presume that P&P also collects data over the same time period for the number of miles flown by the airline and that the daily mean and standard deviation prove to be 1,267.5 and 152.7, respectively. The higher standard deviation for miles flown might suggest that these data exhibit a far greater variation.

However, if we calculate the coefficient of variation for passengers, we find it to be

$$CV = \frac{12.14}{78.70}(100) = 15.43$$

while that for miles is only

$$CV = \frac{152.7}{1267.5}(100) = 12.05$$

It is clear that, in comparing the variation in two vastly different data sets, it is wise to use the coefficient of variation and not just the standard deviation.

Section Exercises

13. A data set for the fill weights of 1000 bags of Happy Pooch dog food has a mean of 50 pounds and a standard deviation of 2.3 pounds. The data are not known to be normally distributed. The makers of Happy Pooch hope that at least 750 of those bags weigh between 45.4 and 54.6 pounds. What assurance can you give them?

14. A normally distributed data set has a mean of 5,000 and a standard deviation of 450. What percentage of the observations lie:

    a. Between 4550 and 5450?
    b. Between 4100 and 5900?
    c. Between 3650 and 6350?
    d. Above 6350?
    e. Below 4550?

15. Shard Lumber cuts logs to a mean length of 20 feet, with a standard deviation of 3.5 feet. If the cuts are normally distributed, what percentage of the logs are less than:

    a. 16.5 feet?
    b. 13 feet?

16. Data on ages of 100 top executives for Fortune 500 firms reveal a mean age of 56.2 years and a standard deviation of 12.7 years. Their mean income is $89,432, with s = $16,097. Which variable, age or income, exhibits the greater variation?

17. If the median income in Exercise 16 is $87,567,

    a. Are the data skewed right, skewed left, or normally distributed?

    b. What is the Perasonian coefficient of skewness?

Solved Problems

1. **Information Pays** A 1996 issue of *Inc. Technology* reported that Information Please, a new firm selling information over the Internet, recorded the number of "hits" it had on an hourly basis as 47, 52, 69, 72, 112, 36, 28, 68, 69, and 41. Presume that the manager wishes to evaluate these data on the basis of their measures of central tendency and measures of dispersion.

   The mean is

$$\bar{X} = \frac{\Sigma X_i}{n} = \frac{594}{10} = 59.4$$

Given the ordered array 28, 36, 41, 47, 52, 68, 69, 69, 72, 112, the median position is

$$\text{Median position} = \frac{n+1}{2} = 5.5$$

and the median is the average of the fifth and sixth observations or $52 + 68/2 = 60$. The mode is the observation that occurred most frequently, 69. The variance is

$$s^2 = \frac{\Sigma(X_i - \bar{X})^2}{n-1} = \frac{5264.4}{9} = 584.933$$

and the standard deviation is $\sqrt{584.933} = 24.185$.

2. **Weighing In** Members of the Heart-to-Heart Health Club are charged dues on the basis of their average weight. Of the 60 members, 12 weighed 110 pounds, 25 weighed 120 pounds, 18 tipped the scale at 150 and the rest registered 180 pounds. If the members must pay $5 for each pound they weigh on the average, how much must each fork over?

   Since each weight category contained a different number of members, the weighted mean is necessary.

Pounds (X)	Number of Members (W)	XW
110	12	1320
120	25	3000
150	18	2700
180	5	900
	60 = ΣW	7920 = ΣXW

$$\bar{X}_w = \frac{\Sigma XW}{\Sigma W} = 132 \text{ pounds}$$

Thus, each member must pay $132 \times 5 = \$660$.

3. **Growing Pains** Employee dissatisfaction at Bates Electronics is reflected in the number of official complaints over the past four months: 23, 41, 37 and 49. Based on these data, what is the average monthly increase in complaints?

The geometric mean, whose job it is to determine average percentage change over time, requires that we first determine what percentage each number is of the previous month:

Month	Complaints	Percentage of Previous Month
1	23	—
2	41	1.78
3	37	0.90
4	49	1.32

Then,

$$GM = \sqrt[n]{(X_i)(X_2)\ldots(X_n)} = \sqrt[3]{(1.78)(0.9)(1.32)} = 128$$

Then, 1.28 − 1.00 = 28 percent mean monthly increase in complaints.

4. **People Who Care** Statisticians for the Meals on Wheels program, which brings hot meals to shut-ins, want to evaluate their services. The number of daily meals they provide is shown in the frequency table below.

Number of Meals Per Day	Number of Days	M	fM	fM^2
0–5	3	2.5	7.5	18.75
6–11	6	8.5	51.0	433.50
12–17	5	14.5	72.5	1,051.25
18–23	8	20.5	164.0	3,362.00
24–29	2	26.5	53.0	1,404.50
30–35	3	32.5	97.5	3,168.75
	27		445.5	9,438.75

The mean, median, and modal number of meals are

$$\bar{X}_g = \frac{\Sigma fM}{n} = \frac{445.5}{27} = 16.5 \text{ meals per day}$$

$$\begin{aligned}\text{Median} &= L_{md} + \left[\frac{n/2 - F}{f_{md}}\right](c)\\ &= 12 + \left[\frac{27/2 - 9}{5}\right](6)\\ &= 17.4 \text{ meals}\end{aligned}$$

$$\begin{aligned}\text{Mode} &= L_{mo} + \left[\frac{D_a}{D_a + D_b}\right](c)\\ &= 18 + \left[\frac{3}{3 + 6}\right](6)\\ &= 20 \text{ meals}\end{aligned}$$

The variance and standard deviation are

$$\begin{aligned}s^2 &= \frac{\Sigma fM^2 - n\bar{X}^2}{n - 1}\\ &= \frac{9438.75 - 27(16.5)^2}{27 - 1}\\ &= 80.31\end{aligned}$$

$$s = \sqrt{80.31} = 8.96 \text{ meals}$$

List of Formulas

[3.1]	$\mu = \dfrac{X_1 + X_2 + X_3 + \cdots + X_N}{N} = \dfrac{\sum_{i=1}^{N} X_i}{N}$	Population mean.
[3.2]	$\bar{X} = \dfrac{X_1 + X_2 + X_3 + \cdots + X_n}{n} = \dfrac{\sum_{i=1}^{n} X_i}{n}$	Sample mean.
[3.3]	$\text{Median position} = \dfrac{n+1}{2}$	Determines the position of the median in an ordered array.
[3.4]	$\bar{X}_w = \dfrac{\Sigma XW}{\Sigma W}$	Determines the weighted mean.
[3.5]	$GM = \sqrt[n]{(X_1)(X_2)\ldots(X_n)}$	Calculates the average percentage change.
[3.6]	$\sigma^2 = \dfrac{\Sigma(X_i - \mu)^2}{N}$	Variance for a population.
[3.7]	$\sigma = \sqrt{\sigma^2}$	Population standard deviation.
[3.8]	$s^2 = \dfrac{\Sigma(X_i - \bar{X})^2}{n}$	Sample variance.
[3.9]	$s = \sqrt{s^2}$	Sample standard deviation.
[3.10]	$\bar{X}_g = \dfrac{\Sigma fM}{n}$	Mean for grouped data.
[3.11]	$\text{Median} = L_{md} + \left[\dfrac{n/2 - F}{f_{md}}\right](C)$	Median for grouped data.
[3.12]	$\text{Mode} = L_{mo} + \left[\dfrac{D_a}{D_a - D_b}\right](C)$	Mode for grouped data.
[3.13]	$s^2 = \dfrac{\Sigma fM^2 - n\bar{X}^2}{n-1}$	Sample variance for grouped data.
[3.14]	$s = \sqrt{s^2}$	Standard deviation of grouped data.
[3.15]	$L_p = (n+1)\dfrac{P}{100}$	Location of a percentile.
[3.16]	$1 - \left[\dfrac{1}{K^2}\right]$	Chebyshev's Theorem.
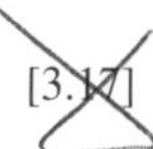 [3.17]	$P = \dfrac{3(\bar{X} - \text{median})}{s}$	Coefficient of skewness.
[3.18]	$CV = \dfrac{s}{\bar{X}}(100)$	Coefficient of variation.

Chapter Exercises

18. Stock prices are quoted in eighths of dollars such that, for example, 5 1/8 is $5.125, 5 1/4 is $5.25, 5 3/8 is $5.375, and so on up to 5 7/8, which is $5.875. Below is a sample of seven closing prices of stocks taken from *The Wall Street Journal* of October 8, 1997.

Wal-Mart	27 3/8	General Mills	69 7/8
Disney	42 5/8	Toys R Us	38 5/8
Mobil	69 7/8	Dow Jones	29 1/4
General Motors	39 1/2		

a. Calculate the mean, the median, and the mode. Interpret each statistic. What does each tell you? Why are they different if they are all averages?
b. Calculate and interpret the variance and the standard deviation.
c. Calculate and interpret the interquartile range.
d. Calculate and interpret the fortieth percentile.

19. The Snowflake markets ski boots in San Luis Obispo, California. Of the last 100 pairs sold, 4 were size 9, 33 were size 9 1/2, 26 were size 10, 29 were size 10 1/2, and 8 were size 13. Comment on the use of the mean, median, and mode as measures of central tendency and the use of each in making decisions regarding sizes to hold in inventory. Calculate each measure.

20. As interest rates fell in early 1997, a sample of mortgage rates for 15-year mortgages at local lending institutions in Peoria, Illinois, was found to be

7.1%, 7.3%, 7.0%, 6.9%, 6.6%, 6.9%, 6.5%, 7.3%, 6.85%

a. Calculate and interpret the mean, the median, and the mode.
b. Are these data skewed left, or right, or are they normally distributed? Calculate the Pearsonian coefficient as a measure of the skewness.
c. Calculate and interpret the variance and the standard deviation.

21. A survey of lending institutions in an urban center near Peoria (see previous problem) revealed mortgage rates of

7.1%, 7.3%, 6.3%, 6.7%, 6.8%, 6.85%, 7.5%

a. Are mortgage rates higher in Peoria or the other urban center?
b. Which city seems to have the most consistent rates among institutions?
c. Calculate and interpret the Pearsonian coefficient of skewness.

22. Alan Munday manufactures a paint sealant for automobiles in the Denver area. He uses four different chemicals in the production process. To make his product, Munday must use 2 gallons of calcimine which costs $2.50 per gallon, 1/2 gallon of kalsolite at $1.25 per gallon, 1 gallon of binder costing $0.75 per gallon, and 3 gallons of drying oil at $2.00 per gallon. Calculate the cost of a gallon of the sealant.

23. The May 31, 1997, issue of *Business Week* reported that the number of transactions in billions performed at the nation's ATM banking facilities were

1991	3.9	1994	4.5
1992	4.1	1995	6.5
1993	4.3	1996	6.5

The banking industry intends to prepare for 8 billion transactions by 1998. Will that be sufficient to handle the level of activity that you predict for that year?

24. The Noah Fence Company sells four types of fencing to local suburbanites. Grade A costs Noah $5.00 per running foot to install, grade B costs $3.50, grade C costs $2.50, and grade D costs $2.00. Yesterday, Noah installed 100 yards of A, 150 yards of B, 75 yards of C, and 200 yards of D. What was Noah's average installation cost per foot?

25. A sample of weekly sales receipts for Pig-In-A-Poke Bar-B-Q are, in hundreds of dollars,

43.3, 54.2, 34.8, 42.9, 49.2, 29.5, 28.6

An advertising program designed to even out sales is implemented. A subsequent sample of sales proves to be

45.5, 39.5, 35.7, 36.7, 42.6, 42.14

Did the advertising campaign achieve its goal of smoothing weekly sales?

26. Bill Karl purchased 20 shares of stock at $15 each, 50 shares at $20, 100 shares at $30, and 75 shares at $35.

a. What is the total amount of his investment?
b. What is the average price per share?

27. The ages of 50 of the nation's CEOs of top corporations reported in the May 24, 1997, issue of *Forbes* produced the following frequency table.

a. Calculate and interpret the mean, the median, and the mode.
b. Calculate and interpret the variance and the standard deviation.

Ages	Frequency
50 and under 55	8
55 and under 60	13
60 and under 65	15
65 and under 70	10
70 and under 75	3
75 and under 80	1

28. The same issue of *Forbes* (see the previous problem) also provided data on salaries in thousands of dollars. The following frequency table resulted:

Salary (in $1,000's)	Frequency
90 and under 440	9
440 and under 790	11
790 and under 1140	10
1140 and under 1490	8
1490 and under 1840	4
1840 and under 2190	3
2190 and under 2540	5

a. Calculate the mean, median, and mode. Interpret your answers.
b. Are salaries as dispersed as ages in the previous problem?

29. Janna Vice uses two different machines to produce paper chutes for Kodak copiers. A sample of the chutes from the first machine measured 12.2, 11.9, 11.8, 12.1, 11.9, 12.4, 11.3, and 12.3 inches. Chutes made with the second machine measured 12.2, 11.9, 11.5, 12.1, 12.2, 11.9, and 11.8 inches. Janna must use the machine with the greater consistency in sizes of the chutes. Which machine should she use?

30. Scores on the first two statistics tests you took were normally distributed and reported means of 90 for test A and 50 for test B. Would you hope for a high or a low standard deviation for test A? Would you want a high or low standard deviation for test B if you feel that you did well on the test? Why? Draw a graph illustrating the logic in your responses.

31. The following sample data have been obtained for the number of daily customers at Rosie's Flower Shoppe:

34, 45, 23, 34, 26, 32, 31, 41

Calculate the variance, the standard deviation, and the interquartile range.

32. The following is a sample of the earnings per share, in dollars, for stocks listed on the New York Stock Exchange:

1.12, 1.43, 2.17, −1.19, 2.87, −1.49

Calculate the variance and the standard deviation and the interquartile range. Interpret each.

33. The hours worked each week by Ronnie over the past two months are

52 48 37 54 48 15 42 12

Assuming these are sample data, calculate:

a. The mean.
b. The median.
c. The mode.
d. Which is probably a better measure of the center point?

34. Using Ronnie's work hours from the previous problem, calculate and interpret:

a. The range.
b. The variance.
c. The standard deviation.
d. The first quartile.
e. The 25th percentile.
f. The interquartile range.

35. The disc jockeys on KAYS claim they play more songs each hour than their crosstown rivals on KROC. Over the last 24 hours, data on the number of songs played for both stations were collected and tabulated. Use the data to prepare a report comparing the two stations. Your finished report is to be submitted to the Federal Communications Commission, and is to contain references to measures of central tendency and measures of dispersion.

Number of Hits per Hour	KAYS	KROC
5–10	2	4
11–16	4	5
17–22	6	7
23–28	8	5
29–34	2	2
35–40	2	1

36. *The Wall Street Journal* described a dispute between management and the local labor union regarding the efficiency and productivity of the workers. Management argued that it was taking the employees more than 20 minutes to complete a certain job task. If 85 employees are

timed, yielding the results tabulated, is management correct based on this sample? Compute all three measures of central tendency.

Class (number of minutes)	Frequency (number of employees)
5 and under 7	2
7 and under 9	8
9 and under 11	10
11 and under 13	15
13 and under 15	17
15 and under 17	14
17 and under 19	7
19 and under 21	9
21 and under 23	3

37. Management in the previous exercise is also worried that employees' performance is too erratic; there is too much variation in the amount of time it takes the workers to complete the task. Identify and compute the statistic that would address management's concern.

38. Given the following nine tests scores for Professor Pundit's economics class, compute the Pearsonian coefficient of skewness. Assume these represent sample data.

80 83 87 85 90 86 84 82 88

39. Unionists at a Ford Motor Company plant in Toledo argue that, in violation of the labor agreement, production line workers average a lower hourly wage with greater variability than do office workers. A sample of $n = 10$ is taken from each class of workers, yielding the following values. Do they support the unionists' charge?

Workers	Production Workers	Office Workers
1	12.15	15.12
2	18.17	18.42
3	19.42	17.12
4	15.17	16.92
5	18.63	18.15
6	16.42	15.81
7	15.49	19.12
8	18.73	19.15
9	19.12	18.73
10	18.36	19.66

40. Two competing brands of running shoes were tested for wear. Each reported the following number of hours of use before significant wear was detected.

Brand A	Brand B
97	78
83	56
75	87
82	54
98	89
65	65
75	

a. Which shoe seems to exhibit the longest wear?
b. Which shoe seems to have a quality control program which produces the most consistency in their wear?

41. Manly Bankford works as a stockbroker for E. F. Hutton. His records show that the rates of return (in percent) on two securities for 10 selected months were

Security 1	5.6	7.2	6.3	6.3	7.1
	8.2	7.9	5.3	6.2	6.2
Security 2	7.5	7.3	6.2	8.3	8.2
	8.0	8.1	7.3	5.9	5.3

a. Which security might be better for those clients interested in a higher return?
b. Which security should Manly advise to those clients who prefer less risk?

42. The price-earning ratios for 30 different stocks trading on the New York Stock Exchange (NYSE) are shown here.

4.8	5.2	7.6	5.7	6.2	6.6	7.5	8.0	9.0	7.7
3.7	7.3	6.7	7.7	8.2	9.2	8.3	7.3	8.2	6.5
5.4	9.3	10.0	7.3	8.2	9.7	8.4	4.7	7.4	8.3

a. Calculate the mean and the standard deviation.
b. According to Chebyshev's Theorem, at least how many price-earnings ratios lie within two standard deviations of the mean?
c. How many actually do lie within two standard deviations of the mean?

43. The local mechanic at Vinney's Auto Shop and Charm School tells you that the repairs on your car will cost $714.12. Industry data show that the average bill for repairs similar to yours in $615, with a standard deviation of $31. What might you conclude about Vinney's rates if you assume that repairs are normally distributed?

44. Given below is the frequency table of monthly sales in dollars for skydiving equipment in the southern California market (figures are in hundreds).

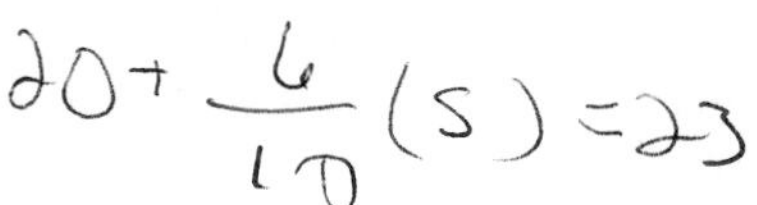

Class (in $100's)	Number of Months
5 and under 10	5
10 and under 15	7
15 and under 20	9
20 and under 25	10
25 and under 30	8
30 and under 35	3
35 and under 40	2

a. You are chief statistician for the Bounce Twice Parachute Company, and your manager requests a breakdown on the frequency of sales. He is interested in that value below which at most 60 percent of the observations fell, along with a complete quartile breakdown.
b. In addition, you feel that it would be useful to determine the values of the 10th and 90th percentiles.

45. A supervisor at an assembly plant received the following efficiency ratings over the 12 months

56, 69, 48, 75, 65, 72, 81, 43, 61, 42, 36, 52

a. If she wishes to create the most favorable impression, should she report the mean, the median, or the modal rating in her annual self-evaluation?
b. How consistent have her ratings been?

Computer Exercises

Access the file OUTPUT from your data disk. It contains 100 observations of weekly output for Leisure Sports, a Cleveland-based manufacturer of sporting goods. Ernst Rawls, Director of Corporate Operations, is concerned about meeting production schedules established at the meeting last November that called for an average weekly output of at least 1000 units. Mr. Rawls must also guard against large variations in output from week to week.

Using your chosen computer software, prepare a report for Mr. Rawls as described in Appendix 1. Include all relevant descriptive statistics, analysis of the findings and your conclusions and recommendations.

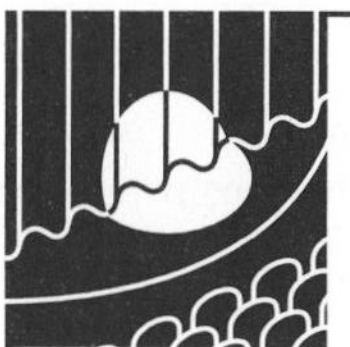

CURTAIN CALL

In Setting the Stage at the beginning of this chapter you were to function as an investment analyst to evaluate the three funds offered by Janus. Assume that the funds yielded the returns shown here.

Year	Venture	Income	Growth
1	14.2%	9.2%	22.2%
2	9.2	10.5	15.1
3	19.9	11.5	10.5
4	21.5	12.4	10.8
5	22.8	15.8	11.8
6	25.1	17.2	12.8

Using as many of the descriptive tools presented in this chapter as possible, provide a thorough comparative description of each fund. Include all the measures of central tendency and measures of dispersion. What conclusions can you reach regarding the performance of each fund?

If your client invested 30 percent of his portfolio in Venture, 50 percent in Income, and the rest in Growth, what would be the average annual return? What would you project the returns for each fund to be in year 7?

From the Stage to Real Life

The common form of reporting mutual fund yields is as 1-year, 3-year, 5-year, and 10-year returns. Here we will look at funds in the Vanguard Group (www.vanguard.com). At the Home Page, select the "mutual funds" icon. Then click on "funds by category." You will find 1-year, 3-year, 5-year, and 10-year returns for individual funds along with the Standard & Poor's index. The Vanguard Funds are grouped into Growth, Growth and Income, and other categories. Choose 5 specific funds from each of the Growth and Growth and Income categories and the Standard & Poor's data at this site. Using descriptive tools in this chapter and in Chapter 2, provide comparative descriptions of each fund to the Standard & Poor's results.

After you have completed your analyses, you might want to compare your techniques to analyses provided by some popular "Investor Guide" sites:

Net Worth Mutual Fund Market Manager	*http://networth.quicken.com/investments*
Mutual Fund Investor's Center	*www.mfea.com*
Tradeline Mutual Fund Center	*http://nestegg.iddis.com*

These sites have links to the home pages of major fund companies. You may wish to compare Vanguard Funds with those of another company like Fidelity or Dreyfus.

CHAPTER 4

Principles of Probability

Chapter Blueprint

Many business decisions rest on the possible outcomes of those decisions. This chapter examines the ways in which we can establish the likelihood associated with those outcomes. By determining the likelihood, or probability, of future events, we can greatly reduce risk in the decision-making process.

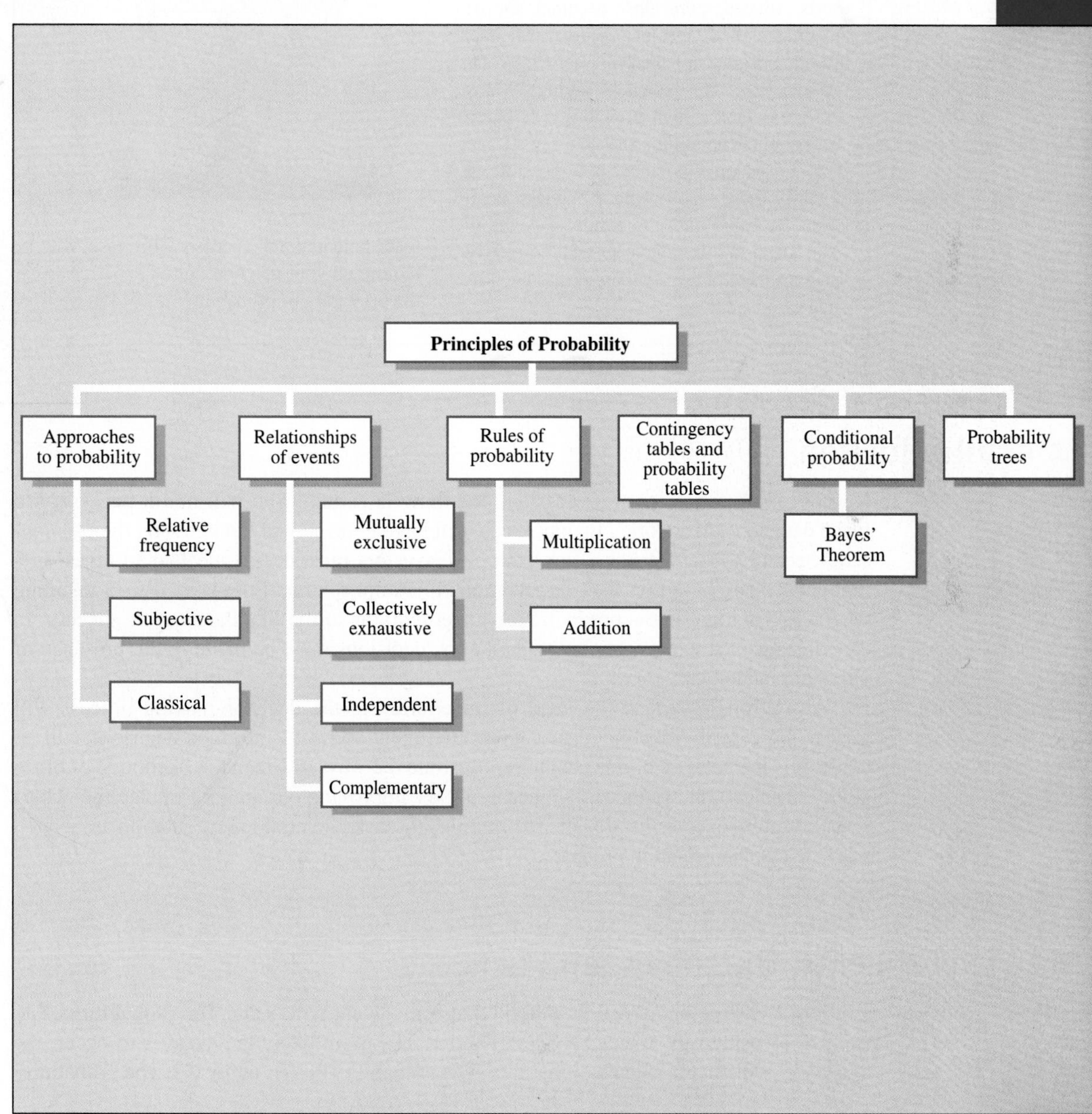

SETTING THE STAGE

The National Ski Association studied the financial impact of location on the 850 ski resorts in the United States (*Forbes,* May 1996). The purpose was to determine whether a resort located close to an urban center attracted more skiers or enjoyed higher profits than one in a more isolated locale. The comparison also included resorts situated quite close to other similar resorts—called cluster resorts. Michael Berry, president of the National Ski Areas Association, was quoted as saying, "Many ski areas face a high probability of bankruptcy in the upcoming seasons."

Based on this study, it is possible to identify those resorts whose financial positions are more likely to exhibit a downhill trend, and to allow them to take corrective actions that might lift their economic fortunes.

As a consultant hired by Berry, you have the job of providing a comparative evaluation of the future of these resorts and

their potential for success. This task will require all your newly acquired expertise in the principles of probability.

4.1 Introduction

Regardless of your chosen profession, one thing is certain. You will find it necessary to make decisions. More often than not, you will have to do so without knowing the full consequences of those decisions. For example, investors must decide whether to invest in a particular stock based on their expectations of future returns. Entrepreneurs, in deciding whether to market a new product, face uncertainty as to the likelihood of its success. In each instance, as with most business matters, decisions must be made in the presence of uncertain outcomes.

Any effort to reduce the level of uncertainty in the decision-making process will greatly increase the likelihood that more intelligent and well-informed decisions will be made. It is the purpose of this chapter to illustrate the ways in which the likelihood or probability of uncertain events can be measured. By improving our ability to judge the occurrence of future events, we are able to minimize the risk and perilous speculation associated with the decision-making process.

4.2 Experiments, Outcomes, and Sets

Probability is the numerical likelihood that some event will occur. The probability of an event is measured by values between 0 and 1. The more likely the event is to occur, the closer to 1 will be its assigned probability. The probability of a certainty is 1. The probability of an impossibility is 0. We could write this as

$$P(\text{certain event}) = 1$$
$$P(\text{impossible event}) = 0$$
$$\text{Thus, } 0 \leq P(E_i) \leq 1$$

where E_i is some event.

The probability that the sun will rise tomorrow is very high—quite close to 1. The probability you will pass this course without studying is, at the other extreme, close to zero.

> **Probability** Probability is the numerical likelihood, measured between 0 and 1, that an event will occur.

The process that produces the event is called an experiment. An **experiment** is any well-defined action leading to a single, well-defined **outcome.** Rolling a die (one-half of a pair of dice) is an experiment. The well-defined outcome is a number from 1 to 6. An experiment might consist of examining a product to determine if it meets certain manufacturing specifications. The outcome is either (1) it is defective or (2) it is not defective.

The set of all possible outcomes for an experiment is the **sample space.** The sample space for rolling a die is

$$\text{SS} = (1,\ 2,\ 3,\ 4,\ 5,\ 6)$$

while the sample space for the experiment of flipping a coin is

$$\text{SS} = (\text{heads},\ \text{tails})$$

The probability that one of the events in the sample space will occur is equal to 1. If a die is rolled, the outcome must be a number between 1 and 6. Since this is a certainty, it can be stated that

$$\sum P(E_i) = 1$$

4.3 Approaches to Probability

Probability theory occupies a prominent position in many business matters. Insurance and actuarial practices are firmly based on the principles of probability theory. The life insurance rates we pay depend on mortality tables, which are based on the probabilities of death at specific ages. Other forms of insurance rates such as property and auto insurance are similarly determined. Probability also plays a role in estimating the number of defective units in the manufacturing process, the likelihood of receiving payments on accounts receivable, and the potential sales of a new product. Even professional odds-makers for sporting events must have firm understanding of probability theory.

Despite the widespread application of the principles of probability, there are only three generally accepted ways to approach probability: (1) the relative frequency (or posterior) approach, (2) the subjective approach, and (3) the classical (or a priori) approach.

The **relative frequency approach** uses past data that have been empirically observed. It notes the frequency with which some event has occurred in the past and estimates the probability of its reoccurrence on the basis of these historic data. The probability of an event based on the relative frequency approach is determined by

Relative frequency	$P(E) = \dfrac{\text{Number of times the event has occurred in the past}}{\text{Total number of observations}}$	[4.1]

For example, assume that during the last calendar year there were 50 births at a local hospital. Thiry-two of the little new arrivals were baby girls. The relative frequency approach reveals that the probability the next birth (or any randomly selected birth) is a girl is

$$P(\text{Girl}) = \frac{\text{Number of girls born last year}}{\text{Total number of births}} = \frac{32}{50}$$

As another example, a New York importer of Irish crystal receives shipments of boxes each containing three items. The data for the past 100 boxes indicating the number of items in each box that were damaged are reported in the table. They show for example, that in 40 of the boxes, no items were damaged while in 12 of the boxes all three items were broken.

Outcome (E_i) (number of defects)	Number of Boxes	$P(E_i)$
0	40	40/100 = 0.40
1	27	27/100 = 0.27
2	21	21/100 = 0.21
3	12	12/100 = 0.12
	100	1.00

In the past, 21 of the total 100 boxes contained exactly two damaged items. The relative frequency approach would then assign a probability that two items in any given box are damaged as $P(2) = 21/100 = 0.21$. The probability for each individual outcome is shown in the last column, which sums to 1.

A common problem with the relative frequency approach results when estimates are made with an insufficient number of observations. For example, assume that both flights you booked on an airline last year were late in arriving at their destinations. You therefore conclude that the flight you are to take next month on the same airline will also be late. Although such inferences are common, there is not sufficient data to draw such a conclusion, and basing decisions on such inferences must be avoided.

In many instances past data are not available. It is therefore not possible to calculate probability from previous performance. The only alternative is to estimate probability on the basis of our best judgment. This **subjective approach** requires the assignment of the probability of some event on the basis of the best available evidence. In many instances, this may be nothing more than an educated guess. The subjective approach is used when we want to assign probability to an event that has never occurred. The probability that a woman will be elected president of the United States is an example. Since there are no past data to rely on, we must examine our opinions and beliefs to obtain a subjective estimation.

Of the three methods of assessing probability, the **classical approach** is the one most often associated with gambling and games of chance. The classical probability of an event

E is determined as

Classical approach	$P(E) = \dfrac{\text{Number of ways the event can occur}}{\text{Total number of possible outcomes}}$	[4.2]

Even without a discussion of classical probability, you may be aware that the probability of getting a head in the single flip of a fair coin is 1/2. This can be illustrated using Formula (4.2) as

$$P(\text{head}) = \frac{\text{Number of ways the event can occur}}{\text{Total number of possible outcomes}} = \frac{1}{2}$$

There is only one way that the event can occur (you get a head), and only two possible outcomes (a head or a tail). In similar fashion, the probability of rolling a 3 with a six-sided die is

$$P(3) = \frac{\text{Number of ways the event can occur}}{\text{Total number of possible outcomes}} = \frac{1}{6}$$

There is only one way that the event can occur (you roll a 3), and six possible outcomes.

Classical probability involves the determination of the probability of some event in an a priori (before the fact) manner. Thus, *before* drawing a card from a deck of 52 cards, it can be determined that the probability of drawing an ace is

$$P(\text{ace}) = \frac{\text{Number of ways the event can occur}}{\text{Total number of possible outcomes}} = \frac{4}{52}$$

Section Exercises

1. Which approach to probability is appropriate for each of the experiments listed below? Explain why you answered as you did.

a. The Dow-Jones Index of stock prices will close up today.
b. A unit of output will be defective.
c. Rolling a 6 with a die.
d. The sun will nova.

2. Cite three business examples for each of the three approaches to probability.

3. The accompanying table shows the number of computers sold daily by a retail store.

Number of Computers Sold	Number of Days
0	12
1	43
2	18
3	20
4	25

Determine the probability that the number sold today is:

a. 2.
b. Less than 3.
c. More than 1.
d. At least 1.

4. During the past four Super Bowls, the coin flip to start the game resulted in heads each time. Your coach tells you that calling tails this time will increase the likelihood you will win the flip. Is he right or wrong? Fully explain your answer.
5. Which approach to probability did you use in the proceding problem? Explain.
6. Over the past year weekly sales at Petunia's Pet Shoppe have been "low" 16 weeks, "fair" 27 weeks and "high" the remaining weeks. What is the probability this week sales are:
   a. Fair.
   b. Low.
   c. High.
   d. At least fair.

4.4 Unions, Intersections, and the Relationships between Events

A **set** is any collection of objects. It is often useful to identify how sets can be related to each other. Assume we have identified two sets *A* and *B*. Each contains numerous elements. It is entirely possible for some elements to be in both sets. For example, assume set *A* consists of all the students in your statistics class, and set *B* consists of all students at your university or college who are majoring in economics. Those elements (students) that are in both sets are the economics majors in your statistics class. These students constitute the intersection of *A* and *B*. The **intersection** of *A* and *B*, written $A \cap B$ and read as "*A* intersection *B*," consists of those elements that are common to both *A* and *B*.

Figure 4.1
A Venn Diagram

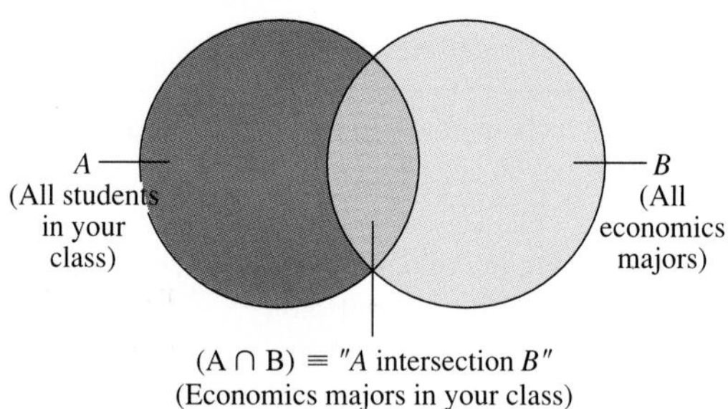

A Venn diagram is a useful tool to portray the relationship between sets. Developed by John Venn (1834–1923), an English mathematician, this pictorial display is shown in Figure 4.1. The two sets, *A* and *B*, can be seen in the diagram. The overlapping area contains elements that are in both sets and constitutes $A \cap B$. These are the students that are in both set *A* (your class) and set *B* (economics majors).

> **Intersection of *A* and *B*** The set of all elements that are in *both A* and *B*.

For $A \cap B$ to occur, **both** "*A* and *B*" must occur. The student must be in your statistics class *and* an economics major. The events *A* and *B* are called **joint** events. Both must occur before the event $A \cap B$ ("*A* and *B*") occurs.

The **union** of *A* and *B*, written $A \cup B$ and read as "*A* union *B*," consists of those elements that are in either *A* or *B* or both. As seen in Figure 4.1, all students who are in your class (set A), regardless of their major, and all economics majors (set B), regardless of whether they are in your class, are elements in $A \cup B$.

> **The Union of *A* and *B*** The set of all elements that are in *A* or *B*.

For an element to be in $A \cup B$, it need only be in set A or set B or both.

A complete understanding of probability cannot be acquired without a comprehension of the ways in which events can be related. Two events are said to be **mutually exclusive** if the occurrence of one event prohibits the occurrence of the other. A classic example of mutually exclusive events is flipping a head and a tail in the single flip of a coin. If a head occurs, a tail cannot occur. Selecting a unit of output and finding it defective or not defective are mutually exclusive events.

Drawing a card from a deck that is a queen and an ace are also mutually exclusive events. However, drawing a queen and a heart are not, since both would occur if the queen of hearts were drawn. In the opening case at the beginning of this chapter, the National Ski Association is to study the locations of ski resorts. Selecting a resort that is (1) in an isolated area and (2) located near an urban center are mutually exclusive events. If it is isolated, it is not near a large city. On the other hand, a ski resort located (1) near a city and (2) near other similar ski resorts are not mutually exclusive, since there are numerous resorts in the Chicago area.

Collectively exhaustive events consist of all possible outcomes of an experiment and constitute its sample space. The collectively exhaustive events of rolling a die are 1, 2, 3, 4, 5, and 6. Further, since it is a *certainty* that one of these events will occur, their combined probability is equal to one:

$$P(1 \text{ or } 2 \text{ or } 3 \text{ or } 4 \text{ or } 5 \text{ or } 6) = 1$$

Of the 500 employees at King Dynamics, Inc., 170 are classified as staff workers, 290 are line workers, and the remaining 40 workers are auxiliary employees. The collectively exhaustive events are S, L, and A. If an employee is selected at random, the

$$P(S) = 170/500 = 0.34$$
$$P(L) = 290/500 = 0.58$$
$$P(A) = 40/500 = 0.08$$

Since it is a certainty that the employee selected will come from one of these three collectively exhaustive categories, $P(S \text{ or } L \text{ or } A) = 0.34 + 0.58 + 0.08 = 1.00$.

Independent events are events such that the occurrence of one has no bearing on the occurrence of the other. Examples include the outcome of a coin flip and rolling a die. The result of the coin flip does not affect the die. Two successive flips of a coin are also independent events.

Are the results of drawing two cards from a deck independent events? That is, does the outcome of the first draw affect the probability of the second outcome? It depends on whether the first card is replaced before the second is drawn. Let the first event be drawing a queen and the second event be drawing an ace. According to the classical approach, the probability of drawing a queen on the first draw is $P(Q) = 4/52$.

The probability of drawing an ace on the second draw depends on whether the first card is replaced before the second is drawn. Assume that a queen, or any card other than an ace, was drawn the first time. If that card is held out of the deck on the second draw, the probability of drawing an ace is $P(A) = 4/51$ since 4 of the remaining 51 cards are aces. If the first card is returned to the deck before the second is drawn, the probability of an ace on the second draw is $P(A) = 4/52$.

When drawing from a finite set, such as a deck of cards, two events are independent if and only if the drawing is done *with replacement.* However, if the first element is not replaced before the second is drawn, the two events are dependent.

If *two* workers are selected at King Dynamics, the probability the first is a staff worker is $P(S) = 170/500 = 0.34$. If this selection is *not* replaced, the probability the second is a line worker is $P(L) = 290/499$, not $290/500$.

Complementary events are events such that if one event does not occur, the other must. If event A is rolling an even number with a die (2, 4, or 6), the complement is rolling an odd number (1, 3, or 5). If you do not get an even number, you must get an odd number. The complement of A is written $\bar{A}$, and is referred to as "not A."

Of course, complementary events are also collectively exhaustive, because if A does not occur, $\bar{A}$ must occur. Thus,

$$P(A) + P(\bar{A}) = 1$$

and

$$P(A) = 1 - P(\bar{A})$$

If a staff worker is not selected at King Dynamics, then either a line or an auxiliary worker must be. The probability of a staff worker is $P(S)$ and the probability of a line or auxiliary worker is $P(\bar{S})$. Then, $P(S) + P(\bar{S}) = 1$.

Section Exercises

7. Given a deck of 52 cards, set A consists of all 13 hearts and set B is all four aces. Identify which cards are included in $(A \cup B)$ and $(A \cap B)$.

8. Construct a Venn diagram for the preceding exercise.

9. Some of the male and female workers at a large plant have a high school education. Set A consists of all male workers, set B is female workers, set C is those with a high school education, and set D is those workers without a high school education. Identify and explain $(A \cup C)$, $(B \cup D)$, and $(A \cap C)$.

10. For the preceding problem, what is the difference between $(B \cup D)$, and $(B \cap D)$?

11. Given the conditions in Exercise 9, identify events that are:

a. Mutually exclusive.
b. Collectively exhaustive with respect to gender.
c. If 300 of the 1000 workers are male, what is the probability a worker is female, $P(F)$? What role did the rule of complementarity play in your answer?
d. What is the difference between $P(F)$ and $P(\bar{M})$?

12. Describe three business-related examples in which the events are independent.

4.5 Contingency Tables and Probability Tables

Contingency tables and probability tables are useful in calculating the probability of events. Returning to our example of King Dynamics, presume that the contingency table for all 500 employees appears as Table 4.1.

The table shows, for example, that of the 170 staff workers, 120 are male and 50 are female. A probability table can be formed by dividing each of the entries in the Table 4.1 by the total, 500 workers. The results are seen in Table 4.2.

Table 4.1
Contingency Table for King Dynamics

	Classification of Employees			
Gender	Staff	Line	Auxiliary	Total
Male	120	150	30	300
Female	50	140	10	200
Total	170	290	40	500

Table 4.2
Probability Table for King Dynamics

	Classification of Employees			
Gender	Staff	Line	Auxiliary	Total
Male	120/500 = **0.24**	150/500 = 0.30	30/500 = 0.06	300/500 = **0.60**
Female	50/500 = 0.10	140/500 = 0.28	10/500 = 0.02	200/500 = 0.40
Total	170/500 = 0.34	290/500 = **0.58**	40/500 = 0.08	500/500 = 1.00

The values in the margins of the table are called *marginal probabilities*. For example, the probability of selecting a line worker at random is $P(L) = 0.58$ and the probability of selecting a male is $P(M) = 0.60$. The *joint probabilities* in the cells in the main body of the table show the probability of the intersection of two events. For example, the probability of selecting a male staff worker, that is, a worker who is staff *and* male, is $P(M \cap S) = 0.24$. A marginal probability is found as the sum of the corresponding joint probabilities. Thus, $P(M) = P(M \cap S) + P(M \cap L) + P(M \cap A) = 0.24 + 0.30 + 0.06 = 0.60$.

Section Exercises

13. You collected data from 500 economists in academe, private industry, and government concerning their opinions on whether the economy would prove stable, would expand, or would enter a period of contraction in the near future. However, part of the information was lost, resulting in the partial contingency table seen below. Based on the remaining data, create a probability table.

	Economy			
Economists	Stable	Expansion	Contraction	Total
Academe	125		100	
Private industry		35		110
Government	25	40		65
Total	200			

From the probability table, find:

a. $P(A)$.
b. $P(G)$.
c. $P(A \cap S)$.
d. $P(A \cap E)$.
e. $P(G \cap C)$.

14. *Forbes* (February 1997) ranked 120 U.S. cities as to their quality of life based in part on the percentage of employees with college degrees. The results are seen in the partial contingency table below, where A is less than 15 percent with college degrees, B is 15 percent to 20 percent have college degrees and C is over 20 percent have college degrees. Form a probability table and answer the questions presented below the table.

	Quality of Life			
Percentages with College Degrees	**Poor**	**Good**	**Excellent**	**Total**
A	10	20		40
B			20	
C		10		20
Total	20	60		

a. $P(A)$?
b. $P(P \cap B)$?
c. $P(E \cap C)$?
d. $P(A \cap G)$?

15. Based on your probability table in the previous exercise, write a report to the chair of the committee to select a new site for the company headquarters. Include and evaluate all relevant comparisons, based on the percentage/quality factors. What conclusion do you reach?

4.6 Conditional Probability

We often want to determine the probability of some event given, or on the *condition*, that some other event has already occurred. Logically, this is called **conditional probability.** It is denoted as $P(A \mid B)$ and is read as the "probability of A given B."

> **Conditional Probability** The probability that event *A* will occur given, or on the condition that, event *B* has already occurred.

Conditional probability is commonly used in a business setting to *revise* the probability of some event given that additional information has been gathered. For example, you may estimate the probability that you will make a sale (S) to a long-time customer to be $P(S) = 0.80$. However, if you subsequently learn that this customer is now buying from one of your competitors, you may revise the probability you will make a sale given that the competitor (C) has submitted an offer as only $P(S \mid C) = 0.30$.

To illustrate with a simple example, we already know the probability of drawing a jack from a deck of 52 cards is $P(J) = 4/52$ since there are four jacks in the deck. However, suppose you wanted to know the probability the card drawn was a jack given the additional information that it is a face card (F). That is, $P(J \mid F)$. Because 4 of the 12 face cards in a deck are jacks, $P(J \mid F) = 4/12$, not 4/52. This is the general formula for conditional probability of event A given that event B is already known to have occurred:

The conditional probability of A given B

$$P(A \mid B) = \frac{P(A \cap B)}{P(B)} = \frac{P(A)P(B \mid A)}{P(B)} \qquad [4.3]$$

Thus,

$$P(J \mid F) = \frac{P(J \cap F)}{P(F)} = \frac{P(J)P(F \mid J)}{P(F)} = \frac{(4/52)(1)}{12/52} = 4/12$$

The $P(F \mid J)$ is 1 because all jacks are face cards. Although in this rather simple example it was possible to determine $P(J \mid F)$ without the use of Formula (4.3), there are many instances in which the formula is necessary. To illustrate the value of Formula (4.3), return for a moment to Table 4.2 for King Dynamics. We can see that the probability a worker picked at random is a male is $P(M) = 0.60$. However, if we wanted to calculate the probability the worker was a male given he is a staff worker $P(M \mid S)$ can be found only as

$$P(M \mid S) = \frac{P(M \cap S)}{P(S)} = \frac{0.24}{0.34} = 0.71$$

Section Exercises

16. From the probability table you created in Exercise 13,

a. Find $P(S \mid A)$.

b. If you are an academic economist, are you more likely to forecast a stable economy than if you work for the government?

c. Given you work in private industry, are you more likely to forecast a contraction than an academician?

d. If you work for the government, which of the three forecasts are you most likely to make?

17. Based on the probability table you created in Exercise 14,

a. Given a rank of Excellent, which of the three percentage categories is most likely to occur?

b. If 19 percent of a city's employees have a college degree, is the quality of life most likely to be ranked Poor, Good, or Excellent?

c. If over 20 percent of the employees of a city have degrees, how likely is the city to be ranked as Excellent?

d. If a city is ranked as Excellent, how likely is it that over 20 percent of its employees have college degrees?

4.7 The Two Rules of Probability

There are only two basic rules to follow to calculate the probability of more complex events: The multiplication rule and the addition rule. Each is used for specific purposes. The multiplication rule is used to determine the probability of "*A* and *B*," $P(A \cap B)$, and the addition rule is used to calculate the probability of "*A* or *B*," $P(A \cup B)$.

A. The Multiplication Rule

The purpose of the **multiplication rule** is to determine the probability of the joint event $P(A \cap B)$. That is, to find the probability of "*A* and *B*," simply multiply their respective probabilities. The exact procedure depends on whether *A* and *B* are dependent or independent. Events *A* and *B* are independent if $P(A) = P(A \mid B)$. That is, the probability of *A* is the same whether or not event *B* is considered. Similarly, if *A* and *B* are independent, $P(B) = P(B \mid A)$.

For *independent* events the joint probability of the two events becomes

Probability of independent events	$P(A \cap B) = P(A) \times P(B)$	[4.4]

The probability of the two independent events of rolling a 3 with a die and flipping a head with a coin is

$$P(3 \cap H) = P(3) \times P(H) = (1/6) \times (1/2) = 1/12$$

Since these two events are independent, merely multiply their individual probabilities. Similarly, the probability of drawing one of the 13 hearts from a deck of 52 cards and rolling an even number with a die is $P(H \cap E) = P(H) \times P(E) = 13/52 \times 3/6 = 39/312$.

In order to attract customers, Norman, owner of the Bates Motel, has modernized his facilities. He observes that 20 percent of all the cars passing by stop to rent a room. What is the probability that the next two cars will stop? Assuming these events are independent, $P(S_1 \cap S_2) = P(S_1) \times P(S_2) = (0.20)(0.20) = 0.04$. The probability that both of the next two cars will rent a room from Norman is 4 percent. What is the probability that the first car will stop and the second will not? $P(S_1 \cap \bar{S}_2) = P(S) \times P(\bar{S}_2) = (0.20) \times (0.80) = 0.16$.

If the events are *dependent,* then, by definition, we must consider the first event in determining the probability of the second. That is, the probability of event B depends on the condition that A has already occurred. The principle of conditional probability is required. The probability of the joint events A and B is

Probability of dependent events	$P(A \cap B) = P(A) \times P(B \mid A)$	[4.5]

Return to our probability table for King Dynamics, Table 4.2. The marginal probability in the first row clearly shows that $P(M) = 0.60$ regardless of whether the worker is staff, line, or auxiliary. However, the joint probability of male *and* staff is seen to be $P(M \cap S) = 0.24$.

We can also calculate this probability using Formula (4.5); $P(M \cap S) = P(M) \times P(S \mid M)$. The last term is conditional probability, which we determined earlier to be

$$P(S \mid M) = \frac{P(S \cap M)}{P(M)} = \frac{0.24}{0.60} = 0.40$$

Then,

$$P(M \cap S) = P(M) \times P(S \mid M) = (0.60) \times (0.40) = 0.24$$

Although the use of a table can simplify probability computations, there are instances in which the formation of a table is quite difficult, thereby requiring use of the formulas. Example 4.1 illustrates this.

Example 4.1 The credit manager at Dollar-Wise Department Store collects data on 100 of her customers. Of the 60 men, 40 have credit cards (C). Of the 40 women, 30 have credit cards (C). Ten of the men with credit cards have balances due (B), while 15 of the women have balances (B). The credit manager wants to determine the probability that a customer selected at random is:

a. A woman with a credit card.
b. A woman with a balance.
c. A man without a balance.
d. A man with a balance.

Solution: Creating a probability table is difficult since there are three factors: gender, credit card, and a balance on the card. The use of Formula (4.5) is perhaps the preferred approach.

a. $P(W \cap C) = P(W) \times P(C \mid W)$. Clearly $P(W) = 40/100$. Further, of the 40 women, 30 have cards. Thus, given that the customer is a woman, the probability that she has a card is $P(C \mid W) = 30/40$. Then, $P(W \cap C) = P(W) \times P(C \mid W) = (40/100) \times (30/40) = 0.30$.

b. $P(W \cap B) = P(W) \times P(B \mid W)$. Of the 40 women, 15 have balances. Given that the customer is a woman, the probability that she has a balance is $15/40$. So, $P(W \cap B) = P(W) \times P(B \mid W) = (40/100)(15/40) = 0.15$.

c. $P(M \cap \overline{B}) = P(M) \times P(\overline{B} \mid M)$. Since 50 of the 60 men do not have balances, $P(\overline{B} \mid M) = 50/60$. Then, $P(M \cap \overline{B}) = P(M) \times P(\overline{B} \mid M) = (60/100)(50/60) = 0.50$.

d. $P(M \cap B) = P(M) \times P(B \mid M)$. Of the 60 men, 10 have balances. $P(B \mid M) = 10/60$. Thus, $P(M \cap B) = P(M) \times P(B \mid M) = (60/100)(10/60) = 0.10$.

Interpretation: The probabilities of other joint events that would help the credit manager determine store policies and lead to increased sales can be determined.

B. The Addition Rule

The **addition rule** is used to determine the probability of *A or B*, $P(A \cup B)$.

Probability of event *A* or event *B* (when the events are *not* mutually exclusive)	$P(A \cup B) = P(A) + P(B) - P(A \cap B)$	[4.6]

Recall that events *A* and *B* are not mutually exclusive if they can both occur at the same time. In this case the formula requires that we subtract the probability of the joint event *A* and *B*. The probability of drawing either an ace *or* one of the 13 hearts from a deck of cards is $P(A) + P(H) - P(A \cap H)$. Events *A* and *H*, $P(A \cap H)$, are not mutually exclusive, since both would occur if the ace of hearts were drawn. Thus, $P(A) + P(H) - P(A \cap H) = (4/52) + (13/52) - (1/52) = 16/52$.

The reason we must subtract the joint probability when the events are not mutually exclusive is to avoid *double counting*. When we counted all four aces, we included the ace of hearts. When we counted all 13 hearts, we included the ace of hearts a second time. Since there is only one ace of hearts, it is necessary to subtract it out one time.

In the King Dynamics example, the probability that an employee is either a male worker or a staff worker is $P(M) + P(S) - P(M \cap S) = (0.60) + (0.34) - (0.24) = 0.70$. Again, we must subtract out the joint probability $P(M \cap S)$, because we included staff workers when we counted all males, and we included males when we counted all staff workers. Male staff workers were counted twice.

Example 4.2 Most service stations sell three grades of gasoline, regular, super, and premium. Often, some of each grade is enriched with ethanol. The contingency table shown below illustrates the percentages of customers who prefer each.

	Regular	Super	Premium	Total
Ethanol	0.05	0.10	0.05	0.20
No ethanol	0.15	0.40	0.25	0.80
Total	0.20	0.50	0.30	1.00

Determine the probability that the next customer prefers:

a. Regular or ethanol; $P(R \cup E)$.
b. Super or no ethanol; $P(S \cup \overline{E})$.
c. Premium or ethanol; $P(P \cup E)$.
d. Premium or no ethanol; $P(P \cup \overline{E})$.

Solution:

a. $P(R \cup E) = P(R) + P(E) - P(R \cap E)$
$= 0.20 + 0.20 - 0.05 = 0.35$

b. $P(S \cup \overline{E}) = P(S) + P(\overline{E}) - P(S \cap \overline{E})$
$= 0.50 + 0.80 - 0.40 = 0.90$

c. $P(P \cup E) = P(P) + P(E) - P(P \cap E)$
$= 0.30 + 0.20 - 0.05 = 0.45$

d. $P(P \cup \overline{E}) = P(P) + (P\overline{E}) - P(P \cap \overline{E})$
$= 0.30 + 0.80 - 0.25 = 0.85$

Interpretation: Other probabilities could be determined to compare the popularity of consumer preferences and thereby formulate a marketing program designed to increase overall sales.

Remember, the examples above relate to two events that are not mutually exclusive. If A and B *are* mutually exclusive, $P(A \cap B) = 0$. By definition, they cannot occur simultaneously. Since there is no sense in subtracting zero, Formula (4.6) reduces to

Probability of event A or event B (when the events are mutually exclusive)	$P(A \cup B) = P(A) + P(B)$	[4.7]

The probability a customer prefers regular or super (mutually exclusive events since he or she cannot prefer both) is $P(R \cup S) = P(R) + P(S) = 0.20 + 0.50 = 0.70$.

Some instances may require the use of both the multiplication rule and the addition rule. Presume that we flip a coin three times and want to determine the probability that we get two heads. We must ask, How can the event (2 out of 3 are heads) happen? We can get two heads if:

Only the third flip is a tail	$P(H_1 \text{ and } H_2 \text{ and } T_3) = 1/2 \times 1/2 \times 1/2 = 1/8$
Only the second flip is a tail	$P(H_1 \text{ and } T_2 \text{ and } H_3) = 1/2 \times 1/2 \times 1/2 = 1/8$
Only the first flip is a tail	$P(T_1 \text{ and } H_2 \text{ and } H_3) = 1/2 \times 1/2 \times 1/2 = 1/8$
	$3/8$

Because the event can happen either the first way *or* the second way *or* the third way, we must add their respective probabilities. Thus, the probability that three coin flips can produce two heads is $3/8$. Example 4.3 further demonstrates this.

Example 4.3 Of 10 computer chips, 4 are defective. What is the probability of selecting 3 without replacement, only one of which is defective?

Solution: You must ask yourself, "How can the event happen?" There are only three ways in which just one can be defective: (1) only the first is defective, (2) only the second is defective, and (3) only the last is defective. According to the rule of multiplication,

The first way is $P(D_1 \cap \overline{D}_2 \cap \overline{D}_3) = (4/10)(6/9)(5/8) = 120/720$.
The second way is $P(\overline{D}_1 \cap D_2 \cap \overline{D}_3) = (6/10)(4/9)(5/8) = 120/720$.
The last way is $P(\overline{D}_1 \cap \overline{D}_2 \cap D_3) = (6/10)(5/9)(4/8) = 120/720$.

Since the event "only one is defective" can happen the first way, the second way, or the third way, we must add the three probabilities according to the rule of addition. P(only one is defective) $= 120/720 + 120/720 + 120/720 = 360/720 = 0.50$.

Interpretation: Many companies base product warranties on the probability that a certain number of units sold will be defective. If this probability is too high, proving costly, the companies will be forced to offer less attractive warranties.

Section Exercises

18. Based on your probability table in Exercise 13, find

a. $P(A \cup S)$.
b. $P(P \cup C)$.
c. $P(E \cup G)$.
d. $P(G \cup E)$.
e. $P(A \cup G)$.

19. Wally, owner of Wally's Workout World, wants to construct a profile of the members to develop an advertising campaign that will appeal to potential customers typical of those who currently prefer his health club. Thirty percent of the current members are women, 80 percent of whom are under 30 years of age. Sixty percent of the men are under 30. What is the probability that a member selected at random is:

a. A women under 30?
b. A women over 30?
c. A man over 30 or a woman under 30?
d. Over 30?
e. A man or a woman over 30?

20. Of 1,000 18-year-olds, 600 are employed and 800 are high school graduates. Of the 800 graduates, 500 have jobs. What is the probability that an 18-year-old picked at random is:

a. An employed graduate?
b. Employed but not a graduate?
c. Unemployed or a graduate?
d. Employed or not a graduate?

21. Sammy's Sweat Shop sells two types of running shoes, the Mercury and the Racer. The probabilities that a given customer will buy the Mercury is $P(M) = 0.40$ and the probability he or she will buy the Racer is $P(R) = 0.30$. The probability that he or she will buy both is $P(B) = 0.10$. What is the probability that a customer will buy either M or R?

22. A broker knows from past experience that the probability that a client will buy stock is 65 percent. The probability that the client will buy a government bond if he or she already owns stock is 35 percent.

a. What is the probability that a client owns both?
b. Are B and S independent? Explain.

4.8 Bayes' Theorem

Reverend Thomas Bayes (1702–1761) developed a concept useful in calculating certain probabilities. Assume that Dunham Manufacturing uses two machines to produce its output. Machine A produces 60 percent of the total output, and machine *B* produces the remaining 40 percent. Two percent of the units produced by A are defective, while B has a defect rate of 4 percent.

This is shown in the accompanying *tree diagram* in Figure 4.2. Assume a unit of output is selected at random. The first set of "branches" in the tree, indicating which machine produced the unit, shows that the probability it came from machine A is $P(A) = 0.60$ and that the probability it came from machine B is $P(B) = 40$. The second set of branches indicating quality of the unit tells us that if it came from machine A it can be either defective or not defective. These *conditional probabilities* show that the probability it is not defective given it came from A is $P(\bar{D} \mid A) = 0.98$ and the probability it is defective given it came from A is $P(D \mid A) = 0.02$. The conditional probabilities for B reveal that the probability it is not defective given it came from B is $P(\bar{D} \mid B) = 0.96$ and the probability it is defective on the condition that it came from B is $P(D \mid B) = 0.04$.

Figure 4.2
Tree Diagram for Dunham Manufacturing

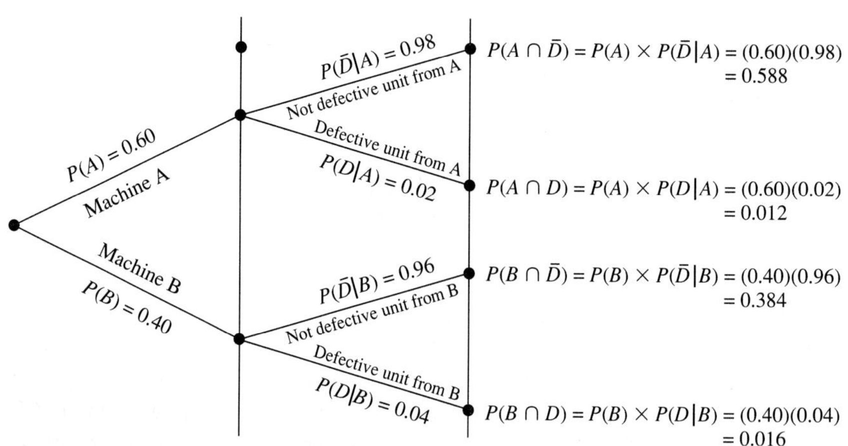

Finally, we see that there are four possible outcomes to the experiment of selecting a unit of output. The probability of each is calculated by multiplying the probabilities on each of the branches leading to it. To illustrate, the first possible outcome is that unit came from A and is not defective, $P(A \cap \bar{D})$. Using the rule of multiplication, $P(A \cap \bar{D}) = P(A) \times P(\bar{D} \mid A) = (0.60)(0.98) = 0.588$. The probabilities of the three remaining outcomes can be determined similarly.

We can see directly Figure 4.2 that $P(A) = 0.60$. Suppose that we are told the unit is defective and we now want to know the probability the unit came from machine A. With this additional information, we can revise the probability the unit was produced by machine A. We now want to determine $P(A \mid D)$, not just $P(A)$.

Recall the rule of conditional probability:

$$P(A \mid D) = \frac{P(A \cap D)}{P(D)} = \frac{P(A) \times P(D \mid A)}{P(D)}$$

However, $P(D)$ is not readily discernible. This is where Bayes' Theorem comes in. There are two ways the unit may be defective. It can come from machine A and be defective, or it can come from machine B and be defective. Using the rule of addition,

$$P(D) = P(A \cap D) + P(B \cap D)$$
$$= P(A) \times P(D \mid A) + P(B) \times P(D \mid B)$$

When we make the substitution in the denominator of the conditional probability formula above for $P(D)$, Bayes' Theorem tells us

Bayes' Theorem

$$P(A \mid D) = \frac{P(A \cap D)}{P(A \cap D) + P(B \cap D)} = \frac{P(A) \times P(D \mid A)}{P(A) \times P(D \mid A) + P(B) \times P(D \mid B)} \quad [4.8]$$

We can now find $P(A \mid D)$ as

$$P(A \mid D) = \frac{P(A \cap D)}{P(D)}$$
$$= \frac{P(A \cap D)}{P(A \cap D) + P(B \cap D)}$$
$$= \frac{(0.012)}{(0.012) + (0.016)}$$
$$= 0.429$$

While $P(A) = 0.60$, the $P(A \mid D) = 0.429$. Notice that $P(A \mid D) < P(A)$ because machine A produces a smaller percentage of defects than does machine B.

Example 4.4 **Bayes' Theorem**

The personnel department for a large firm has found that only 60 percent of the job applicants it interviews are actually qualified (Q) to hold a position in the company. A review of the firm's records shows that of those who were qualified, 67 percent had previous statistical training (T), while 20 percent of those who were not qualified had undergone earlier statistical instruction. That is,

$$P(Q) = 0.60 \qquad P(T \mid Q) = 0.67 \qquad P(T \mid \overline{Q}) = 0.20$$

The personnel director can clearly see that given you are qualified, you are more likely to have some statistical training than if you are not qualified ($0.67 > 0.20$). Because so much time is wasted interviewing applicants who turn out to be unqualified, however, he is considering granting interviews only to those applicants who have prior training in statistics. He hopes to increase the probability of finding applicants qualified to fill a position. The question then becomes, Are you more likely to be qualified given that you have training: $P(Q/T)$? If so, the personnel department could avoid delay and unnecessary cost by restricting interviews to those applicants with previous training in statistical analysis.

Solution: Using the rule of conditional probability

$$P(Q \mid T) = \frac{P(Q \cap T)}{P(T)} = \frac{P(Q) \times (T \mid Q)}{P(T)} = \frac{(0.60) \times (.067)}{P(T)}$$

Because company records do not provide $P(T)$, we must use Bayes' theorem to find the denominator. There are two ways an applicant might have previous training: (1) the applicant might be qualified and have training, $P(Q \cap T)$ and (2) the applicant might not be qualified and have training $P(Q \cap T)$. Thus,

$$\begin{aligned} P(T) &= P(Q \cap T) + P(\overline{Q} \cap T) \\ &= P(Q) \times P(T \mid Q) + P(\overline{Q}) \times P(T \mid \overline{Q}) \\ &= (0.60)(0.67) + (0.40)(0.20) \\ &= 0.482 \end{aligned}$$

Then,

$$\begin{aligned} P(Q \mid T) &= \frac{(0.60)(0.67)}{0.482} \\ &= (0.834) \end{aligned}$$

While $P(Q) = 0.60$, $P(Q \mid T) = 0.834$

Interpretation: To increase the probabilty of interviewing only qualified applicants, personnel should interview only those applicants who have previous training in statisitcal analysis.

Section Exercises

23. James Business Equipment sells a wide range of office supplies to businesses in the Midwest. The sales manager believes she has discovered a trend that could boost sales. The results of a study seem to suggest that law firms are more inclined to place purchase orders than are other business concerns. Her data show that the probability the general business community will buy their supplies is 20 percent, $P(B) = 0.20$. Among customers over the past several months, 50 percent were law firms, while 60 percent of those who did not place an order were law firms. The manager feels that concentrating on law offices will increase the probability that a sales call will result in a purchase. What is your conclusion?
24. A drug company testing a new hay fever remedy finds that 60 percent of all hay fever sufferers enjoy relief from their symptoms within four weeks whether or not they take medication. Of those who obtain relief, 40 percent have taken medication, while 30 percent of those who do not get relief have tried medication. The drug company wants to determine the advisability of taking medication by comparing the probability of getting relief from hay fever symptoms if sufferers do take medication to the probability of relief if sufferers do not take medication.

4.9 Counting Techniques

Many business decisions require that we count the number of subsets we can obtain from a set. From a sales line consisting of 10 products, how many subsets of 3 products can be offered to customers? Seven sales personnel are in a contest to see who wins a free trip to Cancun. How many different orders of finish are there? How many different phone numbers can be assigned to a large office given the digits 0–9? Many other examples abound. We will examine four counting techniques used to answer these and many similar questions: combinations, permutations, multiple choice, and multiplication.

In selecting the elements in the subsets, the distinction between *permutations* and *combinations* depends on whether the order of the selections makes a difference. If a different order is a sufficient to constitute another subset, we are dealing with permutations. If two subsets are considered the same because they have merely rearranged the same elements, combinations are involved.

From the first five letters of the alphabet, A, B, C, D and E, how many different subsets can we get? Two possibilities are: {A, B, C} and {A, C, B}. Both have the same elements and differ only in the order in which the elements were selected. If the two subsets are considered *different* subsets because the order is different, they are seen as permutations. If the two subsets are seen as identical and constitute the same subset because both have the same elements regardless of order, they are called combinations. Simply put, with permutations order makes a difference.

Given a set of n elements, the number of permutations, each of size r, is determined as

The number of permutations of n elements taken r at a time	$${}_nP_r = \frac{n!}{(n-r)!}$$	[4.9]

where $n!$ is read as "n factorial" and means the product of all numbers 1 through n. Thus, $4! = 1 \times 2 \times 3 \times 4 = 24$. By definition $0! = 1$.

The number of combinations of n elements taken r at a time is

The number of combinations of n elements taken r at a time	$${}_nC_r = \frac{n!}{r!\,(n-r)!}$$	[4.10]

Above, we asked, given 10 products, how many subsets of 3 products could we package together and offer our customers? If we feel that the order in which we offer the 3 products will not influence customers, that is, order will not make a difference, we must find the number of combinations of 10 elements taken 3 at a time.

$$
\begin{aligned}
{}_{10}C_3 &= \frac{10!}{3!\,(10-3!)} \\
&= 120
\end{aligned}
$$

There are 120 packages of 3 items we could offer our customers.

Combinations also can be used to calculate the probability that one of the three computer chips from Example 4.3 is defective. Instead of determining the probability of every way that one is defective, we merely find the probability of *one* of the ways a single chip is defective: $P(D_1 \cap \overline{D}_2 \cap \overline{D}_3) = 120/720$. Then count the number of ways one of the three is defective as ${}_3C_1 = 3$, and multiply: $(3)(120/720) = 0.50$.

Example 4.5 A recent court case in Madison County, Kentucky, centered on the hiring practices of the local telephone company. The company planned to hire 3 new employees. There were 8 applicants for the jobs, 6 of whom were men. All 3 of those hired were men. A charge of sex discrimination was levied against the company. How would you decide?

Solution: The decision rests largely on the probability that all 3 hired are men if each applicant is given equal consideration without preference to gender. We must therefore determine the probability that all three are men.

$$P(\text{all three are men}) = \frac{\text{Number of ways all 3 can be men}}{\text{Total number of possible outcomes}}$$

The number of ways 3 of the 6 men and none of the 2 women can be hired is ${}_6C_3 \times {}_2C_0 = 20 \times 1 = 20$. The total number of ways 3 out of all 8 applicants can be hired is ${}_8C_3 = 56$. Thus,

$$P(\text{all three are men}) = \frac{20}{56} = 36\%$$

Interpretation: There is a 36% probability that all 3 employees hired are men if no preference is given to gender. This event could take place roughly one out of every three times. The court ruled that any event that could occur this frequently is not unusual and does not constitute evidence beyond any reasonable doubt. The charge of discrimination was not upheld.

Returning to our problem of determining how many ways we could package 3 of our 10 products, if our research suggested that the order in which we packaged the 3 products would affect sales, we should determine the number of permutations of 10 elements taken 3 at a time.

$$\begin{aligned}{}_{10}P_3 &= \frac{10!}{(10 - 3!)} \\ &= 720\end{aligned}$$

Given values for n and r, ${}_nP_r > {}_nC_r$ since you can get another permutation just by changing the order.

The number of finishing orders of the seven sales personnel vying for the trip to Cancun noted above is ${}_7P_7 = 5{,}040$. There are 5,040 different ways in which those seven people can be ranked or ordered according to their sales records. If the sales manager is to reward three members of the sales force with a trip and the order of finish is important because each got a different percentage of the trip paid for, we find ${}_7P_3 = 210$. On the other hand, if all three were to win the same trip and order wouldn't make a difference, we would have ${}_7C_3 = 35$.

Neither permutations nor combinations permit an element to be selected more than once. If duplication is allowed, the *multiple-choice* method of counting is used. The number of multiple-choice arrangements of n elements taken r at a time is ${}_nM_r = n^r$.

The question above concerning the number of phone lines in a large office requires the multiple-choice approach, since each of the 10 digits can be used more than once. If the office uses only one extension followed by four digits, such as 555-*XXXX*, the number of phone lines is ${}_{10}M_4 = 10^4 = 10{,}000$. If a second extension is used, such as 556-*XXXX*, $({}_{10}M_4)(2)$, or 20,000 lines are possible.

In all of the above cases, selection was made from only one set. The phone numbers came from only one set of 10 elements. If we are to choose one element from two or more sets, the *multiplication* process is appropriate. This principle requires that we simply multiply the number of elements in each set. George intends to buy a new automobile for his vacation to Piney Flats. He can chose from three colors, two engine sizes, and four different interior designs. How many different modes of transport are available to George? According to the multiplication principle, since the three sets contain three elements, two elements, and four elements, respectively, George must make a choice from $3 \times 2 \times 4 = 24$ different ways of reaching his destination.

Section Exercises

25. From the 15 members on the board of directors of a large corporation, how many 5-member committees can be selected if order is not important?
26. Of 10 executives, 3 are to be selected to serve as a president, vice-president, and treasurer. How many different selections are possible?
27. Your two sick roommates send you to the student center to bring back dinner for each of them. If you may choose from five selections, in how many ways can you feed your companions? (Hint: Does order make a difference? Can you duplicate?)
28. As a construction engineer for Base Electronics, you must determine how many different compact disk (CD) players you can assemble composed of a speaker system, a disk track, and a tuning mechanism if you can choose from among three different speaker systems, four tracks, and two tuning mechanisms.
29. Of the 12 employees at Worldwide Travel Services, 7 have had special training. If 5 employees are to be sent to Europe, what is the probability that 3 will be among those with the special training?

Solved Problems

1. **Basic Probabilities** Ortez Exports, based in Brazil, ships frozen meat products to customers in North America (N), Europe (E) and Asia (A). The protective packages are either deluxe (D) or standard (S). The probability table below shows the relative frequencies of many of the most recent shipments.

	Europe	North America	Asia	Total
Deluxe	0.083	0.167	0.167	0.417
Standard	0.167	0.167	0.250	0.584
Total	0.250	0.334	0.417	1.000

To finalize several pending business decisions, Mr. Ortez must determine the likelihood of shipping to the three destinations with either of the two package options.

a. Deluxe to Europe $= P(D \cap E) = 0.083$, as seen in the first cell showing the joint probability of the two events deluxe and Europe.

b. Is Mr. Ortez more likely to ship a D to E or an S to A? $P(S \cap A) = 0.25 > 0.083$.

c. Standard or either package to North America:

$$P(S \cup N) = P(S) + P(N) - P(S \cap N) = 0.584 + 0.334 - 0.167 = 0.751$$

d. $P(N \cup D) = P(N) + P(D) - P(N \cap D) = 0.334 + 0.417 - 0.167 = 0.584.$

2. **Using Bayes' Theorem** Only 60 percent of the students in Professor Harmond's statistics class pass the first test. Of those who pass, 80 percent studied; 20 percent of those who didn't pass studied. Should you study for his tests?

This can be determined by calculating the probability that you would pass, given that you studied. From the information above: $P(P) = 0.60$, $P(S \mid P) = 0.80$, and $P(S \mid \overline{P}) = 0.20$. Then

$$P(P \mid S) = \frac{P(P \cap S)}{P(S)} = \frac{P(P) \times P(S \mid P)}{P(P) \times P(S \mid P) + P(\overline{P}) \times P(S \mid \overline{P})}$$

$$= \frac{(0.60)(0.80)}{(0.60)(0.80) + (0.40)(0.20)}$$

$$= \frac{0.48}{(0.48) + (0.08)}$$

$$= 0.857 > P(P) = 0.60$$

3. **How Can the Event Occur?** The probability that John can solve a particular statistics problem is 40 percent. There is a 70 percent chance that Fred can solve it. What is the probability it is solved? Assume that John and Fred work separately and the outcomes are therefore independent.

   It can be solved if John solves it (and Fred doesn't), if Fred solves it (and John doesn't), or if both solve it.

$$\begin{aligned} P(S) &= P(J \cap \bar{F}) + P(\bar{J} \cap F) + P(J \cap F) \\ &= (0.40)(0.30) + P(0.60)(0.70) + (0.40)(0.70) \\ &= 0.82 \end{aligned}$$

4. **A Simplification Using Combinations** Harry sells to 30 percent of the customers he calls on. If he makes three calls today what is the probability he will make exactly one sale?

   Harry can sell to any one of the three customers:

$$\begin{aligned} P(1) &= S \cap \bar{S} \cap \bar{S} = (0.30)(0.70)(0.70) = 0.147 \\ &+ \bar{S} \cap S \cap \bar{S} = (0.70)(0.30)(0.70) = 0.147 \\ &+ \bar{S} \cap \bar{S} \cap S = (0.70)(0.70)(0.30) = 0.147 \\ &= 0.441 \end{aligned}$$

   As an alternative, determine the probability that a sale is made to any one of the three, and then multiply by the number of ways one sale can be made.

$$\begin{aligned} P(1) &= [(S \cap \bar{S} \cap \bar{S})] \times {}_3C_1 \\ &= 0.147 \times 3 \\ &= 0.441 \end{aligned}$$

List of Formulas

[4.1]	$P(E) = \dfrac{\text{Number of times the event has occurred in the past}}{\text{Total number of observations}}$	Relative frequency
[4.2]	$P(E) = \dfrac{\text{Number of way the event can occur}}{\text{Total number of possible outcomes}}$	Classical approach
[4.3]	$P(A \mid B) = \dfrac{P(A \cap B)}{P(B)}$	Conditional probability
[4.4]	$P(A \cap B) = P(A) \times P(B)$	Probability of independent events
[4.5]	$P(A \cap B) = P(A) \times P(B \mid A)$	Probability of dependent events
[4.6]	$P(A \cup B) = P(A) + P(B) - P(A \cap B)$	Probability of events that are not mutually exclusive

[4.7]	$P(A \cup B) = P(A) + P(B)$	Probability of mutually exclusive events
[4.8]	$P(A \mid D) = \dfrac{P(A \cap D)}{P(A \cap D) + P(B \cap D)} = \dfrac{P(A) \times P(D \mid A)}{P(A) \times P(D \mid A) + P(B) \times P(D \mid B)}$	Bayes' Theorem
[4.9]	${}_nP_r = \dfrac{n!}{(n-r)!}$	Permutations
[4.10]	${}_nC_r = \dfrac{n!}{r!\,(n-r)!}$	Combinations

Chapter Exercises

30. Dell Publishing has 75 different book titles classified by type and cost as follows:

	Cost		
Type	**$10**	**$15**	**$20**
Fiction	10	8	3
Biography	12	10	9
Historical	4	17	2

Find the probability that a book selected at random is:

a. Fiction or costs $10.
b. Historical and costs $20.
c. Historical and costs either $10 or $15.
d. Fiction and costs less than $20.
e. Biographical or costs $15.
f. Biographical or costs more than $10.

31. The management department at State University has access to three fax machines. The probability that each is out of service is 20/100, 25/100, and 30/100, respectively. Assuming independence, find the probability that:

a. The first and the second are out of service.
b. The first and the third are out of service.
c. All are out of service.
d. None are out of service.
e. One is out of service.
f. Two are out of service.
g. Two or more are out of service.

32. Mark buys three different stocks. The probability the first will rise in value is 1/3, the probability the second will rise is 3/4, and the probability the third rise is 1/10. Determine the probability that:

a. All will rise in value.
b. None will rise.
c. One will rise.
d. Two will rise.
e. At least two will rise.
f. At least one will rise.

33. A local construction company found that only 20 percent of all jobs were completed on time, while 30 percent of all jobs suffered cost overruns. In addition, cost overruns occurred 75 percent of the time that a job was completed on time. The owner of the firm wants to find the probability that a job suffers a cost overrun:

a. And is done on time.

b. Or is done on time.

34. From the previous problem, how can you prove that cost overruns and the probability that a job is done on time are not mutually exclusive events?

35. *Fortune* magazine found that 10 percent of workers in upper-level corporate executive positions were women, and that 3 percent of those in the upper level were women with MBA degrees. The board of directors of a large corporation, whose executive profile fits this description, wishes to select one of their executive women at random. How likely is it that they will select an MBA?

36. Ten units of output are selected from the production line. Three of these 10 are defective. If 5 are to be drawn from the 10, what is the probability that 2 are defective?

37. Biggie Burger offers their burgers with a selection of five different condiments: mustard, pickle, ketchup, onion, and tomatoes. How many different burgers can you buy?

38. Auto license plates in Illinois consist of three letters followed by three numbers. How may different license plates can be made?

39. Randy Rusty, owner of Rusty Cars, Inc., offers his customers cars with eight color options, four interior packages, and three different sunroof designs. From how many different automobiles can Randy's customers choose?

40. Studies by the National Education Association show that 30 percent of the nation's teachers leave the profession within 10 years. Furthermore, of those who leave, 60 percent have an advanced degree, while of those who do not leave, 20 percent have an advanced degree. Mr. Chips, the students' favorite teacher, just got his advanced degree. What is the probability he will leave the students behind and take a different job?

41. A manufacturing firm has plants in Chicago and Houston. The Chicago plant produces 40 percent of the total output, with a 10 percent defect rate. The Houston plant has a 20 percent defect rate. If a single unit is found to be defective, is it more likely to have come from Chicago or from Houston?

42. The president must select 5 members from a list of 12 senators, of whom 7 support him and 5 oppose him. If he picks at random, what is the probability that a majority of the committee support the president?

43. Kelly Katz sells mobile telephones offering five styles, four colors, and seven service options. How many different phones can Ms. Katz offer her customers?

CURTAIN CALL

In the case presented in Setting the Stage at the beginning of this chapter, you are retained by Michael Berry, president of the National Ski Areas Association, to analyze the financial conditions of the 850 ski resorts in the nation. Berry provides you with the following information, which he has collected: none of the urban resorts are facing bankruptcy, 635 of all the resorts are urban, 17 of the isolated resorts are facing bankruptcy, 765 of all resorts are not facing bankruptcy, and 60 of all the resorts are located in isolated areas.

Using this limited data set, provide a response to Berry containing all the relevant facts you can contribute to his efforts to improve financial conditions for the resorts. The report should contain a contingency table and a probability table. What conclusions can you reach and what specific results do you think would be most useful to Berry? Berry is especially interested in which location is more likely to suffer bankruptcy.

Formalize your results in the form of a business report, as described in Appendix 1.

From the Stage to Real Life

In the *Curtain Call* analysis of ski resorts, we saw that a location near a major urban area was an important factor in their financial success. Can you think of reasons for this? Can you think of additional factors that would contribute to the financial success of ski resorts?

The World Ski Association (*www.worldski.com*) is a sport membership organization that arranges travel packages for skiers at resorts all over the world. At this site, visit the "Directory of Benefits" and review some of the resort packages available to members. What is a common element to all of these package arrangements? Do you think that discount arrangements would be a factor in the success of a ski resort?

The National Ski Areas Association maintains *The Official Ski Resort Guide* (*www.skifun.com*). In the descriptions of the resorts found at this site, what features attract you to different resorts? The U.S. Collegiate Ski Association (*www.beater.com/uscsa*) lists scheduled ski competitions by team, date, and location. Could ski competitions influence your selection of a resort?

CHAPTER 5

Probability Distributions

Chapter Blueprint

This chapter examines how probability distributions can be used to solve many common business problems. Both discrete and continuous variables are used in the illustrations.

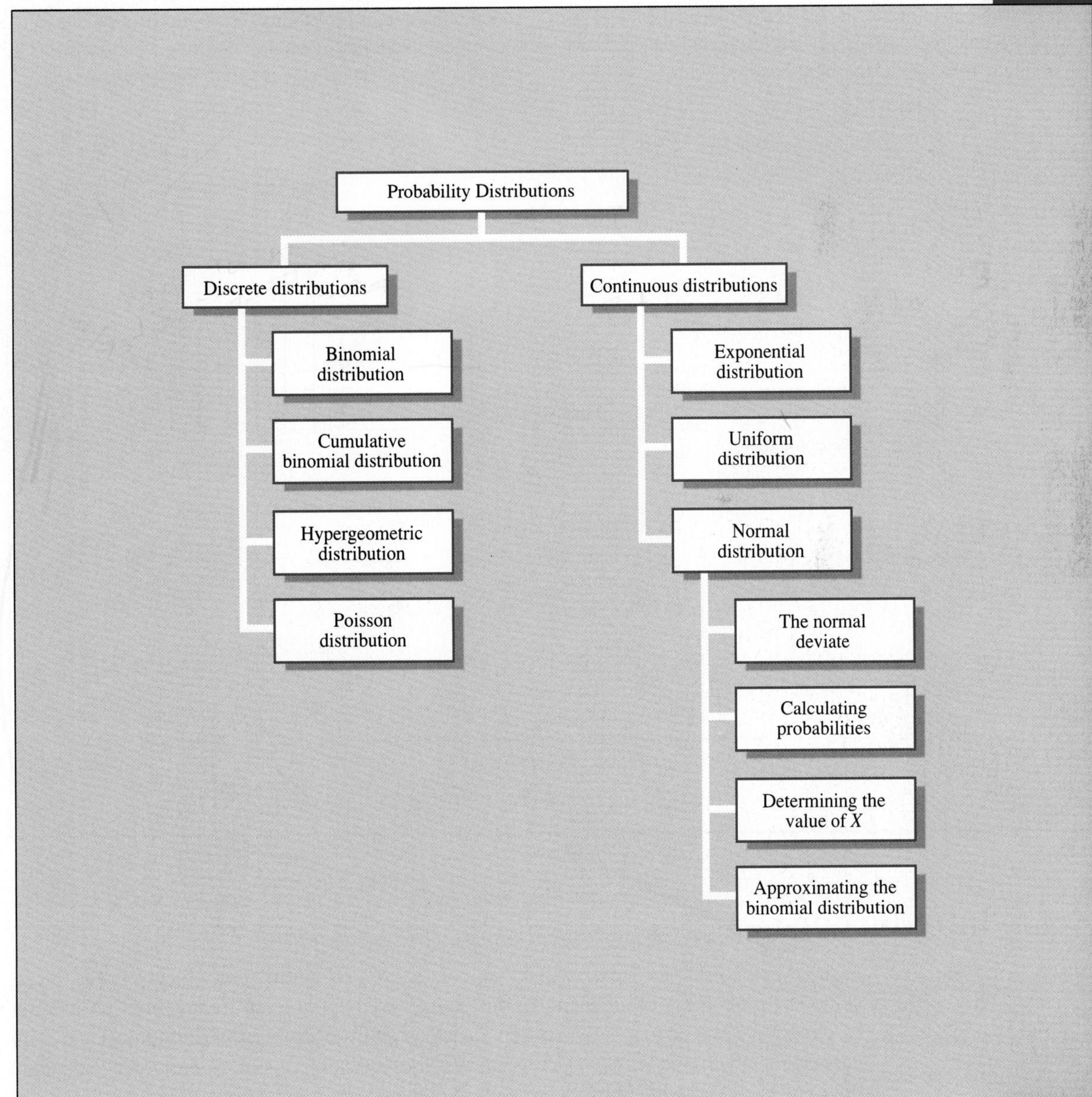

SETTING THE STAGE

A feasibility study by professors in the College of Business at Bradley University in Peoria, Illinois, revealed that on Friday and Saturday nights the response time to 911 calls ranged from 1.2 minutes to 4.6 minutes and proved to be roughly uniformly distributed. Calls were Poisson distributed and arrived at the mean rate of 9 per hour. If the city police were in response to more than 3 calls at any one time, they could call on the assistance of the state police.

The mayor of the city wanted to reduce the mean response time to 2 minutes. It was estimated that the cost of more patrol cars, fire units, and personnel would be $575,000 for every reduction of 30 seconds. The cost was to be borne by a property tax on homes above $70,000 in assessed value. Houses in Peoria average $45,750 in value with a standard deviation of $15,110, and appeared to be normally distributed. At the time of the study there were 42,089 houses in the city's boundaries.

The study submitted to the mayor's office was designed to evaluate the city's response to emergencies as well as the feasibility of achieving the mayor's goal of response-time reduction. The final report required the application of numerous probability distributions as well as an assessment as to the potential of enacting a surcharge on property taxes to finance the program improvements.

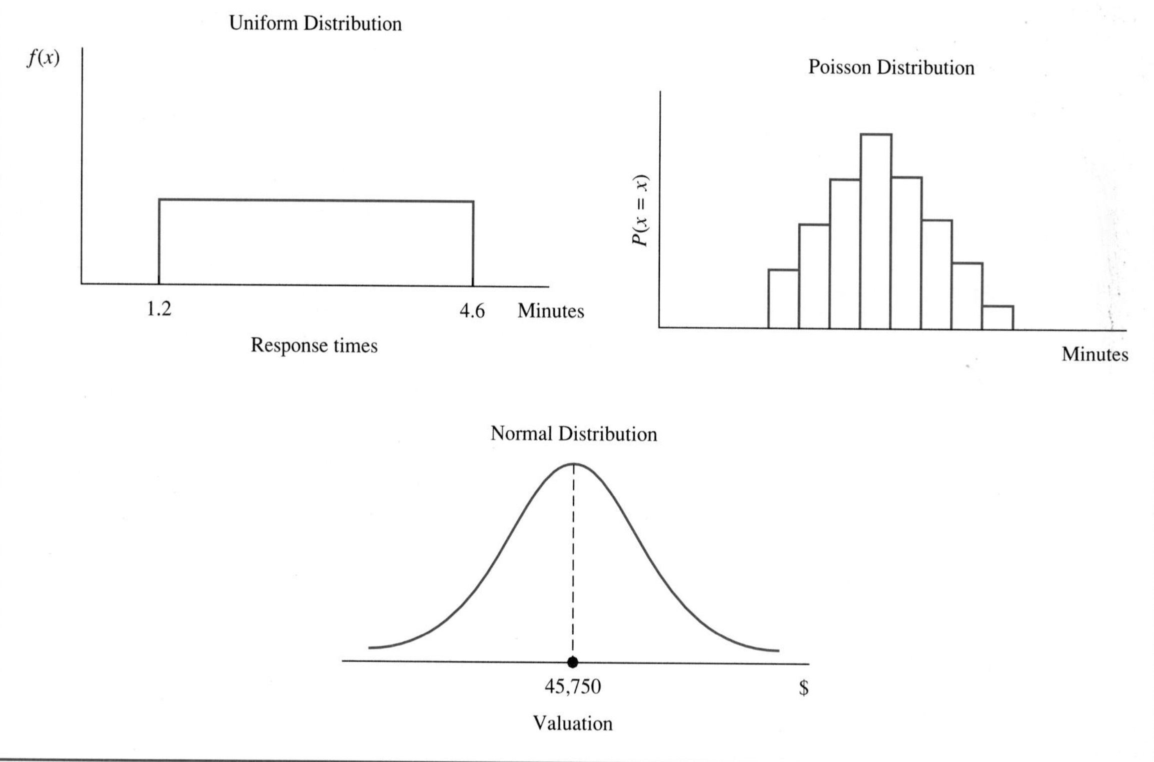

5.1 Introduction

In the previous chapter we examined the concept of probability. Our objective was to calculate the probability of an event. In this chapter we continue our treatment of probability by examining the concepts of random variables and probability distributions. A **random variable** is a variable whose value is the result of a random event. Suppose we flip a coin three times and note the number of heads that occur. The possible outcomes are, of course,

0 heads, 1 head, 2 heads, or 3 heads. The random variable is the number of heads that occur, and the possible outcomes are the values of the random variable. As a second example, the shipping weights of containerized spring water randomly range from 10 to 25 pounds. The actual weights of the containers, in pounds, are the values of the random variable "weight."

As these two examples suggest, random variables may be either discrete or continuous. A **discrete random variable** may take on only certain values, often whole numbers, and results primarily from counting. The number of heads in the coin-flip experiment is an example of a discrete random variable. The values of the random variable are restricted to only certain numbers: 0, 1, 2, and 3. The result of the roll of a die, the number of delivery trucks arriving per hour at the loading dock, and the number of library patrons lining up to check out their favorite books are other examples of discrete random variables.

A **continuous random variable** results primarily from measurement and can take on any value, at least within a given range. The weights of the spring water is an example because the containers can take on any value between 10 and 25 pounds. Other examples of continuous random variables include the heights of customers at a clothing store, the incomes of employees at the local shopping mall and the time between the arrival of the library patrons. In each case, the random variable can be measured at any value, including fractional units. Although monetary units cannot be broken down into a continuous or infinite number of subdivisions (the dollar can be subdivided only 100 times), they are commonly treated as continuous probability distributions.

A **probability distribution** is a display of all possible outcomes of an experiment along with the probabilities of each outcome. From our work in Chapter 4, we can determine that the probability of flipping a coin three times and getting (1) no heads is 1/8, (2) 1 head is 3/8, (3) 2 heads is 3/8 and (4) 3 heads is 1/8. This probability distribution is presented in Table 5.1 which shows all four outcomes and their probabilities. Notice that the probabilities sum to one. The same information can also be shown graphically as in Figure 5.1.

Table 5.1
Discrete Probability Distribution for Flipping Heads

Outcome (heads)	Probability
0	1/8
1	3/8
2	3/8
3	1/8
	1

Figure 5.1
Probability Distribution for Flipping Heads

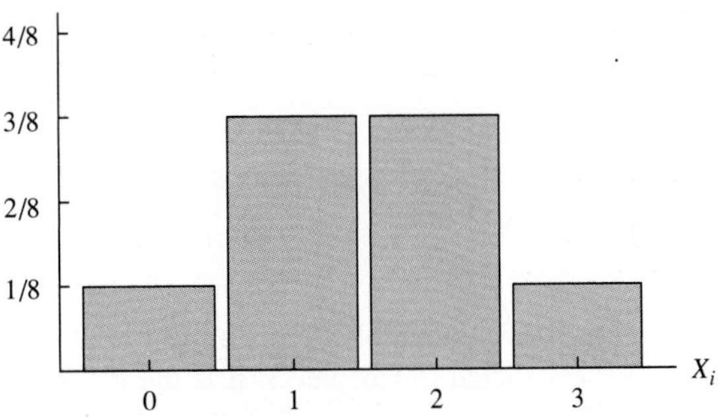

> **Probability Distribution** A list of all possible outcomes of some experiment and the probability associated with each outcome.

The probability that a random variable X can take on some specific value, x_i, is written $P(X = x_i)$. Thus, the probability that three flips of a coin result in two heads is $P(X = 2) = 3/8$. Note that $0 \leq P(X = x_i) \leq 1$ and $\Sigma P(X = x_i) = 1$.

5.2 The Mean and the Variance of Discrete Distributions

Just as we calculated the mean of a data set in Chapter 3, we can also determine the mean of a probability distribution. The mean of a probability distribution is called the **expected value** $E(X)$, and is found by multiplying each possible outcome by its probability and summing the results, as shown in Formula (5.1).

Mean or expected value of a discrete probability distribution

$$\mu = E(X) = \Sigma[(x_i)P(x_i)] \qquad [5.1]$$

where x_i are the individual outcomes

Table 5.2
The Discrete Probability Distribution for Rolling a Die

(1) Outcome (x_i)	(2) $P(x_i)$	(3) $(x_i) \cdot P(x_i)$	(4) $(x_i - \mu)^2 \cdot P(x_i)$
1	1/6	1/6	$(1 - 3.5)^2 \cdot 1/6 = 1.042$
2	1/6	2/6	$(2 - 3.5)^2 \cdot 1/6 = 0.375$
3	1/6	3/6	$(3 - 3.5)^2 \cdot 1/6 = 0.042$
4	1/6	4/6	$(4 - 3.5)^2 \cdot 1/6 = 0.042$
5	1/6	5/6	$(5 - 3.5)^2 \cdot 1/6 = 0.375$
6	1/6	6/6	$(6 - 3.5)^2 \cdot 1/6 = 1.042$
	1.00	$3.5 = \mu = E(X)$	$2.92 = \sigma^2$

The probability distribution for the experiment of rolling a die is shown in the first two columns of Table 5.2. Column (3) illustrates the calculation of the expected value for the experiment using Formula (5.1). Each outcome is multiplied by its respective probability, and the results are summed, yielding $\mu = E(X) = 3.5$. Does this suggest that if we roll a die we can expect to get a 3.5? Hardly. It means that if we average the results of rolling a die many times (theoretically, an infinite number), we will get 3.5.

> **Expected Value** The expected value of a discrete random variable is the weighted mean of all possible outcomes in which the weights are respective probabilities of those outcomes.

The variance of a probability distribution is conceptually the same as the variance we calculated in Chapter 3. It is the mean of the squared deviations from the mean. The variance may be written as:

Variance of a probability distribution	$\sigma^2 = \Sigma[(x_i - \mu)^2 P(x_i)]$	[5.2]

Formula (5.2) measures the difference between each of the outcomes and their mean. These differences are squared and multiplied by their respective probabilities. The results are then summed. As column (4) of Table 5.2 reveals, $\sigma^2 = 2.92$.

The standard deviation is $\sigma = \sqrt{\sigma^2} = \sqrt{2.92} = 1.71$. The variance and the standard deviation carry the same interpretation as they did in Chapter 3. They measure the dispersion of the outcomes around their mean. The variance is expressed in units squared, but the standard deviation is expressed in the same units as the random variable and thus often carries a more rational interpretation.

Example 5.1 The number of houses sold each month by Ponder Real Estate, which has varied from 5 to 20, is reported, along with the frequency of each sales level, in the first two columns of the table shown below.

(1) Number of Months	(2) Houses (x_i)	(3) $P(x_i)$	(4) $(x_i)P(x_i)$	(5) $(x_i - \mu)^2 P(x_i)$
3	5	3/24 = 0.125	0.625	$(5 - 10.912)^2(0.125) = 4.369$
7	8	7/24 = 0.292	2.336	$(8 - 10.912)^2(0.292) = 2.476$
4	10	4/24 = 0.167	1.670	$(10 - 10.912)^2(0.167) = 0.139$
5	12	5/24 = 0.208	2.496	$(12 - 10.912)^2(0.208) = 0.246$
3	17	3/24 = 0.125	2.125	$(17 - 10.912)^2(0.125) = 4.633$
2	20	2/24 = 0.083	1.660	$(20 - 10.912)^2(0.083) = 6.855$
24		1.000	$10.912 = \mu$	$18.718 = \sigma^2$

Mr. Ponder hopes these numbers reflect an increase in the average number of sales over the 7.3 he sold in earlier months and a reduction in the variability of monthly sales that had been $\sigma = 5.7$. If not, he has decided to sell the business and become a rodeo clown. What advice can you offer Mr. Ponder?

Solution: You must first determine the probability of each level of sales, as shown in column (3). For example, in 3 of the 24 months, 5 houses were sold: $P(x_i = 5) = 0.125$. The expected value, or mean, is calculated by multiplying these probabilities by their respective sales levels. It is shown in column (4) to be $\mu = 10.912$ houses per month. The variability is measured by the variance and is displayed in the last column. The squared difference between each observation and the mean of 10.912 is multiplied by the appropriate probabilities and summed to yield $\sigma^2 = 18.718$ houses squared, with $\sigma = 4.236$ houses.

Interpretation: Mr. Ponder can relax. He has increased his mean monthly sales and reduced their variability. He should remain in real estate.

Section Exercises

1. Give several examples of both discrete and continuous probability distributions that might commonly appear in a business setting. What is the difference between a discrete and a continuous probability distribution?

2. Are the following random variables discrete or continuous? In each case why did you answer the way you did?
   a. Cars sold by Honest Harry.
   b. The revenue Harry earns.
   c. Completion times for a particular job task.
   d. The employees required to complete that job task.
3. Calculate and interpret the expected value, the variance, and the standard deviation of the experiment of flipping a coin three times and noting the number of heads.
4. The number of employee complaints at Fidelity Services has ranged from 0 to 6 each day, as shown in the table below. Calculate and interpret the expected value, the variance, and the standard deviation.

Complaints	Number of Days	Complaints	Number of Days
0	3	4	2
1	4	5	1
2	3	6	4
3	6		

5. To gather data for a research project, a marketing major at a small university in the Midwest counted the number of students in 50 business courses who had recently purchased CDs. He found no students had made such a purchase in 12 classes, 3 students had in 8 classes, 4 had in 9 classes, 5 had in 15 classes, and 7 students in the remaining 6 classes had recently added to their music collections. The student wanted to begin his research by summarizing his data. How can you help?

A surprisingly large number of business decisions depend on the prevailing probability distribution. One of the more important is the binomial distribution.

5.3 The Binomial Distribution—a Discrete Probability Distribution

The experiment with the coin flip discussed above has only two possible outcomes; (1) head and (2) tail. The probability of each is known and constant from one trial (flip) to the next and the experiment can be repeated many times. Experiments of this type follow a **binomial distribution.** Based on the Bernoulli process, named for Jacob Bernoulli (1654–1705), a member of a family of Swiss mathematicians, a binomial distribution exhibits four properties:

1. There must be only two possible outcomes. One is identified as a success, the other as a failure. However, you are warned not to attach any connotation of "good" or "bad" to these terms. They are quite objective, and a "success" does not necessarily imply a desirable outcome.
2. The probability of a success, π, remains constant from one trial to the next, as does the probability of a failure, $1 - \pi$.
3. The probability of a success in one trial is totally independent of any other trial.
4. The experiment can be repeated many times.

It should be apparent why the coin flip fits the requirements for a binomial distribution.

Many business-related examples can also be cited. Labor unions often want to know how many workers (1) are interested in joining a union, as opposed to those who (2) are not interested. Bankers may survey economic experts as to whether they feel interest rates (1) will go up or (2) will not go up. Marketing personnel want to know if a person (1) does or (2) does not prefer a certain product. The application of the binomial distribution to business settings is almost unlimited.

A Binomial Distribution Each trial in a binomial distribution results in one of only two mutually exclusive outcomes, one of which is identified as a success and the other as a failure. The probability of each outcome remains constant from one trial to the next.

If we know the probability that any given trial will result in a success, it is possible to estimate how many successes there will be in a given number of trials. For example, if the probability that any single worker is interested in joining a union is known, then the probability that any given number of workers in the labor force would be interested in joining can be estimated. The probability that out of n number of workers, a given number x would be interested in joining is

The binomial formula

$$P(x) = \frac{n!}{x!\,(n-x)!}\pi^x(1-\pi)^{n-x} = {}_nC_x(\pi)^x(1-\pi)^{n-x} \qquad [5.3]$$

Although the formula looks rather formidable, do not despair. Probabilities for different values of π, x, and n have been calculated for you and tabulated in Appendix III, Table B, in the back of the book.

Consider the following situation. A credit manager for American Express has found that $\pi = 10$ percent of the company's card users do not pay the full amount of indebtedness during any given month. She wants to determine the probability that of $n = 20$ accounts randomly selected, $x = 5$ of them are not paid. This can be written as $P(X = 5 \mid n = 20, \pi = 0.10)$, which is read as "the probability of five successes given that there are 20 trials and the probability of a success of any one trial is 10 percent."

The probability that 5 accounts out of the 20 sampled remain unpaid can be calculated by using Formula (5.3). Where $n = 20$, $X = 5$, and $\pi = 0.10$, we have

$${}_{20}C_5(0.10)^5(0.90)^{20-5} = (15504)(0.00001)(0.2058911) = 0.0319$$

If the probability that any one account is not paid in full is $\pi = 0.10$, then there is a 3.19 percent chance that exactly 5 of 20 accounts selected at random will retain a positive balance.

This information is more readily attained by using Table B. Notice that the first two columns in the table show possible values for n and x. Locate the value of 20 for n since there are 20 trials (accounts) in our experiment. Since the credit manager seeks the probability $x = 5$ successes (unpaid accounts), locate the row containing probability values for $x = 5$. Proceed across that row until you find the column headed by $\pi = 0.10$. There you will find the value 0.0319, the answer to the credit manager's question.

Consider another example of binomial distribution. Sales personnel for Widgets, Inc., make a sale to 15 percent of the customers on whom they call. If a member of the sales staff calls on 15 customers today, what is the probability he or she will sell exactly two widgets? Given $\pi = 0.15$, $n = 15$, and $x = 2$, locate the value for $n = 15$, then the row pertaining to $x = 2$. In that row headed by the column $\pi = 0.15$, you will find $P(x = 2 \mid n = 15, \pi = 0.15) = 0.2856$. There is a 28.56 percent chance that exactly two sales will be made out of 15 sales calls.

Example 5.2 According to the *Journal of Higher Education,* 40 percent of all high school graduates work during the summer to earn money for college tuition for the upcoming fall term. If 7 graduates are selected at random, what is the probability that (*a*) 5 have summer jobs, (*b*) none work, (*c*) all work?

Solution:

a. Locate the value for $n = 7$ and $\pi = 0.40$. The row corresponding to $x = 5$ yields a value of .0774. There is a 7.74 percent probability that 5 of the 7 graduates have taken summer jobs to earn tuition money.

b. Given $n = 7$ and $\pi = 0.40$, the probability that none work is shown in the table to be $P(x = 0) = 0.0280$.

c. The probability that all students work is seen to be $P(x = 7 \mid n = 7, \pi = 0.4) = 0.0016$.

Interpretation: It is highly unlikely that none of the students work.

The binomial table includes values of π only up to 0.5. What do we do if the probability of a success is higher? Presume that 70 percent of all the residents of Flatbush have home computers hooked to the Internet. What is the probability that out of 10 residents chosen at random, 6 are "plugged in"? Since $\pi > 0.5$, we can't use Table B (Appendix III) without some adjustment. However, if the probability of a success (a resident is hooked to the Internet) is $P(S) = 0.70$, the probability he or she is not hooked up is $P(\overline{S}) = 0.30$. Further, if 6 of the 10 residents are Internet users, then 4 are not. That is, 6 successes at $\pi = 0.70$ is the *same* as 4 failures at $\pi = 0.30$. Instead of finding x successes at π, we find $n - x$ failures at $1.00 - \pi$.

This practice can be illustrated by constructing two ordered arrays like those seen here, one from 0 to 10 at $\pi = 0.70$ and one from 10 to 0 at $\pi = 0.30$.

0	1	2	3	4	5	**6**	7	8	9	10	($\pi = 0.70$)
10	9	8	7	6	5	**4**	3	2	1	0	($\pi = 0.30$)

This more clearly reveals that $P(X = \mathbf{6} \mid n = 10, \pi = \mathbf{0.70}) = P(X = \mathbf{4} \mid n = 10, \pi = \mathbf{0.30})$. From Table B (Appendix III), this is seen to be 0.2001.

A. The Mean and the Variance of a Binomial Distribution

Earlier we saw how to determine the mean and the variance of a discrete distribution using Formulas (5.1) and (5.2). However, if there are only two possible outcomes, as with a binomial distribution, the mean and variance can more readily be determined as

Mean of a binomial distribution

$$E(X) = \mu = n\pi \tag{5.4}$$

and

Variance of a binomial distribution	$\sigma^2 = n\pi(1 - \pi)$	[5.5]

For the Flatbush residents, if $n = 10$, $E(X) = (10)(0.70) = 7$. Out of 10 people selected at random, we would expect 7 to be on the Internet. The variance is $\sigma^2 = (10)(0.70)(0.30) = 2.1$ and the standard deviation is $\sigma = 1.45$.

B. Cumulative Binomial Distributions

Given the data in Example 5.2 for the students' summer jobs, suppose that we wanted to determine the probability that 3 or fewer students worked. This problem involves a *cumulative* binomial distribution since we are interested in a *range* of values (0 to 3) rather than a single, specific number. The ordered array below illustrates this point. The probability of event A (0 to 3 work) is $P(A) = P(X \leq 3)$.

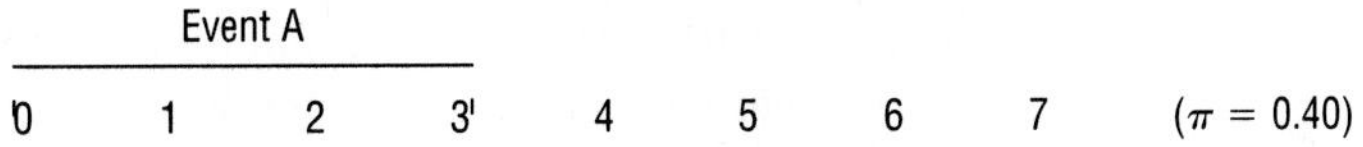

Event A (0 through 3)

0 1 2 3 4 5 6 7 ($\pi = 0.40$)

In Table B (Appendix III), this can be found by summing up $P(X = 0) + P(X = 1) + P(X = 3) + P(X = 3) = 0.7102$. For convenience, these summations are compiled in Table C, which shows the probability of the number of successes being equal to *or less than* some amount. In our present case, we have $P(X \leq 3 \mid n = 7, \pi = 0.40) = 0.7102$.

Remember, Table C provides the probability that the number of successes is equal to or less than some amount. Suppose we want to know $P(A) = P(X \geq 5)$. Table C will not directly yield the probability a number of successes is equal to *or greater than* some amount. Take a look at the ordered array.

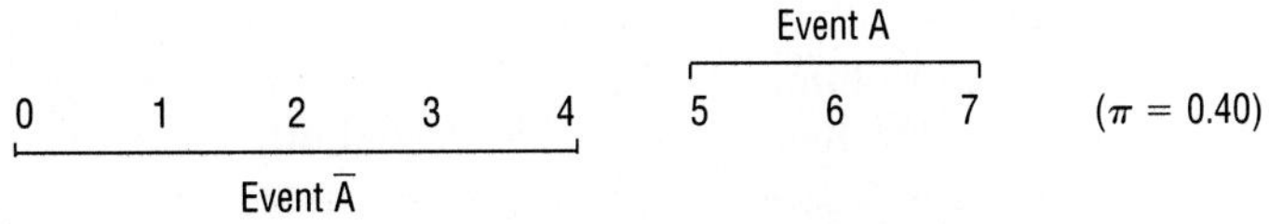

Event A (5 through 7)

0 1 2 3 4 5 6 7 ($\pi = 0.40$)

Event $\bar{A}$ (0 through 4)

If event A is $P(X \geq 5)$, then not $\bar{A}$ is 4 or less, which can be found in Table C. We know that $P(A) = 1 - P(\bar{A})$. Then, $P(X \geq 5 \mid n = 7, \pi = 0.40) = 1 - P(X \leq 4 \mid n = 7, \pi = 0.40)$. From Table C, we see this is $1 - 0.9037 = 0.0963$. The probability that at least 5 of the 7 students have summer jobs is 9.63 percent.

Suppose we needed to determine the probability that between 3 and 5 students, inclusive, worked. Again, the array proves useful.

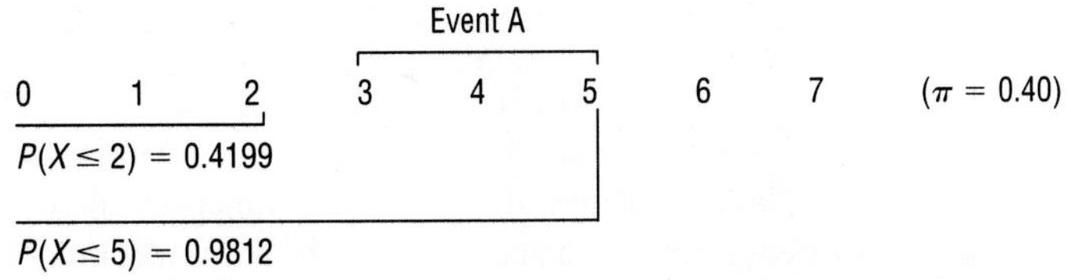

Event A (3 through 5)

0 1 2 3 4 5 6 7 ($\pi = 0.40$)

$P(X \leq 2) = 0.4199$

$P(X \leq 5) = 0.9812$

$P(3 \leq X \leq 5) = P(X \leq 5) - P(X \leq 2) = 0.9812 - 0.4199 = 0.5613$

$P(3 \leq X \leq 5 \mid n = 7, \pi = 0.40)$ must be determined in two steps. First, we determine the probability that the number of students with jobs is 0 to 5 (which includes the 3 to 5 interval we seek), and then we subtract out the probability that the number of enterprising students is 2 or less. Then $P(3 \leq X \leq 5) = P(0 \leq X \leq 5) - P(0 \leq X \leq 2) = 0.9812 - 0.4199 = 0.5613$.

If $\pi > 0.50$, we need two ordered arrays. Assume that 80 percent of all graduates took summer jobs. An array for $\pi = 0.80$ and one for $1 - \pi = 0.20$ must be constructed.

Event A								
0	1	2	3	4	5	6	7	($\pi = 0.80$)
7	6	5	4	3	2	1	0	($\pi = 0.20$)
Event A				Event $\bar{A}$				

If, as before, we want the probability that 3 or fewer students work, we must find $P(A) = P(X \leq 3 \mid n = 7, \pi = 0.80)$. Since Table C does not contain values for $\pi > 0.50$, we must turn to the ordered array for $\pi = 1 - 0.80 = 0.20$. We see that the probability 3 or fewer work at $\pi = 0.80$ is the *same* as the probability that 4 or more do not work. That is, if 3 of the 7 work, 4 do not; if 2 of the 7 work, 5 do not, and so on. Thus, $P(A)$ is also equal to $P(X \geq 4 \mid n = 7, \pi = 0.20)$. However, we still have a problem. Table C will not directly yield the probability that X is equal to or greater than some value, such as 4 in this case. The solution to this nagging dilemma is the same as before: we find the probability of $\bar{A}$, that is, 3 or less, and subtract from 1. $P(X \leq 3 \mid n = 7, \pi = 0.80) = 1 - P(X \leq 3 \mid n = 7, \pi = 0.20) = 1 - 0.9667 = 0.0333$.

C. Using the Computer

Both Minitab and Excel easily compute these binomial probabilities. To use Minitab to determine the probabilities for the summer jobs in Example 5.2, enter the values for X in the cells of column (1) (or any other column). In this case, enter 5, 0, and 7 in the first three cells of column (1). Then choose **Calc > Probability Distributions > Binomial > Probability.** Enter the number of trials, 7 in this case, in the **Number of Trials** box, 0.40 in the **Probability of a Success** box, and *C*1 (where you earlier entered the values for X) in the **Input Column** box. The resulting printout is seen in Display 5.1. Had you chosen **Cumulative Probability** instead of **Probability** above, Minitab would have returned the cumulative probabilities as they appear in Table C.

Minitab Display 5.1

```
Probability Density Function

Binomial with n = 7 and p = 0.400000
          x          P(X = x)
       5.00           0.0774
       0.00           0.0280
       7.00           0.0016
MTB >
```

Excel works similarly. Place the cursor in the cell of the worksheet where you want the answer to appear. Then choose **Insert > Function > Statistical** (from the function category box) > **Binomdist** (from the function name box). Click on **Next.** Enter 5 in the **Numbers** box (for 5 successes), 7 in the **Trials** box, 0.4 in the **Probability** box, and False in the **Cumulative** box. Select **Finish.** The answer will appear in the **Value** box in the upper right corner and in the cell you designated in the worksheet. If you had entered True in the **Cumulative** box, the cumulative probability for 5 successes would be reported as they appear in Table C.

Section Exercises

6. What are the four characteristics of a binomial distribution? Give at least three business-related examples.

7. Ten percent of the computer disks produced by a new process are defective. If there 20 disks in a box;
   a. How many would you expect to be defective?
   b. What is the probability that the number of defective disks equals the expected number you determined in your answer to part *a*?

8. From the problem above, what variation would you expect to find in defective disks from one box to another?

9. Only 20 percent of the civilian employees at a restricted military base carry their personal identification. If 10 employees arrive, what is the probability that the security guard will find:
   a. 8 employees with identification?
   b. 4 employees with identification?
   c. At least 4 employees with identification?
   d. At most 5 employees with identification?
   e. Between 4 and 7 employees with identification?

10. Answer the above question if 60 percent of all employees carry identification.

11. You have hired eight telephone receptionists to take telephone orders for a sporting goods line your company is marketing. A receptionist is busy cataloguing an order 30 percent of the time. You do not want the probability that a customer's call is met with a busy signal to exceed 50 percent. Should you have hired more receptionists if three customers call?

12. A student must get at least 60 percent on a true-false test with 18 questions to pass. If the student flips a coin to determine the answer to each question, what is the probability the student will pass?

5.4 The Hypergeometric Distribution

As we just learned, the binomial distribution is appropriate only if the probability of a success remains constant for each trial. This will occur if the sampling is done with replacement or from an infinite (or very large) population. However, if the population is rather small and sampling occurs without replacement, the probability of a success will vary. If the probability of a success is not constant, the **hypergeometric distribution** is particularly useful. The probability function for the hypergeometric distribution is

Hypergeometric distribution

$$P(x) = \frac{{}_{r}C_{x} \; {}_{N-r}C_{n-x}}{{}_{N}C_{n}} \qquad [5.6]$$

where N is the population size
r is the number in the population identified as a success
n is the sample size
x is the number in the sample identified as a success

The Hypergeometric Distribution If a sample is selected without replacement from a known finite population and contains a relatively large proportion of the population, such that the probability of a success is measurably altered from one selection to the next, the hypergeometric distribution should be used.

Assume a racing stable has $N = 10$ horses, and $r = 4$ of them have a contagious disease. What is the probability of selecting a sample of $n = 3$ in which there are $x = 2$ diseased horses?

$$\begin{aligned} P(X = 2) &= \frac{{}_4C_2 \; {}_{10-4}C_{3-2}}{{}_{10}C_3} \\ &= \frac{6 \times 6}{120} \\ &= 0.30 \end{aligned}$$

There is a 30 percent probability of selecting three racehorses, two of which are ill.

Example 5.3 **Use of the Hypergeometric Distribution to Examine Discrimination**

In a recent case in Johnson District Court in Kansas City, three women brought suit against a local utility company, charging sex discrimination. Of nine people who were eligible for promotion, four were women. Three of the nine were actually given promotions; only one of those promoted was a woman. The other three eligible women sued the utility. A major consideration in the case hinged on what the probability was that out of the three people promoted, no more than one woman would be chosen by chance. That is, if gender was not a factor, what is the probability that no more than one of the three promotions would go to a woman?

Solution: An economic consultant specializing in legal matters was called in by the defense attorney to address the charges. The economist calculated the probability that, in the absence of discrimination, only one of the women would be promoted. This calculation was based on

$N = 9$; the number of people eligible for promotion

$r = 4$; the number in the population identified as successes (women)

$n = 3$; the number in the sample (those chosen for promotion)

$x \leq 1$; the number of successes (women) in the sample

The probability that no more than one woman was promoted is $P(X = 0) + P(X = 1)$.

$$P(X = 1) = \frac{{}_4C_1 \, {}_5C_2}{{}_9C_3} = \frac{4 \times 10}{84} = 0.4762$$

$$P(X = 0) = \frac{{}_4C_0 \, {}_5C_3}{{}_9C_3} = \frac{1 \times 10}{84} = 0.1190$$

Thus, $P(X \leq 1) = 0.4762 + 0.1190 = 0.5962$.

Interpretation: There was almost a 60 percent probability that without any consideration given to gender, no more than one woman would be promoted. On the basis of these findings, as well as other evidence presented in the case, the court ruled that there was not sufficient evidence of discrimination.

A. Using the Computer

Excel works almost like magic in solving hypergeometric distributions. Simply click on **INSERT > FUNCTION > STATISTICAL > HYPERGEOMETRIC.** Then enter the values for x, n, r, and N. The answer will appear in the **Value** box.

Section Exercises

13. As assistant manager at your commodities firm, you must hire 10 people from 30 applicants, 22 of whom have college degrees. What is the probability that 5 of those you hire have a degree?

14. Of the 15 senior executives in an import-export business, 12 are to sent to Japan to study a new production process. Eight of the executives already have some training in the process. What is the probability that 5 of those sent have some knowledge of the process before leaving for the Far East?

15. Forty workers in your office have just been given new computers. Twenty-seven have the new MMX technology. If 10 are selected at random, what is the probability that 3 are equipped with MMX?

16. A survey in *Fortune* magazine (March 17, 1997) serves as the source for this problem, which you are asked by your supervisor to solve. Of 10 male employees, 7 had working wives. What is the probability that at most one husband has a wife who is employed outside the home if 3 are randomly chosen?

17. From the problem above, the survey revealed that 6 of the 10 employees made in excess of $95,000 per year. Of the 3 selected, what is the probability that all 3 make over $95,000?

5.5 The Poisson Distribution

A discrete random variable that is highly useful in measuring the relative frequency of an event over some unit of time or space is the **Poisson distribution.** It is often used to describe the number of arrivals of customers per hour, the number of industrial accidents each month, the number of defective electrical connections per mile of wiring in a city's power system, or the number of machines that break down and are awaiting repair.

> **Poisson Distribution** Developed by the French mathematician Simeon Poisson (1781–1840), the Poisson distribution measures the probability of a random event over some interval of time or space.

Two assumptions are necessary for the application of the Poisson distribution:

1. The probability of the occurrence of the event is constant for any two intervals of time or space.
2. The occurrence of the event in any interval is independent of the occurrence in any other interval.

Given these assumptions, the Poisson probability function can be expressed as

Poisson probability function	$$P(x) = \frac{\mu^x e^{-\mu}}{x!}$$	[5.7]

where x is the number of times the event occurs
μ is the mean number of occurrences per unit of time or space
e = 2.71828, the base of the natural logarithm system

Suppose we are interested in the probability that exactly five customers will arrive during the next hour (or any given hour) of business. Simple observation over the past 80 hours has shown that 800 customers have entered our business. Thus, $\mu = 10$ per hour. Using Formula (5.7),

$$P(5) = \frac{(10)^5 \times 2.71828^{-10}}{5!} = 0.0378$$

Since this formula is a little awkward, probabilities for selected values are given in Table D. Go across the top of the table until you find $\mu = 10$. Go down that column to the row where $x = 5$. There you will find 0.0378. There is a 3.78 percent chance that exactly five customers will enter the store during the next hour.

A local paving company obtained a contract with the county to maintain roads servicing a large urban center. The roads recently paved by this company revealed an average of two defects per mile after use for one year. If the county retains this paving company, what is the probability of 3 defects in any given mile of road after carrying traffic for one year?

$$P(1) = \frac{2^3 \times 2.71828^{-2}}{3!} = 0.1804$$

or 18.04 percent. To use Table D, find the column where $\mu = 2$ and the row where $x = 3$. There you will find the value 0.1804.

Presume for the moment that we wish to know the probability of 3 defects in 0.5 miles. Since the mean is given in occurrences per *one mile* (2 per one mile) it is necessary to adjust μ to fit the stipulation in the problem of 0.5 miles. We must determine what percentage 0.5 miles is of 1 mile: $0.5/1 = 0.5$. Then, the mean number of occurrences for this problem is $\mu = (0.5)(2 \text{ occurrences}) = 1$. If the average is 2 per mile, it is going to be 1 per one-half mile. Thus, $P(X = 3 \mid \mu = 1) = 0.0613$. Take a look at Example 5.4, especially part *c*.

You should also realize that if the values in the problem exceed the limited ranges in Table D, it is possible to work the problem with most handheld calculators by remembering the rule of exponents: $e^{-\mu} = 1/e^{\mu}$. Then,

$$\begin{aligned} P(X = 3 \mid \mu = 1) &= \frac{\mu^x e^{-\mu}}{x!} \\ &= \frac{1^3\, 2.71828^{-1}}{3!} \\ &= \frac{(1)\left[\dfrac{1}{2.71828^1}\right]}{3!} \\ &= 0.0613 \end{aligned}$$

Example 5.4 **A Poisson Distribution for Prudent Students**

Professor Bradley encourages his statistics students to "act in a prudent manner" by consulting the tutor if they have any questions as they prepare for the final exam. It appears that students' arrival at the tutor's office fits a Poisson distribution, with an average of 5.2 students every 20 minutes. Professor Bradley is concerned that if too many students need the tutor's services, a crowding problem may develop.

a. The tutor must determine the probability that four students will arrive during any 20-minute interval, which could create the crowding problem Professor Bradley fears. If this probability exceeds 20 percent, a second tutor will be hired.

b. The tutor must also calculate the probability that more than four students will arrive during any 20-minute period. If it is greater than 50 percent, the tutor's office hours will be extended, allowing students to spread out the times they come to see the tutor.

c. If the probability that more than seven students arrive during any 30-minute time period exceeds 50 percent, Professor Bradley himself will offer additional tutoring.

Solution: *a.* $P(X = 4 \mid \mu = 5.2) = 0.1681$

b. $P(X > 4 \mid \mu = 5.2)$

$$= 1 - P(X \leq 4 \mid \mu = 5.2)$$

$$= 1 - [P(X = 0) + P(X = 1) + P(X = 2) + P(X = 3) + P(X = 4)]$$

$$= 1 - [0.0055 + 0.0287 + 0.0746 + 0.1293 + 0.1681]$$

$$= 0.5938$$

c. It is given that $\mu = 5.2$ for every 20 minutes. The good professor's stipulation covers a 30-minute period. We must determine what percentage 30 is of 20: $30/20 = 1.5$. Then, μ for every 30 minutes is $5.2(1.5) = 7.8$. Thus,

$$\begin{aligned} P(X > 7 \mid \mu = 7.8) &= 1 - [P(X \leq 7)] \\ &= 1 - [P(X = 0) + \cdots + P(X = 7)] \\ &= 0.5133 \end{aligned}$$

Interpretation: Since $P(X = 4) = 0.1681 < 20$ percent, a second tutor is unnecessary. $P(X > 4) = 0.5938 > 50$ percent; the tutor's office hours will be extended. And $P(X > 7) = 0.5133 > 50$ percent; Professor Bradley will assist in the tutoring efforts.

A. Using the Computer

Poisson probabilities can also be obtained using Minitab and Excel. Suppose we want to determine the probability that 4 students will arrive at the tutor's office in part *a* of Example 5.4. To get the Poisson probabilities with Minitab, enter 4 in column (1) of the worksheet. Choose **Calc** > **Probability Distribution** > **Poisson** > **Probability.** Enter 5.2 in the **Mean** box and C1 in the **Input Column** box.

To use Excel, choose **Insert** > **Function** > **Statistical** > **Poisson.** Click on **Next.** Enter 4 in the **x** box, 5.2 in the **Mean** box and False in the **Cumulative** box. The answer will appear in the **Value** box in the upper right-hand corner.

Section Exercises

18. Calls come in to a switchboard at the company home office at the rate of two each minute on the average and are known to be Poisson distributed. If the operator is distracted for one minute, what is the probability the number of unanswered calls is:

a. Zero?
b. At least one?
c. Between 3 and 5, inclusive?

19. What are the probabilities in Exercise 18 if the operator is distracted for 4 minutes?

20. A manufacturing process used to make authentic plastic Incan artifacts suffers a defect rate of 5 per 100 units. The units are shipped to dealers in lots of 200. If the probability that more than 3 are defective exceeds 30 percent, you plan to stock T-shirts of the Grateful Dead instead. Which item do you add to inventory?

21. You purchase bicycle parts from a supplier in Toledo that has 3 defects per 100 parts. You are in the market for 150 parts but will not accept a probability of more than 50 percent that more than two parts are defective. Do you buy from this supplier?

5.6 The Exponential Distribution

As we just saw, the Poisson distribution is a discrete distribution that measures the number of occurrences over some interval of time or space. It describes, for example, the number of customers who might arrive during some given period. The **exponential distribution,** on the other hand, is a continuous distribution. It measures the passage of time between those occurrences. While the Poisson distribution describes arrival rates (of people, trucks, telephone calls, etc.) within some time period, the exponential distribution estimates the lapse of time between those arrivals. If the number of occurrences is Poisson distributed, the lapse of time between occurrences will be exponentially distributed.

The probability that the lapse of time is less than or equal to some amount x is

Exponential distribution

$$P(X \leq x) = 1 - e^{-\mu t} \qquad [5.8]$$

where t is the time lapse
e is the base of the natural logarithm system, 2.71828
μ is the mean rate of occurrence

The distribution of an exponential random variable is displayed in Figure 5.2. The continuously declining curve shows that as lapsed time X increases, the probability decreases.

Figure 5.2
Exponential Distribution

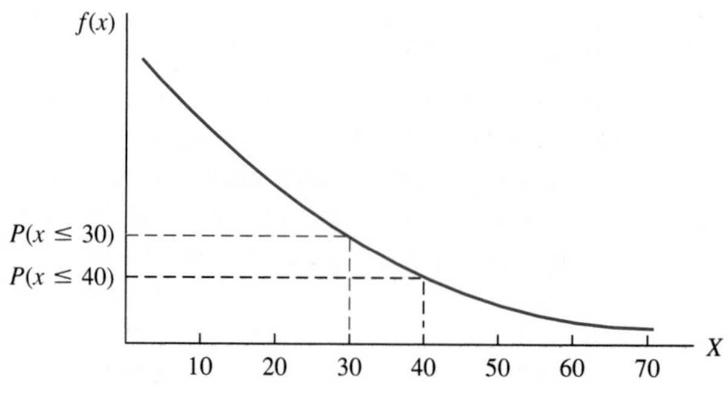

The probability that 30 minutes will lapse between occurrences exceeds the probability that 40 minutes will lapse: $P(X \leq 30) > P(X \leq 40)$. This is because 30 minutes must *always* lapse before 40 minutes can.

Just as we had to adjust the mean arrival rate to fit the stipulation in a Poisson distribution, a similar correction is necessary for exponential distribution. Here, however, it is easier to adjust the value for time t in Formula (5.8) to fit the time frame stipulated in the problem. Assume that the mean arrival rate of customers is $\mu = 1.5$ per hour and we want to know the probability that no more than two hours will lapse between arrivals. Using Formula (5.7), t is 2. Then, $P(X \leq 2) = 1 - e^{-(1.5)(2)} = 1 - e^{-3}$. The solution can be found with most handheld calculators as $e^{-3} = 1/e^3 = 0.0498$. You may want to use the Poisson table (Table D) much as we did in solving Poisson problems. The secret is to set $x = 0$ and to ignore the negative sign for μ. With the value of 3 for the exponent and $x = 0$, Table D reveals $e^3 = 0.0498$. The probability that no more than two hours will lapse between the arrival of customers is $1 - 0.0498 = 0.9502$. There is a 95.02 percent chance that a second customer will enter within two hours of the first if the mean rate of arrivals is 1.5 per hour.

Trucks arrive at the loading dock at the rate of $\mu = 2$ per hour. What is the probability no more than 30 minutes will lapse between arrivals? The mean rate of arrival is given per hour, or 60 minutes, and the problem is stated in minutes (30 of them). To avoid the "apples and oranges thing" we must find *what percentage the 30 minutes is of 60.* Thus, $t = 30/60 = 1/2$. Then, $P(X \leq 30 \text{ min.}) = 1 - e^{-(2)(1/2)} = 1 - e^{-2.}$ Using a calculator, or relying on Table D by setting $x = 0$, we have $1 - 0.1353 = 0.8647$.

Example 5.5 Cross City Cab Company schedules its taxicabs to arrive at the local airport in a Poisson distribution with a mean arrival rate of 12 per hour. You have just landed at the airport and must get into town to close a big business deal. What is the probability you will have to wait no more than 5 minutes to get a cab? Your boss is a tyrant who will not tolerate failure, so if the probability another cab will be along within 5 minutes is less than 50 percent, you will rent a car for the trip to the office.

Solution: Assuming the worst, that the last cab just left, you must determine $P(X \leq 5 \text{ minutes})$. Since $\mu = 12$ per 60 minutes, you must determine what percentages the 5 minutes is of the 60: $5/60 = 1/12$. Therefore, $t = 1/12$ and $P(X \leq 5) = 1 - e^{-(12)(1/12)} = 1 - e^{-1}$. With a calculator or using Table D, you determine $P(X \leq 5) = 1 - 0.3679 = 63.21\%$.

Interpretation: You can relax and wait for the cab. There is a 63.21 percent (> 50 percent) chance that one will be along within 5 minutes.

While waiting for the cab, you might consider that the probability one will arrive between 5 and 10 minutes is equal to $P(X \leq 10) - P(X \leq 5)$. You may also want to kill some time by reviewing your algebraic rules of exponents in case the exponent for e does not conveniently work out to a nice respectable whole number as it did above. Recall that $e^{-3} = \frac{1}{e^3}$ and $e^{-0.4} = e^{-4/10} = 1/\sqrt[10]{e^4}$.

A. Using the Computer

Excel again proves its worth in calculating exponential probabilities. Merely click on **Insert > Function > Statistical > Expondist.** Entered the *adjusted* value for t in the **x** box, the mean in the **Lambda** box and True in the **Cumulative** box. Presto, the answer appears in the **Value** box.

Section Exercises

22. Planes arrive at the small airport in Puerto Vallarta, Mexico, at the rate of two per hour. It will take one hour to repair a ramp used to disembark passengers. What is the probability that a plane will arrive while the ramp is under repair?
23. The university's main computer goes off line three times per week. Professor Mundane must complete a project this week which requires the computer. What is the probability the computer will be down all week?
24. In Exercise 23, what is the probability the computer will be down for any two-week period?
25. During a typical 8-hour workday, the computers used to monitor the cooling stage in the production of automobile tires signal that the temperature is improperly maintained 30 times. Mr. Radial, the company's CEO, is to drop by for a 30-minute inspection of the plant. What is the probability he will be there when the computer's signal is activated?
26. In Exercise 25, what is the probability Mr. Radial's visit will be uninterrupted by the computer's signal?

5.7 The Uniform Distribution

The **uniform probability distribution** is a distribution in which the probabilities of all the outcomes are the same. The experiment of rolling a die shown in Table 5.2 is an example. All six outcomes had a 1/6 probability of occurrence. Figure 5.3 shows a uniform distribution in which all outcomes over the distribution's entire range of possibilities from its minimum of a to its maximum of b are equally likely.

Uniform Distribution The probabilities in a uniform distribution are the same for all possible outcomes.

The mean, or expected value, of a uniform distribution is halfway between its two end points. Thus,

Mean of a uniform distribution
$$E(x) = \mu = \frac{a + b}{2} \qquad [5.9]$$

where a and b are the lowest and highest values, respectively.

Figure 5.3
A Uniform Distribution

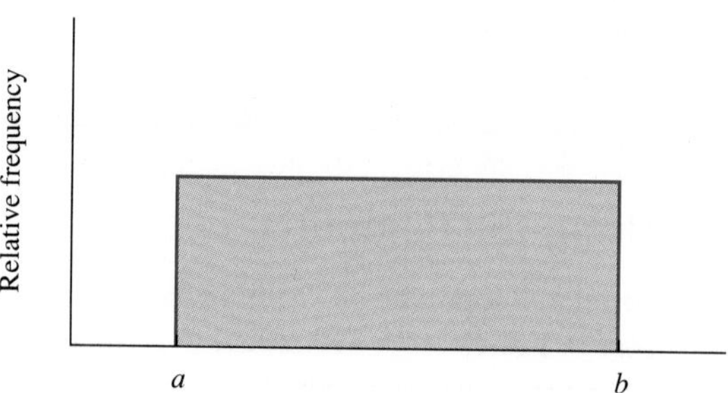

The variance is found as

Variance of a uniform probability distribution	$\sigma^2 = \dfrac{(b - a)^2}{12}$	[5.10]

The total area under the curve, as is the case with all continuous probability distributions, must equal 1, or 100 percent. Since the area is height times width, the height is

$$\text{Height} = \frac{\text{Area}}{\text{Width}}$$

and, therefore,

$$\text{Height} = \frac{1}{b - a} \qquad [5.11]$$

where $b - a$ is the width or range of the distribution.

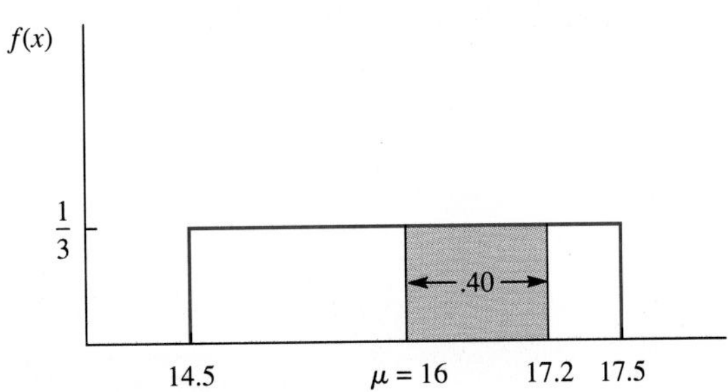

Figure 5.4
A Uniform Distribution of Canned Products

Suppose the contents of the 16-ounce cans of fruit produced by Del Monte range anywhere from 14.5 ounces to 17.5 ounces and fit a uniform distribution. This is displayed in Figure 5.4. The mean is

$$\mu = \frac{14.5 + 17.5}{2} = 16 \text{ ounces}$$

and the height is

$$\text{Height} = \frac{1}{17.5 - 14.5} = 1/3$$

Assume that Del Monte wanted to find the probability a single can weighed between 16 and 17.2 ounces. This value is provided by the area within that range as shown in Figure 5.4. The probability that a single observation will fall between two values X_1 and X_2 is

Probability an observation falls between two values	$P(X_1 \leq X \leq X_2) = \dfrac{X_2 - X_1}{\text{Range}}$	[5.12]

For the Del Monte can, it becomes

$$P(16 < X < 17.2) = \frac{17.2 - 16}{17.5 - 14.5} = 0.40$$

Example 5.6 Dow Chemical produces inorganic lawn fertilizer for homeowners who fertilize their grass so they can mow it more often. One type of fertilizer is sold in bags with uniformly distributed weight, with a mean of 25 pounds and a range of 2.4 pounds. Harry Homeowner needs 23 pounds to fertilize his lawn, but he is hesitant to buy only one bag since they deviate from 25 pounds over a range of 2.4 pounds. He is also curious about the probability of buying a bag with more than 25.5 pounds.

Solution: If the bags average 25 pounds over a range of 2.4 pounds, then one-half of that range, or 1.2 pounds, must be below 25, and the other half, above 25 pounds. Therefore, the lowest weight is $25 - 1.2 = 23.8$ pounds, and the highest weight is $25 + 1.2 = 26.2$ pounds, as seen in the figure. The probability of selecting a single bag that contains between 25.5 and 26.2 pounds is

$$P(25.5 < X < 26.2) = \frac{26.2 - 25.5}{2.4} = 0.2917$$

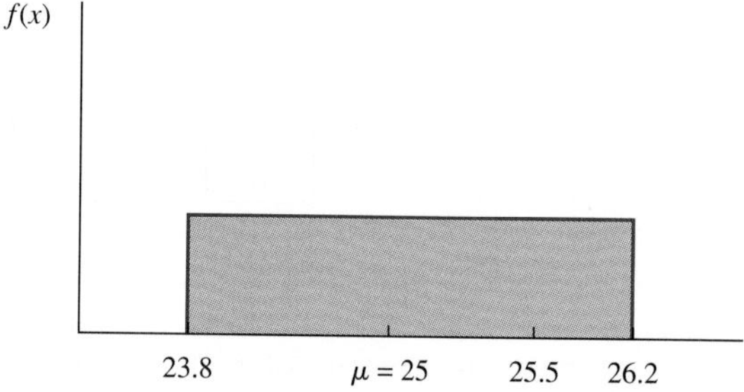

Interpretation: Harry need not worry. The lightest bag he could buy is 23.8 pounds. He will definitely get at least the 23 pounds he needs for his lawn. In addition, the probability of selecting a bag with more than 25.5 pounds is 29.17 percent.

A. Using the Computer

Minitab can be used effectively to determine uniform probabilities. Enter the values for which you want to find probabilities in Column (1). Click on **Calc** > **Probability Distributions** > **Uniform** > **Cumulative Probability.** Enter the lowest and highest values and *C*1 in the **Input Column** box.

Section Exercises

27. It usually takes you somewhere between 1.2 and 1.7 hours to do your statistics homework. The times are uniformly distributed. How likely are you to finish in time to meet your buddies 1.4 hours from now?

28. Cans of Happy-Tale Dog Food average 16 ounces, with a range of 4.2 ounces.

a. What is the smallest can in ounces you can buy for Weiner, your toy poodle? What is the largest can you can buy for your wolfhound, Killer?

b. If you pick a can at random, what is the probability it will weigh between 15.8 and 16.5 ounces?

29. Water used by Auto-Brite to wash cars averages 30 gallons per car. The least it ever takes is 27 gallons, and usage is uniformly distributed. A survey shows that cars don't get clean unless 32 gallons of water are used for the wash. What percentage of cars leaving Auto-Brite are clean?

30. The time required to get a lane at the local bowling alley ranges from 23.5 to 40.5 minutes. Assuming a uniform distribution, if the probability that you have to wait more than 30 minutes exceeds 60 percent, you plan to play golf instead. Should you put your golf bag or your bowling bag in your trunk?

31. Since you decided to play golf, given your answer to the previous question, you learn that the average time to play 18 holes at this course is 4.2 hours. The fastest it has ever been finished was by Rapid Roy Parr, who took 2.9 hours. If times are uniformly distributed, what is the probability you will finish in time to get home to see the football game between the Pittsburgh Steelers and the Denver Broncos, which starts in 4 hours?

5.8 The Normal Distribution

Of all the probability distributions we will examine, none is more important than the normal distribution. In Chapter 3 you were introduced to the basic nature of the normal distribution, its characteristic bell-shaped symmetry, and the manner in which it related to the Empirical Rule. At this time, you should recall that the normal distribution is a continuous (not discrete) distribution. It is used to reflect the distribution of variables such as heights, weights, distances, and other measurements that are infinitely divisible. Such continuous variables are generally the result of measurement.

Consider for a moment a case in which ToppsWear, a large clothing manufacturer, wished to study the distribution in peoples' heights. ToppsWear recognized that the public is ever-changing in its physical size and proportions. In the effort to produce better-fitting clothing, management felt that a thorough analysis was needed of current trends in fashion sizes. Presume that if ToppsWear were to measure the heights of all their potential customers, they would find that these heights are normally distributed around some mean—of, say, 67 inches. That is, while the heights average 67 inches, some people are of course taller than that, and some are shorter. This dispersion above and below the mean could be measured by the standard deviation that we calculated back in Chapter 3. Assume that the standard deviation in customers' heights is found to be 2 inches.

A graph of these heights would produce the customary bell shape. Figure 5.5 shows this graph, placing the individual observations on the horizontal axis, and the frequency

Figure 5.5
A Normal Distribution of Heights for ToppsWear

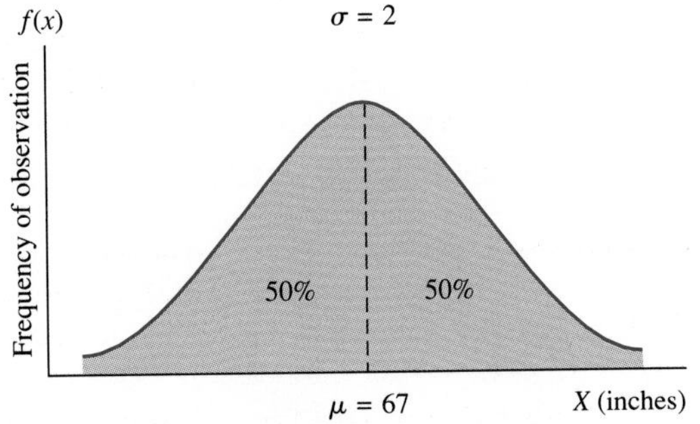

with which each of these observations occurred on the vertical axis. If the values are indeed normal (i.e., normally distributed), then the bell-shaped curve will emerge. Recall further that 50 percent of the observations (heights) are above the mean and 50 percent are below the mean. Similarly, of all the area under the normal curve, 50 percent of it is to the right of the mean, and 50 percent of that area is to the left of the mean. This too is shown in Figure 5.5.

A. A Comparison of Normal Distributions

The shape and position of a normal distribution are determined by two parameters: its mean μ and standard deviation σ. Figure 5.6 shows three different normal distributions of the sizes that ToppsWear might find in their study of fashion trends. The first (I) is the distributions described above, which has a mean of $\mu = 67$ and a standard deviation of $\sigma = 2$. It is centered at 67 with one-half of the observations above 67 and one-half below. The standard deviation of 2 indicates the degree to which the individual observations are spread out above and below 67.

A second distribution (II) has a higher mean, of $\mu = 79$, but the same standard deviation of $\sigma = 2$. It is therefore centered farther to the right directly above 79. But since it has the same degree of dispersion ($\sigma = 2$), it takes the same shape as the first distribution.

A third distribution (III) has the same mean as the first ($\mu = 67$) and is therefore centered at the same place. However, its measure of dispersion is greater as indicated by the standard deviation of $\sigma = 4$. The observations vary above and below that mean of 67 to a greater degree than do those observations in the first distribution. Distribution III is therefore flatter and more spread out above and below the mean of 67.

Figure 5.6 The Empirical Rule

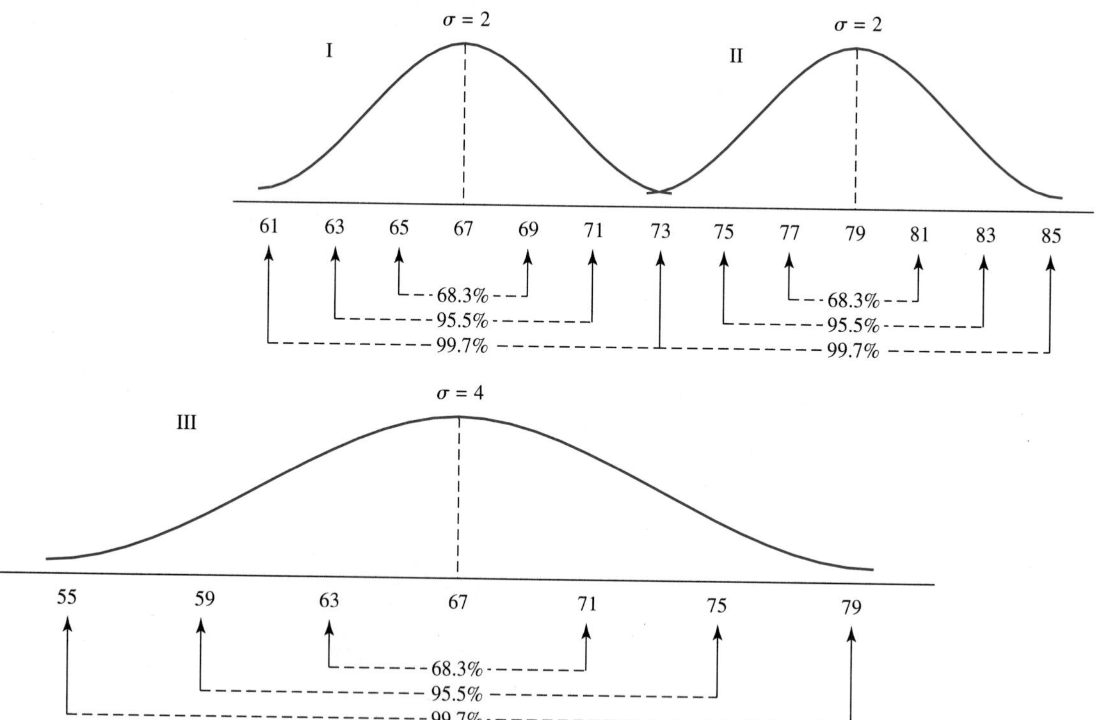

Despite their differences, all three of these are normal distributions. They are all symmetrical and bell-shaped. Furthermore, as normally distributed data sets, the Empirical Rule that we first examined back in Chapter 3 applies to each distribution. The **Empirical Rule** specifies that, regardless of the value of the mean or the standard deviation,

68.3 percent of all the observations lie within one standard deviation of the mean.

95.5 percent of all the observations lie within two standard deviations of the mean.

99.7 percent of all the observations lie within three standard deviations of the mean.

Figure 5.6 illustrates the Empirical Rule. Notice that for all three data sets, regardless of the value for μ or σ, 68.3 percent of all the observations are within one σ of μ. Compare the first distribution (I) to that of the third distribution (III). Since the third distribution is more highly dispersed, it is necessary to take in a wider interval in order to encompass the same proportion of the observations. While the first distribution encloses 68.3 percent of all the observations within the interval 65 to 69, the third distribution can encompass this same percentage only within the wider interval 63 to 71.

Remember that to enclose a certain percentage of all the observations within some interval means also to encompass that same percentage of all the area under the curve within that interval. Thus, while the interval 65 to 69 contains 68.3 percent of all the observations in the first distribution, that same interval also contains 68.3 percent of all the area under the normal curve.

B. The Normal Deviate

There can exist an infinite number of possible normal distributions, each with its own mean and standard deviation. Since we obviously cannot examine such a large number of possibilities, we need to convert all these normal distributions into one standard form. This conversion to the **standard normal distribution** is done with the **conversion formula** (or Z-formula)

The normal deviate or Z-formula	$Z = \dfrac{X - \mu}{\sigma}$	[5.13]

where Z is the **normal deviate** and X is some specified value for the random variable. After this conversion process, the mean of the distribution is 0 and the standard deviation is 1. That is, regardless of what the mean and standard deviation are as measured in the original units in the distribution, after the conversion formula is applied the mean is 0 and the standard deviation is 1.

Figure 5.7 illustrates use of the ToppsWear data. The top axis measures the observations of height X in inches. The mean is $\mu = 67$ inches, and the standard deviation is $\sigma = 2$ inches. The bottom axis reflects these heights in terms of their Z-values.

Tom Typical is 67 inches tall—the mean height of all the consumers in the ToppsWear clothing market. Using Formula (5.13), the Z-value associated with a height of $X = 67$ is

$$\begin{aligned} Z &= \frac{X - \mu}{\sigma} \\ &= \frac{67 - 67}{2} \\ &= 0 \end{aligned}$$

Figure 5.7
Converting
Customer Heights

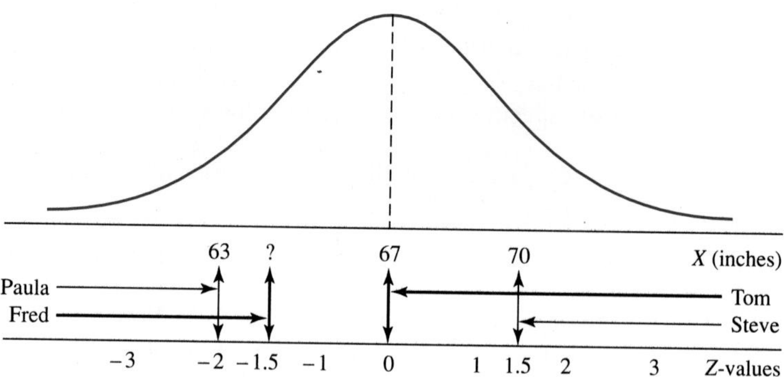

This is seen on the bottom axis, or Z-axis, in Figure 5.7. After applying the conversion formula, we find that the mean height of 67 inches has a Z-value of 0. If we were to convert the heights of all the consumers in the entire market, we would find that all the resulting Z-values would have a mean of zero and a standard deviation of 1.

Z, the *normal deviate,* is defined as "the number of standard deviations an observation lies from the mean." Paula Petite is 63 inches tall. Her Z-value is

$$Z = \frac{63 - 67}{2}$$
$$= -2$$

As Figure 5.7 shows, 63 inches is 4 inches, or 2 standard deviations, below the mean. Converting $X = 63$ inches to its Z-value yields -2.00.

Z-Value The number of standard deviations an observation is above or below the mean.

Steve Stretch is 70 inches in height. Figure 5.7 reveals that converting 70 inches to a Z-value yields

$$Z = \frac{70 - 67}{2}$$
$$= 1.5$$

Steve's Z-value is 1.5. He is 3 inches, or 1.5 standard deviation, above the mean height of 67 inches. How tall is Fred if his Z-value is -1.5?

C. Calculating Probabilities with the Normal Deviate

Standardizing a normal distribution allows us to more easily determine the probability a certain event will occur. ToppsWear personnel can find the probability a single customer is between, say, 67 and 69 inches tall, $P(67 \leq X \leq 69)$, by simply finding the area under the normal curve between 67 and 69. That is, if they know the area, they will know the probability.

Think of it in this sense. Presume you are shooting at a target, two-thirds of which is painted green and one-third red. You have the same chance of hitting any point on the target as you do any other point. You are not necessarily shooting at the bull's eye, just the target in general. The probability that you will hit green is two-thirds. Why? Because two-thirds of its area is green. Since you know area, you know probability. The same can be said for the area under the normal curve.

The area associated with a given Z-value can be found in Table E in Appendix III. Figure 5.8(*a*) illustrates this process. We want the area between 67 and 69. The Z-value for 69 is

$$Z = \frac{69 - 67}{2}$$
$$= 1.00$$

Table E gives the area under the curve *from the mean to some value above it or below it.* This is just the area we want. In Table E, find the Z-value of 1.0. Move to the right to the next column headed by 0.00 to get $Z = 1.00$. There you will find the entry 0.3413. That is, 34.13 percent of the area under the curve is between 67 and 69. There is a 34.13 percent chance that a customer picked at random in between 67 and 69 inches tall.

Although Table E gives only the area from the mean to some value above it or below it, other probabilities can be easily found. Presume ToppsWear must determine the probability that a customer is taller than 69 inches. As Figure 5.8(*b*) shows, we have already determined that 34.13 percent of all the customers are between 67 and 69 inches tall. Furthermore, we also know that 50 percent of all the customers are above the mean of 67. That leaves $0.5000 - 0.3413 = 0.1587$ in the area in the tail beyond $Z = 1.00$. There is a 15.87 percent chance that a randomly chosen customer is taller than 69 inches.

Figure 5.8
Areas under the Normal Curve

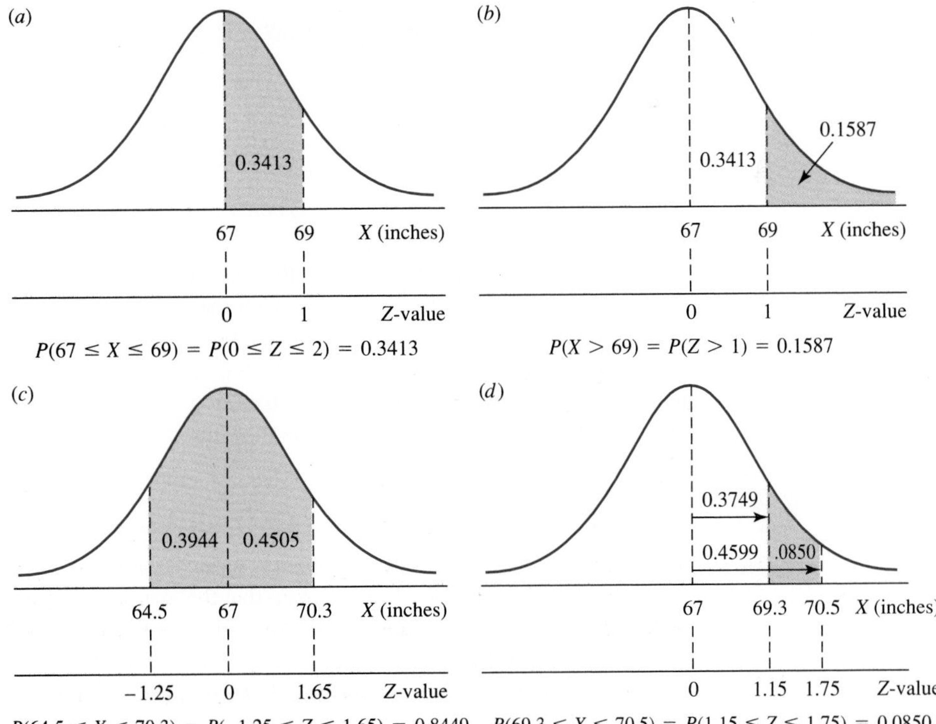

Figure 5.8(c), which seeks the area between 64.5 and 70.3, requires that we calculate two Z-values. Since the table will give only the area from the mean to some value above it or below it, we must determine the areas (1) between 64.5 and 67 and (2) between 67 and 70.3 and add them together.

$$Z = \frac{64.5 - 67}{2}$$
$$= -1.25$$

A Z-value of 1.25 (we can ignore the negative sign since the curve is symmetrical and the right half is the same as the left half) yields an area of 0.3944. For the area between 67 and 70.3, we find

$$Z = \frac{70.3 - 67}{2}$$
$$= 1.65$$

Table E reveals that the area is 0.4505. Thus, $P(64.5 \leq X \leq 70.3) = 0.3944 + 0.4505 = 0.8449$. The probability a customer is between 64.5 and 70.3 inches tall is 84.49 percent.

To determine $P(69.3 \leq X \leq 70.5)$ also requires two calculations of Z, as shown in Figure 5.8(d). We must determine the area from 67 to 70.5, which includes the area we want and some we do not want. Then calculate the area from 67 to 69.3 and subtract it out.

$$Z = \frac{70.5 - 67}{2}$$
$$= 1.75$$

A Z-value of 1.75 yields an area of 0.4599. Then,

$$Z = \frac{69.3 - 67}{2}$$
$$= 1.15$$

which produces an area of 0.3749. Then $P(69.3 \leq X \leq 70.5) = 0.4599 - 0.3749 = 0.0850$.

Notice that the larger the Z-value, the less area left in the tail of the distribution. Table E shows that as Z approaches 3.99, the encompassed area is virtually the entire 50 percent above the mean, leaving very little in the tail beyond $Z = 3.99$. Therefore $P(Z > 3.99) \approx 0$.

Incidentally, $P(X < x) = P(X \leq x)$, where x is any given value. This is because the normal distribution is a continuous distribution. There is an infinite number of possible values X can take. Therefore, to *include* the value of x does not increase the probability the event will occur.

Example 5.7 TelCom Satellite provides communication services to businesses in the Chicago metropolitan area. Company officers have learned that the average satellite transmission is 150 seconds, with a standard deviation of 15 seconds. Times appear to be normally distributed.

To properly estimate customer demand for its services and establish a rate structure which will maximize corporate profits, TelCom must determine how likely some calls are to happen. The director of services wants you to provide estimates of the probability that a call will last:

a. Between 125 and 150 seconds.

b. Less than 125 seconds.

c. Between 145 and 155 seconds.

d. Between 160 and 165 seconds.

Solution: *a.*

$$Z = \frac{125 - 150}{15}$$
$$= -1.67$$

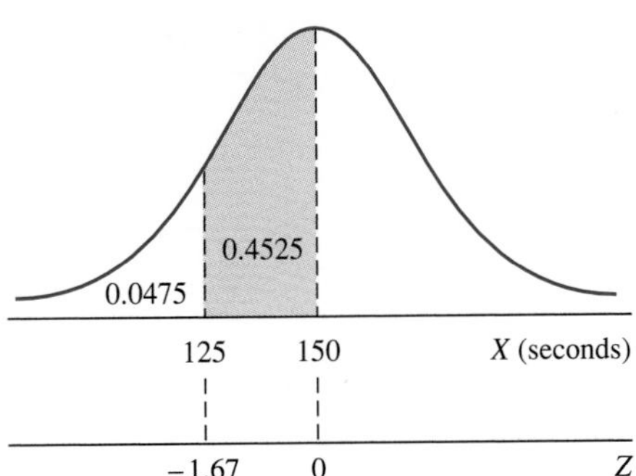

From Table E, a Z-value of 1.67 yields an area of 0.4525. Therefore the probability that a transmission will take between 125 and 150 seconds is 45.25 percent.

b. If 45.25 percent of the area is between 125 and 150, then $0.5000 - 0.4525 = 0.0475$, or 4.75 percent of all transmissions require less than 125 seconds. The probability that any transmission selected at random requires 125 seconds or less is 4.75 percent.

c.

$$Z = \frac{145 - 150}{15}$$
$$= -0.33$$

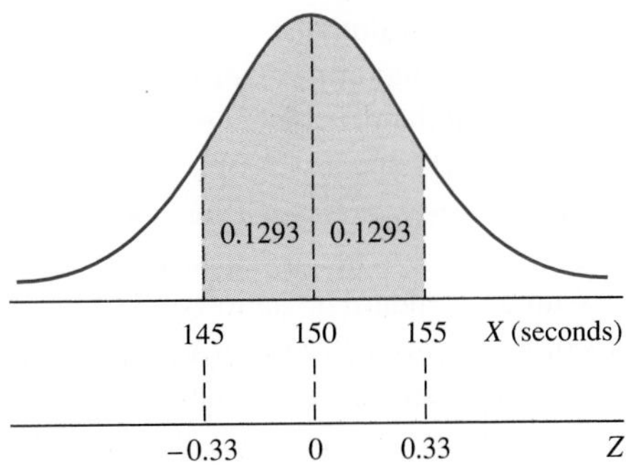

Given $Z = -0.33$, the area between 145 and 150 is 0.1293. Since 155 is as far above the mean of 150 as 145 is below the mean, the area between 150 and 155 is also 0.1293. Therefore, $P(145 \leq X \leq 155) = 0.1293 + 0.1293 = 0.2586$.

d.

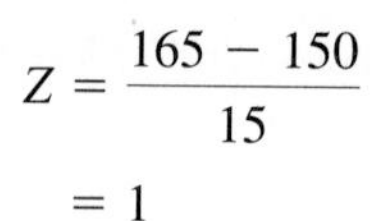

$$Z = \frac{165 - 150}{15}$$
$$= 1$$

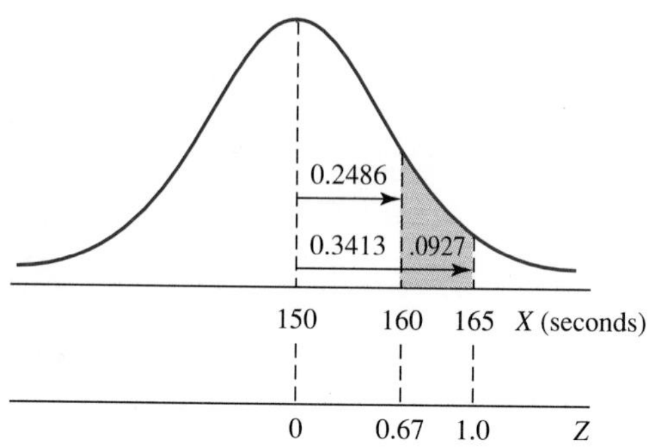

With $Z = 1$, the area is 0.3413. To find the area between 150 and 160,

$$Z = \frac{160 - 150}{15}$$
$$= 0.67$$

for an area of 0.2486. Therefore, $P(160 \leq X \leq 165) = 0.3413 - 0.2486 = 0.0927$.

Interpretation: Based on these probabilities, it is possible for TelCom to develop a sense of the demand for its services that will aid in establishing policies regarding customers' use of the facilities, as well as an optimal rate structure that TelCom can charge.

D. Calculating an X-Value from a Known Probability

In the previous section, you were asked to calculate a probability given some value of X. That is, you were given a value X for the random variable, and you wished to find the area between that value and the mean. However, sometimes you may know what probability you require, and must determine what value of X will yield that probability. For example, assume that the president's economic advisors propose a welfare program to aid the disadvantaged, which consists of a money payment to the nation's poorest 15 percent. The question then arises as to what income level separates the lower 15 percent of the people from the rest. In 1996, mean disposable personal income measured in 1982 dollars was $13,812. Assume a standard deviation of $3,550. This is shown in Figure 5.9. There is some level of income shown as "?" which separates the lowest 15 percent from the upper 85 percent. Assume that incomes are normally distributed.

As shown in Figure 5.9, we know the area and seek the corresponding value for X that is shown by the question mark. In the earlier problems, we calculated a Z-value and used it

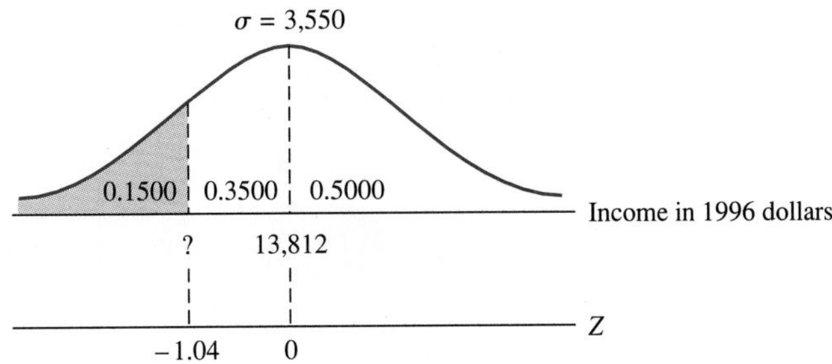

Figure 5.9
Incomes of the Poorest 15 Percent

to look up an area in the table. This time we have an area, and we can use Table E to look up the corresponding Z-value. Although we are interested in the value of 0.15, we must look up 0.3500(0.5 − 0.15), since only the area from the mean to some value above or below it is given in the table. We search out in the main body of Table E the area of 0.3500. The closest we can get is 0.3508, which corresponds to a Z-value of 1.04. (Extrapolation can be used when a greater degree of accuracy is required.) Since

$$Z = \frac{X - \mu}{\sigma}$$

and a Z-value of 1.04 was found, we have

$$-1.04 = \frac{X - 13{,}812}{3{,}550}$$

We then solve for X and get X = \$10,120. Anyone with an income of \$10,120 or less will receive the government subsidy.

Notice the negative sign for the Z-value. The algebraic sign of Z was unimportant in earlier problems because we merely used the Z-value to look up an area in Table E. However, such is not the case now. In this instance, the Z-value is used for further mathematical calculations in solving for X. Hence, its sign is of importance. The rule of thumb is, if we are working in the area to the left of the mean, the sign is always negative.

Example 5.8 **Improving Urban Fire Prevention**

A state commission has been formed to reduce response times of local fire departments. A group of experts is attempting to identify those city fire departments whose response time is either in the lowest 10 percent, or who take longer than 90 percent of all fire departments in the study. Those in the first group are to serve as models for the less efficient fire units in the second group.

Data show that the mean response times for a certain class of fire departments is 12.8 minutes, with a standard deviation of 3.7 minutes.

Solution: Assuming that response times are normally distributed, the accompanying figure illustrates the problem. It must determine two response times. The first is so short that only 10 percent of all fire units arrive at the fire within that time. The second is so long that only 10 percent of all fire units take more time. The Z-formula is used to determine each X value. To ascertain the quicker response time, we look up 0.4000 in the main body of Table E. Although we are concerned about the bottom 10 percent, we must look up 0.4000, since that is what the table is designed to reveal. The entry 0.3997 is the closest, yielding a Z-value of 1.28.

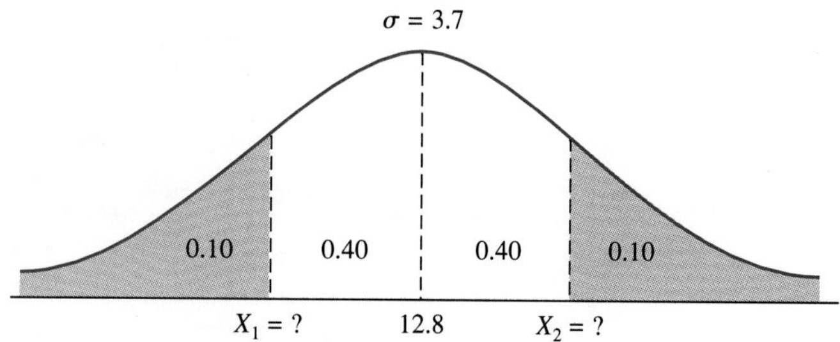

Since we are seeking a value for X in the left tail, the Z-value is given the appropriate negative sign.

$$Z_1 = \frac{X_1 - \mu}{\sigma}$$

$$-1.28 = \frac{X_1 - 12.8}{3.7}$$

$$X_1 = 8.06 \text{ minutes}$$

and

$$Z_2 = \frac{X_2 - \mu}{\sigma}$$

$$1.28 = \frac{X_2 - 12.8}{3.7}$$

$$X_2 = 17.54 \text{ minutes}$$

The Z-value for X_2 is given a positive sign since we seek a value in the right tail greater than the mean.

Interpretation: Only 10 percent of the fire departments in this classification responded to fire calls in less than 8.06 minutes. These fire units will serve as model programs for the 10 percent of fire departments whose fire runs exceeded 17.54 minutes.

E. Normal Approximation to the Binomial Distribution

The binomial distribution, you recall, involves a series of n trials that can produce (1) a success or (2) a failure. The probability of a success is indicated as π. The answers can often be found in the binomial table or by using the binomial formula, Formula (5.3). However, if n is too large, it may exceed the confines of any table and the formula may be excessively cumbersome. An alternative method must be devised. The solution can be found in the use of the normal distribution to approximate the binomial distribution. This approximation is considered sufficiently accurate if $n\pi \geq 5$ and $n(1 - \pi) \geq 5$ and if π is close to 0.50.

Consider a labor union in which 40 percent of the members favor a strike. If 15 members are selected at random, what is the probability that 10 support a strike? From the binomial table we find

$$P(X = 10 \mid n = 15, \ \pi = 0.40) = 0.0245$$

If we were unable to use the table, we could approximate the answer using the normal distribution. We must first find the mean μ and the standard deviation σ of the normal distribution as

$$\mu = n\pi \qquad \text{and} \qquad \sigma = \sqrt{n(\pi)(1 - \pi)}$$

In our present case, $\mu = (15)(0.40) = 6$ and $\sigma = \sqrt{15(0.40)(0.60)} = 1.897$.

Because there is an infinite number of possible values in a normal distribution (or any continuous distribution), the probability that the random variable is exactly equal to some specific value such as 10 is zero. When using a continuous distribution to estimate a discrete random variable, a slight adjustment is therefore necessary. This adjustment, called the *continuity correction factor,* requires that we treat the probability of exactly 10 members as the interval between 9.5 members and 10.5 members. This is illustrated in Figure 5.10, which shows the probabilities for each value of the random variable (number of members) taken from Table B.

Figure 5.10
Normal Approximation of the Binomial

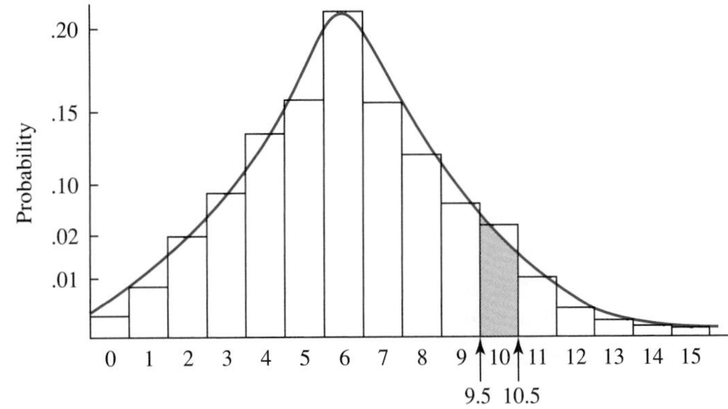

The probability that exactly 10 members favor a strike is shown by the area of the rectangle centered at 10. Notice that the rectangle extends from 9.5 to 10.5. The normal curve is superimposed over the rectangles.

Using the normal distribution to find $P(9.5 \leq X \leq 10.5)$, we have

$$Z = \frac{9.5 - 6}{1.897} = 1.85$$

for an area of 0.4678, and

$$Z = \frac{10.5 - 6}{1.897} = 2.37$$

for an area of 0.4911. Then, $P(9.5 \leq X \leq 10.5) = 0.4911 - 0.4678 = 0.0233$, which is a close approximation of the 0.0245 found in Table B.

Section Exercises

32. General Mills packages Cheerios in 36-ounce boxes that have a standard deviation of 1.9 ounces. Weights are thought to be normally distributed. If you select one box at random, what is the probability the box will weigh:

a. Less than 34.8 ounces?
b. More than 34.8 ounces?

c. Between 34.3 ounces and 38.9 ounces?
d. Between 39.5 ounces and 41.1 ounces?

33. As a construction engineer, you purchase bags of cement averaging 50 pounds, with a standard deviation of 5.2 pounds. The doctor told you not to lift anything over 60 pounds since your mountain climbing accident. Should you pick up a bag?

34. The brakes on new Lambourginis are advertized to last an average 35,000 miles with a standard deviation of 1,114 miles. What is the probability the one you just bought will last:

a. Over 35,000 miles?
b. Less than 33,900 miles?
c. Less than 37,500 miles?
d. Between 35,200 and 36,900 miles?

35. Cost overruns for computer upgrades at your firm have averaged \$23,500, with a standard deviation of \$9,400. As executive director of the Research Division, you do not want to risk more than a 34 percent chance that the overrun on a newly proposed upgrade will exceed \$25,000. Should you implement the upgrade?

36. Wages at the commercial banks in Illinois average \$22.87 per hour, with a standard deviation of \$5.87. What must your hourly wage be if you want to earn:

a. More than 80 percent of all employees?
b. More than 30 percent of all employees?
c. Less than 20 percent of all employees?
d. More than 50 percent of all employees?

37. Employees at Coopers-Price and Lybrand work an average of 55.8 hours per week, with a standard deviation of 9.8 hours. Promotions are more likely for those employees in the upper 10 percent of the time they spend working. How long must you work to improve your chances of promotion?

38. Records show that 45 percent of all automobiles produced by Ford Motor Company contain parts imported from Japan. What is the probability that out of the next 200 cars, 115 contain Japanese parts?

Solved Problems

1. Binomial Distribution A manufacturer in California supplies you with a prototype design for an aircraft part your business requires. This new product, which is shipped in lots of $n = 12$, suffers a 40 percent defect rate.

a. If you do not want to risk more than a 10 percent chance that 5 of the 12 are defective, should you buy from this supplier?

From Table B, $P(X = 5 \mid n = 12, \pi = 0.40) = 0.2270 > 10\%$. Do not buy.

b. If you do not want to face more than a 20 percent chance that more than 5 are defective, should you purchase from this supplier?

From Table C, $P(X > 5 \mid n = 12, \pi = 0.40) = 1 - P(X \leq 5 \mid n = 12, \pi = 0.40) = 1 - 0.6652 = 0.3348 > 20\%$. You still shouldn't buy from this supplier.

2. Hypergeometric Distribution A sporting goods store has $N = 20$ ski boots in stock, $r = 8$ of which are in your size. If you select $n = 3$ pairs that you like, what is the probability that $x = 1$ will fit you?

$$P(X = 1) = \frac{{}_rC_x \; {}_{N-r}C_{n-x}}{{}_NC_n}$$

$$= \frac{{}_8C_1 \; {}_{12}C_2}{{}_{20}C_3} = 0.4632$$

3. **Poisson Distribution** Wire cable used to secure bridge structures has an average of 3 defects per 100 yards. If you require 50 yards, what is the probability there will be one defect?

   Since the mean is given in terms of 100 yards, we must determine what percentage 50 yards is of 100: $50/100 = 0.50$. Then, the mean number of defects per 50 yards is $(3)(0.50) = 1.5$. From Table D, $P(X = 1 \mid \mu = 1.5) = 0.3347$, or, using the formula,

$$P(x) = \frac{\mu^x e^{-\mu}}{x!} = \frac{1.5^1\, e^{-1.5}}{1!} = \frac{1.5^1 \frac{1}{e^{1.5}}}{1!} = 0.3347$$

4. **Exponential Distribution** As manager of Burger Heaven, you observe that customers enter your establishment at the rate of 8 per hour. What is the probability that more than 15 minutes pass between the arrival of 2 customers?

   Although the mean rate is originally given as 8 per 60 minutes, we want to know the probability that 15 minutes will lapse. We must determine what percentage the 15 minutes is of the 60: $15/60 = 0.25$. Thus, t is 0.25 and $-\mu t = -8(.25) = -2$. To determine $P(X > 15)$, we should first find $P(X \leq 15)$ and subtract from 1.00. If we let $x = 0$ and $\mu t = 2$, Table D shows $P(X \leq 15) = 1 - e^{-8(0.25)} = 1 - e^2 = 1 - 0.1353 = 0.8647$. Then, $P(X > 15) = 1 - 0.8647 = 0.1353$.

   If we use Formula (5.8) instead of the table,

$$P(X \leq 15) = 1 - e^{-\mu t} = 1 - e^{-8(0.25)} = 1 - 0.1353 = 0.8647$$

   Then, $P(X > 15) = 1 - 0.8647 = 0.1353$.

5. **Uniform Distribution** The completion times for a job task range from 10.2 minutes to 18.3 minutes and are thought to be uniformly distributed. What is the probability that it will require between 12.7 and 14.5 minutes to perform this task?

$$P(X_1 \leq X \leq X_2) = \frac{(X_2 - X_1)}{\text{Range}} = \frac{14.5 - 12.7}{8.1} = 0.2222$$

6. **Normal Distribution** The U.S. Department of Agriculture has learned from a study of crop yields that the daily rainfall in parts of Hawaii appears to be normally distributed with a mean of 2.2 inches during the rainy season. The standard deviation was determined to be 0.8 inches.

   a. What is the probability it will rain more than 3.3 inches on any one day during the rainy season?

$$Z = \frac{X - \mu}{\sigma} = \frac{3.3 - 2.2}{0.8} = 1.38$$

   As seen in the accompanying graph, a Z-value of 1.38 yields an area of 0.4162. Thus, $P(X > 3.3) = 0.5000 - 0.4162 = 0.0838$.

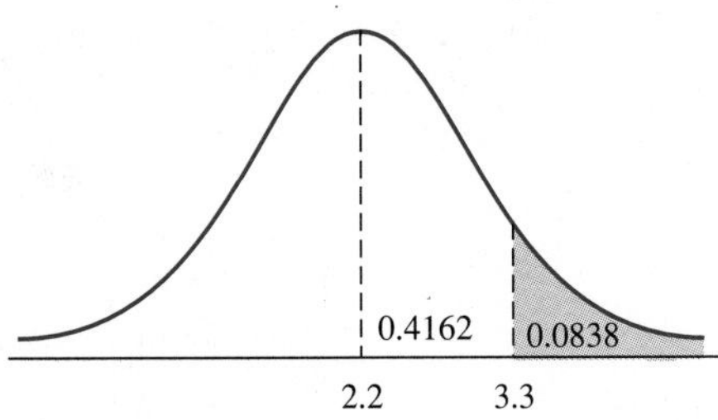

b. Find the probability that it will rain more than 1.3 inches.

$$Z = \frac{X - \mu}{\sigma} = \frac{1.3 - 2.2}{0.80} = -1.13$$

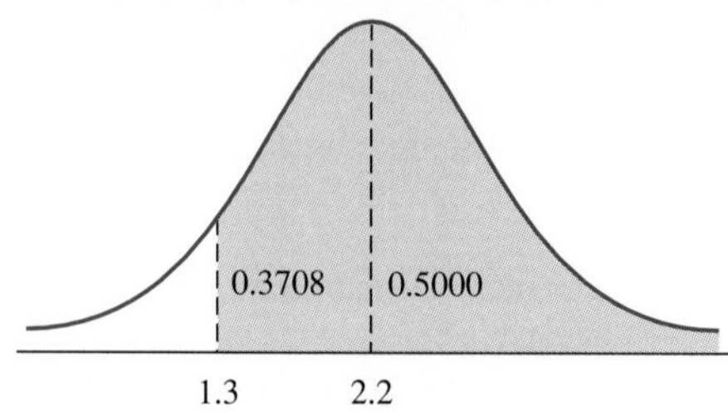

The Z-value of -1.13 produces an area of 0.3708, and the $P(X > 1.3) = 0.5000 + 0.3708 = 0.8708$.

c. What is the probability that the rainfall will be between 2.7 and 3.0 inches?

$$Z_1 = \frac{3.0 - 2.2}{0.80} = 1.00 \qquad \text{for an area of } 0.3412$$

$$Z_2 = \frac{2.7 - 2.2}{0.80} = 0.63 \qquad \text{for an area of } 0.2389$$

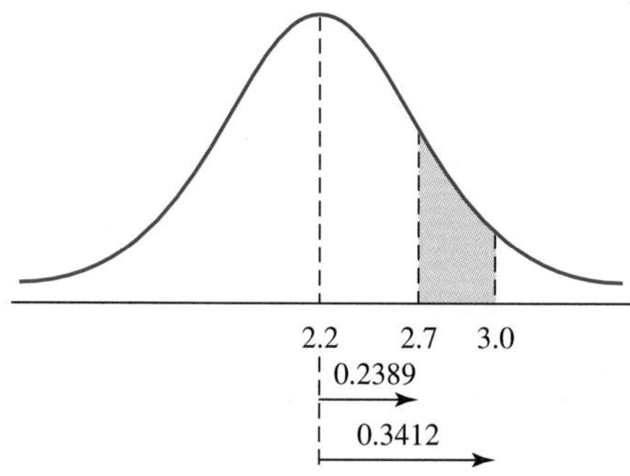

Therefore, $P(2.7 \leq X \leq 3.0) = 0.3412 - 0.2389 = 0.1023$.

d. How much rainfall must occur to exceed 10 percent of the daily precipitation?

As seen in the graph, an area of 0.40 is associated with a Z-value of -1.28. Therefore,

$$-1.28 = \frac{X - 2.2}{0.80}$$

$$X = 1.176 \text{ inches}$$

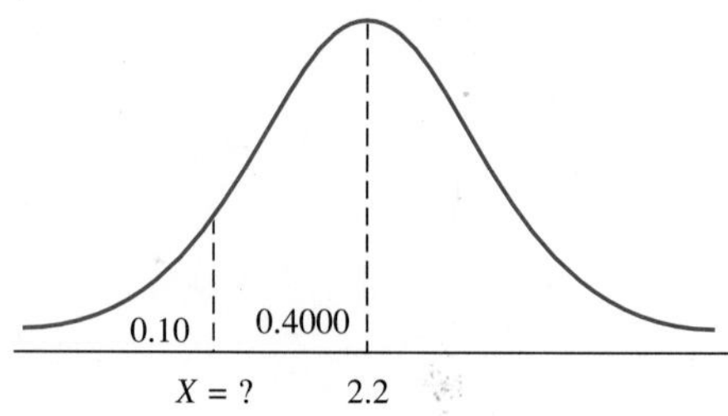

7. **Normal Approximation of the Binomial Distribution** Forty-five percent of all the employees in the management training center at Condor Magnetics have college degrees. What is the probability that, of 150 employees selected at random, 72 have college degrees?

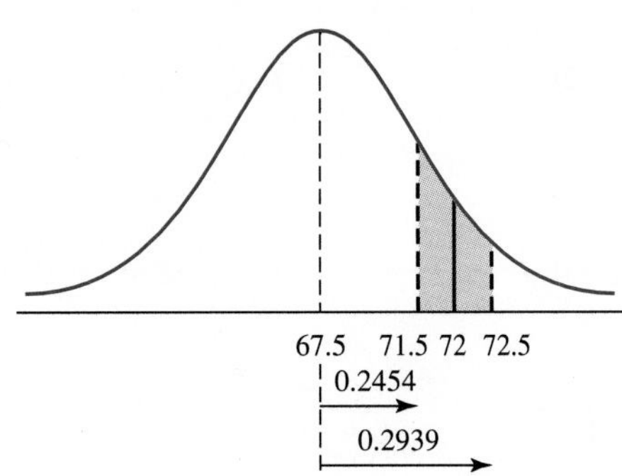

The mean and standard deviation are $\mu = (n)(\pi) = (150)(0.45) = 67.5$ and $\sigma = \sqrt{(n)(\pi)(1 - \pi)} = \sqrt{(150)(0.45)(0.55)} = 6.09$. Then, $P(71.5 \leq X \leq 72.5)$ is found as

$$Z_1 = \frac{72.5 - 67.5}{6.09} = 0.82 \qquad \text{for an area of } 0.2939$$

$$Z_2 = \frac{71.5 - 67.5}{6.09} = 0.66 \qquad \text{for an area of } 0.2454$$

$$P(71.5 \leq X \leq 72.5) = 0.2939 - 0.2454 = 0.0485$$

List of Formulas

[5.1]	$\mu = E(X) = \Sigma[(x_i)P(x_i)]$	Mean or expected value of a discrete distribution
[5.2]	$\sigma^2 = \Sigma[(x_i - \mu)^2 P(x_i)]$	Variance of a probability distribution
[5.3]	$P(x) = {}_nC_x(\pi)^x - (1 - \pi)^{n-x}$	Binomial distribution
[5.4]	$E(X) = \mu = n\pi$	Mean of a binomial distribution
[5.5]	$\sigma^2 = n\pi(1 - \pi)$	Variance of a binomial distribution
[5.6]	$P(x) = \dfrac{{}_rC_x \; {}_{N-r}C_{n-x}}{{}_NC_n}$	Hypergeometric distribution
[5.7]	$P(x) = \dfrac{\mu^x e^{-\mu}}{x!}$	Poisson distribution
[5.8]	$P(X \leq x) = 1 - e^{-\mu t}$	Exponential distribution
[5.9]	$E(x) = \mu = \dfrac{a + b}{2}$	Expected value for a uniform distribution

[5.10]	$\sigma^2 = \dfrac{(b-a)^2}{12}$	Variance for a uniform distribution
[5.11]	$\text{Height} = \dfrac{1}{b-a}$	Height of a uniform distribution
[5.12]	$P(X_1 \leq X \leq X_2) = \dfrac{X_2 - X_1}{\text{Range}}$	Probability a value falls within a certain range in a uniform distribution
[5.13]	$Z = \dfrac{X - \mu}{\sigma}$	Normal deviate

Chapter Exercises

39. A trucking company finds that 30 percent of its shipments arrive late. If eight shipments are scheduled, what is the probability that:

a. Three will arrive late?
b. Three or more will arrive late?
c. Three or less will arrive late?
d. Between three and five inclusive will arrive late?

40. A survey reveals that 60 percent of households prefer a certain brand of sports gear. If 12 households are surveyed, what is the probability that this sports gear will be the choice of:

a. 7 households?
b. Less than 6 households?
c. 10 or more households?
d. More than 2 households?

41. Temps Ltd, dispatched nine temporary day workers to the Bank of America in San Francisco. Only six of them are actually qualified to do the job to which they might be assigned. The accounting department selects five of the nine employees at random. What is the probability that:

a. All five are qualified?
b. Four are qualified?
c. At least three are qualified?

42. The board of directors for ABC, Inc. consists of four economists, three accountants, and five engineers. If a committee of seven is to be selected at random, what is the probability it will consist of two economists, two accountants, and three engineers?

43. Airplanes arrive at Chicago's O'Hare airport at the average rate of 5.2 per minute. Air traffic controllers can safely handle a maximum of seven airplanes per minute. What is the probability that airport safety is jeopardized? Arrivals are thought to be Poisson distributed.

44. *Business Week* reported that 80 percent of the population thinks congressional salaries are too high. If 15 people are chosen to form a committee to decide by majority vote whether these salaries should be raised, what is the probability the vote will be to not increase them?

45. Trucks arrive for loading at the rate of 9.3 per hour on the average. The dock foreman knows that if six or fewer trucks arrive, only one loading dock is necessary. If more than six arrive, a second dock must be opened. Should he open a second dock?

46. A company suffering a 10 percent defect rate sells its product in lots of 15 units. It offers a $100 discount if more than three units are defective. How much discount should the company expect for every 50 shipments?

47. Janet Powell is the chief accountant for a large clothing store in a major shopping mall. She completes the payrolls for all 11 employees, but seven contain errors. Janet's boss, Martha Holt, has become displeased with Janet's work lately and selects five payroll records to examine. It is found that three contain errors. Janet defends herself by arguing that the 3 errors were all that she made in the 11 records. Is this a good argument?

48. The mean time between failures for General Electric's new light bulb is 10 weeks. What is the probability that one light bulb will fail within 15 weeks?

49. Customers enter a local restaurant at the rate of 10 per hour. What is the probability that 30 minutes will lapse between the arrivals of any two customers?

50. The weights contained in boxes of cereal are uniformly distributed with a mean of 35 ounces and a range of 3.4 ounces.

    a. What are the smallest and the largest weights in the boxes?
    b. What is the probability that a single box contains between 32 and 33 ounces?

51. Over the past 20 years Fred has driven to work in San Francisco every day. The quickest he has made the trip is 63 minutes. The longest it has ever taken him is 110 minutes. If driving times are uniformly distributed:

    a. What is Fred's average time spent in traffic?
    b. What is the probability he can make it within 1.5 hours?

52. Reports show that five homicides are committed each hour in our nation's largest cities, and that the distribution fits a Poisson distribution. If true, what is the probability that in the next 30 minutes, three people will be murdered?

53. A manufacturing process produces 1.2 defects per 100 units of output, and follows a Poisson distribution. What is the probability that the next 500 units will show three defects?

54. It normally takes two weeks to train a worker to use a computerized drill press. What is the probability a worker can be trained in 1.5 weeks?

55. In the effort to reduce costs, Wendy's International Inc., a popular fast-food restaurant, examined the tendency for its automatic processors to determine the weights of hamburger in their quarter-pound burgers. It was found that the weights ranged from 3.2 ounces to 4.9 ounces. A uniform distribution was assumed. What percentage of the burgers are more than one-quarter of a pound?

56. Is the normal distribution a discrete or a continuous distribution? Defend your answer. If two normally distributed data sets have the same mean but different standard deviations, how will the range that encompasses 68.3 percent of all the observations compare from one data set to the other? Draw the necessary figures to illustrate how the Empirical Rule can apply to both distributions.

57. Monthly production costs for a print shop in Toledo have averaged \$410, with a standard deviation of \$87. The manager promises the shop owner to hold costs below \$300 this month. If costs are normally distributed, can the owner believe the manager?

58. The accounting firm of Dooit and Quick finds that the time it takes to complete an auditing process is approximately normally distributed, with a mean time of 17.2 days and a standard deviation of 3.7 days. Mr. Dooit promises to start an auditing job for your firm within 20 days, but must finish the one he has just begun. How likely is it he will keep his promise?

59. Runners at a local marathon finished the course in an average time of 180.3 minutes; $s = 25.7$. How fast must you run to finish in the top 10 percent?

60. Electrical connectors last an average of 18.2 months, and $s = 1.7$. The seller agrees to replace one if it fails within 19 months. Out of 500 units, how many must he replace on the average?

61. Barry's sales average \$500, with $s = \$15.2$. He gets a \$100 commission only if the sale exceeds \$530. On the average, what is his commission out of every 25 sales?

62. Daily production at the local plant averages 7,300 tons, with $s = 125$ tons. On the average, out of 100 days how many times will output exceed 7,000 tons?

63. Daily receipts at one of the attractions at Dollywood in Tennessee average $1,012 with a standard deviation of $312. What is the probability that today the attraction will take in more than $1,100?

64. Students taking the Graduate Management Aptitude Test averaged 812 with a standard deviation of 145. Only those in the top 20 percent can apply for a particular scholarship. Gus Genius received a 900 on the test. Can he apply?

65. Storage units at Stor-N-Loc average 82.3 square feet, with $s = 53.7$ square feet. How many square feet must a unit have to be larger than 90 percent of all units?

66. According to *National Geographic,* 32 percent of the Australians living in the outback drink "tinnies," a form of local beer. Out of 500 Aussies selected at random, what's the probability that at least 150 have been known to quaff a tinnie?

67. The *Chicago Tribune* reported that 69 percent of Russians were worse off economically after the revolution. Out of 800 selected at random, what is the probability that fewer than 580 suffer more trying conditions?

68. The *Chicago Tribune* reported that 56 percent of all seven-year-olds believe that Cinderella was a real person. What is the probability that at least 50 percent of 120 seven-year-olds believe so?

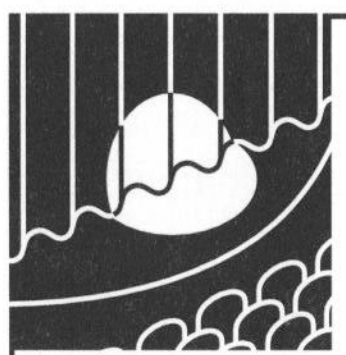

CURTAIN CALL

In response to the mayor's request, as set forth in Setting the Stage at the beginning of this chapter, the researchers had to determine the mean response time and the variation in those response times. They also had to calculate the probability that the response time would exceed (1) 1.5 minutes, (2) 2 minutes, and (3) 3 minutes.

The mayor was also interested in the probability that the assistance of the state police would be needed as well as the probability that 10 minutes and 15 minutes would lapse between calls. The researchers also had to address the cost to each household with assessed valuation over $70,000 to achieve the goal of reducing the mean response time to 2 minutes.

Prepare the report you would submit in accord with the format set out in Appendix I. Address each of these points along with any others you feel are pertinent.

From the Stage to Real life

Median housing values are as major in economic importance to individual consumers as they are to local governments. The median price of a single family home is a gauge to how much house a consumer can afford to buy; that is, age of house, square footage, number of bathrooms, number of bedrooms, and so on. The U.S. Department of Housing and Urban Development makes median housing values available on a national basis (*www.huduser.org*). At this site, click on "Publications," then click on "Housing Markets and Demographics." In the next list, click on "U.S. Housing Market Conditions," and then on "Current Issue." In the Historical Data section, Tables 8A and 8B provide you with price data for new and existing single family homes from the 1960s to the present. Note the most current median price of each type.

The National Association of Realtors provides a selection of listings of homes for sale across the nation (*www.realtorads.com*). Think of three areas of the country where you might wish to live. At the Realtors site, for each of your desired three areas, use the national median housing prices to see listings of available houses. Are the houses desirable to you? Would you prefer something less or more expensive? Are there major differences among the three areas in the "amount of house" you can purchase at the median prices?

Note, that mortgage rates determine in part the price of a house you can afford. The Mortgage Loan Directory (*www.mortgageloan.com*) provides a selection of current mortgage rates by state.

CHAPTER 6

Sampling Distributions

Chapter Blueprint

This chapter offers an introduction to the all-important concept of sampling and the manner in which samples are used to draw inferences about the population.

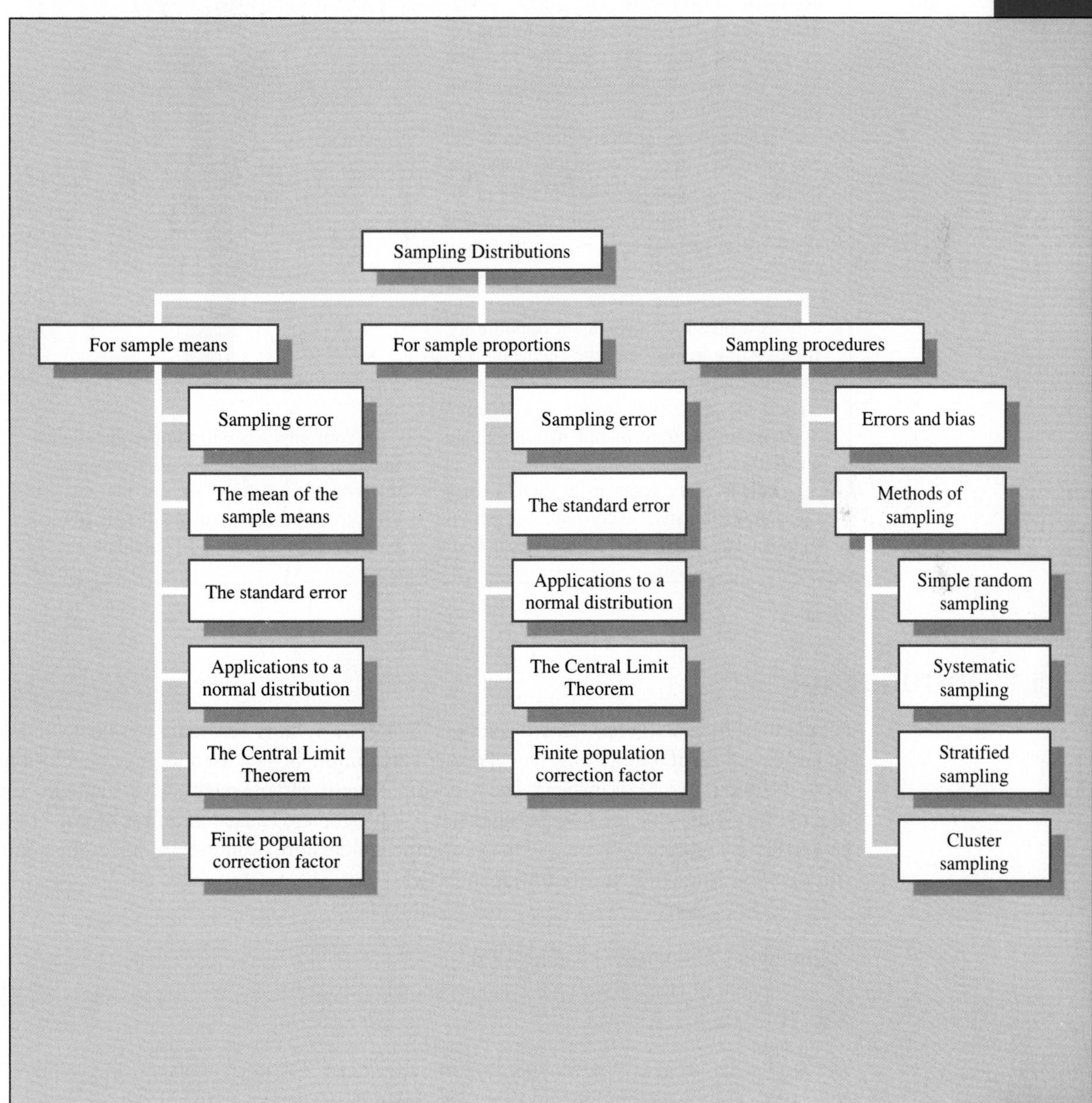

SETTING THE STAGE

Several wealthy clients have chosen you as their investment analyst to evaluate three vastly different industries. Their intention is to identify which industry they should invest in. Currently, they are considering the sports and leisure industry, which seems to enjoy prosperity during recessionary periods as people seek relief from their economic misfortunes. The clients anticipate a downturn in the economy during the next several years and therefore feel that funds invested in this area could produce significant returns.

Due to the aging of the population and the increased need for medical care, the health care industry is a second area of interest to your clients. The threat to our nation's social security system and the failure to institute a national health care plan have also stimulated the clients' interest in this area as a potential investment opportunity. By investing in this field, the clients hope to capitalize on a persistent demographic trend and, at the same time, mitigate a growing threat to the welfare of our nation's aging population.

Finally, they want an evaluation of a large group of firms that concentrate on environmental protection and preservation of our nation's wetlands. They feel that not only could such an investment generate financial rewards, but also they would be providing a significant contribution to posterity for many generations well into the future.

Your analysis will require the application of much of the information presented in this chapter on sampling distributions and the probability for successful investment portfolios for these important clients.

6.1 Introduction

Populations are usually too large to study in their entirety. It is necessary to select a representative sample of a more manageable size. This sample is then used to draw conclusions about the population. For instance, we may calculate the sample mean, the statistic $\overline{X}$, and use it as an estimate of the population mean μ. The statistic is used as an **estimator** of the parameter. By relying on a sample to draw some conclusion, or inference, about the population, we are engaging in **inferential statistics.**

> **Inferential Statistics** Inferential statistics involves the use of a statistic to form a conclusion, or inference, about the corresponding parameter.

The inferential process is extremely important in many statistical analyses. In Chapters 7 and 8 dealing with estimation and hypothesis testing, inferential statistics proves essential.

However, the value of the statistic depends on the sample taken. From any given population of size N, it is possible to get many different samples of size n. Each sample may well have a different mean. In fact, it is possible to get an entire distribution of different $\bar{X}$'s from the various possible samples.

6.2 Sampling Distributions

In a study of the firms on the Fortune 500 list of the nation's largest businesses, we might want to take a sample of, say, $n = 50$. From this sample we could calculate the mean rate of return $\bar{X}$ for these 50 firms. This sample mean would then serve as an estimate of μ, the population mean rate of return for all 500 firms.

From this list of 500 firms, it would be possible to get many different samples of size 50. Specifically, we could get ${}_{500}C_{50}$ different samples of size $n = 50$. Since ${}_{500}C_{50}$ is a rather large number, let us assume instead, for the sake of simplicity in our discussion, that we have a population of $N = 4$ incomes for four college students. These incomes are \$100, \$200, \$300, and \$400. The mean income can be calculated as $\mu = \$250$. However, to make matters even simpler, we may feel that calculating the mean of four observations requires too much effort. As an alternative, we decide to select a sample of $n = 2$ observations in order to estimate the "unknown" μ. We would then randomly select one sample from the ${}_4C_2 = 6$ possible samples. These six different samples and their means are shown in Table 6.1.

Table 6.1
All Possible Samples of Size $n = 2$ from a Population of $N = 4$ Incomes

Sample	Sample Elements X_i	Sample Means $\bar{X}$
1	100,200	150
2	100,300	200
3	100,400	250
4	200,300	250
5	200,400	300
6	300,400	350

With the exception of the third and fourth samples, each sample has a different mean. Assuming each sample is equally likely to be chosen, the probability of selecting a sample that yields an $\bar{X}$ equal to the population mean of 250 is only $2/6 = 33.3\%$. Four of the six samples will result in some error in the estimation process. This **sampling error** is the difference between μ and the sample mean we use to estimate it, $(\bar{X} - \mu)$.

> **Sampling Error** The difference between the population parameter and the sample statistic used to estimate the parameter.

Due just to the luck of the draw, we may select a sample of $n = 2$ consisting of \$100 and \$300. The resulting mean of $\bar{X} = \$200$ produces a sampling error of \$250 − \$200 = \$50. Of course, we can never really calculate the size of the sampling error since the population mean remains unknown. However, we must be aware that some sampling error is likely to occur.

Table 6.2
Sampling Distribution for Samples of Size $n = 2$ from a Population of $N = 4$ Incomes

Sample Mean $\bar{X}$	Number of Samples Yielding $\bar{X}$	Probability $P(\bar{X})$
150	1	1/6
200	1	1/6
250	2	2/6
300	1	1/6
350	1	1/6
		1

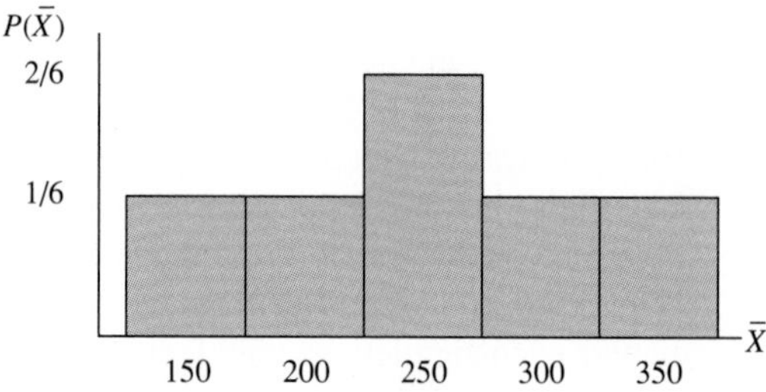

Figure 6.1
Sampling Distribution for Samples of Size $n = 2$ from a Population of $N = 4$ Incomes

With a population of only $N = 4$, we can list every possible sample mean shown in Table 6.1, along with its respective probability. Such a listing is called a **sampling distribution,** and is shown in Table 6.2 and as a histogram in Figure 6.1.

> **Sampling Distribution** A list of all possible values for a statistic and the probability associated with each value.

A. The Mean of the Sample Means

Notice that the sampling distribution of sample means is merely a list of all possible sample means. These sample means, like *any* list of numbers, have a mean called the "mean of the sample means" or the **grand mean.** This mean of the means is calculated in the usual fashion: the individual observations (sample means) are summed and the result is divided by the number of observations (samples). Using $\bar{\bar{X}}$ (pronounced *X*-double bar) as the symbol for the grand mean,

The mean of the sample means

$$\bar{\bar{X}} = \frac{\Sigma \bar{X}}{K} \qquad [6.1]$$

where K is the number of samples in the sampling distribution. Since there are 6 samples in the present sampling distribution, we have

$$\bar{\bar{X}} = \frac{150 + 200 + 250 + 250 + 300 + 350}{6} = 250$$

Notice further that the mean of the sampling distribution $\bar{\bar{X}}$ is equal to the mean of the original population $\mu = 250$. This is no coincidence! The mean of the sampling distribution will always equal the mean of the population ($\overline{\overline{X}} = \mu$). Do not confuse n, the number of observations in a single sample, with K, the number of samples in the sampling distribution. From the population of $N = 4$ in our present case, samples of size $n = 2$ yielded ${}_4C_2$ = K = 6 different samples in the sampling distribution.

B. The Variance and the Standard Error of the Sampling Distribution

The distribution of the sample means also has a variance. This variance in the sample means is like any other variance. It measures the dispersion of the individual observations (sample means) around their mean (the grand mean). Furthermore, this variance is calculated like any other variance. It is the mean of the squared deviations from the mean. It is found by

1. Determining the amount by which each of the observations (sample means) differs from their mean (the grand mean).
2. Squaring those deviations.
3. Averaging the squared deviations by dividing by the number of sample means, K.

Thus, where $\sigma_{\bar{x}}^2$ is the variance of the sampling distribution of sample means, we find

Variance of the sampling distribution of sample means

$$\sigma_{\bar{x}}^2 = \frac{\Sigma(\overline{X} - \overline{\overline{X}})^2}{K} = \frac{\Sigma(\overline{X} - \mu)^2}{K} \qquad [6.2]$$

Given the six sample means above,

$$\sigma_{\bar{x}}^2 = \frac{(150 - 250)^2 + (200 - 250)^2 + (250 - 250)^2 + (250 - 250)^2 + (300 - 250)^2 + (350 + 250)^2}{6}$$

$$= 4{,}167 \text{ dollars squared}$$

If we were to take the square root of the variance in the distribution of these sample means, we would have the **standard error of the sampling distribution, $\sigma_{\bar{x}}$**. Thus,

Standard error of the sampling distribution of sample means

$$\sigma_{\bar{x}} = \sqrt{\sigma_{\bar{x}}^2} \qquad [6.3]$$

In our present case

$$\sigma_{\bar{x}} = \sqrt{4{,}167}$$
$$= 64.55 \text{ dollars}$$

The standard error of the sampling distribution (or standard error) is a measure of the dispersion of the sample means around μ. It is analogous to the standard deviation we calculated in Chapter 3, which measured the dispersion of individual observations around their mean. Since the difference between $\overline{X}$ and μ is the *sampling error,* any measure of the tendency for the sample mean to deviate from μ is rightfully called the *standard error.* Thus, the standard error $\sigma_{\bar{x}}$ measures the tendency to suffer sampling error in our effort to estimate μ.

Example 6.1 Sales for East Coast Manufacturing (ECM) over the past five months in thousands of dollars have been 68, 73, 65, 80, and 72. Assuming these five months constitute the population, the mean is clearly $\mu = 71.6$. As marketing director for ECM, you wish to estimate this "unknown" μ by taking a sample of size $n = 3$. You hope that the sampling error you will likely suffer is relatively small. Create the sampling distribution and comment on the likely sampling error.

Solution: There are ${}_5C_3 = 10$ samples in the sampling distribution:

Sample Number	Sample Elements X_i	Sample Mean $\bar{X}$	Sample Number	Sample Elements X_i	Sample Mean $\bar{X}$
1	68,73,65	68.67	6	68,80,72	73.33
2	68,73,80	73.67	7	73,65,80	72.67
3	68,73,72	71.00	8	73,65,72	70.00
4	68,65,80	71.00	9	73,80,72	75.00
5	68,65,72	68.33	10	65,80,72	72.33

The sampling distribution is:

$\bar{X}$	$P(\bar{X})$
68.67	1/10
73.67	1/10
71.00	2/10
68.33	1/10
73.33	1/10
72.67	1/10
70.00	1/10
75.00	1/10
72.33	1/10

The mean of the sampling distribution is

$$\bar{\bar{X}} = \frac{68.67 + 73.67 + 71.00 + 71.00 + \cdots + 72.33}{10} = 71.6 = \mu$$

The variance and the standard error of the sampling distribution are

$$\sigma_{\bar{x}}^2 = \frac{\Sigma(\bar{X} - \mu)^2}{K}$$

$$= \frac{(68.68 - 71.6)^2 + (73.67 - 71.6)^2 + \cdots + (72.33 - 71.6)^2}{10}$$

$$= 4.31 \quad \text{thousand dollars squared}$$

$$\sigma_{\bar{x}} = \sqrt{\sigma_{\bar{x}}^2} = \sqrt{4.31} = 2.08 \quad \text{thousand dollars}$$

Interpretation: The mean of the sampling distribution equals the mean of the original population $\mu = 71.6$. No surprise there. The standard error, which measures the degree of dispersion of the 10 sample means around μ, thus indicates how far the sample mean may vary from the population mean. Is this what you had in mind when you hoped for a "relatively small" sampling error?

As you may have noticed by now, Formula (6.2) requires a lot of third-grade arithmetic to calculate the variance of the sampling distribution. A close approximation can be obtained by

$$\sigma_{\bar{x}}^2 = \frac{\sigma^2}{n}$$

and

$$\sigma_{\bar{x}} = \frac{\sigma}{\sqrt{n}} \quad [6.4]$$

This, of course, requires the assumption that the population variance σ^2 is known.

Formula (6.4) is appropriate only if sampling is done *with replacement*, or if the sample is taken from a very large (virtually infinite) population. If sampling is done without replacement *and* if the sample size is more than 5 percent of the population, $n > 0.05N$, the **finite population correction factor (fpc)** must be applied. The proper formula for the standard error then becomes

Standard error using the fpc

$$\sigma_{\bar{x}} = \frac{\sigma}{\sqrt{n}}\sqrt{\frac{N-n}{N-1}} \quad [6.5]$$

where $\sqrt{\frac{N-n}{N-1}}$ is the fpc.

If n is small relative to N (less than 5 percent), the fpc approaches 1 and is therefore unnecessary since multiplying by 1 does not change the value of the standard error.

C. The Impact of Sample Size on the Standard Error

Given a population of size $N = 1000$, do you think you would get a more accurate estimate of the population mean μ with a sample of size $n = 100$ or a larger sample of size $n = 900$? Unquestionably, a more exact estimate is likely with a larger sample. This presumption is verified by examining Formula (6.3). It can be seen that as n increases, $\sigma_{\bar{x}}$ will decrease. The fact that larger samples lead to smaller sampling errors will become increasingly important as we progress in our study of inferential statistics.

Section Exercises

1. Define the following terms in your own language. Give examples of each.
   a. Sampling distribution.
   b. Mean of the means.
   c. Variance and standard error of the sampling distribution.
2. A population of weekly factory outputs in thousands of tons is 200, 250, 150, 200, and 300. Develop a sampling distribution and calculate the mean of the means and the standard error for samples of size $n = 2$.

3. What will happen to the standard error in the preceding exercise if $n = 3$? Why is there a difference?
4. Samples of $n = 40$ are taken from a large population with a mean of 100 and standard deviation of 25. Calculate and interpret the standard error.
5. Repeat the preceding exercise with $n = 100$. Discuss the difference.

6.3 The Central Limit Theorem

From our discussion thus far, it should be evident that it is possible to take many samples of some given size from any population. These samples give rise to an entire distribution of sample means. If the original population is normally distributed, the distribution of sample means will also be normally distributed. That is, all the sample means will themselves graph as a normal distribution.

This is seen in Figure 6.2. The top graph shows the distribution of the individual observations X_i in the population to be normally distributed centered at a mean $\mu = 500$ with a standard deviation $\sigma = 50$. Notice that the individual observations X_i are measured on the horizontal axis.

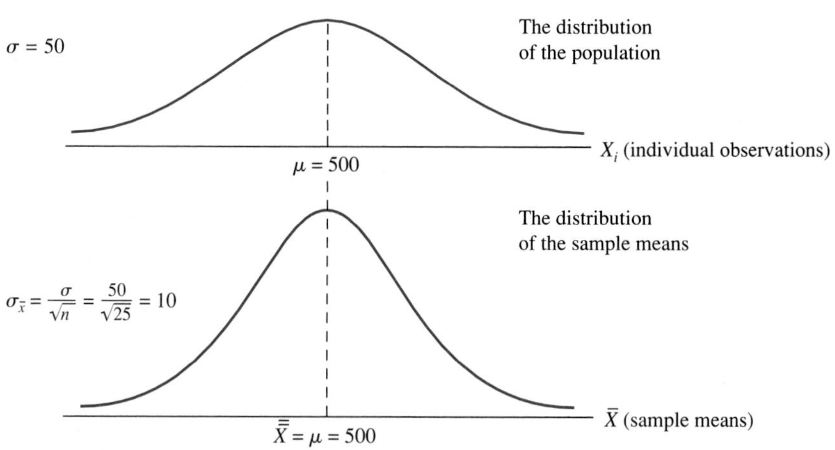

Figure 6.2 A Distribution of Sample Means from a Normal Population

The bottom graph of Figure 6.2 reflects the distribution of the sample means that will result if all samples of size $n = 25$ are taken. Notice that the sample means $\bar{X}_s$ are measured on the horizontal axis. These sample means are also normally distributed and centered at the population mean since $\bar{\bar{X}} = \mu = 500$. That is, the mean of the sample means equals the mean of the population. Notice further that the dispersion of the original population $\sigma = 50$ is greater than the dispersion of the sample means $\sigma_{\bar{x}} = \sigma/\sqrt{n} = 50/\sqrt{25} = 10$. The X_i are more spread out than the $\bar{X}_s$ since $\sigma_{\bar{x}} = \sigma/\sqrt{n}$.

The question might arise as to what the distribution of sample means looks like if the original population is *not* normally distributed. The answer is provided by the **Central Limit Theorem.** The central limit theorem states that for *any* population, as n gets larger, the distribution of sample means approaches a normal distribution with a mean $\bar{\bar{X}} = \mu$ and a standard error $\sigma_{\bar{x}} = \sigma/\sqrt{n}$.

> **Central Limit Theorem** As n gets larger, the distribution of sample means will approach a normal distribution with a mean $\bar{\bar{X}} = \mu$ and a standard error $\sigma_{\bar{x}} = \sigma/\sqrt{n}$.

Thus, even if the population is not normally distributed, the sampling distribution of sample means will be normal if n is large enough. The standard rule of thumb is that if n is at least 30, the central limit theorem will ensure a normal distribution in the sample means even if the population is not normal.

Take a look at Figure 6.3. Assume that the population in the top graph, which is clearly not normally distributed, has a mean of $\mu = 1000$ with a standard deviation of $\sigma = 100$. The center graph displays the distribution of the sample means that would result if samples of size $n = 50$ were taken. The distribution of sample means *is* normally distributed and centered at $\bar{\bar{X}} = \mu = 1000$. Moreover, the dispersion of the sample means as measured by the standard error is $\sigma_{\bar{x}} = \sigma/\sqrt{n} = 100/\sqrt{50} = 14.14$. Notice that the $\bar{X}_s$ are less dispersed than the individual observations in the original population: $\sigma > \sigma/\sqrt{n}$.

Figure 6.3
A Distribution of Sample Means from a Nonnormal Population

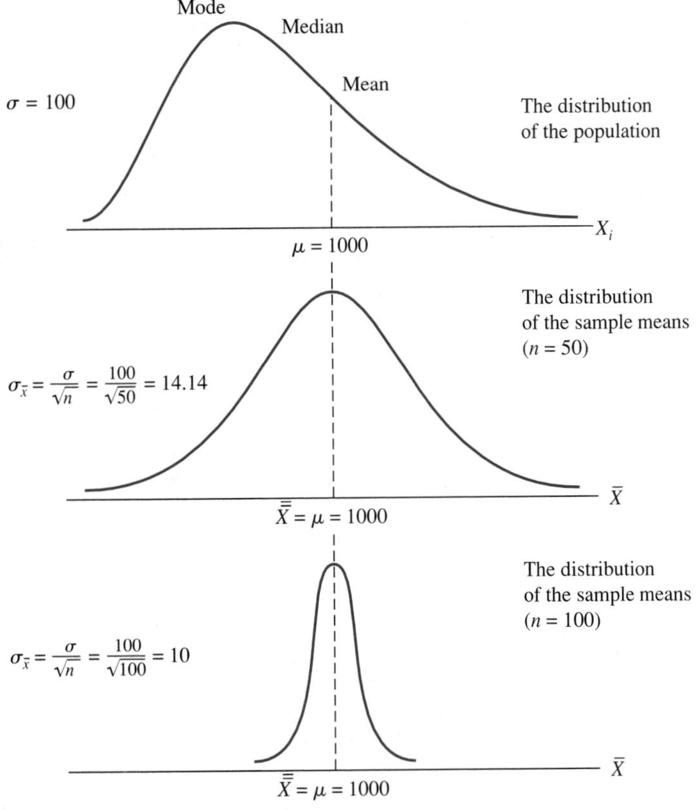

The bottom graph of Figure 6.3 illustrates what happens to the distribution of $\bar{X}_s$ as the sample size increases. If the sample size is increased to $n = 100$, the standard error becomes $\sigma_{\bar{x}} = \sigma/\sqrt{n} = 100/\sqrt{100} = 10$. The sample means are more tightly compacted around the population mean $\mu = 1000$. Since more of the sample means are closer to the population mean, the standard error suffered in the effort to estimate μ is less. This is why larger samples are likely to produce more accurate estimates of the population mean.

Section Exercises

6. State the Central Limit Theorem in your own words.
7. What is meant by the standard deviation of the population and the standard error of the sampling distribution of sample means? How do they relate and how do they compare in size? Draw graphs in your response.
8. What happens to the standard error as the sample size increases? Draw graphs to illustrate.

6.4 Using the Sampling Distribution

The importance of the foregoing discussion can be recognized only if we recall that many decisions are made on the basis of sample results. A business manager may sample a product to determine whether certain production specifications are being met. A government official will take a sample of residents to decide whether a certain tax plan or welfare program will produce the desired results. Academicians often sample students to ascertain the impact of instructional efforts.

Generally speaking, samples have a very direct and consequential impact on decisions that are made. Therefore, any conclusion we can draw or knowledge we have regarding a sample is quite important. An extremely common and quite useful application of a sampling distribution is to determine the probability that a sample mean will fall within a given range. Given that the sampling distribution will be normally distributed because (1) the sample is taken from a normal population, or (2) $n \geq 30$ and the Central Limit Theorem ensures normality in the sampling process, the normal deviate may be used to gain information essential to the decision-making process.

In Chapter 5 we determined the probability of selecting one observation that would fall within a given range. Recall from Example 5.7 that TelCom recorded telephone messages for its customers that averaged 150 seconds, with a standard deviation of 15 seconds. TelCom wished to determine the probability that one single call lasted between 125 and 150 seconds. This was done using the conversion formula, or *Z*-formula,

$$Z = \frac{X - \mu}{\sigma}$$

in which X is a single observation of interest and σ is the population standard deviation.

However, many business decisions depend on an entire sample—not just one observation. In this case, the conversion formula must be altered to account for the fact that we are interested not in one observation X but in the mean of several observations, $\bar{X}$. Therefore, when sampling is done, the conversion formula becomes

$$Z = \frac{\bar{X} - \mu}{\sigma_{\bar{x}}} \qquad [6.6]$$

The value of interest in the numerator is not a single observation X_i, but the mean of n observations $\bar{X}$. Furthermore, the denominator is not the population standard deviation σ, but the standard error of the sampling distribution $\sigma_{\bar{x}}$. Instead of determining the probability of the duration of a single call, we can calculate the probability that the mean of n calls will last a certain length of time.

For example, TelCom can find the probability that a single call would last between 150 and 155 seconds as

$$Z = \frac{X - \mu}{\sigma} = \frac{155 - 150}{15} = 0.33 \qquad \text{for an area of } 0.1293$$

Thus, $P(150 \leq X \leq 155) = 0.1293$. This is shown in the top graph of Figure 6.4.

Figure 6.4
Probabilities for TelCom

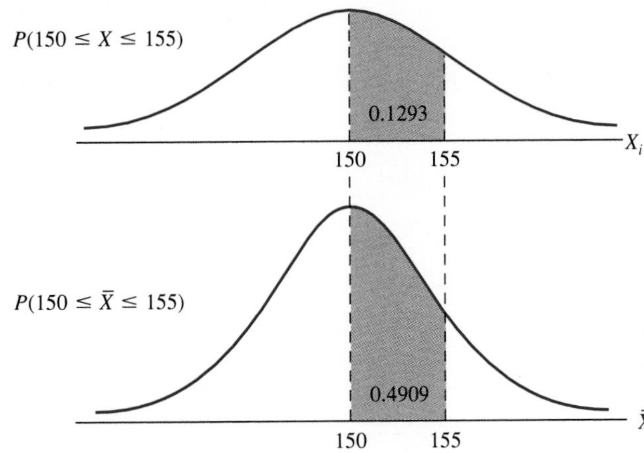

Presume that TelCom now wants to know the probability that the mean of $n = 50$ calls will be between 150 and 155 seconds.

$$Z = \frac{\bar{X} - \mu}{\frac{\sigma}{\sqrt{n}}} = \frac{155 - 150}{\frac{15}{\sqrt{50}}} = 2.36 \qquad \text{for an area of } 0.4909$$

Thus, $P(150 \leq \bar{X} \leq 155) = 0.4909$. This is seen in the bottom graph of Figure 6.4. The large difference in the probabilities is due to the facts that the sample means are less dispersed than the individual observations and that the $\bar{X}_s$ are more compact around $\mu = 150$, as shown by the graphs.

Many business decisions depend on the values of important statistical measures. Consider Example 6.2.

Example 6.2 TelCom plans to install new equipment that would improve the efficiency of its operations. However, before executives can decide whether such an investment would be cost-effective, they must determine the probability that the mean of a sample of $n = 35$:

a. Is between 145 and 150.
b. Is greater than 145.
c. Is less than 155.
d. Is between 145 and 155.
e. Is greater than 155.

Solution: *a.* $P(145 \le \overline{X} \le 150)$

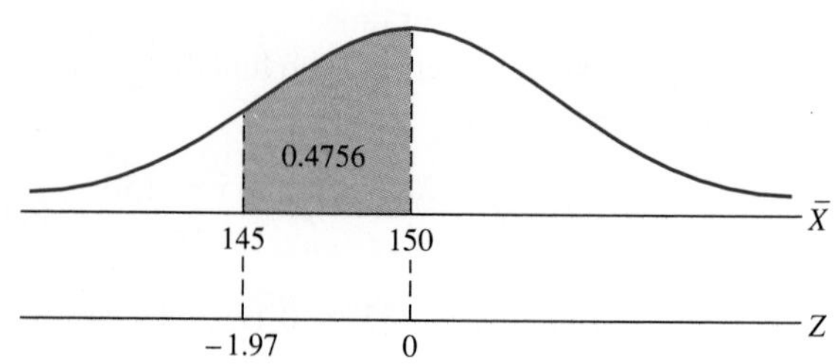

$$Z = \frac{\overline{X} - \mu}{\sigma_{\overline{x}}} = \frac{145 - 150}{15/\sqrt{35}} = -1.97 \qquad \text{or an area of } 0.4756$$

$$P(145 \le \overline{X} \le 150) = P(-1.97 \le Z \le 0) = 0.4756$$

b. $P(\overline{X} \ge 145)$

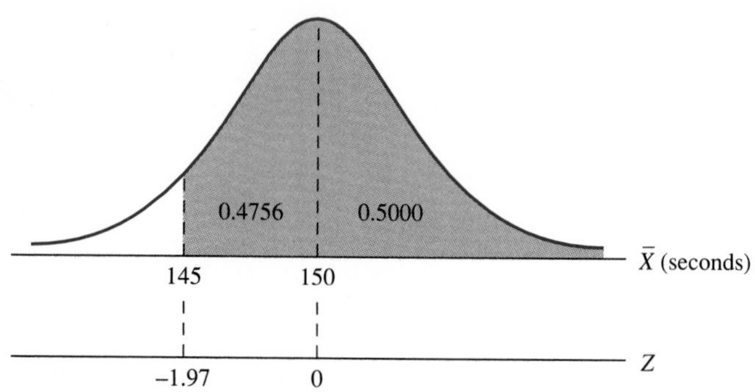

$$Z = \frac{\overline{X} - \mu}{\sigma_{\overline{x}}} = \frac{145 - 150}{2.54} = -1.97 \qquad \text{or an area of } 0.4756$$

$$\begin{aligned} P(\overline{X} \ge 145) &= P(Z \ge -1.97) \\ &= 0.4756 + 0.5000 \\ &= 0.9756 \end{aligned}$$

c. $P(\overline{X} \le 155)$

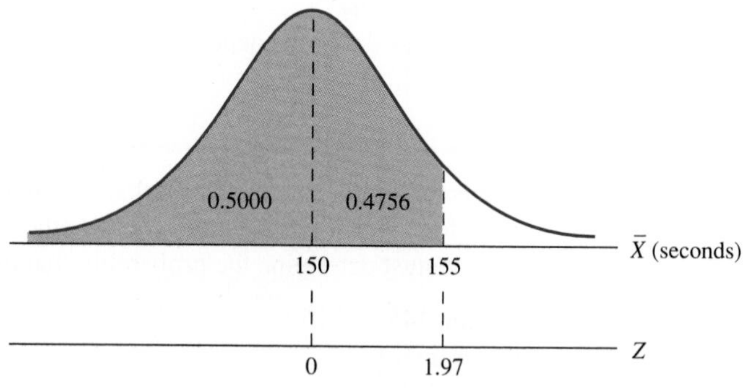

$$Z = \frac{\overline{X} - \mu}{\sigma_{\overline{x}}} = \frac{155 - 150}{2.54} = 1.97 \qquad \text{or an area of } 0.4756$$

$$P(\overline{X} \leq 155) = P(Z \leq 1.97)$$
$$= 0.4756 + 0.5000$$
$$= 0.9756$$

d. $P(145 \leq \overline{X} \leq 155)$. We must find the area between 145 and 150, and add it to the area between 150 and 155.

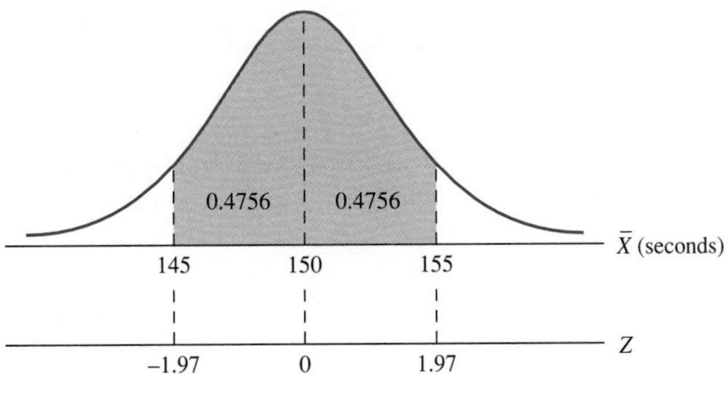

$$Z_1 = \frac{\overline{X} - \mu}{\sigma_{\bar{x}}} = \frac{145 - 150}{2.54} = -1.97 \quad \text{or an area of } 0.4756$$

$$Z_2 = \frac{\overline{X} - \mu}{\sigma_{\bar{x}}} = \frac{155 - 150}{2.54} = 1.97 \quad \text{or an area of } 0.4756$$

$$P(145 \leq \overline{X} \leq 155) = P(-1.97 \leq Z \leq 1.97)$$
$$= 0.4756 + 0.4756$$
$$= 0.9512$$

e. $P(\overline{X} \geq 155)$

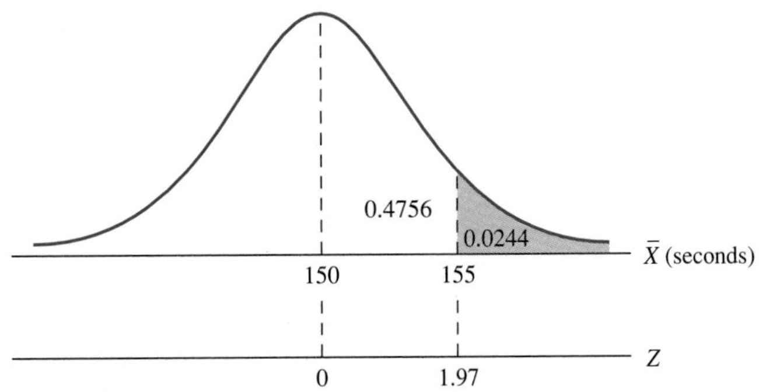

$$Z = \frac{\overline{X} - \mu}{\sigma_{\bar{x}}} = \frac{155 - 150}{2.54} = 1.97 \quad \text{or an area of } 0.4756$$

$$P(\overline{X} \geq 155) = P(Z \geq 1.97)$$
$$= 0.5000 - 0.4756$$
$$= 0.0244$$

Interpretation: On the basis of this information, TelCom can make more intelligent decisions regarding the need for new equipment.

If you are able to predict the likelihood that a certain statistic will fall within a given range, decision making becomes more precise and scientific. It is possible, for example, to determine the probability of error. Consider a population with a mean of $\mu = 25$ and a standard deviation $\sigma = 8.5$. As shown in Figure 6.5, if a sample of $n = 50$ is taken, a sampling error of 2 or more will occur if the sample mean is 27 or more or 23 or less. Thus, $P(\text{error} \geq 2) = P(\overline{X} \geq 27) + P(\overline{X} \leq 23)$.

$$Z = \frac{\overline{X} - \mu}{\frac{\sigma}{\sqrt{n}}} = \frac{27 - 25}{\frac{8.5}{\sqrt{50}}} = 1.66 \qquad \text{for an area of } 0.4515$$

$P(\overline{X} \geq 27) = 0.5000 - 0.4515 = 0.0485$. Then the $P(\text{error} \geq 2) = 0.0485 \times 2 = 9.7\%$. There is almost a 10 percent chance that the sampling error resulting from an attempt to estimate μ will be at least two.

Figure 6.5
The Probability of Error

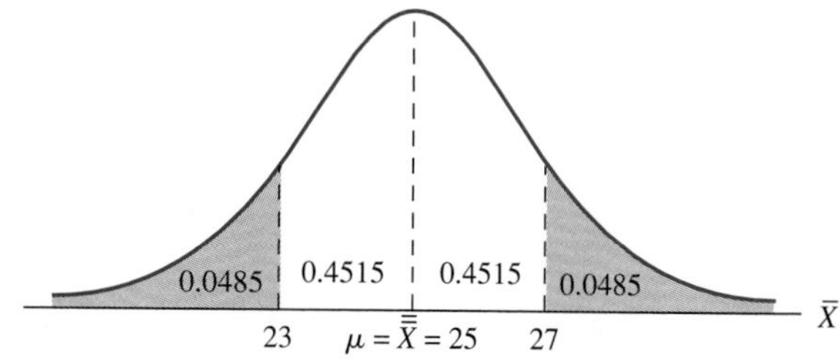

Example 6.3 The Paper House sells invitations, party favors, and other paper products for festive occasions. Presume that the unknown mean weekly hours employees work at the store is $\mu = 36.7$, with a standard deviation of $\sigma = 3.5$. Jill Ramsey, owner of The Paper House, wants to be at least 90 percent confident that her estimate of the mean hours worked per employee each week is within 1 hour of the true population mean. A sample of $n = 36$ weeks is selected. What is the probability Ramsey will not be disappointed in her estimate?

Solution: As seen in the figure below, $P(\text{error} \leq 1) = P(35.7 \leq \overline{X} \leq 37.7)$.

$$Z = \frac{37.7 - 36.7}{\frac{3.5}{\sqrt{36}}} = 1.71 \qquad \text{for an area of } 0.4564$$

$$P(35.7 \leq \overline{X} \leq 37.7) = 0.4564 \times 2 = 91.28\%$$

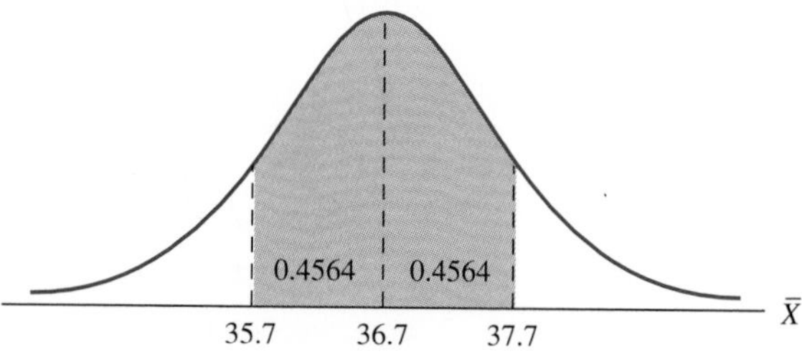

Interpretation: There is 91.28 percent chance that Ramsey's estimate will be within the tolerable error of 1 hour.

Section Exercises

9. The population of miles driven by truckers for Over the Road Van Lines exhibits a mean of 8,500, with a standard deviation of 1,950. If a sample of $n = 100$ drivers is taken, what is the probability the mean will:
   a. Exceed 8,900?
   b. Be less than 8,000?
   c. Be between 8,200 and 8,700?
   d. Be between 8,100 and 8,400?
10. Cans of soda sold at Minute Mart average 16.1 ounces, with a standard deviation of 1.2 ounces. If a sample of $n = 200$ is taken, what is the probability that the mean will be:
   a. Less than 16.27?
   b. At least 15.93?
   c. Between 15.9 and 16.3?
11. A survey by the National Education Association revealed that high school seniors watch an average of 37.2 hours of television per week. Assume a standard deviation of 5.4 hours. In a sample of $n = 500$ students, how likely is it the sample mean will be:
   a. More than 38 hours?
   b. Less than 36.6 hours?
   c. Between 36.4 and 37.9 hours?
12. Daily water consumption in Dry Hole, Texas, averages 18.9 gallons per household, with a standard deviation of 3.6 gallons. The city commissioner wishes to estimate this unknown mean with a sample of 100 households. How likely is it the sampling error will exceed 0.5 gallons?

6.5 The Sampling Distribution for Proportions

Although our discussion thus far has focused exclusively on means, many business matters are concerned with the population proportion π. A marketing firm may want to know whether a customer (1) buys or (2) does not buy the product. A bank must often determine whether a depositor will (1) ask or (2) not ask for a car loan. Many business firms must determine the probability that a capital budgeting project (1) will or (2) will not generate a positive return. In these cases the sample proportion p is used to estimate the unknown parameter π.

The sampling process for proportions is much like that for means. From any population it is possible to get many different samples of some given size. Each sample will have its own proportion of "successes," p. However, as with means, the expected value of the sampling distribution of sample proportions will equal the proportion of successes in the population: $E(p) = \pi$.

Lugget Furniture asks the entire population of all $N = 4$ customers whether they saw the Lugget advertisement in this morning newspaper. A response of "yes" is recorded as a success, and "no" as a failure. The four customers respond Y_1, N_2, N_3, and Y_4. The population proportion of successes is $\pi = 0.50$. Samples of size $n = 2$ are taken, and the proportion of successes is recorded in Table 6.3.

The expected value (mean) of the sampling distribution of sample proportions is

The expected value of the sampling distribution

$$E(p) = \frac{\Sigma p}{K} \qquad [6.7]$$

Table 6.3 The Sampling Distribution of Proportions

X_i	Number of Successes	p (Proportion of successes)
Y_1, N_2	1	0.50
Y_1, N_3	1	0.50
Y_1, Y_4	2	1.00
N_2, N_3	0	0.00
N_2, Y_4	1	0.50
N_3, Y_4	1	0.50
		3.00

and the standard error is

$$\sigma_p = \sqrt{\frac{(\pi)(1-\pi)}{n}} \qquad [6.8]$$

As with means, if $n > 0.05N$, the fpc is required and the standard error becomes

$$\sigma_p = \sqrt{\frac{(\pi)(1-\pi)}{n}}\sqrt{\frac{N-n}{N-1}} \qquad [6.9]$$

In our present case with Lugget Furniture,

$$E(p) = \frac{\Sigma p}{K} = \frac{3}{6} = 0.50 = \pi$$

and, using the fpc

$$\begin{aligned}\sigma_p &= \sqrt{\frac{(\pi)(1-\pi)}{n}}\sqrt{\frac{N-n}{N-1}}\\ &= \sqrt{\frac{(0.50)(1-0.50)}{2}}\sqrt{\frac{4-2}{4-1}}\\ &= 0.289\end{aligned}$$

Our newly developed tools for sample proportions allow us to determine probabilities that can prove very useful in making important business decisions. This is accomplished by applying the normal deviate to the sampling distribution for proportions:

$$Z = \frac{p-\pi}{\sigma_p} \qquad [6.10]$$

Example 6.4 BelLabs obtains components for its cellular telephones in lots of 200 from a firm in Palo Alto. The component has a defect rate of 10 percent. A policy recently established by BelLabs states that if the next shipment has:

a. More than 12 percent defects, it will definitely find a new supplier.

b. Between 10 percent and 12 percent defects, it will consider a new supplier.

c. Between 5 percent and 10 percent defects, it will definitely not get a new supplier.

d. Less than 5 percent defects, it will increase their orders.

Which decision is BelLabs most likely to make?

Solution: Since the population size N is not give, it is reasonable to assume that BelLabs buys many components and the sample size of $n = 200$ is less than $0.05\ N$ and the fpc is therefore not needed.

$$\sigma_p = \sqrt{\frac{(0.1)(0.9)}{200}} = 0.021$$

a. $P(p > 0.12)$:

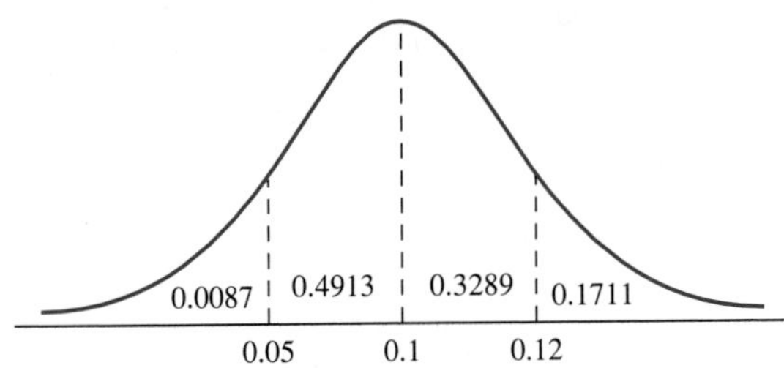

$$Z = \frac{0.12 - 0.10}{0.021} = 0.95 \qquad \text{for an area of } 0.3289$$

$$P(p > 0.12)\text{: } 0.5000 - 0.3289 = 0.1711$$

b. From part *a*, $P(0.10 \leq p \leq 0.12) = 0.3289$.

c. $P(0.05 \leq p \leq 0.10)$:

$$Z = \frac{0.05 - 0.10}{0.021} = -2.38 \qquad \text{for an area of } 0.4913$$

d. From part *c*, $P(p < 0.05) = 0.0087$.

Interpretation: Since part c has the highest probability, BelLabs will stay with its current supplier.

Section Exercises

13. An opinion poll of 1000 residents of a large city asks whether they favor a rise in taxes to pay for a new sports stadium. If more than 85 percent support the tax, a referendum will be introduced in the city's next election. If the unknown population proportion of all residents who favor the tax is $\pi = 0.82$, 82 percent, what is the probability it will be placed on the next ballot?

14. Thirty percent of all employees have advanced training. If, in a sample of 500 employees, less than 27 percent are adequately prepared, all new hirees will be required to enroll in a training program. What is the probability the program will be initiated?

15. Based on a sample of 100 teachers, a study is undertaken to analyze their preference of the current Teachers' Insurance Annuity Fund-College Retirement Equity Fund (TIAA-CREF) retirement program available to them. If fewer than 60 percent are satisfied with TIAA-CREF, an alternative will be found. Assuming $\pi = 65$ percent, what is the probability the current plan will be supplemented?

16. The proportion of all customers at Pizza Hut who eat on-site is 75 percent. In a sample of 100 patrons, what is the probability that less than 20 percent take their meal home?

17. Sixty percent of all cattle in a large herd have anthrax. Out of 100 cattle chosen at random, what is the probability that at least 50 will have to be cut from the herd?

6.6 Sampling Methods

We have repeatedly emphasized the need to select a sample representative of the population. A sample that misrepresents the population will introduce sampling error and produce inaccurate estimates of the population parameters.

There are two basic sources of sampling error. The first is just plain bad luck. Due to the "luck of the draw," our sample might contain elements that are not characteristic of the population. Fate may dictate that certain selections in the sample are atypically larger than most of those in the population, which would result in an overestimation of the parameter. Or perhaps many of the sample elements tend to be smaller than what are typically found in the population, in which case an underestimation would result.

A second source of sampling error is *sampling bias*. Bias results from the tendency to favor the selection of certain samples over others in the collection of our sample data. A classic example of sampling bias occurred in the 1936 presidential election. Franklin D. Roosevelt was running on the Democratic ballot against Alf Landon, the Republican candidate. A survey of voters conducted by the *Literary Digest* (which long ago ceased publication) revealed that Landon would win in a veritable landslide. When the smoke lifted after the election, the editors of *Literary Digest* tried courageously to determine how they could have been so wrong!

They soon discovered their blunder. In selecting the people for their sample, they took names from two sources: the phone book and their own subscription rolls. Remember, in 1936 the nation was in the midst of the Great Depression. Most people, rightfully or wrongfully, blamed the Republicans for this economic catastrophe and steadfastly refused to vote for anyone with that party affiliation. *Literary Digest* chose people who were less affected by harsh financial conditions and could actually afford a telephone and a regular subscription to a magazine. The people used in the survey were therefore *not* representative of the nation as a whole. The sample tended to favor in its selection those voters who were not so adamantly opposed to the Republicans. No wonder the magazine is no longer in circulation.

There are many other instances in which the selection of the sample can result in error. It is therefore wise to ensure that the collection of sample data follows a prescribed method that has proved its ability to minimize such error. Although an exhaustive examination of sampling methods is beyond the scope of this text, a brief look at proper sampling procedures is warranted at this point.

A. Simple Random Sample

As we have seen, several different samples can be selected from any population. Taking a **simple random sample** ensures that each sample of some given size has the *same* probability of being selected. Assume a national fast-food chain wishes to randomly select 5 of the 50 states to sample consumers' taste. A simple random sample will guarantee that the ${}_{50}C_5 = 2{,}118{,}760$ samples of size 5 will all have the same likelihood of being used in the study.

A simple random sample can be obtained by merely listing the observations on identical pieces of paper, placing them in a hat and drawing out the desired number. In addition, a *random numbers table* may also be used. The table is often generated by a computer in which each of the 10 digits (0–9) has an equal probability of being selected. If a three-digit table is desired, the computer might randomly select 4, 2, 7, 5, 2, 6, 1, 0, 5, and so on, forming the random numbers 427, 526, and 105. A random numbers table is provided in Table A.

B. Systematic Sampling

A systematic sample is formed by selecting every *i*th item from the population. If i is set equal to 10, a systematic sample consists of every tenth observation in the population. The population must be ordered or listed in a random fashion.

The first selection must be randomly determined, and if $i = 10$, it will be somewhere within the first 10 observations. The exact starting point can be identified either by selecting a number between 1 and 10 drawn from a hat, or by using a table of random numbers. In any event, every tenth observation thereafter is selected.

The process of systematic sampling is advantageous in that it doesn't require a highly skilled expert to count to 10 and record the outcome. In addition, the method permits flexibility in that i can be set to 10, 100, 1,000, or any other desired number. Determination of the proper value for i is also quite easy. If we wish to select a sample of size 100 from a population of 1,000, i must be 10.

The primary danger that must be avoided is the occurrence of a pattern in the ordering of the population. For example, listing the population alphabetically assumes a random distribution throughout the alphabet.

C. Stratified Sampling

The U.S. Department of Agriculture recently became interested in the impact of drought conditions on the production of wheat. Of particular concern was the rate of bankruptcies causing farmers to lose their land. It was felt that an account of the production levels by farmers in Kansas, Oklahoma, Nebraska, and South Dakota, the four states hardest hit by the drought, might prove useful in devising a relief program. The department decided that a sample of this year's harvest should be taken for several hundred farmers from each state.

However, it was noted that the number of farmers was quite different in each state. If a simple random sample was taken from all four states as a whole, it might very well include proportionately too few farmers from some states and too many from others. This would result in a nonrepresentative sample, which would increase the sampling error.

The Department of Agriculture decided to take a **stratified sample** by dividing all the farmers into subgroups or strata (hence the term *stratified sampling*). In this case, the logical subgroups would be the four states in question. The proportion of farmers included in the sample from each state would be set equal to those proportions of all farmers in each state: If Kansas farmers made up 30 percent of all the farmers in all four states, then 30 percent of the farmers in the sample would be randomly selected from Kansas.

A stratified sample is taken by forcing the proportions of the sample from each strata to conform to the pattern of the population. It is commonly employed when the population is heterogeneous, or dissimilar, yet certain homogeneous subgroups can be isolated. In this manner the researcher can increase accuracy beyond that obtained by a simple random sample of similar size.

D. Cluster Sampling

Another alternative technique, **cluster sampling,** offers certain advantages over other methods. It consists of dividing the entire population into clusters, or groups, and then selecting a sample of these clusters. All observations in these selected clusters are included in the sample. To illustrate, consider the following example. The U.S. Department of Agriculture, in its study of drought conditions, might decide that a cluster sample is preferable. A cluster sample is taken by identifying the counties in each state as clusters. A sample of these counties (clusters) is then chosen randomly by using a table of random numbers or some other generally accepted means. All farmers in the counties selected in this manner are included in the sample. This procedure is often easier and quicker than simple random sampling or stratified sampling. For example, if it is necessary to travel to each farm in the sample to observe the effects of the drought, it is easier to visit several farmers in the same county.

It is also possible to combine stratified sampling with cluster sampling. In our agricultural example, it might be wise to select for our sample a number of counties from each state proportional to the total number of counties in all four states.

Certain problems can arise in the use of cluster sampling. If an abnormally large (or small) percentage of the farmers in a selected cluster tend to use irrigation to enhance crop yields, the sample results may be biased.

This discussion is in no way a complete account of sampling methods or the problems that can arise in the process of searching for a representative sample to be used to draw statistical inferences. A study of sampling techniques constitutes an entire course in and of itself and is beyond the scope of this text. However, due to the importance of the sampling process, even the beginning student should be aware of sampling fundamentals.

Solved Problems

1. Investment records show that the mean rate of return for firms in the consumer goods industry is 30 percent, with a standard deviation of 12 percent. If a sample of 250 such firms is selected, what is the probability that the mean of these firms will exceed 31 percent?

As the graph shows, the probability that the sample mean is between 30 percent and 31 percent is

$$Z = \frac{0.31 - 0.30}{\frac{0.12}{\sqrt{250}}} = 1.32 \qquad \text{for an area of } 0.4066$$

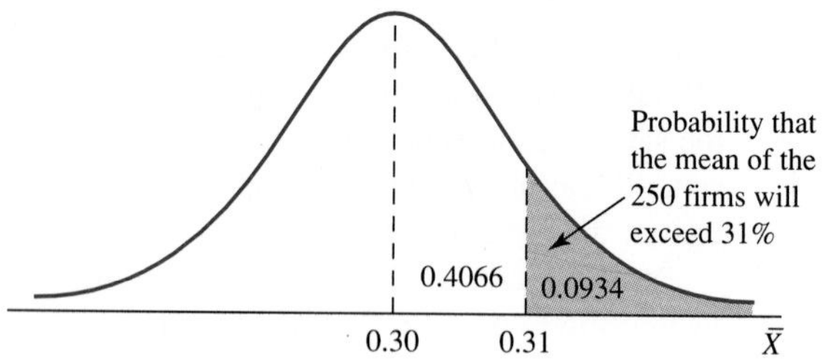

Thus, $P(\bar{X} > 0.31) = 0.5000 - 0.4066 = 0.0934$.

2. Only 22 percent of all the firms in the consumer goods industry market their products directly to the final consumer. If a sample of 250 firms reveals a proportion of more than 20 percent who engage in direct marketing, you plan to make your next purchase from the firms in this industry. How likely are you to spend your hard-earned money elsewhere?

$$Z = \frac{0.20 - 0.22}{\sqrt{\frac{(0.22)(0.78)}{250}}} = -0.76 \qquad \text{for an area of } 0.2764$$

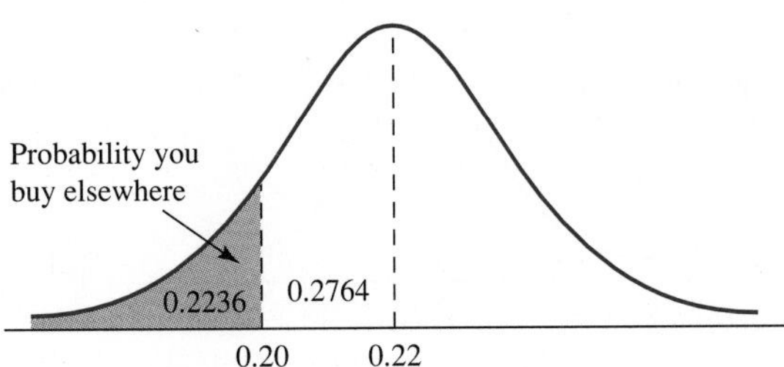

Thus, $P(p > .20) = 0.7765$, and the probability you do not buy from these firms is $1.00 - 0.7765 = 0.2236$.

List of Formulas

[6.1]	$\bar{\bar{X}} = \frac{\Sigma \bar{X}}{K}$	Mean of the sample means
[6.2]	$\sigma_{\bar{x}}^2 = \frac{\Sigma(\bar{X} - \mu)^2}{K}$	Variance of the sampling distribution of sample means
[6.3]	$\sigma_{\bar{x}} = \sqrt{\sigma_{\bar{x}}^2}$	Standard error of the sampling distribution of sample means
[6.4]	$\sigma_{\bar{x}} = \frac{\sigma}{\sqrt{n}}$	Standard error of the sampling distribution
[6.5]	$\sigma_{\bar{x}} = \frac{\sigma}{\sqrt{n}}\sqrt{\frac{N-n}{N-1}}$	Standard error with finite population correction factor
[6.6]	$Z = \frac{\bar{X} - \mu}{\sigma_{\bar{x}}}$	Normal deviate for means
[6.7]	$E(p) = \frac{\Sigma p}{K}$	Expected value of proportions
[6.8]	$\sigma_p = \sqrt{\frac{(\pi)(1-\pi)}{n}}$	Standard error of proportions
[6.9]	$\sigma_p = \sqrt{\frac{(\pi)(1-\pi)}{n}}\sqrt{\frac{N-n}{N-1}}$	Standard error with finite population correction factor
[6.10]	$Z = \frac{p - \pi}{\sigma_p}$	Normal deviate for proportions

Chapter Exercises

18. If a sample is taken in which $n < 30$, what problem might we have in working with it?

19. If several samples of a given size are taken from a population, what will influence the variability of those sample means? What happens to that variability as n increases?

20. From a single population, two sampling distributions are formed by taking all possible samples of a given size to get sampling distribution A, and all possible samples of a different size to get sampling distribution B. These distributions are graphed below. Which distribution contains the larger sample size? How can you tell?

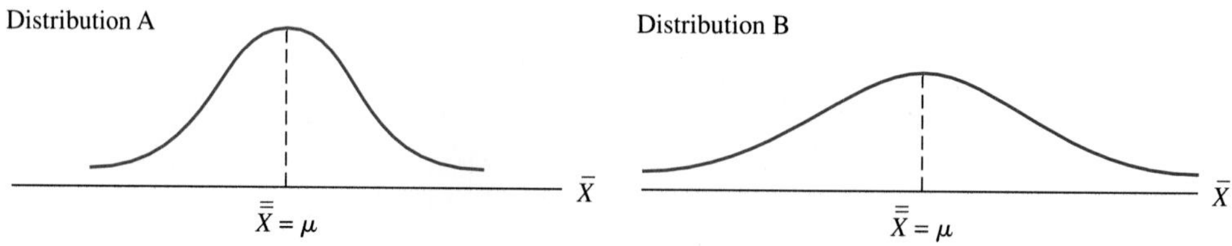

21. A population of weekly sales (in $1,000's) at Blazing Salads, a vegetarian restaurant in Chicago, is 27, 32, 17, 21, and 32.

a. Calculate and interpret σ.
b. Set $n = 2$ and develop the sampling distribution.
c. Calculate and interpret $\sigma_{\bar{x}}$. How does it relate to σ?
d. Calculate and interpret μ.
e. Calculate and interpret $\overline{\overline{X}}$ How does it compare with μ.

22. Using the data in Exercise 21, set $n = 3$ and

a. develop the sampling distribution.
b. calculate $\overline{\overline{X}}$ and $\sigma_{\bar{x}}$. How do they differ from the values in Exercise 21, and why?

23. A sample of $n = 50$ is taken from a large population with a mean of 12.2 and a standard deviation of 4.1. What are the mean and the standard error of the sampling distribution of sample means?

24. Customers at the Madison Hair Garden, a beauty shop in Madison, Connecticut, average 40.7 per day, with a standard deviation of 12.9. If a sample of 100 days is taken, what is the probability that the mean number of customers will exceed 43?

25. Jim Sears manufactures farm equipment. His work requires the use of steel bars which must have a mean length of at least 50 inches. The bars can be purchased from a supplier in Kansas City whose bars average only 47 inches, with a standard deviation of 12 inches, or from a supplier in Dallas whose bars average 49 inches, with a standard deviation of 3.6 inches. If Sears is to buy 81 bars, should he use the supplier in Kansas City or the one in Dallas?

26. According to *Business Week*, the average years of experience of airline pilots is 25.2. Assume a standard deviation of 12 years. This year you must make 36 business flights. You hope the average length of experience for the pilots of your flights is over 30. How likely is it that $\overline{X} > 30$?

27. The mean deposits at First of America Bank in Peoria are $7,012, with a standard deviation of $532, and they are normally distributed.

a. If one deposit is selected at random, what is the probability that it exceeds $6,911?
b. If a sample of $n = 35$ deposits is randomly selected, what is the probability that the mean will exceed $6,911?

c. Why does taking a sample decrease your answer? Draw graphs, one directly above the other, to illustrate.

28. The mean production level at a local manufacturing plant is 47.3 units per day, with a standard deviation of 12.7. The plant manager will take a sample of 100 days. If the sample mean exceeds 49, she promises to give all employees a Christmas bonus. How likely are the employees to enjoy a merry Christmas?

29. Incomes for production line workers in Chicago average $21.15 per hour with a standard deviation of $5.15. These incomes are skewed left. Describe the sampling distribution of incomes for sample size 100. Draw the distributions for both the original population and the sampling distribution.

30. If the sample size in Exercise 29 was 64, how would the sampling distribution compare? Graph both.

31. A local mechanic charges $110 on the average to complete a certain repair. Records show a standard deviation of $21.50 in billings. A customer recently complained that his bill of $115.50 was excessive. After considerable haggling, the mechanic agreed to refund the money if a sample of 36 similar jobs revealed a mean billing less than the customer's bill. Do you think the mechanic was wise in offering this settlement?

32. A manufacturing process produces units that average 10 inches in length with a standard deviation of 3.2 inches. If only those units between 9.5 and 10.5 inches can be used, how many out of a sample of 100 must be thrown away?

33. In a computer assignment given a sophomore statistics class, the students averaged 14.2 errors, with a standard deviation of 4.3.

a. What is the probability that you (or any given single student) will have more than 13 errors in your assignment if errors are known to be normally distributed?

b. If errors are not known to be normally distributed, what is the probability that a sample of 36 students will average more than 13 errors?

c. Why are your answers different? Draw two graphs, one directly above the other, to illustrate.

d. Why was the assumption of normality required in part *a* and not in part *b*?

34. The standard deviation in the amount of time it takes to train a worker to perform a task is 40 minutes. A random sample of 64 workers is taken.

a. What is the probability the sample mean will exceed the population mean by more than 5 minutes?

b. What is the probability the sample mean is more than 8 minutes less than the population mean?

35. A random sample of 81 purchases at a local department store was taken to estimate the mean of all purchases. It is known that the population standard deviation is $25.

a. What is the probability the sample mean will not overstate the population mean by more than $4?

b. What is the probability the sample mean will understate the population mean by more than $1?

36. The average retirement fund in TIAA for a population of teachers is $40,715, with a standard deviation of $19,015. Find the probability that a sample of 75 teachers will yield a sampling error less than $1,000.

37. National figures show that 32 percent of all students fail their first statistics test. If 100 students are selected at random, what is the probability more than 40 fail?

38. An industrial process generates 8 percent defective units. You purchase 100 units. What is the probability that less than 10 percent are defective?

39. From the same industrial process cited in the previous exercise, you again purchase 100 units. What is the probability that less than 10 percent are defective?

40. A producer of VCRs advertises that 28 percent of the VCRs sold on the market are its brand. Of 150 recent sales, exactly 40 were produced by this company. How do you feel about the company's claim?

41. Your customers require that at least 90 percent of your products are without defects. A sample of 500 reveals 31 defects. Are you meeting customers' specifications?

42. The maker of a new computer proves to you that you will experience only 9 percent downtime for repairs and maintenance with their new model. A check of your current hardware reveals that out of the last 90 hours, 12 hours were downtime. Is the new computer more reliable than your current model?

43. Five cards are laid out on a table face down. Your friend claims he has ESP. You select a card at random without revealing your choice to your friend. Out of 200 attempts, he correctly identifies 54 cards. Do you believe your friend has ESP?

44. A corporation is going to float a new stock issue. Law requires that current stockholders be given the first opportunity to buy any new issue. Management feels that 45 percent of current stockholders will want to make a purchase. A random sample of 130 stockholders is selected, 63 of whom express a desire to buy.
    a. What is the standard error of the sample proportion?
    b. What is the mean of the sampling distribution of sample proportions?
    c. What is the probability of obtaining the results described in the problem if $\pi = 0.45$?

45. Sears has determined that 17 percent of all purchases made during the Christmas season are returned. If a store sells 150 video games, what is the probability that at most 20 percent will be returned?

46. Without working the problem, explain what would happen to the answer in the previous problem if n increased to 200. Why?

CURTAIN CALL

In Setting the Stage at the beginning of this chapter, you were charged with the responsibility of analyzing three industries to identify in which one several of your important clients might invest their funds. The three areas in which your clients are interested are sports and leisure, the health care field, and environment protection. Presume that the unknown mean rates of return in these three fields are 8 percent, 23 percent, and 15 percent respectively, and that the standard deviation in these returns are 3 percent, 5 percent, and 7 percent. Bankruptcy rates are 12 percent, 7.5 percent, and 3 percent in the three industries, respectively.

The clients are concerned most about the mean rate of return their investment will yield as well as the risk of default they will have to bear due to bankruptcy. Your analysis is to include your estimates of the probabilities of default and the potential rates of return. Your clients are very cautious investors and are also requesting estimates of the probability of any errors in your analysis. You plan to sample 50 firms from the sports and leisure industry, 150 firms in the health care industry, and 250 firms concerned with wildlife management. Fully explain and justify any additional assumptions you must make to complete the analysis. Prepare your final report in accord with the rules set out in Appendix I for report writing.

From the Stage to Real Life

As an individual investor, you are able to learn a great deal about specific companies on the Internet. If you are considering companies you have heard tips about, a good place to begin your information gathering is at the companies' web sites. Marriott Hotels (*www.marriott.com*) is a major corporation in the leisure industry. What information does its web site provide you about its consumer services? What investor information is provided at this site? Similarly, Aetna (*www.aetnaushc.com*) is a major managed health care provider. What information is made available at this site for its customers? For its investors? Finally, Environment One Corporation (*www.eone.com*) manufactures pollution control equipment. What information does this company make available to its customers? Its investors?

You can look up specific corporation financial data on the Edgar database maintained by the Securities and Exchange Commission (*www.sec.gov*).

CHAPTER 7

Estimating with Confidence Intervals

Chapter Blueprint

Chapter 6 showed how sampling distributions of the population mean and the population proportion can be used to generate point estimates of μ and π. This chapter shows how interval estimates can be formed for these two parameters and how levels of confidence can be assigned to these intervals.

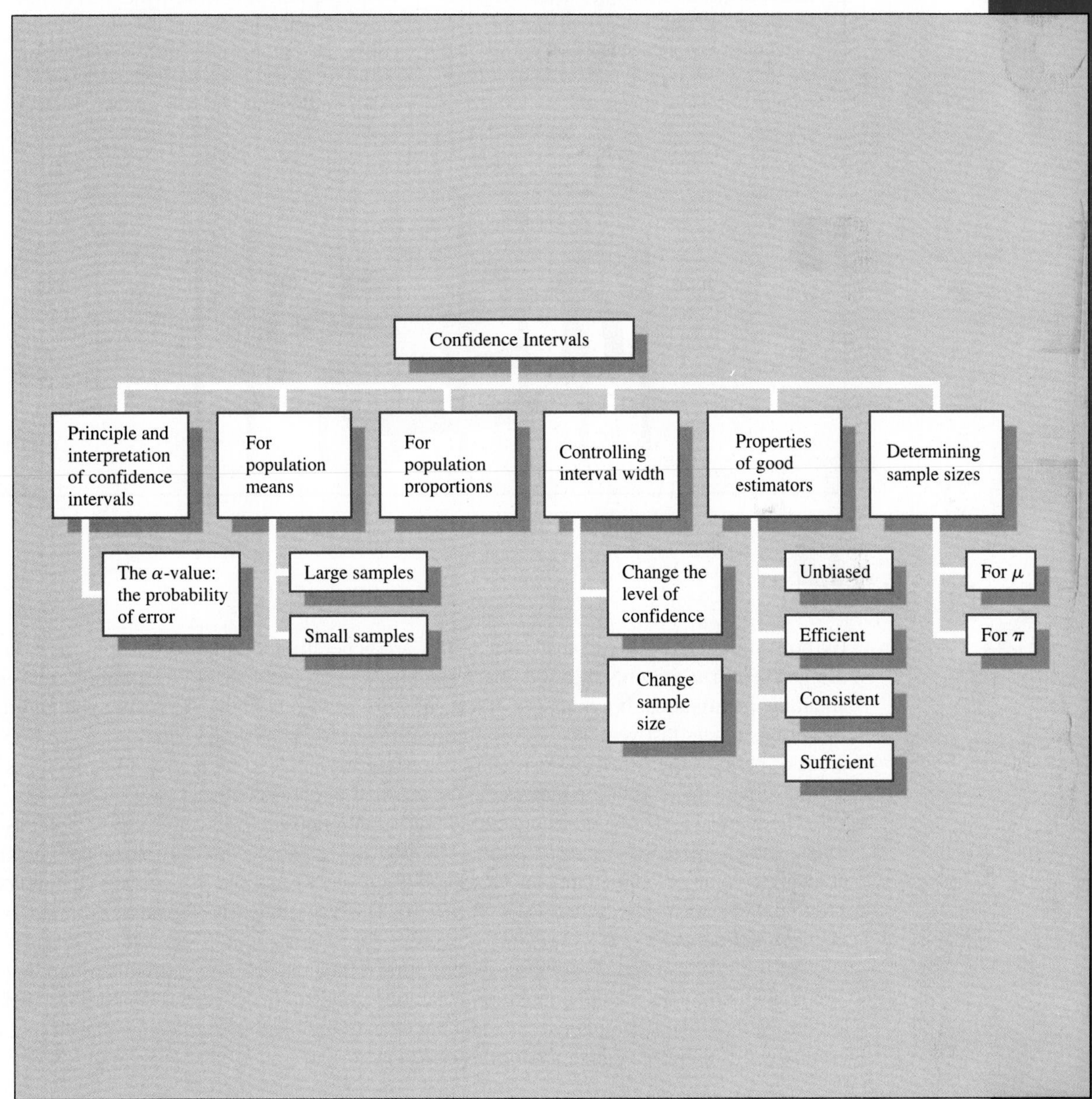

SETTING THE STAGE

In 1997 the Federal Bureau of Investigation (FBI) implemented revolutionary procedures to facilitate the apprehension of people wanted for serious crimes. A spokesperson from the Bureau's Crime Statistics Division appeared on the *Larry King Live* show on Cable News Network (CNN) to discuss the procedures that would make our streets safer. She cited several statistics the FBI collected describing motives, techniques and frequencies of crimes that she felt were useful in profiling at-large criminals the bureau desperately wanted to capture.

Her discussion focused on the bureau's efforts to maintain a large database on crime statistics that could be used to predict criminal activity and thus to better anticipate where and when an unlawful act might take place. She cited several cases that had been solved due in large part to work by professional statisticians to provide estimates of recidivism rates of offenders as well as other activities that could provide some clue that might aid in their arrest. This information proved extremely useful to agents in the field whose job it is to locate those on the FBI's Most Wanted List.

7.1 Introduction

By now you are well aware that populations are generally too large to study in their entirety. Their size requires that we select samples, which we then use to draw inferences about the populations. If a manager of a retail store wished to know the mean expenditure by her customers last year, she would find it difficult to calculate the average of the hundreds or perhaps thousands of customers who shopped in her store. It would be much easier to estimate the population mean with the mean of a representative sample.

There are at least two types of estimators commonly used for this purpose: a point estimate and an interval estimate. A **point estimate** uses a statistic to estimate the parameter at a single value or point. The store manager may select a sample of $n = 500$ customers and find the mean expenditure to be $\overline{X} = \$37.10$. This value serves as the point estimate for the population mean.

An **interval estimate** specifies a range within which the unknown parameter may fall. The manager may decide the population mean lies somewhere between \$35 and \$38. Such an interval is often accompanied by a statement as to the level of confidence placed in its accuracy. It is therefore called a **confidence interval.**

Estimates A point estimate uses a single number or value to pinpoint an estimate of the parameter. A confidence interval denotes a **range** within which the parameter might be found, and the level of confidence that the interval contains the parameter.

Actually there are three levels of confidence commonly associated with confidence intervals: 99, 95, and 90 percent. There is nothing magical about these three values. We could calculate an 82 percent confidence interval if we so desired. These three levels of confidence, called **confidence coefficients,** are simply conventional. The manager referred to above might be 95 percent confident that the population mean is between \$35 and \$38.

Interval estimates enjoy certain advantages over point estimates. Due to sampling error, $\bar{X}$ will likely not equal μ. However, we have no way of knowing how large the sampling error is. Intervals are therefore used to account for this unknown discrepancy.

We begin with a discussion of what a confidence interval is and how to interpret it.

A. The Principle of a Confidence Interval

A confidence interval has a **lower confidence limit** (LCL) and an **upper confidence limit** (UCL). These limits are found by first calculating the sample mean, $\bar{X}$. A certain amount is then added to $\bar{X}$ to get the UCL, and the same amount is subtracted from $\bar{X}$ to get the LCL. The determination of that amount is the subject of this chapter.

How can we construct an interval and then argue that we can be 95 percent confident that it contains μ if we don't even know what the population mean is? Recall from our discussion of the Empirical Rule that 95.5 percent of all sample means lie within two standard errors of the population mean. Then, the population mean lies within two standard errors of 95.5 percent of all sample means. Therefore, starting with any sample mean, if we move two standard errors above that mean and two standard errors below that mean, we can be 95.5 percent confident that the resulting interval contains the unknown population mean.

Remember, our discussion of sampling distributions showed that, from any population, we can get many different samples of some given size, each with its own mean. Figure 7.1 on page 170 shows six of these possible sample means. If our sample yields $\bar{X}_1$, an interval extending two standard errors above and two standard errors below $\bar{X}_1$ does indeed include the unknown value of the population mean. Similarly, if our sample had yielded a mean of $\bar{X}_2$, the resulting interval would also include the population mean. Notice that only $\bar{X}_3$ and $\bar{X}_5$ lie so far from the population mean that an interval ± 2 standard errors does not include the population mean. All other sample means will produce an interval that contains the population mean. The key to remember, then, is this: Since the population mean lies within two standard errors of 95.5 percent of all these sample means, then, given *any* sample mean, we can be 95.5 percent certain that the interval of two standard errors around that sample mean contains the unknown population mean.

If we wish to construct the more conventional 95 percent interval (rather than the 95.5 percent discussed above), how many standard errors must we move above and below the sample mean? As Figure 7.2 shows, because the Z-table contains values only for the area above *or* below the mean, we must divide the 95 percent by 2, yielding 0.4750. We then find the Z-value corresponding to an area of 0.4750, which is $Z = 1.96$. Thus, to construct a 95 percent confidence interval, we simply specify an interval 1.96 standard errors above and below the sample mean. This value of 95 percent is called the **confidence coefficient.**

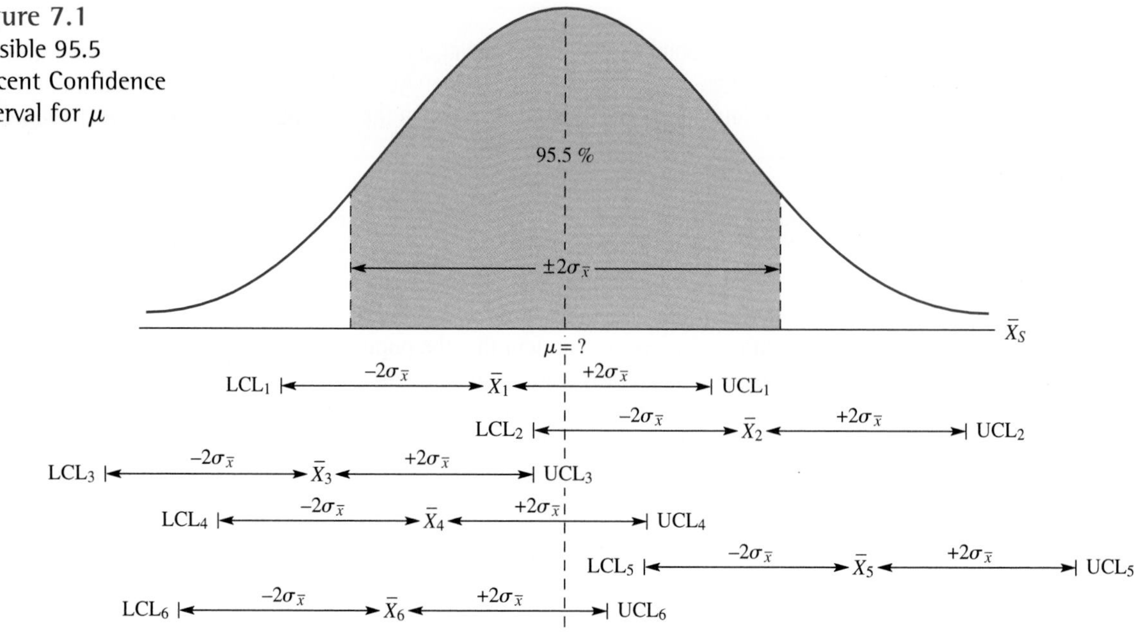

Figure 7.1
Possible 95.5 Percent Confidence Interval for μ

Confidence Coefficient The confidence coefficient is the level of confidence we have that the interval contains the unknown value of the parameter.

Perhaps we can best illustrate using an example. We begin by developing an interval estimate of the population mean with a large sample ($n \geq 30$).

7.2 Confidence Interval of Population Mean—Large Sample

One of the most common uses of confidence intervals is to estimate the population mean. A manufacturer may want to estimate the mean monthly output of his plant; a marketing representative may be concerned about the drop in mean weekly sales; the chief financial officer of a Fortune 500 firm may wish to estimate the mean quarterly returns earned on corporate operations. The number of circumstances commonly en-countered in the business world requiring an estimate of the population mean is almost unlimited.

Recall that the interval is formed by using the sample mean as a point estimate to which a certain value is added and from which it is subtracted to get the upper and lower bounds, respectively, of the confidence interval. Thus, the interval is

Confidence interval for μ when σ is known

$$\text{C.I. for } \mu = \bar{X} \pm Z\sigma_{\bar{x}} \qquad [7.1]$$

How much is to be added and subtracted depends in part on the desired level of confidence stipulated by the Z-value in Formula (7.1). A 95 percent level of confidence requires a Z-value of 1.96 ($0.95/2 = 0.4750$). The area of 0.4750 corresponds to a Z-value of 1.96.

Consider a real estate developer who intends to build a large shopping mall. He may estimate the mean family income in the area as an indicator of expected sales. A sample of

Figure 7.2
A 95 Percent Confidence Interval for the Population Mean

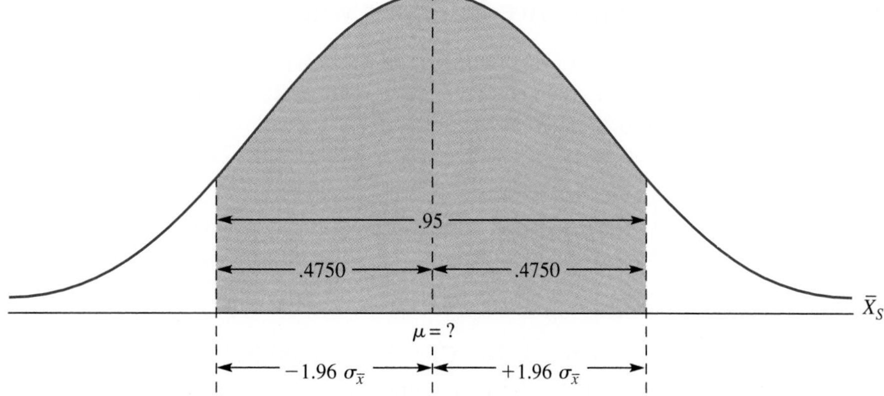

$n = 100$ families yields a mean of $\bar{X} = \$35{,}500$. Presume the population standard deviation is $\sigma = \$7{,}200$. Given that $\sigma_{\bar{x}} = \dfrac{\sigma}{\sqrt{n}}$, a 95 percent interval is estimated as

$$\begin{aligned}\text{C.I. for } \mu &= 35{,}500 \pm (1.96)\frac{7{,}200}{\sqrt{100}} \\ &= 34{,}088.80 \leq \mu \leq 36{,}911.20\end{aligned}$$

A. Interpretation of the Confidence Interval

The developer can interpret the results of his confidence interval in two ways. The first, and most common, interpretation states that the developer is "95 percent confident that the true unknown population mean is between \$34,088.80 and \$36,911.20." Although the true value for the population mean remains unknown, the developer is 95 percent confident that it is somewhere between these two values.

The second interpretation recognizes that many different confidence intervals can be developed. Another sample would likely produce a different sample mean due to sampling error. With a different $\bar{X}$, the interval would have different upper and lower bounds. Therefore, the second interpretation states that if all ${}_NC_n$ confidence intervals are constructed, 95 percent of them will contain the unknown population mean.

If a second sample yields a mean of \$35,600 instead of \$35,500, the interval is

$$\begin{aligned}\text{C.I. for } \mu &= \$35{,}600 \pm (1.96)\frac{\$7{,}200}{\sqrt{100}} \\ &= \$34{,}188.80 \leq \mu \leq \$37{,}011.20\end{aligned}$$

The developer can be 95 percent certain that the population mean is between \$34,188.80 and \$37,011.20. If all possible intervals were constructed based on all the different sample means, 95 percent of them would contain the unknown population mean.

This means, of course, that 5 percent of all the intervals would be wrong—they would not contain the population mean. This 5 percent, found as (1 − confidence coefficient), is called the **alpha value** and represents the probability of error. The alpha value is the probability that any given interval does not contain the population mean.

> **Alpha value** The probability of error, or the probability that a given interval does not contain the unknown population mean.

B. Confidence Intervals when σ Is Unknown

Formula (7.1) requires the improbable assumption that the population standard deviation σ is known. In the likely event σ is unknown, the sample standard deviation must be substituted:

Confidence interval for μ when σ is unknown	C.I. for $\mu = \bar{X} \pm Zs_{\bar{x}}$	[7.2]

where $s_{\bar{x}} = s/\sqrt{n}$

Gerry Gerber, CPA, has just finished filing the tax returns for his clients. He wishes to estimate the mean amount they owe the Internal Revenue Service. Of the 50 clients he selects in his sample, the mean amount owed is \$652.68. Since the standard deviation of all his clients σ is unknown, Gerber must estimate σ with the sample standard deviation of $s = \$217.43$. If a 99 percent level of confidence is desired, the proper Z-value is 2.58 ($0.99/2 = 0.4950$). From the Z-table, an area of 0.4950 reveals $Z = 2.58$. Using Formula (7.2),

$$\begin{aligned} \text{C.I. for } \mu &= \bar{X} \pm Zs_{\bar{x}} \\ &= \$652.68 \pm 2.58 \frac{\$217.43}{\sqrt{50}} \\ &= \$573.35 \leq \mu \leq 732.01 \end{aligned}$$

Mr. Gerber can be 99 percent confident that the mean amount all his clients owe the IRS is somewhere between \$573.35 and \$732.01.

What would happen to this interval if Mr. Gerber were willing to accept a 95 percent level of confidence? With a Z-value of 1.96, the interval would become

$$\$652.68 \pm 1.96 \frac{\$217.43}{\sqrt{50}}$$

$$\$592.41 \leq \mu \leq \$712.96$$

The results are both good and bad. The good news is that the 95 percent interval is narrower and exhibits more **precision.** A wide interval is not particularly useful. It would reveal very little if your professor told you that the mean on the next test would be between 0 percent and 100 percent. The narrower the interval, the more meaningful it is.

The bad news is that Mr. Gerber is now only 95 percent certain that the interval actually does contain μ. There is a trade-off. Although the interval is more precise (narrower), the probability that it contains μ has dropped from 99 percent to 95 percent. Mr. Gerber had to give up some confidence to gain more precision.

Display 7.1

```
MTB > ZInterval 99.0  217.434338  C1.

Confidence Intervals

The assumed sigma = 217

Variable      N      Mean      StDev   SE Mean         99.0 % C.I.
TXRET        50     652.7      217.4      30.7     (   573.4,    731.9)
```

Display 7.1 shows Mr. Gerber's Minitab printout for tax returns (TXRET). By clicking on **Stat > Basic Statistics > 1-sample Z** and entering 99 percent for the **Confidence Interval Level** and 217.43 for **Sigma,** Mr. Gerber obtains his interval estimate, which differs only slightly from his hand calculations above due to rounding.

Example 7.1 Checkered Cabs plans to buy a fleet of new taxis for its operations in Miami. The decision depends on whether the make of car under consideration gets at least 27.5 miles per gallon of gasoline. The 36 cars the company tests report a mean of 25.6 miles per gallon (MPG), with a standard deviation of 3.5 MPG. At the 99 percent level of confidence, what would you advise Checkered to do?

Solution: The confidence interval is found as

$$\text{C.I. for } \mu = 25.6 \pm (2.58)\frac{3.5}{\sqrt{36}}$$

$$= 24.10 \leq \mu \leq 27.11$$

Interpretation: You can be 99 percent certain that the mean MPG of this make of car is less than the minimum of 27.5 that is required. You would advise Checkered to seek an alternative model.

Section Exercises

1. How do point estimates differ from interval estimates?
2. If the population mean is unknown, how is it possible to attach a level of confidence to its interval estimate? Provide a graph in your answer.
3. A 90 percent interval for the mean weight gain of laboratory mice ranges from 0.93 ounces to 1.73 ounces. How would you interpret these results? What Z-value was used in the estimate?
4. One hundred 16-ounce cans of Jake's Mom's Tomato Sauce average 15.2 ounces. The population standard deviation in weight is known to be 0.96 ounces. At the 95 percent level of confidence, do the cans seem to be filled with a mean of 16 ounces?
5. To estimate the mean expenditure of customers at a local McDonald's, students in a statistics class sample 200 customers and find a mean expenditure of $5.67, with a standard deviation of $1.10. What is the 95 percent interval for the mean expenditures of all customers? Interpret your results.
6. A study by professors at a university in Kansas is designed to offer inferences about unemployment rates by county in the United States. A sample of 200 counties reports a mean rate of 6.2 percent, with a standard deviation of 1.7 percent. At the 90 percent level of confidence, what is the estimate of the mean unemployment rate by county in the nation? Interpret your results.
7. After watching 50 television programs selected at random, the National Education Association (NEA) reported an average of 32.7 acts of violence in 1997. Assume a sample standard deviation of 10.1. What would be your 95 percent estimate of the mean number of violent acts per program children watch on TV?
8. A local movie theater wants to develop an interval for the mean boxes of popcorn sold per movie. If records kept for 70 movies reveal a mean of 54.98 boxes and a standard deviation of 12.7, calculate and interpret the 92 percent confidence interval for the population mean.
9. A sample of 121 calls to the 900 number you operate has a mean duration of 16.6 minutes and a standard deviation of 3.63 minutes. You intend to discontinue the service unless the mean duration exceeds 18 minutes. At the 90 percent level of confidence, what is your decision?
10. What would be your decision in the previous problem at the 95 percent level? Why are the intervals different?
11. How would you decide if Exercise 9 used a sample of 200 calls? Why are the intervals different?

7.3 Small Sample Intervals for the Mean—the t-Distribution

In all the previous examples, the sample size was larger ($n \geq 30$). However, it may not always be possible to obtain at least 30 observations. For an insurance company testing the crash resistance of automobiles, purposely destroying 30 luxury vehicles can get a bit expensive. A medical researcher testing a new drug may not find 30 people willing to act as human guinea pigs. In many cases a large sample is not possible.

When a small sample must be taken, the normal distribution may not apply. The Central Limit Theorem ensures normality in the sampling process only if the sample is large. When a small sample is used, an alternative distribution, the **Student's *t*-distribution** (or simply the t-distribution), may be necessary. Specifically, the t-distribution is used when three conditions are met: (1) the sample is small, (2) σ is unknown, and (3) the population is normal or near normal. If σ is known, the Z-distribution is even if the sample is small. Further, if a normally distributed population cannot be assumed, we increase the sample size to use the Z-distribution or to rely on *nonparametric* tests.

The Student's t-distribution was developed in 1908 by William S. Gosset (1876–1937), who worked as a brewmaster for Guinness Breweries in Dublin, Ireland. Guinness would not allow its employees to publish their research, so when Gosset (who liked to "toy with numbers for pure relaxation") first reported on his t-distribution, he published under the pseudonym "Student" to protect his job.

Like the Z-distribution, the t-distribution has a mean of zero, is symmetrical about the mean, and ranges from $-\infty$ to $+\infty$. However, while the Z-distribution has a variance of $\sigma^2 = 1$, the variance of the t-distribution is greater than 1. It is therefore flatter and more dispersed than the Z-distribution. The variance for the t-distribution is

Variance for the t-distribution

$$\sigma^2 = \frac{n - 1}{n - 3} \qquad [7.3]$$

Actually, the t-distribution is a family of distributions each with its own variance. The variance depends on the *degrees of freedom* (d.f.), defined as the number of observations that can be freely chosen. It is the number of observations minus the number of constraints placed on those observations, where a constraint is some value those observations must generate. Presume we have $n = 4$ observations that must produce a mean of 10. The mean of 10 serves as a constraint and there are $n - 1 = 3$ degrees of freedom. Thus, we can choose any three observations; we might choose 8, 9, and 11. After these three values are selected, we are not free to choose the last observation. The fourth value *must* be 12 if they are to average 10. Note in Figure 7.3 that as n increases, the t-distribution approaches the Z-distribution. That's why we can use the Z-distribution when $n \geq 30$.

Figure 7.3
A Family of t-Distributions

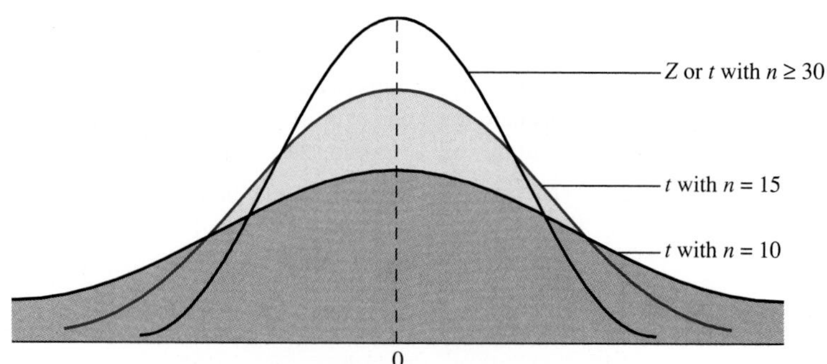

> **Degrees of freedom** The number of observations minus the number of constraints placed on those observations.

As we shall see shortly, for any given set of conditions the t-distribution will produce a wider interval than would the Z-distribution if it were used. This additional width is necessary, since some accuracy is lost because σ is unknown and must be estimated.

The t-statistic is calculated much as the Z-statistic is.

$$t = \frac{\overline{X} - \mu}{s_{\overline{x}}} \qquad [7.4]$$

Rewriting (7.4) algebraically to express it as a confidence interval for μ, we have

Confidence interval for the population mean—small samples

$$\text{C.I. for } \mu = \overline{X} \pm (t)(s_{\overline{x}}) = \overline{X} \pm t\frac{s}{\sqrt{n}} \qquad [7.5]$$

The proper t-value can be found from Table F in Appendix III. To illustrate, assume you want a 95 percent confidence interval and have a sample of 20 observations. Since $n = 20$, the degrees of freedom are d.f. $= n - 1 = 19$. Move down the first column in Table F under "d.f." to 19. Move across that row to the column headed by a confidence level of 0.95 for two-tailed tests. (Ignore the two rows concerning one-tailed tests. They will be dealt with in Chapter 8.) The resulting entry of 2.093 is the proper t-value for a 95 percent confidence interval with a sample size of 20 (d.f. $= 19$).

Consider the following problem taken from *The Wall Street Journal.* A construction firm was charged with inflating the expense vouchers it files for construction contracts with the federal government. The contract stated that a certain type of job should average \$1,150. In the interest of time, the directors of only 12 government agencies were called on to enter court testimony regarding the firm's vouchers. If a mean of \$1,275 and a standard deviation of \$235 are discovered from testimony, would a 95 percent confidence interval support the firm's legal case? Assume voucher amounts are normal.

A 95 percent level of confidence with d.f. $= 12 - 1 = 11$ yields from Table F a t-value of 2.201. Then

$$\begin{aligned}\text{C.I. for } \mu &= \overline{X} \pm t\frac{s}{\sqrt{n}}\\ &= 1275 \pm (2.201)\frac{235}{\sqrt{12}}\\ &= 1275 \pm 149.31\\ \$1{,}125.69 \le \mu &\le \$1{,}424.31\end{aligned}$$

The court can be 95 percent confident that the mean voucher was between \$1,125 and \$1,424. This interval contains the agreed-on \$1,150 strengthening the firm's defense.

Notice that the t-value for a 95 percent interval is 2.201 (given d.f. $= 11$), while a large-sample 95 percent interval uses a Z-value of 1.96. The interval based on a t-value is therefore wider.

Example 7.2 The labor agreement between the United Auto Workers (UAW) and Ford Motor Company (FMC) required that the mean output for a particular production section be held at 112 units per month per employee. Disagreement arose between UAW and FMC as to whether this standard was being maintained. The labor agreement specified that if mean production levels dropped below the stipulated amount of $\mu = 112$, FMC was permitted to take "remedial action." Due to the cost involved, only 20 workers were tested, yielding a mean of 102 units. Assume that a standard deviation of 8.5 units was found and that output levels are normally distributed. Does a 90 percent confidence interval tend to suggest a violation of the labor contract, thereby allowing the remedial action?

Solution: With a 90 percent level of confidence and $n - 1 = 19$ d.f., Table F yields a t-value of 1.729.

$$\text{C.I. for } \mu = \bar{X} \pm t\frac{s}{\sqrt{n}}$$

$$= 102 \pm (1.729)\frac{8.5}{\sqrt{20}}$$

$$= 102 \pm 3.29$$

$$98.71 \leq \mu \leq 105.29$$

The mean output level of 112 units specified in the labor contract is not in the confidence interval.

Interpretation: There is a 90 percent level of confidence that the contract is being violated. FMC is within its rights to pursue a remedy for lagging productivity.

Figure 7.4
Selecting the Proper Test Statistic for μ

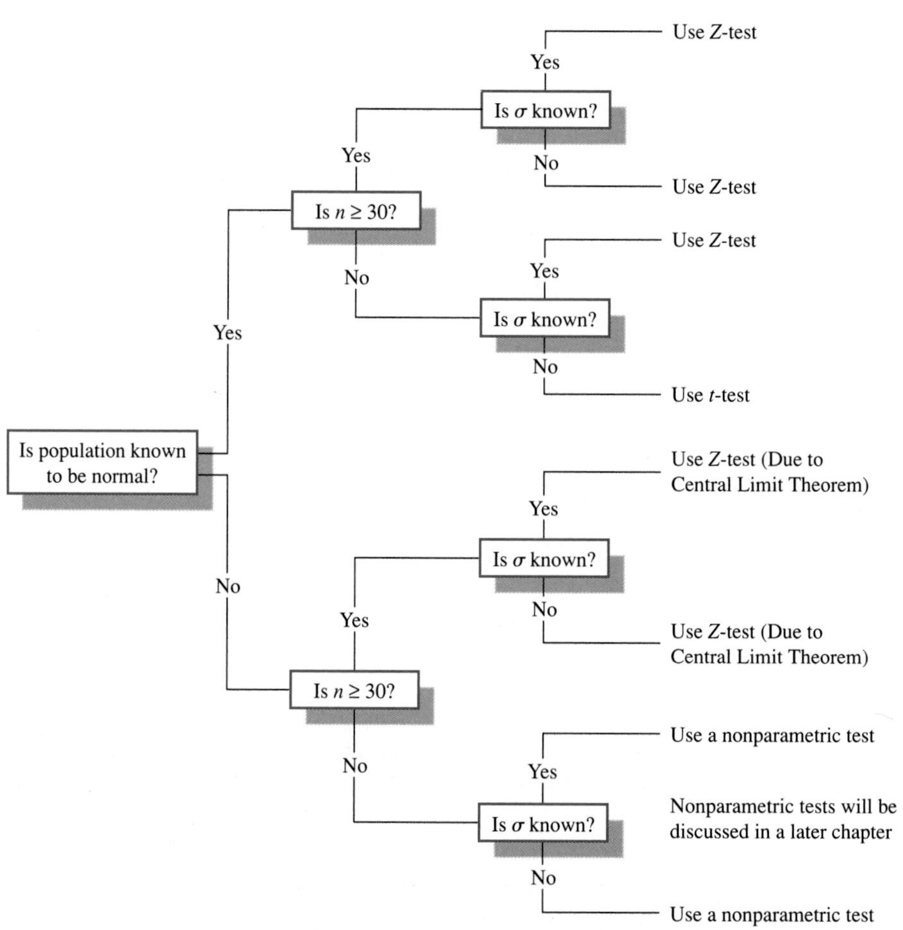

Obviously, deciding whether to use a t-test or a Z-test is crucial. Figure 7.4 will aid in selecting the proper test statistic. Remember that the t-distribution should be used when all three of these conditions are present: (1) the population is normal, (2) a small sample is taken, and (3) σ is unknown.

Section Exercises

12. What three conditions must be met before the t-distribution can be used?

13. How does the variance of the t-distribution differ from that of the Z-distribution? If a data set has 17 observations, what is the variance of the t-distribution?

14. The Lucky Lady, a popular student hangout, sells 16-ounce glasses of beer. Ten students purchase a total of 22 glasses, and, using their own measuring cup, estimate the mean contents. The sample mean is 15.2 ounces, with $s = 0.86$. At the 95 percent level of confidence, are the students getting their money's worth? Interpret the interval.

15. Dell Publishing samples 23 shipments to estimate the mean postal cost. The sample mean is \$23.56, with $s =$ \$4.65.

    a. The senior editor for Dell hopes to keep the mean cost under \$23.00. Calculate and interpret the 99 percent interval. Will the editor be happy?
    b. Compare the results in part *a* to the 99 percent interval, if $s =$ \$2.05. Explain why there is a difference.
    c. Retaining $s =$ \$4.65, compare the results in part *a* to a 95 percent interval. Explain the difference.

16. The signing bonuses for 10 new players in the National Football League are used to estimate the mean bonus for all new players. The sample mean is \$65,890 with $s =$ \$12,300. What is your 90 percent interval estimate of the population mean?

17. A sample of 25 calls to the Psychic Friends Network reveals a mean cost of \$23.87. If the standard deviation is \$9.56, what is the 98 percent interval estimate of the mean cost of all those who call to learn about their future?

18. Greenleaf Lawn Care finds that the mean cost of landscaping 20 homes in the area is \$2,365, with $s =$ \$983. At the 99 percent level of confidence, what would you estimate the mean cost of landscaping for all homes in the area to be?

7.4 Confidence Intervals for Population Proportions

Decisions often depend on parameters that are binary—parameters with only two possible categories into which responses may fall. In this event, the parameter of concern is the population *proportion*. A firm may want to know what proportion of its customers pay on credit as opposed to those who use cash. Corporations are often interested in what percentage of their products are defective as opposed to the percentage that is not defective, or what proportion of their employees quit after one year in contrast to that proportion who do not quit after one year. In each of these instances, there are only two possible outcomes. Concern is therefore focused on that proportion of responses that fall into one of these two outcomes.

In the previous chapter we found that if $n\pi$ and $n(1 - \pi)$ are both greater than 5, the distribution of sample proportions will be normal. The sampling distribution of sample proportions will have a mean equal to the population proportion π and a standard error of

The standard error of the sampling distribution of sample proportions	$\sigma_p = \sqrt{\frac{\pi(1-\pi)}{n}}$	[7.6]

However, Formula (7.6) requires π, the parameter we wish to estimate. Therefore, the sample proportion p is used as an estimator for π.

Formula (7.6) can be restated as

Estimate of the standard error of sampling distribution of sample proportions	$s_p = \sqrt{\frac{p(1-p)}{n}}$	[7.7]

The confidence interval is then

Confidence interval for population proportion	$\text{C.I. for } \pi = p \pm Zs_p$	[7.8]

The manager of a TV station must determine what percentage of households in the city have more than one TV set. A random sample of 500 homes reveals that 275 have two or more sets. What is the 90 percent confidence interval for the proportion of all homes with two or more sets? Given these data, $p = 275/500 = 0.55$, and

$$s_p = \sqrt{\frac{(0.55)(0.45)}{500}}$$

$$= 0.022$$

Table E yields a Z of 1.65 for a 90 percent confidence interval.

$$\text{C.I. for } \pi = 0.55 \pm (1.65)(0.022)$$

$$= 0.55 \pm 0.036$$

$$0.514 \leq \pi \leq 0.586$$

The manager can be 90 percent confident that between 51.4 percent and 58.6 percent of the homes in the city have more than one TV set.

Example 7.3 Executive search firms specialize in helping corporations locate and secure top-level management talent. Called "headhunters," these firms are responsible for the placement of many of the nation's top CEOs. *Business Week* recently reported that "one out of every four CEOs is an outsider—an executive with less than five years at the company he runs." If, in a sample of 350 U.S. corporations, 77 have outsider CEOs, would a 99 percent confidence interval support the quote?

Solution:

$$p = \frac{77}{350} = 0.22$$

$$s_p = \sqrt{\frac{(0.22)(0.78)}{350}} = 0.022$$

$$\begin{aligned}\text{C.I. for } \pi &= p \pm Zs_p \\ &= 0.22 \pm (2.58)(0.022)\end{aligned}$$

$$0.163 \leq \pi \leq 0.277$$

Interpretation: We are confident at the 99 percent level that between 16.3 percent and 27.7 percent of U.S. corporations have outside CEOs. The quote is supported by these findings, since 25 percent is contained within the interval.

Section Exercises

19. What is s_p and what does it measure?

20. CNN reported that 68 percent of all high school students had computers in their homes. If a sample of 1,020 students reveals that 673 have home computers, does a 99 percent interval support CNN?

21. In response to the new fad of cigar smoking sweeping the nation, the National Heart Institute surveyed women to estimate the proportion who smoke an occasional cigar. Of the 750 respondents, 287 reported that they had done so. Based on these data, what is your 90 percent estimate of the proportion of all women who engage in this habit?

22. The National Travel Association sampled vacationers in Ireland to estimate the frequency with which Americans visit the Emerald Isle. What is the 96 percent interval of the proportion of tourists who are American if 1,098 of the 3,769 surveyed held U.S. passports?

23. Of the 1,098 American tourists, 684 had booked their trip through a professional travel agent. Calculate and interpret the 95 percent interval for the proportion of all Americans who use professional travel services in Ireland.

24. If 896 of those American tourists would recommend the trip to their friends, what percentage of all American tourists would do so at the 99 percent level of confidence?

25. If 796 of the 1,098 American tourists plan return trips to Ireland, at the 92 percent level of confidence, what proportion of all American tourists would repeat their vacations?

7.5 Controlling the Interval Width

As noted earlier, a narrower interval is preferable because of the additional precision it provides. There are two principal methods of achieving a more precise interval: (1) decreasing the level of confidence and (2) increasing the sample size.

A. Decreasing the Level of Confidence

We have already seen from Mr. Gerber's attempt to estimate the mean tax return of his clients that an increase in precision can be gained by accepting a lower level of confidence. His 99 percent interval ranged from \$573 to \$732, while the 95 percent interval was narrower at \$594 to \$712. This resulted from the fact that the 99 percent interval required a *Z*-value of 2.58 instead of the 1.96 the 95 percent interval uses.

However, there was a cost involved in achieving this greater precision: the level of confidence fell to 95 percent, resulting in a 5 percent probability of error instead of the 1 percent associated with the 99 percent interval. Is there any way we can narrow the interval without suffering a loss of confidence? Yes, by increasing the sample size.

B. Increasing the Sample Size

By increasing the sample size, we can decrease the standard error $\sigma/\sqrt{n}$. If Mr. Gerber's sample size is increased to 80, the 99 percent interval exhibits a degree of precision similar to the narrower 95 percent interval without any loss of confidence. With $n = 80$, the 99 percent interval is

$$\text{C.I. for } \mu = \$652.68 \pm \frac{\$217.43}{\sqrt{80}}$$

$$\$589.96 \leq \mu \leq \$715.39$$

This is very close to the more precise 95 percent interval of \$594 to \$712 but retains a 99 percent level of confidence.

Unfortunately, this advantage is not gained without a price. The larger sample size means more time and more money must be spent in collecting and managing the data. Again, a trade-off must be made. It becomes a managerial decision as to which approach to take.

7.6 Determining the Proper Sample Size

The size of the sample plays an important role in determining the probability of error as well as the precision of the estimate. Once the desired level of confidence has been chosen, two factors are particularly instrumental in influencing the sample size: (1) the variance of the population σ^2 and (2) the size of the *tolerable error* the researcher is willing to accept. While the first factor is beyond the control of the researcher (there is nothing that can be done about the variance of the population), it is possible to limit the size of the error.

The extent of error a researcher can tolerate depends on how critical the work is. Some tasks are extremely delicate and require exacting results: vital medical procedures upon which lives may depend, or the production of machine parts that must meet precise measurements, can tolerate only a small error. In other instances, larger errors may be of less consequence.

Presume that in manufacturing a part for compact disk (CD) players, an error of 2 centimeters (cm) in diameter will cause no problem. Any error in excess of 2 cm will, however, result in a defective disk player. If the part can vary above and below some desired mean diameter by 2 cm, an interval of 4 cm is allowed. Any given interval is twice the tolerable error. See Figure 7.5 for an illustration.

Figure 7.5
The Tolerable Error Is One-Half the Interval

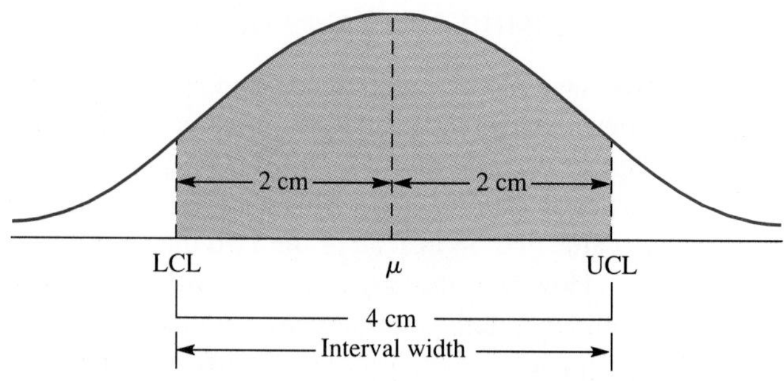

The remainder of this section considers the determination of the proper sample size under various conditions.

A. Sample Size for μ

Recall that the normal deviate Z can be expressed as

$$Z = \frac{\bar{X} - \mu}{\sigma_{\bar{x}}} = \frac{\bar{X} - \mu}{\sigma/\sqrt{n}}$$

This can be rewritten algebraically as

Sample size for intervals of the population mean	$n = \dfrac{Z^2\sigma^2}{(\bar{X} - \mu)^2}$	[7.9]

where the difference between the sample mean and the population mean $(\bar{X} - \mu)$ is the error. In the example above for the CD players with a tolerable error of 2 cm, Formula (7.9) would be written as

$$n = \frac{Z^2\sigma^2}{(2)^2}$$

The value of Z depends on the level of confidence required. This leaves only σ^2 to be determined in order to calculate the proper sample size. In the likely event σ^2 is unknown, it can be estimated by the sample standard deviation s using a **pilot sample** of any reasonable size ($n \geq 30$). The variance calculated from this preliminary sample can then be used in Formula (7.9).

Assume, for example, that the manufacturer of the disk players wishes to construct a 95 percent interval for the mean size of the part. A pilot sample has revealed a standard deviation of 6 cm. How large should the sample be? A 95 percent interval calls for a Z-value of 1.96. Thus,

$$n = \frac{(1.96)^2(6)^2}{(2)^2} = 34.5 \text{ or } 35$$

The manufacturer should select a sample of 35 parts. From this sample, a 95 percent interval could be constructed for the mean size. This interval would have an error not greater than 2 cm.

Example 7.4 The owner of a small ski resort in southern Wisconsin is considering the purchase of a snowmaking machine to assist Mother Nature in providing a proper base for ski enthusiasts. If the average snowfall seems insufficient, he feels that the machine should soon pay for itself. He plans to estimate the average snowfall in the area, but has no idea how large his sample should be. He only knows that he wants to be 99 percent confident of his findings and that the error should not exceed 1 inch. The owner promises you season lift tickets if you can help him.

Solution: You begin with a large ($n \geq 30$) pilot sample that produces a standard deviation of 3.5 inches. Thus,

$$n = \frac{Z^2(s)^2}{(\text{error})^2}$$

$$= \frac{(2.58)^2(3.5)^2}{(1)^2}$$

$$= 81.5$$

or 82 snowfalls over the past several years.

Interpretation: You can now collect the data on 82 past snowfalls that will be used to estimate the average snowfall. With this information the owner can determine whether Mother Nature needs help. More important, you can spend the rest of the winter skiing for free.

B. Sample Size for π

In the Chapter 6, we found that

$$Z = \frac{p - \pi}{\sigma_p}$$

where

$$\sigma_p = \sqrt{\frac{\pi(1 - \pi)}{n}}$$

We can rewrite this to produce an expression for sample size.

Sample size for intervals of the population proportion	$n = \dfrac{Z^2(\pi)(1 - \pi)}{(p - \pi)^2}$	[7.10]

where $(p - \pi)$ is the difference between the sample proportion and the population proportion, and is therefore the error.

Formula (7.10) requires a value for π. However, π is the parameter we wish to estimate, and is unknown. This problem can be handled in one of two ways. We could take a pilot sample to obtain a preliminary value for π, as we did in our efforts to determine the proper sample size for the mean. Or, we might merely set $\pi = 0.5$ for the purpose of determining sample size. This approach is often preferred because it is very "safe" or conservative—it will ensure the largest possible sample size given any desired level of confidence and error. This larger sample results from the fact that the numerator of Formula (7.10), which contains $\pi(1 - \pi)$, will be maximized (thus, n will be maximized) if $\pi = 1 - \pi = 0.5$. There is no value other than 0.5 which you could assign to π that would make $\pi(1 - \pi)$ larger. If $\pi = 0.5$, then $\pi(1 - \pi) = 0.25$. Any value other than 0.5 would result in $\pi(1 - \pi) < 0.25$. Thus, n would be smaller.

Wally Simpleton is running for governor. He wants to estimate within 1 percentage point the proportion of people who will vote for him. He also wants to be 95 percent confident of his findings. How large should the sample size be?

$$n = \frac{(1.96)^2(0.5)(0.5)}{(0.01)^2}$$

$$= 9{,}604 \text{ voters}$$

A sample of 9,604 voters will permit Wally to estimate π within 1 percent at the 95 percent level of confidence.

Example 7.5 The city council is planning an ordinance prohibiting smoking in all public buildings including restaurants, taverns, and theaters. Only private housing will be exempt. However, before such an ordinance is brought before the council, this august body wishes to estimate the proportion of residents who support such a plan. Lacking any statistical skills, the council hires you as a consultant. Your first step will be to determine the necessary sample size. You are told that your error should not exceed 2 percent and that you must be 95 percent confident of your results.

Solution: Since no pilot survey was previously taken, you must temporarily set π at 0.5 for the purpose of resolving the sample size.

$$n = \frac{Z^2\pi(1-\pi)}{(\text{error})^2}$$

$$= \frac{(1.96)^2(0.5)(0.5)}{(.02)^2}$$

$$= 2{,}401 \text{ citizens}$$

Interpretation: With the data supplied by 2,401 people you can proceed with your estimate of the proportion of all residents who might favor the ordinance. The council can then make its determination regarding the citywide smoking policy.

Section Exercises

26. Days Inn wants to develop a 99 percent interval for the mean number of rooms occupied each night at its locations around the nation. How many nights must be included in the sample if an error of 50 rooms can be tolerated and a pilot sample reveals $s = 165$ rooms?

27. What would happen to your answer if $s = 265$? Why?

28. How large a sample is required to provide a 90 percent estimate of the mean number of graduates from our nation's colleges and universities with an error of 2,000 students if a pilot sample reports $s = 8{,}659$?

29. A study you are conducting requires a 95 percent interval for the mean rate of return your firm earns on its capital budgeting projects. How many projects must you sample if your supervisor specifies an interval of only 5 percent and $s = 2.3$ percent? What is the size of the tolerable error?

30. As a newly hired employee in the marketing division for a large retail concern, you have been assigned the task of estimating the proportion of consumers who prefer your product over the competitor's. How many consumers must you sample if you want to restrict the error to 10 percent and still provide a 99 percent level of confidence?

31. How large must the sample be in the previous problem if the error is restricted to 5 percent? Explain the difference.

32. The credit division for a large commercial bank wants to estimate at the 99 percent level of confidence the proportion of its consumer loans that are in default. If the interval width is to be 7 percent, how many loans must be examined? What is the tolerable error?

7.7 Properties of Good Estimators

A distinction should be drawn between an estimator and an estimate. An **estimator** is the rule or procedure, usually expressed as a formula, that is used to derive the **estimate.** For example,

$$\bar{X} = \frac{\Sigma X_i}{n}$$

is the estimator for the population mean. If the value of the estimator $\overline{X}$ is found to be, say, 10, then 10 is the estimate of the population mean.

Estimators and Estimates An estimator is the process by which the estimate is obtained. An estimate is the numerical result of the estimator.

To perform reliably, estimators must be (1) unbiased, (2) efficient, (3) consistent, and (4) sufficient. Each property is discussed in turn in this section.

A. An Unbiased Estimator

As we saw in Chapter 6, it is possible to construct a sampling distribution by selecting all possible samples of a given size from a population. An estimator is unbiased if the mean of the statistic computed from all these samples equals the corresponding parameter.

Let θ (Greek letter *theta*) be the parameter we are trying to estimate by $\hat{\theta}$ (read "theta hat"). Then $\hat{\theta}$ is an unbiased estimator if its mean, or expected value, $E(\hat{\theta})$, equals θ. That is,

$$E(\hat{\theta}) = \theta$$

To cite a specific example, $\overline{X}$ is an unbiased estimator of μ because the mean of the sampling distribution of sample means, $\overline{\overline{X}}$, equals μ. Thus,

$$E(\overline{X}) = \overline{\overline{X}} = \mu$$

Unbiased Estimator An estimator is unbiased if the mean of the sampling distribution equals the corresponding parameter.

Figure 7.6 illustrates how the mean of a sampling distribution must equal the corresponding parameter to ensure an unbiased estimator.

Figure 7.6
Distributions for Biased and Unbiased Estimators

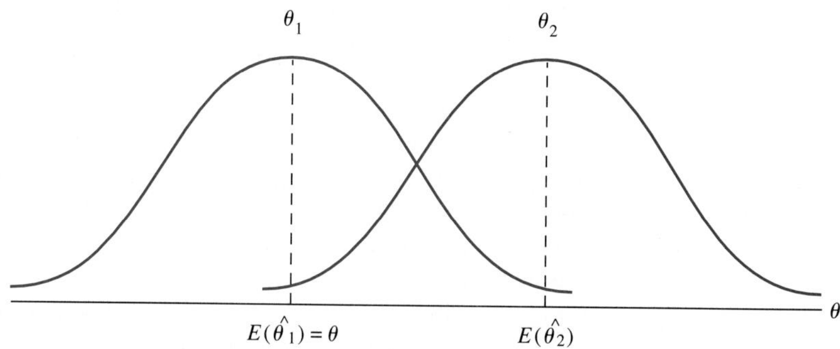

Here, $\hat{\theta}_1$ is an unbiased estimator of θ since its distribution is centered over θ. Thus, $E(\hat{\theta}_1) = \theta$. If many different samples were taken, yielding many different values for $\hat{\theta}_1$, their mean would equal θ. Conversely, if many samples were taken and $\hat{\theta}_2$ was calculated each time, their mean would exceed θ. Thus, $\hat{\theta}_2$ is a biased (upward) estimator of θ. The measure of bias is the difference between the mean of $\hat{\theta}_2$ and θ. Note that

$$E(\hat{\theta}_1) - \theta = 0$$

while

$$E(\hat{\theta}_2) - \theta \neq 0$$

B. An Efficient Estimator

The efficiency of an estimator depends on its variance. Let $\hat{\theta}_1$ and $\hat{\theta}_2$ be two unbiased estimators of θ. Then $\hat{\theta}_1$ is a more efficient estimator if, in repeated sampling with a given sample size, its variance is less than that of $\hat{\theta}_2$. It is only logical that an estimator with a smaller variance will more closely estimate the parameter. Consider Figure 7.7, which shows the sampling distributions with a given sample size of two statistics, $\hat{\theta}_1$ and $\hat{\theta}_2$. Both $\hat{\theta}_1$ and $\hat{\theta}_2$ are unbiased estimators of θ because their sampling distributions are centered above θ, and

$$E(\hat{\theta}_1) = E(\hat{\theta}_2) = \theta$$

However, the variance of the sampling distribution of $\hat{\theta}_1$, is less than that of $\hat{\theta}_2$. Possible values for $\hat{\theta}_2$ are more dispersed. Any estimate of θ using $\hat{\theta}_2$ is likely to produce a larger sampling error than an estimate of θ using $\hat{\theta}_1$.

Figure 7.7
The Variance of Estimators

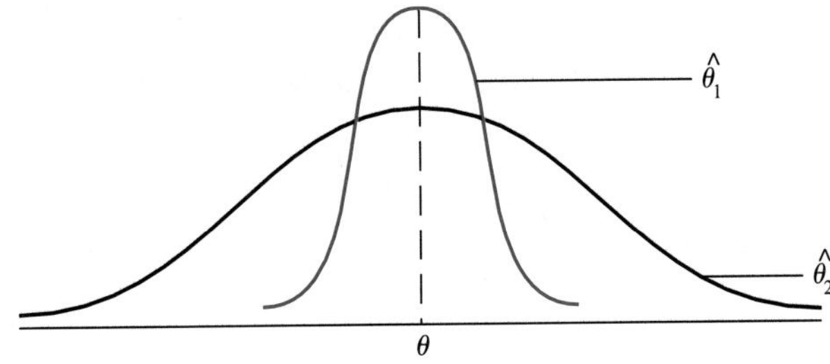

An Efficient Estimator Given any unbiased estimators, the most efficient estimator is the one with the smallest variance.

C. A Consistent Estimator

An estimator is consistent when, as n increases, the estimator approaches the value of the parameter.

Consistent Estimator An estimate is consistent if, as n increases, the value of the statistic approaches the parameter.

For an estimate to be consistent, it must be unbiased and its variance must approach zero as n increases. The variance of the sampling distribution of the sample means, $\sigma_{\bar{x}}^2$, is σ^2/n. As n gets larger, $\sigma_{\bar{x}}^2$ will approach zero. Therefore, it can be said that $\overline{X}$ is a consistent estimator of μ.

If a statistic is not a consistent estimator, taking a larger sample to improve your estimate will prove fruitless.

D. A Sufficient Estimator

An estimator is sufficient if it uses all relevant information about the parameter contained in the sample. If an estimator is sufficient, nothing can be gained by using any other estimator.

Sufficient Estimator An estimator is sufficient if no other estimator could provide more information about the parameter.

This discussion of estimator properties is by no means a complete account. It does, however, provide a sufficient foundation for an examination of estimating parameters by constructing confidence intervals.

Solved Problems

Artesian Spring Water provides bottled drinking water to homes in the tri-county area in 15-gallon containers. The manager wants to estimate the mean number of containers the typical home uses each month. A sample of 75 homes is taken and the number of containers is recorded. The mean is $\overline{X} = 3.2$, with $s = 0.78$.

a. What would a 92 percent interval reveal?

Solution: The Z-value for a 92 percent interval is found by first dividing 0.92 by 2: as $0.92/2 = 0.46$. The area of 0.46 requires a Z-value of 1.75. Then,

$$\text{C.I. for } \mu = \overline{X} \pm (Z)s_{\overline{x}}$$

$$= 3.2 \pm (1.75)\frac{0.78}{\sqrt{75}}$$

$$3.04 \leq \mu \leq 3.36$$

The manager can be 92 percent certain that the mean containers per month is between 3.04 and 3.36.

b. However, the manager feels this interval is too wide. How many homes must he sample to be 99 percent confident that the interval is not in error by more than 0.10 containers?

Solution:

$$n = \frac{Z^2s^2}{(\text{error})^2} = \frac{(2.58)^2(0.78)^2}{(0.1)^2} = 405$$

A sample of 405 would permit a 99 percent interval, with an error not exceeding 0.10 containers.

c. A smaller sample of 10 homes is selected to estimate the mean number of family members per house. The results are 1, 3, 4, 7, 2, 2, 3, 5, 6, and 6 people in each house. What are the results of a 99 percent interval for the mean number of family members?

Solution: The sample standard deviation is $s = 2.02$ with a mean of 3.9. Given the small sample, a t-value of $t_{0.01,9} = 3.250$ must be used. Therefore,

$$\text{C.I. for } \mu = \overline{X} \pm ts_{\overline{x}}$$

$$= 3.9 \pm (3.250)\frac{2.02}{\sqrt{10}}$$

$$1.82 \leq \mu \leq 5.98 \text{ people}$$

d. Of the 75 homes in the sample, 22 have in-home water softeners. What is the 95 percent interval estimate of the proportion of all homes in the tri-county area with softeners?

Solution: Since the sample proportion is $p = 22/75 = 0.29$, the standard error is

$$s_p = \sqrt{\frac{(p)(1-p)}{n}} = \sqrt{\frac{(0.29)(0.71)}{75}} = 0.052$$

Then,

$$\text{C.I. for } \pi = p \pm Zs_p$$
$$= 0.29 \pm (1.96)(0.052)$$
$$0.188 \leq \pi \leq 0.392$$

e. If an interval ranging from 18.8 percent to 39.2 percent of all homes that have softeners lacks precision, how large a sample must be taken to produce an interval of only 10 percent?

Solution: If the interval is to be 10 percent, the error can be only 5 percent. Then,

$$n = \frac{Z^2(0.5)(0.5)}{(\text{error})^2} = \frac{(1.96)^2(0.5)(0.5)}{(0.05)^2} = 385 \text{ homes}$$

List of Formulas

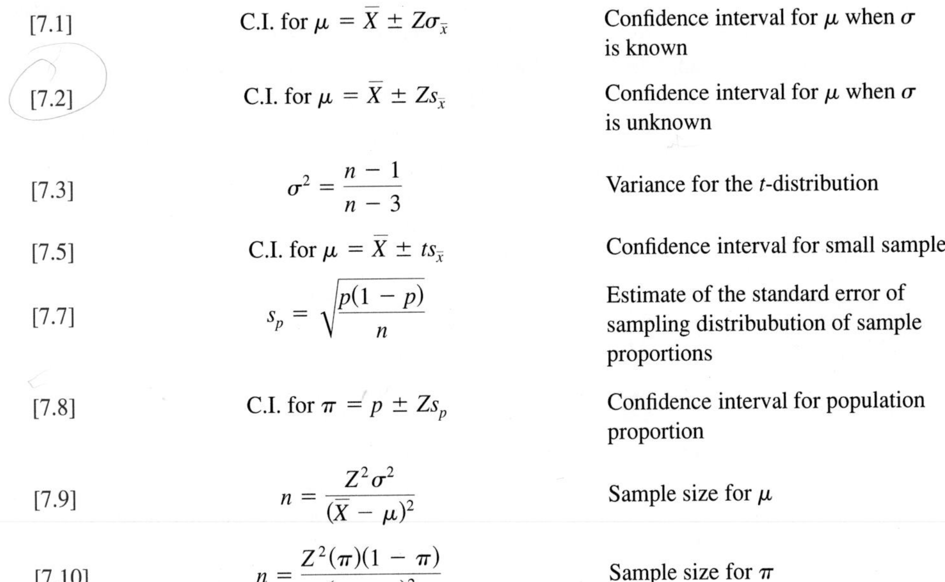

[7.1]	$\text{C.I. for } \mu = \bar{X} \pm Z\sigma_{\bar{x}}$	Confidence interval for μ when σ is known
[7.2]	$\text{C.I. for } \mu = \bar{X} \pm Zs_{\bar{x}}$	Confidence interval for μ when σ is unknown
[7.3]	$\sigma^2 = \dfrac{n-1}{n-3}$	Variance for the *t*-distribution
[7.5]	$\text{C.I. for } \mu = \bar{X} \pm ts_{\bar{x}}$	Confidence interval for small samples
[7.7]	$s_p = \sqrt{\dfrac{p(1-p)}{n}}$	Estimate of the standard error of sampling distribubution of sample proportions
[7.8]	$\text{C.I. for } \pi = p \pm Zs_p$	Confidence interval for population proportion
[7.9]	$n = \dfrac{Z^2\sigma^2}{(\bar{X}-\mu)^2}$	Sample size for μ
[7.10]	$n = \dfrac{Z^2(\pi)(1-\pi)}{(p-\pi)^2}$	Sample size for π

Chapter Exercises

33. A 95 percent confidence interval is constructed, yielding a lower confidence limit of 62 and an upper confidence limit of 69. Can you conclude from this that there is a 95 percent probability the parameter is between 62 and 69? Explain.

34. In a survey of 500 managers, Posner Products found 200 managers lacked sufficient statistical training.

a. What is the point estimate of the proportion of all Posner managers who require additional work in statistical analysis?

b. What is the estimate of the standard error of the proportion?

c. What is the 90 percent confidence interval for the population proportion? Interpret your answer.

35. Jose has a thriving business in Acapulco selling authentic plastic Inca relics to American tourists. He selects $n = 60$ days to estimate his daily profit. However, Jose does not know whether the population of daily profits is normally distributed, and is uncertain how to proceed. What should he do?

36. As a quality control expert, you want to estimate the mean thickness of optical lenses produced by your firm. A sample of 120 lenses reveals a mean of 0.52 millimeter (mm). The population standard deviation is known to be 0.17 mm. You feel that you can risk a probability of error of only 1 percent. Construct the appropriate confidence interval.

37. How would the previous problem change if σ was unknown and the sample standard deviation was 0.17 mm? Calculate the interval.

38. Georgia Pacific (GP), a major U.S. paper company, decides to harvest a timber stand if it can get an average of at least 700 board feet per tree (bf). A sample of 1,000 trees yields a mean of 695 bf, with a standard deviation of 22.1 bf.

    a. Calculate the 90 percent confidence interval.
    b. Interpret your answer.
    c. Should GP harvest the stand?

39. In a survey of 6,000 people, *U.S. News & World Report* found that, in his or her lifetime, the average American spends six months sitting at stoplights. Taking this as the sample mean, and assuming the standard deviation is 2.2 months, what is the 90 percent confidence interval for the population mean? Interpret your answer.

40. *The Journal of Retail Management* reported that a sample of 600 shoppers spent an average of 1.79 hours in a shopping mall per visit. The standard deviation was 0.83 hour. What is the interval estimate of the average number of hours all shoppers spend in the mall? Set $\alpha = 0.10$.

41. Your product requires that a certain component used in its manufacture average 15.2 grams. If you purchase 100 components and find $\bar{X} = 14.8$ grams, with $s = 3.2$ grams, what would a confidence interval tell you about the advisability of buying more from this supplier? Your product is very delicate, and you feel you can tolerate only a 1 percent probability of error.

42. If, given the conditions in the previous problem, the sample had yielded a mean of 14.1 grams, what would you conclude?

43. Wally wants to buy his wife a brand-new septic tank for her birthday. Being a careful shopper, he examines 40 different models and finds a mean price of \$712, with a standard deviation of \$215. What is the 95 percent confidence interval for the mean price of all septic tanks?

44. A manufacturer of snow skis wants to estimate the mean number of ski trips taken by avid skiers. A sample of 1,100 skiers yields $\bar{X} = 15.3$ trips per season, with $s = 5.1$ trips. What is the 99 percent confidence interval for the population mean?

45. Consider the data in the previous exercise:

    a. Without working the problem, explain what would happen to the interval if the level of confidence were decreased to 90 percent.
    b. Work the problem with $\alpha = 0.10$ and show how the answer supports your response to part *a*.

46. A researcher found that a sample of 100, with $\bar{X} = 50.3$ and $s = 10.1$, generated a confidence interval of 48.3204 to 52.2796. What level of confidence can be attributed to this interval?

47. The weights of 25 packages shipped through United Parcel Service (UPS) had a mean of 3.7 pounds and a standard deviation of 1.2 pounds. Find the 95 percent confidence interval for the mean weight of all packages. Package weights are known to be normally distributed.

48. A sample of 12 donations by political action committees (PACs) to congressional campaign funds was recorded, in thousands of dollars, as 12.1, 8.3, 15.7, 9.35, 14.3, 12.9, 13.2, 9.73, 16.9, 15.5, 14.3, and 12.8. Calculate the 90 percent confidence interval for the mean donation by PACs. Donations are assumed to be normal.

49. The earnings per share for 10 industrial stocks listed on the Dow-Jones were \$1.90, \$2.15, \$2.01, \$0.89, \$1.53, \$1.89, \$2.12, \$2.05, \$1.75, and \$2.22. Calculate a 99 percent confidence interval for the EPS of all the industrials listed in the DJIA. What assumption must you make?

50. Dr. Bottoms, the local proctologist, found that the average age of 75 of his patients was 47.3 with a standard deviation of 10.9 years. Calculate the 99 percent confidence interval for the mean age of all his patients under the assumption that the ages are not normally distributed.

51. During the last Superbowl Sunday, Sammy Salami and his buddies ordered 27 pizzas from Pizzas On Wheels. The average delivery time proved to be 23.7 minutes, with a standard deviation of 10.7 minutes. Feeling this was far too long a delay in their culinary pursuits,

Sammy and his friends decided to buy the 28th pizza elsewhere if it appeared that the delivery time for POW exceeded 30 minutes. Set alpha at 1 percent. Will they order elsewhere?

52. A large public accounting firm hired an industrial psychologist to measure the job satisfaction of its senior partners. Seventeen partners were given a test to measure satisfaction; they scored an average of 83.2 out of a possible 100. From previous studies the firm knows that the test scores are normal and the variance for all its partners is 120. What is the 90 percent confidence interval for the mean score?

53. To estimate how many of the 350,000 residents of Peoria desire a new civic center, the mayor finds that 1,570 out of the 2,100 residents sampled expressed support. Help the mayor construct and interpret the 90 percent confidence interval.

54. Of 209 customers, 183 expressed satisfaction with the banking services offered by First of America in Peoria, Illinois. How does this compare with the results of an earlier study by River Valley Savings, which estimated at the 99 percent level of confidence that somewhere between 74.1 and 83.7 percent of its customers were satisfied?

55. A textile firm found that it suffered an overall 19 percent waste factor. A new process was implemented and a sample of 1,376 units revealed an average waste factor of 11.1 percent, with a standard deviation of 1.12 percent. What conclusion can be made with a 95 percent confidence interval about the benefit of the new process?

56. Professional golfers were asked to rate a new graphite club on a scale of 0 to 10. Twenty-five pros generated a mean rating of 7.3, with $s = 1.01$. Construct and interpret the 90 percent confidence interval.

57. Named after Malcolm Baldrige, who served as secretary of commerce in the late 1980s, the Baldrige National Quality Award is a highly sought recognition of a corporation's commitment to a total quality management (TQM) system. Seven criteria are specified by which the corporations are judged. One such criterion, leadership, allows organizations to collect up to 100 points toward achieving this honor. Chrysler Corporation sampled 19 plants and found an average of 73.2 points, with $s = 10.1$. Construct and interpret the 99 percent confidence interval for all of Chrysler's plants.

58. The Pizza Pub is considering increasing the price of its large sausage pizza if the average price of its competitors exceeds Pizza Pub's price of $12.95. Thirty-seven other pizza places report a mean price of $12.50, with a standard deviation of $1.01. Pizza Pub wants to be 90 percent confident of its findings.

59. In a survey of 673 retail stores, 521 reported a problem with employee thefts. Can you conclude, with 99 percent confidence, that these data suggest that 78 percent of all stores have similar difficulty—as reported in a recent CNN account?

60. Wok and Roll, a Chinese takeout restaurant, wanted to determine what percentage of its customers chose birds' nest soup as part of their dining pleasure.

a. In a sample of 320 customers, 220 took home this delicacy. Calculate and interpret the 99 percent interval.

b. Using the above data, construct the 90 percent interval.

c. Why did you get a smaller interval? Wouldn't it always be desirable to reduce the interval width in this manner?

61. The Jesse James First National Bank has hired you as a statistical consultant to analyze operations of its automatic teller machines. A sample of 15 showed mean transactions of $4,810, with a standard deviation of $1,202 per day. Your supervisor insists that you must be 99 percent confident of your estimate of the average daily volume. What do you tell her?

62. The owner of a small business wishes to estimate the average time required to complete a certain job task. He must ensure that he is 90 percent confident that the error is less than 0.5 minutes. The standard deviation is known to be 3.2 minutes. How many observations of completion times must he make?

63. The dean of a private university wants an estimate of the number of out-of-state students enrolled. She must be 95 percent confident that the error is less than 3 percent. How large a sample must she take? If the sample reveals a proportion of 31 percent out-of-staters, and there are 12,414 students, how many students do you estimate come from other states?

64. The director of a branch bank is asked to estimate the average time a customer spends in the drive-through facility. He must be 99 percent confident that the estimate is not in error by more than 15 seconds. How many observations must he collect if the standard deviation is known to be 2.7 minutes?

65. In an effort to reduce insider trading, the Securities and Exchange Commission (SEC) requested information regarding the proportion of bank holding companies whose officers hold more than 50 percent of their banks' outstanding stock. Of 200 companies selected at random, 79 reported that insiders held a majority of their stock. What is the 90 percent confidence interval for the proportion of all bank holding companies whose officers hold at least 50 percent of stock?

66. A researcher for the Federal Aviation Administration (FAA) was quoted in a February issue of *The Washington Post* as saying that, of 112 airline accidents, "73 involved some type of structural problem with the aircraft." If these figures are representative, what is the confidence interval for the proportion of accidents involving such a structural defect? Set $\alpha = 0.01$.

67. United Airlines surveyed 93 passengers on a flight from Cincinnati to Atlanta. Sixty-four said they would like to have been on a later flight had space been available. United had decided that if more than 50 percent of the passengers expressed interest in departures later in the day, they would consider making such flights available. Given the results of the survey, does a 90 percent confidence interval suggest they should do so?

68. *The Wall Street Journal* reported efforts by Nestlé, the world's largest food company, to introduce a new product. Management decided to use the Chicago area as a test market. If more than 30 percent of the people expressed a desire for the product, they would consider marketing it in a wider area. Of 820 people tested, 215 expressed a positive reaction. Would a 90 percent confidence interval for the proportion of all consumers who prefer the product encourage management to continue with their marketing plans?

69. *Business Week* carried a story about efforts by the 12 member countries of the Common Market to curtail a growing wave of mergers thought to be "economically undesirable to international interests." A sample is to be selected to estimate the mean size of firms (as measured in corporate net worth) involved in mergers. If the interval is to be \$5.2 million and carry a level of confidence of 95 percent, how large should the sample be if the standard deviation of corporate net worth is deemed to be \$21.7 million?

70. Your division director requests that you, as a newly hired marketing analyst, estimate average weekly sales. He cautions you to keep your error within \$100 and retain a 90 percent level of confidence. How many weeks of data must you collect if the standard deviation is \$750?

71. A survey of violence in schools is designed to estimate the percentage of male students who were threatened with violence on school grounds over the past year. The tolerable error is set at 1 percent, and the level of confidence is to be 99 percent. What is the proper sample size?

72. The Student Finance Association at Faber College is planning a "spring fling," at which they intend to sell T-shirts imprinted with their logo. The treasurer wants an estimate of the proportion of students who will buy one of the T-shirts. The estimate is to provide a 90 percent level of confidence and the error should not exceed 3 percent. How large a sample must be taken?

73. If a manufacturer wishes to develop a 99 percent interval of the proportion of defects that is in error by less than 1 percent, how large a sample is required?

Computer Exercise

Telmark Technologies recently instituted new company goals to increase the average size of sales per customer and to improve the service offered their customers. Last quarter sales averaged \$373.10 per customer order and it took an average of 4.5 days to delivery the shipment to the customers. In addition, top executives at Telmark want to reduce the average weight of shipments below the mean of 55.8 pounds to decrease shipping costs. Hal Ketchum, Vice-President for Product Relations, has been charged with the responsibility of achieving these objectives. He directs his statistical staff to collect the necessary data and prepare a report detailing the current conditions.

Access the file TELMARK from your data disk. It contains data for sales orders from 75 customers. The size of sales in hundreds of dollars is recorded as Size, the number of days each order took to be shipped to the customers is recorded as Days and the variable Weight provides data for the weights of the shipments in pounds. Finally, the variable SAT indicates whether the customer was satisfied with the service from Telmark. It is encoded as a "1" if the customer was satisfied and a "0" if not satisfied.

Using the data in the TELMARK file, provide interval estimates for Size, Days and Weight of shipments. What conclusions do you reach? Compute the interval estimate for the proportion of satisfied customers. Present your finalized statistical report as described in the appendix. Include all relevant findings, conclusions and recommendations.

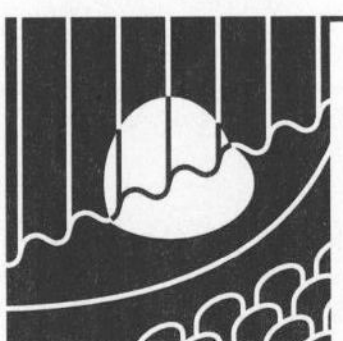

CURTAIN CALL

For many years the Federal Bureau of Investigation has served as a model for law enforcement agencies. Revolutionary efforts by the FBI to more fully integrate the use of statistical analysis in crime fighting efforts were mentioned in Setting the Stage at the beginning of this chapter.

The statistical-based approach to crime fighting includes data on a wide variety of crimes as well as the personal characteristics and habits of the offenders. Although the spokesperson on Larry King Live offered no specifics, she stated that data were kept on the number of crimes each lawbreaker commits, the number of days that pass between crimes, and the number who are killed by law enforcement in the arrest attempt.

Let us assume that the data for a sample of 1,000 felons are collected. The data reveal that, on the average, criminals commit 12.4 unlawful acts with a standard deviation of 4.7 before finally being apprehended or killed. In addition, the data report that an average of 19.6 days lapse between criminal acts, with a standard deviation of 11.5 days. In addition, 212 of the 1,000 felons in the database lost their lives trying to elude police.

Assume further that a smaller sample of a specific type of criminal is taken. Fifteen observations for armed robbery report the following amounts, in thousands of dollars, were taken in the robbery: 45.6, 23.8, 45.3, 27.9, 54.3, 27.5, 63.4, 12.6, 75.9, 64.6, 54.7, 17.5, 21.4, 56.4, and 34.9.

Based on these data and the tools learned in this chapter, provide a profile of criminal activity across the nation like that you think a statistician for the FBI might prepare. Select and justify your own levels of confidence, and calculate and interpret all confidence intervals. Comment on the sample sizes. Are they sufficient to achieve your objective? Clearly specify what sample sizes are needed to achieve the level of confidence and tolerable error you require. Present your final account in the form of a business report as described in Appendix I.

From the Stage to Real Life

The FBI web site (*www.fbi.gov*) provides selected crime statistics similar to those used in the *Curtain Call* analysis. From the FBI home page, click on "Publications." Under the Uniform Crime Statistics heading, click on "Final 19xx Crime Statistics" (most recent full year data). Make a list of the categories of crime statistics available at this site.

Look up information on burglary and on aggravated assaults. Note both the crime counts and the rate per 100,000 population for these two categories. What information is given on the increase or decrease in the type of crime over the previous year? Are these data a sample or a census? Does the available data provide enough detail for you to test if the change from the previous year is statistically significant? If not, what further information would you need to construct such a test?

CHAPTER 8

Hypothesis Testing

Chapter Blueprint

A hypothesis is an assumption or an inference about the unknown value of a parameter. This chapter examines how we can test hypotheses and thereby draw some conclusions about the population.

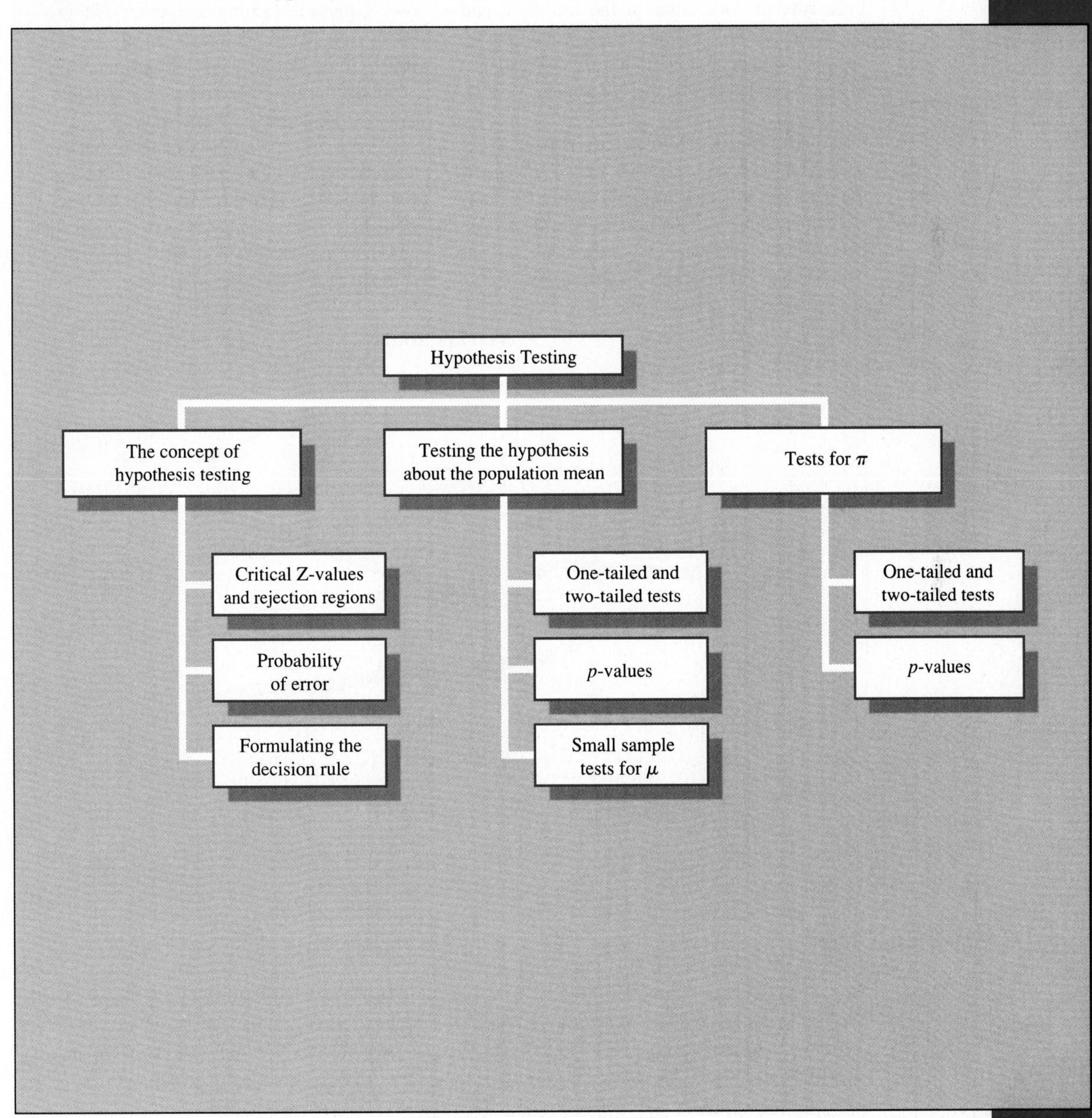

SETTING THE STAGE

Over the past several years the American banking system has undergone considerable deregulation. Much of this deregulation has come in the form of the relaxation of laws governing the performance and operations of commercial banks and other financial institutions. First Bank of America has just merged with Great Lakes National, a smaller competitor in the Midwest, and management is planning several policy changes that could dramatically affect banking operations (*Chicago Tribune,* June 5, 1997).

Lawrence Hopkins, divisional manager of customer relations, has been charged with the responsibility of providing estimates of many of the important indicators of consumer attitudes toward these anticipated changes. Of special concern is the bank's intention to base fees and other charges on the depositor's average daily checking accounts balance. Due to the merger, the bank feels its market position is strong enough to impose a fee increase without undue customer backlash. Records show that average deposits have been rising and that First Bank has gained a larger market share over the past two years relative to their two biggest remaining competitors, Magna Bank and City National. As the graph shows, First Bank's share of total bank deposits in the fourth quarter of 1998 (1998-IV) is estimated to be 70 percent.

This chapter explores the tools that can be used to prepare a report that could prove very beneficial in making many of the decisions First Bank must address in its effort to continue the success and prosperity it has enjoyed over the past several years.

Market Share

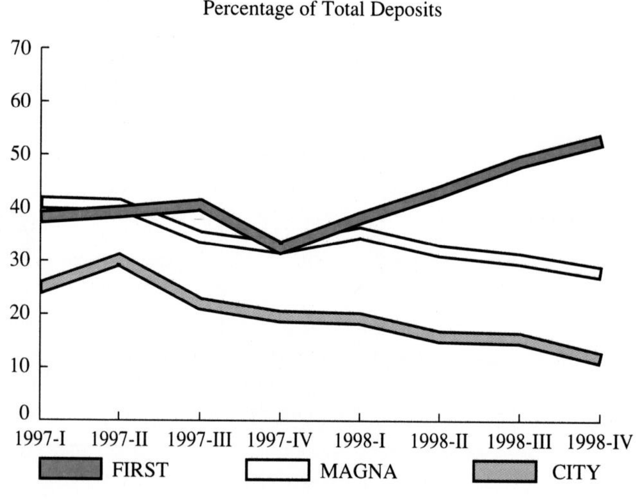

8.1 Introduction

The purpose of statistical analysis is to reduce the level of uncertainty in the decision-making process. Business managers can make better decisions only if they have more information at their disposal. Hypothesis testing is a very effective analytical tool for obtaining this valuable information under a wide variety of circumstances. Common business examples abound:

- A bottler of soft drinks must determine whether the mean fill-weight in its bottles is 16 ounces ($\mu = 16$ ounces).
- A producer of computer software wishes to certify that the proportion of its products that are defective is less than 3 percent ($\pi < 0.03$).
- A manufacturer of sports equipment wants to see whether there is evidence that a production process has reduced mean production costs below their current level of $5 per unit ($\mu < 5$).

Illustrations of this nature are virtually limitless in a business setting. If answers to these questions and many others like them can be obtained with some degree of assurance, decision making becomes more certain and less likely to lead to costly error.

8.2 The Concept of Hypothesis Testing

To conduct a hypothesis test, we make some inference or educated guess about the population. The bottler of soft drinks cited above may assume, or hypothesize, that the mean fill is 16 ounces ($\mu = 16$). This **null hypothesis** (H_0:) is tested against the **alternative hypothesis** (H_A:) stated to the contrary. In this case the mean fill is *not* 16 ounces ($\mu \neq 16$). Thus, we would have

$$H_0: \mu = 16 \qquad H_A: \mu \neq 16$$

The word *null* implies none or nil. The term arises from its earliest applications by agricultural researchers who tested the effectiveness of a new fertilizer to determine its impact on crop yield. They assumed that the fertilizer made no difference in yield until it caused some effect. Thus, the null hypothesis traditionally contains some reference to an equal sign such as " $=$ ", " $\geq$ ", " $\leq$ ". We explore this idea more fully later in our discussion of one-tailed hypothesis tests.

Based on sample data, this null is either rejected or not rejected. We can never "accept" the null as true. Failure to reject the null only means that the sample evidence is not strong enough to lead to its rejection. Even if $\overline{X} = 16$, it does not prove that $\mu = 16$. It could be that μ is 15.8 (or anything else), and due to sampling error the sample mean just happened to equal the hypothesized value of 16. An analogy is that testing a hypothesis is like putting a person on trial. The accused is found either guilty or not guilty. Never is a verdict of "innocent" handed down. A not-guilty verdict simply means the evidence is not strong enough to find the defendant guilty. It does not mean that he or she is innocent.

When conducting a hypothesis test, the null is presumed "innocent" (true) until a preponderance of evidence indicates that it is "guilty" (false). Just as in a legal setting, the evidence of guilt must be established beyond any reasonable doubt. Before the null is rejected, the sample mean must differ from the hypothesized population mean significantly. That is, the evidence must be quite convincing and conclusive. A conclusion based on a rejection of the null is more meaningful than one that results in a decision to not reject.

Presume that we take a sample of n bottles and find a mean of $\overline{X} = 16.15$ ounces. Can we conclude the population mean is not 16? After all, 16.15 is not 16! Probably not. This small difference could be *statistically insignificant* in that it could easily be explained away as a mere sampling error. That is, due to sampling error it may be possible to enter a population with a mean of 16 and emerge with a sample mean of $\overline{X} = 16.15$. Due to the luck of the draw, some of the bottles in the samples may have been somewhat overfilled, causing the sample mean to slightly overestimate the population mean. The sample evidence $\overline{X} = 16.15$ is not strong enough to lead to a rejection of the null hypothesis that $\mu = 16$.

> **Statistically Insignificant Difference** A difference between the hypothesized population mean and the sample mean that is small enough to attribute to sampling error.

If the difference between the hypothesized mean of 16 and the sample finding of 16.15 is insufficient to reject the null, the question then becomes just how large the difference must be to be statistically significant and to lead to a rejection of the null. Recall from our discussion of sampling distributions that we can transform any unit of measurement, such as the ounces for the bottler, to corresponding Z-values with the Z-formula:

$$Z = \frac{\overline{X} - \mu}{\sigma_{\overline{x}}} = \frac{\overline{X} - \mu}{\frac{\sigma}{\sqrt{n}}}$$

If σ is unknown, the sample standard deviation s is used.

The resulting normal distribution of Z-values has a mean of zero and a standard deviation of one. The empirical rule tells us 95 percent of the $\overline{X}$'s in the sampling distribution are within 1.96 standard errors of the unknown population mean, as shown in Figure 8.1.

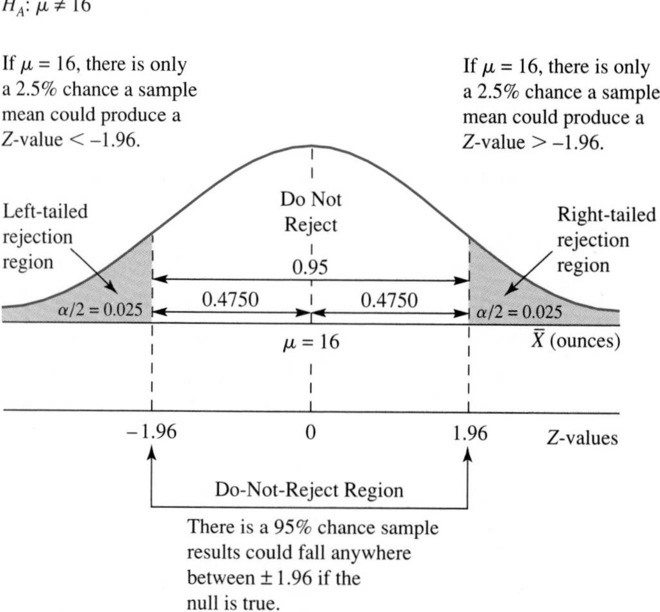

H_0: μ = 16
H_A: $\mu \neq$ 16
If μ = 16, there is only a 2.5% chance a sample mean could produce a Z-value < –1.96.
If μ = 16, there is only a 2.5% chance a sample mean could produce a Z-value > –1.96.
Left-tailed rejection region
Do Not Reject
0.95
Right-tailed rejection region
$\alpha/2 = 0.025$
0.4750
0.4750
$\alpha/2 = 0.025$
μ = 16
$\overline{X}$ (ounces)
–1.96
0
1.96
Z-values
Do-Not-Reject Region
There is a 95% chance sample results could fall anywhere between ±1.96 if the null is true.

Figure 8.1
Critical Values for Z and the Rejection Regions

A. Critical Z-Values and the Rejection Regions

These Z-values of ±1.96 are the **critical values** indicating the rejection regions. To find them, divide the 95 percent by 2. From the Z-table, the area of 0.95/2 = 0.4750 produces a Z-value of 1.96. The remaining 5 percent is distributed in the two tails, with 2.5 percent in each rejection region. This 5 percent is the **level of significance,** or the alpha-value, of the test.

In Figure 8.1 note that if the bottler's hypothesis is correct and $\mu = 16$ ounces, it is unlikely (only a 5 percent chance) that any sample could produce a Z-value falling in either rejection region. Thus, if a Z-value *greater* than 1.96 or *less* than -1.96 does occur, it is unlikely that the distribution is centered at $\mu = 16$, and the null should be rejected.

These critical Z-values of ± 1.96 allow us to establish a **decision rule** that tells us whether to reject the null. The decision rule is:

Decision Rule Do not reject the null if the Z-value is between ± 1.96. Reject if the Z-value is less than -1.96 or greater than $+1.96$.

The logic behind this decision rule, which is based simply on probabilities, should be clear. If the null is true, it is unlikely that a Z-value greater than 1.96 or less than -1.96 could possibly result. Only 5 percent of all the samples in the sampling distribution could produce a Z-value greater than 1.96 or less than -1.96. Therefore, if such a Z-value occurs, it is unlikely that $\mu = 16$, and the null should be rejected.

B. The Level of Significance and the Probability of Error

In testing a hypothesis, we can make two types of mistakes. A **Type I error** is rejecting a true hypothesis. In Figure 8.1, if the bottler's hypothesis is true and $\mu = 16$, there is still a 5 percent chance that a sample mean could fall in either rejection region, causing us to incorrectly reject the null. Of all the sample means in the sampling distribution, 2.5 percent produces a Z-value >1.96 in the right-tailed rejection region and 2.5 percent produces a Z-value < -1.96 in the left-tailed rejection region. This 5 percent is the *level of significance,* or alpha-value (α-value) and represents the probability of a Type I error.

Type I Error Rejecting a true hypothesis. The probability of a Type I error equals the level of significance, or α-value, at which the hypothesis is tested.

A **Type II error** is not rejecting a false hypothesis. If the null hypothesis H_0: $\mu = 16$ is *not* correct, but our test fails to detect this, we commit a Type II error. While the probability of a Type I error is equal to the selected alpha value, the probability of a Type II error, signified as β, is not easily determined. We cannot assume that $\alpha + \beta = 1$.

Levels of significance, or α-values, commonly selected for hypothesis tests are 10 percent, 5 percent, and 1 percent. However, as with confidence intervals, there is nothing special or magical about these alpha-values. We could test a hypothesis at the 4 percent level of significance if we chose to. The selection of an alpha-value depends on which error, Type I or Type II, we most want to avoid. Recall that the alpha-value of the test is the probability of a Type I error. If rejecting a true hypothesis (Type I error) is more serious than not rejecting a false hypothesis (Type II error), you would want to chose a low alpha-value, such as 1 percent or 5 percent, to minimize the probability of committing a Type I error. On the other hand, if not rejecting a false hypothesis (Type II error) is more serious, a higher alpha-value, such as 10 percent, might be preferable.

Assume that the soft-drink bottler rejects the null H_0: $\mu = 16$ and shuts down the bottling process to adjust the fill level. If the mean is indeed 16 ounces, however, the bottler has committed a Type I error. If this is more costly than a Type II error, allowing the process to continue when $\mu \neq 16$, the bottler would want to select a low alpha-value, such as 1 percent, for the test.

8.3 A Two-Tailed Test for μ

We are now ready to conduct the hypothesis test. There are four steps involved in the test:

Step 1: State the hypotheses.

Step 2: Based on the sample results, calculate the value of the test statistic, Z_{test}.

Step 3: Determine the decision rule based on the critical Z-values.

Step 4: Note the findings and conclusion.

Presume that the bottler wants to test the hypothesis that the population mean is 16 ounces and chooses a 5 percent level of significance. Since it is hypothesized that $\mu = 16$, the null and alternative hypotheses are

$$H_0: \mu = 16$$
$$H_A: \mu \neq 16$$

To test the hypothesis, the test statistic, Z_{test}, is calculated and compared to the critical Z-values.

The Z_{test}-value used to test the hypothesis when σ is known	$Z_{\text{test}} = \dfrac{\overline{X} - \mu_H}{\dfrac{\sigma}{\sqrt{n}}}$	[8.1]

where $\overline{X}$ is the sample mean
μ_H is the hypothesized value for the population mean
$\sigma/\sqrt{n}$ is the standard error of the sampling distribution

When σ is unknown, we use the sample standard deviation and the Z_{test} becomes

The Z_{test}-value used to test the hypothesis when σ is unknown	$Z_{\text{test}} = \dfrac{\overline{X} - \mu_H}{\dfrac{s}{\sqrt{n}}}$	[8.2]

where s is the sample standard deviation.

If the bottler selects a sample of $n = 50$ bottlers with a mean $\overline{X} = 16.357$ ounces and a standard deviation of $s = 0.866$ ounces, the Z_{test} is

$$Z_{\text{test}} = \frac{16.357 - 16}{\dfrac{0.866}{\sqrt{50}}}$$
$$= 2.91$$

In Figure 8.2, the level of significance of 5 percent is divided in the two tails. The remaining 95 percent is divided by 2 to find the area of 0.4750. From the Z-table this area of 0.4750 yields critical Z-values of ± 1.96. The decision rule becomes

Decision Rule Do not reject the null if $-1.96 \leq Z_{\text{test}} \leq 1.96$. Reject if $Z_{\text{test}} < -1.96$ or $Z_{\text{test}} > 1.96$.

Figure 8.2
Hypothesis Test for the Mean Fill Level

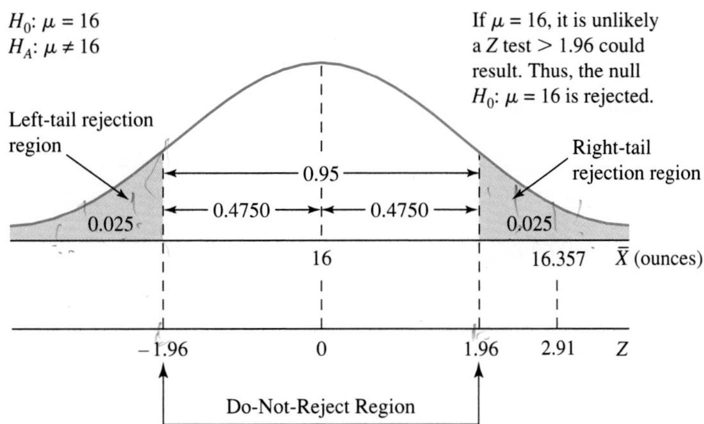

Notice the rejection regions in both tails. If $Z_{\text{test}} > 1.96$ or $Z_{\text{test}} < -1.96$, the null is rejected. For this reason this is referred to as a two-tailed test.

The final step in the hypothesis test is to note the findings and determine whether the null should be rejected. Our sample findings of 16.357 ounces produced a $Z_{\text{test}} = 2.91 > 1.96$ and fall in the right-tailed rejection region. We may interpret these results as "the null is rejected at the 5 percent level of significance." It just isn't likely that a population with a mean of 16 could yield a sample that would produce a $Z_{\text{test}} > 1.96$. There is *only* a 2.5 percent probability that Z_{test} could exceed 1.96 (and only a 2.5 percent chance that $Z_{\text{test}} < -1.96$) if μ is really 16. Thus, the null hypothesis H_0: $\mu = 16$ should be rejected at the 5 percent level of significance.

Does this mean that μ is *not* 16? Not at all. If $\mu = 16$, 2.5 percent of all the samples of size $n = 50$ would still generate a $Z_{\text{test}} > 1.96$. The population mean could be 16, in which case we have committed a Type I error by rejecting it. But this *is not* likely since $P(Z_{\text{test}} > 1.96 \mid \mu = 16)$ is only 2.5 percent.

Display 8.1

Z-Test

```
Test of mu = 16.000 vs mu not = 16.000
The assumed sigma = 0.866

Variable    N     Mean    StDev   SE Mean      Z    P-Value
Ounces     50   16.357    0.866     0.122   2.91     0.0037
```

The Minitab printout in Display 8.1 provides the results of this test. Assuming 50 observations are entered in column 1, merely click on **STAT** > **Basic Statistics** > **1-Sample Z,** and enter 16 for **Test Mean** and the standard deviation for our sample data of 0.866. Notice that the sample mean, standard deviation, and Z-value of 2.91 are given. We will discuss the all-important *p*-value later.

Example 8.1 As noted in "Setting the Stage" at the opening of this chapter, management at First Bank of America is planning to base the fees charged for checking accounts on their average daily balances. The senior accounts manager wants to test the hypothesis that the accounts average \$312. A sample of 200 accounts is selected, yielding a mean of \$298.10 with

s = \$97.30. To minimize the probability of a Type I error, an alpha-value of 1 percent is chosen. (Notice the four steps in conducting the test.)

Solution: The null and alternative hypotheses are

$$H_0: \mu = 312$$
$$H_A: \mu \neq 312$$

The Z_{test} is

$$Z_{\text{test}} = \frac{\overline{X} - \mu_H}{\frac{s}{\sqrt{n}}} = \frac{298.10 - 312}{\frac{97.30}{\sqrt{200}}} = -2.02$$

As the accompanying figure shows, an $\alpha = 0.01$ requires critical Z-values of ± 2.58. The 0.01 is evenly divided in the two rejection regions, leaving an area of 0.4950 which corresponds to critical Z-values of ± 2.58.

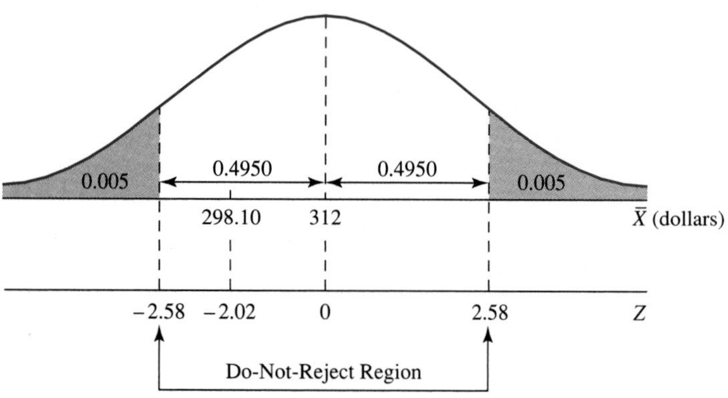

Decision Rule Do not reject if $-2.58 \leq Z_{\text{test}} \leq +2.58$. Reject if $Z_{\text{test}} < -2.58$ or $Z_{\text{test}} > 2.58$.

If the null is true, there is only a 1 percent chance that a sample could result in a Z_{test} value less than -2.58 or greater than 2.58. Thus, if Z_{test} falls in either tail, it is unlikely that $\mu = 312$ and the null should be rejected. Our $Z_{\text{test}} = -2.02$ is in the do-not-reject region.

Interpretation: The difference between the hypothesized value of \$312 and the sample findings of \$298.10 is statistically insignificant. It could result merely from sampling error. In fact, if μ = \$312, 99 percent of all the samples of size $n = 200$ would produce Z_{test} values between ± 2.58. Thus, a value of -2.02 is not unexpected.

Section Exercises

1. What are the four steps to a hypothesis test?
2. Explain in your own words why the decision rule should be used to determine whether the null should be rejected. What is the role of probability in this decision?
3. What is meant by an "insignificant difference" between the hypothesized population mean and the sample mean?

4. Why can we never "accept" the null as true?
5. What role do the critical Z-values perform in the testing process? How are they determined? Draw a graph in your response.
6. What is the "level of significance" in a test? How does it influence the critical Z-values? Draw a graph in your response.
7. Distinguish between a Type I error and a Type II error. Give an example.
8. Using a graph, clearly illustrate how the probability of a Type I error is equal to the level of significance (α-value) of a test.
9. If a Type II error is considered more serious in a certain situation, would you choose a high or a low alpha value? Explain.
10. As the purchasing manager for a large insurance firm, you must decide whether to upgrade the office computers. You have been told that the average cost of desktop computers is \$2,100. A sample of 64 retailers reveals a mean price of \$2,251, with a standard deviation of \$812. At the 5 percent level of significance, does it appear that your information is correct?
11. Enticed by commercials, you have been persuaded to purchase a new automobile. You think you will have to pay \$25,000 for the car you want. As a careful shopper, you price 40 possible vehicles and find a mean cost of \$27,312, with a standard deviation of \$8,012. Wishing to avoid a Type II error, you test the hypothesis that the mean price is \$25,000 at the 10 percent level of significance. What is your conclusion?
12. Due to excessive commute times, the office where you work in downtown Chicago is considering staggered work hours for its employees. The manager feels that it takes an average of 50 minutes for employees to get to work. Seventy employees average 47.2 minutes with a standard deviation of 18.9 minutes. Set alpha at 1 percent and test the hypothesis.
13. In 1997 the investment firm of Goldman Sachs reported that Americans invest an average of \$18.6 million every month in the bond market. Is this claim supported at the 5 percent level if a sample of 36 months finds a mean of \$17.1 million and a standard deviation of \$2.4 million?
14. Returning home from the mines, the seven dwarfs tell Snow White that they excavate a weekly average of 12 tons of gold. Unwilling to believe this without proof, Miss White collects data for 49 weeks and finds a mean of 11.5 tons and a standard deviation of 1.1 tons. At the 10 percent level does it appear that the dwarfs are correct?
15. Before publishing a new cookbook, Bantam Books wants to test the hypothesis at the 2 percent level of significance that the average price of such books is \$35.00. Is this claim supported if a sample of 50 cookbooks has a mean of \$32.97 and a standard deviation of \$12.87?
16. The local supermarket spent many weeks and thousands of dollars remodeling. Although the disruption temporarily drove away customers, the store manager hopes that the customers will now return to enjoy the new conveniences. Before the remodeling, store receipts averaged \$32,533 per week. Now that the remodeling has been completed, the manager takes a sample of 36 weeks to see whether the construction in any way affected business. A mean of \$34,166 is reported and the standard deviation is \$12,955. At the 1 percent level, what can the manager decide?

8.4 One-Tailed Tests for μ

The tests conducted above were all *two-tailed* tests because there were rejection regions in *both* tails. As Figure 8.3(A) shows, the test of the bottler's hypothesis that $\mu = 16$ would be rejected if the sample findings are either too high or too low. Either way, it appears that μ is not 16 and the null is rejected.

However, there are times when we are interested in only one extreme or the other. A fresh seafood restaurant in Kansas City is not concerned about how quickly the lobsters arrive from the East Coast. They worry only if it takes too long for the shipment to arrive. A retail outlet will become alarmed only if revenues fall to disturbingly low levels. Particularly high sales are no problem. In each of these cases, concern is focused on one extreme or the other and a one-tailed test is conducted.

Instead of hypothesizing that the mean fill level is exactly 16 ounces, suppose our bottler feels that the mean fill level is "at least 16 ounces." The null hypothesis becomes H_0: $\mu \geq 16$; that is, 16 or more. The alternative hypothesis is stated to the contrary, and the entire set of hypotheses is

$$H_0: \mu \geq 16 \qquad H_A: \mu < 16$$

Figure 8.3(B) shows that the hypothesis H_0: $\mu \geq 16$ is not rejected if the sample findings are above 16. The hypothesis H_0: $\mu \geq 16$ allows for values above 16. Sample means such as 16.3 or 16.5 or even 17 and 18 support, not refute, the claim that $\mu \geq 16$. Only values significantly *below* 16 can cause a rejection of the null. Thus, a rejection region appears in only the left tail and the full amount of the alpha-value is placed in this single rejection region.

Figure 8.3
A Comparison of Two-Tailed and One-Tailed Tests

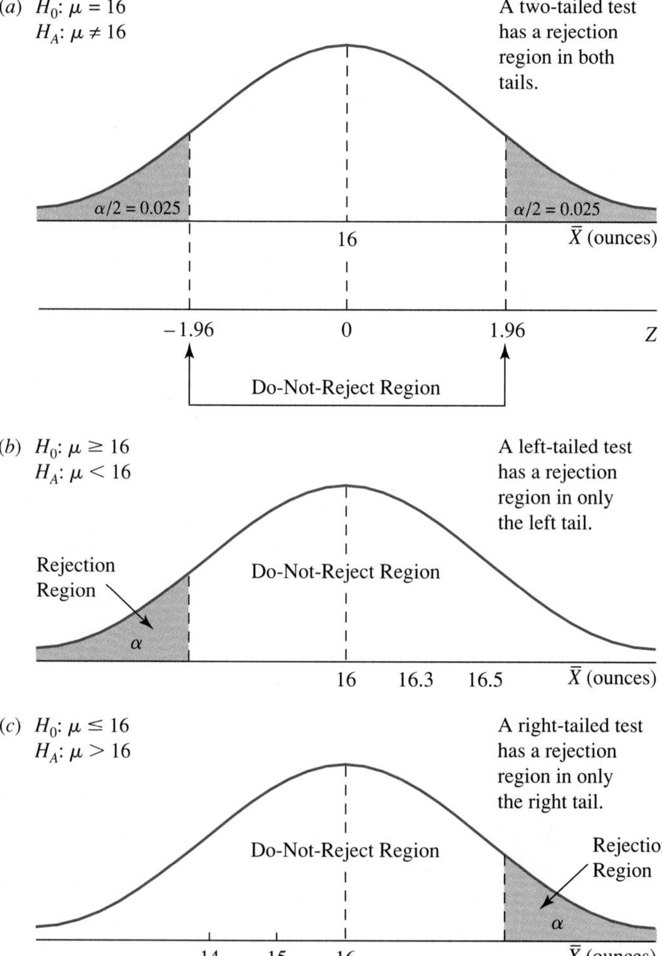

Presume the bottler claims that the mean fill level "is at most 16." The null is now written as H_0: $\mu \leq 16$. The hypotheses are

$$H_0: \mu \leq 16 \qquad H_A: \mu > 16$$

Figure 8.3(C) shows that now low values for the sample findings will *not* result in a rejection. The null hypothesis H_0: $\mu \leq 16$ permits findings below 16. Sample means such as 15 or even 14 support the claim that $\mu \leq 16$. Only values significantly above 16 will cause a rejection. Thus, there is a rejection region in only the right tail. The full value for alpha is placed in this single rejection region.

Notice that in both a left-tailed and a right-tailed test, the equals sign is placed in the null hypothesis. This is because the null hypothesis is being tested at a *specific* alpha value (such as 5 percent) and the equals sign gives the null a *specific* value (such as 16) to test. Example 8.2 illustrates a one-tailed test.

Example 8.2 In a monthly briefing to the corporate office, the manager for the Embassy Suites hotel in Atlanta reports that the mean number of rooms rented out per night is at least 212. That is, $\mu \geq 212$. One of the corporate officials feels that this number might be somewhat overstated. A sample of 150 nights produces a mean of 201.3 rooms and a standard deviation of 45.5 rooms. If these results suggest the manager has "padded" his report, he will be severely admonished. At the 1 percent level, what is the manager's fate?

Solution: The manager's statement that $\mu \geq 212$ contains the equals sign and thus serves as the null hypothesis:

$$H_0: \mu \geq 212 \qquad H_A: \mu < 212$$

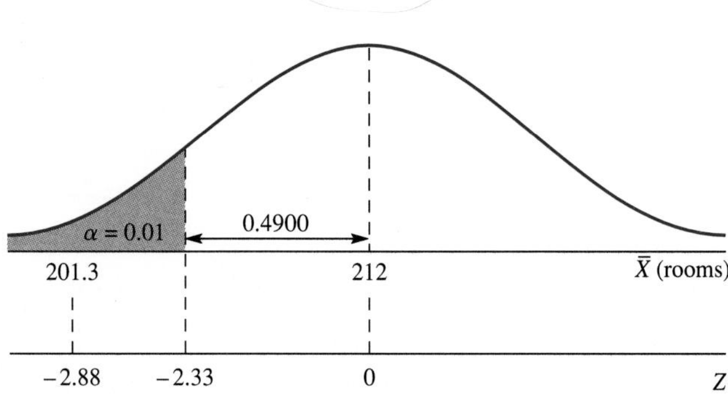

Values above 212 will not cause us to reject the null, which clearly allows for values in excess of 212. Only values significantly below 212 will lead to a rejection of $\mu \geq 212$. Thus, this is a left-tailed test. The Z_{test} is

$$Z_{\text{test}} = \frac{201.3 - 212}{\dfrac{45.5}{\sqrt{150}}} = -2.88$$

As the figure shows, a 1 percent level of significance leaves an area of 0.4900 that, from the Z-table, calls for a critical Z-value of -2.33. The decision rule is

Decision Rule Do not reject if $Z_{test} \geq -2.33$. Reject if $Z_{test} < -2.33$.

The Z_{test} of -2.88 is clearly in the rejection region. The null hypothesis H_0: $\mu \geq 212$ is not supported.

Interpretation: It appears the manager has overstated his occupancy rate and will apparently receive a reprimand from the home office.

Consider this next right-tailed test.

Example 8.3 A survey by the National Collegiate Students' Association showed that students at our nation's colleges and universities spend on average more than \$75 a month for general entertainment. If you can find evidence to support this claim, you intend to use it to request additional support money from home. From 100 students you sample, you find a mean of \$80.23 with a standard deviation of \$45.67. At the 2 percent level of significance, have you found justification for your request?

Solution: The claim that the mean is more than \$75.00 serves as the *alternative* hypothesis since $\mu > 75$ does not contain the equal sign. The hypotheses are then

$$H_0: \mu \leq 75 \qquad H_A: \mu > 75$$

and a right-tailed test is required since lower values would not result in a rejection of the null. Then,

$$Z_{test} = \frac{80.23 - 75}{\frac{45.67}{\sqrt{100}}} = 1.15$$

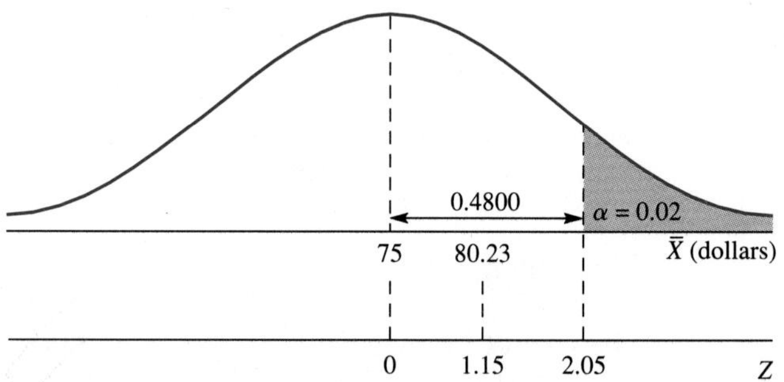

The area shown in the figure of 0.4800 indicates a critical Z-value of 2.05. The decision rule is

Decision Rule Do not reject if $Z_{test} \leq 2.05$. Reject if $Z_{test} > 2.05$.

Since $Z_{test} = 1.15 < 2.05$, the null H_0: $\mu \leq 75$ is not rejected. It appears that the mean cost of entertainment is not more than \$75.

Interpretation: Despite your decadent lifestyle, the typical student does not spend more than \$75. You are going to have to find another way to squeeze more money from home.

Section Exercises

17. Explain the difference between one-tailed and two-tailed hypotheses tests in your own words. Give examples of both.

18. Why does the equals sign always go in the null hypothesis?

19. Explain clearly why a null hypothesis of H_0: $\mu \leq 10$ requires a right-tailed test, while a null hypothesis of H_0: $\mu \geq 10$ requires a left-tailed test.

20. Over the past several months Raynor & Sons has heavily advertised its electrical supply business. Mr. Raynor hopes that the result has been to increase mean weekly sales above the \$7,880 the company experienced in the past. A sample of 36 weeks shows a mean of \$8,023 with a standard deviation of \$1,733. At the 1 percent level of significance, does it appear the advertising paid off?

21. In the fall of 1997, Hardee's, the fast-food giant, was purchased by a company in California that plans to remove the fried-chicken line from the menu. The claim was that recently revenues have slipped below the \$4,500 mean they displayed in the past. Does this seem like a wise decision if 144 observations reveal of mean of \$4,477 and a standard deviation of \$1,228? Management is willing to accept a 2 percent probability if committing a Type I error.

22. According to *The Wall Street Journal* (May 12, 1997) many sportswear companies are trying to market to the younger age groups. The article suggested that the mean age of the consumers has fallen below the 34.4 years that characterized the earlier part of the decade. If a sample of 1,000 customers reports a mean of 33.2 years and a standard deviation of 9.4, what do you conclude at the 4 percent level of significance?

23. The July 1997 issue of *Forbes* reported on exclusive "hideaways" in upper New York State and surrounding areas used by rich executives to escape the tedium of their stressful daily lives. The cost is quite reasonable, the article reported. You can hire weekend accommodations for less than \$3,500. Is this "reasonable" figure supported at the 5 percent level if a sample of 60 resorts average \$3,200 and $s = \$950$?

24. In the early 1990s, Hyundai, the Korean automobile manufacturer, suffered a severe drop in sales below its monthly peak of 25,000 units in May 1988. *Hyundai Motor America* (Summer 1997) reported that sales had slipped to less than 10,000 units. During a 48-month period starting in January 1990, the average sales were 9,204 units. Assume a standard deviation of 944 units. At the 1 percent level, does it appear that the mean number of units has fallen below the 10,000 mark?

25. Baskin-Robbins, the ice-cream franchise, claims that the number of outlets it opens has increased above the weekly mean of 10.4 experienced in leaner times (*The Wall Street Journal,* February 1997). Is there evidence to support this claim if 50 weeks show a mean of 12.5 and a standard deviation of 0.66 outlets? Management is willing to accept a 4 percent probability of rejecting the null if it is true.

26. A recent advertisement claims that the amount of property and marine insurance written by Atlantic Mutual is at least \$325,500 per month. Forty months report a mean of \$330,000 and $s = \$112,300$. At the 5 percent level of significance, does Atlantic Mutual's claim seem to be valid?

8.5 p-Values: Their Interpretation and Use

To test a hypothesis, as we have seen, we calculate a Z_{test} value and compare it to a critical Z-value based on our selected level of significance. While the p-value of a test can serve as an alternative method of hypothesis testing, it is really much more than that.

In this section we develop a strict definition of the p-value and the role it can play in hypothesis testing. You should fully understand *why* the p-value can be defined in the manner it is. We also explain how to calculate the p-value for both two-tailed and one-tailed tests.

The p-value for a test is the probability of getting sample results at least as extreme as those we obtained given that the null is true. It is found as the area in the tail *beyond* the sample findings. Let us begin with a one-tailed test. Chuck Cash is a personnel manager. From a brief examination of employee records, Chuck feels that the employees have an average of more than \$31,000 in their retirement accounts ($\mu > 31{,}000$). Sampling 100 employees, Chuck finds a mean of \$31,366, with $s = \$1{,}894$.

Suppose Chuck wants to calculate the p-value associated with this right-tailed test. The hypotheses are

$$H_0\text{: } \mu \leq 31{,}000 \qquad H_A\text{: } \mu > 31{,}000$$

The Z_{test} is

$$Z_{\text{test}} = \frac{31366 - 31000}{\dfrac{1894}{\sqrt{100}}} = 1.93$$

Figure 8.4
Chuck's Test of a One-Tailed Hypothesis

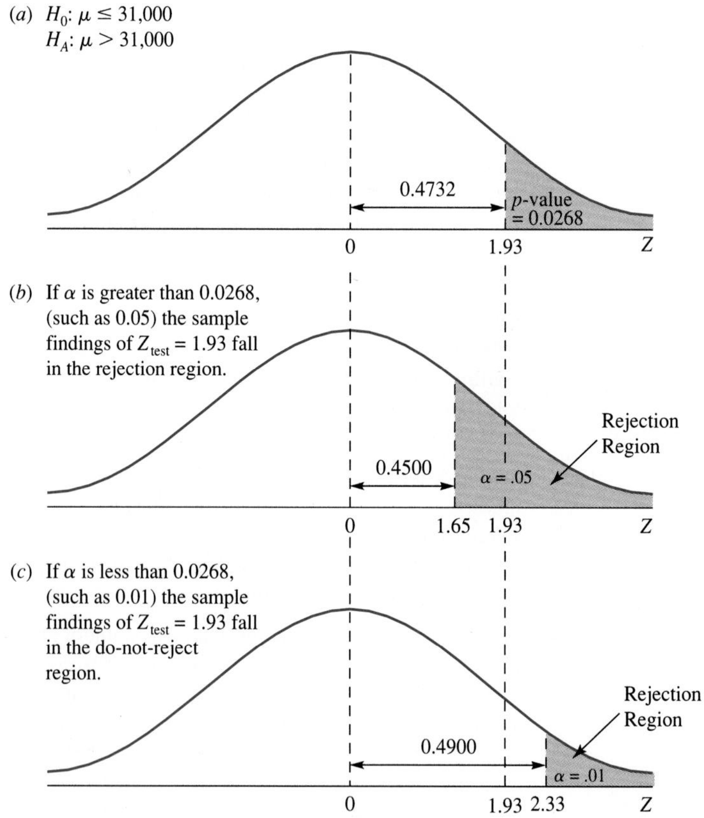
(a) H_0: $\mu \leq 31{,}000$
H_A: $\mu > 31{,}000$
0.4732
p-value = 0.0268
0
1.93
Z
(b) If α is greater than 0.0268, (such as 0.05) the sample findings of $Z_{\text{test}} = 1.93$ fall in the rejection region.
Rejection Region
0.4500
$\alpha = .05$
0
1.65 1.93
Z
(c) If α is less than 0.0268, (such as 0.01) the sample findings of $Z_{\text{test}} = 1.93$ fall in the do-not-reject region.
Rejection Region
0.4900
$\alpha = .01$
0
1.93 2.33
Z

The p-value is the area in the tail beyond the sample finding of $Z_{test} = 1.93$. As Figure 8.4(A) illustrates, a Z_{test} of 1.93 yields an area of 0.4732. The p-value, the area in the tail beyond the sample findings of 1.93, is $0.5000 - 0.4732 = 0.0268$, or 2.68 percent.

> ***p*-Value** The lowest level of significance (α-value) at which the null can be rejected. It is the area in the tail beyond the sample findings.

What exactly does this p-value of 2.68 percent tell Chuck? The ***p*-value** is defined as the lowest level of significance (lowest alpha-value) he can set and still reject the null. For example, Figure 8.4(B) shows that if α is set at some value greater than 0.0268, such as 0.05, the area of 0.4500 calls for a critical Z-value of 1.65. Thus, the sample findings of $Z_{test} = 1.93$ fall in the rejection region. On the other hand, as Figure 8.4(C) reveals, if an α-value less than 0.0268 is selected, such as 0.01, the resulting area of 0.4900 specifies a critical Z-value of 2.33 and the sample findings of $Z_{test} = 1.93$ fall in the do-not-reject region. Thus, Chuck can lower the α-value for the test down to 0.0268 without placing the sample findings in the do-not-reject region. That is, an α-value of 0.0268 is the lowest α-value Chuck can set and still reject the null.

The p-value tells Chuck what decision he would reach at any selected alpha-value. Simply put, if the p-value is less than the alpha-value, the null will be rejected.

Display 8.2

```
Z-Test

Test of mu = 31000 vs mu > 31000
The assumed sigma = 1894

Variable     N      Mean     StDev     SE Mean      Z      P-Value
Amount     100     31366     1894      189        1.93     0.0268
```

Minitab Display 8.2 provides the printout for Chuck's one-tailed test. The Z-value and p-value he calculated can be easily obtained by clicking on **Stat** > **Basic Statistics** > **1-Sample Z.** Set the confidence level and enter the hypothesized value for the mean. Select **greater than** for the alternative. Finally, enter 1894 for sigma. Caution: Many computer programs report only p-values for two-tailed tests. If you are conducting a one-tailed test, divide the reported p-value by 2 to get the one-tailed value. However, if you follow the directions above, Minitab will report the one-tailed value.

A. p-Value for Two-Tailed Tests

Calculating the p-value of a two-tailed test is quite similar, with a slight twist at the end. Presume that Chuck also suspects that the employees invest an average of \$100 each month in the company's stock option plan ($\mu = 100$). Sampling 100 employees, Chuck finds a mean of \$106.81 with a standard deviation of \$36.60. He now wants to determine the p-value associated with the hypothesis test

$$H_0\text{: } \mu = 100 \qquad H_A\text{: } \mu \neq 100$$

The Z_{test} is

$$Z_{test} = \frac{106.81 - 100}{\frac{36.60}{\sqrt{100}}} = 1.86$$

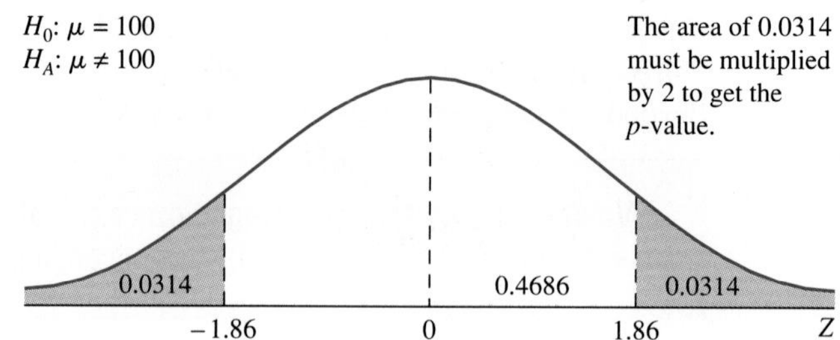
H_0: μ = 100
H_A: $\mu \neq$ 100
The area of 0.0314 must be multiplied by 2 to get the p-value.
0.0314
0.4686
0.0314
−1.86
0
1.86
Z

Figure 8.5
Chuck's Two-Tailed Hypothesis Test

To calculate the p-value, Chuck determines the area in the tail beyond the sample findings of $Z_{\text{test}} = 1.86$. In Figure 8.5 this area is 0.0314. Unlike a one-tailed test, this area must be multiplied by 2 to get the p-value. This is necessary because in a two-tailed test the alpha-value is divided into the two rejection regions. The p-value is $0.0314 \times 2 = 0.0628$. Remember, the p-value is the lowest alpha-value at which the null is rejected. If the alpha-value is set lower than the p-value, the null is not rejected.

Display 8.3

```
Z-Test

Test of mu = 100.00 vs mu not = 100.00
The assumed sigma = 36.6

Variable      N      Mean     StDev    SE Mean        Z     P-Value
Dollars     100    106.81     36.60       3.66     1.86       0.063
```

Minitab Display 8.3 shows the results of Chuck's two-tailed test. Notice that the p-value of 0.063 is for a two-tailed hypothesis and it is not necessary to multiply by 2.

Example 8.4 In May 1997 Congress approved a federal budget containing several provisions for tax cuts. Analysts claimed it would save the average taxpayer \$800 per year. Calculate and interpret the p-value if a sample of 500 taxpayers shows a mean savings of \$785.10 with a standard deviation of \$187.33.

Solution:

$$H_0: \mu = 800 \qquad H_A: \mu \neq 800$$

The Z_{test} is

$$Z_{\text{test}} = \frac{785.10 - 800}{\dfrac{187.33}{\sqrt{500}}} = -1.78$$

The p-value is determined by finding the area beyond the sample findings of -1.78; as the figure shows, $0.5000 - 0.4625 = 0.0375$. Then, $0.0375 \times 2 = 0.0750 = p$-value.

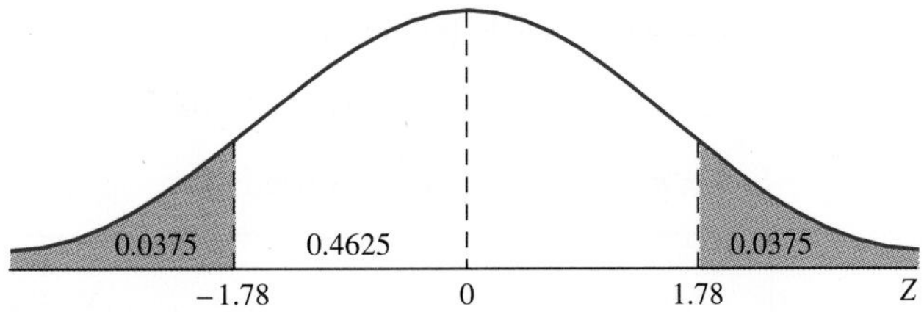

Interpretation: The p-value shows that the lowest alpha-value that could be set and still reject the null is 7.5 percent. That's why we do not reject it here at an alpha-value of 5 percent.

Section Exercises

27. Define the p-value associated with a hypothesis test. Use a graph to explain clearly why the p-value is defined in this manner and how it can be used to test a hypothesis. Do so for both a one-tailed and a two-tailed test.
28. In the summer of 1997 Congress approved a federal budget containing several provisions for tax reductions. Analysts claimed it would save the average taxpayer \$800. A sample of 500 taxpayers showed a mean reduction in taxes of \$785.10 with a standard deviation of \$277.70. Test the hypothesis at the 5 percent level. Calculate and interpret the p-value.
29. Using the data from the previous problem, compare the alpha-value of 5 percent to the p-value you calculated, and explain why you did or did not reject the null. Use a graph in your response.
30. In the early 1990s Sony Corporation introduced its 32-bit PlayStation in the home video game market. Management hoped the new product would increase monthly U.S. sales above the \$283 million Sony had experienced in the previous decade. A 40-month sample reported a mean of \$297 million. Assume a standard deviation of \$97 million. Test the hypothesis at the 1 percent level. Calculate and interpret the p-value.
31. In the fall of 1996, Joe Galli, president of the Black and Decker (B&D) global power tool business, attended a convention in Kansas City's Kemper Arena and announced to those present that B&D's sales had reached a new high of \$7.7 million per week during the current decade. (*Forbes,* September 1996). Is Galli's statement supported at the 1 percent level if two years of data yields a mean of \$8.2 million and $s = \$1.8$ million? What is the lowest level of significance Galli can set and still reject the null?
32. *Forbes* (September 1996) reported that Freddie McMann, manager for the pop singer Madonna, estimated the daily sales of her new album would exceed that of her biggest 1994 hit, *Like a Virgin,* which averaged 27,400. Is Freddie correct at the 10 percent level if 50 observations (days) produced a mean of 28,788 copies with a standard deviation of 3,776? Calculate and interpret the p-value.

8.6 Small-Sample Tests for μ

As with confidence intervals, if the sample is small, σ is unknown, and the population is normal or near-normal in its distribution, the small sample t_{test} can be used. The students in a statistics class at State University question the claim that McDonald's puts 0.25 pounds of beef in their "quarter-pounders." Some students argue that more is actually used, while others insists it is less. To test the advertising claim that the mean weight is 0.25 pounds, each student buys a quarter-pounder and brings it to class, where it is weighed on a scale provided by the instructor. The sample results are $\overline{X} = 0.22$ pounds and $s = 0.09$. If there are 25 students in class, what conclusions did they reach at the 5 percent level of significance? The hypotheses are

$$H_0: \mu = 0.25 \qquad H_A: \mu \neq 0.25$$

Since, $n < 30$, the t_{test} is calculated as

Small sample test for the mean

$$t_{\text{test}} = \frac{\bar{X} - \mu_H}{\frac{s}{\sqrt{n}}} \qquad [8.3]$$

Given our present data, we find

$$t_{\text{test}} = \frac{0.22 - 0.25}{\frac{0.09}{\sqrt{25}}} = 1.667$$

The t_{test} value of 1.667 is compared to a critical t-value with $n - 1 = 24$ degrees of freedom and an alpha-value of 5 percent. From the t-table for *two-tailed tests*, $t_{.05,24} = 2.064$. The decision rule, as reflected in Figure 8.6, is

Decision Rule Do not reject if t_{test} is between ± 2.064. Reject if t_{test} is less than -2.064 or greater than $+2.064$.

Figure 8.6
Two-Tailed t_{test} for the Population Mean

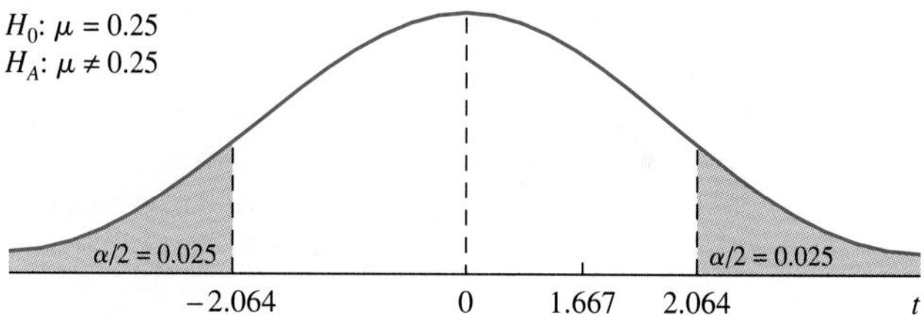

Since $t_{\text{test}} = 1.667$ is between ± 2.064, the null is not rejected. The test evidence supports McDonald's claim that its quarter-pounders contain 0.25 pounds of beef.

As you might expect by now, a one-tailed test is similar, but with one slight alteration. When using the t-table, we must use the values for one-tailed tests. The American Kennel Club (AKC) reported in its bimonthly publication *American Dog Owners* (April 1997) that one-year-old water cocker spaniels should weigh "slightly over 40 pounds ($\mu > 40$) if they have received the proper nutrition." To test the hypothesis

$$H_0: \mu \leq 40 \qquad H_A: \mu > 40$$

Hill's, maker of dietary dog foods, weighs 15 one-year-old cockers and finds a mean of 41.17 pounds, with $s = 4.71$ pounds. Selecting a 1 percent probability of a Type I error, it finds

$$t_{\text{test}} = \frac{41.17 - 40}{\frac{4.71}{\sqrt{15}}} = 0.96$$

From the *t*-table for *one*-tailed tests, $t_{0.01,14} = 2.624$. The decision rule, as reflected in Figure 8.7, is

Decision Rule Do not reject if $t_{\text{test}} \le 2.624$. Reject if $t_{\text{test}} > 2.624$.

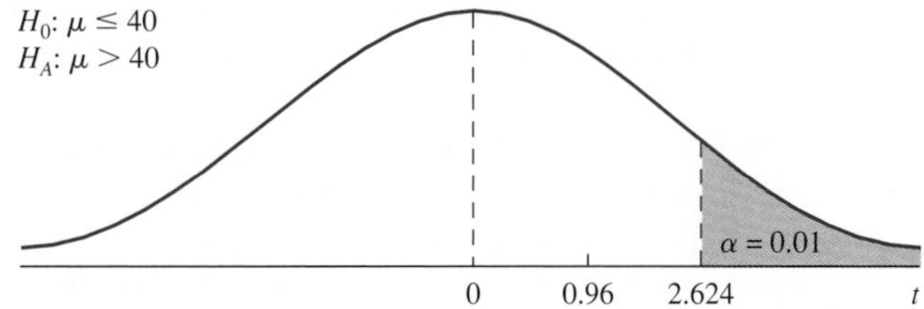

Figure 8.7
One-Tailed t_{test} for the Population Mean

The t_{test} value of 0.96 clearly falls in the do-not-reject region. The null H_0: $\mu \le 40$ is not rejected. The sample evidence suggests that the AKC's claim is not supported.

Display 8.4

T-Test of the Mean

```
Test of mu = 40.00 vs mu > 40.00
```

Variable	N	Mean	StDev	SE Mean	T	P-Value
Weight	15	41.17	4.71	1.22	0.96	0.18

Minitab Display 8.4 shows the test results for the cocker spaniel hypothesis. The *t*-value is 0.96 along with *p*-value of $0.18 > 0.01$. Calculating the *p*-value from a *t*-table requires more guesswork than using a *Z*-table because the *t*-table is less detailed. Do not attempt hand calculation of *p*-values for small samples; rely strictly on the computer for this information.

Section Exercises

33. A beverage distributor hypothesizes that sales average $12,000 per month. Ten months selected as a sample report a mean of $11,277 and a standard deviation $3,772. If an alpha-value of 5 percent is used, what can you conclude about the distributor's impression of business conditions?

34. The records kept by a large department store indicate that, in the past, weekly sales have averaged $5,775. In order to increase sales, the store recently began an aggressive advertising campaign. After 15 weeks, sales average $6,012 with $s = \$977$. Should the store continue the advertising program? Set alpha at 1 percent.

35. Stan and Ollie sell ice cream from a pushcart in New York's Central Park. Stan tells Ollie that they sell an average of at least 15 pounds of vanilla when the temperature exceeds 80 degrees. Ollie disagrees. If 20 days of 80 degrees or more reveals an average of 13.9 pounds and $s = 2.3$ pounds, who's right, Stan or Ollie? Set alpha at 5 percent.

36. A new light bulb by Sun Systems is designed to increase the average life of bulbs over the 5,000-hours currently in existence. Does Sun's new product offer an improvement if 25 bulbs burn an average of 5,117 hours with $s = 1,886$ hours? Set alpha at 5 percent.

37. A postal delivery company assures your firm that it can reduce the average time required to receive a package below the 2.5 days you currently experience. After using the new company 17 times, the average delivery time was 2.2 days and the standard deviation was 0.9 days. Should your firm switch to the new delivery company? Let alpha equal 1 percent.

38. As production supervisor, it is your responsibility to ensure that the bags of grass seed your firm sells average 25 pounds. Prompted by concern that this weight specification is not being met, you select 25 bags and find a mean of 23.8 pounds with a standard deviation of 6.6 pounds. Should you order that the assembly line be shut down and adjustments be made in the filling process? To minimize a Type I error, choose an alpha value of 1 percent.

39. You have just been hired as a management trainee for a West Coast manufacturer of computer parts. In your first job assignment, you need to monitor the time required for workers to complete a certain job task that is supposed to take an average of 15 minutes. Your immediate supervisor is concerned that a labor shortage requiring the use of untrained workers has increased the completion time above the 15-minute mandate. You sample 20 workers and find a mean of 17.3 minutes and $s = 1.9$ minutes. At an alpha-value of 1 percent, what do you report back to your supervisor?

40. An electrical contractor has concluded that the average home uses 500 yards of electrical wiring. You find that a sample of 15 homes used 545.3 yards with $s = 166.4$ yards. At an alpha-value of 5 percent, do you agree with the contractor?

8.7 Tests for π

Many business decisions depend on the proportion or percentage of the population that fits some characteristic. A marketing specialist may want to know the proportion of the residents in a large city that fit the target market. Managers are often concerned about the percentage of employees who feel that company rules are too oppressive. Financial and economic analysts may need to estimate the portion of capital projects that suffer cost overruns. Many other illustrations, can be cited.

The process of testing a hypothesis regarding the population proportion π is quite similar to that of testing μ. A Z_{test} value calculated from the sample findings is compared to a critical Z-value based on the selected alpha value. The Z_{test} is calculated as

Hypothesis test for the population proportion

$$Z_{test} = \frac{p - \pi_H}{\sigma_p} \qquad [8.4]$$

where p is the sample proportion of observations that are considered "successes"
π_H is the hypothesized value for the population proportion
σ_p is the standard error of the sampling proportion.

As a standard error, σ_p measures the tendency for the sample proportions to deviate from the unknown population proportion. It is calculated as

Standard error of the sampling distribution of sample proportions

$$\sigma_p = \sqrt{\frac{\pi_H(1 - \pi_H)}{n}} \qquad [8.5]$$

As the director of marketing operations for a large retail chain, you believe that 60 percent of the firm's customers are college graduates. You intend to establish an important policy decision regarding pricing structure on this proportion. A sample of 800 customers reveals that 492 have college degrees, yielding a sample proportion of $p = 492/800 = 0.615$. At the 5 percent level, what can you conclude about the proportion of all customers who have graduated from college? Your hypotheses are

$$H_0: \pi = 0.60 \qquad H_A: \pi \neq 0.60$$

The standard error is

$$\sigma_p = \sqrt{\frac{0.60\,(1 - 0.60)}{800}} = 0.017$$

Then,

$$Z_{\text{test}} = \frac{0.615 - 0.60}{0.017} = 0.88$$

In Figure 8.8, the α-value of 5 percent is divided in the two rejection regions, placing 2.5 percent in each tail. The remaining 95 percent divided by 2 yields an area of 0.4750; which, using the Z-table, requires critical Z-values of ± 1.96. The decision rule is therefore

Decision Rule Do not reject if Z_{test} is between ± 1.96. Reject if Z_{test} is greater than $+1.96$ or less than -1.96.

Figure 8.8
Hypothesis Test for the Proportion of Customers with College Degrees

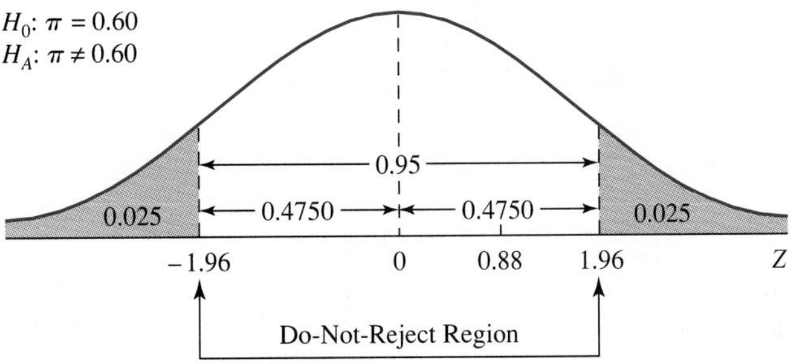

The Z_{test} of 0.88 is in the do-not-reject region. The sample evidence supports the hypothesis that $\pi = 0.60$. It is now possible for you to develop your pricing policy based on this conclusion.

Returning to the Z-table, it is possible to calculate the p-value associated with this test. Remember, the p-value is the lowest alpha-value at which the null can be rejected. It is found as the area in the tail beyond the sample findings. Figure 8.9 shows this area to be

Figure 8.9
The p-Value for the Proportion of Customers with College Degrees

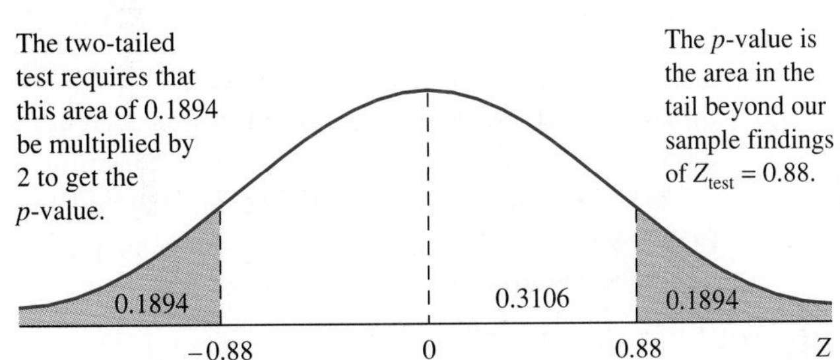

$0.5000 - 0.3106 = 0.1894$. However, since this is a two-tailed test, the p-value is $0.1894 \times 2 = 0.3788$. Since the alpha-value of 5 percent is less than 37.88 percent, the null is not rejected.

As with tests for means, one-tailed hypotheses tests for proportions can be either right-tailed or left-tailed. Consider this left-tailed test. The management director for a large manufacturing firm must ensure that at least 75 percent of his employees have completed an advanced training course. Of 1,200 employees selected at random, 875 have done so. The director enlists your assistance to test this hypothesis and to calculate the p-value. At the 5 percent level of significance, what findings do you include in your report?

Since at least 75 percent is written $\pi \geq 0.75$, the hypotheses are

$$H_0: \pi \geq 0.75 \qquad H_A: \pi < 0.75$$

and require a left-tailed test. Given,

$$\sigma_p = \sqrt{\frac{(0.75)(1 - 0.75)}{1200}} = 0.0125$$

and $p = 875/1200 = 0.729$, the Z_{test} becomes

$$Z_{\text{test}} = \frac{0.729 - 0.75}{0.0125} = -1.68$$

In Figure 8.10(A), by placing the full amount of α-value of 0.05 in the single rejection region, the area of 0.4500 requires a critical Z-value of -1.65. The decision rule is

Decision Rule Do not reject if Z_{test} is ≥ -1.65. Reject if $Z_{\text{test}} < -1.65$.

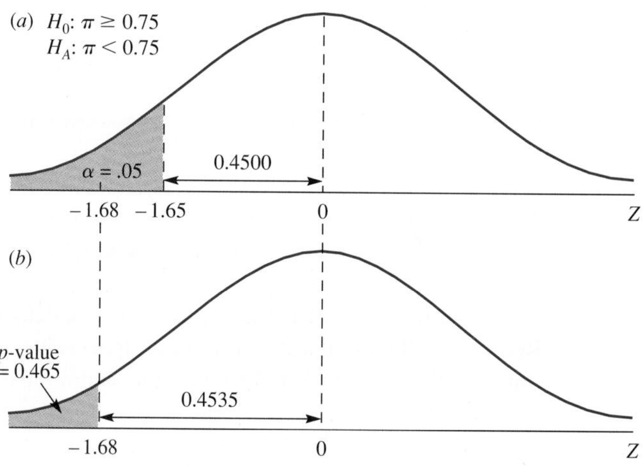

Figure 8.10
Hypothesis Test for the Proportion of Employees with Advanced Training

Since $Z_{\text{test}} = -1.68 < -1.65$, the null is rejected. The director must take action to increase the proportion of employees given further training to enhance job skills.

The p-value is the area in the tail beyond the sample findings of $Z_{\text{test}} = -1.68$. In Figure 8.10(B), a Z-value of -1.68 yields an area of 0.4535. Thus, the p-value is $0.5000 - 0.4535 = 0.0465$.

Section Exercises

41. A 1982 study revealed that 78 percent of those responding felt they were better off financially than their parents. A more recent study (*The Wall Street Journal,* April 1997) found that 370 of the 500 respondents thought their financial fortunes were better than their parents'. Does this suggest a decrease in the proportion of people who feel they are more financially stable than their parents were? Test the hypothesis at 1 percent and calculate the p-value.
42. Traditionally, 35 percent of all the loans by the Jesse James National Bank have been to members of minority groups. During the past year, the bank has undertaken efforts to increase this proportion. Of 150 loans currently outstanding, 56 are identified as having been made to minorities. Has the bank been successful in its efforts to attract more minority customers? Test the hypothesis at 5 percent. Calculate the p-value.
43. Midwest Productions plans to market a new product only if at least 40 percent of the public like it. The research department selects 500 people and finds that 225 prefer it over the nearest competitor. At the 2 percent level, should Midwest market the product?
44. Radio Shack, the home electronics retailer, announced that it sells 21 percent of all home computers. Is this claim supported if 120 out of 700 computer owners bought from Radio Shack? Set alpha at 5 percent, and calculate and interpret the p-value.
45. Director Steven Spielberg, the second-highest-paid entertainer (at \$30 million) in 1997, appeared on the Oprah Winfrey show. Winfrey is the highest-paid entertainer (at \$97 million). Spielberg stated that about "75 percent of the general public" had seen his movie *Jurassic Park.* Oprah took a survey of the 200 people in the audience that day and found that 157 had seen the movie. Is Spielberg's claim supported at the 1 percent level?
46. *The Wall Street Journal* (March 1997) reported that job dissatisfaction was reaching epidemic proportions. An estimated 70 percent of U.S. workers would switch jobs if they could. If this is true of the workers at your firm, you plan to institute a program to improve employee morale. You find that 1,020 workers from a sample of 1,500 at your firm expressed job dissatisfaction. At the 2 percent level of significance, should you implement the program?
47. Midlakes Commuter Service voluntarily ceased flight operations out of its Chicago offices (*Chicago Tribune,* June 10, 1997). It was estimated that more than 18 percent of Midlakes flights involved airplanes with mechanical faults. Is this estimate supported at the 5 percent level if 24 planes used for 120 flights showed mechanical problems?

Solved Problem

In 1997 the Illinois legislature debated various proposals to reform state school funding (*Peoria Journal Star,* May 1997). It was alleged that the average amount Illinois spent per pupil was less than the U.S. average of \$5,541. A study by Quality Counts, a citizens-based educational "watchdog" in the state, reported a mean of \$5,015 per pupil.

House speaker Michael Madigan (D-Chicago) reported that more than 40 percent of the general populace supported Governor Jim Edgar's plan to raise state income tax by more than 25 percent to fund education. However, Senate President James Philip (R-Wood Dale) claimed that support was not that pervasive. House Republican Leader Lee Daniels (R-Elmhurst) reported that an average of \$2.5 million was being spent per school in Illinois.

Mark Boozell, the governor's advisor on education, undertook an extensive survey of public opinion. He found an average of \$5,112 was spent on a sample of 1,200 students to match others in the study. Assume a standard deviation of \$1,254. Boozell also found that 25 schools studied reported a mean of \$2.2 million. Assume a standard deviation of \$900,000. Boozell further learned that of

1,000 taxpayers questioned, 355 supported the governor's plan to raise taxes to pay for the educational reform.

a. Test the allegation that the mean expenditure in Illinois is less than the U.S. average of $5,541 at the 5 percent level, and calculate the *p*-value.

Solution:

$$H_0\text{: } \mu \geq 5541 \qquad H_A\text{: } \mu < 5541$$

$$Z_{\text{test}} = \frac{5112 - 5541}{\frac{1254}{\sqrt{1200}}} = -11.85$$

Decision Rule Do not reject if $Z_{\text{test}} \geq -1.65$. Reject otherwise.

Since $Z_{\text{test}} = -11.85 < -1.65$, the null $H_0\text{: } \mu \geq 5541$ is rejected. The data support the claim that Illinois funding is below the national average.

As the figure below shows, the *p*-value, the area in the tail beyond the sample findings of -11.85, is virtually zero.

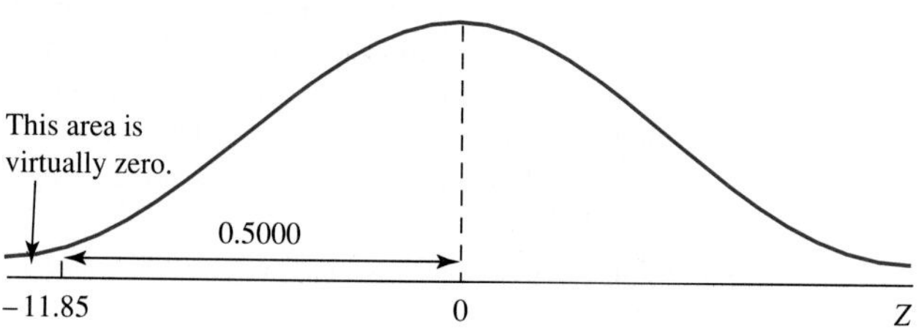

b. Test the hypothesis by Quality Counts at the 1 percent level. Calculate the *p*-value.

Solution:

$$H_0\text{: } \mu = 5015 \qquad H_A\text{: } \mu \neq 5015$$

$$Z_{\text{test}} = \frac{5112 - 5015}{\frac{1254}{\sqrt{1200}}} = 2.68$$

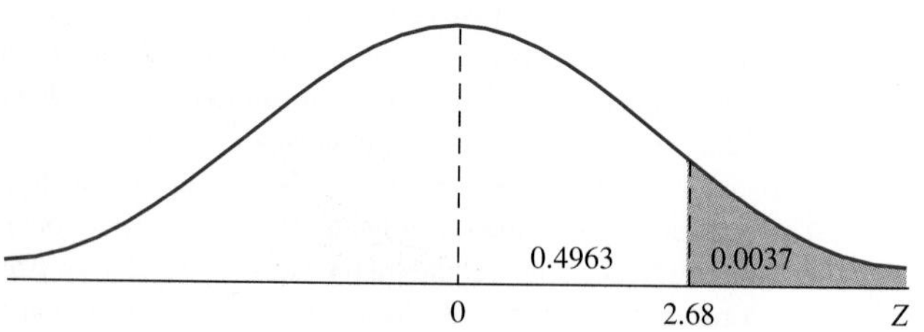

Decision Rule Do not reject if $-2.58 \leq Z_{\text{test}} \leq 2.58$. Reject otherwise.

Since $Z_{\text{test}} = 2.68 > 2.58$, reject the null H_0: $\mu = 5015$. Quality Counts seems to have understated expenditures. As the figure shows, the p-value is $0.0037 \times 2 = 0.0074$.

c. Test Madigan's claim at the 5 percent level.

Solution:

$$H_0: \pi \leq 0.40 \qquad H_A: \pi > 0.40$$

$$Z_{\text{test}} = \frac{0.355 - 0.40}{\sqrt{\dfrac{(0.40)(0.60)}{1000}}} = -2.90$$

Decision Rule Do not reject if $Z_{\text{test}} \leq 1.65$. Reject otherwise.

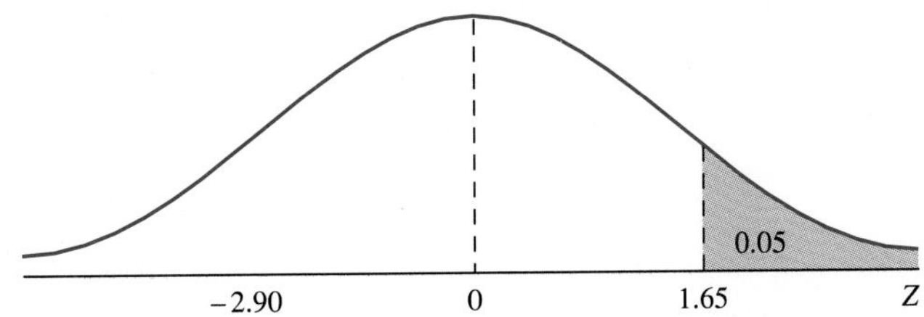

Since, as the figure shows, $Z_{\text{test}} = -2.90 < 1.65$, the null H_0: $\pi \leq 0.40$ is not rejected. Madigan's claim that more 40 percent of the people favor the governor's proposal is not supported.

d. Compare the results of Madigan's claim above to Philip's. Retain an alpha of 5 percent

Solution:

$$H_0: \pi \geq 0.40 \qquad H_A: \pi < 0.40$$

Decision Rule Do not reject if $Z_{\text{test}} \geq -1.65$. Reject otherwise.

As seen in the figure, since $Z_{\text{test}} = -2.91 < -1.65$, the null H_0: $\pi \geq 0.40$ is rejected. Philip's claim that less than 40 percent of the people favor the governor's proposal is supported.

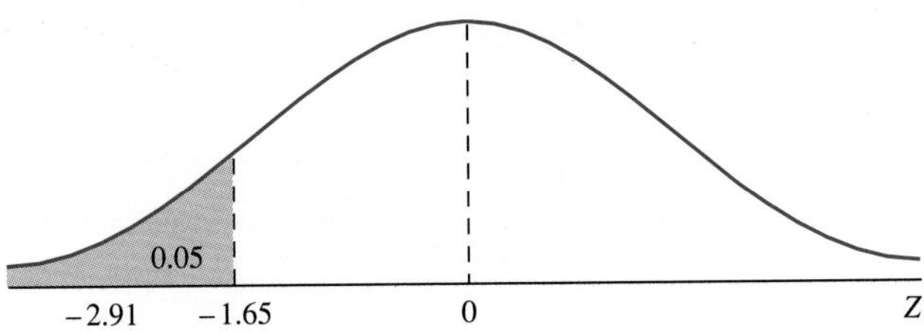

e. Test Daniel's hypothesis at the 5 percent level.

Solution:

$$H_0: \mu = 2.5 \qquad H_A: \mu \neq 2.5$$

$$t_{\text{test}} = \frac{2.2 - 2.5}{\frac{0.9}{\sqrt{25}}} = 1.667$$

Decision Rule Do not reject if $-2.064 \leq t_{\text{test}} \leq 2.064$. Reject otherwise.

Since $t_{\text{test}} = 1.667$, do not reject H_0: $\mu = 2.5$. Daniel's claim is supported.

List of Formulas

[8.1] $$Z_{\text{test}} = \frac{\bar{X} - \mu_H}{\frac{\sigma}{\sqrt{n}}}$$ Z_{test} for μ when σ is known.

[8.2] $$Z_{\text{test}} = \frac{\bar{X} - \mu_H}{\frac{s}{\sqrt{n}}}$$ Z_{test} for μ when σ is unknown.

[8.3] $$t_{\text{test}} = \frac{\bar{X} - \mu_H}{\frac{s}{\sqrt{n}}}$$ t_{test} for μ with small sample.

[8.4] $$Z_{\text{test}} = \frac{p - \pi_H}{\sigma_p}$$ Z_{test} for π.

[8.5] $$\sigma_p = \sqrt{\frac{\pi_H(1 - \pi_H)}{n}}$$ Standard error of the sample proportions.

Chapter Exercises

48. Ralph Root works in the garden center at the local Kmart. In the effort to estimate the mean growth rate of the pansies they sell, Ralph is at a loss in trying to explain the role of the critical value in a hypothesis test. Help poor Ralph out.

49. Ralph (from the previous question) must determine whether a supplier is meeting required production specifications. If he is not, and Ralph continues to buy from him, serious consequences will result. If he is but Ralph decides to buy from someone else, little is lost. State the hypotheses Ralph must use. Should he use a large or small significance level? Why?

50. Describe the effect of an increase in the sample size on the:

a. Probability of a Type I error.
b. Critical values.

Illustrate your answer with the proper graphical work.

51. What is a Type II error, and what is its relationship to a Type I error? Does $P(\text{Type I}) + P(\text{Type II}) = 1$?

52. Why does an extremely low p-value mean that the null hypothesis will likely be rejected? Use a graph in your response.

53. A labor-management contract calls for an average daily output of 50 units. A sample of 150 days reveals a mean of 47.3, with a standard deviation of 5.7 units. Set $\alpha = 5$ percent and determine whether this contract provision is fulfilled. Calculate the p-value.

54. The Colonial Canning Company of Claremont, California, uses a machine to fill its 18-ounce cans of kumquats. If the machine performs improperly, it is readjusted. A sample of 50 cans is found to have a mean of 18.9 ounces with a standard deviation of 4.7 ounces. Should the machine be readjusted? Set $\alpha = 5$ percent. Calculate the p-value.

55. From the previous problem, if a sample of 500 cans was taken, yielding the same mean and standard deviation as the smaller sample, should the machine be readjusted?

56. A *Fortune* article discussing the rising trend for employees to sue their companies for failure to meet promises regarding proposed health benefits concluded the average lawsuit was for $115,000. Forty-two suits averaged $114,412. Assume a standard deviation of $14,000. Is the hypothesis supported at the 7 percent level? Calculate the p-value.

57. Members of the Strain and Sweat Health Club are distressed by a decision by the owner to limit racketball court reservations to an unacceptable time restriction. They claim that the average set of games lasts two hours. From 27 recent sets a mean of 1.82 hours is found with a standard deviation of 0.32 hour. The manager agrees to remove the time limit if members are correct in their assertion. Set $\alpha = 2$ percent. What should the manager do?

58. *Sports Illustrated* discussed the problems TV networks were having telecasting professional football games, due to variations in the amount of time it takes to play a game. Games that took additional time due to high scoring or numerous time-outs often ran into the time slot for the next program, while games that required less time left the networks with time gaps to fill. NBC decided to test the hypothesis that it should allot exactly 3.1 hours for a game. To test this hypothesis, times for 12 games were selected. The results, in hours, are shown below. If $\alpha = 1$ percent, what should NBC do?

Times (in hours) for 12 Professional Football Games on NBC in 1997

2.91	3.19	3.05
3.21	3.09	3.19
3.12	2.98	3.17
2.93	2.95	3.14

59. The Santa Clara, California, police department has found that traffic officers should write an average of 27 traffic tickets per month. If an officer writes more than that, he is likely too zealous in the performance of his duties. If fewer tickets are handed out, the officer may not be doing a thorough job. To evaluate his officers, the police chief noted the number of tickets written by 15 officers. The results are shown below. At the 5 percent level, does it appear the police force is performing satisfactorily?

28	34	30
31	29	33
22	32	38
26	25	31
25	24	31

60. A company policy at State Farm Insurance is to restrict the proportion of claims settled in favor of the insured to 25 percent. Of the past 1,122 policies, 242 fully compensated the insured. If $\alpha = 0.10$, is the policy being observed? Calculate the p-value.

61. Due to grade inflation in which professors have been giving too many high grades, the dean insists that each professor fail 30 percent of his or her students. In a sample of 315 recent students, Professor Nodoze failed 112 students. Is the professor fulfilling the dean's requirement? Set $\alpha = 0.05$. Calculate the p-value.

62. Given the dean's stipulation in the previous problem, the faculty argues that it unduly restricts their grading authority. The dean relaxes his requirement by stating that the faculty must fail an average of 30 percent of the students. The failure rates for eight faculty members are

$$0.27, 0.31, 0.32, 0.25, 0.33, 0.25, 0.26, 0.31$$

Is the dean going to be happy with these data? Set $\alpha = 0.01$.

63. A weight-reduction plan stipulates that 75 percent of the people placed on the plan should lose between 5 percent and 12 percent of their body weight within the first six weeks. If more than 75 percent lose the stipulated amount, the diet is too severe. If fewer than 75 percent of the participants lose the required amount, the diet is too lax. Of 450 people surveyed, 347 lost an amount within the tolerable range. At the 5 percent level, what does this say about the diet?

64. The manager for the Whatchaneed market feels that 50 percent of his customers spend less than \$10 during any visit to the store. Many of his pricing decisions are based on this assumption. He decides to test this assumption by sampling 50 customers whose total expenditures are shown here. What do these data reveal about the manager's pricing decisions? Set $\alpha = 5$ percent.

Customers' Expenditures				
\$18.17	\$21.12	\$ 4.12	\$ 8.73	\$ 8.42
7.17	17.18	27.18	2.17	7.12
2.08	6.12	2.17	6.42	9.17
4.17	2.12	8.15	12.18	2.63
18.02	9.99	3.02	8.84	21.22
8.73	10.00	0.65	17.17	18.42
4.12	5.12	11.12	11.17	4.82
8.15	5.12	3.32	17.89	5.55
5.15	12.12	4.83	11.12	11.11
17.15	18.17	10.12	8.92	17.83

65. Brach's Candies mixes its jelly bean candy so that 20 percent of the bags contain at least five colors of beans. Quality control examines 400 bags and finds that 87 contain more than five colors. At the 1 percent level, is this quality feature being met? Calculate the p-value.

66. Biggie Burger claims that its deluxe special has at least 0.25 pounds of beef. A sample of 100 burgers had a mean of 0.237 pounds, with a standard deviation of 0.04 pounds. Is Biggie Burger guilty of false advertising at the 5 percent level of significance?

67. Minit-Mart, a nationwide convenience store chain, stated in *The Wall Street Journal* that it will not open a store in any location unless median income in the neighborhood is at least \$12,000. A survey of 200 families in a given neighborhood produces a mean income of \$11,852 with a standard deviation of \$1,517. Should Mini-Mart open the store if all other criteria for a desirable location are met? Set $\alpha = 1$ percent.

68. A tire manufacturer has been making snowtires in Akron, Ohio, for over 40 years. His best tire has averaged 52,500 miles with a standard deviation of 7,075 miles. A new tread design is thought to add additional wear to the tires. Sixty tires with the new design are tested, revealing a mean of 54,112 miles, with a standard deviation of 7,912 miles. At the 5 percent level, can it be said that the new tread adds to tire wear? (Note: In addition to the sample standard deviation of 7,912, the population standard deviation of 7,075 is also known, which one should be used in the calculations? Why?)

69. Industrial espionage is a growing problem. *Business Week* reported that former employees of Du Pont demanded that the chemical firm pay a ransom of $10 million, or competitors would be given the company's secret for making Lycra, the popular fiber used in underwear, bathing suits, and other clothing. It has been estimated that corporate extortion costs companies an average of more than $3.5 million. If 75 cases of this nature are examined and found to average $3.71 million with a standard deviation of $1.21 million, is that estimate supported at the 10 percent level? Calculate the *p*-value.

70. Rex Cutshall, National Director for MultiMedia Entertainment, wants to ensure that episodes of *Star Trek: The Next Generation* average no more than 57 minutes in length. Eighty episodes yield a mean of 63.2 minutes with a standard deviation of 23.7 minutes.

a. At the 1 percent level, should Rex alter the length of the programs?
b. What is the lowest level of significance at which Rex can reject the hypothesis?

71. Vince Showers, managing director for Sleaz Entertainment, claims that the average age of Sleaz customers is at least 23. If this is not the case, Showers will face charges of violating local ordinances regarding public decency. One hundred customers averaged 19.7 years with $s = 10.2$. Set alpha at 1 percent.

a. State and test the hypotheses. Must Showers appear in court?
b. Calculate and interpret the *p*-value.

72. Your firm has determined in the past that exactly 53 percent of the people in your marketing area prefer your product. Several thousand dollars is spent on an advertising program to increase your market share. Afterward, a sample of 622 reveals that 348 prefer your product. At the 4 percent level of significance, was the money well spent?

73. You have been working for an advertising firm in Chicago for five years. Now you are thinking of starting your own company, but you are worried about losing many of your clients. You decide to go it alone only if at least 30 percent of those accounts you now handle will leave with you and follow you to your new business. As a test, you find that 14 out of 54 accounts you sample express their desire to go with you if you leave the company. At the 7 percent level, should you start your own firm?

74. As a recently hired marketing analyst for Griffin Industries, you are given the responsibility of ensuring that more than 10 percent of the population is aware of your new product line. Of 300 people, 36 express an awareness. Set alpha at 4 percent.

a. State and test the proper hypotheses. Have you done your job?
b. What is the lowest alpha-value at which you can reject the null?

75. Your position as Marketing Representative for Wakco Wheels, a manufacturer of toy cars and trucks for children under five, requires that you test the durability of your product. Your company claims that the Richard Petty Rapid Roller will endure at least 200 pounds of pressure per square inch without breaking. You test 100 of these models and find a mean breaking point of 195 pounds, with a standard deviation of 22.2 pounds.

a. At the 5 percent level of significance, is your company's claim supported?
b. If the claim is true, what is the probability of getting a Z_{test} value as low or lower than that obtained by the sample?

76. A supplier for Ralph's Tanning Parlor and Quickie Car Wash Emporium insists that no more than 33 percent of Ralph's customers spend less than \$20 on the average per visit. Of 80 customers pooled randomly, 29 spend less than \$20.

a. At the 1 percent level, is the supplier correct?
b. What is the lowest α-value at which the supplier would be deemed wrong?

77. Weight Watchers claims that those people who use their program lose an average of 42 pounds. A sample of 400 determined dieters lost an average of 43.17 pounds, with a standard deviation of 8.7 pounds.

a. Is the claim supported at the 5 percent level?
b. What is the lowest α-value at which the claim could be rejected?

78. Hilda Radner owns a publishing company in Palo Alto, California. Business has improved recently, and Hilda thinks that daily revenues are higher than the \$500 they were last year. A sample of 256 days reveals a mean of \$520 and a standard deviation of \$80.70.

a. At the 1 percent level of significance, is Hilda correct?
b. If mean revenues are actually \$507, what is the probability of committing a Type II error? Draw the proper normal curves to illustrate.

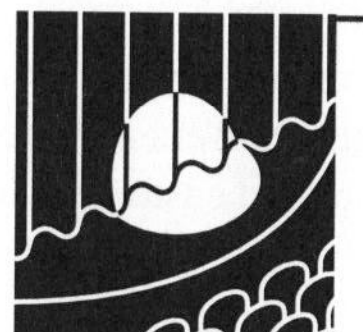

CURTAIN CALL

As we saw in Setting the Stage at the opening of this chapter, First Bank of America is planning an extensive statistical analysis of its operations. Mr. Hopkins must perform tests on several different aspects of First Bank's operations. The results of these tests are to assist in the formulation of many operational policies. Mr. Hopkins samples 1,200 customers and finds that 850 object to a new policy to charge \$2 each month to return depositors' canceled checks with their monthly statements. These 1,200 customers have a mean deposit in their saving accounts of \$4,533, with a standard deviation of \$1,776. Mr. Hopkins also found that 27 local businesses average balances of \$344,500, with a standard deviation of \$104,600.

Based on these data, Mr. Hopkins determines that if more than 65 percent of the depositors object to the \$2 charge, the policy will not be implemented. Further, if savings accounts of individual depositors average \$4,500, he plans to offer a graduated interest rate schedule with higher rates for larger accounts. Finally, if business accounts are at least \$340,000, Mr. Hopkins will establish a separate administrative division to handle business accounts.

Assist Mr. Hopkins in his efforts. Offer all the relevant findings and conclusions including p-values where appropriate. Present your findings as specified in Appendix I.

From the Stage to Real Life

Market share data on banking deposits is obtained from the ratio of an individual bank's total deposits to the aggregate deposits in all domestic commercial banks. If you were Lawrence Hopkins at First Bank of America, where would you obtain data for the market share analysis in the chapter opening "Setting the Stage"? Would you expect to have difficulty learning the total deposits in your own bank? Where would you look for the aggregate industry figures?

Surprisingly, the aggregate figures you would need are readily available on the Internet from the Board of Governors of the Federal Reserve System (*www.bog.frb.fed.us*). At the Board of Governors Home Page, scroll down to the heading, Domestic and International Research. Under this heading, click on "Statistics: Releases and historical data." Here you can choose to look at a variety of aggregate U.S. banking data. Select "H.8 Assets and Liabilities of Commercial Banks in the United States—Historical data." Here you will find approximately 10 years of monthly and weekly data on deposits, current within about one month of the date of your search. Contrast the ease of obtaining data from the Board of Governors to the American Banking Association (*www.aba.com*).

CHAPTER 9

Two Population Tests

Chapter Blueprint

Many business problems require the comparison of two populations. This chapter discusses the situations in which such a comparison can be made. Illustrations show the circumstances in which it is essential to compare two populations, and the proper manner in which to make these comparisons.

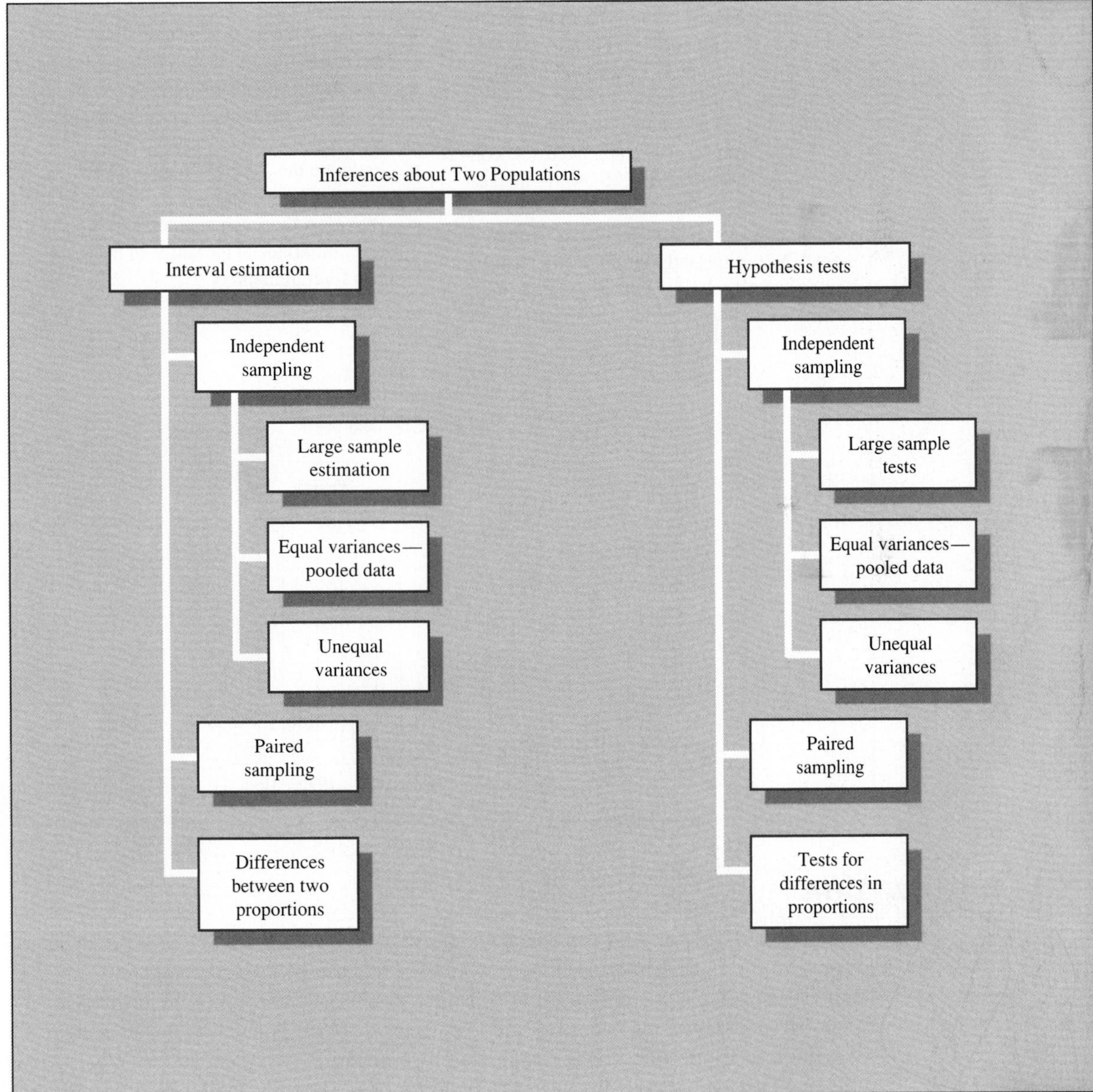

SETTING THE STAGE

Fortune (October 1996) carried a series of articles discussing trends in U.S. foreign trade. These articles focused on the huge sums of money involved in international transactions and the roles Europe and Asia play as competing sites for U.S. investment. American investment in Europe totaled $364 billion in 1996, rising 17 percent over the record level established just the year before. There occurred a 16 percent increase in U.S. business involvement in Asia, elevating the level of investment in that region to over $100 billion. These trends are reflected in the accompanying figure.

The articles also challenged the conventional wisdom that U.S. firms increasingly prefer to invest in Asia's growing economies over Europe's huge existing market. They suggested that domestic business interests still consider Europe to offer a more lucrative opportunity for corporate growth.

As an international analyst for your firm, you must prepare an extensive report detailing the comparative advantages between involvement in these two geopolitical areas. This report is to be presented at a meeting of many of the firm's divisional directors. The purpose of the meeting is to decide the future course of the firm's foreign investment activity over the next several years. This will require that you:

- Compare the mean return on investment in Europe to that in Asia.
- Determine which area has a lower percentage of defaults on investment projects.
- Estimate the average level of investment in Europe and Asia.
- Provide a thorough comparison of all relevant financial measures in these two foreign markets.

U.S. Investments Abroad

(Billions of Dollars)

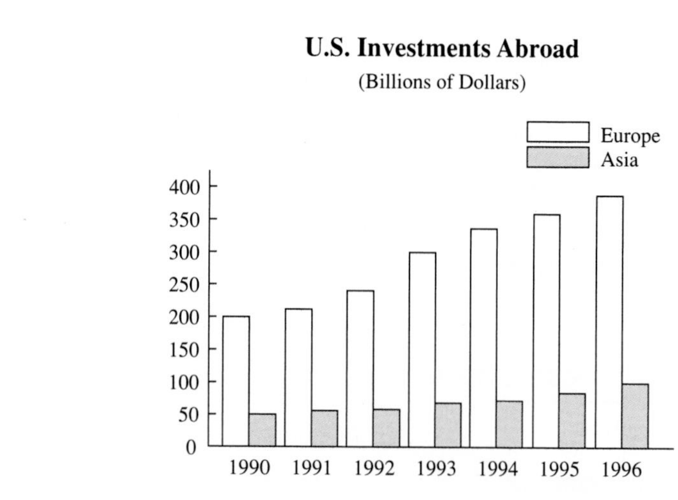

9.1 Introduction

Chapters 7 and 8 showed how to construct interval estimates and test hypotheses for a single population. This chapter examines how these tools can be used to compare two populations. For example, we may want to construct an interval estimate of the difference between two population means or test the hypothesis that two population means are equal. Many important questions can be addressed by comparing two populations. What is the difference, if any, between the average durability of ski boots made by North Slope and those made by Head? Do workers in one plant produce more on the average than workers in a second plant? Is there a difference between the proportion of defective units produced by one method and that produced by an alternative method?

The exact procedure to follow in conducting these tests depends on the sampling technique that is used. Samples for two-population tests can be either (1) independent or (2) paired. As the term implies, independent sampling is done by collecting separate samples from each population. The samples do not even have to be the same size. With paired sampling, observations from each population are matched up. This will be more fully described later. Let us begin with a discussion of independent sampling.

9.2 Interval Estimates with Independent Sampling

Our interest here lies in estimating the difference between two population means $(\mu_1 - \mu_2)$. The proper approach depends on the sizes of the samples n_1 and n_2. If *both* n_1 and n_2 are large (at least 30), the technique differs somewhat from that when either or both sample sizes are less than 30. Let us first examine the approach when both samples are large.

A. Large Sample Estimation

The point estimate of the difference between $(\mu_1 - \mu_2)$ is provided by the difference between the two sample means $(\overline{X}_1 - \overline{X}_2)$. Given that many different samples can be taken from each population, there results an entire distribution of differences in these sample means. If both n_1 and n_2 are large, this distribution in the differences in sample means $(\overline{X}_1 - \overline{X}_2)$ is a normal distribution centered at $(\mu_1 - \mu_2)$ as displayed by Figure 9.1.

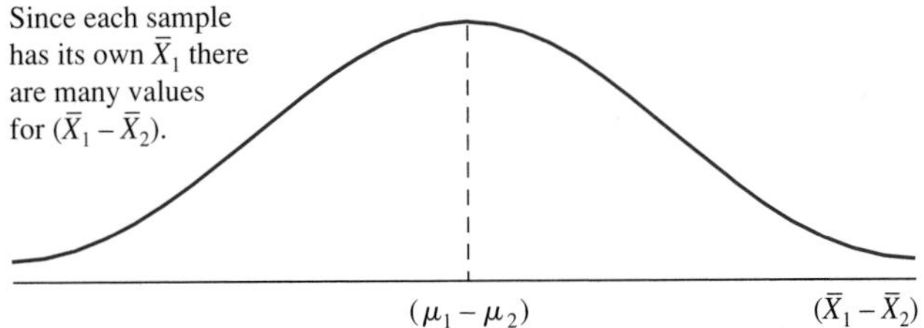
Since each sample has its own $\overline{X}_1$ there are many values for $(\overline{X}_1 - \overline{X}_2)$.
$(\mu_1 - \mu_2)$
$(\overline{X}_1 - \overline{X}_2)$

Figure 9.1 The Sampling Distribution of the Differences in Sample Means $(\overline{X}_1 - \overline{X}_2)$

Given this normal distribution in the differences between sample means, the normal deviate Z can be used to construct the interval. The procedure is much like that developed in Chapter 7 for a single population. Using $(\overline{X}_1 - \overline{X}_2)$ as the point estimate of the difference between the two population means, a confidence multiplier is applied to obtain the upper and lower boundaries of the interval.

Confidence interval for the difference between two population means—large samples

$$\text{C.I. for } (\mu_1 - \mu_2) = (\overline{X}_1 - \overline{X}_2) \pm Z\sigma_{\bar{x}_1 - \bar{x}_2} \qquad [9.1]$$

where $\sigma_{\bar{x}_1 - \bar{x}_2}$ is the standard error of the differences between sample means. As with any standard error, $\sigma_{\bar{x}_1 - \bar{x}_2}$ measures the tendency for the differences between sample means to vary. It is found as

Standard error of the differences between sample means	$\sigma_{\bar{x}_1-\bar{x}_2} = \sqrt{\dfrac{\sigma_1^2}{n_1} + \dfrac{\sigma_2^2}{n_2}}$	[9.2]

where σ_1^2 *and* σ_2^2 are the two population variances. In the likely event σ_1^2 *and* σ_2^2 are unknown, the sample variances s_1^2 *and* s_2^2 must be used. The estimate of the standard error becomes

Estimate of the standard error of the difference between sample means	$s_{\bar{x}_1-\bar{x}_2} = \sqrt{\dfrac{s_1^2}{n_1} + \dfrac{s_2^2}{n_2}}$	[9.3]

The interval for the difference in sample means is then

Confidence interval when population variances are unknown	$\text{C.I. for } (\mu_1 - \mu_2) = (\bar{X}_1 - \bar{X}_2) \pm Zs_{\bar{x}_1-\bar{x}_2}$	[9.4]

Note that we are not interested in the value of either population mean, but only in the difference between the two population means.

Transfer Trucking transports shipments between Chicago and Kansas City via two routes. A sample of 100 trucks sent over the northern route revealed a mean transit time of $\bar{X}_N = 17.2$ hours with a standard deviation of $s_N = 5.3$ hours, while 75 trucks using the southern route required an average of $\bar{X}_S = 19.4$ hours and a standard deviation of $s_S = 4.5$ hours. Delmar, the dispatcher for Transfer Trucking, wants to develop a 95 percent confidence interval for the difference in the mean time between these two alternate routes.

Since the population standard deviations are unknown, the standard error is

$$s_{\bar{x}_N-\bar{x}_S} = \sqrt{\frac{(5.3)^2}{100} + \frac{(4.5)^2}{75}} = 0.742$$

A 95 percent interval requires a Z-value of 1.96. The interval is then

$$\text{C.I. for } (\mu_N - \mu_S) = (17.2 - 19.4) \pm (1.96)(0.742)$$
$$-3.7 \le (\mu_N - \mu_S) \le -0.75$$

The results can be interpreted as either:

1. Delmar can be 95 percent certain that $(\mu_N - \mu_S)$ is somewhere between -3.7 hours and -0.75 hours.

Or, since Delmar subtracted the mean of the southern route from that of the northern route and got negative numbers,

2. Delmar can be 95 percent confident that the southern route takes between 0.75 hours and 3.7 hours longer.

Example 9.1 Charles Schwab, the discount brokerage service, recently instituted two training programs for newly hired telephone marketing representatives. To test the relative effectiveness of each program, 45 representatives trained by the first program were given a proficiency test.

The mean score was $\bar{X}_1 = 76.00$ points with $s_1 = 13.50$ points. The 40 people trained under the second program reported a mean score of $\bar{X}_2 = 77.97$ and $s_2 = 9.05$. Management wants to know if one training program is more effective than the other. As the one selected to make this determination, you decide to construct a 99 percent confidence interval for the difference between the mean proficiency scores of the employees trained under each program. You are also charged with the responsibility of recommending which training program the company should use exclusively.

Solution: The standard error of the difference between sample means is

$$s_{\bar{x}_1-\bar{x}_2} = \sqrt{\frac{(13.50)^2}{45} + \frac{(9.05)^2}{40}} = 2.47$$

The 99 percent interval is found as

$$\text{C.I. for } (\mu_1 - \mu_2) = (76.00 - 77.97) \pm (2.58)(2.47)$$
$$-8.34 \le (\mu_1 - \mu_2) \le 4.40$$

Interpretation: You can be 99 percent certain that $(\mu_1 - \mu_2)$ is between -8.34 points and 4.40 points. Expressed differently, you can report with 99 percent confidence that the mean scores of those trained by program 2 is between 4.40 points less and 8.34 points more than those trained by program 1. Of importance, since the interval contains zero, you can be 99 percent confident that there is no difference in the mean scores. You may conclude that either program can be used to train all newly hired representatives.

Section Exercises

1. Clark Insurance sells policies to residents throughout the Chicago area. The owner wants to estimate the difference in the mean claims between people living in urban areas and those residing in the suburbs. Of the 180 urban policies selected for the sample, a mean claim of \$2,025 was reported, with a standard deviation of \$918. The 200 suburban policies revealed a mean claim of \$1,802 and $s = \$512$. What does a 95 percent interval tell the owner about the mean claims filed by these two groups?

2. Two production processes are used to produce steel pipe. A sample of 100 pipes taken from the first production process has a mean length of 27.3 inches and $s = 10.3$ inches. The corresponding figures for 100 pipes produced by the second method are 30.1 and 5.2. What does a 99 percent interval reveal about the difference in the mean lengths of pipe produced by these two methods?

3. Chapman Industries uses two telephone answering devices. Chuck Chapman wishes to determine whether customers who call in are kept waiting longer on the average with one or the other of the systems. If 75 calls on the first system reported a mean wait time of 25.2 seconds with $s = 4.8$ seconds and 70 calls on the second system yielded a mean of 21.3 seconds with $s = 3.8$ seconds, what recommendation would you offer Chuck if he wants to minimize wait time based on a 90 percent interval estimate of the difference in mean wait times?

4. Two production designs are used to manufacture a certain product. The mean time required to produce the product using the old design was 3.51 days with $s = 0.79$ days. The new design required an average of 3.32 days with $s = 0.73$ days. Equal size samples of 150 were used for both designs. What would a 99 percent interval estimate of the difference

between the mean times required to produce the product reveal about which design should be used?

5. Explain precisely what the standard error of the difference between sample means actually measures.

B. Small Sample Estimation: The t-Distribution

If either sample is small (less than 30), we cannot assume that the distribution of the differences in sample means $(\bar{X}_1 - \bar{X}_2)$ fits a normal distribution. The normal deviate Z therefore cannot be used. Instead, if

1. The populations are normally or near-normally distributed, and
2. The population variances are unknown,

we must turn to the *t*-distribution.

To apply the *t*-distribution properly, we must also determine whether the variances of the two populations are equal. How can we presume these variances are equal if, as just noted above, we don't know what they are? Many assembly line processes use machines to fill product containers such as cans, bottles, and boxes. When the machines are periodically adjusted to ensure proper operation, it is assumed that the mean fill level has changed but the variance in the fill levels before and after adjustment, although unknown, remains unchanged. Other instances also prevail in which the assumption of equal variances is reasonable. A method is presented later in this chapter to test for the equality of two variances. For now, let us examine confidence intervals when (1) the variances are assumed equal and when (2) the variances cannot be assumed equal.

1. The Assumption of Equal but Unknown Variances $\sigma_1^2 = \sigma_2^2$ If the two population variances are equal, there is some variance σ^2 common to both populations. That is, $\sigma_1^2 = \sigma_2^2 = \sigma^2$. However, due to sampling error, if a sample is taken from each population, the two sample variances will likely differ from each other as well as from the common variance σ^2. But since the populations have a common variance, the data from both samples can be *pooled* to obtain a single estimate of σ^2. This is done by computing the weighted average of the two sample variances where the weights are the degrees of freedom $n - 1$ for each sample. This **pooled estimate** of the common population variance s_p^2 is

Pooled estimate of the variance common to both populations

$$s_p^2 = \frac{s_1^2(n_1 - 1) + s_2^2(n_2 - 1)}{n_1 + n_2 - 2} \qquad [9.5]$$

The confidence interval for the difference between the two population means is then found as a *t*-test with $n_1 + n_2 - 2$ degrees of freedom.

Interval for the difference in population means using pooled data

$$\text{C.I. for } (\mu_1 - \mu_2) = (\bar{X}_1 - \bar{X}_2) \pm t\sqrt{\frac{s_p^2}{n_1} + \frac{s_p^2}{n_2}} \qquad [9.6]$$

A vending machine in the student cafeteria dispenses drinks into paper cups. A sample of 15 cups yields a mean of 15.3 ounces with a variance of 3.5. After adjusting the machine, a sample of 10 cups produces an average of 17.1 ounces with a variance of 3.9. If σ^2 is assumed to be constant before and after the adjustment, construct a 95 percent confidence interval for the difference in mean fills. Assume the amounts dispensed are normally distributed.

Then

$$s_p^2 = \frac{3.5(14) + 3.9(9)}{15 + 10 - 2}$$

$$= 3.66$$

With $\alpha = 0.05$ (a 95 percent level of confidence) and $n_1 + n_2 - 2 = 23$ d.f., the t-table reveals a value of 2.069.

$$\text{C.I. for } \mu_1 - \mu_2 = (15.3 - 17.1) \pm 2.069\sqrt{\frac{3.66}{15} + \frac{3.66}{10}}$$

$$= -1.8 \pm 1.61$$

$$-3.41 \leq \mu_1 - \mu_2 \leq -0.19$$

Subtracting the mean fill level after adjustment (17.1) from the mean fill level before adjustment (15.3) resulted in negative values for both the lower and upper ends of the interval. That is, the interval does not contain zero. We can therefore be 95 percent confident that the adjustment increased the mean fill level between 0.19 ounce and 3.41 ounces.

Example 9.2 Wage negotiations between your firm and the union representing your workers are about to collapse. There is considerable disagreement about the mean wage level of workers in the plant in Atlanta and the plant in Newport News, Virginia. Wages were set by the old labor agreement reached three years ago and are based strictly on seniority. Since wages are closely controlled by the labor contract, it is assumed that the variation in wages is the same at both plants and that the wages are normally distributed. However, it is felt that there is a difference between the mean wage levels due to differing patterns of seniority between the two plants.

Management's head labor negotiator wants you to develop a 98 percent confidence interval for the difference between the mean wage levels. If a difference exists in the means, wage adjustments must be made to bring the lower wages up to the level of the higher ones. Given the data below, what adjustments, if any, are called for?

Solution: Samples of workers taken from each plant reveal the following information.

Atlanta Plant	Newport News Plant
$n_A = 23$	$n_N = 19$
$\overline{X}_A = \$17.53$ per hour	$\overline{X}_N = \$15.50$
$s_A^2 = 92.10$	$s_N^2 = 87.10$

Then

$$s_p^2 = \frac{92.10(22) + 87.1(18)}{23 + 19 - 2}$$

$$= 89.85$$

Given $\alpha = 0.02$ and d.f. $= 23 + 19 - 2 = 40$, Table F in Appendix III reveals a t-value of 2.423.

$$\text{C.I. for } \mu_1 - \mu_2 = (17.53 - 15.5) \pm 2.423\sqrt{\frac{89.85}{23} + \frac{89.85}{19}}$$

$$= 2.03 \pm 7.12$$

$$-5.09 \leq \mu_1 - \mu_2 \leq 9.15$$

Interpretation: You can be 98 percent confident that the mean wage in Atlanta is between \$9.15 more than Newport News and \$5.09 less than Newport News. Since this interval contains \$0, the conclusion that no difference exists is possible. No adjustment is warranted.

---

2. Unequal Variances If the population variances are unequal or there is no evidence to assume an equality, the procedures described above do not apply directly, because the distribution of differences between sample means does not fit a t-distribution with $n_1 + n_2 - 2$ d.f. In fact, no exact distribution has been found to adequately describe this sampling process, and only approximations have been developed. One such approximation has been proposed using the t-statistic with d.f. slightly altered. In the event $\sigma_1^2 \neq \sigma_2^2$, the degrees of freedom can be found as

Degrees of freedom when population variances are not equal

$$\text{d.f.} = \frac{(s_1^2/n_1 + s_2^2/n_2)^2}{(s_1^2/n_1)^2/(n_1 - 1) + (s_2^2/n_2)^2/(n_2 - 1)} \qquad [9.7]$$

Since d.f. is calculated in this altered manner, the t-statistic is symbolized as t'. The confidence interval is then calculated as

Interval for difference in population means

$$\text{C.I. for } \mu_1 - \mu_2 = (\bar{X}_1 - \bar{X}_2) \pm t'\sqrt{\frac{s_1^2}{n_1} + \frac{s_2^2}{n_2}} \qquad [9.8]$$

The Wall Street Journal described two training programs used by IBM. Twelve executives who were given the first type of training scored a mean of 73.5 on an achievement test. Although the news article did not report the standard deviation for these 12 employees, let us assume that the variance in test scores for this group was 100.2. Fifteen executives to whom the second training program was administered scored an average of 79.8. Assume a variance of 121.3 for this second group. Develop a 95 percent confidence interval for the difference in the mean scores of all executives entered in these programs.

$$\begin{aligned}\text{d.f.} &= \frac{(100.2/12 + 121.3/15)^2}{(100.2/12)^2/11 + (121.3/15)^2/14} \\ &= 24.55\end{aligned}$$

If d.f. is fractional, round down to the next lowest whole integer. Thus, d.f. = 24. A 95 percent confidence interval with 24 degrees of freedom calls for a t'-value of 2.064.

$$\begin{aligned}\text{C.I. for } \mu_1 - \mu_2 &= (\bar{X}_1 - \bar{X}_2) \pm t'\sqrt{\frac{s_1^2}{n_1} + \frac{s_2^2}{n_2}} \\ &= (73.5 - 79.8) \pm 2.064\sqrt{\frac{100.2}{12} + \frac{121.3}{15}} \\ &= -6.3 \pm 8.36 \\ -14.66 \leq \mu_1 - \mu_2 &\leq 2.06\end{aligned}$$

Since the interval contains zero, there is no strong evidence that there exists any difference in the effectiveness of the training programs.

Example 9.3 Acme Ltd. sells two types of rubber baby buggy bumpers. Wear tests for durability revealed that 13 of type 1 lasted an average of 11.3 weeks with a standard deviation of 3.5 weeks, while 10 of type 2 lasted an average of 7.5 weeks with a standard deviation of 2.7 weeks. Type 1 costs more to manufacture, and the CEO of Acme doesn't want to use it unless it averages at least eight weeks longer than type 2. The CEO will tolerate a probability of error of only 2 percent. There is no evidence to suggest that variances in wear for the two products are equal.

Solution:

$$\bar{X}_1 = 11.3 \qquad \bar{X}_2 = 7.5$$
$$n_1 = 13 \qquad n_2 = 10$$
$$s_1 = 3.5 \qquad s_2 = 2.7$$

$$\text{d.f.} = \frac{(s_1^2/n_1 + s_2^2/n_2)^2}{(s_1^2/n_1)^2/(n_1 - 1) + (s_2^2/n_2)^2/(n_2 - 1)}$$

$$= \frac{[(3.5)^2/13 + (2.7)^2/10]^2}{\dfrac{[(3.5)^2/13]^2}{12} + \dfrac{[(2.7)^2/10]^2}{9}}$$

$$= 20.99 \approx 20$$

A 98 percent confidence interval ($\alpha = 0.02$) with 20 d.f. requires a t'-value of 2.528.

$$\text{C.I. for } \mu_1 - \mu_2 = (11.3 - 7.5) \pm 2.528\sqrt{\frac{(3.5)^2}{13} + \frac{(2.7)^2}{10}}$$
$$= 3.8 \pm 3.3$$
$$0.5 \leq \mu_1 - \mu_2 \leq 7.1 \text{ weeks}$$

Interpretation: Acme can be 98 percent confident that type 1 lasts between 0.5 and 7.1 weeks longer than type 2. Since the required eight-week difference is not in the interval, the CEO can be 98 percent confident he does not want to use type 1.

Section Exercises

6. What conditions must be present before the t-distribution can be used?
7. Seventeen cans of Croc Aid report a mean of 17.2 ounces with a standard deviation of 3.2 ounces, and 13 cans of Energy Pro produce a mean of 18.1 ounces and $s = 2.7$ ounces. Assuming equal variances and normal distributions in population weights, what conclusion can you draw regarding the difference in mean weights based on a 98 percent confidence interval?
8. Grow-rite sells commercial fertilizer produced at two plants in Atlanta and Dallas. Recent customer complaints suggest that the Atlanta shipments are underweight, compared to the Dallas shipments. If 10 boxes from the Atlanta plant average 96.3 pounds with $s = 12.5$ and 15 boxes from the Dallas plant average 101.1 with $s = 10.3$, does a 99 percent interval support this complaint? Assume equal variances.
9. Opus, Inc. has developed a process to make gold from seawater. Fifteen gallons taken from the Pacific Ocean produced a mean of 12.7 ounces of gold per gallon with $s = 4.2$ ounces,

and 12 gallons of water from the Atlantic Ocean yielded similar figures of 15.9 and 1.7. Based on a 95 percent interval, what is your estimate of the difference in the mean ounces of gold from these two sources? There is no reason to assume the variances are equal.

10. Ralphie is off to college next fall. He samples apartments in both the north and the south ends of town to see if there is any difference in mean rents. Those in the north report rents of $600, $650, $530, $800, $750, $700, and $750, and those in the south report $500, $450, $800, $650, $500, $500, $450, and $400. If there is no evidence that variances are equal, what does a 99 percent interval tell Ralphie about the difference in mean rents?

11. Bigelow Products wishes to develop a 95 percent interval for the difference in mean weekly sales in two target markets. A sample of 9 weeks in market 1 produced a mean and standard deviation, in hundreds of dollars, of 5.72 and 1.008 respectively. Comparable figures for market 2, based on a sample of 10 weeks, were 8.72 and 1.208. If the assumption of equal variances is made, what results do you report?

12. U.S. Manufacturing purchases raw materials from two suppliers. Management is concerned about production delays due to failure to receive shipments on time. A sample of 10 shipments from supplier A has a mean delivery time of 6.8 days with $s = 2.57$ days, while 12 shipments from supplier B have a mean of 4.08 days and $s = 1.93$. If the variances cannot be assumed equal, what recommendation would you make based on a 90 percent interval estimate of the difference in mean delivery times?

9.3 Interval Estimates with Paired Sampling

Also called matched pairs, **paired sampling** involves a procedure in which several pairs of observations are matched up as closely as possible in terms of relevant characteristics. The two sets of observations are different in only one respect or "treatment." Any subsequent differences in the two groups are attributed to that treatment. The advantages of paired sampling are that (1) smaller samples can be used, (2) smaller variances are encountered, (3) fewer degrees of freedom are lost in the analysis, and (4) a smaller sampling error results (the variation between observations is reduced since they are matched up as closely as possible). For these reasons, paired sampling is often preferred if its application is possible.

Paired Samples Matched pairs are two observations that are as similar as possible to each other. They differ in only one relevant aspect.

Assume a medical researcher wishes to test the effects of new drugs on patients' blood pressure levels. Twenty people in one group are paired off as closely as possible with 20 people in a second group in terms of weight, age, sex, level of activity, cholesterol, and any other factor that might affect blood pressure. We then have 20 pairs of "identical twins." One group is given one new drug, and the other group receives the other drug. No one except the researcher knows which group gets which medication. Any subsequent differences, good or bad, in the twins' blood pressures is attributed to the drugs, since we have "corrected" for all other relevant factors affecting blood pressure (such as age and sex); that is, we have matched up pairs of observations (twins) that are identical in terms of these other relevant factors.

Another method of using paired samples involves the examination of the same observations before and after treatment. A common practice in industry is to test employees before and after a training program. We then have a "before" test score and an "after" test score for each observation (employee). Any change in the score can be attributed to the training. (The researcher should be cautioned that some bias may affect the sampling because the employees may resent being tested or may remember their answers from the first test and try to be consistent in their responses.)

Paired sampling has certain advantages in that smaller samples will often lead to more accurate results; by controlling for the other relevant factors the researcher does not have to rely on the use of large samples to reduce sampling error.

To illustrate, assume that we have test scores for 10 employees before and after they are given additional on-the-job training. The scores are shown in Table 9.1.

Table 9.1
Before and After Test Scores

Employee	Score before OJT	Score after OJT	d_i	d_i^2
1	9.0	9.2	−0.2	0.04
2	7.3	8.2	−0.9	0.81
3	6.7	8.5	−1.8	3.24
4	5.3	4.9	0.4	0.16
5	8.7	8.9	−0.2	0.04
6	6.3	5.8	0.5	0.25
7	7.9	8.2	−0.3	0.09
8	7.3	7.8	−0.5	0.25
9	8.0	9.5	−1.5	2.25
10	7.5	8.0	−0.5	0.25
	74.0	79.0	−5.0	7.38

Let d_i be the difference between any matched pair. The mean of the differences between all pairs is then

Mean difference in paired observations

$$\bar{d} = \frac{\Sigma d_i}{n} \qquad [9.9]$$

$$= \frac{-5.0}{10} = -0.5$$

The standard deviation of these differences is

Standard deviation of the differences in paired observations

$$s_d = \sqrt{\frac{\Sigma d_i^2 - n\bar{d}^2}{n-1}} \qquad [9.10]$$

$$= \sqrt{\frac{7.38 - 10(-0.5)^2}{9}}$$

$$= 0.736$$

Since $n < 30$ and the standard deviation of the differences in scores, σ_d, is unknown, use of the t-statistic is required. If n had been greater than 30 or σ_d was known, the Z-statistic could have been used. Furthermore, it must be assumed that the d-values are normally distributed. The distribution of the raw scores themselves is immaterial, but the d-values must be normal.

Then, for a 90 percent confidence level and $n - 1 = 9$ degrees of freedom, a confidence interval for the mean of the difference in scores before and after training is

Interval for difference in means of paired observations	$\text{C.I. for } \mu_d = \bar{d} \pm t\frac{s_d}{\sqrt{n}}$	[9.11]

$$= -0.5 \pm (1.833)\frac{0.736}{\sqrt{10}}$$

$$-0.927 \leq \mu_d \leq -0.073$$

Since we subtracted the after test scores from the before test scores yielding negative values, we can be 90 percent confident that the mean of the after test scores is between 0.073 points and 0.927 points higher.

Example 9.4 Vicki Peplow, regional director of Medicare payments for Aetna Insurance in Peoria, Illinois, became aware that two different hospitals seemed to charge vastly different amounts for the same medical procedure. She collected observations of billing costs for 15 identical procedures from each hospital, and constructed a 95 percent confidence interval for the difference between the mean costs submitted by each hospital. Paired sampling was used because Vicki corrected for all relevant factors other than cost.

If a difference does exist, Ms. Peplow plans to report this matter to Medicare authorities. Should she make such a report?

Hospital 1	Hospital 2	d_i	d_i^2
465	512	−47	2,209
532	654	−122	14,884
426	453	−27	729
543	521	22	484
587	632	45	2,025
537	418	−119	14,161
598	587	−11	121
698	376	−322	103,684
378	529	−151	22,801
376	517	−141	19,881
524	476	48	2,304
387	519	−132	17,424
429	587	−158	24,964
398	639	−241	58,081
412	754	−342	116,964
		$-1{,}698 = \Sigma d_i$	$400{,}716 = \Sigma d_i^2$

Solution: Given the data above, we have

$$\bar{d} = \frac{\Sigma d_i}{n} = \frac{-1{,}698}{15} = -113.2$$

$$s_d = \sqrt{\frac{\Sigma d_i^2 - n\bar{d}^2}{n - 1}} = \sqrt{\frac{400{,}716 - (15)(113.2)^2}{15 - 1}}$$

$$= 122.037$$

$$\text{C.I. for } \mu_1 - \mu_2 = \bar{d} \pm (t)s_d/\sqrt{n}$$
$$= -113.2 \pm (2.145)122.037/\sqrt{15}$$
$$= -113.2 \pm 67.5886$$
$$-180.79 \le \mu_1 - \mu_2 \le -45.61$$

Interpretation: Since negative values resulted when the charges of the second hospital were subtracted from those of the first hospital, Vicki can be 95 percent certain that the second hospital is charging somewhere between \$45.61 and \$180.79 more than the first hospital for the same services. A report to the proper Medicare administrators seems in order.

Figure 9.2 will aid in deciding which formula and which approach should be used in constructing these intervals.

Figure 9.2
Calculating Intervals for the Difference in Two Population Means

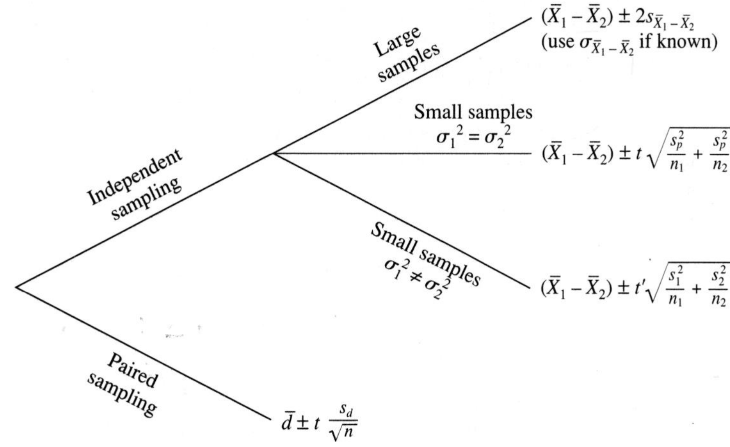

Section Exercises

13. Rankin Associates will accept bids from two construction companies on a remodeling job in its home office. The decision about which offer to accept depends in part on the mean completion times of similar jobs by each company. Data are collected and paired for several remodeling jobs. Based on a 99 percent level of confidence, which company would you recommend?

Company 1	Company 2	Company 1	Company 2
10.0	9.2	12.5	7.2
12.2	10.0	7.3	8.4
15.3	9.2	9.4	10.5
9.6	10.5	8.7	6.2
8.6	9.5	9.1	8.1
9.4	8.4		

14. On his recent trip to Las Vegas, Lucky Louie played 15 games of blackjack at the Golden Nugget and 15 games at the Flamingo. To compare his mean winnings, Louie subtracted his "take" at the Flamingo from that at the Nugget and found $\Sigma d_i = 40$ *and* $\Sigma d_i^2 = 415$. Using a 95 percent confidence interval, where should Louie play most often if he wants to maximize his mean winnings?

15. The annual marathon run is coming up this weekend. You have recorded your time over the course for the past five races using two types of running shoes. Determined to win the race

this year, you want to estimate the difference in your mean times using these two types of footgear. Subtracting the times you recorded using SpeedBurst Shoes from the times running in RocketMaster yielded, in minutes, $\Sigma d_i = 8$ *and* $\Sigma d_i^2 = 24$. At the 90 percent level of confidence, which shoe, if either, is preferred?

16. As an investment analyst, you must compare the mean returns of two types of bonds your client is interested in purchasing. The data below are for 12 bonds of each type. What recommendation would you offer based on a 99 percent interval estimate of the difference between the mean returns of each type of bond? Assume the observations are paired.

Bond 1	Bond 2	Bond 1	Bond 2
3.21%	6.39%	6.58%	4.58%
6.50	8.69	4.58	4.00
8.25	7.89	7.80	7.80
9.32	9.58	4.60	9.88
5.26	6.57	5.89	6.58
4.58	7.48	6.66	7.89

17. The monthly starting salaries in thousands of dollars of 12 business graduates from Tech U are compared to those from State U using the data shown below. Develop and interpret a 95 percent interval for the difference in mean starting salaries obtained by subtracting State salaries from Tech salaries.

Tech	State	Tech	State
3.7	5.6	2.5	8.8
3.6	6.8	3.5	9.5
5.2	8.5	3.9	7.5
1.2	6.5	8.2	6.5
1.6	5.5	4.5	4.5
5.2	4.8	1.2	8.7

18. Using the data from the previous problem, calculate and interpret the 95 percent interval for the difference in mean salaries obtained by subtracting Tech from State. What differences do you find?

9.4 Confidence Intervals for the Difference between Two Proportions

Occasions often arise in which we must compare the proportions of two different populations. Firms continually examine the proportion of defective products produced by different methods. Medical researchers are concerned about the proportion of men who suffer heart attacks as opposed to the percentage of women. In general, many business matters are determined by the estimation of the relative proportions of two populations.

The procedure should be familiar to you by now. The standard error of the difference between two sample proportions $(p_1 - p_2)$ is estimated by

Standard error of the difference in two sample proportions

$$s_{p_1-p_2} = \sqrt{\frac{p_1(1-p_1)}{n_1} + \frac{p_2(1-p_2)}{n_2}} \qquad [9.12]$$

The term $s_{p_1-p_2}$ recognizes that if several pairs of samples were taken from each population, $(p_1 - p_2)$ would vary. Formula (9.12) accounts for that variation. The confidence interval is

Interval for the difference in population proportions	$\text{C.I. for } \pi_1 - \pi_2 = (p_1 - p_2) \pm (Z)s_{p_1-p_2}$	[9.13]

A firm conducts a study to determine whether absenteeism of day workers is different from those who work the night shift. A comparison is made of 150 workers from each shift. The results show that 37 day workers have been absent at least five times over the past year, while 52 night workers have missed at least five times. What does this reveal about the tendency for absenteeism among the workers? Calculate a 90 percent confidence interval of the difference in the proportion of workers on the two shifts who missed five times or more.

$$p_1 = \frac{37}{150} = 0.25, \qquad p_2 = \frac{52}{150} = 0.35$$

$$s_{p_1-p_2} = \sqrt{\frac{(0.25)(0.75)}{150} + \frac{(0.35)(0.65)}{150}}$$

$$= 0.0526$$

$$\text{C.I. for } \pi_1 - \pi_2 = (p_1 - p_2) \pm (Z)s_{p_1-p_2}$$

$$= (0.25 - 0.35) \pm (1.65)(0.0526)$$

$$= -0.10 \pm 0.087$$

$$-18.7\% \leq (\pi_1 - \pi_2) \leq -1.3\%$$

Since the proportion of night workers who were absent five times or more (p_2) was subtracted from the proportion of day workers who were absent, the firm can be 90 percent certain that the proportion of night workers absent five or more times is between 1.3 percent and 18.7 percent higher than that for day workers.

Example 9.5 provides another look at an interval estimation of the difference between proportions.

Example 9.5 Your firm uses two different machines to cut Spandex costumes worn by performers in Ice Capades extravaganzas. Problems have developed in proper fittings, due to the performance of the machines. As the director of quality control, your job is to estimate the difference in the proportion of defects produced by each machine. Samples of sizes $n_1 = 120$ and $n_2 = 95$ were taken: The first machine produced 38 percent defects and the second, 43 percent defects. Set alpha at 5 percent. If the evidence suggests that the difference in the proportion of defects exceeds 5 percent, all costumes will be produced on the machine that seems to have a lower defect rate. What decision will you make?

Solution:

$$s_{p_1-p_2} = \sqrt{\frac{(0.38)(0.62)}{120} + \frac{(0.43)(0.57)}{95}}$$

$$= 0.0677$$

$$\begin{aligned}\text{C.I. for } \pi_1 - \pi_2 &= (0.38 - 0.43) \pm (1.96)(0.0677)\\ &= -0.05 \pm 0.1327\\ &= -0.1827 \leq (\pi_1 - \pi_2) \leq 0.0827\end{aligned}$$

Interpretation: You can be 95 percent certain that the proportion of defects produced by the first machine is somewhere between 18.27 percent lower and 8.27 percent higher than the second machine. Since the interval contains zero, there is no evidence that there is any difference in the proportion of defects produced by the machines. Your decision is that it makes no difference which machine you use, and you might as well continue to use both.

Section Exercises

19. Of 150 men and 130 women, 27 percent and 35 percent respectively stated that they used credit cards to purchase Christmas gifts. Calculate and interpret the 99 percent confidence interval for the difference in the proportion of men and women who relied on credit.

20. Records show that, of 1000 out-of-state students, 40 percent went home for spring break, while 47 percent of the 900 in-state students did so. What is the 95 percent confidence interval for the difference in the proportion of students who went home?

21. Of 50 graduate students, 10 went to a warm climate for spring break, while 24 out of 75 undergraduates did so. Construct the 95 percent interval.

9.5 Selecting the Proper Sample Size

It is often necessary to determine the proper sample size needed to conduct a study. As with single populations, the required sample size depends on (1) the variances of the populations, and (2) the desired degree of accuracy. This section examines how to determine the appropriate sample size for studies involving both means and proportions.

A. Sample Size for $\mu_1 - \mu_2$

The proper sample size is found by Formula (9.14).

Sample size for difference in population means	$n = \dfrac{Z^2(\sigma_1^2 + \sigma_2^2)}{(\text{error})^2}$	[9.14]

An economist at the University of Texas at Arlington has been asked by the Texas Economic Planning Commission to develop a 99 percent confidence interval for the difference between the mean length of service by public employees and that of workers in the private sector. The commission desires an interval width of three years. Pilot samples yield variances of 15 and 21, respectively. How large should the samples taken from each population be?

Since the interval is to be 3 years, the error is one-half of that, or 1.5 years. Then

$$\begin{aligned}n &= \frac{(2.58)^2(15 + 21)}{(1.5)^2}\\ &= 106.5, \text{ or } 107\end{aligned}$$

Thus, 107 employees should be selected from the public sector and 107 should be selected from the private sector in order to make the comparison.

B. Sample Size for $\pi_1 - \pi_2$

The correct sample size to estimate the difference between two population proportions is found by Formula (9.15).

Sample size for difference in population proportions	$n = \dfrac{Z^2[\pi_1(1-\pi_1)+\pi_2(1-\pi_2)]}{(\text{error})^2}$	[9.15]

Wally Simpleton, the leading candidate in the governor's race, wants to develop a confidence interval with a width of 3 percentage points and a 99 percent level of confidence for the difference between the proportion of men and the proportion of women who favor his candidacy. How large should the samples be? A pilot sample for men and women revealed $p_m = 0.40$ and $p_w = 0.30$. If the interval width is 0.03, the error is $0.03/2 = 0.015$.

$$n = \frac{(2.58)^2[(0.4)(0.6)+(0.3)(0.7)]}{(0.015)^2}$$

$$= 13{,}312 \text{ men and } 13{,}312 \text{ women}$$

9.6 Tests of Hypotheses about Two Means with Independent Sampling

Tests of hypotheses for differences in means follow a procedure much like that for intervals, in that sampling is either (1) independent or (2) paired. In this instance, however, unlike the instance of interval estimation, we are not interested in the size of the difference in means, but only in whether a difference does or does not exist. A two-tailed test, for example, would be expressed as

$$H_o\text{: } \mu_1 = \mu_2$$
$$H_A\text{: } \mu_1 \neq \mu_2$$

or the equivalent

$$H_o\text{: } \mu_1 - \mu_2 = 0$$
$$H_A\text{: } \mu_1 - \mu_2 \neq 0$$

This section examines tests with independent sampling for both large and small samples.

A. Large Sample Tests

The hypothesis test for the difference in two population means is much like that for a single population. The same four steps are involved:

1. The hypotheses are stated.
2. A Z-test or a t-test statistic is calculated.
3. A decision rule is formed.
4. The findings and conclusion are offered.

The Z-test value is

Z-test statistic for large samples	$Z_{\text{test}} = \dfrac{(\bar{X}_1 - \bar{X}_2) - (\mu_1 - \mu_2)}{s_{\bar{x}_1 - \bar{x}_2}}$	[9.16]

where $s_{\bar{x}_1-\bar{x}_2}$ is the estimate for the standard error of the differences in sample means, just as it was for interval estimation. Of course, if the population variances are known, $\sigma_{\bar{x}_1-\bar{x}_2}$ should be used.

Weaver Ridge Golf Course wants to see whether the mean time men require to play 18 holes is different from that required by women. Fifty foursomes of men and 45 of women are timed, yielding

Men	Women
$\bar{X} = 3.5$ hours	$\bar{X} = 4.9$ hours
$s = 0.9$ hours	$s = 1.5$ hours

Recall from our discussion of interval estimates that

$$s_{\bar{x}_1-\bar{x}_2} = \sqrt{\frac{(0.9)^2}{50} + \frac{(1.5)^2}{45}} = 0.257$$

Then,

$$Z_{\text{test}} = \frac{(3.5 - 4.9) - 0}{0.257} = -5.45$$

If $\alpha = 0.05$, the critical Z-value is ± 1.96 and the decision rule is:

Decision Rule Do not reject if Z_{test} is between ± 1.96. Reject if Z_{test} is less than -1.96 or more than $+1.96$.

As Figure 9.3 shows, the null is rejected. Since the null of equality is rejected and $\bar{X}_w > \bar{X}_m$, the evidence suggests that women take longer on the average. Notice also that the p-value associated with the test is virtually zero.

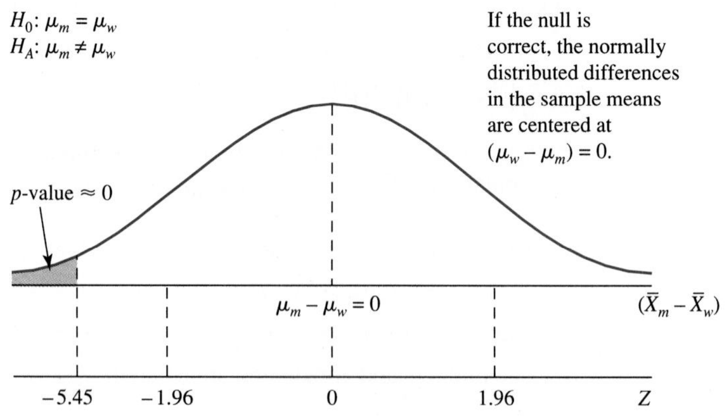

Figure 9.3 Hypothesis Test for the Equality of Golfing Times

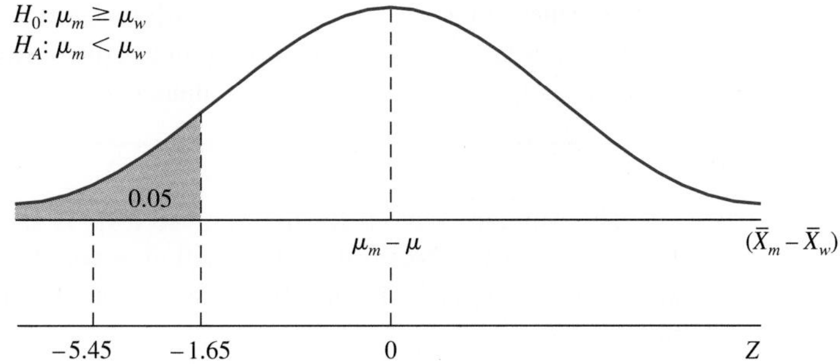

Figure 9.4
A One-Tailed Test for Mean Golf Times

If the golf course had hypothesized that men take less time, ($\mu_m < \mu_w$), the hypotheses would be stated as

$$H_o\colon \mu_m \geq \mu_w$$
$$H_A\colon \mu_m < \mu_w$$

and a left-tailed test as seen in Figure 9.4 would be conducted. If $\alpha = 0.05$ is retained, the left-tailed test calls for a critical Z-value of -1.65. The Z_{test} value of -5.45 does not change and again falls in the rejection region.

Example 9.6 In Example 9.1 above, managers at Charles Schwab constructed a 99 percent interval estimate of the difference between the mean proficiency levels of two groups of employees. The result was $-8.34 \leq (\mu_1 - \mu_2) \leq 4.40$. Suppose instead they wanted to test the hypothesis that the mean proficiencies were equal.

Solution: The hypotheses are

$$H_o\colon \mu_1 = \mu_2$$
$$H_A\colon \mu_1 \neq \mu_2$$

Given the data from Example 9.1,

$$Z_{\text{test}} = \frac{(76 - 77.97) - 0}{2.47} = 0.79$$

If $\alpha = 0.01$, the decision rule is

Decision Rule Do not reject if Z_{test} is between ± 2.58. Reject otherwise.

As the figure shows, since $Z_{\text{test}} = 0.79$, the null is not rejected. Further, the p-value is found to be $0.5000 - 0.2852 = 0.2148 \times 2 = 0.43$.

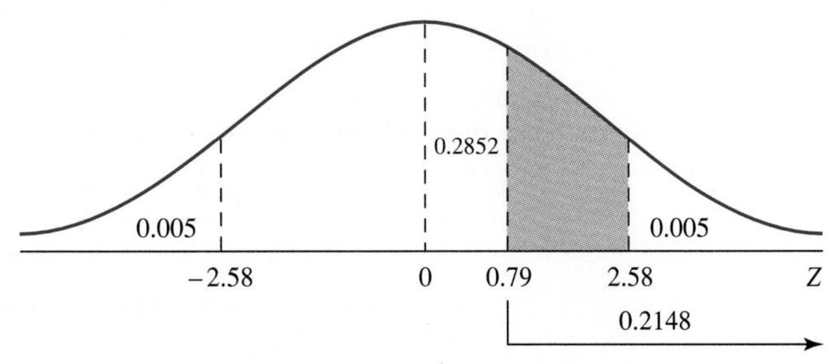

Interpretation: The evidence suggests that there is no difference in the mean proficiency of the groups of employees trained under the two programs. This position is supported by the fact that the interval calculated in Example 9.1 contained zero, indicating no difference.

The Minitab printout for the Schwab tests is seen in Display 9.1. Click on **Stat > Basic Statistics > 2-sample t.** This will give you the results of both the interval estimate and the hypothesis test. Notice the 99 percent confidence interval as well as the *t*-value and the *p*-value.

Display 9.1

Two Sample T-Test and Confidence Interval

```
Twosample T for Prog 1 vs Prog 2
          N       Mean      StDev    SE Mean
Prog 1   45       76.0       13.5        2.0
Prog 2   40      77.97       9.05        1.4

99% C.I. for mu Prog 1 - mu Prog 2:  ( -8.4,    4.6)
T-Test mu Prog 1 = mu Prog 2 (vs not  =): T= -0.78 P=0.44 DF= 77
```

B. Small Sample Tests: The t-Distribution

As was the case with confidence intervals, tests involving small samples depend on whether the population variances can be assumed equal, thereby permitting pooled data. If the assumption of equal variances is permitted, the *t*-test becomes

Small sample hypothesis test with pooled data

$$t_{\text{test}} = \frac{(\bar{X}_1 - \bar{X}_2) - (\mu_1 - \mu_2)}{\sqrt{\dfrac{s_p^2}{n_1} + \dfrac{s_p^2}{n_2}}} \qquad [9.17]$$

Return to Example 9.2. A 98 percent interval estimate of the difference in mean wages of workers in Atlanta and Newport News was calculated based on

Atlanta	Newport News
$n = 23$	$n = 19$
$\bar{X} = \$17.53$	$\bar{X} = \$15.50$
$s^2 = 92.10$	$s^2 = 87.10$

The interval was $-5.09 \leq (\mu_1 - \mu_2) \leq 9.15$. If, instead of an interval estimate, we had wanted to conduct a hypothesis test for equal means, we would have

$$H_o\text{: } \mu_A = \mu_N$$
$$H_A\text{: } \mu_A \neq \mu_N$$

Applying these data to Formula (9.17), we have

$$t_{\text{test}} = \frac{(17.53 - 15.5) - 0}{\sqrt{\dfrac{89.85}{23} + \dfrac{89.85}{19}}} = 0.69$$

Given that alpha is 2 percent and there are 23 + 19 − 2 = 40 degrees of freedom, the critical t-value is ±2.423. The null is therefore not rejected. It would appear that there is no difference in the mean wage. This conclusion is supported by the fact that the interval contained zero.

If the assumption of equal variance is not made, we find

Small sample test with unequal variances	$$t_{\text{test}} = \frac{(\overline{X}_1 - \overline{X}_2) - (\mu_1 - \mu_2)}{\sqrt{\frac{s_1^2}{n_1} + \frac{s_2^2}{n_2}}}$$	[9.18]

The t_{test} is compared to a critical t-value based on degrees of freedom determined by Formula (9.7). In Example 9.3, a 98 percent interval for the difference in the mean durability of two types of rubber baby buggy bumpers was estimated to be

$$0.5 \text{ weeks} \le (\mu_1 - \mu_2) \le 7.1 \text{ weeks}$$

These results were based on the data

$$\overline{X}_1 = 11.3 \text{ weeks} \qquad \overline{X} = 7.5 \text{ weeks}$$
$$n_1 = 13 \qquad n_2 = 10$$
$$s_1 = 3.5 \text{ weeks} \qquad s_2 = 2.7 \text{ weeks}$$

A hypothesis test for equal means would appear as

$$H_o\text{: } \mu_1 = \mu_2$$
$$H_A\text{: } \mu_1 \ne \mu_2$$

The t_{test} is

$$t_{\text{test}} = \frac{(11.3 - 7.5) - 0}{\sqrt{\frac{(3.5)^2}{13} + \frac{(2.7)^2}{10}}} = 2.94$$

If $\alpha = 0.02$ and the degrees of freedom are 20 based on Formula (9.7), the decision rule is

Decision Rule Do not reject if t_{test} is between ±2.528. Reject otherwise.

Since 2.94 > 2.528, the null of equality is rejected. Given $\overline{X}_1 > \overline{X}_2$, the evidence suggests that Type 1 rubber baby buggy bumpers exhibit greater durability. Again, this assertion is supported by the fact that the interval in Example 9.3 did not contain zero.

9.7 Hypotheses Tests with Paired Data

Pairing samples to conduct a hypothesis test offers the same advantages as it does in the construction of confidence intervals. Less sampling error is suffered due to the reduction in variation between observations since they are matched up as closely as possible.

The t_{test} is

Hypothesis test for matched pairs	$$t_{test} = \frac{\bar{d} - (\mu_1 - \mu_2)}{\frac{s_d}{\sqrt{n}}}$$	[9.19]

where $\bar{d}$ is the mean of the differences in the paired observations and s_d is the standard error of those differences and is found using Formula (9.10).

In Example 9.4, Vicki Peplow prepared a 95 percent interval estimate of the difference in costs for identical procedures at two hospitals. The result was

$$-\$180.79 \leq (\mu_1 - \mu_2) \leq -45.61$$

based on $n = 15$, $\Sigma d_i = -1{,}698$, and $\Sigma d_i^2 = 400{,}716$. If Ms. Peplow were to test a hypothesis of equality, she would find

$$H_o\text{: } \mu_1 = \mu_2$$
$$H_A\text{: } \mu_1 \neq \mu_2$$

and

$$t_{test} = \frac{-113.2 - 0}{\frac{122.037}{\sqrt{15}}} = -3.59$$

Given $t_{.05,14} = \pm 2.145$, the decision rule is:

Decision Rule Do not reject if t_{test} is between ± 2.145. Reject otherwise.

This results in a rejection of the null.

Section Exercises

22. Samples of sizes 50 and 60 reveal means of 512 and 587 and standard deviations of 125 and 145, respectively. At the 2 percent level, test the hypothesis that $\mu_1 = \mu_2$.
23. At the 1 percent level, test for the equality of means if samples of 10 and 8 yield means of 36 and 49 and standard deviations of 12 and 18, respectively. Assume that variances are not equal.
24. Answer the previous problem if it is assumed that variances are equal.
25. Matched pairs of sizes 81 yielded a mean of the differences of 36.5 and a standard deviation of the differences of 29.1. Test for the equality of means. Set $\alpha = 0.01$.
26. Test H_o: $\mu_1 \leq \mu_2$ if sample sizes of 64 and 81 produce means of 65.2 and 58.6 and standard deviations of 21.2 and 25.3. Set $\alpha = 5\%$.
27. Test H_o: $\mu_1 \geq \mu_2$ if samples of 100 produce means of 2.3 and 3.1 with standard deviations of 0.26 and 0.31. Set $\alpha = 1\%$.
28. Paired samples of sizes 25 reported a mean difference of 45.2 and a standard deviation of the differences of 21.6. Test for the equality of means at the 5% level.

9.8 A Test for the Difference between Two Proportions

Problems often arise in the business world requiring the comparison of two different population proportions: the proportion of defects produced by one method compared to that produced by a second, or the proportion of bad debts in one firm compared to that in another.

The test for proportions is performed as

Test for the difference of two proportions	$Z_{\text{test}} = \dfrac{(p_1 - p_2) - (\pi_1 - \pi_2)}{s_{p_1-p_2}}$	[9.20]

where p_1 and p_2 are the proportions of successes in the samples and $s_{p_1-p_2}$ is the standard error in those differences. It is calculated with Formula (9.12) we used in the construction of confidence intervals.

To illustrate, a retailer wants to test the hypothesis that the proportion of his male customers who buy on credit equals the proportion of women who use credit. He selects 100 male customers and finds that 57 bought on credit while 52 of the 110 women did so. The hypotheses are

$$H_o\text{: } \pi_m = \pi_w$$
$$H_A\text{: } \pi_m \neq \pi_w$$

At the 1 percent level the decision rule is:

Decision Rule Do not reject if $-2.58 \leq Z_{\text{test}} \leq 2.58$. Reject otherwise.

$$s_{p_1-p_2} = \sqrt{\frac{p_1(1-p_1)}{n_1} + \frac{p_2(1-p_2)}{n_2}}$$
$$= \sqrt{\frac{(0.57)(0.43)}{100} + \frac{(0.473)(0.527)}{110}}$$
$$= 1.05$$

Then,

$$Z_{\text{test}} = \frac{(0.57 - 0.473) - 0}{1.05}$$
$$= 0.092$$

Since Z_{test} is between ± 2.58, the null is not rejected. The retailer cannot conclude at the 1 percent level that the proportions of men and women who buy on credit differ.

Example 9.7 Johnson Manufacturing has recently suffered an increase in the number of defective units. The production supervisor feels that the night shift produces a higher proportion of defects than does the day shift: $\pi_N > \pi_D$. To compare the proportion of defects, a sample of 500 units taken from the daytime production reveals 14 defects. A sample of 700 units from the night shift has 22 defects. If a larger proportion of defects originates from nighttime production, the supervisor intends to institute a training program for those workers to improve their job skills. At the 5 percent level, should such a program be implemented?

Solution: Since it is thought that the night workers suffer a higher proportion of defects, the hypotheses are

$$H_o\colon \pi_N \leq \pi_D$$
$$H_A\colon \pi_N > \pi_D$$

and a right-tailed test is required. The decision rule is:

Decision Rule Do not reject if $Z_{\text{test}} \leq 1.65$. Reject if $Z_{\text{test}} > 1.65$.

The proportion of defects from the night shift is $p_N = 22/700 = 0.031$ and that of the day shift is $p_D = 14/500 = 0.028$; then

$$s_{p_1-p_2} = \sqrt{\frac{(0.031)(0.969)}{700} + \frac{(0.028)(0.972)}{500}}$$
$$= 0.0099$$

and

$$Z_{\text{test}} = \frac{(0.031 - 0.028) - 0}{0.0099}$$
$$= 0.303$$

Interpretation: Since Z_{test} is less than 1.65, the null that $\pi_N \leq \pi_D$ is not rejected. The evidence is not strong enough to conclude that the nighttime defect rate is greater than that of the daytime workers. The training program should not be instituted.

Section Exercises

29. Samples of sizes 120 and 150 produced proportions of 0.69 and 0.73. Test for the equality of population proportions at the 5 percent level.

30. Two samples of sizes 500 each are used to test the hypothesis that $H_o\colon \mu_1 \leq \mu_2$. The sample proportions are 14 percent and 11 percent. At the 10 percent level, what is your conclusion?

31. Samples of sizes 200 and 250 reveal sample proportions of 21 percent and 26 percent. Test the hypothesis that $H_o\colon \pi_1 \geq \pi_2$. Set alpha at 1 percent.

9.9 Comparing the Variance of Two Normal Populations

Several of the statistical tests discussed earlier required the assumption of equal population variances. At the time you were asked to blindly accept this equality, with the promise that at a later time you would be shown how to test for it. That time has come: This section demonstrates how to determine if the assumption of equal variances is reasonable. This test is based on the F-distribution, which was named after Sir Ronald A. Fisher (1890–1962) in 1924.

When comparing the variances of two populations, a sample is taken from each population. The sample variances serve as estimates of their respective population variances. An

F-distribution is then formed by the ratio of these two sample variances. The F-ratio is

F-ratio used to compare two population variances	$$F = \frac{s_L^2}{s_s^2}$$	[9.21]

where s_L^2 is the larger of the two sample variances and s_s^2 is the smaller of the two sample variances.

Assume that the variance of the second sample exceeds that of the first. In that case, the F-ratio is $F = s_2^2/s_1^2$. The more s_2^2 exceeds s_1^2, the less likely it is that $\sigma_1^2 = \sigma_2^2$ and the larger will be the F-ratio. Therefore, a large F-value will lead to a rejection of the null H_o: $\sigma_1^2 = \sigma_2^2$.

Manipulating the F-ratio to ensure that the higher sample variance is placed in the numerator will make sure that the F-value will always be greater than 1. Notice from Figure 9.5 that the F-distribution is not symmetrical and is bounded by zero on the lower end.

Figure 9.5
The F-Distribution

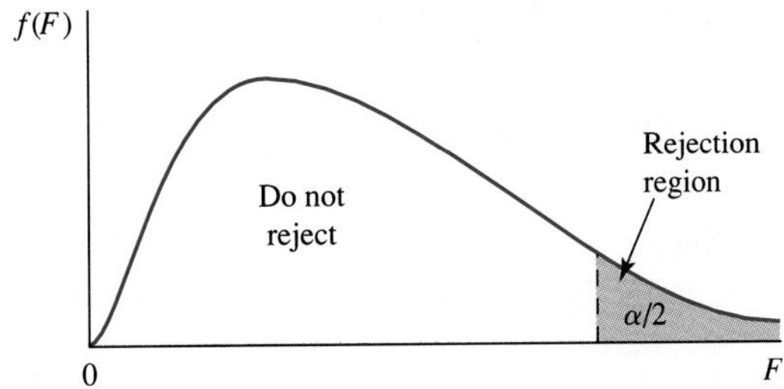

Since the F-ratio is restricted to always exceed 1, there results only one rejection region in the right tail. Any rejection region that might have otherwise appeared in the left tail is prohibited. Thus, only one-half as much of the area under the distribution is accessible as a rejection region. Therefore, it is necessary to divide the chosen alpha-value by 2 and identify a single rejection region in the right tail with an area equal to $\alpha/2$ as shown in Figure 9.5.

The α-value When controlling the F-ratio to ensure $F > 1$, we are conducting the two-tailed test of the hypothesis H_o: $\sigma_1^2 = \sigma_2^2$ as if it were a one-tailed test. It is therefore necessary to divide the α-value by 2.

Suppose an alpha-value of 10 percent is originally chosen. Dividing by 2, $\alpha/2 = 0.05$, requires that we consult that portion of Table G (Appendix III) that pertains to an α of 5 percent. Further, the F-distribution carries two degrees of freedom: one for the numerator, which is equal to $n_1 - 1$ and one for the denominator, which equals $n_2 - 1$, where n_1 and n_2 are the sample sizes in the numerator and the denominator respectively. Notational convenience allows us to express the critical F-value as $F_{\alpha/2,\, n_1-1,\, n_2-1}$.

A management consultant wishes to test a hypothesis regarding two population means. However, before doing so, he must decide whether there is evidence to suggest that the population variances are equal. In collecting his data, the consultant finds:

	Sample 1	Sample 2
Sample size	10	10
Standard deviation	12.2	15.4
Variance	148.84	237.16

He wishes to test

$$H_o\colon \sigma_1^2 = \sigma_2^2$$
$$H_A\colon \sigma_1^2 \neq \sigma_2^2$$

Using Formula (9.21), and ensuring the higher variance is in the numerator, he finds

$$F = \frac{s_1^2}{s_2^2} = \frac{(15.4)^2}{(12.2)^2} = 1.59$$

If alpha is set equal to 5 percent, $F_{.05/2,9,9} = 3.72$. This is found from Table G (Appendix III) by locating that portion of the table dealing with an alpha of $0.05/2 = 0.025$. Move across the top row for 9 degrees of freedom for the numerator and then down the column to 9 degrees of freedom for the denominator. There the value 3.72 is found. As shown by Figure 9.6, the decision rule is therefore:

Decision Rule Do not reject if $F \leq 3.72$. Reject if $F > 3.72$.

Since $F = 1.59 < 3.72$, the null $H_o\colon \sigma_1^2 = \sigma_2^2$ is not rejected. The consultant can proceed with the hypothesis test regarding population means under the assumption that the variances are equal.

Figure 9.6
The *F*-Distribution for Equality of Variances

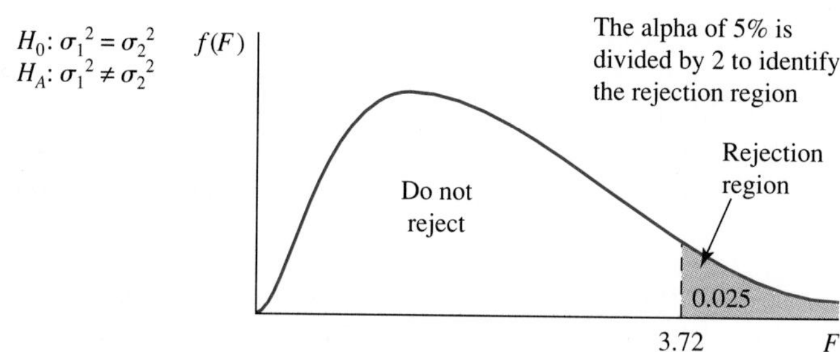

Solved Problems

1. **The Yuppies' Work Ethic** An April 1991 issue of *Fortune* carried a story about workaholic baby boomers, ages 25 to 43, who have corporate managerial jobs. The article compared the work life of these young executives who had placed themselves on the fast corporate track with workers who committed less time to their jobs. While those in the success-oriented mode often reported 70, 80, or even 90 hours on the job each week, about 60 was typical. The data were gathered from interviews of corporate employees. Letting group 1 be the fast-trackers and group 2 be those who spent less time on the job, assume the interviews revealed the following statistics regarding weekly work schedules:

Group 1	Group 2
$\bar{X}_1 = 62.5$ hours	$\bar{X}_2 = 39.7$ hours
$s_1 = 23.7$ hours	$s_2 = 8.9$ hours
$n_1 = 175$	$n_2 = 168$

Construct and interpret a 90 percent interval estimate of the difference in mean work hours and test the hypothesis of equal means at the 10 percent level.

Solution: Given

$$s_{\bar{x}_1-\bar{x}_2} = \sqrt{\frac{s_1^2}{n_1} + \frac{s_2^2}{n_2}} = \sqrt{\frac{(23.7)^2}{175} + \frac{(8.9)^2}{168}}$$
$$= 1.92$$

Then,

$$\text{C.I. for } (\mu_1 - \mu_2) = (\bar{X}_1 - \bar{X}_2) \pm Zs_{\bar{x}_1-\bar{x}_2}$$
$$= (62.5 - 39.7) \pm (1.65)(1.92)$$
$$19.63 \le (\mu_1 - \mu_2) \le 65.67$$

You can be 90 percent confident that the fast trackers work an average of 19.63 hours to 65.67 hours longer.

The hypothesis test is

$$H_o\text{: } \mu_1 = \mu_2$$
$$H_A\text{: } \mu_1 \ne \mu_2$$

$$Z_{\text{test}} = \frac{(62.5 - 39.7) - 0}{1.92} = 11.88$$

The decision rule is:

Decision Rule Do not reject if Z_{test} is between ± 1.65. Reject otherwise.

Since $Z_{\text{test}} = 11.88 > 1.65$, the null is rejected.

2. **Inflation and Market Power** Many economic studies focus on industries in which a good deal of market power is concentrated in the hands of just a few firms. It is feared that powerful firms in such highly concentrated industries will dominate the market to their own selfish advantage. Firms in nine concentrated industries were paired with firms in an equal number of industries in which economic power was more dispersed. Industries in each group were matched with respect to foreign competition, cost structures, and all other factors that can affect industry prices. The average price increases in percentages in each industry are shown here. Does it appear at the 5 percent level that concentrated industries exhibit more pronounced inflationary pressures than do less concentrated industries? Construct the appropriate interval and test the appropriate hypothesis.

Industry Pairings	Concentrated Industries (%)	Less Concentrated Industries (%)	d_i (%)	d_i^2
1	3.7	3.2	0.5	0.25
2	4.1	3.7	0.4	0.16
3	2.1	2.6	−0.5	0.25
4	−0.9	0.1	−1.0	1.00
5	4.6	4.1	0.5	0.25
6	5.2	4.8	0.4	0.16
7	6.7	5.2	1.5	2.25
8	3.8	3.9	−0.1	0.01
9	4.9	4.6	0.3	0.09
			2.0	4.42

Solution:

$$\bar{d} = \frac{\Sigma d_i}{n} = \frac{2}{9} = 0.22$$

$$s_d = \sqrt{\frac{\Sigma d_i^2 - n\bar{d}^2}{n-1}} = \sqrt{\frac{4.42 - 9(0.22)^2}{8}}$$

$$= 0.706$$

$$\text{C.I. for } (\mu_1 - \mu_2) = \bar{d} \pm t\frac{s_d}{\sqrt{n}}$$

$$= 0.22 \pm (1.860)\frac{0.706}{\sqrt{9}}$$

$$-0.218 \leq \mu_d \leq 0.658$$

We are 95 percent confident that the mean price increase in less concentrated industries is 0.658 percent lower to 0.218 percent higher.

The hypothesis test is:

$$H_o\colon \mu_1 = \mu_2$$

$$H_A\colon \mu_1 \neq \mu_2$$

$$t_{\text{test}} = \frac{\bar{d} - (\mu_1 - \mu_2)}{\frac{s_d}{\sqrt{n}}} = \frac{0.22 - 0}{\frac{0.706}{\sqrt{9}}}$$

$$= 0.935$$

The decision rule is:

Decision Rule Do not reject if t_{test} is between ± 1.860. Reject otherwise.

Since $0.935 < 1.860$, do not reject the null.

3. **Small-Sample *t*-Tests** A drilling company tests two drill bits by sinking wells to a maximum of 112 feet and recording the number of hours the procedure took. The first bit was used in 12 cases, resulting in a mean time of $\bar{X}_1 = 27.3$ hours and $s_1 = 8.7$ hours. Ten wells were dug with the second bit, producing an $\bar{X}_2 = 31.7$ hours and $s_2 = 8.3$ hours.

   Does it appear that one bit is more effective than the other? Set $\alpha = 0.10$. No evidence suggests variances are equal. Respond by constructing the appropriate interval and testing the appropriate hypothesis.

Solution:

$$\text{d.f.} = \frac{[s_1^2/n_1 + s_2^2/n_2]^2}{\frac{(s_1^2/n_1)^2}{(n_1 - 1)} + \frac{(s_2^2/n_2)^2}{(n_2 - 1)}}$$

$$= \frac{[(8.7)^2/12 + (8.3)^2/10]^2}{\frac{[(8.7)^2/12]^2}{11} + \frac{[(8.3)^2/10]^2}{9}} = \frac{174.15}{8.89}$$

$$= 19.59$$

$$\approx 19$$

With d.f. = 19, and $\alpha = 0.10$, $t' = 1.729$.

$$\text{C.I. for } (\mu_1 - \mu_2) = (\bar{X}_1 - \bar{X}_2) \pm t'\sqrt{\frac{s_1^2}{n_1} + \frac{s_2^2}{n_2}}$$

$$= (27.3 - 31.7) \pm (1.729)\sqrt{\frac{(8.7)^2}{12} + \frac{(8.3)^2}{10}}$$

$$-10.68 \leq (\mu_1 - \mu_2) \leq 1.88$$

We can be 90 percent confident that drill 1 takes between 1.88 hours more and 10.68 hours less.

The hypothesis test is:

$$H_o\text{: } \mu_1 = \mu_2$$

$$H_A\text{: } \mu_1 \neq \mu_2$$

$$t_{\text{test}} = \frac{(27.3 - 31.7) - 0}{\sqrt{\frac{(8.7)^2}{12} + \frac{(8.3)^2}{10}}}$$

$$= -1.211$$

The decision rule is:

Decision Rule Do not reject if t_{test} is between ± 1.729. Reject otherwise.

Since $t_{\text{test}} = -1.211 > -1.729$, do not reject the null.

All the wells were dug with the same drilling team and in the same soil. If for these reasons, or any others that might be cited, the drilling company felt drilling times had equal variances, how would the test differ from part? Equal variances allow the pooling of sample data.

$$s_p^2 = \frac{s_1^2(n_1 - 1) + s_2^2(n_2 - 1)}{n_1 + n_2 - 2}$$

$$= \frac{(8.7)^2(12 - 1) + (8.3)^2(10 - 1)}{12 + 10 - 2}$$

$$= 72.63 \text{ hours squared}$$

With degrees of freedom equal to $n_1 + n_2 - 2 = 12 - 10 - 2 = 20$, $t_{0.10,20} = 1.725$. Then

$$\text{C.I. for } (\mu_1 - \mu_2) = (\bar{X}_1 - \bar{X}_2) \pm t\sqrt{\frac{s_p^2}{n_1} + \frac{s_p^2}{n_2}}$$

$$= (27.3 - 31.7) \pm (1.725)\sqrt{\frac{72.63}{12} + \frac{72.63}{10}}$$

$$-10.69 \leq (\mu_1 - \mu_2) \leq 1.89$$

4. **The Credit Crunch** A study in *Retail Management* revealed that 131 of 468 women who made retail purchases did so using a particular credit card, while 57 of 237 men used the same card. Is there evidence to suggest a difference in the proportion of women and men who use that card? Let $\alpha = 0.05$. Construct the interval and test the hypothesis.

Solution:

$$s_{p_1-p_2} = \sqrt{\frac{p_1(1-p_1)}{n_1} + \frac{p_2(1-p_2)}{n_2}}$$

$$= \sqrt{\frac{(0.28)(0.72)}{468} + \frac{(0.24)(0.76)}{237}}$$

$$= 0.035$$

$$\text{C.I. for } (\pi_w - \pi_m) = (0.28 - 0.24) \pm (1.96)(0.035)$$

$$-0.029 \leq (\pi_w - \pi_m) \leq 0.109$$

There appears to be no difference in the proportion of men and women who use credit.

The hypothesis test is:

$$H_o\text{: } \pi_w = \pi_m$$

$$H_A\text{: } \pi_w \neq \pi_m$$

$$Z_{\text{test}} = \frac{(0.28 - 0.24) - 0}{0.035} = 1.14$$

The decision rule is:

Decision Rule Do not reject if Z_{test} is between ± 1.96. Reject otherwise.

Since $Z_{\text{test}} = 1.14$, do not reject the null.

List of Formulas

[9.1]	$(\bar{X}_1 - \bar{X}_2) \pm Z\sigma_{\bar{x}_1-\bar{x}_2}$	Confidence interval for the difference between two population means—large samples
[9.2]	$\sigma_{\bar{x}_1-\bar{x}_2} = \sqrt{\frac{\sigma_1^2}{n_1} + \frac{\sigma_2^2}{n_2}}$	Standard error of the differences between sample means
[9.3]	$s_{\bar{x}_1-\bar{x}_2} = \sqrt{\frac{s_1^2}{n_1} + \frac{s_2^2}{n_2}}$	Estimate of the standard error of the difference between sample means
[9.4]	$(\bar{X}_1 - \bar{X}_2) \pm Zs_{\bar{x}_1-\bar{x}_2}$	Confidence interval when population variances are unknown
[9.5]	$s_p^2 = \frac{s_1^2(n_1 - 1) + s_2^2(n_2 - 1)}{n_1 + n_2 - 2}$	Pooled estimate of the variance common to both populations
[9.6]	$(\bar{X}_1 - \bar{X}_2) \pm t\sqrt{\frac{s_p^2}{n_1} + \frac{s_p^2}{n_2}}$	Interval for the difference in means using pooled data
[9.7]	$\frac{(s_1^2/n_1 + s_2^2/n_2)^2}{(s_1^2/n_1)^2/(n_1 - 1) + (s_2^2/n_2)^2/(n_2 - 1)}$	Degrees of freedom when population variances are not equal
[9.8]	$(\bar{X}_1 - \bar{X}_2) \pm t'\sqrt{\frac{s_1^2}{n_1} + \frac{s_2^2}{n_2}}$	Interval for difference in population means
[9.9]	$\bar{d} = \frac{\Sigma d_i}{n}$	Mean difference in paired observations

[9.10]	$s_d = \sqrt{\dfrac{\Sigma d_i^2 - n\bar{d}^2}{n-1}}$	Standard deviation of the differences in paired observations
[9.11]	$\bar{d} \pm t\dfrac{s_d}{\sqrt{n}}$	Interval for difference in means of paired observations
[9.12]	$\sqrt{\dfrac{p_1(1-p_1)}{n_1} + \dfrac{p_2(1-p_2)}{n_2}}$	Standard error of the difference in two sample proportions
[9.13]	$(p_1 - p_2) \pm (Z)s_{p_1-p_2}$	Interval for the difference in population proportions
[9.14]	$\dfrac{Z^2(\sigma_1^2 + \sigma_2^2)}{(\text{error})^2}$	Sample size for difference in population means
[9.15]	$\dfrac{Z^2[\pi_1(1-\pi_1) + \pi_2(1-\pi_2)]}{(\text{error})^2}$	Sample size for difference in population proportions
[9.16]	$Z_{\text{test}} = \dfrac{(\bar{X}_1 - \bar{X}_2) - (\mu_1 - \mu_2)}{s_{\bar{x}_1-\bar{x}_2}}$	Hypothesis test for difference in means—large samples
[9.17]	$t_{\text{test}} = \dfrac{(\bar{X}_1 - \bar{X}_2) - (\mu_1 - \mu_2)}{\sqrt{\dfrac{s_p^2}{n_1} + \dfrac{s_p^2}{n_2}}}$	Small sample hypothesis test with pooled data
[9.18]	$t_{\text{test}} = \dfrac{(\bar{X}_1 - \bar{X}_2) - (\mu_1 - \mu_2)}{\sqrt{\dfrac{s_1^2}{n_1} + \dfrac{s_2^2}{n_2}}}$	Small sample test with unequal variances
[9.19]	$t_{\text{test}} = \dfrac{\bar{d} - (\mu_1 - \mu_2)}{\dfrac{s_d}{\sqrt{n}}}$	Hypothesis test for matched pairs
[9.20]	$Z_{\text{test}} = \dfrac{(p_1 - p_2) - (\pi_1 - \pi_2)}{s_{p_1-p_2}}$	Test for the difference of two proportions
[9.21]	$F = \dfrac{s_L^2}{s_s^2}$	The F-ratio used to compare two population variances

Chapter Exercises

32. An accountant for a large corporation in the Midwest must decide whether to select AT&T or Sprint to handle the firm's long-distance telephone service. Data collected for many calls using both services are reported here.

	AT&T	Sprint
Number of calls	145	102
Mean cost	\$4.07	\$3.89
Standard deviation	\$0.97	\$0.85

What does a 95 percent interval reveal about the difference in the population means?

33. The Metro Pet Center compares telephone costs using two different billing programs. Under the first program, Metro found that over 100 weeks the mean bill was \$32.40, with $s =$ \$15.10. A sample of 150 weeks using the second program yielded a mean of \$47.30, with

s = \$13.20. Calculate and interpret the 95 percent confidence interval for the difference between the means of the two programs.

34. In an article on business travel, *U.S. News & World Report* stated that the mean cost for one national hotel chain was \$45.12 per night, and a second chain was \$42.62 per night. Assume these statistics are based on samples of 82 and 97, respectively, and that population variances for each chain are known to be 9.48 and 8.29 dollars squared, respectively. You must determine which chain of hotels your company will use. At the 1 percent level, what does the confidence interval indicate your decision should be? Does it make a difference which you use?

35. Assume the sample sizes in the previous problem are $n_1 = 182$ and $n_2 = 197$.

a. Without working the problem, explain what would happen to the interval with these larger samples. Why does it happen?

b. Work the problem with these larger samples and see if you were right.

36. A recent issue of *Business Week* discussed efforts by a major car company to determine whether one type of vehicle was withstanding the wear and tear of daily use more than a second type. A finance major who has just graduated from a local university was hired to determine whether any difference exists in mean life. She collects data on the mean number of months a vehicle is in service before the first major repair is necessary, and finds the following information: vehicle 1: $\overline{X}_1 = 27.3$ months, $s_1 = 7.8$ months, and $n_1 = 82$ vehicles; vehicle 2: $\overline{X}_2 = 33.3$ months, $s_2 = 10.4$ months, and $n_2 = 73$ vehicles. At the 2 percent level, construct the confidence interval and interpret its results.

37. Professor James wants to estimate the difference in the mean time two organizations require to decide on grant requests submitted to them. If 14 grant requests to the National Science Foundation (NSF) took an average of 45.7 weeks with a standard deviation of 12.6 weeks, and 12 requests to Health and Human Services (HHS) exhibited respective values of 32.9 and 16.8 weeks, calculate and interpret the 90 percent confidence interval for the difference between the means. If NSF takes more than five weeks longer than HHS, James plans to submit her requests to the latter. Should she do so? Assume that the variances are equal.

38. To compare the means of daily sales revenues, a retailer selects a sample size of 12 weeks from one store, with mean revenues of \$125.40 and a standard deviation of \$34.50, and a sample of 15 weeks from another store, with a mean of \$117.20 and standard deviation of \$21.50. Calculate and interpret the 99 percent confidence interval for the difference between the population means. Set $\sigma_1^2 = \sigma_2^2$.

39. A management team was asked to solve 10 different quality control problems commonly encountered in their work. A second management team was asked to solve the same problems. Solution times in minutes required by each team are shown below. Calculate and interpret the 90 percent confidence interval for the difference between the population mean times required for the two teams. What can you conclude about the relative problem-solving ability of the two teams?

Problem	Team 1	Team 2
1	12	25
2	15	26
3	14	21
4	21	23
5	19	31
6	12	19
7	25	35
8	18	28
9	17	27
10	20	26

40. *The Wall Street Journal* reported that Ford Motor Company became interested in the mean salaries of its executives stationed overseas as opposed to those based stateside. The mean salary for 87 executives posted abroad was \$78,010, with a standard deviation of \$15,700. The same number of executives placed in domestic service revealed a mean and standard deviation of \$69,410 and \$10,012. Develop and interpret the 97 percent interval for mean differences.

41. Sammy Shopper wishes to compare the costs of 10 different services offered by new car dealers in his area. The data are displayed here. Calculate and interpret the 90 percent confidence interval for the difference between the population means. If quality of service is the same, which dealer should Sammy use—or does it make a difference?

Service	Dealer 1	Dealer 2
1	\$54	\$36
2	56	35
3	59	34
4	65	39
5	62	37
6	43	32
7	38	31
8	48	30
9	46	29
10	59	45

42. *The Wall Street Journal* reported that concern has been raised regarding the environment in which beef cattle are kept prior to slaughter. Supposedly, stress-free surroundings promote growth and quality of the meat. A beef grower in northern California even advertises that he "treats his cattle to a spectacular seaside view" before preparing them for the meat counter at the local grocery store. Assume 50 cattle raised in this vacationlike setting gain an average of 112 pounds with $s = 32.3$ pounds over a given time period. During the same time, 50 cows with a view of the slaughterhouse gain 105.7 pounds on the average with $s = 28.7$ pounds. Calculate and interpret the 90 percent interval.

43. Several Christmases ago a portion of Santa Claus's elves unionized. Since that time Santa has wondered whether there was any difference in mean productivity of unionized elves and nonunionized elves. A sample of 150 unionized elves reported a mean output of 27.3 toys per week per elf, with a standard deviation of 8.7 toys. A sample of 132 nonunionized elves revealed a mean of 29.7 toys per week per elf, with $s = 10.7$. What does a 90 percent interval tell Mr. Claus about the difference in mean output?

44. Twenty-six mutual funds, each with \$5,000 invested in them, are selected for comparison. Of the 26 funds, 12 are income oriented, and yielded a mean return of \$1,098,60 (including capital gains), with a standard deviation of \$43.20. The remaining funds are growth oriented, and generated a mean return of \$987.60 (including capital gains), with a standard deviation of \$53.40.

a. Calculate and interpret the 80 percent confidence interval for the difference between the population mean returns. There is no reason to believe that the variances are equal.

b. What sample size is necessary to be 95 percent certain that the error does not exceed \$10.00?

45. The Baldwin Piano Company has long argued that their method of teaching people to play the piano is superior to that of its competitors. To estimate any difference in the length of time required to learn the basic techniques, as the new staff analyst for Baldwin, you select 100 students who used your method and find the mean time was 149 hours with $s = 37.7$ hours.

The corresponding statistics for 130 students using the competitor's method prove to be 186 and 42.2.

a. At the 99 percent level of confidence, what can you conclude about the difference in the mean learning times? Does it appear that your company offers a better method?

b. What sample size is needed to be 99 percent certain that the error does not exceed 5 hours?

46. While serving as a summer intern for a major insurance company, a management major at the local university performed a study to measure the mean life expectancy of alcoholics as opposed to those who do not drink excessively. The company felt that insurance costs were affected by the shorter life span of heavy drinkers.

The mean age at death for 100 alcoholics was found to be 63.7 years with $s = 17.7$, while 100 moderate and nondrinkers lived an average of 75.2 years with $s = 8.7$. How would you interpret a 95 percent confidence interval for the difference in the mean life of the two groups?

47. A pricing experiment was conducted by a national chain of stereo equipment outlets. For one weekend, the price of their top compact disk players was raised by 4 percent in 35 stores and lowered by a like amount in 35 other randomly selected stores. Changes in sales revenue were noted in each case. In those stores raising their price, revenues on the CD players increased by an average of \$842, with $s = \$217$. The mean increase in revenues in those stores lowering prices was \$817, with $s = \$202$. The marketing manager for the firm has always felt that an increase in price would raise revenues more than would a decrease (a concept economists call elasticity of demand). What does a 99 percent interval tell the manager about the mean increases in revenue?

48. A controversial theory in finance holds that stocks traded on the organized exchanges always increase more on Fridays than on Mondays due to the timing of Treasury auctions. As his senior project, a finance major at a large university randomly selects 302 stocks trading on the New York Stock Exchange on Friday and finds the average price change to be 0.375 point, with a standard deviation of 0.075. The 412 stocks randomly selected on Monday's trading yielded a mean price change of -0.25 point, with a standard deviation of 0.05. How would you suggest the finance major interpret the results of a 99 percent interval?

49. You have just graduated from college and been hired as a quality control analyst for Electric Charlie's, a large producer of lighting equipment. Currently, Electric Charlie's uses two methods to produce their Bright-Spot home lighting system. To determine whether one method is better, you select 50 systems from each production method. Those from the first method continue providing light for a mean time of 45.5 hours, with $s = 12.4$ hours. Those produced using the second method burn for an average of 41.2 hours, with $s = 15.3$.

a. Calculate and interpret the 95 percent confidence interval for the difference between the population mean service times. Your supervisor wants you to make a recommendation. What will it be?

b. Are your samples large enough to be 90 percent certain that the error does not exceed two hours? How large should the sample be?

50. As a new analyst in the financial analysis division of a Florida-based firm making jet skis, you must determine whether the firm should concentrate its efforts on supplying customers on the West Coast or those in Florida. The decision will rest in part on which market is paying the higher price. The CEO feels that the average price on the West Coast is more than \$15 above what the firm can receive from Florida customers. Using these data, interpret for the CEO the results of a 95 percent interval.

	West Coast Orders	Florida Orders
Number of orders	37	41
Mean price	\$418.10	\$397.20
Standard deviation	73.00	62.10

51. Seven Asian nations reported a mean increase in per capita income over the last year of \$121.20, with a standard deviation of \$23.30. Nine European countries reported corresponding figures of \$111.10 and \$19.10. Calculate and interpret the 90 percent confidence interval for the difference between the population mean increases in income. Can you conclude that one continent seems to have generated larger increases than the other? It does not appear that the standard deviations are equal.

52. Six economists working for the government are asked to predict inflation rates for the upcoming year. Eight economists who work for private concerns are given the same task. The six government economists report rates of 4.2 percent, 5.1 percent, 3.9 percent, 4.7 percent, 4.9 percent, and 5.8 percent. The eight privately employed economists forecast rates of 5.7 percent, 6.1 percent, 5.2 percent, 4.9 percent, 4.6 percent, 4.5 percent, 5.2 percent, and 5.5 percent. What is your estimate of the difference in the mean predictions of the two groups of economists? Set alpha at 10 percent and assume equal variances.

53. Many economic impact studies have been done to determine the effect of labor unions on wage rates. To address this important issue, an economist examines 10 union shops where a mean wage rate of \$22.07 and $s = \$8.12$ are found. Twelve nonunion shops reveal a mean of \$24.17 and $s = \$9.07$. Use a 99 percent interval to estimate any difference in the mean wage levels. Should your shop unionize? Assume equal variances.

54. *The Wall Street Journal* reported that a food distributor in the Midwest examined the effects of two sales programs on per capita milk consumption. Ten cities were treated to extensive TV advertising, and the subsequent increase in mean daily consumption of 0.25 gallon and a standard deviation of 0.09 gallon was recorded. Twelve other cities were saturated with newspaper advertisements. There resulted an increase of 0.02 gallon in mean consumption, per capita, with $s = 0.02$ gallon. If variances are assumed to be equal, how would you interpret the results of a 90 percent interval?

55. As production director for Maxx Manufacturing, you must decide which of two plants should be given the responsibility of producing the wine corks used by Paul Masson Wineries. This decision is to be based on productivity levels. A sample of 67 days at the Northridge plant produced a mean of 92.2 thousand corks per day with $s = 12.2$ thousand. The Southridge plant produced an average 89.2 thousand with $s = 15.4$, over 54 days.

    a. Test the hypothesis of equality of means at the 10 percent level of significance.
    b. How large must the samples be to be 90 percent confident that the error does not exceed 5,000 corks?

56. Many corporate finance decisions are based on cash flows. An old machine your firm is currently using generated a mean positive net cash flow of \$15.6 thousand with a standard deviation of \$2.3 thousand over an 18-week period. A new machine used by your competitor recently provided respective values of \$12.1 and \$3.4 thousand over a 13-week period. Test the hypothesis of equality of means at the 2 percent level of significance. Based on this analysis, what would you recommend? Assume $\sigma_1^2 \neq \sigma_2^2$.

57. Many European countries use a value-added tax (VAT), which is a tax on the value added to a good at each stage of production. Eight countries using a consumption-type VAT reported a mean per capita weekly revenue of \$1,142, with $s = \$312$. Ten countries using a gross-income-type VAT reported a mean per capita weekly tax take of \$1,372, with $s = \$502$. If $\alpha = 0.05$ and $\sigma_1 \neq \sigma_2$, how would you interpret the results of a hypothesis for $\mu_1 = \mu_2$?

58. The impact of different pay methods on productivity and workers' levels of satisfaction has always been of interest to labor economists. *Fortune* reported that a sporting goods company experimented with the effects of two methods of payment on employee morale in an Ohio plant. Fourteen workers paid a fixed salary were given a test measuring morale and scored a mean of 79.7 with $s = 8.2$. Twelve workers paid on a commission achieved a mean of 72.7 with $s = 5.1$. Set $\alpha = 0.10$ and assume $\sigma_1 \neq \sigma_2$. What can be concluded regarding the relative merits of the two pay systems based on the resulting hypothesis test?

59. The chief financial officer (CFO) for a Fortune 500 firm must decide whether debt financing or equity financing would prove less costly. She examines recent market transactions for firms similar to hers and finds that 17 firms using bonds (debt financing) experienced a mean cost of 17.3 percent with $s = 3.7$ percent, and 10 recent stock issues (equity financing) resulted in figures of 22.7 percent and 4.7 percent, respectively. Help her test the appropriate hypothesis at the 5 percent level of significance, if $\sigma_1^2 \neq \sigma_2^2$. Does this study provide any evidence as to the lower-cost method of financing?

60. B. F. Skinner, a noted behavior theorist, espoused the use of positive reinforcement to shape work attitudes. Texaco, Inc., has long used Skinner's techniques. A sample of 45 employees who were treated to this positive treatment averaged a score of 5.5 out of 10 on an attitude test, with $s = 1.2$. Sixty employees working in an area not receiving positive reinforcement averaged 4.8 on the test, with $s = 1.9$.

a. Calculate and interpret the 98 percent confidence interval for the difference between the population means. Do the results seem to support Skinner's theories?

b. What are the proper sample sizes if you want to be 95 percent certain the error is less than 1 point?

61. A plumbing contractor wishes to estimate the difference in the proportion of construction jobs that require a second visit to the construction site before the job is completed. The contractor intends to submit his work to that plumbing firm with the lower level of repeated visits. Of 50 jobs completed by the Alpha Plumbing Corporation, 39 required a second visit, while the Omega Plumbing Group made a second visit on 67 percent of its 60 jobs. What can you conclude about the difference in the proportions of jobs requiring a second effort based on a 95 percent interval? Which company should the contractor use, or does it make a difference?

62. Two "identical" sets of 50 employees are put through two different training programs and subsequently given aptitude tests. The mean difference in the scores is 13.5, with a standard deviation in those differences of 4.3. What would a 95 percent interval conclude about the relative effectiveness of the training programs?

63. Snow White buys her seven dwarfs new shovels for Christmas. The amounts that each dwarf could dig in the mine with the old shovels and the new shovels are shown here. Test the proper hypothesis at the 10 percent level. Did Snow White's gift to her seven little buddies improve output?

	Daily Output in Tons	
Dwarf	**Old Shovels**	**New Shovels**
Doc	1.7	1.9
Happy	1.4	1.5
Grumpy	2.1	2.2
Bashful	1.9	2.0
Sleepy	2.2	2.2
Dopey	1.4	1.5
Sneezy	1.9	1.8

64. In finance, an efficient market is defined as one that allocates funds to the most productive use. A considerable body of literature exists that is designed to determine whether securities markets are indeed efficient. *Business Week* recently surveyed financial analysts. Of 110 analysts who work for private manufacturing firms in the effort to sell their firms' securities, 42 felt markets were efficient, while 31 of 75 analysts who work for brokerage houses who assist in these sales agreed that markets were efficient. Test the hypothesis at the 5 percent level; does there appear to be a difference in the proportion of these two types of analysts who accept the concept of market efficiency?

65. Two drugs are to be tested for patients' adverse reactions. Accura is given to 37 patients and it is found that 25 percent have a reaction. Of the 55 people who receive Tardi, 29 percent experience a reaction. Set alpha at 1 percent. What can you conclude from the resulting interval?

66. Many large companies use assessment centers in the employee selection process. To test the benefit of these centers, IBM recently compared 100 employees hired through their main assessment center with 150 employees hired in a less formal manner. The results showed that 55 percent of those in the first group failed to advance to mid-level management within seven years of employment, while the corresponding figure for the second group was 60 percent. What can you conclude about the difference in the effectiveness of these two hiring methods based on a 98 percent interval?

67. Each strategic business unit (SBU) within a company is responsible for developing its own strategy. In that effort, Whirlpool Corporation was one of the first American companies to emphasize strategic marketing strategy. A common approach was through a consumer survey. If Whirlpool found that 28 percent of the 70 men who were surveyed stated their approval of tinted appliances, while 34 percent of the 80 women did so, what does a 90 percent interval reveal about the difference in proportion of men and women who prefer tinted washers and dryers?

68. Of 35 people on one weight-reduction plan, 70 percent reach their goal. A second plan works for 65 percent of the 50 people who use it.

a. Does a 99 percent interval indicate a significant difference in the success rate of the plans?

b. How large must the samples be to ensure with 99 percent confidence that the error does not exceed 5 percent?

69. United Airlines finds that one-half of a sample of 150 flights are on time when flying from east to west. Of 160 east-bound flights, 72 are on time. Set alpha at 10 percent.

a. What does the resulting interval say about the relative likelihood of arriving on time depending on the direction of the flight?

b. Your boss, who is flying on United this week, wants to be 90 percent certain the error in this estimation does not exceed 10 percent. How large should your samples be?

70. As part of her senior project, a marketing major at North Texas State University in Denton, Texas, surveyed 100 men and 100 women at a local shopping mall regarding their buying habits. Of the men, 79 said they had used a credit card to make a purchase over $10 in the past month, while 84 of the women admitted to this type of purchase. The student was attempting to refute the notion that women are more likely to use credit. At the 5 percent level, did she do so? State and test the appropriate hypotheses.

71. A term paper by a computer science major at Ohio State University, entitled "Your Chip Is About to Come In," examined the quality of computer chips manufactured by two companies. Of 453 chips made by company 1, 54 proved defective. Of 317 made by company 2, 43 proved defective. If $\alpha = 0.10$, is there evidence to suggest that one firm maintains stricter quality control than the other, based on the appropriate hypothesis test?

72. Denny Dimwit, a securities analyst for Your Bottom Dollar, Inc. has always felt that convertible bonds are more likely to be overvalued than are income bonds. Of 312 convertible bonds examined last year, Denny found 202 to be overvalued, while 102 of the 205 income bonds proved to be overvalued. Do these data support Denny's assumption? Set $\alpha = 0.10$, and test the hypothesis.

73. Two production methods are used to assemble compact disk players. The average time required by both methods has been estimated to be about 5.6 minutes. However, studies seem to suggest that the variances in those times differ. It is important to maintain similar production schedules in order to coordinate the production schedules. Determine whether the variances in production times are dissimilar. Fifteen players produced by the first method report a standard deviation of 5.4 minutes, and 17 players from the second method report a standard deviation of 4.8 minutes. At the 5 percent level of significance, what do you conclude from the appropriate hypothesis test?

74. Data are collected to determine whether there is a difference in the variances of daily revenues at two stores. Given the data below, what is your conclusion based on a hypothesis test with alpha set at 1 percent?

Store 1	Store 2	Store 1	Store 2
$45.78	$67.89	$12.55	$34.91
34.66	76.45	37.77	56.88
65.89	87.12	21.87	45.99
54.78	98.65	23.45	
98.66	65.87	56.98	

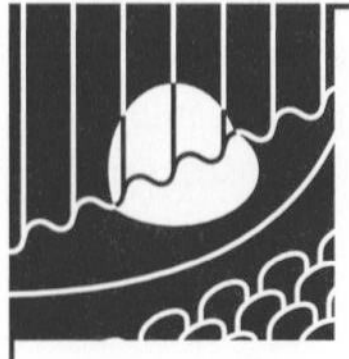

CURTAIN CALL

The opening scenario in "Setting the Stage" described your job task as an international analyst: you are to compare investment opportunities in Europe and Asia. You must prepare a report to be used by your firm's directors to decide in which area the majority of investments should be made. The decision will rest on several factors. Your firm wishes to concentrate where conditions are most favorable with respect to highest mean (1) rates of return, (2) profit levels, (3) investment levels, (4) economic growth rates, and (5) measures of political stability. The mean rates of default on loans and investments are also a consideration. Estimates of the differences between these means are also critical.

The data shown below are contained in a file called ABROAD on your data disk. They were collected by your firm's Data Analysis Section for quarterly data over the past 20 quarters. RETE and RETA are the rates of return in Europe and Asia measured in percentages, respectively. Similarly, INVE and INVA are investments in billions of dollars, PROE and PROA are profits in billions of dollars, GROE and GROA are economic growth rates in percentages. LICE and LICA are area evaluations of political stability measured on a Likert scale from 1 to 10 provided by 20 political analysts. Each analyst was asked to rate both Europe and Asia as to the extent of political stability. The lower the rating, the less stable foreign governments are judged to be.

Of 25 recent investments in Europe, two suffered defaults resulting in a complete loss of all money invested. In Asia, 27 investment projects showed seven defaults.

Provide all necessary statistical analysis and a complete discussion of the interpretation and results. Clearly state your conclusions and recommendation as to the area, Europe or Asia, in which your firm should concentrate its investment activity.

RETE	RETA	INVE	INVA	PROE	PROA	LICE	LICA	GROE	GROA
20	15	250	52	10	3	5	2	9	9
25	17	240	54	14	6	8	4	8	8
27	14	210	74	15	5	7	2	9	5
26	12	195	84	17	2	5	3	12	7
12	8	174	147	21	5	6	6	15	5
15	9	154	54	25	4	9	2	14	6
16	7	214	95	21	7	8	1	17	5
24	5	187	87	26	8	5	5	14	8
26	14	165	85	18	9	4	2	12	5
29	14	240	96	17	5	7	3	11	9
31	15	287	74	15	4	8	2	15	11
14	18	247	35	19	7	5	5	12	12
15	5	265	68	14	8	6	4	14	8
14	8	187	54	15	5	8	1	16	9
18	7	198	78	18	11	5	2	10	6
9	12	177	104	12	10	6	5	11	8
8	14	154	108	21	14	8	6	12	7
15	10	147	147	11	15	4	1	14	11
16	11	165	158	10	9	7	4	11	5
24	11	147	211	9	8	8	5	11	4

From the Stage to Real Life

A visit to the U.S. Census Bureau (*www.census.gov*) will help you to become more familiar with foreign trade as a component of the U.S. economy. From the Census Bureau Home Page, select "Subjects from A to Z." Here, move through the index to "foreign trade" and click on it. Select "Trade Balances with U.S. Trading Partners" under the features list. Next, under the heading, Trade Balances with Partner Countries—Current Year, click on "Try it out." (An advanced version of Netscape might automatically skip the page with the "Try it out" step.) Then go to the area "Select an item for which you want the trade balance."

You will be able to select a particular country from a list and view its monthly data on exports, imports, and trade balances with the United States Data are for 12 months and annual figures are provided. Pick two each of African, Asian, and European countries. Examine the monthly data for each country. Do the trade balances change frequently from positive to negative? Note your observations and the annual trade balance for each country. How similar are the U.S. trade balances of the two African countries? The two Asian countries? The two European countries? Compare the African, Asian, and European trade balances taking two countries at a time from different areas in each comparison. Are you able to detect any patterns either by the size or the direction of the annual balances?

In this same area on the web site, detailed information about goods traded with each country is also available. Look for the heading, Country Detail, and then click on the most current year. Here, look up and click on each of the six countries for which you obtained trade balance information. Are there notable differences between the countries in the goods they trade with the United States?

CHAPTER 10

Analysis of Variance

Chapter Blueprint

Analysis of variance is used to test hypotheses about the equality of three or more population means. By comparing sample variances, it is possible to draw some conclusion or inference about the relative sizes of population means.

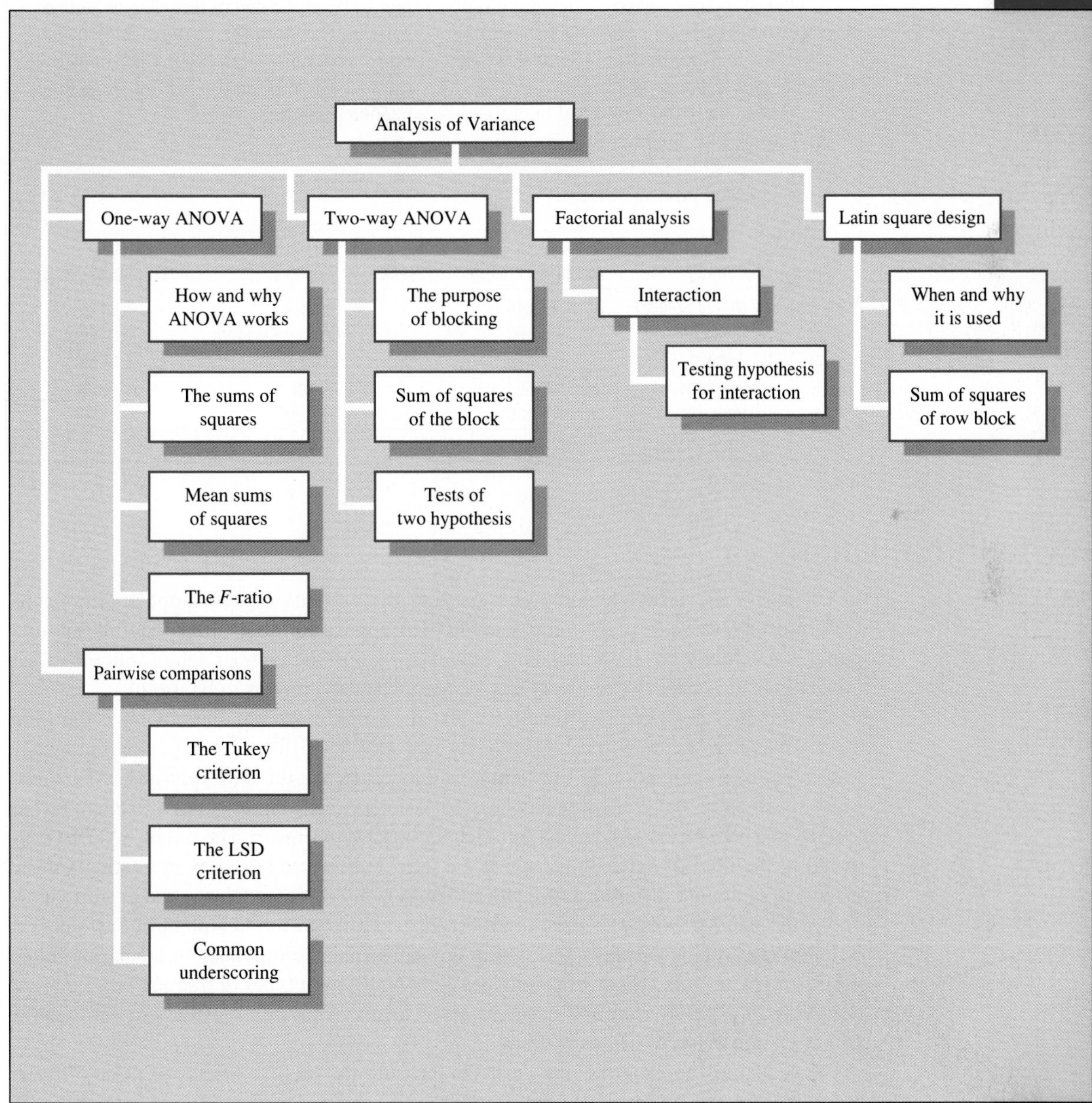

SETTING THE STAGE

The June 1997 issue of *U.S. News and World Report* carried a report by the Central Intelligence Agency (CIA) detailing the economic performance of the world's largest economies in 1995. The Group of Seven (G-7), called the Summit of the Eight since Russia's inclusion, met in Denver in 1997 to discuss ways to combat world poverty. Interest focused on the changing status of world economies and the establishment of economic and political policies that would further global development.

The table below, compiled by the CIA prior to the G-7 Summit, provides a list of the world's 10 largest economies with real gross domestic product (GDP).

Since there have been several position changes among the nations over the past few years, discussion in Denver centered on shifts in the world economic order. A question was raised as to whether there was any "real significant difference in the sizes of the economics from top to bottom." Leaders of the G-7 nations felt that levels of inflation and unemployment rates listed in the "Curtain Call" at the end of this chapter were of particular importance in measuring a nation's economic well-being. The material presented in this chapter will prove helpful in addressing these issues.

Rank	Country	GDP (billions of U.S.$)	Rank	Country	GDP (billions of U.S.$)
1	United States	$7,248	6	France	$1,173
2	China	3,500	7	United Kingdom	1,138
3	Japan	2,679	8	Italy	1,089
4	Germany	1,452	9	Brazil	977
5	India	1,409	10	Russia	796

10.1 Introduction

In Chapter 9 we tested hypotheses regarding the equality of two populations means. Unfortunately, these tests were restricted in their application to a comparison of only two populations. Many business decisions, however, require the comparison of more than two populations. It is here that analysis of variance (ANOVA) proves to be useful.

ANOVA is designed specifically to test if two or more populations have the same mean. Even though the purpose of ANOVA is to test for differences in population means, it involves an examination of the sample variances; hence the term *analysis of variance.* More specifically, the procedure can be used to determine if a particular "treatment" when applied to a population will have a significant impact on its mean. The use of ANOVA originated in the field of agriculture, where the term *treatment* is used as in treating various parcels of land with different fertilizers and noting any discrepancies in mean crop yields. Today the word *treatment* is used quite broadly, to refer to the treatment of customers to different advertising displays and noting any subsequent differences in mean purchases, the treatment of three groups of employees to three different types of training programs and observing any differences that occur in mean levels of productivity, or any situation in which a comparison of means is desired.

Consider, as an example, the desire to measure the relative effects of three different training programs on employee output. These different types of training may be (1) self-taught, (2) computer instructed, or (3) taught by a supervisor. In an ANOVA study, the **experimental units** are the objects receiving the treatment. In our training example, the employees constitute the experimental units. The **factor** is the force or variable whose impact on these experimental units we wish to measure. In this case, "training" is the factor of interest. Finally, the three types of training constitute the **treatments,** or factor levels, of the factor "training."

The manner in which treatments are selected determines whether we are using a **fixed-effects model** or a **random-effects model.** The model described above for the employees' training program is a fixed-effects model. The three training programs were chosen, or fixed, prior to conducting the study. We know which three programs we want to test from the outset of the study. The conclusions from the study are applicable only to the three programs included in the study.

Fixed-Effects Model Specific treatments are chosen or fixed in advance of the study.

In contrast, suppose Apex Manufacturing had many different training programs, and wanted to know whether training programs in general had different effects on employee performance. These three training programs used in the study are seen as only a sample of all training programs that might be used by the firm. It doesn't matter which three training methods we use in the study to make the comparison. Any conclusions from the study are seen as applicable to the entire population of all training programs. This procedure would produce a random-effects model.

Random-Effects Model The levels (treatments) used in the study are chosen randomly from a population of possible levels.

A thorough study of random-effects models is beyond the scope of this text. Our attention in this chapter will focus on fixed-effects models.

Three assumptions are essential for the application of ANOVA:

1. All the populations involved are normal.
2. All the populations have the same variance.
3. The samples are independently chosen.

If the number of treatments is designated as c, the set of hypotheses to test is

$$H_0\!: \mu_1 = \mu_2 = \mu_3 \cdots = \mu_c$$
$$H_A\!: \text{Not all means are equal}$$

The letter c is used for the number of treatments because in an ANOVA table, which we will devise shortly, each treatment is specified in its own column.

You might argue that it would be possible to test the equality of several means by using several two-sample t-tests as we did in Chapter 9. However, certain complications arise that render this approach ineffective. For example, if a manufacturer wishes to compare the mean daily output for three plants, he might test all three of the following sets of hypotheses:

$$H_0\!: \mu_1 = \mu_2$$
$$H_A\!: \mu_1 \neq \mu_2$$

and

$$H_0: \mu_1 = \mu_3$$
$$H_A: \mu_1 \neq \mu_3$$

and

$$H_0: \mu_2 = \mu_3$$
$$H_A: \mu_2 \neq \mu_3$$

If the null is not rejected in each of the tests, he might conclude that all three means are equal.

At least two problems emerge with this approach. First, as the number of populations (plants) increases, the number of required tests rises markedly. If there are four plants the manufacturer wants to compare, the number of individual tests doubles from 3 to ${}_4C_2 = 6$ tests. The second problem is perhaps even more disturbing. It arises due to a compounding of the α-value, which is the probability of a Type I error. If the tests are to be conducted at the 5 percent level, and if there are three populations requiring three separate hypotheses tests, the probability of a Type I error is far in excess of 5 percent. It can be calculated as

$$\begin{aligned} P(\text{Type I}) &= [1 - (1 - 0.05)(1 - 0.05)(1 - 0.05)] \\ &= 1 - (0.95)^3 \\ &= 0.1426 \end{aligned}$$

While we wanted to test at the 5 percent level, the need to make three tests increased the probability of the Type I error beyond acceptable limits.

10.2 One-Way ANOVA: Completely Randomized Design

There are several ways an ANOVA experiment can be designed. Perhaps the most common is the *completely randomized design* or *one-way ANOVA*. The term comes from the fact that several subjects or experimental units are randomly assigned to different levels of a single factor. For example, several employees (the experimental units) may be randomly chosen to participate in different types (the different levels) of a training program (the factor).

The management director for a large industrial firm wants to determine whether three different training programs have different effects on employees' productivity levels. These programs are the treatments that ANOVA can evaluate. Fourteen employees are randomly selected and assigned to one of the three programs. Upon completion of the training, each employee is given a test to determine his or her proficiency. Four employees are placed in the first training program, and five in each of the other two. Each of these three groups is treated as a separate sample. The test scores are shown in Table 10.1, along with a few basic calculations.

Of the 15 *cells* in the table, 14 have entries. The last cell in the first treatment is an empty cell. A cell identified as X_{ij} where i is the row and j is the column in which the cell is located. X_{32} is the entry in the third row and second column. It is seen to be 81. X_{51} is the empty cell. The number of rows in each column is indicated by r and the number of columns or treatments is indicated by c. In our present case, $r = 5$ and $c = 3$.

As seen in Table 10.1, the mean is calculated for each treatment (column). Since the columns are identified by the subscript j, the column mean is represented as $\overline{X}_j$. Finally, the

Table 10.1
Employee Test Scores

	Treatments		
	Program 1	Program 2	Program 3
	85	80	82
	72	84	80
	83	81	85
	80	78	90
	**	82	88
Column means $\bar{X}_j$	$\bar{X}_1 = 80$	$\bar{X}_2 = 81$	$\bar{X}_3 = 85$

grand mean $\bar{\bar{X}}$ is calculated for all n observations.

The grand mean for all observations in the experiment

$$\bar{\bar{X}} = \frac{\Sigma X_{ij}}{n} \qquad [10.1]$$

$$\bar{\bar{X}} = \frac{85 + 72 + 83 + \cdots + 90 + 88}{14}$$

$$= 82.14$$

ANOVA is based on a comparison of the amount of variation in each of the treatments. If the variation from one treatment to the next is significantly high, it can be concluded that the treatments are having dissimilar effects on the populations. In Table 10.1 we can identify three types, or sources, of variation. Note that the first variation is the sum of the other two.

1. There is variation among the total number of all 14 observations. Not all 14 employees scored the same on the test. This is called the **total variation.**
2. There is variation between the different treatments (samples). Employees in program 1 did not score the same as those in programs 2 or 3. This is called **between-sample variation.**
3. There is variation within any one given treatment (sample). Not all employees in the first sample, for instance, scored the same. This is called **within-sample variation.**

It is by comparing these different sources of variation that ANOVA can be used to test for the equality in means of different populations. Any difference that the treatments may have in employee productivity will be detected by a comparison of these forms of variation.

A. The Principle behind ANOVA

To determine whether the different treatments have different effects on their respective populations, a comparison is made between the variation within samples (W/S) and the variation between samples (B/S). The variation in scores within any given sample can be caused by a variety of factors: native ability of employees in that sample, personal motivation, individual efforts and skill, blind luck, and a host of other random circumstances. The treatment itself will not produce any variation in the observations within any sample because all observations in that sample receive the same treatment.

It is a different matter with the variation between samples. The variation in scores between samples (from one sample to the next) can be caused by the same random factors as the variation within a sample (motivation, skill, luck, etc.), plus any additional influence that the different treatments may have. There can be a ***treatment effect*** between samples because each sample gets a different treatment.

> **Treatment Effect** Since different samples get different treatments, variation between samples can be caused by the different treatment effects.

If a treatment effect exists, it can then be detected by comparing between-sample and within-sample variation. If the variation between samples is significantly greater than the variation within samples, a strong treatment effect is present. This difference between variation *between* samples and variation *within* samples is precisely what ANOVA measures. ANOVA is a ratio of the variation between samples to the variation within samples. If the different treatments are having different effects, the variation between samples will rise, causing the ratio to increase. This ratio is based on the F-ratio introduced in the previous section.

> **The F-Ratio as Used in ANOVA** The F-ratio is a ratio of the variation between samples to the variation within samples.

Again, the variation between samples can be caused in part by different treatments. Variation within a given sample can be caused only by random factors such as the luck, skill, and motivation of the employees. Such variation is independent of the treatment (since all observations within a sample get the same treatment) and is the result only of **randomized sampling error** within the sample.

> **The F-Ratio** When population means are different, a treatment effect is present, and the deviations between samples will be large compared with the error deviation within a sample. Thus, the F-value, which is a ratio of the treatment variation to the error variation, will rise.

The total variation is equal to the variation caused by the different treatments plus the variation caused by the random error elements within treatments such as skill, luck, and motivation. That is,

$$\text{Total variation} = \text{Treatment variation} + \text{Error variation}$$

B. The Sums of Squares

Recognition of these three sources of variation allows us to *partition the sums of squares*, a procedure necessary for ANOVA. Each of the three types of variation gives rise to a sum of squares. There is (1) the total sum of squares (SST), (2) the treatment sum of squares ($SSTR$), and (3) the error sum of squares (SSE). As you might expect,

$$SST = SSTR + SSE$$

This illustrates that SST can be partitioned into its two component parts: $SSTR$ and SSE.

We can use these sums of squares to test the equality of population means. Recall from Chapter 3 that the sample variance is calculated as

The sample variance	$s^2 = \dfrac{\Sigma(X_i - \overline{X})^2}{n - 1}$	[10.2]

The numerator is the sum of the squares of the deviations from the mean. In this manner, the sum of squares is used to measure variation. The denominator is the number of degrees of freedom. This equation serves as a pattern that can be applied to the sums of squares in ANOVA.

Let X_{ij} be the *i*th observation in the *j*th sample. For example, X_{21} is the second observation in the first sample. In Table 10.1, $X_{21} = 72$, $X_{32} = 81$, $X_{43} = 90$, and so on. Then,

Total sum of squares	$SST = \sum_{i=1}^{r}\sum_{j=1}^{c}(X_{ij} - \overline{\overline{X}})^2$	[10.3]

The grand mean is subtracted from each of the 14 observations. The differences are squared and summed. As shown by the double summation sign in Formula (10.3), this is done across all rows and across all columns. Hereafter, the notation for the summation signs is dropped in the interest of simplicity. Using the data in Table 10.1, we have

$$\begin{aligned} SST &= (85 - 82.14)^2 + (72 - 82.14)^2 + (83 - 82.14)^2 \\ &\quad + (80 - 82.14)^2 + (80 - 82.14)^2 + (84 - 82.14)^2 \\ &\quad + \cdots (90 - 82.14)^2 + (88 - 82.14)^2 \\ &= 251.7 \end{aligned}$$

It should be noted that *SST* is merely the variation of the observations around the grand mean.

For the treatment sum of squares we have

Treatment sum of squares	$SSTR = \Sigma r_j(\overline{X}_j - \overline{\overline{X}})^2$	[10.4]

The number of observations, or rows, in each treatment, r_j, is multiplied by the squared differences between the mean for each treatment, $\overline{X}_j$, and the grand mean. The results are summed for all treatments. Formula (10.4) tells us to multiply the number of rows in the *j*th column (remember, *j* denotes a column) by the squared deviation of the mean of that column from the grand mean. Table 10.1 yields

$$\begin{aligned} SSTR &= 4(80 - 82.14)^2 + 5(81 - 82.14)^2 + 5(85 - 82.14)^2 \\ &= 65.7 \end{aligned}$$

SSTR reflects the variation in the column means around the grand mean.

The error sum of squares is expressed as

Error sum of squares	$SSE = \Sigma\Sigma(X_{ij} - \overline{X}_j)^2$	[10.5]

The mean of a treatment, $\overline{X}_j$, is subtracted from each observation in that treatment. The differences are squared and summed. This is done for all treatments, and the results are summed. Using the data in Table 10.1 again, we have

$$\begin{aligned} SSE &= (85-80)^2 + (72-80)^2 + (83-80)^2 + (80-80)^2 \\ &\quad \text{for the first treatment} \\ &\quad + (80-81)^2 + (84-81)^2 + (81-81)^2 + (78-81)^2 + (82-81)^2 \\ &\quad \text{for the second treatment} \\ &\quad + (82-85)^2 + (80-85)^2 + (85-85)^2 + (90-85)^2 + (88-85)^2 \\ &\quad \text{for the third treatment} \\ &= 186.0 \end{aligned}$$

SSE measures the random variation of the values within a treatment around their own mean.

A quick check of all these calculations can be done as

$$SST = SSTR + SSE$$
$$251.7 = 65.7 + 186.0$$

If you trust your arithmetic, you can find *SSE* as simply

$$SSE = SST - SSTR = 251.7 - 65.7 = 186.0$$

C. The Mean Sums of Squares

As Formula (10.2) for the variance tells us, after we have obtained the sums of squares, each one is divided by its degrees of freedom. A sum of squares divided by its degrees of freedom results in a *mean sum of squares*. That is, if we average a sum of squares over its degrees of freedom, we get a mean sum of squares.

Recall from Chapter 7 that we defined the degrees of freedom as the total number of observations in the data set minus any "constraints" that might apply. A constraint was any value that was computed from the data set.

In that regard, notice that in calculating *SST*, we used the entire data set of n observations to calculate one value. That one value was the grand mean $\overline{\overline{X}}$, which represents one constraint. Therefore, *SST* carries $n - 1$ degrees of freedom.

The calculation of *SSTR* involved the use of the $c = 3$ sample means from which the grand mean can be computed. The sample means are therefore seen as individual data points and the grand mean is taken as a constraint. *SSTR* then has $c - 1$ degrees of freedom.

Finally, we calculated *SSE* above by noting the deviation of the $n = 14$ observations from the $c = 3$ sample means. Thus, *SSE* has $n - c$ degrees of freedom.

Note that

$$\text{d.f. for } SST = \text{d.f. for } SSTR + \text{d.f. for } SSE$$
$$n - 1 = c - 1 + n - c$$

Since, as noted above, a sum of squares divided by its degrees of freedom produces a mean sum of squares, we find the total mean square, or mean square of the total deviation, *MST*, as

Total mean squares $$MST = \frac{SST}{n-1} \qquad [10.6]$$

the treatment mean square (*MSTR*) as

Mean square treatment	$MSTR = \dfrac{SSTR}{c-1}$	[10.7]

and the error mean square (*MSE*) as

Mean square error	$MSE = \dfrac{SSE}{n-c}$	[10.8]

Using our data from Table 10.1, we have

$$MST = \frac{SST}{n-1} = \frac{251.7}{14-1} = 19.4$$

$$MSTR = \frac{SSTR}{c-1} = \frac{65.7}{3-1} = 32.9$$

$$MSE = \frac{SSE}{n-c} = \frac{186.0}{14-3} = 16.9$$

These three mean squares are patterned after Formula (10.2). They are sums of squares divided by their degrees of freedom, and as such they are measures of variances. It is the ratio of the last two, *MSTR* and *MSE*, that is used as the basis of ANOVA to test the hypothesis regarding the equality of means. As noted above, this ratio fits the *F*-distribution, and is expressed as

F-ratio for a test of means	$F = \dfrac{MSTR}{MSE}$	[10.9]

In our present case it becomes

$$F = \frac{32.9}{16.9} = 1.94$$

MSTR measures the variation between treatments. If the treatments are having different effects, *MSTR* will reflect this by increasing. The F-ratio itself will then increase. Thus, if the F-ratio becomes "significantly" large because *MSTR* exceeds *MSE* by such a great amount, we must recognize that treatment effects probably exist. It is likely that the different treatments are having different effects on the means of their respective populations, and the null hypothesis that $\mu_1 = \mu_2 = \mu_3$ must be rejected.

The critical value for F that is deemed significantly large can be found in Table G (Appendix III) as before. Assume that the management director wishes to test the following hypothesis at the 5 percent level:

$$H_0\text{: } \mu_1 = \mu_2 = \mu_3$$

$$H_A\text{: Not all means are equal}$$

Since *MSTR* has $c - 1 = 3 - 1 = 2$ degrees of freedom and *MSE* has $n - c = 14 - 3 = 11$ degrees of freedom, the critical F-value is found from the table to be $F_{0.05,2,11} = 3.98$. The 2 is listed before the 11 in the statement of the degrees of freedom because *MSTR* is in the numerator.

Figure 10.1
The Effects of Training

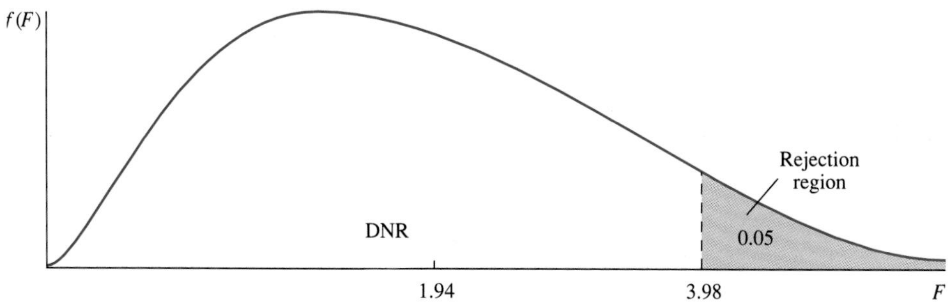

The decision rule, depicted in Figure 10.1, is

Decision Rule Do not reject the null if $F \leq 3.98$. Reject the null if $F > 3.98$.

Since the F-value was calculated to be $1.94 < 3.98$, the director should not reject the null. She can reject at the 5 percent level the hypothesis that the mean test scores are the same for all three training programs. There is no significant treatment effect associated with any of the programs.

D. An ANOVA Table

It is customary to summarize the ANOVA calculations in a table. The general form of the ANOVA table is shown in Table 10.2(A), while Table 10.2(B) contains the specific values pertaining to the training program example.

Notice that the relevant sources of variation are listed, and the F-value of 1.94 is shown in the extreme right column. Example 10.1 provides a more concise illustration of ANOVA.

Table 10.2
An ANOVA Table Summarizing ANOVA Calculations

A. The Generalized ANOVA Table

Source of Variation	Sum of Squares	Degrees of Freedom	Mean Squares	*F*-value
Between samples (treatment)	$SSTR$	$c - 1$	$SSTR/(c-1)$	$MSTR/MSE$
Within samples (error)	SSE	$n - c$	$SSE/(n-c)$	
Total variation	SST	$n - 1$		

B. ANOVA Table for Employee Training Programs

Source of Variation	Sum of Squares	Degrees of Freedom	Mean Squares	*F*-value
Between samples (treatment)	65.7	2	32.9	1.94
Within samples (error)	186.0	11	16.9	
Total variation	251.7	13		

H_0: $\mu_1 = \mu_2 = \mu_3$
H_A: Not all means are equal
Decision Rule: Do not reject if $F \leq 3.98$. Reject if $F > 3.98$.
Conclusion: Since $F = 1.94 < 3.98$, do not reject the null.

Example 10.1 Robert Shade is vice president for marketing at First City Bank in Atlanta. Recent promotional efforts to attract new depositors include certain games and prizes at the bank's four branch locations. Shade is convinced that different types of promotional prizes would appeal to different income groups. People at one income level might prefer gifts, while another income group might be more attracted by free trips to favorite vacation spots. Shade decides to use size of deposits as a proxy measure for income. He wants to determine whether there is a difference in the mean level of deposits between the four branches. If a difference is found, Shade will offer a variety of promotional prizes.

Solution: Seven deposits are randomly selected from each branch and are displayed here, rounded to the nearest \$100. There are $c = 4$ treatments (samples) and $r_j = 7$ observations in each treatment. The total number of observations is $n = rc = 28$.

Deposit	Branch 1	Branch 2	Branch 3	Branch 4
1	5.1	1.9	3.6	1.3
2	4.9	1.9	4.2	1.5
3	5.6	2.1	4.5	0.9
4	4.8	2.4	4.8	1.0
5	3.8	2.1	3.9	1.9
6	5.1	3.1	4.1	1.5
7	4.8	2.5	5.1	2.1
$\bar{X}_j$	4.87	2.29	4.31	1.46

$$\bar{\bar{X}} = \frac{\Sigma X_{ij}}{n}$$

$$= \frac{(5.1 + 4.9 + 5.6 + \cdots + 2.1)}{28}$$

$$= 3.23$$

Shade wants to test the hypothesis at the 5 percent level that

$$H_0\text{: } \mu_1 = \mu_2 = \mu_3 = \mu_4$$
$$H_A\text{: Not all means are equal}$$

Using Formulas (10.3) to (10.5), he would have

$$
\begin{aligned}
SST &= \Sigma\Sigma(X_{ij} - \bar{\bar{X}})^2 \\
&= (5.1 - 3.23)^2 + (4.9 - 3.23)^2 + (5.6 - 3.23)^2 \\
&\quad + \cdots + (2.1 - 3.23)^2 \\
&= 61.00 \\
SSTR &= \Sigma\, r_j(\bar{X}_j - \bar{\bar{X}})^2 \\
&= 7(4.87 - 3.23)^2 + 7(2.29 - 3.23)^2 \\
&\quad + 7(4.31 - 3.23)^2 + 7(1.46 - 3.23)^2 \\
&= 55.33 \\
SSE &= \Sigma\Sigma(X_{ij} - \bar{X}_j)^2 \\
&= (5.1 - 4.87)^2 + \cdots + (4.8 - 4.87)^2 && \text{for the first treatment} \\
&\quad + (1.9 - 2.29)^2 + \cdots + (2.5 - 2.29)^2 && \text{for the second treatment} \\
&\quad + (3.6 - 4.31)^2 + \cdots + (5.1 - 4.31)^2 && \text{for the third treatment} \\
&\quad + (1.3 - 1.46)^2 + \cdots + (2.1 - 1.46)^2 && \text{for the fourth treatment} \\
&= 5.67
\end{aligned}
$$

Formulas (10.7) and (10.8) for the mean squares yield

$$
\begin{aligned}
MSTR &= \frac{55.33}{3} \\
&= 18.44 \\
MSE &= \frac{5.67}{24} \\
&= 0.236
\end{aligned}
$$

Then the F-ratio is

$$
\begin{aligned}
F &= \frac{MSTR}{MSE} \\
&= \frac{18.44}{0.236} \\
&= 78.14
\end{aligned}
$$

Shade must use 3 and 24 degrees of freedom, since d.f. for $SSTR = 3$ and d.f. for $SSE = 24$. If he wants an α of 5 percent, he finds from Table G (Appendix III) that $F_{0.05,3,24} = 3.01$. The ANOVA table summarizes these figures as

Source of Variation	Sum of Squares	Degrees of Freedom	Mean Squares	F-value
Between samples (treatment)	55.33	3	18.44	78.14
Within samples (error)	5.67	24	0.236	
Total variation	61.00	27		

H_0: $\mu_1 = \mu_2 = \mu_3 = \mu_4$
H_A: Not all means are equal
Decision Rule: Do not reject if $F \leq 3.01$. Reject if $F > 3.01$.
Conclusion: Since $F = 78.14 > 3.01$, reject the null.

The test is demonstrated in the following figure.

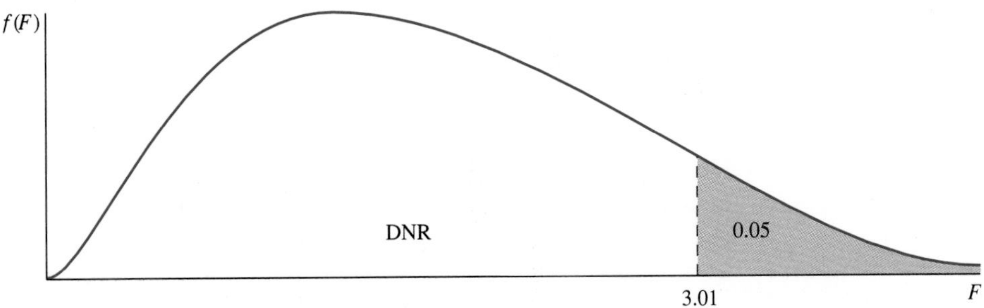

Interpretation: Since $F = 78.14$, Shade must reject the null. He can be 95 percent confident that the mean deposits at all the branch banks are not equal. If he feels that different income groups are attracted by different types of promotional games, he should devise alternative schemes for each branch to entice new depositors.

10.3 Tests for Differences between Individual Pairs

As you can see from the discussion above, ANOVA tells us whether all means are equal. However, when the null hypothesis is rejected, ANOVA does not reveal which mean(s) is (are) different from the rest. We must use other statistical tests to make this determination. These tests rely on a pairwise comparison of all possible pairs of means. If the absolute value (ignoring signs) of the difference between any two sample means is greater than some standard, it is seen as a significant difference, and we conclude that the respective population means are different.

We can determine this standard by a variety of statistical procedures including the Tukey's (Too′ Key) method and the least significant difference (LSD).

A. Test for Balanced Designs

Both the Tukey method and the first of two LSD methods shown here are used if there is an equal number of observations in each sample. Such ANOVA designs are said to be *balanced.* If the design is unbalanced in that the samples are of different sizes, an alternative LSD approach (to be illustrated shortly) must be used.

> **ANOVA Designs** In a balanced ANOVA design, each sample has the same number of observations. If one or more samples have a different number of observations, the design is said to be unbalanced.

In Example 10.1, Mr. Shade found that not all four of his branch banks had the same deposit levels. The next logical step is to determine which ones are different. Since there is an equal number of observations in all four samples ($r = 7$), either the Tukey method or the first LSD approach can be used.

The Tukey Approach Tukey's method, developed by J. W. Tukey in 1953, requires the calculation of the Tukey criterion, T, as shown in Formula (10.10).

Tukey criterion for pairwise comparisons	$$T = q_{\alpha,c,n-c}\sqrt{\frac{MSE}{r}}$$	[10.10]

where q is a **studentized range distribution** with c and $n - c$ degrees of freedom and α is the selected alpha value. Recall that c is the number of samples or treatments (columns), and n is the total number of observations in all samples combined. These values are 4 and 28 in Shade's branch banking problem.

Table L (Appendix III) gives the critical values for q with $\alpha = 0.01$ and $\alpha = 0.05$. If α is set at 0.05, Shade wants the value for $q_{0.05,4,24}$. From that portion of Table L for values with $\alpha = 0.05$, move across the top row for the first degrees of freedom of 4 and down that column to the second degrees of freedom of 24. There you will find the value 3.90. Then

$$\begin{aligned} T &= 3.90\sqrt{\frac{0.236}{7}} \\ &= 0.716 \end{aligned}$$

This Tukey standard criterion of 0.716 is then compared with the absolute difference between each pairwise comparison of sample means. If any pair of sample means has an absolute difference greater than the T-value of 0.716, we can conclude at the 5 percent level that their respective population means are not equal. The difference between the sample means is too great to conclude that they came from similar populations. There is only a 5 percent chance that populations with equal means could yield samples of these sizes with means that differ by more than 0.716.

$$\begin{aligned} |\overline{X}_1 - \overline{X}_2| &= |4.87 - 2.29| = 2.58 > 0.716^* \\ |\overline{X}_1 - \overline{X}_3| &= |4.87 - 4.31| = 0.56 < 0.716 \\ |\overline{X}_1 - \overline{X}_4| &= |4.87 - 1.46| = 3.41 > 0.716^* \\ |\overline{X}_2 - \overline{X}_3| &= |2.29 - 4.31| = 2.02 > 0.716^* \\ |\overline{X}_2 - \overline{X}_4| &= |2.29 - 1.46| = 0.83 > 0.716^* \\ |\overline{X}_3 - \overline{X}_4| &= |4.31 - 1.46| = 2.85 > 0.716^* \end{aligned}$$

In comparing the absolute values of each pairwise difference in sample means to $T =$ 0.716, Shade can be 95 percent confident that only branches 1 and 3 have equal mean deposit levels. All the other differences exceed the T-criterion.

These results can be summarized by **common underscoring** in which connecting lines are drawn under those means that do *not* differ significantly. The sample means must first be put into an *ordered array,* usually from lowest to highest as shown here. Since only branches 1 and 3 do not differ significantly, they are the only ones connected by a common underscore.

$\overline{X}_4$	$\overline{X}_2$	$\overline{X}_3$	$\overline{X}_1$
$\underline{1.46}$	$\underline{2.29}$	$\underline{4.31 \quad 4.87}$	

Least Significant Difference The least significant difference approach is quite similar to the Tukey method. It compares the LSD criterion to the absolute difference in sample means.

If the design is balanced, the *LSD* criterion is

Least significant difference	$$LSD = \sqrt{\frac{2(MSE)F_{\alpha,1,n-c}}{r}}$$	[10.11]

Note that in using the *LSD* approach, F has 1 and $n - c$ degrees of freedom. In Shade's case this is 1 and $n - c = 28 - 4 = 24$ degrees of freedom. From the F-table, $F_{0.05,1,24} = 4.26$. Then

$$LSD = \sqrt{\frac{2(0.236)4.26}{7}}$$
$$= 0.536$$

In comparing the *LSD* of 0.536 with each of the absolute differences figured above, Shade finds that all values, including the last one, suggest different population means. The *LSD* approach is more conservative in that, given any set of conditions, the *LSD* criterion will be less than the Tukey value.

The extensive mathematic calculations required by ANOVA can be facilitated with the use of modern software packages. Display 10.1 shows the printout for Example 10.1 in which Mr. Shade at First City Bank had to decide whether mean deposits at four branch banks were the same. The upper portion shows the F-value of 78.09, which is comparable to the 78.14 we calculated by hand. The p-value of 0.000 reveals why we rejected the null at the 5 percent level.

The bottom portion of the printout provides the common underscoring. In accord with the Tukey criterion, it can be seen that only branches 1 and 3 overlap.

Display 10.1

One-Way Analysis of Variance

```
Analysis of Variance on C1
Source      DF        SS        MS        F        P
C2           3    55.333    18.444    78.09    0.000
Error       24     5.669     0.236
Total       27    61.001
                                    Individual 95% CIs For Mean
                                    Based on Pooled StDev
 Level       N      Mean     StDev  --+---------+---------+---------+----
     1       7    4.8714    0.5469                              (---*--)
     2       7    2.2857    0.4259            (--*--)
     3       7    4.3143    0.5210                          (--*--)
     4       7    1.4571    0.4392   (--*--)
                                    --+---------+---------+---------+----
Pooled StDev =    0.4860             1.2       2.4       3.6       4.8
MTB >
```

With either method, what may appear to be inconsistencies may arise. Assume for the sake of simplicity that there are only three populations under study, requiring three pairwise comparisons:

$$|\bar{X}_1 - \bar{X}_2| \qquad |\bar{X}_1 - \bar{X}_3| \qquad |\bar{X}_2 - \bar{X}_3|$$

You may find that 1 does not differ significantly from 2, and that 2 does not differ significantly from 3, but that 1 does differ significantly from 3. This may seem contradictory. According to the rule of transitivity, if 1 equals 2 and 2 equals 3, then 1 must equal 3. However, pairwise comparisons do not involve equalities. In comparing the three populations, we are merely examining statistical evidence to determine if it is sufficiently strong to reject the null. To conclude that 1 does not differ significantly from 2 simply means that we have insufficient evidence to conclude that they are different. If we conclude, as we did here, that 1 does differ from 3, it can be assumed that evidence comparing these two samples was stronger.

B. Tests for Unbalanced Designs

If the design is unbalanced, the Tukey approach and the LSD method discussed above do not apply. Instead, an alternate LSD approach can be used.

Alternate LSD Approach To compare the jth and kth samples, the equation for LSD becomes

Least significant difference for unbalanced design

$$LSD_{j,k} = \sqrt{\left[\frac{1}{r_j} + \frac{1}{r_k}\right](MSE)F_{\alpha,c-1,n-c}} \quad [10.12]$$

where r_j is the number of observations in the jth sample and r_k is the number of observations in the kth sample. The LSD value will be different for each pair of pairwise comparisons, since the number of observations is not the same in every sample.

Example 10.2 As more Americans seek escape from urban pressures, the burden on our national parks has shown a marked increase with the rise in weekend campers. *Outdoor World* recently reported that the Yosemite National Park in California's High Sierras hired an economic consultant to study the financial position of the park.

Part of the consultant's effort required the comparison of park revenues from various sources, including camping fees, fishing licenses, and boating. Displayed here are the data for several randomly selected visitors. Determine whether there is a difference in the mean revenues the park receives from these three activities.

Visitor	Camping	Fishing	Boating
1	$38.00	$30.00	$19.00
2	32.00	25.00	35.00
3	35.00	31.00	20.00
4	36.00	35.00	22.00
5	38.00	**	25.00
6	32.00	**	**
$\bar{X}_j$	$35.17	$30.25	$24.20

Solution: Assuming α is set at 5 percent, then $F_{\alpha,c-1,n-c} = F_{0.05,2,12} = 3.89$. The ANOVA table would appear as

Source of Variation	Sum of Squares	Degrees of Freedom	Mean Squares	F-value
Between samples (treatment)	328.0	2	164.0	7.74
Within samples (error)	254.4	12	21.2	
Total variation	582.4	14		

H_0: $\mu_1 = \mu_2 = \mu_3$
H_A: Not all means are equal
Decision Rule: Do not reject if $F \leq 3.89$. Reject if $F > 3.89$.
Conclusion: Reject null since $F = 7.74 > 3.89$.

Since the null hypothesis that mean revenues from all three activities is rejected, the consultant would want to use pairwise comparisons to determine which ones differ from the rest. If α is 5 percent, $F_{0.05,c-1,n-c} = F_{0.05,2,12} = 3.89$. The comparison for the first (camping) and the second (fishing) activities, using Formula (10.12) to calculate *LSD*, is:

$$LSD_{C,F} = \sqrt{\left[\frac{1}{6} + \frac{1}{4}\right](21.2)(3.89)}$$
$$= 5.85$$

A comparison of camping and boating reveals

$$LSD_{C,B} = \sqrt{\left[\frac{1}{6} + \frac{1}{5}\right](21.2)(3.89)}$$
$$= 5.48$$

The last comparison of fishing and boating produces

$$LSD_{F,B} = \sqrt{\left[\frac{1}{4} + \frac{1}{5}\right](21.2)(3.89)}$$
$$= 6.08$$

The differences in the means and whether they exceed their respective *LSD* value are

$$|\overline{X}_c - \overline{X}_f| = |35.17 - 30.25| = 4.92 < 5.85$$
$$|\overline{X}_c - \overline{X}_b| = |35.17 - 24.20| = 10.97 > 5.48$$
$$|\overline{X}_f - \overline{X}_b| = |30.25 - 24.20| = 6.05 < 6.08$$

Only camping and boating differ significantly. The results can be summarized with common underscoring after the means have been placed in an ordered array as

$\overline{X}_b$	$\overline{X}_f$	$\overline{X}_c$
24.2	30.25	35.17

Interpretation: We can conclude at the 5 percent level of significance that only boating and camping differ significantly. The park can use this information in making decisions to relieve the financial strain on resources and provide an outdoor experience for modern-day pioneers.

It might seem that the common underscoring in the example is self-contradictory. It shows that boating and fishing are not different and fishing and camping are not different, yet boating and camping are different. Doesn't the algebraic rule of transitivity say that if A equals B and B equals C, then A must equal C? Yes, but we are not dealing with equalities in this example. We are simply saying that the difference between boating and fishing is not significant and the difference between fishing and camping is not significant, yet the difference between boating and camping is large enough to be significant.

Section Exercises

1. A producer of house paints wants to compare the brightness factor of his paint using four different emulsions. Five boards are painted with each type of emulsion and the rating given to each is shown here.

	Emulsion			
Boards	**1**	**2**	**3**	**4**
1	79	69	83	75
2	82	52	79	78
3	57	62	85	78
4	79	61	78	73
5	83	60	75	71

   a. At the 1 percent level does it appear that a difference in mean rating exists?
   b. Use Tukey's method to test for differences and determine if there is one type the producer should use or avoid using. Summarize with common underscoring.

2. A recent study by the American Assembly of Collegiate Schools of Business compared starting salaries of new graduates in several fields. A portion of their results is depicted in the table. At the 5 percent level, does there appear to be a difference in the mean salaries (in thousands of dollars) of graduates in different fields? (CIS is computer information systems, and QM is quantitative methods.)

	Field of Study			
Graduate	**Finance**	**Marketing**	**CIS**	**QM**
1	23.2	22.1	23.3	22.2
2	24.7	19.2	22.1	22.1
3	24.2	21.3	23.4	23.2
4	22.9	19.8	24.2	21.7
5	25.2	17.2	23.1	20.2
6	23.7	18.3	22.7	22.7
7	24.2	17.2	22.8	21.8

3. Considering your results from the previous problem, use Tukey's method to determine which means are different. Do you get the same results with the LSD approach? Keep $\alpha = 0.05$. Summarize the results with common underscoring.

4. A medical supply firm wishes to compare the mean daily output of its three plants in Toledo, Ohio; Ottumwa, Iowa; and Crab Apple Cove, Maine. Data were collected for each site and are listed here. At the 10 percent level, is there a difference in the means? The figures are in units of output.

   Toledo: 10, 12, 15, 18, 9, 17, 15, 12, 18

   Ottumwa: 15, 17, 18, 12, 13, 11, 12, 11, 12

   Crab Apple Cove: 12, 17, 15, 15, 18, 12, 13, 14, 14

5. Ralph works as a waiter to put himself through taxidermy college. Tips he recently received at three restaurants are shown here.

Beef & Boar	Sloppy Sam's	Crazy Charlie's
$5.12	$5.60	$6.00
6.18	4.25	5.00
4.25	6.25	2.00
5.00	7.25	4.50
6.00	5.00	6.50
3.25	4.00	5.50

At which place should he work if he wants to maximize his tips, or does it seem to make a difference? Set alpha at 5 percent.

6. Since stockbrokers work for the most part on strict commission, they are interested in trading activity on the market. A study was done to determine whether there is a difference in the mean commissions paid based on the day of the week, and the data shown here in hundreds of dollars were collected. At the 1 percent level, what days seem to pay the most? Use Tukey's criterion. Summarize with common underscoring.

Monday	Tuesday	Wednesday	Thursday	Friday
$21	28	11	15	25
26	21	14	14	23
24	19	12	12	26
32	15	10	12	28
25	12	10	16	24
26	10	12	13	25
24	13	15	18	29

10.4 Two-Way ANOVA: The Randomized Block Design

With one-way ANOVA, only one factor is thought to influence the experimental units—such as the deposits in the branch banks, or the revenues of the park activities. However, we often find that a second, *extraneous* influence may impact on the experimental units. For example, our interest may be to compare the mean productivity of three different types of machines (treatments). However, we realize that in testing these machines, the operators' skill and experience may affect machine output, causing some confusion about which machine is really best. Thus, to get a clear, uncontaminated view of machine capability, we must in some way eliminate, or correct for, the operators' influence on final output. This simultaneous consideration of two forces requires **two-way ANOVA.**

In order to obtain a decisive measure of machine capability, we must "block" on the extraneous factor by placing the observations in homogeneous groups based on years of experience. Thus, the observations are classified by both blocks and treatments. The purpose of blocking is to decrease the variation within a treatment (type of machine). This experimental design is called a **randomized block design.**

If blocking is done effectively and is based on a factor (such as experience) that truly does affect productivity, a purer measure of the treatment effect is obtained. However, if the factor selected for blocking does not affect productivity (such as a worker's social security number, hair color, or sex), the results can be quite misleading. It is important to determine whether blocking is done correctly, and if the factor upon which blocking is based does have an impact.

To illustrate, a large accounting firm is trying to select an office-integrated computer system from three models currently under consideration. The final choice will depend on the systems' productivity. Five operators are selected at random to operate each system. It is important to realize that the level of experience the employees have in operating computers may affect the outcome of the test. There is therefore a need to account for the impact of experience in determining the relative merits of the computer systems. The resulting levels of output measured in units per hour are recorded in Table 10.3. A higher-coded value for experience indicates more years of training.

Table 10.3
Output Levels for Computer Systems

	Systems (Treatments)			
Experience Level	1	2	3	$\bar{X}_i$
1	27	21	25	24.33
2	31	33	35	33.00
3	42	39	39	40.00
4	38	41	37	38.67
5	45	46	45	45.33
$\bar{X}_j$	36.5	36.0	36.2	
				$\bar{\bar{X}} = 36.27$

Within any given sample (system) there will occur variation in output due to operator experience, proficiency, state of health at the time, and other random error factors. In one-way ANOVA, we identified this as error variation. If any of these random factors associated with the operators materially affect the level of output, the accounting firm must correct for them. The firm may feel that an operator's years of experience would significantly affect his or her productivity. However, the firm is interested in the productivity of the computer systems, not that of their employees. It must therefore adjust for employee productivity by eliminating the effect of operator variability in order to get a more accurate, uncontaminated measure of system quality.

With two-way ANOVA, the total sum of squares is partitioned into three parts: the treatment sum of squares (*SSTR*), the error sum of squares (*SSE*), and the block sum of squares (*SSBL*). Thus,

$$SST = SSTR + SSE + SSBL$$

SST and *SSTR* are calculated in the same manner as in one-way ANOVA. However, *SSE* is subdivided into a measure for *SSE* and *SSBL*, where

Sum of squares of the block

$$SSBL = \Sigma c_i(\bar{X}_i - \bar{\bar{X}})^2 \qquad [10.13]$$

The number of treatments in each block, c_i, is multiplied by the squared difference between the mean for each block, $\bar{X}_i$, and the grand mean. The results are then summed for all blocks. The symbol c_i is used to indicate the number of treatments in a block (row) because the treatments are recorded in columns. From Table 10.3,

$$\begin{aligned} SSBL &= 3(24.33 - 36.27)^2 + 3(33 - 36.27)^2 + 3(40 - 36.27)^2 \\ &\quad + 3(38.67 - 36.27)^2 + 3(45.33 - 36.27)^2 \\ &= 765.04 \end{aligned}$$

The sum of squares of the block measures the degree of variation of the block (row) means around the grand mean.

Formulas (10.3) and (10.4) yield

$$SST = 806.93 \qquad \text{and} \qquad SSTR = 0.93$$

SSE is calculated as

Error sum of squares	$SSE = SST - SSTR - SSBL$	[10.14]

$$= 806.93 - 0.93 - 765.04$$
$$= 40.96$$

Where there are r blocks and c treatments, there are $n = rc$ observations. The degrees of freedom for each of the sums of squares for the values in Formula (10.14) are

$$\begin{aligned} SSE &= \quad SST \quad - \; SSTR \; - \; SSBL \\ (r-1)(c-1) &= (n-1) - (c-1) - (r-1) \\ (5-1)(3-1) &= (15-1) - (3-1) - (5-1) \\ 8 &= \quad 14 \quad - \quad 2 \quad - \quad 4 \end{aligned}$$

The mean square total and the mean square treatment are, as before, the sum of their squares divided by their degrees of freedom. Thus,

$$\text{Mean square total} = MST = \frac{SST}{n-1} = \frac{806.93}{14} = 57.64$$

$$\text{Mean square treatment} = MSTR = \frac{SSTR}{c-1} = \frac{0.93}{2} = 0.47$$

In two-way ANOVA,

Mean square error	$MSE = \dfrac{SSE}{(r-1)(c-1)}$	[10.15]

$$= \frac{40.96}{8} = 5.1$$

Mean square block	$MSBL = \dfrac{SSBL}{r-1}$	[10.16]

$$= \frac{765.04}{4} = 191.26$$

Table 10.4
Two-Way ANOVA for the Computer Systems

Source of Variation	Sum of Squares	Degrees of Freedom	Mean Squares	*F*-value
Between samples (treatment)	0.93	2	0.47	0.09
Between blocks	765.04	4	191.26	37.50
Within samples (error)	40.96	8	5.10	
Total variation	806.93	14		

These calculations are summarized in Table 10.4. The F-values are calculated in the same manner as in one-way ANOVA:

$$F = \frac{MSTR}{MSE} = \frac{0.47}{5.1} = 0.09$$

$$F = \frac{MSBL}{MSE} = \frac{191.26}{5.1} = 37.50$$

Notice that two F-values are computed—one using $MSTR$ and one for $MSBL$. The F-value for $MSBL$ is calculated in order to determine whether blocking was done effectively. Recall that if blocking is based on a factor that does not affect operator productivity, the results can be misleading. The accounting firm must therefore test to see whether there is a significant difference between block (row) means. If there is no significant difference between mean levels of output based on experience blocks (rows), then experience is not a critical factor. In this event, two-way ANOVA should be abandoned, and a return to one-way ANOVA with no distinction between experience levels is called for. At the 5 percent level, the critical F-value for $MSBL$ with 4 and 8 degrees of freedom is found from Table G to be $F_{0.05,4,8} = 3.84$. The degrees of freedom of 4 and 8 are used because the F-ratio for blocks uses $MSBL$ with $r - 1 = 4$ degrees of freedom and MSE with $(r - 1)(c - 1) = 8$ degrees of freedom.

The accounting firm must first test the hypothesis that the mean level of output for each experience level is the same. If it is, then experience is not a factor in determining output, and blocking on it would prove useless at best. If the mean levels of output of the different experience levels are not the same, then the accounting firm must block on experience in order to correct for its impact and thereby obtain a more accurate measure of the differences in computer system quality. The hypothesis to test is

$$H_0\text{: } \mu_1 = \mu_2 = \mu_3 = \mu_4 = \mu_5$$

$$H_A\text{: Not all row means are equal}$$

where μ_i are the mean levels of output for each experience (row) level.

Decision Rule Do not reject the null if $F \leq 3.84$. Reject the null if $F > 3.84$.

Since $F = 37.50$, the null should be rejected, and the firm should conclude that experience levels have an effect on rates of output. It must correct for experience by using two-way ANOVA.

The firm is now ready to test the hypothesis in which it was originally interested. Is there a difference in the mean output of the computer systems (treatments)? If the α-value of 5 percent is retained, the $F_{\alpha,(c-1),(r-1)(c-1)} = F_{0.05,2,8} = 4.46$ is found from the table. The degrees of freedom of 2 and 8 are used because the F-ratio for the treatments used *MSTR* with 2 degrees of freedom and *MSE* with 8 degrees of freedom. The set of hypotheses is

$$H_0\colon\ \mu_1 = \mu_2 = \mu_3$$
$$H_A\colon\ \text{Not all column means are equal}$$

where μ_i are the column means for the three computer systems.

Decision Rule Do not reject the null if $F \leq 4.46$. Reject the null if $F > 4.46$.

Table 10.4 reveals that $F = 0.09 < 4.46$. The null is not rejected, and the firm concludes that the mean output levels of the three computer systems do not differ once a correction has been made for experience. Employees of different experience levels perform equally well on all machines. It doesn't matter which computer system they buy.

Example 10.3 provides another illustration of two-way ANOVA.

Example 10.3 A recent issue of *Fortune* magazine described efforts by a major electronics firm to develop a system in which employees would be given the opportunity to evaluate the performance of their supervisors and other managerial personnel. Assume five employees are selected at random and asked to evaluate four of their managers on a scale of 10 to 50. The results, along with row and column means, might appear as in the accompanying table.

	Manager (Treatment)				
Employee	**1**	**2**	**3**	**4**	$\bar{X}_i$
1	31	35	46	38	37.50
2	29	32	45	36	35.50
3	13	17	35	20	21.25
4	28	38	52	39	39.25
5	14	20	40	20	23.50
$\bar{X}_j$	23	28.4	43.6	30.6	$\bar{\bar{X}} = 3.14$

The management director for the electronics firm wants to know whether there is a difference in the mean ratings of the four managers.

Solution: The director decides to use two-way ANOVA to test the means.

$$\begin{aligned} SST &= \Sigma\Sigma(X_{ij} - \bar{\bar{X}})^2 \\ &= (31 - 31.4)^2 + (29 - 31.4)^2 + \cdots + (39 - 31.4)^2 \\ &\quad + (20 - 31.4)^2 \\ &= 2344.8 \end{aligned}$$

$$
\begin{aligned}
SSTR &= \Sigma r_j(\bar{X}_j - \bar{\bar{X}})^2 \\
&= 5(23 - 31.4)^2 + 5(28.4 - 31.4)^2 + 5(43.6 - 31.4)^2 \\
&\quad + 5(30.6 - 31.4)^2 \\
&= 1145.2 \\
SSBL &= \Sigma c_i(\bar{X}_i - \bar{\bar{X}})^2 \\
&= 4(37.5 - 31.4)^2 + 4(35.5 - 31.4)^2 \\
&\quad + 4(21.25 - 31.4)^2 + 4(39 - 31.4)^2 \\
&\quad + 4(23.5 - 31.4)^2 \\
&= 1124.3 \\
SSE &= SST - SSTR - SSBL \\
&= 2344.8 - 1145.2 - 1124.3 \\
&= 75.3
\end{aligned}
$$

The two-way table becomes

Source of Variation	Sum of Squares	Degrees of Freedom	Mean Squares	*F*-value
Between samples (treatment)	1,145.2	3	381.73	60.79
Between blocks	1,124.3	4	281.08	44.76
Within samples (errors)	75.3	12	6.28	
Total variation	2,344.8	19		

The director can now determine whether there is a significant difference in the mean ratings given by each of the five employees (rows), which would require blocking on the employees. The hypotheses are

$$H_0\text{: } \mu_1 = \mu_2 = \mu_3 = \mu_4 = \mu_5$$
$$H_A\text{: Not all row means are equal}$$

If $\alpha = 1$ percent is retained, the proper F-value is $F_{0.01,4,12} = 5.41$. The F-value associated with the test on blocks is shown in the ANOVA table to be $44.76 > 5.41$. The null is rejected, and the director determines at the 1 percent level of significance that the mean ratings by the five employees (rows) are different and blocking is required.

The director can now test his primary hypothesis regarding the mean ratings of the four managers (columns). The hypotheses are

$$H_0\text{: } \mu_1 = \mu_2 = \mu_3 = \mu_4$$
$$H_A\text{: Not all column means are equal}$$

The F-value of $F_{0.01,3,12} = 5.95$ is less than 60.79. The null hypothesis must be rejected at the 1 percent level of significance.

Interpretation: By including a blocking factor, the director was able to detect a significant difference in the mean rating of the managers by the five employees. Without the blocking factor, the variation in the ratings due to the blocks (differences in employee attitudes) would have been included in the error factor *SSE*. This would have the effect of increasing *SSE* and *MSE*.

The F-value would therefore be lower since $F = MSTR/MSE$. As the F-value goes down, there is a greater likelihood of not rejecting the null.

However, with the two-way ANOVA, the MSE is subdivided into variation due to blocks ($MSBL$) and variation due to error within samples (MSE).

Now that the director knows that not all managers' ratings are the same, he can use Tukey's method or LSD to determine which are different. In applying these tools to a two-way test, certain changes must be made in the degrees of freedom associated with the Tukey method. Rather than explore that involved adjustment, the LSD method as demonstrated earlier can be used with two-way ANOVA.

Display 10.2

Two-Way Analysis of Variance

```
Analysis of Variance for rating
Source          DF          SS          MS
Employee         4     1124.30      281.08
Manager          3     1145.20      381.73
Error           12       75.30        6.28
Total           19     2344.80

                                Individual 95% CI
 Employee          Mean    ----------+---------+----------+---------+-
        1          37.5                                 (----*---)
        2          35.5                              (---*----)
        3          21.2     (---*----)
        4          39.2                                        (---*----)
        5          23.5         (---*----)
                           ----------+---------+----------+---------+-
                                   24.0      30.0       36.0      42.0

                                Individual 95% CI
 Manager           Mean    -+---------+---------+----------+---------+
        1          23.0    (---*--)
        2          28.4            (---*--)
        3          43.6                                  (---*--)
        4          30.6               (---*--)
                           -+---------+---------+----------+---------+-
                          21.0      28.0      35.0       42.0      49.0
MTB >
```

Display 10.2 shows the Minitab printout for Example 10.3. The top portion provides the ANOVA table. However, as the Minitab manual notes, you cannot specify whether the effects are random or fixed with the **TWOWAY** command. Thus, Minitab does not provide F-values or p-values. Minitab apparently expects you to calculate these by hand. The hypothesis for row means (blocking on employees)

$$H_0\colon \mu_1 = \mu_2 = \mu_3 = \mu_4 = \mu_5$$

carries an F-value of

$$\frac{MSBL}{MSE} = \frac{281.08}{6.28} = 44.76 > F_{0.05,4,12} = 3.49$$

The null of equal row means is rejected at the 5 percent level, and two-way ANOVA is used to test the primary hypothesis of equal mean ratings for the managers:

$$H_0\colon \mu_1 = \mu_2 = \mu_3 = \mu_4$$

The F-value is

$$\frac{MSTR}{MSE} = \frac{381.73}{6.28} = 60.79 > F_{0.05,\,3,\,12} = 3.26$$

The null of equal mean ratings for the managers is rejected at the 5 percent level. The pairwise comparisons are shown in the remaining portions of the printout.

The results of the test for row (employee) means are found in the middle section of the printout. Notice that not all means are equal. The means of employees 3 and 5 are less than the other three. The results for the primary hypothesis regarding manager ratings are found in the last portion of the printout. Manager 3 has the highest rating and manager 1 has the lowest. There does not appear at the 5 percent level of significance to be any difference in the mean ratings of managers 2 and 4.

Section Exercises

7. As a recent graduate with a degree in marketing, you have just landed a big job with a major cosmetics firm in New York. You must assist in the analysis of the effectiveness of three advertising displays. Five consumers are randomly selected. Each is shown an advertisement and asked to rate it. The results are shown here. Your supervisor is unsure how to proceed, but your vast knowledge of statistical analysis based on your college course work tells you that two-way ANOVA is appropriate since each consumer (block) rated all three displays (treatments). Is there a significant difference in consumers' attitudes? Set $\alpha = 0.01$.

	Display		
Consumer	**1**	**2**	**3**
1	50	45	45
2	45	30	35
3	30	25	20
4	45	35	40
5	40	30	35

8. Debits and Credits, Inc., an accounting firm in Rocky Top, Tennessee, has a policy of evaluating each new employee by having him or her complete several accounting statements and compiling any errors. You and two other new members of the firms, Seymore Nueshaum and Gretchen Nordick, must fill out six statements. They are examined by a senior partner in the firm, and the errors each of you made are displayed in the table. Does it appear that one of you might be either more or less efficient in your accounting skills? Set $\alpha = 0.05$. If so, which one? It is decided to block on each statement to account for any differences in difficulty that may exist.

	Numbers of Errors		
Statement	**You**	**Seymore**	**Gretchen**
1	2	2	3
2	1	3	4
3	0	1	4
4	4	6	5
5	2	3	4
6	1	4	3

9. Current negotiations between union and management focus on the effect on worker output of methods of payment. A large firm has five plants. In each one, workers are paid by commission, straight salary, or a bonus plan. Three workers are randomly selected out of all plants, with each paid by a different method. Their daily output measured in units is shown here. It is thought necessary to block on plants, correcting for any differences that might exist in mean plant output.

Based on these data, which payment plan would you suggest to management if the objective was to maximize output? Set $\alpha = 0.05$.

	Payment Method		
Plant	**Commission**	**Salary**	**Bonus**
1	25	25	37
2	35	25	50
3	20	22	30
4	30	20	40
5	25	25	35

10. A coal company in West Virginia plans to test the mean production of three mines. Four work crews will work in each mine and record in tons the resulting output of coal. Since each crew will work in each mine, two-way ANOVA will be used by blocking on crews. As the new management supervisor, you must determine if any difference exists in productivity of the mines. Let $\alpha = 0.01$. Reflect which mines are more productive with common underscoring.

Crew	Mine 1	Mine 2	Mine 3
1	42.7	54.1	56.9
2	47.1	59.2	59.2
3	32.1	53.1	58.7
4	29.2	41.1	49.2

11. Speedo manufactures touring bikes for the serious rider. The chief quality control engineer decides to compare the top speeds obtained using three different gearing mechanisms. Five experienced riders are timed using each of the three mechanisms; the results are shown here. Do the data suggest a difference in the average speeds at the 1 percent level?

	Mechanism		
Rider	**1**	**2**	**3**
1	40	51	37
2	42	49	38
3	37	53	38
4	45	57	41
5	42	42	40

12. The U-Plant'um Nursery must determine whether there is a difference in the growth rate of saplings that have been treated with different chemical formulas. Since soil condition is a consideration, saplings treated with each formula are planted in each of three types of soil. The resulting growth rates over a given period are shown here. Does a difference appear to exist in the growth factor of the formulas after correcting for soil? Set alpha at 1 percent.

	Formula			
Soil Type	1	2	3	4
Sandy	10	8	5	7
Clay	12	15	17	14
Rocky	17	16	15	15

13. Curly, Moe, and Larry are selling electric forks door to door. Each goes into four neighborhoods independently and delivers his own sales pitch. The numbers of forks sold are recorded here. At the 5 percent level, does it appear one of the salesmen has a brighter future than the others? If so, which one? Since each salesman called on all neighborhoods, test to see whether blocking should be used.

Neighborhood	Curly	Moe	Larry
1	15	12	19
2	27	25	12
3	24	29	30
4	32	31	29

14. The National Health Institute surveyed 1,060 adults to determine how they spent their leisure time. The data have been broken down by age groups and condensed to only 16 observations for computational purposes. Does there appear to be any difference in the mean time spent at the different pursuits? The observations are hours per week. Test to determine whether blocking should be used. Set $\alpha = 0.05$

	Pursuit			
Respondents (by age)	TV	Read	Sports	Quality Time with Family
15–18	35	12	10	6
19–25	22	13	12	8
26–35	25	15	8	15
36 and up	27	20	5	20

10.5 Factorial Analysis

In our discussion of two-way ANOVA we recognized the presence of a second factor that would influence the experimental units. Since we had no interest in analyzing this second force, we sought to eliminate its impact. In our earlier example on system productivity, we feared that experience would contaminate our results of the study, and so we blocked on the experience level.

Assume now that we want not only to test the computer system, but also to compare the effect of two different software packages on output. Thus, we wish to test simultaneously the effect on output of two different factors: computer system and software package. The proper experimental design to employ is called **factorial analysis**, or two-factor ANOVA.

> **Factorial Analysis** Examination of two factors of interest at the same time.

In factorial analysis we can conduct a **main-effects** test for each factor. Each test is much like those presented earlier: they are designed to determine if different levels of either factor impact on the experimental units in a different manner. If no main effects are found for a factor, the null is not rejected.

Main-Effects Test Tests on both factors to determine whether different levels of the factor impact on the units differently.

Notice that in factorial analysis there are two factors we wish to consider. Each factor has more than one level. We can say that factor A has *a* levels and factor B has *b* levels. In our particular case we want to compare three computer systems and two software packages. Therefore, factor A has three levels and factor B has two levels. There are $a \times b$, or six system/package combinations. This is referred to as a 3×2 factorial design. Each combination is called a *treatment*. There are now six different treatments under consideration. Each treatment, or system/package combination, is shown in one of the six cells that will appear in the table.

In our earlier studies of ANOVA each cell contained only one observation. For example, only one person with a given amount of experience recorded his or her output in the appropriate cell. However, to conduct factorial analysis, more than one observation *must* appear in each cell. The number of observations within a cell is often called the number of **replicates,** *r*. Table 10.5 illustrates. In each of the six cells, the output of several experimental units (employees) will appear. The first employee working in system 1 and package 1 (S1/P1) might produce 27 units of output. If two other employees are chosen to work on S1/P1, they might produce 26 and 25 units, respectively. The mean of that cell, μ_{11}, equals 26. The test must be designed so that each cell has the same number of observations. An unequal number is beyond the scope of this text. The entire table might appear as Table 10.5. With three observations in each of the six cells, there are 18 experimental units.

Table 10.5
Cell Configuration for Factorial Analysis

		FACTOR A (Computer System) Three Levels of Factor A		
		1	2	3
Factor B (Software Package)	1	27 26 25 $\mu_{11} = 26$	20 22 21 $\mu_{12} = 21$	30 26 28 $\mu_{13} = 28$
Two Levels of Factor B	2	28 27 29 $\mu_{21} = 28$	20 26 23 $\mu_{22} = 23$	30 31 29 $\mu_{23} = 30$

The design is said to be *completely randomized* if the 18 units are randomly assigned three to a cell. On the other hand, assume only three employees are randomly chosen, and each will perform on all six system/software combinations. In this case the cells would be homogeneous and we would block not only on the columns but also on the rows. This is called a *blocking design* in factorial analysis. We will concentrate here on the random configuration.

Factorial analysis has the advantage of being less costly. We can study two factors with one experiment instead of conducting two separate tests. Thus, not only do we save time and effort, but we achieve the same degree of accuracy using fewer experimental units, since both tests are conducted at the same time.

Of perhaps even greater value is the fact that by using a factorial design we can identify any interaction between the two factors that might exist. This interaction would be impossible to detect if the experiments were conducted separately or if each cell had only one observation.

Recall that in factorial analysis, each factor has several levels. Our computer system, factor A, has three levels and the software packages, factor B, have two levels. Interaction is said to exist if one level of factor A works differently (either better or worse) with different levels of factor B. For example, computer system 1 might be more (or less) productive with software package 1, while computer system 3 might work better with software package 2. Thus, the total impact of factor A (system) on productivity depends on which level of factor B (software) is used. The two factors are said to *interact* in their impact on productivity.

> **Interaction** The relationship between factor A and the variable under analysis (productivity in this case) depends on the level of factor B that is used.

Interaction can be detected by examining the mean differences between the levels of one factor relative to different levels of the other factor. If these mean differences are the same across all levels of both factors, interaction does not exist. On the other hand, interaction does exist if the mean differences between levels of one factor are not the same for all levels of the other factor.

> **Interaction** Interaction occurs when the differences in the mean responses for two levels of one factor are not the same across all levels of the second factor.

This can best be shown by using a system of graphs. Let us begin with a factorial design that does *not* exhibit interaction. Consider again the data in Table 10.5. The means of all cells are shown in Figure 10.2. Notice that the lines do not intersect. Level 2 of the factor package is higher than level 1 for all three levels of the factor system. In fact, level 2 of package adds 2 units over level 1 for all three levels of the factor system. A graph with parallel line segments like these evidences the **absence** of interaction. We say that the effects are **additive.**

Figure 10.2
Factorial Analysis without Interaction

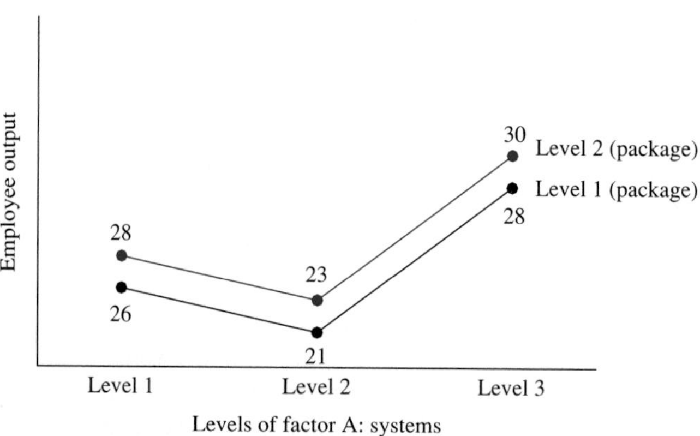

Now assume that the tests produced the results shown in Table 10.6. The graph of the cell means appears in Figure 10.3. Notice now that the lines do cross. There is not a constant addition between levels of the package factor across all levels of the system factor. While level 2 of package adds 2 units to level 1 at the first level of system (28 > 26), this

Table 10.6
Factorial Analysis with Interaction

		FACTOR A (Computer System) Three Levels of Factor A		
		1	2	3
Factor B (Software Package)	**1**	28 26 24 $\mu_{11} = 26$	25 23 27 $\mu_{11} = 23$	30 29 28 $\mu_{11} = 29$
Two Levels of Factor B	**2**	28 27 29 $\mu_{11} = 28$	29 31 27 $\mu_{11} = 29$	28 27 26 $\mu_{11} = 27$

Figure 10.3
Factorial Analysis Evidencing Interaction

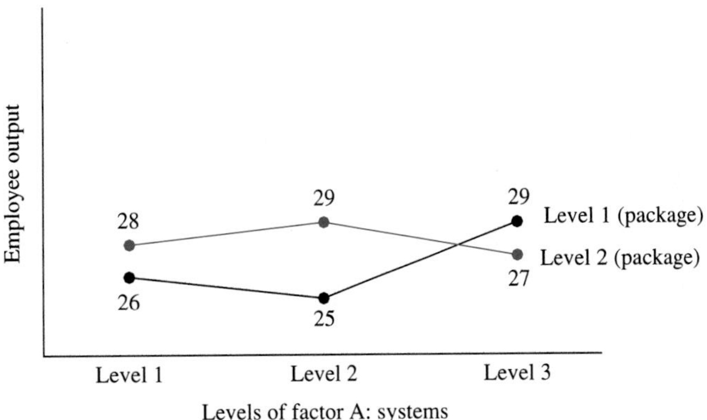

pattern does not continue. In fact, package level 1 varied from low to high depending on which level of system it was paired with. We could say, for example, that output benefited from the interaction derived from a pairing of system level 3 and package level 2.

As noted earlier, the absence of interaction is evidenced by parallel lines. However, the lines need not be perfectly parallel to conclude interaction is not present. To illustrate, when we test the hypothesis that $\mu = 100$, we do not need a sample mean of exactly 100 to not reject the null. Values close to 100 are sufficient to not reject. In the same manner, graphs with lines that are approximately parallel offer support for the null.

A more compelling method of detecting interaction relies on tests of hypotheses. We can identify three hypotheses that we must test:

H_0: The column means are all equal (Main-effects test for the systems factor)

H_0: The row means are all equal (Main-effects test for the package factor)

H_0: No interaction is present

The alternative hypotheses for each test are stated to the contrary, as is the usual case.

As with one-way and two-way ANOVA, we are now ready to partition the sums of squares and construct the factorial table to test the hypotheses. The necessary calculations are quite tedious when done by hand; we will rely solely on computer analysis to accomplish this task.

Given the data in Table 10.5, Minitab is used to generate the factorial table in Display 10.3. The test for interaction is $F = 0.00/2.83 = 0 < F_{0.05,2,12} = 3.89$. The hypothesis of no interaction is not rejected. The impact of the computer system on productivity does not depend on which software program is used. The test for a difference in software is $F = 18.00/2.83 = 6.36 > F_{0.05,1,12} = 4.75$. The null that the row means are equal is rejected. Finally, the test for a difference in system means is $F = 78.00/2.83 = 27.56 > F_{0.05,2,12} = 3.89$ and the null is rejected.

Display 10.3

Two-Way Analysis of Variance

```
Analysis of Variance for Product
Source          DF        SS        MS
Software         1     18.00     18.00
System           2    156.00     78.00
Interaction      2      0.00      0.00
Error           12     34.00      2.83
Total           17    208.00

MTB >
```

On the other hand, presume that the test of computer systems and software packages produced the data shown in Table 10.6. The resulting Minitab printout, Display 10.4, shows that interaction is present. The F-value of $14.0/2.40 = 5.60 > F_{0.05,2,12} = 3.89$.

Display 10.4

Two-Way Analysis of Variance

```
Analysis of Variance for Product
Source          DF        SS        MS
Software         1      8.00      8.00
System           2      4.00      2.00
Interaction      2     28.00     14.00
Error           12     30.00      2.50
Total           17     70.00

MTB >
```

10.6 Latin Square Design

Another type of blocking design allows us to block on two extraneous variables at the same time. Recall our example of computer systems in which we wanted to block on experience level to remove its extraneous influence. Assume now that we also want to correct for the time of day the work is done, since we know that employees' productivity varies throughout the day. Some employees are more effective during the morning, others during the afternoon, and still others are "night people." Now we have two variables on which we must block. We wish to eliminate the influence of two extraneous elements to capture a more precise impression of true system capability. The proper experimental scheme is the **Latin square design.**

One of the blocking variables is assigned to the rows and the second to the columns. The treatments are arranged to occur once in each row and in each column. Therefore, the number of rows, the number of columns, and the number of treatments must all be the same.

> **Latin Square Design** Used when we want to block out the extraneous effect of two variables that might cause equivocal results.

The Latin square design allows the researcher to gain more information with a smaller sample size, since it removes even more of the extraneous variation by blocking on two variables. Unlike factorial analysis, the Latin square design contains only one element per treatment per cell.

As just noted, if there are r treatments under examination, we must have r levels for each of the blocking variables. Hence, we have $r \times r = r^2$ elements, thereby suggesting the term *square*. The design is called *Latin square* because Latin letters such as A, B, and C are used to denote the treatments.

Since there are three computer systems we wish to test, we will now select three employees to work on each system during each of the three time periods. We have three treatments (computer systems) and three levels for each block: that is, three levels of experience and three time periods. We say that we have a 3 × 3 Latin square. The three computer systems (treatments) will be identified as A, B, and C. Each treatment will appear in every row and every column of the square.

We must now partition the sums of squares among the rows, the columns, and the treatments. This is accomplished using the following set of formulas. The sum of the squares of the row block (*SSRB*) is found as

Sum of squares of the row block

$$SSRB = \frac{\Sigma(\text{Row sum})^2}{r} - \frac{(\Sigma X_i)^2}{r^2} \quad [10.17]$$

where (Row sum) is the sum of each row
r is the number of treatments
X_i is each of the observations

The sum of the squares of the column block (*SSCB*) is

Sum of squares of the column block

$$SSCB = \frac{\Sigma(\text{Col sum})^2}{r} - \frac{(\Sigma X_i)^2}{r^2} \quad [10.18]$$

where (Col sum) is the sum of each column.

The sum of the squares of the treatment (*SSTR*) is

Treatment sum of squares

$$SSTR = \frac{\Sigma(TRT_i\ \text{sum})^2}{r} - \frac{(\Sigma X_i)^2}{r^2} \quad [10.19]$$

where (TRT_i sum) is the sum of each of the treatments, A, B, and C.

The total sum of squares is

Total sum of squares

$$SST = \Sigma(X_i)^2 - \frac{(\Sigma X_i)^2}{r^2} \quad [10.20]$$

where $(X_i)^2$ is the square of all nine values of output. Last, for the error sum of squares, we have

Sum of the squared errors

$$SSE = SST - SSTR - SSCB - SSRB \quad [10.21]$$

Assume that the experiment produced the data shown in Table 10.7. The first cell of B/15 means that the first employee working in the morning produced 15 units of output on machine B. The upper right cell of C/11 means that the first employee working in the evening produced 11 units of output on machine C.

Table 10.7
Data for a Latin Design

	Time			
Employee	Morning	Afternoon	Evening	Row Totals
1	B/15	A/18	C/11	44
2	C/12	B/20	A/9	41
3	A/17	C/19	B/10	46
Column Totals	44	57	30	131

$\Sigma A = 44$
$\Sigma B = 45$
$\Sigma C = 42$

Applying Formulas (10.17) to (10.21), we have

$$SSRB = \frac{(44)^2 + (41)^2 + (46)^2}{3} - \frac{(131)^2}{3^2}$$

$$= 4.222$$

$$SSCB = \frac{(44)^2 + (57)^2 + (30)^2}{3} - \frac{(131)^2}{3^2}$$

$$= 121.5556$$

$$SSTR = \frac{(44)^2 + (45)^2 + (42)^2}{3} - \frac{(131)^2}{3^2}$$

$$= 1.5556$$

$$SST = (15)^2 + (12)^2 + (17)^2 + \cdots + (10)^2 - \frac{(131)^2}{3^2}$$

$$= 138.222$$

Therefore, $SSE = 10.89$. The table would appear as Table 10.8.

Table 10.8
Latin Square Design for the Computer Test

Source of Variation	Sum of Squares	Degrees of Freedom	Mean Square	*F*-value
Row blocks	4.222	2	2.111	0.3877
Column blocks	121.555	2	60.778	11.1621
Treatments	1.555	2	0.7775	0.1428
Error	10.890	2	5.445	
Total	138.222			

H_0: $\mu_1 = \mu_2 = \mu_3$ The mean outputs of all three computers are equal.
$F = 0.1428 < F_{0.05,2,2} = 19$; do not reject null.

Setting alpha at 5 percent, the F-value for $F_{0.05,2,2} = 19 > 0.1428$, and we therefore do not reject the null hypothesis that there is no difference in the mean output of the computers after adjusting for employee experience and time of day.

Section Exercises

15. A producer of metal wires wants to compare the tensile strength of wire made with three different chemical mixes: A, B, and C. It is necessary to control for the type of oven used to "fire" the mix, and the temperature at which it was fired. Using the data below, what conclusion can you reach for the producer? Set alpha at 1 percent.

	Temperature		
Oven	Low	Medium	High
1	A/40	B/42	C/18
2	B/70	C/19	A/45
3	C/20	A/51	B/27

16. As marketing director, you are interested in comparing the revenues of three brands—"good," "better," "best"—of electric forks your firm sells. To do so, you want to correct for the area of the country in which the store is located, and the type of store at which the sale was made. Your assistant collects the data for monthly sales in hundreds of dollars seen here, but has no idea what to do with them. Conduct the test yourself and inform the assistant of the findings. Set alpha at 1 percent.

	Area		
Store	Northeast	Southeast	Midwest
Discount	Good/4.2	Better/9.0	Best/12.9
Convenience	Better/7.3	Best/11.1	Good/11.3
Mall	Best/8.0	Good/9.4	Better/10.7

17. A researcher collects data on faculty salaries to determine whether there is a difference in the mean incomes of those in business, the social sciences, and the natural sciences. She must eliminate the extraneous effects of rank and size of school. Using the information seen here for salaries in thousands of dollars, what do you suppose are her results? Set alpha at 1 percent and interpret.

	Size		
Rank	Small	Medium	Large
Assistant professor	Bus/65	SS/60	NS/78
Associate professor	SS/72	NS/81	Bus/79
Full professor	NS/82	Bus/73	SS/79

Solved Problems

1. **Fleecing the Motorist** *Consumers' Research* published the results of a survey on U.S. driving habits. The data contained gasoline taxes per household for all 50 states. Six states are randomly chosen from the four regions of the country to determine whether there is any difference in the annual mean gasoline tax within the regions. The results follow, rounded to the nearest dollar.

State	Region (treatment)			
	North (1)	South (2)	West (3)	Midwest (4)
1	\$293	\$121	\$114	\$136
2	280	116	176	164
3	283	223	224	117
4	242	238	183	153
5	268	118	159	152
6	184	222	149	108
$\overline{X}_j$	258.3	173.0	167.5	138.3
$\overline{\overline{X}} = 184.3$				

An economist wanted to test at the 5 percent level the hypothesis that, on the average, residents in all four regions pay the same amount in federal gasoline taxes.

Solution:

$$\begin{aligned} SST &= \Sigma\Sigma(X_{ij} - \overline{\overline{X}})^2 \\ &= (293 - 184.3)^2 + \cdots + (108 - 184.3)^2 \\ &= 83{,}515 \end{aligned}$$

SSTR is found as

$$\begin{aligned} SSTR &= \Sigma r_j(\overline{X}_j - \overline{\overline{X}})^2 \\ &= 6(258.3 - 184.3)^2 + \cdots + 6(138.3 - 184.3)^2 \\ &= 48{,}023 \end{aligned}$$

SSE is

$$\begin{aligned} SSE &= \Sigma\Sigma(X_{ij} - \overline{X}_j)^2 \\ &= (293 - 258.3)^2 + \cdots + (108 - 138.3)^2 \\ &= 35{,}492 \end{aligned}$$

Then,

$$\begin{aligned} MSTR &= \frac{SSTR}{c - 1} \\ &= \frac{48{,}023}{4 - 1} \\ &= 16{,}008 \end{aligned}$$

$$\begin{aligned} MSE &= \frac{SSE}{n - c} \\ &= \frac{35{,}492}{24 - 4} \\ &= 1{,}775 \end{aligned}$$

If α is set at 5 percent, $F_{0.05,3,20} = 3.10$ as seen here. The hypothesis is H_0: $\mu_1 = \mu_2 = \mu_3 = \mu_4$.

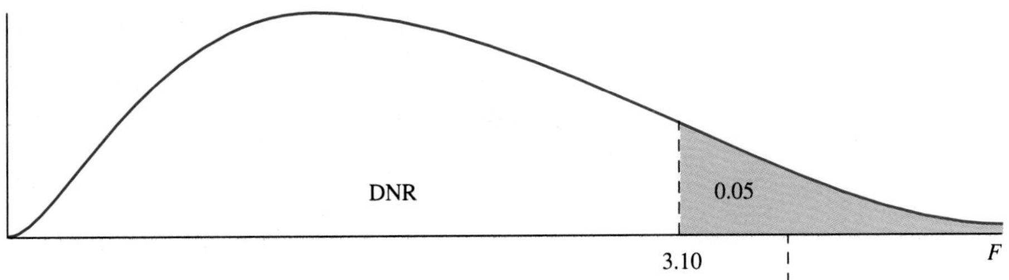

The ANOVA table is

Source of Variation	SS	d.f.	MS	F-value
Between samples (treatment)	48,023	3	16,008	9.02
Within samples (error)	35,492	20	1,775	
Total variation	83,515	23		

H_0: $\mu_1 = \mu_2 = \mu_3 = \mu_4$
H_A: Not all means are equal
Decision Rule: Do not reject the null if $F \leq 3.10$. Reject if $F > 3.10$.
Conclusion: Reject the null.

It can be concluded at the 5 percent level of significance that the mean tax bite is not the same in all four regions.

2. **Who Gets Bitten the Hardest?** To formulate an effective tax system, the government must now determine which regions pay more and which pay less. Using both Tukey's method and the LSD approach, the computations would proceed as shown here.

Solution: It is first necessary to find the absolute differences in the sample means of the taxes paid in each pair of the four regions.

$$|\bar{X}_1 - \bar{X}_2| = |258.3 - 173.0| = 85.3$$
$$|\bar{X}_1 - \bar{X}_3| = |258.3 - 167.5| = 90.8$$
$$|\bar{X}_1 - \bar{X}_4| = |258.3 - 138.3| = 120.0$$
$$|\bar{X}_2 - \bar{X}_3| = |173.0 - 167.5| = 5.5$$
$$|\bar{X}_2 - \bar{X}_4| = |173.0 - 138.3| = 34.7$$
$$|\bar{X}_3 - \bar{X}_4| = |167.5 - 138.3| = 29.2$$

Tukey's criterion is

$$T = q_{\alpha,c,n-c}\sqrt{\frac{MSE}{r}}$$

If α is set at 5 percent, $q_{0.05,4,20} = 3.96$,

$$T = 3.96\sqrt{\frac{1{,}775}{6}}$$
$$= 68.11$$

Any absolute difference between the sample means greater than 68.11 is significant and suggests that their respective populations' means are different. There is only a 5 percent chance that two populations could have the same mean and generate samples of these sizes with means in excess of 68.11. Comparing 68.11 to the six pairs of sample means above, it can be seen that population 1 (North) has a mean different from the other three; μ_1 is assumed to be higher since $\bar{X}_1$ is significantly higher than the rest.

Using the LSD method, we have

$$LSD = \sqrt{\frac{2(MSE)F_{\alpha,1,n-c}}{r}}$$

$F_{0.05,1,20} = 4.35$. Then

$$LSD = \sqrt{\frac{2(1{,}775)(4.35)}{6}}$$
$$= 50.73$$

The *LSD* criterion is compared with the absolute differences in sample means above. Any differences greater than 50.73 are significant. Again, it is seen that those motorists in the North endure the heaviest tax burden.

3. **Acme, Ltd.** As a production supervisor for Acme Ltd., Melvin Moore wishes to compare production levels of Acme's four plants. Data on the weekly levels in tons are collected over a given seven-week period including the four weeks in August and the first three in September. The results are shown in the table.

	Plant (treatment)				
Week	**1**	**2**	**3**	**4**	$\bar{X}_i$
1	42.7	38.3	42.9	30.1	38.5
2	47.3	35.1	38.2	37.5	39.5
3	57.3	42.7	49.9	47.8	49.4
4	63.1	58.2	59.3	53.9	58.6
5	49.2	32.7	45.7	33.8	40.4
6	51.2	30.1	48.3	38.7	42.1
7	48.0	31.1	45.2	39.7	41.0
$\bar{X}_j$	51.3	38.3	47.1	40.2	
$\bar{\bar{X}} = 44.23$					

Melvin conducts a one-way ANOVA and finds a significant difference in mean output levels. However, before submitting his report to higher management, Melvin comes to an important realization: The seven weeks were not picked randomly for each plant. Data for the same seven weeks were used for all four plants. Perhaps he should block on weeks to eliminate any variation due to the time period. Since the same weeks were recorded for each plant, blocking on weeks is possible.

Solution: *SST* and *SSTR* are calculated in the same fashion as in Solved Problem 1 and are found to be 2,276.1 and 761.4, respectively. In addition,

$$SSBL = \Sigma c_i(\bar{X}_i - \bar{\bar{X}})^2$$
$$= 4(38.5 - 44.23)^2 + 4(39.5 - 44.23)^2$$
$$+ \cdots + 4(41 - 44.23)^2$$
$$= 1{,}276.6$$

$$SSE = SST - SSTR - SSBL$$
$$= 238.1$$
$$MSTR = \frac{SSTR}{c - 1}$$
$$= \frac{761.4}{4 - 1}$$
$$= 253.8$$
$$MSBL = \frac{SSBL}{r - 1}$$
$$= \frac{1{,}276.6}{7 - 1}$$
$$= 212.8$$
$$MSE = \frac{SSE}{(r - 1)(c - 1)}$$
$$= \frac{238.1}{(7 - 1)(4 - 1)}$$
$$= 13.2$$

These calculations are summarized in the two-way ANOVA table:

Source of Variation	*SS*	d.f.	*MS*	*F*-value
Between samples (treatment)	761.4	3	253.8	19.23
Between blocks	1,276.6	6	212.8	16.12
Within samples (error)	238.1	18	13.2	
Total variation	2,276.1	27		

Melvin must first determine whether blocking on weeks is effective. He sets α at 5 percent. The F-value for blocks is $MSBL/MSE$, and since $MSBL$ has $r - 1 = 6$ d.f. and MSE has $(r -)(c - 1) = 18$ d.f., $F_{0.05,6,18} = 2.66$ is found to be the critical F-value. Since $F = 16.12 > 2.66$, Melvin concludes that the mean output between weeks is different. Blocking is therefore necessary to correct for variation from one week to the next. Melvin should continue with his two-way test.

He can now test the primary hypothesis on mean plant output levels.

$$H_0\text{: } \mu_1 = \mu_2 = \mu_3 = \mu_4$$
$$H_A\text{: Not all means are equal}$$

The F-value for treatments has $c - 1 = 3$ and $(r - 1)(c - 1) = 18$ d.f. $F_{0.05,3,18} = 3.16 < 19.23$. The hypothesis is rejected, and Melvin concludes that there is some difference in plant output levels on the average. He can now use *LSD* to determine which ones are different.

4. **Driving in Circles** Circle Trucking Company wishes to determine if the mean driving time is the same for three different routes. The traffic director for Circle feels that it is necessary to correct for weather conditions as well as the proficiency of the drivers. Three levels of weather conditions are identified: poor, fair, and good. Three drivers with varying abilities are selected and each covers all three routes under each of the three weather conditions. The results are reported in the Latin square shown here. Recall that the Latin letters indicate the variables under examination—in this case, routes. Times are recorded in minutes.

Driver	Weather: Poor	Fair	Good	Row Totals
1	A/20	C/18	B/17	55
2	C/22	B/10	A/10	42
3	B/18	A/9	C/8	35
Column Totals	60	37	35	132
	ΣA = 39	ΣB = 45	ΣC = 48	

Solution: Using the Latin square design since there are two extraneous variables to correct for (skills and weather), the calculations appear as

$$SSRB = \frac{(55)^2 + (42)^2 + (35)^2}{3} - \frac{(132)^2}{9}$$

$$= 68.667$$

$$SSCB = \frac{(60)^2 + (37)^2 + (35)^2}{3} - \frac{(132)^2}{9}$$

$$= 128.667$$

$$SSTR = \frac{(39)^2 + (45)^2 + (48)^2}{3} - \frac{(132)^2}{9}$$

$$= 14$$

$$SST = (20)^2 + (22)^2 + \cdots + (8)^2 - \frac{(132)^2}{9}$$

$$= 230$$

$$SSE = 230 - 14 - 128.667 - 68.667$$

$$= 18.663$$

Source of Variation	Sum of Squares	Degrees of Freedom	Mean Square	*F*-value
Row blocks (Driver)	686.667	2	34.33	3.679
Column blocks (Weather)	128.667	2	64.33	6.895
Treatment (Route)	14.000	2	7.00	0.750
Error	18.663	2	9.33	
Total	230.000			

If the hypothesis is to be tested at the 5 percent level, $F_{0.05,2,2} = 19 > 0.750$. Therefore, Circle should not reject the null.

List of Formulas

[10.1] $$\overline{\overline{X}} = \frac{\Sigma X_{ij}}{n}$$ Grand mean of all observations in the experiment

[10.2] $$s^2 = \frac{\Sigma(X_i - \overline{X})^2}{n - 1}$$ The sample variance

[10.3]	$SST = \sum_{i=1}^{r}\sum_{j=1}^{c}(X_{ij} - \bar{\bar{X}})^2$	Total sum of squares is the variation of the values around $\bar{\bar{X}}$
[10.4]	$SSTR = \Sigma r_j(\bar{X}_j - \bar{\bar{X}})^2$	Treatment sum of squares measures the variation in the column means around the grand mean
[10.5]	$SSE = \Sigma\Sigma(X_{ij} - \bar{X}_j)^2$	Error sum of squares reflects the variation of the values within a treatment around their own mean
[10.6]	$MST = \dfrac{SST}{n - 1}$	Total mean squares
[10.7]	$MSTR = \dfrac{SSTR}{c - 1}$	Mean square treatment
[10.8]	$MSE = \dfrac{SSE}{n - c}$	Mean square error
[10.9]	$F = \dfrac{MSTR}{MSE}$	F-ratio for the test of means
[10.10]	$T = q_{\alpha,c,n-c}\sqrt{\dfrac{MSE}{r}}$	Tukey criterion measures the critical amount for difference between means
[10.11]	$LSD = \sqrt{\dfrac{2(MSE)F_{\alpha,1,n-c}}{r}}$	LSD criterion measures critical difference between two means—for balanced designs
[10.12]	$LSD_{j,k} = \sqrt{\left[\dfrac{1}{r_j} + \dfrac{1}{r_k}\right](MSE)F_{\alpha,1,n-c}}$	LSD criterion measures critical difference between two means—for unbalanced designs
[10.13]	$SSBL = \Sigma c_i(\bar{X}_i - \bar{\bar{X}})^2$	Sum of the squares of the block measures the deviations of the row means around the grand mean
[10.14]	$SSE = SST - SSTR - SSBL$	Error sum of squares measures the random variation of the observations around their treatment means
[10.15]	$MSE = \dfrac{SSE}{(r - 1)(c - 1)}$	Mean sum of squares in two-way ANOVA
[10.16]	$MSBL = \dfrac{SSBL}{r - 1}$	Mean square block
[10.17]	$SSRB = \dfrac{\Sigma(\text{Row sum})^2}{r} - \dfrac{(\Sigma X_i)^2}{r^2}$	Sum of squares of the row block for Latin square design
[10.18]	$SSCB = \dfrac{\Sigma(\text{Col sum})^2}{r} = \dfrac{(\Sigma X_i)^2}{r^2}$	Sum of squares of the column block for Latin square design

[10.19]	$SSTR = \frac{\Sigma(TRT \text{ sum})^2}{r} - \frac{(\Sigma X_i)^2}{r^2}$	Treatment sum of squares for Latin design
[10.20]	$SST = \Sigma(X_i^2) - \frac{(\Sigma X_i)^2}{r^2}$	Total sum of squares for Latin design
[10.21]	$SSE = SST - SSTR - SSCB - SSRB$	Error sum of squares for Latin design

Chapter Exercises

18. As a marketing analyst you want to determine whether there is a difference in mean sales in three markets: Pittsburgh, Toledo, and Columbus. Why not eliminate the need for ANOVA by just testing for the equality between each pair of markets? If each hypothesis is not rejected, may you then conclude that all three markets have the same mean?

19. Why does a *high* F-value result in a rejection of the null of equal means?

20. What is the difference between a fixed-effects model and a random-effects model?

21. What is the difference between one-way ANOVA and two-way ANOVA?

22. Under what conditions would you use factorial analysis? A Latin square design?

23. What is the difference between a balanced design and an unbalanced design?

24. According to an article in *Fortune,* smaller manufacturing companies are having increasing difficulty receiving orders from their suppliers within a reasonable time. As the economy heats up and production capacity is strained, orders tend to backlog. As a production supervisor for Novelties, Inc., you wish to test mean delivery time in days for orders you place with three different suppliers of an important component of your firm's deluxe whoopie cushion. Delivery times are shown here. At the 5 percent level, is there a difference in mean times?

Supplier 1: 5, 6, 6, 5, 6, 6, 7

Supplier 2: 5, 4, 5, 5, 6, 5, 4

Supplier 3: 4, 5, 2, 6, 5, 2, 4

25. Given the results from the previous problem, which supplier(s) would you recommend? Which one(s) would you recommend be avoided? Set $\alpha = 0.01$. Summarize the results with common underscoring.

26. A discussion in *American Agriculture* drew attention to concern about the effect of different food grain supplements on the growth rates of commercially raised chickens. At Charlie's Chicken Ranch, a test was performed in which 18 chickens were evenly divided into three groups, and each group was fed a particular supplement. The resulting increases in growth over a six-week period as measured in pounds are shown here. At the 10 percent level, does there appear to be evidence indicating which supplement Charlie should use in the future?

	Supplement		
Chicken	Grow-Big	Cluckers Choice	Cock of the Walk
1	2.2	3.7	3.8
2	2.4	2.1	4.1
3	2.7	3.2	3.9
4	3.8	2.9	2.7
5	3.2	3.9	4.1
6	3.9	3.8	3.2

27. There are many aspects to consider in developing marketing strategy. Store location is a major concern. PDQ, a convenience chain throughout the Southeast, reported the results in an in-house publication of a survey of weekly revenues from stores with urban, suburban, and rural locations. The data, which have been somewhat simplified for our purposes, are shown below. Can any conclusions be reached regarding prime locations for stores? Determine which location(s) if any are better. Set $\alpha = 0.05$. Display the results with common underscoring.

	Location		
Store	Urban	Suburban	Rural
1	789	612	718
2	762	655	655
3	722	725	725
4	745	609	645
5	802	632	622

28. A recent issue of *Bicycling* discussed the use of computer-coded programs in the development of a training regimen. One such computer-based program tested several cyclists who were in superior physical condition and concluded that, to be most beneficial, extended workouts should be done at 60 to 70 percent of the individual's maximum heart rate (approximately 220 beats per minute minus the person's age). More intense workouts of a shorter duration should reach 80 to 90 percent of that maximum.

    Three training programs were devised to determine optimal training techniques. Assume five individuals were placed in each program, and at the end of six weeks, final heart rates were monitored. The data, as recorded here, represent percentages of recommended maximum rates. At the 5 percent level, does there appear to be a difference in the mean maximum rates?

	Training Program		
Cyclist	1	2	3
1	0.62	0.68	0.72
2	0.73	0.52	0.69
3	0.59	0.59	0.73
4	0.82	0.63	0.74
5	0.79	0.61	0.68

29. Complete the calculations from the previous problem, setting $\alpha = 0.10$. Draw graphs for the F-distributions in each case, showing a comparison of the tests for each α-value.

30. *Business Week* quoted John F. Akers, CEO of IBM, as saying that he felt it was unlikely that in the near future, IBM's annual growth in sales of 6.1 percent could keep pace with the overall industry's growth of 9.2 percent. This lag in receipts was due in part to IBM's reliance on mainframes, the market for which has fallen to third behind PCs and minicomputers in world sales.

    Quarterly data for percentage increase in sales for five periods have been collected for each of the three hardware markets. The results are

    Mainframes: 3.2, 4.8, 4.1, 4.2, 3.9

    PCs: 8.7, 9.2, 9.3, 8.3, 8.9

    Minicomputers: 9.1, 9.4, 8.7, 9.5, 9.9

    Do these data show any significant difference in mean increases in sales at the 1 percent level?

31. *USA Today* printed a story about the use of private detectives for the purpose of uncovering any facts that might make a firm less desirable from the standpoint of a merger or acquisition. "M & A work," says J. B. Kroll, head of Kroll and Associates, a New York-based detective firm, "accounts for at least 20 percent of the $50 million Kroll should gross this year." Petrochemicals, banking, computers, and electronics are particularly fertile industries for M & A business.

    Assume that six firms in each industry are randomly surveyed to determine the amounts involved in the takeover bids, and the results are as shown below. Can it be concluded at the

5 percent level that any differences exist in mean tender offers among these industries? Values are in millions of dollars.

Tender Offer	Petrochemicals	Banking	Computers	Electronics
1	919.3	842.7	647.3	743.7
2	874.2	1,144.7	873.2	747.3
3	832.7	942.3	714.4	812.5
4	732.9	747.1	652.8	643.7
5	893.2	812.7	855.6	682.1
6	1,321.4	855.6	642.1	632.1

32. The Big Bad Wolf wants to fatten up the Three Little Pigs for the holiday brunch. His data show the amount of food in pounds each piggy has eaten for a sample of five days.

Piggy 1	Piggy 2	Piggy 3
12	14	19
15	16	18
14	15	17
16	18	16
13	12	18

a. At the 5 percent level, is there a difference in the mean amount of food eaten by the piggies?
b. Use Tukey's criterion to determine which piggy or piggies might get fattened up first. Summarize with common underscoring.
c. Perform the same pairwise tests using the LSD method. Summarize with common underscoring.

33. When President Clinton removed the trade embargo on Vietnam in 1994, many U.S. companies initiated trading relations. Data are shown here for trading amounts (in billions of dollars) for four industries. Set alpha at 1 percent. What is your conclusion concerning a difference in the mean trading levels of these four industries? Use Tukey's method to draw conclusions on pairwise comparisons. Summarize with common underscoring.

Petroleum	Soft Drinks	Construction Equipment	Computers
2.1	5.6	1.5	4.5
2.5	6.2	1.0	4.2
2.6	7.8	1.8	4.1
2.1	6.8	1.9	4.6
3.5	5.4	1.7	4.2

34. An economist for the U.S. State Department specializing in demographics obtained the following data showing annual in-migration in millions of people from four different countries for a sample of five years. If alpha is 1 percent, what conclusion can you draw regarding a comparison of means?

England	Mexico	Canada	France
1.5	2.5	0.9	0.8
1.6	2.6	1.1	0.6
1.8	2.7	0.8	0.8
1.7	2.9	1.1	0.7
1.6	2.5	0.9	0.9

35. Use both Tukey and LSD to make pairwise comparisons on the results in the previous problem. Complete with common underscoring.

36. A management consulting firm tests three different methods of decision making by comparing the amount of time required by management teams using each of these methods to complete financial projects. Based on the data shown here, does it appear that the method of decision making affects the time needed to complete the project? Set alpha at 10 percent. Times are measured in days to completion of the project.

	Method		
Management Team	1	2	3
1	40	37	43
2	31	31	32
3	27	49	43
4	52	28	44
5	63	37	32
6	57	27	37

37. As director of advertising for your firm, you wish to compare the effectiveness of various advertising formats. Three advertisements are shown to several shoppers, who subsequently rate them on a scale of 10 to 50. The results are shown here. Which advertisement(s) would you choose, if any, over the others for mass distribution? Set $\alpha = 0.10$. Summarize the results with common underscoring.

	Advertisements		
Shopper	1	2	3
1	45	40	30
2	40	30	35
3	35	30	30
4	35	35	30
5	40	40	35
6	35	25	30
7	30	25	30

38. An informal survey of students' dating habits was taken at a state university. The results, which record the number of dates per month, are shown here. At the 5 percent level, does there appear to be any difference by class in frequency of dates? If so, use both the Tukey approach and LSD to determine which are different. Summarize the results with common underscoring.

	Class			
Student	Fr	So	Ju	Sr
1	2	2	3	4
2	2	0	5	2
3	1	2	6	5
4	2	6	4	3
5	0	4	3	3
6	3	4	6	4

39. As the wave of hostile takeovers reached a frenzy in the late 1980s, many corporations reported the use of "poison pills" to make themselves less attractive to other firms looking for prospective acquisitions. The pills were actions taken to discourage a takeover, and included debt-retirement plans, stock-option policies, and golden parachutes for retiring executives, all of which were unfavorable to the acquiring firm. An informed study designed to measure the comparable effects of these three actions recorded changes in stock prices of several firms that used them. The data are shown here. At the 5 percent level, does it appear some pills are more effective at lowering firms' stock prices?

Firm	Debt Retirement Plans	Stock Options	Golden Parachutes
1	−1.55	−2.10	0.20
2	−2.54	−3.20	−1.10
3	−3.55	−1.47	1.55
4	−2.10	1.01	−1.25
5	1.50	−3.55	2.10
6	−2.17	−2.99	1.20

40. Using data from the previous problem, which pill(s) would you recommend to your board of directors if they desired to reduce stock prices to make your firm less attractive? Set $\alpha = 0.05$. Display the appropriate common underscoring.

41. A national firm marketing tanning lotion randomly selects five people to test three tanning formulas. Each lotion is applied to different parts of the body on all test subjects. After a designated time in the sun, the tanning factor is measured using a scale developed by a noted dermatologist.

	Tanning Formulas		
Test Subjects	Tan Your Hide	Burn Not	Tanfastic
1	3	4	5
2	5	4	4
3	4	3	4
4	4	5	3
5	3	2	4

Set $\alpha = 0.01$ and determine whether any formula promotes tanning more than the others. If so, identify which ones. Given the test subjects' differences in natural tanning ability, test to determine whether blocking is needed.

42. A taxicab company is attempting to construct a route system that will minimize the time spent driving to certain locations. Four routes are under revision. You are hired as a statistical consultant to assist. Five cabbies drive each of the routes and record their times in minutes. At the 5 percent level, can you identify which route(s) is (are) quicker? Should you block on driver? Which route(s) would you advise the company to use?

	Route			
Cabbie	1	2	3	4
1	12	15	17	13
2	18	18	18	17
3	10	11	15	9
4	13	12	12	15
5	18	14	12	15

43. Four quality control inspectors have just completed a training course. Each inspects the same 5 units of finished product and is asked to rate them. At the 5 percent level, does it seem the inspectors assign the same average ratings?

	Inspector			
Product	Fred	Sam	Terri	Minerva
1	55	45	52	51
2	87	86	78	82
3	69	68	67	62
4	75	71	72	68
5	69	71	75	68

44. A local consumer group is interested in determining whether stores in different localities throughout the city offer the same prices for food. A sample market basket of five items was priced at three locations in the city. At the 1 percent level, does it seem that prices on the average are the same for all three locations?

	Location		
Product	**Midtown**	**Suburb**	**Outlying**
1	2.92	3.15	4.35
2	1.21	1.32	1.10
3	5.12	4.79	5.20
4	0.98	1.00	0.98
5	1.50	1.45	1.50

45. The owner of Stop & Shop has tried four different check cashing policies to reduce the large number of bad checks his stores receive. He wants to know which policy, if any, minimizes the problem. Since the area of town in which a store is located may affect the number of bad checks, records are kept for the daily number of checks returned for insufficient funds under each policy at all five store locations. The results are shown here. Set alpha at 1 percent. Is one policy better than another?

	Policy			
Location	**A**	**B**	**C**	**D**
1	22	35	47	43
2	27	28	31	47
3	20	17	15	12
4	18	20	23	17
5	15	18	18	19

46. D. Bumstead works as an advertising agent for Dithers & Company. Mr. Bumstead must determine whether three different advertising announcements evoke the same response from viewers. Sensing that time of day might influence attitudes, Mr. Bumstead wisely chooses to test each announcement at the same three time periods during a 24-hour period. Do the results shown below tell Mr. Bumstead that a difference exists in mean viewer ratings? Assume an alpha value of 1 percent.

	Announcement		
Time Period	**A**	**B**	**C**
Morning	10	15	12
Afternoon	2	2	3
Evening	2	1	2

47. Bantam Books uses three different printing techniques. A quality control study found excessive printing errors such as smudges, overprints, blurred type, and some pages were even left blank. To determine whether there is a difference in the mean number of errors based on printing method, a certain passage was printed using each method on the four different types of paper Bantam uses. Do the results indicate one or more of the methods are better? Set alpha at 5 percent.

	Printing Method		
Type of Paper	**A**	**B**	**C**
W	2	1	1
X	3	3	2
Y	5	6	3
Z	4	4	4

Computer Exercise

Given your considerable experience in the investment industry, you decide to establish your own brokerage company. Your first task is to compare the mean returns of three different industries. Access the file ANOVA from your data disk. The first column of data ("Rate") is the growth rate for several companies in the three industries you wish to examine. The second column ("Ind") identifies each industry and is encoded as a 1 for the electronics industry, a 2 for the insurance industry, and a 3 for the banking industry.

You also want to compare the mean returns of different investors based on the size of their investment. The third column of the data set is the rate of return ("ROR") investors have earned over the past year. The fourth column identifies the size of the investment as small, medium, and large encoded as 1, 2, and 3, respectively. You also feel it necessary to correct for the level of activity in the account in comparing mean returns of different size investment. Therefore, the fifth column is encoded 1 through 5 to distinguish between the less actively traded accounts and those that exhibit a greater level of activity. The higher the coded value, the more actively the account is traded.

Prepare all the necessary analysis and present your findings in the form of a statistical report, as discussed in Appendix I.

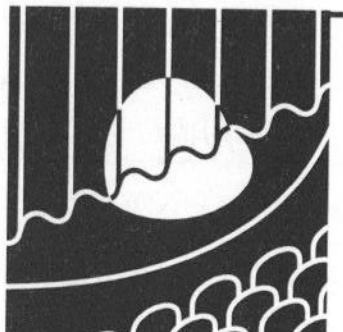

CURTAIN CALL

John S. Mill recently received a research-oriented master's degree in economics and for the last 18 months has been working with the Central Intelligence Agency as an economic analyst. He accompanied the U.S. delegation to Denver for the G-7 talks mentioned in "Setting the Stage" at the beginning of this chapter. His current project is to search for identifying characteristics that might serve as predictors of future political turmoil within a foreign country. Once those factors have been isolated, countries exhibiting such tendencies will be targeted for further study and analysis.

John's economic background has taught him that nations with high unemployment and other unfavorable economic conditions are often more likely to suffer political unrest. The Data Analysis Division of the CIA provides John with unemployment figures and inflation rates for several countries in four areas worldwide. These values are shown here with the unemployment rate first and the rate of inflation second. Thus, an entry such as "17.5% & 20.2%" means the country had an unemployment rate of 17.5 percent and an inflation rate of 20.2 percent.

Country	Middle East	Eastern Europe	Far East	Central America
1	17.5% & 20.2%	10.2% & 8.2%	18.1% & 9.7%	27.8% & 50.2%
2	16.1% & 10.2%	8.4% & 7.3%	30.2% & 17.5%	39.7% & 40.3%
3	12.5% & 8.7%	7.2% & 6.3%	25.3% & 21.2%	37.8% & 47.3%
4	15.2% & 17.1%	7.5% & 5.3%	19.7% & 10.2%	42.1% & 80.7%
5	22.3% & 18.7%	9.2% & 6.1%	21.3% & —	37.0% & 38.9%
6	18.3% & 23.7%	10.7% & —	22.0% & —	48.0% & 73.1%
7	19.2% & —	17.1% & —	24.1% & —	38.7% & 63.2%

The agency has budgeted $4.7 million for the acquisition of additional intelligence-gathering equipment over the next several months. John must prepare a report indicating roughly how these funds should be allocated. How can John use these data in the decision-making process regarding proper allocation of the money? John's superiors have warned him that, at all costs, he must avoid rejecting the hypothesis of no significant differences in these countries if indeed none exists.

From the Stage to Real Life

Yes, the CIA does have a public Internet site (www.odci.gov/cia). When you visit this site, you will need to click on a "continue" area to get to the features page. There, select "Publications," and then select the "World Fact Book." In this area, you will find similar information to that used in the "Curtain Call" analysis. This site provides unemployment, inflation, and GDP data by country for most countries around the globe. By clicking on either "all countries" or on particular regions, look up the most current data on these three economic indicators for each of the 10 countries in the table in the chapter opening "Setting the Stage." Note that the data available at this site is about two years behind current times and that only one year's data is provided.

Alternatively, international data on key economic indicators that are up to date, and provide the most current three years of data, are available from the U.S. State Department (www.state.gov). This economic summary information is part of comprehensive business research reports on individual countries. For your choice of three of the 10 countries listed in the chapter opening "Setting the Stage," look up the economic summary data provided at this site. At the U.S. State Department Home Page, select "Services." Scroll down to the heading Business, and then click on "Country Commercial Guides." Next select a geographic region, and then select a country of interest. In the country's commercial profile, scroll down to Section X: Appendices to find summary information on the domestic economy. As you scroll through this report, make notes on the other major sections of these profiles.

If you were doing comparative international research, which of the sites, the CIA or the U.S. State Department, would be your first choice and why?

CHAPTER 11

Simple Regression and Correlation

Chapter Blueprint

This chapter examines two of the most important and useful tools of statistical analysis: regression and correlation. These powerful techniques illustrate the manner in which relationships between two variables can be analyzed to predict future events.

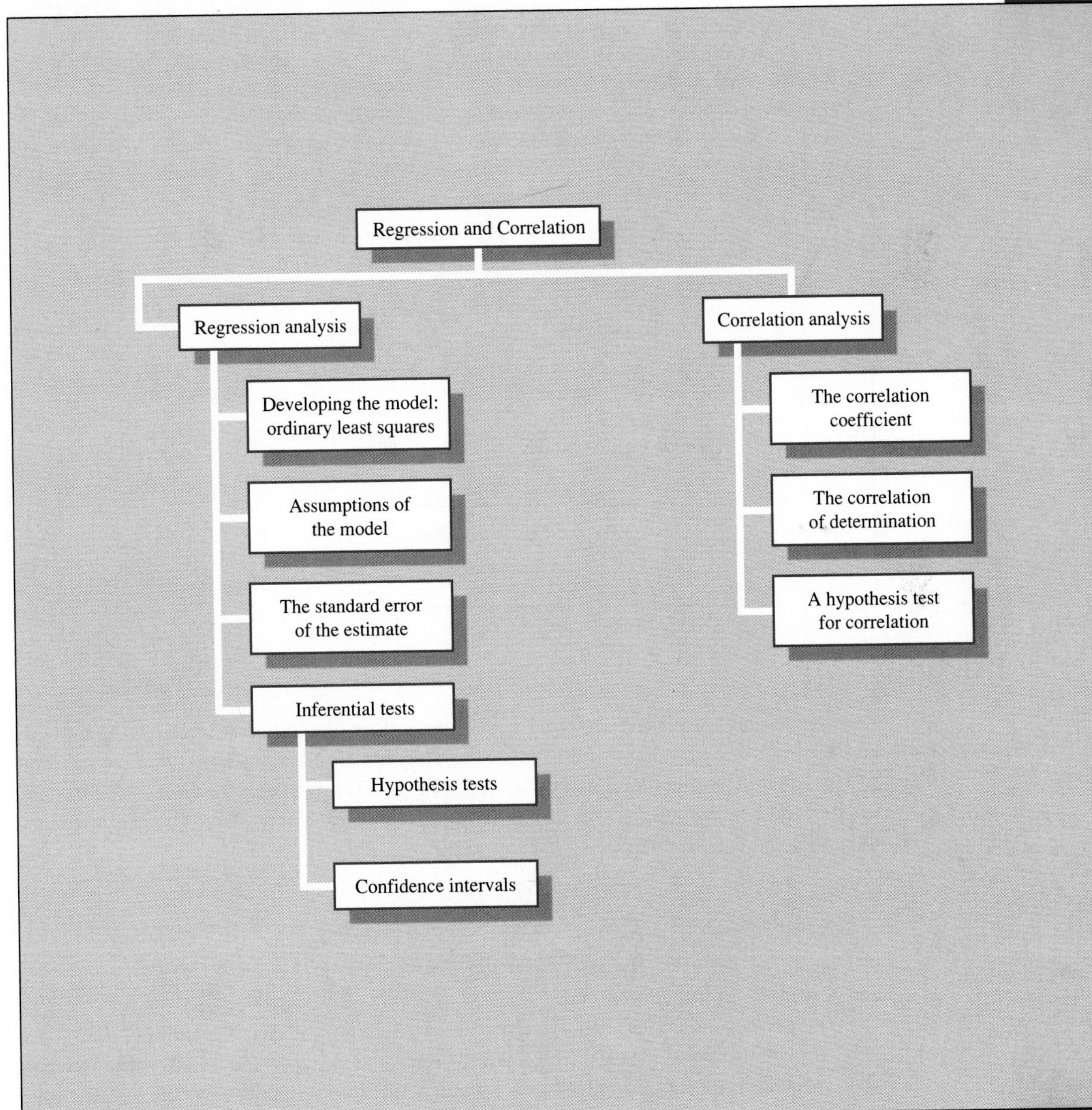

SETTING THE STAGE

Competition in the soft-drink industry has always been intense. Recently, the struggle between Coca-Cola and Pepsi-Cola to increase their respective shares of the \$27 billion domestic soft-drink market has been particularly heated. Each company has offered its own brand of promotional flair in a continual effort to reorder its marketing mix and promote its respective product. Coke currently enjoys a 21.7 percent market share, with Pepsi close behind at 18.9 percent.

No doubt marketing executives, management specialists, and statisticians alike are hard at work for both companies, trying to surpass their competitive-minded counterparts. So far they have agreed on very little other than that sales seem to increase with soaring summer temperatures.

Predicting trends in market share is a particularly difficult and hazardous task. Many executives have lost careers in the frustrating attempt to correctly anticipate the behavior of fickle consumers.

Regression and correlation analysis are two of the most powerful and useful tools analysts of all types have at their disposal to peer into the murky future. In this chapter we will examine these statistical procedures and learn how they can lead business professionals down a successful career path.

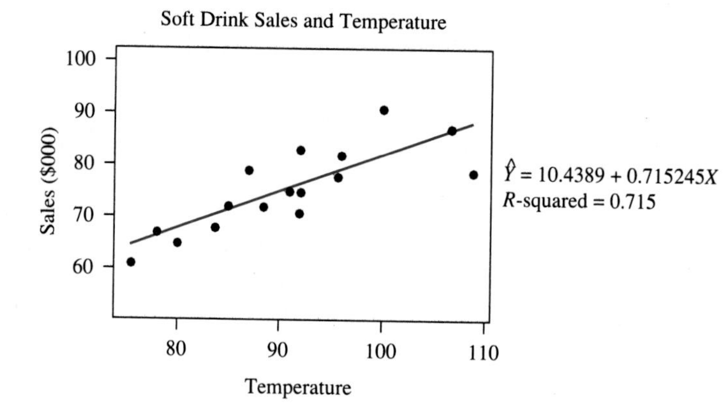

11.1 Introduction

Regression and correlation are two of the most powerful and versatile statistical tools we can use to solve common business problems. They are based on the belief that we can identify and quantify some functional relationship between two or more variables. One variable is said to depend on another. We might say Y depends on X where Y and X are any two variables. This may be written as

Y is a function of X.	$Y = f(X)$	[11.1]

and is read "Y is a function of X."

Since Y depends on X, Y is the **dependent variable** and X is the **independent variable.** It is important to identify which is the dependent variable and which is the independent variable in the regression model. This depends on logic and what the statistician is trying to measure. The dean of the college wishes to examine the relationship between students' grades and the time they spend studying. Data are collected on both variables. It is only logical to presume that grades depend on the amount of quality time students spend with the books! Thus, "grades" is the dependent variable and "time" is the independent variable.

Dependent variable The variable we wish to explain or predict; also called the *regressand* or *response variable.*

The independent variable X is used to explain Y.

Independent variable The independent variable is also called the *explanatory variable* or the *regressor.*

It is said that "Y is regressed on X."

Regression analysis was first developed by the English scientist Sir Francis Galton (1822–1911). His earliest experiments with regression began with an analysis of the hereditary growth patterns of sweet peas. Encouraged by the results, Sir Francis extended his study to include the hereditary patterns in the heights of adult humans. He found that children who have unusually tall or short parents tended to "regress" back toward the average height of the adult population. With this humble beginning, regression analysis exploded into one of the most powerful statistical tools at our disposal.

We should distinguish between simple regression and multiple regression. In **simple regression,** Y is said to be a function of only one independent variable. Often referred to as *bivariate* regression because there are only two variables, one dependent and one independent, simple regression is represented by Formula (11.1). In a **multiple regression** model, Y is a function of two or more independent variables. A regression model with k independent variables can be expressed as

In a multiple regression model Y is a function of two or more independent variables.

$$Y = f(X_1, X_2, X_3, \ldots, X_k) \qquad [11.2]$$

where $X_1, X_2, X_3, \ldots, X_k$ are independent variables used to explain Y.

A distinction must also be made between linear regression and curvilinear (nonlinear) regression. In a **linear regression** model, the relationship between X and Y can be represented by a straight line. It holds that as X changes, Y changes by a constant amount. **Curvilinear regression** uses a curve to express the relationship between X and Y. It maintains that as X changes, Y changes by a *different* amount each time.

Some of these relationships are depicted in Figure 11.1 showing **scatter diagrams** that plot the paired observations for X and Y. It is customary to put the independent variable on the horizontal axis. Figure 11.1(a) suggests a linear and positive relationship between X and Y. It is positive because X and Y seems to move in the same direction. As X goes up (down), Y goes up (down). It is linear because the relationship can be defined by the straight line drawn through the scatter points. Figure 11.1(b) shows a linear and negative relationship between X and Y because the two variables seem to move in opposite directions. Figure 11.1(c) and 11.1(d) indicate curvilinear relationships. The pattern of

Figure 11.1
Scatter Diagrams

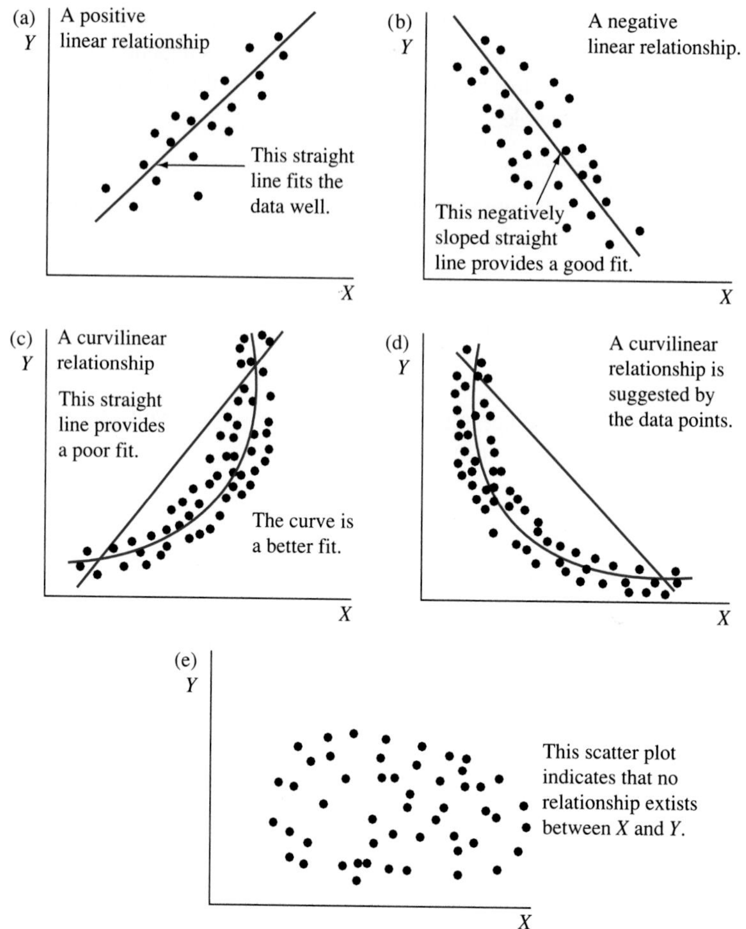

scatter points is not well described by the straight line, but is more accurately defined by the curve which provides a much better fit. Finally, it is difficult to observe any relationship between X and Y in Figure 11.1(e). The absence of any detectable pattern suggests that no relationship exists between X and Y.

Linear and Curvilinear Relationships If X and Y are related in a linear manner, then, as X changes, Y changes by a constant amount. If a curvilinear relationship exists, Y will change by a different amount as X changes.

11.2 Determining the Simple Linear Regression Model

Our interest throughout this chapter will focus on simple linear regression. Only two points are needed to draw the straight line representing this linear relationship. The formula for a straight line can be expressed as

Formula for a straight line. $$Y = b_0 + b_1X \qquad [11.3]$$

where b_0 is the vertical intercept and b_1 is the slope of the line. If we find, for example, that

$$Y = 5 + 2X$$

then, as seen in Figure 11.2, the line intersects the vertical axis at 5. Furthermore, the slope of the line is found as

$$b_1 = \text{slope} = \frac{\text{vertical change}}{\text{horizontal change}} = \frac{2}{1} = 2$$

For every one-unit change in X, Y changes by two units.

Notice that as X increases from 2 to 3 (a one-unit increase), Y increases from 9 to 11 (a two-unit increase). Figure 11.3(a) shows a graph in which $b_1 < 0$ such as

$$Y = 10 - 3X$$

It reveals that a negative relationship exists between X and Y such that for every one unit increase (decrease) in X, Y will decrease (increase) by 3 units. If the slope of the line is $b_1 = 0$ as in Figure 11.3(b), then a change of X has no relationship with a change in Y. Thus, X cannot be used as an explanatory variable for Y.

Relationships between variables are either **deterministic** or **stochastic** (random). A deterministic relationship can be expressed by the formula that converts speed in miles per hour (mph) into kilometers per hour (kph). Since 1 mile equals approximately 1.6 kilometers, this model is 1 mph = 1.6 kph. Thus, a speed of 5 mph = 5(1.6) kph = 8.0 kph. This is a deterministic model because the relationship is exact and there is no error (except for rounding).

Figure 11.2
A Straight Line with a Positive Slope

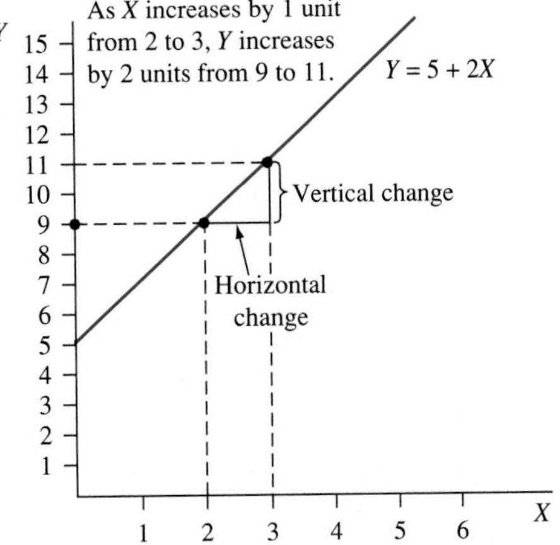

Figure 11.3
Graphing Straight Lines

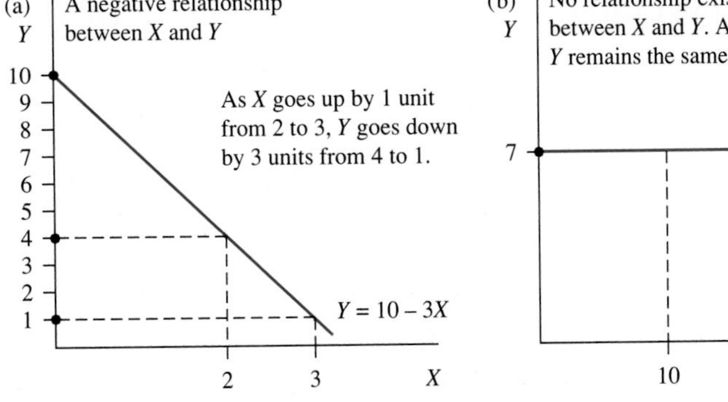

Unfortunately, few relationships in the business world are that exact. We often find that, in using one variable to explain another, there is some variation in the relationship. Presume, for example, that the management of Vita+Plus, Inc., distributors of health products, wants to develop a regression model in which advertising is used to explain sales revenues. They will likely find that when advertising is set at a certain amount, X_i, sales will take on some value, Y_i. However, the next time advertising is set equal to that same amount, sales may very well be some other value. The dependent variable (sales, in this case) exhibits some degree of randomness. Thus, there will be some *error* in our attempt to explain or predict sales. A model of this nature is said to be stochastic due to the presence of random variation, and can be expressed as

A linear model.	$Y = \beta_0 + \beta_1 X + \varepsilon$	[11.4]

Formula (11.4) is the population (or true) relationship when we regress Y on X. Further, $\beta_0 + \beta_1(X)$ is the deterministic portion of the relationship, while ε (the Greek epsilon) represents the randomness displayed by the dependent variable and therefore denotes the error term in the expression. The parameters β_0 and β_1, like most parameters, will remain unknown and can be estimated only with sample data. This is expressed as

A linear model based on sample data.	$Y = b_0 + b_1 X + e$	[11.5]

where b_0 and b_1 are the estimates of β_0 and β_1, respectively, and e is the random term. Customarily referred to as the *residual* when using sample data, e recognizes that not all observations fall exactly on a straight line. If we knew the exact value of e, we could calculate Y precisely. However, since e is random, Y can only be estimated. Our regression model therefore takes the form

The estimated regression model.	$\hat{Y} = b_0 + b_1 X$	[11.6]

where $\hat{Y}$ (read Y-hat) is the *estimated* value of Y, and b_0 and b_1 are the intercept and slope of the estimated regression line. That is, $\hat{Y}$ is merely the estimated value for sales based on the regression model.

11.3 Ordinary Least Squares: The Line of Best Fit

The purpose of regression analysis is to identify a line that fits the sample data better than any other line that can be drawn. To illustrate, presume that Vita+Plus, Inc. collects data for advertising expenditures and sales revenue for 5 months, as shown in Table 11.1.

Table 11.1
Sales Data for Vita+Plus, Inc.

Month	Sales ($000s)	Advertising ($00s)
1	$450	$50
2	380	40
3	540	65
4	500	55
5	420	45

Figure 11.4
Data for Vita + Plus, Inc.

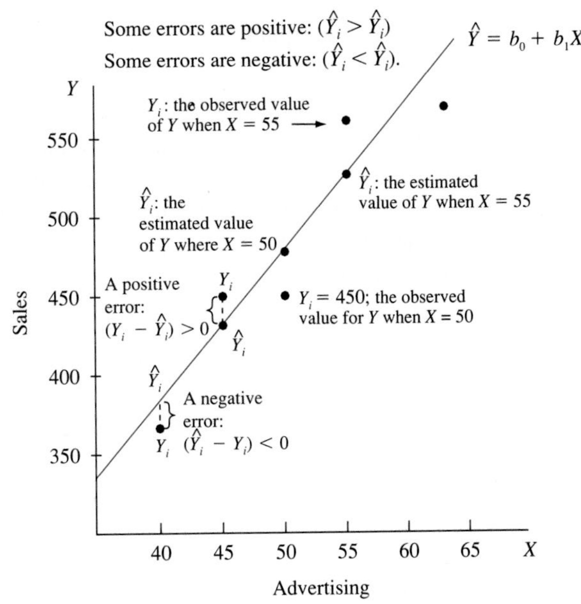

Although a sample of only 5 data points would most likely be insufficient, it will serve our purposes for the moment.

These five data points and the line that best fits them are shown in Figure 11.4. This line is determined by calculating b_0 and b_1. The mathematical procedure used to calculate these values is called **ordinary least squares (OLS)**. OLS will produce a line that extends through the middle of the scatter diagram coming closer to all the data points than any other line. Return to Figure 11.4. The 5 data points, Y_i, in the scatter diagram are the actual, observed data values for Y in Table 11.1. The $\hat{Y}$ values are provided by the regression line and represent our estimate of sales. The difference between what Y actually was, Y_i, and what we estimate it to be, $\hat{Y}_i$, is our error.

The error term is the is the difference between the actual values of Y (Y_i), and our estimate of Y ($\hat{Y}_i$).	Error $= (Y_i - \hat{Y}_i)$	[11.7]

If the actual value of Y, Y_i, is greater than our estimate, then $(Y_i > \hat{Y}_i)$ and the error is positive. This is the case in Figure 11.4, where advertising is 55. Conversely, if we overestimate sales, then $(Y_i < \hat{Y}_i)$ and the error is negative. This occurs where advertising is 50. Since some of the errors are negative and some are positive, OLS will produce a line such that the sum of these errors is zero:

$$\Sigma(Y_i - \hat{Y}_i) = 0$$

OLS will also insure that the sum of these squared errors is minimized. That is, if we take all five vertical differences between the actual values of Y and the regression line, $(Y_i - \hat{Y}_i)$, square these vertical differences, and sum them up, the resulting number will be smaller than what we would get if we did this with any other line. That is, OLS will minimize the *sum of the squared errors*. That is why it is called ordinary least squares; it produces a line such that the sum of squared errors is less than it would be with any other line. See Formula [11.8].

The sum of the squared errors is minimized.	$\Sigma(Y_i - \hat{Y}_i)^2 = \text{min}$	[11.8]

where $(Y_i - \hat{Y}_i)$ is the error for each data point and *min* is the minimum value.

To determine this *line of best fit,* OLS requires that we calculate the *sum of the squares and cross-products*. That is, we must compute the sum of the squared X values (SSx), the sum of the squared Y values (SSy) and the sum of X times Y ($SSxy$). These are shown as Formulas (11.9) through (11.11).

Sum of the squares for X.	$SSx = \Sigma(X_i - \overline{X})^2 = \Sigma X^2 - \dfrac{(\Sigma X)^2}{n}$	[11.9]

Sum of the squares for Y.	$SSy = \Sigma(Y_i - \overline{Y})^2 = \Sigma Y^2 - \dfrac{(\Sigma Y)^2}{n}$	[11.10]

and

Sum of the cross-products of X and Y.	$SSxy = \Sigma(X_i - \overline{X})(Y_i - \overline{Y}) = \Sigma XY - \dfrac{(\Sigma X)(\Sigma Y)}{n}$	[11.11]

Notice that the first portions of each of these formulas,

$$SSx = \Sigma(X_i - \overline{X})^2$$
$$SSy = \Sigma(Y_i - \overline{Y})^2$$

and

$$SSxy = \Sigma(X_i - \overline{X})(Y_i - \overline{Y})$$

illustrate how the OLS line is indeed based on the deviations of the observations from their mean. SSx, for example, is found by (1) calculating the amount by which each of the observations for $X(X_i)$ deviates from their mean ($\overline{X}$), (2) squaring those deviations, and (3) summing those squared deviations. However, these computations are quite tedious when done by hand. We will therefore generally use the second portion of each of these formulas in our calculations.

Given the sums of squares and cross-products, it is then a simple matter to calculate the slope of the regression line, called the *regression coefficient,* and the intercept as

The slope of the regression line.	$b_1 = \dfrac{SSxy}{SSx}$	[11.12]

and

The vertical intercept of the regression line.	$b_0 = \bar{Y} - b_1\bar{X}$	[11.13]

where $\bar{Y}$ and $\bar{X}$ are the means of the Y-values and the X-values.

A word of caution: These calculations are extremely sensitive to rounding. This is particularly true for the calculation of the coefficient of determination, which is demonstrated later in this chapter. You are therefore advised in the interest of accuracy to carry out your calculations to five or six decimal places.

Section Exercises

1. What is the difference between simple regression and multiple regression?

2. What is the difference between linear regression and curvilinear regression? In what way does Y change when X changes in each case?

3. Distinguish between the stochastic and the random components of a regression model.

4. Why is the ordinary least squares method of determining the regression model called "ordinary least squares"? What role does the error play in this analysis?

5. Identify the dependent and the independent variable in each of these cases

a. Time spent working on a term paper and the grade received.
b. Height of the son and height of the father.
c. A woman's age and the cost of her life insurance.
d. Price of a product and the number of units sold.
e. Demand for a product and the number of consumers in the market.

6. Given the following data for X and Y:

$$X \quad 28, 54, 67, 37, 41, 69, 76$$
$$Y \quad 14, 21, 36, 39, 18, 54, 52$$

a. Construct a scatter diagram for the data.
b. What do the data suggest about a relationship between X and Y?
c. Draw a straight line to approximate the relationship.

7. What is the difference between $\hat{Y}_i$ and Y_i in regression analysis?

8. What is the ε (epsilon) term in the regression model and why does it occur?

11.4 An Example Using OLS

The management of Hop Scotch Airlines, the world's smallest air carrier, believes that there is a direct relationship between advertising expenditures and the number of passengers who choose to fly Hop Scotch. To determine whether this relationship does exist and, if so, what its exact nature might be, the statisticians employed by Hop Scotch set out to use OLS procedures to determine the regression model.

Monthly values for advertising expenditures and numbers of passengers are collected for the $n = 15$ most recent months. The data are shown in Table 11.2, along with other calculations necessary to compute the regression model. You will note that *passengers* is labelled as the Y-variable since it is assumed to depend on advertising.

With this simple set of data, and the subsequent computations for XY, X^2, and Y^2, it is an easy task to determine the regression model by calculating values for the regression

Table 11.2
Regression Data for Hop Scotch Airlines

Observation (Months)	Advertising (in \$1,000's) (X)	Passengers (in 1,000's) (Y)	XY	X^2	Y^2
1	10	15	150	100	225
2	12	17	204	144	289
3	8	13	104	64	169
4	17	23	391	289	529
5	10	16	160	100	256
6	15	21	315	225	441
7	10	14	140	100	196
8	14	20	280	196	400
9	19	24	456	361	576
10	10	17	170	100	289
11	11	16	176	121	256
12	13	18	234	169	324
13	16	23	368	256	529
14	10	15	150	100	225
15	12	16	192	144	256
	187	268	3,490	2,469	4,960

constant and the regression coefficient in the regression line $\hat{Y} = b_0 + b_1X$. The sums of squares and cross-products are

$$SSx = \Sigma X^2 - \frac{(\Sigma X)^2}{n}$$

$$= 2{,}469 - \frac{(187)^2}{15}$$

$$= 137.7333333$$

$$SSy = \Sigma Y^2 - \frac{(\Sigma Y)^2}{n}$$

$$= 4{,}960 - \frac{(268)^2}{15}$$

$$= 171.733333$$

$$SSxy = \Sigma XY - \frac{(\Sigma X)(\Sigma Y)}{n}$$

$$= 3{,}490 - \frac{(187)(268)}{15}$$

$$= 148.933333$$

Using Formula (11.12) the regression coefficient can be calculated as

$$b_1 = \frac{SSxy}{SSx}$$

$$= \frac{148.933333}{137.733333}$$

$$= 1.0813166 \text{ or } 1.08$$

Since

$$\bar{Y} = \frac{\Sigma Y}{n} = \frac{268}{15} = 17.86667$$

and

$$\bar{X} = \frac{\Sigma X}{n} = \frac{187}{15} = 12.46667$$

Formula (11.13) reveals the intercept to be

$$\begin{aligned} b_0 &= \bar{Y} - b_1\bar{X} \\ &= 17.866667 - 1.08(12.46667) \\ &= 4.3865 \text{ or } 4.40 \end{aligned}$$

The regression model is then

$$\hat{Y}_i = 4.40 + 1.08X_i$$

where $\hat{Y}_i$ is the predicted individual value for passengers. Thus, if X_i is set equal to 10,

$$\hat{Y}_i = 4.40 + 1.08(10) = 15.2$$

Since both X and Y are expressed in thousands, this means that if \$10,000 is spent on advertising, the model predicts that 15,200 brave souls will choose to fly Hop Scotch Airlines. The coefficient of 1.08 means that for every one unit increase in X, Y will go up by 1.08 units. Thus, if advertising expenditures are increased by \$1,000, then 1,080 more passengers will board Hop Scotch airplanes.

$$\hat{Y}_i = 4.40 + 1.08(11) = 16.28$$

Figure 11.5 shows the regression line we have estimated. The intercept is seen to be 4.40 and a positive slope is indicated. Display 11.1 is a partial Minitab printout. The intercept, or constant as Minitab calls it, is 4.3863 and the coefficient for advertising is 1.08. We will examine some of the other statistics shown on the printout shortly. The fitted line is shown in Minitab Display 11.2. Notice that the line goes through the middle of the scatter diagram.

Figure 11.5
The Regression Line for Hop Scotch Airlines

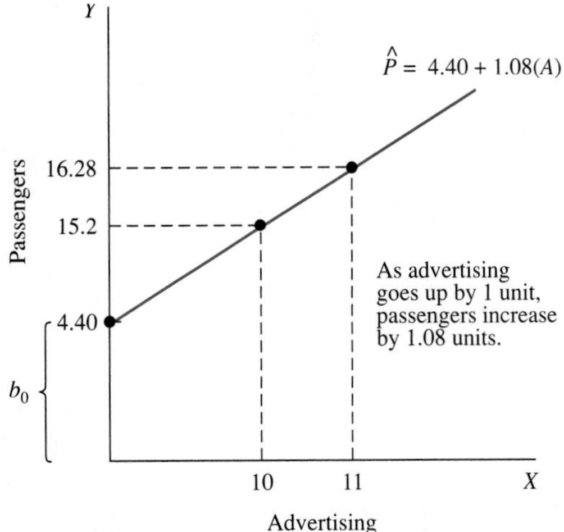

Minitab Display 11.1

```
Regression Analysis
The regression equation is
PASS = 4.39 + 1.08 ADV

Predictor        Coef       Stdev     t-ratio       P
Constant       4.3863      0.9913        4.42   0.001
ADV           1.08132     0.07726       13.99   0.000

s = 0.9068        R-sq = 93.8%        R-sq(adj) = 93.3%
```

Minitab Display 11.2

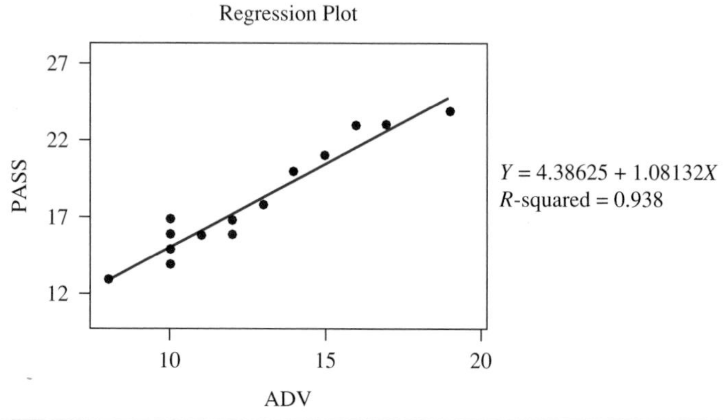

Section Exercises

9. The job placement center at State University wants to determine whether students' grade point averages (GPAs) can explain the number of job offers they receive upon graduation. The data seen here are for 10 recent graduates.

Student	1	2	3	4	5	6	7	8	9	10
GPA	3.25	2.35	1.02	0.36	3.69	2.65	2.15	1.25	3.88	3.37
Offers	3	3	1	0	5	4	2	2	6	2

a. Construct a scatter diagram for the data.
b. Compute and interpret the regression model. What does this model tell you about the relationship between GPA and job offers?
c. If Steve has a GPA of 3.22, how many job offers would you predict he will receive?

10. An economist for the Florida State Department of Human Resources is preparing a study on consumer behavior. He collects the data shown here in thousands of dollars to determine whether there is a relationship between consumer income and consumption levels. Determine which is the dependent variable.

Consumer	1	2	3	4	5	6	7	8	9	10	11	12
Income	24.3	12.5	31.2	28.0	35.1	10.5	23.2	10.0	8.5	15.9	14.7	15
Consumption	16.2	8.5	15	17	24.2	11.2	15	7.1	3.5	11.5	10.7	9.2

a. Construct a scatter diagram for the data.
b. Compute and interpret the regression model. What does this model tell you about the relationship between consumption and income? What proportion of every additional dollar earned is spent for consumption?
c. What consumption would the model predict for someone who earns $27,500?

11. A bank in Atlanta specializing in housing loans intends to analyze the real estate market by measuring the explanatory power interest rates have on the number of houses sold in the area. Data are complied for a 10-month period, as follows:

Month	1	2	3	4	5	6	7	8	9	10
Interest	12.3	10.5	15.6	9.5	10.5	9.3	8.7	14.2	15.2	12
Houses	196	285	125	225	248	303	265	102	105	114

a. Construct a scatter diagram for the data.
b. Compute and interpret the regression model. What does this model tell you about the relationship between interest rates and housing sales?
c. If the interest rate is 9.5 percent, how many houses would be sold according to the model?

12. Overland Group produces truck parts used in large semitrailers. The chief accountant wants to develop a regression model that can be used to predict costs. He selects units of output produced as a predictor variable and collects the data seen here. Costs are in thousands of dollars and units are in hundreds.

Units	12.3	8.3	6.5	4.8	14.6	14.6	14.6	6.5
Cost	6.2	5.3	4.1	4.4	5.2	4.8	5.9	4.2

a. Construct a scatter diagram for the data.
b. Compute and interpret the regression model. What does it tell the accountant about the relationship between output and costs?
c. According to the model, what would it cost to produce 750 units?

13. Professor Mundane has noticed many of his students have been absent from class this semester. He feels that he can explain this sluggish attendance by the distances his students live from campus. Eleven students are surveyed as to how many miles they must travel to attend class and the number of classes they have missed.

Miles	5	6	2	0	9	12	16	5	7	0	8
Misses	2	2	4	5	4	2	5	2	3	1	4

a. Construct a scatter diagram for the data.
b. Compute and interpret the regression model. What has the professor learned?
c. How many classes would you miss if you lived 3.2 miles from campus according to the model?

14. The management director for Bupkus, Inc. obtained data for 100 employees on the entrance tests taken at the time of hiring and the subsequent ratings the employees received from their supervisor one year later. The test scores range from 0 to 10 and the rating is on a 5-point system. The director intends to use the regression model to predict the rating (R) they will receive on the basis of the test score (S). The results are

$$\Sigma S = 522 \qquad \Sigma R = 326 \qquad \Sigma SR = 17{,}325$$

$$\Sigma S^2 = 28{,}854 \qquad \text{and} \qquad \Sigma R^2 = 10{,}781$$

Develop and interpret the regression model. What might the director predict as the rating of an employee who scored 7 on the test?

Note: Retain your computations from Exercises 9 through 14 for use throughout the rest of this chapter. By using the same data, you will avoid the need to calculate SSx, SSy, and $SSxy$ each time. You will gain additional experience with other problems at the end of the chapter.

11.5 Assumptions of the Linear Regression Model

To more fully understand the linear model we must examine the four basic assumptions upon which it is built.

Assumption 1: The error term ε is a normally distributed random variable.

As we noted earlier, if X is set equal to some given value many times, the resulting values of Y will vary. Note observations 1, 5, 7, 10, and 14 in Table 11.2. In each case $X = 10$. However, Y_i is different each time. Sometimes Y_i is above the regression line causing the error term $(Y_i - \hat{Y}_i)$ to be positive while at other times Y_i is less than $\hat{Y}_i$, creating a negative error. It is assumed that these error terms are random and are normally distributed around the population regression line. This is shown in Figure 11.6 for an X-value of 10.

Figure 11.6
The Normal Distribution of y-values Around the Unknown Population Regression Line

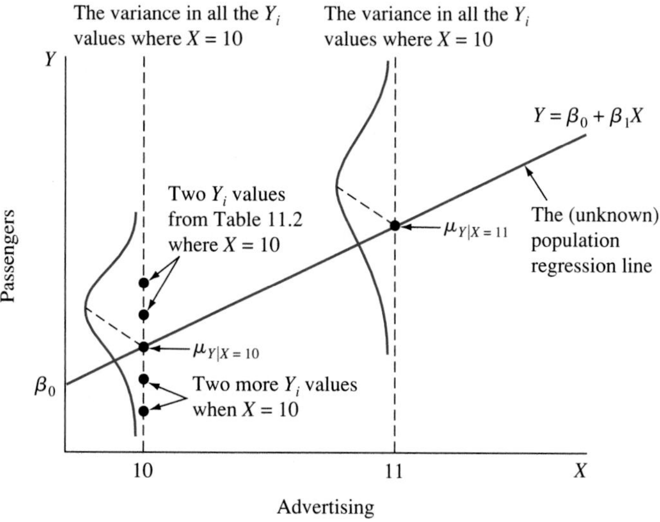

Since Y_i is different every time, the best our regression line can do is estimate the **mean** value of Y. Thus, the population regression line passes through the mean of those Y-values where $X = 10$. This point is indicated as $\mu_{Y|X=10}$ in Figure 11.6. There we see a normal distribution of the error terms above and below the regression line. The same would be true if we were to let $X = 11$ many times. There would result many *different* Y-values. These Y-values are normally distributed above and below the regression line which passes through the mean of those Y-values where $X = 11$, $\mu_{Y|x=11}$.

Assumption 2: Equal variances of the Y-values.

The OLS model assumes that the variance in the Y-values is the same for all values of X. This too is shown in Figure 11.6. The variation in the Y-values above and below the regression line where $X = 10$ is equal to the variation in the Y-values where $X = 11$. This is true for all values of X. This assumption is referred to *homoscedasticity*.

> **Homoscedasticity** The variances in the Y-values are the same at all values of X.

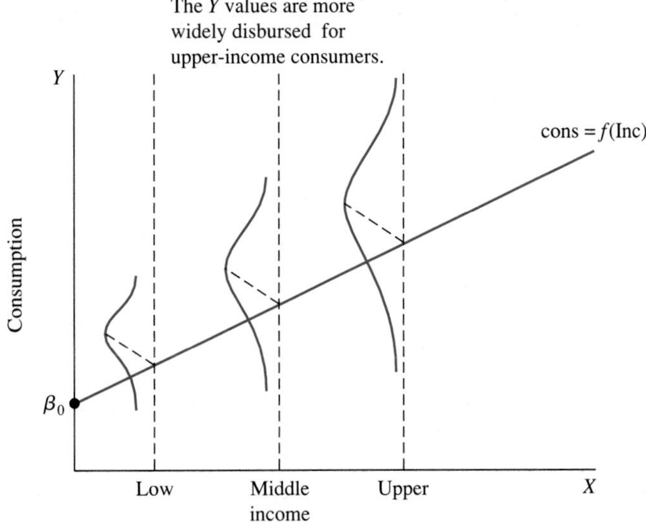

Figure 11.7 Heteroscadasticity in the Variance of the Y Values

Unfortunately, this assumption is often violated when we work with cross-sectional data. Presume, for example, that we wish to develop a regression model in which consumers' incomes are used to predict or explain their consumption expenditures, Cons $= f(\text{Inc})$. If we were to collect data on consumers in different income brackets for some given year we would be using cross-sectional data in that we included observations across different sections of the income strata; the poor, the average and the wealthy. As Figure 11.7 shows, we might find a very narrow range in the values for consumption at low levels of income, while for richer consumers, the variation in their consumption expenditures is much greater. The Y_i-values become more widely dispersed as income rises. This is called *heteroscedasticity.*

Assumption 3: The error terms are independent of each other.

OLS is based on the assumption that the error terms are independent of each other. The error term encountered for one value of Y_i is unrelated to the error term for any other value of Y_i. This hypothesis can be tested by examining a plot of the residuals from the sample data. If no pattern can be observed it may be assumed that the error terms are unrelated.

Minitab Display 11.3

Residual Data for Hop Scotch

ADV	PASS	Y-HAT	RESID
10	15	15.1994	-0.19942
12	17	17.3621	-0.36205
8	13	13.0368	-0.03679
17	23	22.7686	0.23137
10	16	15.1994	0.80058
15	21	20.6060	0.39400
10	14	15.1994	-1.19942
14	20	19.5247	0.47532
19	24	24.9313	-0.93127
10	17	15.1994	1.80058
11	16	16.2807	-0.28074
13	18	18.4434	-0.44337
16	23	21.6873	1.31268
10	15	15.1994	-0.19942
12	16	17.3621	-1.36205

(Continued)

Minitab Display 11.3 (Continued)

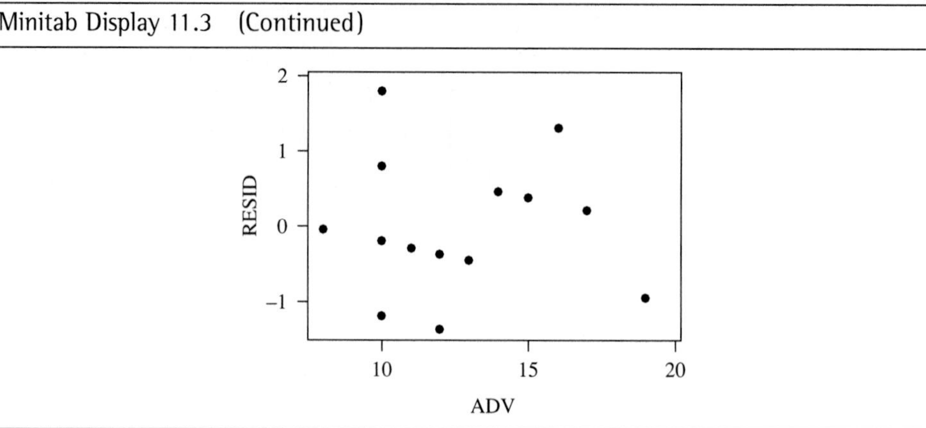

The residual plot and their values for the Hop Scotch data are shown in the Minitab Display 11.3. It is difficult to detect any discernible pattern. This suggests that the errors are indeed independent. Compare this to a residual plot that might appear as Figure 11.8(a). It is apparent that the residuals are not random and that they are clearly related. The pattern begins with several positive residuals, followed by several negative residuals, and then several positive residuals again. In contrast, if you were to flip a coin several times, would you get several heads followed by several tails and then several heads again? It is highly unlikely. While the coin flips are independent events, these residuals are not. They are somehow related. It can be said that the value of a residual is a function of the previous residual. A positive residual is more likely to be followed by another positive residual while a negative residual is associated with a second negative residual. Such a condition, which violates the assumption of independency of errors, is called **positive autocorrelation** because

Figure 11.8
Possible Residual Plots

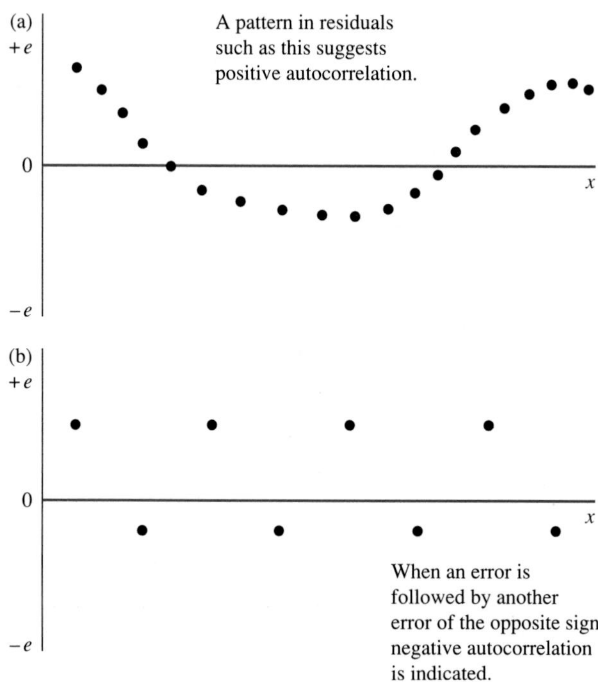

like signs are clustered together. **Negative autocorrelation** is depicted in Figure 11.8(b). Each residual is followed by a residual of an opposite sign. This pattern of alternating signs suggests that the error terms are not independent.

Autocorrelation occurs when the error terms are not independent.

Actually, residual plots are never as obvious or as easy to read as might be suggested by the plots above. Fortunately, there is a more reliable way to detect autocorrelation based on the **Durbin-Watson test.** Autocorrelation is most likely to occur in the use of *time-series* data in which, unlike the cross-sectional data discussed above, observations for some variable are collected over several time periods (weeks, months, years, etc.). For example, we might compile data for the monthly unemployment rate for several months. These data differ from cross-sectional data, which are collected for some specific point in time. The Durbin-Watson statistic is calculated as

The Durbin-Watson statistic. $$d = \frac{\Sigma(e_t - e_{t-1})^2}{\Sigma e_t^2} \qquad [11.14]$$

where e_t is the error in time period t and e_{t-1} is the error in the previous time period. Formula 11.14 (11.14) requires that the error term $(Y_i - \hat{Y}_i)$ be calculated for each time period and is quite difficult to compute by hand. A Minitab computer run revealed that the Durbin-Watson statistic for the Hop Scotch data is 2.48. This value is used to test the hypothesis that no correlation exists between successive error terms, as follows:

$$H_o: \rho_{e_t,e_{t-1}} = 0 \qquad \text{(No autocorrelation exists.)}$$

$$H_A: \rho_{e_t,e_{t-1}} \neq 0 \qquad \text{(Autocorrelation exists.)}$$

where ρ is the correlation coefficient for successive errors. The Durbin-Watson value is compared to critical values taken from Table K in Appendix III for either a 1 percent or a 5 percent level of significance. Suppose we choose an alpha value of 1%. Given that n = 15 and k, the number of independent variables is 1, the lower Durbin-Watson value is $d_L = 0.81$, and the upper Durbin-Watson value is $d_U = 1.07$. These values are then applied to the scale seen in Figure 11.9. If our Durbin-Watson value is less than $d_L = 0.81$, positive autocorrelation is suggested and the null hypothesis is rejected. If it is greater than $(4 - d_L) = 3.19$, negative autocorrelation is suggested and the null is rejected. If it is between $d_u = 1.07$ and $(4 - d_U) = 2.93$, the null is not rejected. If our Durbin-Watson value falls in either of the two remaining regions, the test is inconclusive. In our particular case, the Durbin-Watson value of 2.48 falls in the region of the scale indicating that autocorrelation does not exist and the null is not rejected. Generally speaking, if the Durbin-Watson value is close to 2, the null is not rejected.

Figure 11.9
A Durbin-Watson Test

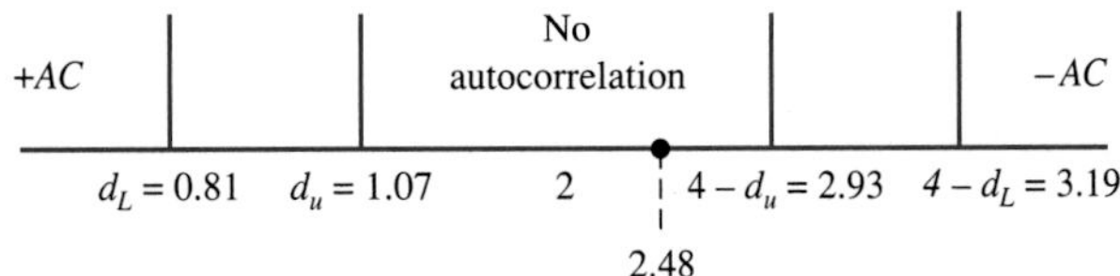

Assumption 4 The assumption of linearity.

As noted in Assumption 1, if X is set equal to some value many times, there will occur a normal distribution of Y-values. This distribution has a mean, $\mu_{Y|X}$. This is true for any value of X. OLS assumes that these means lie on a straight line, as suggested above in Figure 11.6.

Section Exercises

15. What is meant by *homoscedasticity* and *heteroscedasticity?* Draw appropriate graphs to illustrate these two terms.

16. What is meant by *autocorrelation?* Distinguish between *positive autocorrelation* and *negative autocorrelation*. Draw graphs depicting the two types.

17. Explain clearly how the Durbin-Watson test is used to test for autocorrelation. Include a discussion of the nature of the formula used to calculate the Durbin-Watson statistic.

18. What is the nature of the assumption of linearity on the OLS model?

11.6 The Standard Error of the Estimate: A Measure of Goodness-of-Fit

The regression line, as we have already noted, is often called the line of best fit. It fits, or depicts, the relationship between X and Y better than any other line. However, just because it provides the best fit, there is no guarantee that it is any good. We would like to be able to measure just how good our best fit is.

Actually, there are at least two such measures of goodness-of-fit: (1) the standard error of the estimate, and (2) the coefficient of determination. We will defer discussion of the latter concept until we examine correlation analysis later in the chapter. We embark on a description of the standard error of the estimate at this point.

The **standard error of the estimate,** Se, is a measure of the degree of dispersion of the Y_i-values around the regression line. It gauges the variation of the data points above and below the regression line. It reflects our tendency to depart from the actual value of Y when using our regression model for prediction purposes. In that sense, it is a measure of our "typical" error.

If all the data points fell on a perfectly straight line as in Figure 11.10(a), our regression line would pass through each one. In this rather fortunate case we would suffer no error in our forecasts, and the standard error of the estimate would be zero. However, data are seldom that cooperative. There is going to be some scatter in the data, as in Figure 11.10(b). The standard error of the estimate measures this average variation of the data points around

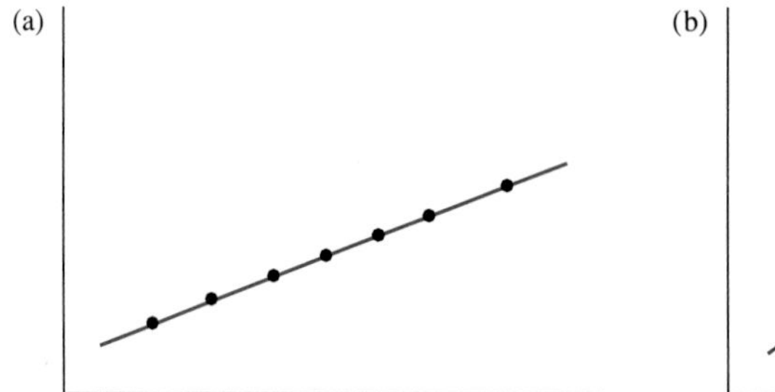

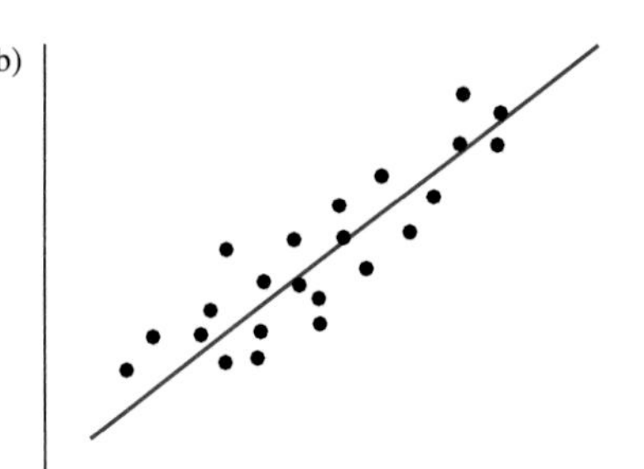

Figure 11.10 Possible Scatter Diagrams

the regression line we use to estimate Y and thus provides a measure of the error we will suffer in that estimation. Formula (11.15) illustrates this principle. Notice that the numerator reflects the difference between the actual values of Y, Y_i, and our estimate $\hat{Y}_i$:

The standard error of the estimate.	$Se = \sqrt{\frac{\Sigma(Y_i - \hat{Y}_i)^2}{n - 2}}$	[11.15]

Unfortunately, Formula (11.15) is computationally inconvenient. It is necessary to develop an easier method of hand calculation. Recall that σ^2 is the variance of the regression errors. One of the basic assumptions of the OLS model is that this variance in the errors around the regression line is the same for all values of X. The smaller the value for σ^2, the less is the dispersion of the data points around the line.

Since σ^2 is a parameter, it will likely remain unknown, and it is necessary to estimate its value with our sample data. An unbiased estimate of σ^2 is the mean square error (*MSE*). In our previous chapter on ANOVA, we learned that the *MSE* is the error sum of squares (*SSE*) divided by the degrees of freedom. In the context of regression analysis, *SSE* is

The sum of the squared errors.	$SSE = SSy - \frac{(SSxy)^2}{SSx}$	[11.16]

In a simple regression model, two constraints are placed on our data set since we must estimate two parameters, β_0 and β_1. There are, therefore, $n - 2$ degrees of freedom, and *MSE* is

The mean squared error.	$MSE = \frac{SSE}{n - 2}$	[11.17]

The standard error of the estimate is then

The standard error.	$Se = \sqrt{MSE}$	[11.18]

In our present case of Hop Scotch Airlines, we have

$$
\begin{aligned}
SSE &= SS_y - \frac{(SS_{xy})^2}{SS_x} \\
&= 171.7333 - \frac{(148.9333)^2}{137.73333} \\
&= 10.6893 \\
MSE &= \frac{10.6893}{15 - 2} \\
&= 0.82226 \\
S_e &= \sqrt{0.82226} \\
&= 0.90678 \text{ or } 0.907
\end{aligned}
$$

Minitab Display 11.4 shows the standard error to be 0.9068.

Minitab Display 11.4

```
Regression Analysis

The regression equation is
PASS = 4.39 + 1.08 ADV

Predictor        Coef        Stdev       t-ratio         p
Constant       4.3863       0.9913          4.42     0.001
ADV           1.08132      0.07726         13.99     0.000

s = 0.9068       R-sq = 93.8%        R-sq(adj)  = 93.3%

Analysis of Variance

SOURCE         DF         SS          MS        F         P
Regression      1     161.04      161.04   195.86     0.000
Error          13      10.69        0.82
Total          14     171.73

Unusual Observations
obs.       ADV        PASS        Fit Stdev.Fit    Residual    St.Resid
10        10.0      17.000     15.199     0.302       1.801       2.11R

R denotes an obs. with a large st. resid.

Durbin-Watson statistic = 2.48

     Fit  Stdev.Fit        95.0% C.I.            95.0% P.I.
  15.199      0.302    (  14.547,  15.852)  ( 13.134,  17.265)

MTB >
```

The standard error is always expressed in the same units as the dependent variable Y, thousands of passengers in this case. Thus, the standard error of 0.907, or 907 passengers, measures the variability of the Y-values around the fitted regression line.

The standard error of the estimate is quite similar to the standard deviation of a single variable that we examined in Chapter 3. If we were to collect data on the incomes for $n = 100$ people, we could easily calculate the standard deviation. This would provide us with a measure of dispersion of the income data around their mean.

In regression analysis we have two variables, X and Y. The standard error of the estimate is thus a measure of the dispersion of the Y-values around their mean, given any specific X-value.

Since the standard error of the estimate is similar to the standard deviation for a single variable, it can be interpreted similarly. Recall that the Empirical Rule states if the data are normally distributed, an interval of one standard deviation above the mean and one standard deviation below the mean will encompass 68.3 percent of all the observations; an interval of two standard deviations on each side of the mean contains 95.5 percent of the observations; and three standard deviations on each side of the mean encompass 99.7 percent of the observations.

The same can be said for the standard error of the estimate. In our present example, where $X = 10$,

$$\begin{aligned}\hat{Y}_i &= 4.4 + 1.08(10)\\ &= 15.2\end{aligned}$$

Remember, this value of 15.2 is the estimate of the mean value we would get for *Y* if we set *X* equal to 10 many times. To illustrate the meaning of the standard error of the estimate, locate the points that are one *Se* (that is, 0.907) above and below the mean value of 15.2. These points are 14.29 (15.2 − 0.907) and 16.11 (15.2 + 0.907). If we draw lines through each point parallel to the regression line as in Figure 11.11, approximately 68.3 percent of the data points will fall within these lines. The remaining 31.7 percent of the observations will be outside this interval. In our case, 68.3 percent of the times when $10,000 is spent on advertising, the number of passengers will be between 14,290 and 16,110. The remaining 31.7 percent of the time, the number of passengers will exceed 16,110 or be less than 14,290.

Figure 11.11
Standard Error of the Estimate

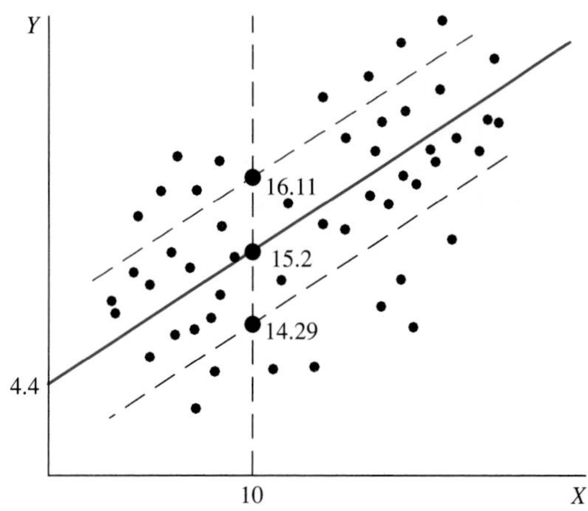

Figure 11.12
A Comparison of the Standard Error of the Estimate

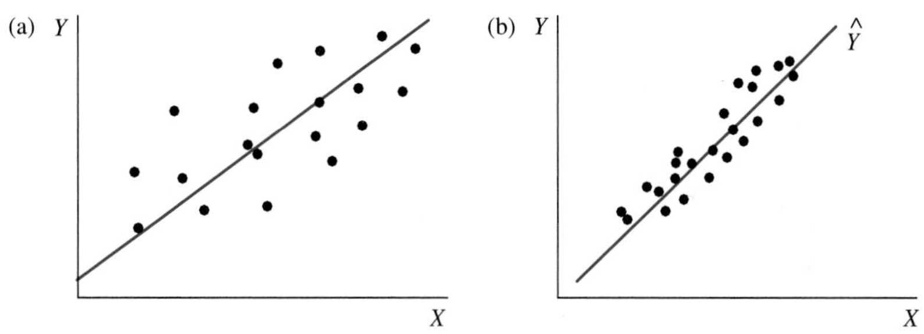

Given our interpretation of *Se*, it follows that the more dispersed the original data are, the larger *Se* will be. The data for Figure 11.12(a) are much more dispersed than those in Figure 11.12(b). The *Se* for Figure 11.12(a) would therefore be larger. After all, if you are to encompass 68.3 percent of the observations within one *Se* of the regression line, the interval must be wider if the data are more spread out.

Section Exercises

19. Using your computations from Exercise 9, calculate and interpret the standard error of the estimate for State University. Draw a graph in the interpretation. How can it be used as a measure of goodness of fit?

20. Based on the data from Exercise 10, what is the standard error of the estimate for the Florida State Department of Human Resources? How would you interpret the results? Use a graph.

21. Calculate and interpret the standard error of the estimate for Exercise 11 for the Atlanta bank.

22. The Overland Group in Exercise 12 now wants to know the standard error of the estimate.

23. What is the standard error of the estimate the professor in Exercise 13 is going to suffer?

11.7 Correlation Analysis

Our regression model has given us a clear picture of the relationship between advertising expenditures by Hop Scotch Airlines and the number of courageous travelers who queue up at the ticket counter. The positive value for b_1 indicates a direct relationship. As advertising goes up, so does the number of passengers. It is now useful to obtain a measure of the strength of that relationship. This is the function of the **correlation coefficient.** Developed by Carl Pearson around the turn of the century, it is sometimes called the Pearsonian product-moment correlation coefficient. Designated as r, the correlation coefficient can take on any value between -1 and $+1$; that is,

$$-1 \leq r \leq +1$$

A value of $r = -1$ indicates a perfect negative relationship between X and Y, as seen in Figure 11.13(a). All the observations lie in a perfectly straight line with a negative slope. Thus, X and Y will move in opposite directions. Figure 11.13(b) shows a perfect positive relationship between X and Y with $r = +1$. As noted earlier, in any relationship between

Figure 11.13
Potential Values for the Correlation Coefficient r

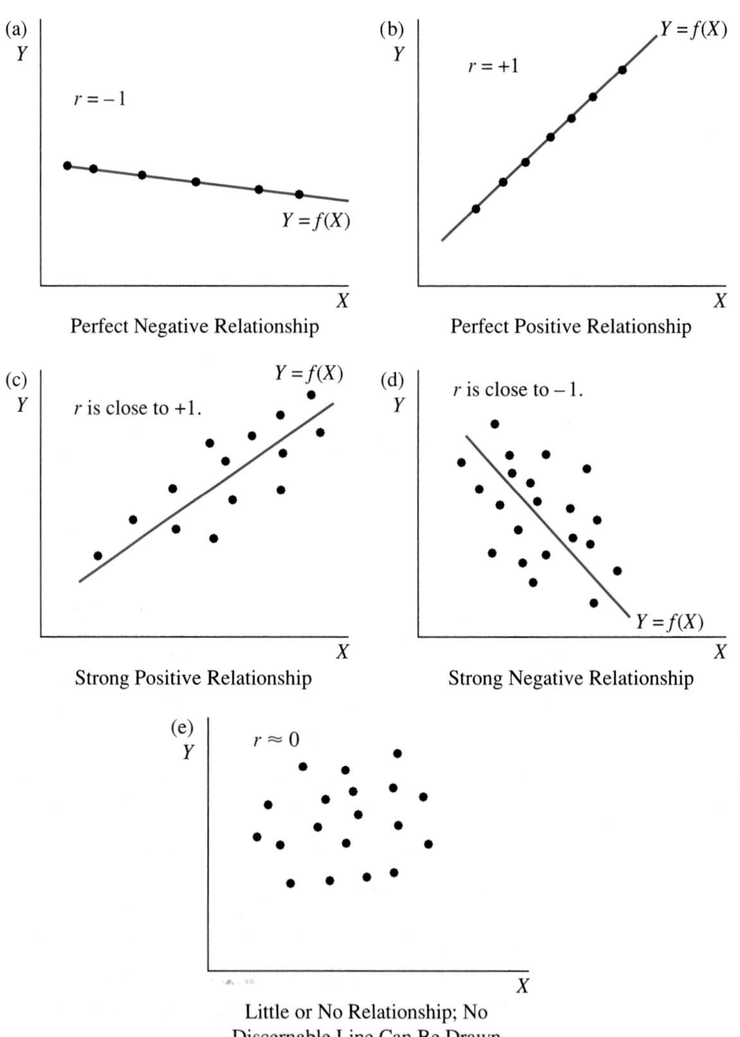

two variables there is likely to be some variation around the regression line. This is seen in Figures 11.13(c) and 11.13(d), which show strong but less than perfect relationships. In both cases the absolute value of r approaches 1. In contrast, Figure 11.13(e) shows little or no relationship between X and Y, and r approaches zero. In general, the higher the absolute value of r, the stronger the relationship between X and Y.

To fully understand what the correlation coefficient measures, we must develop three measures of deviation. The **total deviation** of Y is the amount by which the individual values of Y, (Y_i) vary from their mean $\overline{Y}$, $(Y_i - \overline{Y})$. Using month 13 from the Hop Scotch data in Table 11.2 as an example, Figure 11.14 shows the total deviation to be $(23 - 17.87) = 5.13$. The value of Y_i of 23 lies 5.13 above the horizontal line representing $\overline{Y}$ of 17.87. If all $n = 15$ of these total deviations are calculated and then squared, and the results are summed, we will have the *sum of squares of the total deviations, SST.*

Figure 11.14 Deviations for Hop Scotch Airlines

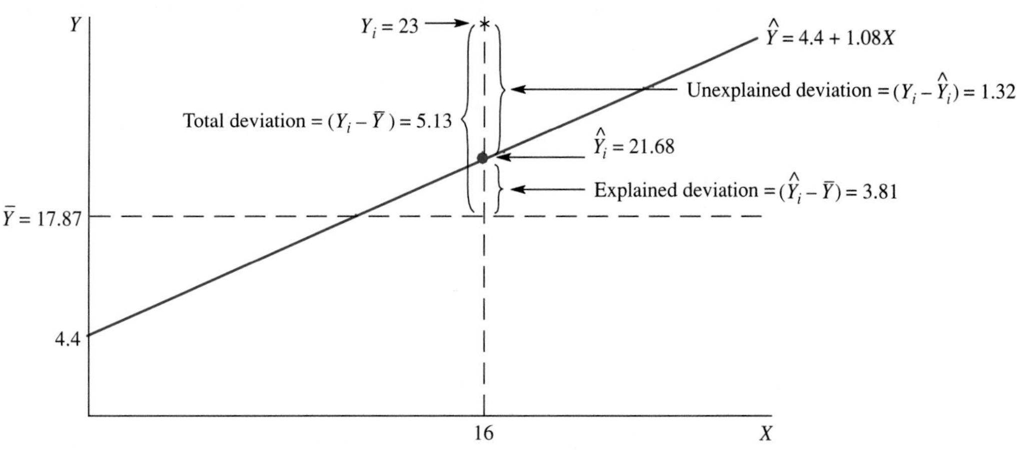

Total sum of squares.	$SST = \Sigma(Y_i - \overline{Y})^2$	[11.19]

This total deviation, as Figure 11.14 shows, can be broken down into the explained deviation and the unexplained deviation. The **explained deviation** is the difference between what our regression model predicts $\hat{Y}_i$, and the mean value of Y, $(\hat{Y}_i - \overline{Y})$. It is that portion of the total deviation that is explained by our regression model. At $X = 16$, $\hat{Y}_i = 4.4 + 1.08(16) = 21.68$. Figure 11.14 shows the explained deviation to be $(21.68 - 17.87) = 3.81$. If this portion of the total deviation, which is explained by our regression model, is calculated for all $n = 15$ observations and then squared, and the results are summed, we will have the *sum of the squares of the regression, SSR*.

Regression sum of squares.	$SSR = \Sigma(\hat{Y}_i - \overline{Y})^2$	[11.20]

The **unexplained deviation** seen in Figure 11.14 is that portion of the total deviation not explained by our regression model. That is, it is the error $(Y_i - \hat{Y}_i)$. Figure 11.14 shows this to be $(23 - 21.68) = 1.32$. If these error terms are calculated for all $n = 15$

observations and then squared, and the results are summed, we will have the sum of the squared errors, *SSE*.

Sum of squared errors.	$SSE = \Sigma(Y_i - \hat{Y}_i)^2$	[11.21]

The correlation coefficient is then calculated as

The correlation coefficient.	$r = \sqrt{\dfrac{\text{Explained variation}}{\text{Total variation}}} = \sqrt{\dfrac{SSR}{SST}}$	[11.22]

Notice precisely what r is measuring. It is comparing the total amount of the deviation around $\overline{Y}$, *SST*, to that portion of it that is explained by our regression model, *SSR*. As the square root of *SSR/SST*, the correlation coefficient provides a relative measure of our model's ability to explain the deviations in the Y_i-values. It thus measures the strength of the relationship between Y and the explanatory variable X.

Formula (11.22) is difficult to compute by hand. A more convenient formula is

The computational form for the correlation coefficient.	$r = \dfrac{SSxy}{\sqrt{(SSx)(SSy)}}$	[11.23]

In our present case for Hop Scotch, we have

$$r = \frac{148.93333}{\sqrt{(137.7333)(171.7333)}} = 0.9683$$

This indicates a strong positive relationship between passengers and the amount of money spent for advertising purposes.

Recall that the standard error of the estimate, *Se*, we calculated earlier is a measure of goodness of fit. It provides a quantifiable measure of how well our model fits the data we have collected.

The **coefficient of determination,** r^2, is another, perhaps more important, measure of goodness of fit. It is found as

The coefficient of determination: a measure of goodness of fit.	$r^2 = \sqrt{\dfrac{\text{explained deviation}}{\text{total deviation}}} = \sqrt{\dfrac{SSR}{SST}}$	[11.24]

A more computationally convenient formula is

Computational formula for the coefficient of determination.	$r^2 = \dfrac{(SSxy)^2}{\sqrt{(SSx)(SSy)}}$	[11.25]

It provides a measure of goodness of fit because it reveals what percentage of the change in Y is explained by a change in X.

The coefficient of determination for Hop Scotch is

$$\begin{aligned} r^2 &= \frac{(SSxy)^2}{(SSx)(SSy)} \\ &= \frac{(148.9333)^2}{(137.7333)(171.7333)} \\ &= 0.93776 \text{ or } 0.94 \end{aligned}$$

As you might expect, r^2 can more easily be determined by simply squaring the correlation coefficient, r.

$$r^2 = (0.9683)^2 = 0.94$$

This states that 94 percent of the change in the number of passengers is explained by a change in advertising. Minitab Display 11.4, presented earlier, shows that r^2 is 93.8 percent.

This r^2 has meaning only for linear relationships. Two variables may have an r^2 of zero and still be related in a curvilinear sense. Further, do not interpret this value as meaning 94 percent of the change in passengers is *caused* by a change in advertising. Correlation does not mean causation. This matter is emphasized in the next section.

Section Exercises

24. How can the coefficient of determination be used as a measure of goodness of fit? Draw a graph to illustrate.
25. What is the strength of the relationship between GPA and job offers in Exercise 9?
26. Calculate and interpret the correlation coefficient and the coefficient of determination for the Florida State Department of Human Resources in Exercise 10.
27. How much of the change in houses sold can be explained by the interest rate in Exercise 11?
28. What is the strength of the model Professor Mundane used in Exercise 13 to explain student absences?

11.8 Limitations of Regression Analysis

Although regression and correlation analysis often prove extremely useful in decision making for a wide variety of business and economic matters, there are certain limitations to their application and interpretation. They cannot determine cause-and-effect relationships. Correlation does not imply causation. This point was dramatically made by a British statistician who "proved" that storks bring babies. He collected data on birthrates and the number of storks in London and found a very high correlation—something like $r = 0.92$. He therefore concluded that the fairy tale about storks and babies was true.

However, as you may have already suspected, that's not really the way it works. It seems that this brand of stork liked to nest in the tops of Londoners' chimneys. Therefore, where population was dense and the birthrate was high, there were many chimneys to attract this fowl—thus, the high correlation between birthrates and storks. Actually, both storks and births were *caused* by a third factor, population density, which the researcher conveniently ignored. Remember, correlation does not mean causation.

Additionally, you must be careful not to use your regression model to predict Y for values of X outside the range of your original data set. Notice that the values for X in the Hop Scotch data set range from a low of 8 to a high of 19. We have isolated the relationship between X and Y only for that range of X-values. We have no idea what the relationship is outside that range. For all we know, it might appear as shown in Figure 11.15. As you can see, for values outside our range of 8 to 19, the X-Y relationship is entirely different from what we might expect given our sample

Figure 11.15
A Possible X-Y Relationship

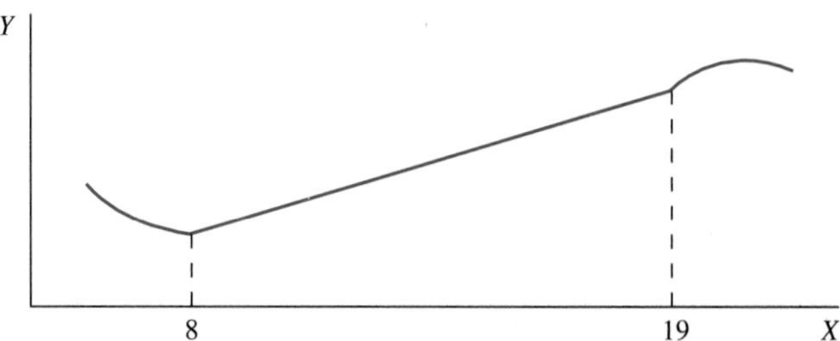

Another failing of regression and correlation analysis becomes apparent when two obviously unrelated variables seem to exhibit some relationship. Assume you wish to examine the correlation between the number of elephants born in the Kansas City Zoo and the tonnage of sea trout caught by sports fishermen in the Gulf off Tallahassee, Florida. You find $r = 0.91$. Would you conclude a relationship? Such a conclusion is obviously bizarre. Despite the r-value, pure logic indicates no relationship between these two variables. You have merely uncovered **spurious correlation,** which is correlation that occurs just by chance. There is no substitute for common sense in regression and correlation analysis.

11.9 Tests for the Population Parameters

Our statistical results suggest a relationship between passengers and advertising for Hop Scotch Airlines. The nonzero values for the regression (slope) coefficient of $b_1 = 1.08$ and the correlation coefficient of $r = 0.968$ indicate that, as advertising expenditures change, the number of passengers changes.

However, these results are based on a sample of only $n = 15$ observations. As always, we ask, is there a relationship at the population level? Could it be that due to sampling error the population parameters are zero and the two variables are not related despite the sample results? To answer this question we must test the population parameters to ensure that the statistical findings differ from zero *significantly.*

A. Tests for β_1

If the slope of the actual but unknown population regression line is zero, there is no relationship between passengers and advertising contrary to the sample results. If we plot the scatter diagram for the population of all X, Y data points, it might appear as Figure 11.16. The absence of any pattern indicates that no relationship exists. In collecting our sample, we might have included only those 15 observations enclosed in the ellipse. Taken by themselves, these data falsely suggest a positive relationship. We must test the hypothesis

$$H_o: \beta_1 = 0$$
$$H_A: \beta_1 \neq 0$$

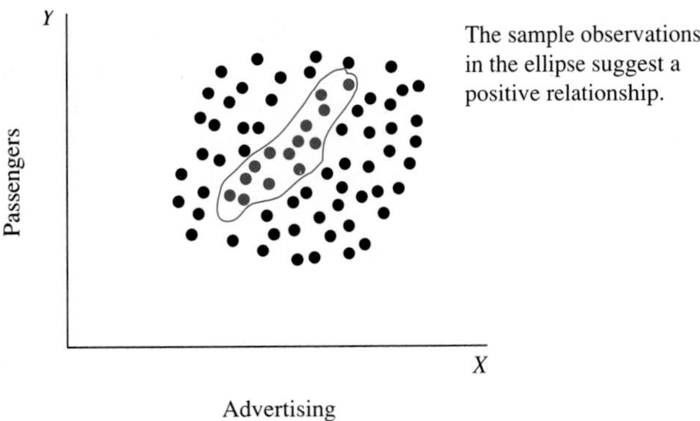

Figure 11.16
A Scatter Diagram for the Population of All X-Y points

This test employs that t-statistic

The t-test for the population regression coefficient.	$t_{\text{test}} = \dfrac{b_1 - \beta_1}{s_{b_1}}$	[11.26]

and carries $n - 2$ degrees of freedom, where s_{b_1} is the standard error of the sampling distribution of b_1. It recognizes that different samples yield different values for b_1. Thus, if β_1 is indeed zero, these values for b_1 would be distributed around zero as shown in Figure 11.17. We can calculate s_{b_1} by

Standard error of the regression coefficient.	$s_{b_1} = \dfrac{Se}{\sqrt{SSx}}$	[11.27]

Given the values for Hop Scotch,

$$s_{b_1} = \frac{0.907}{\sqrt{137.73333}} = 0.07726$$

and

$$t_{\text{test}} = \frac{1.0813 - 0}{0.07726} = 13.995$$

If an alpha value of 5 percent is chosen, $t_{0.05,13} = \pm 2.160$. The decision rule is:

Decision Rule Do not reject if t_{test} is between ± 2.160. Reject otherwise.

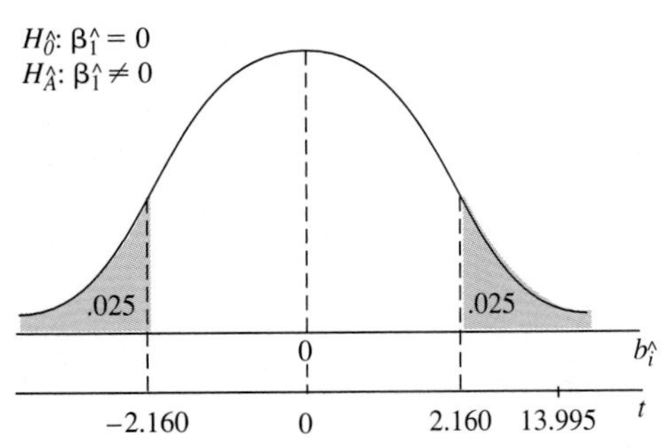

Figure 11.17
A Distribution of b_i if $\beta_1 = 0$.

Since $t_{test} = 13.995$, the null that $\beta_1 = 0$ is rejected. At the 5 percent level a relationship seems to exist between passengers and advertising.This can be confirmed by Minitab Display 11.4 (shown earlier). The p-value of 0.000 is also given in the display.

If the null had not been rejected, we would conclude advertising and passengers are not related. Discarding the model, we would use a different explanatory variable.

Since we have rejected the null that $\beta_1 = 0$, the natural question is, "What is its value?" This question can be answered by computing a confidence interval for β_1.

An interval estimate of β_1.	$\text{C.I. for } \beta_1 = b_1 \pm t(s_{b_1})$	[11.28]

If a 95 percent level of confidence is used,

$$\text{C.I. for } \beta_1 = 1.08 \pm (2.160)(0.07726)$$
$$0.913 \leq \beta_1 \leq 1.247$$

This means that we can be 95 percent certain that the regression coefficient for the entire population of all X, Y values is somewhere between 0.913 and 1.247.

B. Tests for the Population Correlation Coefficient ρ

Much of the work done to test inferences about the regression coefficient can be applied to the correlation coefficient. The purpose and the rationale are much the same. Since our analysis regarding the correlation between passengers and advertising is based on sample data, sampling error could have led us to improper conclusions. That is, the sample data produced a non-zero correlation coefficient of $r = 0.9683$ due to sampling error much like that in Figure 11.16. It might be that the correlation at the population level is zero and a misleading sample caused us to mistakenly assume a relationship. We must therefore test the hypothesis

$$H_o: \rho = 0$$
$$H_A: \rho \neq 0$$

where ρ is the correlation coefficient at the population level. Again, the t-test is used.

A t-test for the population correlation coefficient.	$t_{test} = \dfrac{r - \rho}{s_r}$	[11.29]

where s_r is the standard error of the correlation coefficient and can be figured as

The standard error of the correlation coefficient.	$s_r = \sqrt{\dfrac{1 - r^2}{n - 2}}$	[11.30]

Then,

$$s_r = \sqrt{\frac{1 - 0.93776}{15 - 2}} = 0.069$$

and

$$t_{\text{test}} = \frac{0.9683 - 0}{0.069} = 13.995$$

If alpha is 5 percent, the decision rule is:

Decision Rule Do not reject if t_{test} is between ± 2.160. Reject otherwise.

Because $t = 13.995 > 2.160$, the null is rejected. At the 5 percent level of significance, we conclude that the population correlation coefficient is not zero and that passengers and advertising are related. As with the test for β_1 above, if the null is not rejected we must conclude that advertising carries no explanatory power and a new model will have to the specified.

The fact that the t_{test} value of 13.995 is the same for both β_1 and ρ is not a coincidence. You will always get the identical results from these two hypothesis tests in a simple regression model, and in reality you would not likely conduct tests of hypotheses for both β_1 and ρ. However, you should become accustomed to both tests since this equality will not hold in a multiple regression model, as we will discover in the next chapter.

Section Exercises

29. Using the proper hypothesis test, at the 5 percent level is GPA a significant explanatory variable for job offers in Exercise 9? Be sure to show all four steps.
30. In Exercise 10, is the relationship between the interest rate and housing sales significant? Test the hypothesis at the 1 percent level of significance.
31. In Exercise 11, is the interest rate significant at the 10 percent level? Test the significance of the correlation coefficient at 10 percent. How does this test differ from the one for β_1?
32. Test Professor Mundane's hypothesis for β_1 at the 5 percent level in Exercise 13. What do you conclude? Compare this to his test for ρ.
33. Test the significance of test scores in Exercise 14 at the 5 percent level. What is the p-value for this test?

11.10 Interval Estimation in Regression Analysis

Regression analysis can forecast and predict values for the dependent variable. Once the regression equation has been determined, we can develop a *point* estimate for the dependent variable by substituting a given value for X into the equation and solving for Y.

In addition, the researcher may be interested in *interval* estimates. We have already seen that they are often preferable to mere point estimates. There are at least two such interval estimates commonly associated with regression procedures.

The first one is an interval estimate for the mean value of Y given any X-value. We may estimate the *population* mean for *all* Y-values (not just the $n = 15$ in our sample) when X is equal to some given value. We may want the *average* number of passengers in *all* months we spend \$10,000 on advertising (i.e., $X = 10$). This is called the **conditional mean.**

A second important confidence interval seeks to estimate a *single value* of Y given that X is set equal to a specific amount. This estimate is referred to as a **predictive interval.** Thus, while the conditional mean is an estimate of the average value of Y in all months in which X is equal to a specified amount, the predictive interval estimates Y in any single month in which X is set equal to a given amount.

A. The Conditional Mean for Y

Suppose we wanted to develop an interval estimate for the conditional mean of Y, $\mu_{y|x}$. This is the population mean for all Y-values under the condition that X is equal to a specific value. Recall that if we let X equal some given amount (say $X = 10$) many times, we will get many different values of Y. The interval we are calculating here is an estimate of the mean of all of those Y-values. That is, it is an interval estimate for the mean value of Y on the condition that X is set equal to 10 many times.

Actually, the confidence interval for the conditional mean value of Y has two possible interpretations, just as did those confidence intervals we constructed back in Chapter 7. Assume that we are calculating, for example, a 95 percent confidence interval.

First Interpretation: As noted above, if we let X equal the same amount many times we will get many different Y-values. We can then be 95 percent confident that the mean of those Y-values ($\mu_{y|x}$) will fall within the specified interval.

Second Interpretation: If we were to take many different samples of X and Y values and construct confidence intervals based on each sample, 95 percent of them would contain $\mu_{y|x}$, the true but unknown mean value of Y given $X = 10$.

To calculate this interval for the conditional mean value of Y, we must first determine S_Y, the **standard error of the conditional mean.** The standard error of the conditional mean recognizes that we use a sample to calculate b_0 and b_1 in the regression equation. Thus, b_0 and b_1 are subject to sampling error. If we were to take a different set of $n = 15$ months and determine a regression equation, we would likely get different values for b_0 and b_1. The purpose of S_Y is to account for the different values for b_0 and b_1 resulting from sampling error. It is determined by

Standard error of the conditional mean.

$$S_Y = Se\sqrt{\frac{1}{n} + \frac{(X_i - \overline{X})^2}{SSx}} \qquad [11.31]$$

where Se is the standard error of the estimate

X_i is the given value for the independent variable

The confidence interval for the conditional mean is then

Confidence interval for the conditional mean.

$$\text{C.I. for } \mu_{y|x} = \hat{Y}_i \pm tS_Y \qquad [11.32]$$

in which $\hat{Y}_i$ is the point estimator found from our regression equation. The t-value is based on $n - 2$ degrees of freedom because we must calculate the two values b_0 and b_1 from the sample data.

If Hop Scotch wishes to develop the interval for the conditional mean where $X_i = 10$ and the mean of all 15 X-values is $\overline{X} = 12.47$, Formula (11.31) yields

$$S_y = 0.907\sqrt{\frac{1}{15} + \frac{(10 - 12.47)^2}{137.73333}} = 0.303$$

If a 95 percent level of confidence is used, $t_{0.05,13} = \pm 2.160$. Since

$$\hat{Y}_i = 4.4 + 1.08(10) = 15.2$$

Formula (11.32) finds

$$\text{C.I. for } \mu_{y|x} = 15.2 \pm 2.160(0.303)$$
$$14.55 \leq \mu_{y|x} \leq 15.85$$

Hop Scotch can be 95 percent confident that, if \$10,000 is spent on advertising many times (theoretically, an infinite number of times), there is a 95 percent chance the mean of all the resulting values for passengers will be between 14,550 and 15,850. Minitab will also generate this interval, as seen in Display 11.4 (presented earlier).

Figure 11.18
Confidence Limits for $\mu_{y|x}$

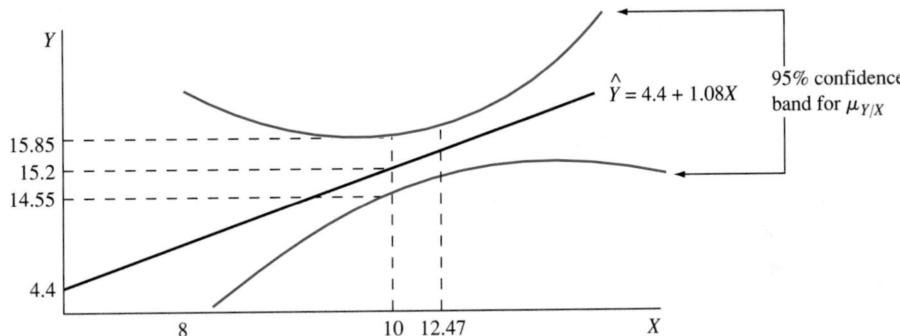

We could calculate the confidence interval for $\mu_{y|x}$ at several different values for X. These intervals would form an entire **confidence band** for $\mu_{y|x}$. Notice in Figure 11.18 that the band becomes wider at each end because regression analysis is based on means and the further we get from the mean of $\overline{X} = 12.47$, the less accurate our result becomes. To retain our 95 percent level of confidence, the band must therefore be wider.

B. The Predictive Interval for a Single Value of Y

The confidence interval constructed above is for the population mean value of all Y-values when X is equal to a given amount many times. At other times it might be useful to construct a confidence interval for a single value of Y that is obtained when X is set equal to some value only once. Hop Sotch may be interested in predicting the number of customers next month if it spends \$10,000 on advertising. This differs from the problem above in which the concern was with the average value of Y if X was set equal to 10 many times.

We now focus on a prediction for a single value of Y if X is set equal to a given amount only once. Instead of trying to predict the mean of many Y-values obtained on the condition that X is set equal to 10 many times, we want to predict a single value for Y obtained if X is set equal to 10 only once. Stop and think about this problem for a minute. Averages tend to be centered around the middle of a data set. They are therefore easier to predict since we know about where they are. Individual values, however, are quite scattered and are therefore much more difficult to predict. Hence, a 95 percent confidence interval for a single value of Y must be wider than that for a conditional mean.

This confidence interval for the predictive interval of Y also carries two interpretations. These interpretations are provided under the assumption that the intervals we calculate are 95 percent intervals, although other levels of confidence may of course be used.

First Interpretation: If we set X equal to some amount just one time, we would get one resulting value of Y. We can be 95 percent certain that single value of Y falls within the specified interval.

Second Interpretation: If many samples were taken and each was used to construct a predictive confidence interval, 95 percent of them would contain the true value for Y.

To calculate this predictive interval, we must first calculate the **standard error of the forecast,** S_{y_i} (not to be confused with the standard error of the conditional mean, S_Y). This standard error of the forecast accounts for the fact that individual values are more dispersed than are means. The standard error of the forecast S_{y_i}, reflects the sampling error inherent in the standard error of the conditional mean S_Y, plus the additional dispersion because we are dealing with an individual value of Y. Formula (11.33) is used in its calculation.

Standard error of the forecast.

$$S_{y_i} = Se\sqrt{1 + \frac{1}{n} + \frac{(X_i - \overline{X})^2}{SSx}} \qquad [11.33]$$

The predictive interval for a single value of Y, Y_x, is then

Confidence interval for the predictive interval

$$\text{C.I. for } Y_x = \hat{Y}_i \pm tS_{Y_i} \qquad [11.34]$$

Let's now construct a 95 percent confidence interval for a single value of Y when $X = 10$ and compare it with the interval for the conditional mean constructed earlier.

$$\begin{aligned} S_{yi} &= Se\sqrt{1 + \frac{1}{15} + \frac{(10 - 12.47)^2}{137.73333}} \\ &= 0.907\sqrt{1.1114} \\ &= 0.956 \end{aligned}$$

Since

$$\begin{aligned} \hat{Y}_i &= 4.4 + 1.08(10) \\ &= 15.2 \end{aligned}$$

we obtain

$$\begin{aligned} \text{C.I. for } Y_x &= \hat{Y}_i \pm tS_{y_i} \\ &= 15.2 \pm (2.160)(0.956) \\ &= 15.2 \pm 2.065 \\ 13.14 &< Y_x < 17.27 \end{aligned}$$

Again, Minitab Display 11.4 confirms this interval. Hop Scotch can be 95 percent certain that if in any single month $X_i = \$10{,}000$, the resulting single value of Y will be between 13,140 and 17,270 passengers.

Figure 11.19 Interval Estimates for $\mu_{y|x}$ and Y_x

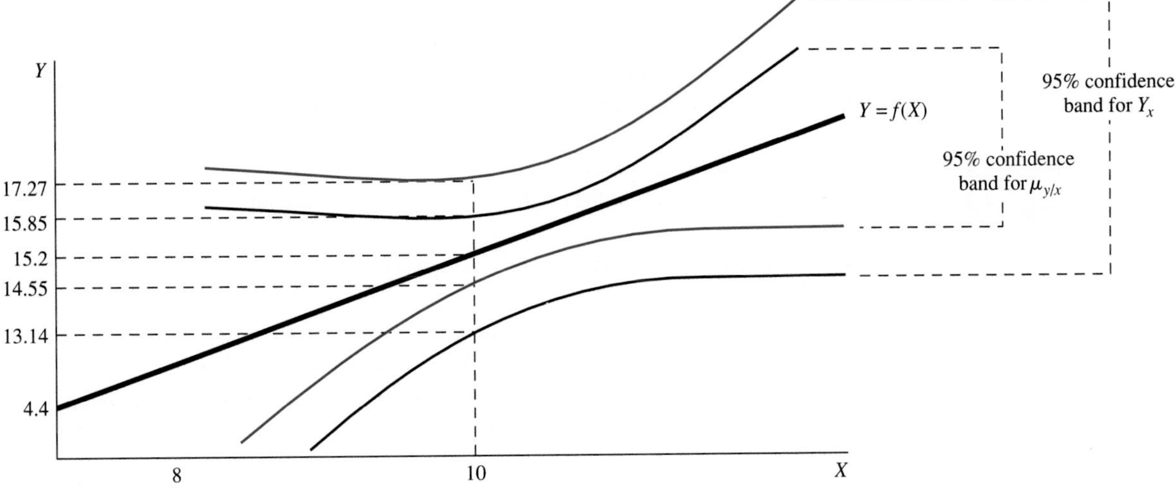

As promised, this interval is wider than the first because we are working with less predictable individual values. The comparison is complete in Figure 11.19.

These confidence bands are seen in Minitab Display 11.5, although the curvatures are not as obvious.

Minitab Display 11.5

Confidence Bands for $\mu_{y|x}$ and Y_x

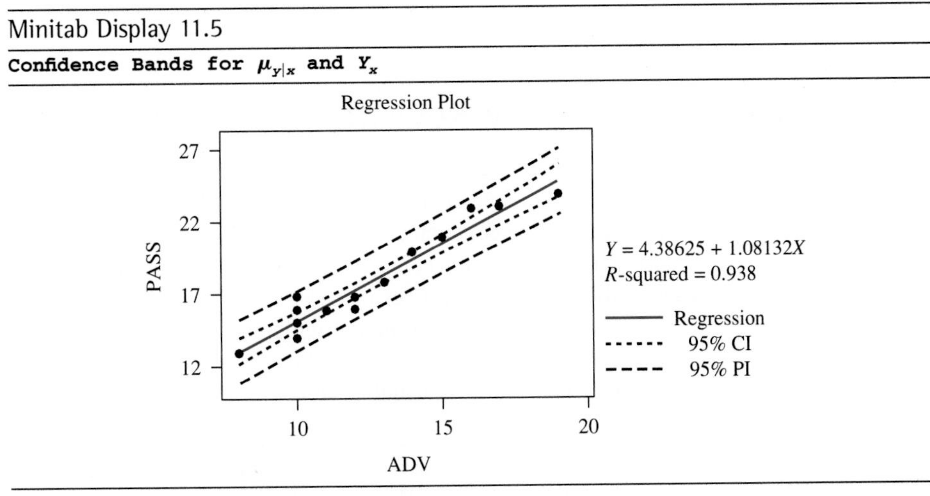

C. Factors Influencing the Width of the Interval

Given a level of confidence, it is preferable to minimize the width of the interval. The narrower the interval, the more accurate is our prediction of $\mu_{y|x}$ or Y_x. However, several forces are working against us in our effort to produce a narrower interval.

The first is the degree of dispersion of the original data. The more dispersed the original data are, the greater will be *Se*, the standard error of the estimate. Given the arithmetic in Formulas (11.31) and (11.33), a higher *Se* results in a wider interval.

Our sample size is a second factor in determining interval width. As we have seen in previous chapters, a large sample size results in a smaller standard error. Again, given the arithmetic described above, a small standard error results in a small interval.

Furthermore, as we have already seen, a value for X relatively close to $\bar{X}$ will produce a small interval since regression is based on averages. Therefore, a third factor influencing interval width is how far the particular value of X that we are interested in is from $\bar{X}$.

Section Exercises

34. What do the standard error of the conditional mean and the standard error of the forecast measure?

35. How does the confidence interval for the conditional mean differ from that of the predictive interval?

36. What do the confidence bands for the conditonal mean and the predictive interval measure and why are they shaped the way they are? What affects the width of these intervals?

37. The placement center at State University in Exercise 9 wants a 95 percent interval estimate of the mean number of job offers many of their graduates will receive who have a GPA of 2.69. Compute and interpret the proper interval.

38. Fred has a GPA of 2.69 (see Exercises 9 and 37). Compute the 95 percent interval for the number of jobs offers he will receive. Why does it differ from your answer in Exercise 37?

39. If the economist for the Florida State Department of Human Resources in Exercise 10 identifies many consumers with incomes of \$14,200, what is the 99 percent interval for the mean consumption of all of those consumers?

40. If the economist in Exercise 39 identifies one consumer with an income of \$14,500,

a. What is the point estimate of his consumption?
b. What is the 99 percent interval estimate of his consumption?

11.11 Analysis of Variance Revisited

The regression model presents a description of the nature of the relationship between our dependent and independent variables. We used a t-test to test the hypothesis that $\beta_1 = 0$. A similar test can be conducted with the use of analysis of variance (ANOVA) based on the F-test. The ANOVA procedure measures the amount of variation in our model. As noted earlier, there are three sources of variation in a regression model: variation explained by our regression (*SSR*), variation that remains unexplained due to error (*SSE*), and the total variation (*SST*), which is the sum of the first two. These can be summarized in an ANOVA table, the general form of which is shown in Table 11.3.

Table 11.3
A General ANOVA Table

Source of Variation	Sum of Squares	Degrees of Freedom	Mean Square	F-ratio
Regression	SSR	k	$MSR = \frac{SSr}{k}$	$\frac{MSR}{MSE}$
Error	SSE	$n - k - 1$	$MSE = \frac{SSE}{n - k - 1}$	
Total	SST	$n - 1$		

The ratio MSR/MSE provides a measure of the accuracy of our model because it is the ratio of the mean squared deviation that is explained by our model and the mean squared deviation left unexplained. The higher this ratio, the more explanatory power our model has. That is, a high F-test signals that our model possesses significant explanatory power. To determine what is high, our F-value must be compared with a critical value taken from Table G of Appendix III.

The computational formula for SSE was given by Formula (11.16). SSR can be calculated as

Regression sum of squares. $$SSR = \frac{(SSxy)^2}{SSx} \qquad [11.35]$$

Using our data for Hop Scotch, Formula 11.16 yields

$$SSE = SSy - \frac{(SSxy)^2}{SSx}$$

$$= 171.73333 - \frac{(148.93333)^2}{137.73333}$$

$$= 10.69$$

and Formula 11.35 produces

$$SSR = \frac{(148.93333)^2}{137.73333}$$

$$= 161.0441$$

SST is found as the sum of SSR and SST, as shown in Table 11.4. The F-value carries 1 and 13 degrees of freedom since it was formed with the mean square regression and the mean square error as seen in Table 11.4. Minitab Display 11.4 also provides the ANOVA table.

Table 11.4
The ANOVA for Hop Scotch Airlines

Source of Variation	Sum of Squares	Degrees of Freedom	Mean Square	*F*-ratio
Regression	161.04	1	161.04	196.39
Error	10.69	13	0.82	
Total	171.73	14		

We can set $\alpha = 0.05$ to test the hypothesis that $\beta_1 = 0$. Then $F_{0.05,1,13} = 4.67$ produces a decision rule stating that we should reject the null if our F-value exceeds 4.67. Since $196.39 > 4.67$, we reject the null and conclude with 95 percent confidence that advertising has explanatory power. This is the same result obtained in our t-test.

Actually, in simple regression, the F-test and the t-test are analogous. Both will give the same results. The F-value is the square of the t-value. In multiple regression, the F-test produces a more general test to determine if any of the independent variables in the model carry explanatory power. Each variable is then tested individually with the t-test to determine whether it is one of the significant variables.

Solved Problems

1. **Keynesian Consumption Function** In his famous 1936 book, *The General Theory of Employment, Interest and Money,* the noted British economist John Maynard Keynes proposed a theoretical relationship between income and personal consumption expenditures. Keynes

argued that as income went up, consumption would rise by a smaller amount. This theoretical relationship has been empirically tested many times since 1936.

Milton Friedman, former professor of economics at the University of Chicago, and winner of the Nobel Prize in economics, collected extensive data on income and consumption in the United States over a long period of time. Shown here are 10 observations on annual levels of consumption and income used by Friedman in his study. Using these data, derive a consumption function under the assumption that there exists a linear relationship between consumption and income. Figures are in billions of current dollars.

Year	Income	Consumption
1950	284.8	191.0
1951	328.4	206.3
1952	345.5	216.7
1953	364.6	230.0
1954	364.8	236.5
1955	398.0	254.4
1956	419.2	266.7
1957	441.1	281.4
1958	447.3	290.1
1959	483.7	311.2

a. Since consumption depends on income, consumption is the Y, or dependent, variable. Friedman sought a consumption function in the form

$$\hat{C} = b_0 + b_1 I$$

where C is consumption and I is income.

$$\Sigma X = 3{,}877.4 \qquad \Sigma XY = 984{,}615.32 \qquad \Sigma Y^2 = 630{,}869.49$$

$$\Sigma Y = 2{,}484.3 \qquad \Sigma X^2 = 1{,}537{,}084.88$$

$$SSx = \Sigma X^2 - \frac{(\Sigma X)^2}{n}$$

$$= 1{,}537{,}084.88 - \frac{(3{,}877.4)^2}{10}$$

$$= 33{,}661.804$$

$$SSy = \Sigma Y^2 - \frac{(\Sigma Y)^2}{n}$$

$$= 630{,}869.49 - \frac{(2{,}484.3)^2}{10}$$

$$= 13{,}694.841$$

$$SSxy = \Sigma XY - \frac{(\Sigma X)(\Sigma Y)}{n}$$

$$= 984{,}615.32 - \frac{(3{,}877.4)(2{,}484.3)}{10}$$

$$= 21{,}352.838$$

$$b_1 = \frac{SSxy}{SSx}$$

$$= \frac{21,352.838}{33,661.804}$$

$$= 0.634$$

$$b_0 = \bar{Y} - b_1\bar{X}$$

$$= 248.43 - (0.634)(387.74)$$

$$= 2.603$$

Therefore,

$$\hat{C} = 2.603 + 0.63I$$

These are not the same values Friedman found because we used only a very small portion of his data set. However, our model bears out Keynes' theory. The coefficient of 0.63 shows that for every $1 (or $1,000,000,000) increase in income, consumption will increase by 63 cents (or $630,000,000). Those of you who have taken an introductory macroeconomics course will recognize 0.63 as marginal propensity to consume. The constant, or intercept term, of 2.603 is the level of consumption when income is zero. Economists often argue that this economic interpretation of the intercept term is invalid since an economic system will always generate positive income. The consumption function is therefore often graphed without the intercept, as in the figure. If $I = 345.5$, as in 1952, our model predicts

$$\hat{C} = 2.603 + 0.63(345.5) = 220.26$$

Consumption was actually 216.7 in 1952, resulting in an error of $3.56 billion.

b. The coefficient of determination is

$$\hat{C} = 2.603 + 0.63(345.5) = 220.26$$

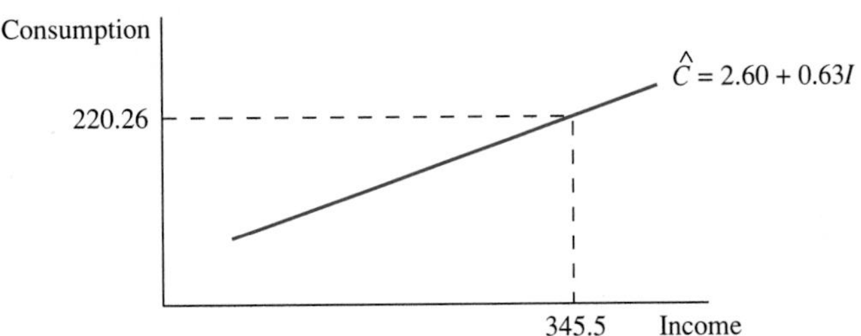

Consumption was actually 216.7 in 1952, resulting in an error of −$3.56 billion.

$$r^2 = \frac{(SSxy)^2}{(SSx)(SSy)}$$

$$= \frac{(21,352.838)^2}{(33,661.804)(13,694.841)}$$

$$= 0.989$$

A change in income explains over 98 percent of the change in consumption. Information concerning the values of b_0, b_1, and r^2 are vital to those who advise Congress and the president on matters of national economics policy.

2. **Federal Reserve Actions to Stem Inflation** After approximately six years of continued expansion, the U.S. economy began to show signs of inflationary pressures in the fall of 1988. An article in a September issue of *The Wall Street Journal* described efforts by the Federal Reserve

Board to cool these inflationary fires. This was to be done by tightening the money supply through a rise in the discount rate commercial banks must pay to borrow from the Federal Reserve. In February 1988, Manuel H. Johnson, vice-chairman of the Fed, told an audience at a Cato Institute conference that Fed actions regarding the discount rate could be predicted on the basis of the federal funds rate, which is the fee banks charge each other for overnight loans. However, throughout the rest of 1988, Fed watchers argued that the federal funds rate was *not* serving as an adequate predictor of the changes in the discount rate, and that this poor performance as a predictor made it difficult for investors trying to predict what interest rate level the Fed would allow.

Shown here are values for the federal funds rate and the discount rate from mid-1987 to mid-1988. Do these data support the charges of the Fed watchers?

Date	Federal Funds Rate(%)	Discount Rate(%)	Date	Federal Funds Rate(%)	Discount Rate(%)
June 1987	8.0	7.5	Dec. 1987	7.0	5.5
July 1987	7.5	7.5	Jan. 1987	6.0	5.5
Aug. 1987	7.0	7.0	Feb. 1987	7.0	5.5
Sept. 1987	6.5	6.5	March 1987	7.5	5.5
Oct. 1987	6.0	6.0	April 1987	7.0	6.0
Nov. 1987	6.0	5.5	May 1987	7.5	6.5
				83.0	74.5

Since Johnson argued that the federal funds rate could explain the behavior of the discount rate, the federal funds rate is seen as the independent variable.

a. The nature of the relationship between the federal funds rate and the discount rate can be examined through regression and correlation analysis.

$$\Sigma X = 83 \qquad \Sigma Y^2 = 469.25$$
$$\Sigma Y = 74.5$$
$$\Sigma XY = 518.5 \qquad \bar{Y} = 6.21$$
$$\Sigma X^2 = 579 \qquad n = 12$$
$$SSx = 4.9166667$$
$$SSy = 6.72917$$
$$SSxy = 3.20833$$
$$b_1 = 0.6525$$
$$b_0 = 1.6949$$

Therefore,

$$\hat{Y} = 1.69 + 0.653\,X$$

The coefficient of determination is

$$r^2 = \frac{(3.20833)^2}{(4.92)(6.73)}$$
$$= 0.3111$$
$$r = 0.56$$

The Fed watchers are correct in their criticism of the federal funds rate as a predictor of changes in the discount rate. Only 31 percent of changes in the discount rate are explained by changes in the federal funds rate.

b. A measure of goodness-of-fit which reflects the ability of the federal funds rate to predict the discount rate is the standard error of the estimate.

The standard error of the estimate is

$$SSE = SSy - \frac{(SSxy)^2}{SSx}$$

$$= 6.7292 - \frac{(3.208)^2}{4.9166}$$

$$= 4.63033$$

$$MSE = \frac{4.63033}{10}$$

$$= 0.463033$$

$$Se = \sqrt{0.463033}$$

$$= 0.6808$$

Typically, the estimate of the discount rate is in error by 0.68 of a percentage point.

c. A test of the significance of the correlation coefficient would prove useful at this point. Set the level of confidence at 95 percent. With 10 degree of freedom the critical value for t is therefore ± 2.228.

The hypotheses are

$$H_0: \rho = 0$$
$$H_A: \rho \neq 0$$

Decision Rule Do not reject H_0 if t is between ± 2.228. Reject otherwise.

$$t = \frac{r}{S_r}$$

$$= \frac{r}{\sqrt{(1 - r^2)/(n - 2)}}$$

$$= \frac{0.56}{\sqrt{(1 - 0.31)/10}}$$

$$= \frac{0.56}{0.2627}$$

$$= 2.13$$

The null hypothesis cannot be rejected. Despite the sample finding of a positive relationship between federal funds rates and the discount rate, the hypothesis that there is no correlation cannot be rejected. The sample correlation coefficient is not significant at the 5 percent level.

d. A test of the significance of the sample regression coefficient of $b_1 = 0.6525424$ is also wise. The test will be conducted at the 99 percent level. With 10 degrees of freedom the critical t-value is ± 3.169.

$$H_0: \beta_1 = 0$$
$$H_A: \beta_1 \neq 0$$

Decision Rule Do not reject if t is between ± 3.169. Reject otherwise. The test requires

$$t = \frac{b_1}{S_{b_1}}$$

where

$$S_{b_1} = \frac{Se}{\sqrt{SSx}}$$
$$= 0.681/\sqrt{4.92} = 0.307$$
$$= \frac{0.652542}{0.307}$$
$$= 2.126$$

The hypothesis that $\beta_1 = 0$ cannot be rejected. The value for b_1 is not significantly different from zero at the 1 percent level. There is little or no confidence in the federal funds rate as a predictor of the discount rate. Investors would be unwise to rely on the federal funds rate as an indicator of what the discount rate and other interest rates will do.

3. **A Further Examination of the Discount Rate** Based on the results of Problem 4, professional bankers and investors can find little comfort in the ability of the federal funds rate to predict the discount rate. Using the regression model to develop a point estimate of the discount rate does not appear wise. To further examine the relationship between these two variables, if any exists, we can calculate interval estimates of the discount rate.

a. People employed in banking and finance would be interested in an interval estimate for the mean value of the discount rate if the federal funds rate was held constant for several months. This is, of course, an interval estimate of the conditional mean of the discount rate:

$$\text{C.I. for } \mu_{y|x} = \hat{Y} \pm tS_Y$$

and requires calculation of the standard error of the conditional mean, S_Y, and $\hat{Y}$ as the point estimator of the discount rate. Since the federal funds rate seemed to move around 7 percent quite often, it is at this rate that the confidence interval will be calculated.

To calculate S_Y and $\hat{Y}$, we have

$$S_Y = Se\sqrt{\frac{1}{n} + \frac{(X - \overline{X})^2}{SSx}}$$
$$= 0.681\sqrt{\frac{1}{12} + \frac{(7 - 6.9167)^2}{4.92}}$$
$$= 0.1982$$

Also,

$$\hat{Y} = b_0 + b_1X$$
$$= 1.6949 + 0.6525424(7)$$
$$= 6.2627$$

If the interval is calculated at a 95 percent level of confidence, the critical t-value is $t_{0.05,n-2} = \pm 2.228$. We then have

$$\text{C.I. for } \mu_{y|x} = \hat{Y} \pm tS_Y$$
$$= 6.2627 \pm (2.228)(0.1982)$$
$$5.82 < \mu_{y|x} < 6.70$$

Bankers can be 95 percent confident that if the federal funds rate is 7 percent for several months, the mean discount rate they must pay to borrow money from the Fed will fall between 5.82 percent and 6.70 percent. Their plans and policies can be formulated according to this expectation.

b. If a banker wished to make plans for next month, he or she would be interested in what the discount rate might be in that month, given that the federal funds rate was

7 percent. The banker would therefore calculate a predictive interval for next month as follows:

$$\text{C.I. for } Y_x = \hat{Y} \pm tS_{y_i}$$

This requires calculation of the standard error of the forecast, S_{y_i}. Assuming a 95 percent level of significance and a federal funds rate of 7 percent, the banker would proceed as follows:

$$S_{y_i} = Se\sqrt{1 + \frac{1}{n} + \frac{(X - \bar{X})^2}{SS_x}}$$

$$= 0.70927$$

Since $\hat{Y} = 6.2627$, we have

$$\text{C.I. for } Y_x = 6.2627 \pm (2.228)(0.70927)$$

$$4.68 < Y_x < 7.85$$

The banker could formulate plans for next month's operations on the realization that he or she could be 95 percent confident that if the federal funds rate was 7 percent, the discount rate would fall between 4.68 percent and 7.85 percent. This is a wider range than that found for the conditional mean of the discount rate.

It would certainly appear that Johnson's statement concerning the use of the federal funds rate to estimate or predict the discount rate is questionable. The r^2 is rather low, and the tests for significance of ρ and β_1 suggest that the hypotheses $\rho = 0$ and $\beta_1 = 0$ cannot be rejected at any acceptable levels of significance.

In all fairness, it might be argued that the federal funds rate should be lagged one month. That is, the discount rate in any month (time period t) is a function of the federal funds rate for the previous month (time period $t - 1$). This would allow the Fed time to adjust the discount rate to last month's federal funds rate, since the Fed cannot respond immediately to changes in the federal funds rate. This is expressed as

$$DR_t = f(FF_{t-1})$$

where DR is the discount rate and FF is the federal funds rate. This lagged model yields

$$\hat{Y} = 0.6 + 0.8X$$

with $r^2 = 60$ percent and $Se = 0.47$. This represents a major improvement over the naive model, which does not include the lagged variable.

4. **The Effect of Productivity on Real GNP** A recent issue of *Fortune* magazine reported on the relationship between worker productivity and rates of change in the nation's level of output measured in real terms. The message was that the increase in productivity during the 1980s could serve as an explanatory factor for GNP growth. With both productivity growth and changes in GNP measured in percentages, and GNP as the dependent variable, annual data for that time period can be summarized as follows:

$$\Sigma X = 32.5 \qquad \Sigma Y^2 = 483.72$$

$$\Sigma Y = 62.2 \qquad n = 9$$

$$\Sigma XY = 255.4 \qquad \Sigma X^2 = 135.25$$

The model is

$$\hat{Y} = 0.69596273 + 1.721118X$$

indicating that if productivity increased one percentage point, real GNP will increase by 1.72 percent. The r^2 is 0.98407, and $Se = 0.35$.

For the purpose of formulating national tax policy, which some supply-side economists argue has a direct impact on worker productivity, Washington planners tested the significance of both the sample correlation coefficient and the sample regression coefficient. Each proved significant at the 10 percent level.

The same planners then requested a confidence interval for each population coefficient at the 10 percent level:

$$\text{C.I. for } \beta_1 = b_1 \pm tS_{b_1}$$

$$S_{b_1} = \frac{Se}{\sqrt{SS_x}} = 0.08275$$

$$\text{C.I. for } \beta_1 = 1.72 \pm (1.895)(0.08275)$$

$$1.56 < \beta_1 < 1.88$$

The planners can then base the formulation of national tax policy on the condition that they can be 90 percent certain that the population regression coefficient is between 1.56 and 1.88.

List of Formulas

[11.3]	$Y = b_0 + b_1X$	Formula for a straight line showing the intercept, b_0, and the slope, b_1.
[11.9]	$SSx = \Sigma X^2 - \frac{(\Sigma X)^2}{n}$	Sum of the squares for X.
[11.10]	$SSy = \Sigma Y^2 - \frac{(\Sigma Y)^2}{n}$	Sum of the squares for Y.
[11.11]	$SSxy = \Sigma XY - \frac{(\Sigma Y)(\Sigma X)}{n}$	Sum of the cross-products.
[11.12]	$b_1 = \frac{SSxy}{SSx}$	The slope of the regression line measures the unit change in Y given a one-unit change in X.
[11.13]	$b_0 = \overline{Y} - b_1\overline{X}$	The intercept is the value of Y when X is set equal to zero.
[11.14]	$d = \frac{\Sigma(e_t - e_{t-1})^2}{\Sigma e_t^2}$	The Durbin-Watson statistic.
[11.15]	$Se = \sqrt{\frac{\Sigma(Y_i - \hat{Y}_i)^2}{n - 2}}$	The standard error of the estimate is the measure of the dispersion of the Y-values around their mean.
[11.16]	$SSE = SSy - \frac{(SSxy)^2}{SSx}$	Error sum of squares.
[11.17]	$MSE = \frac{SSE}{n - 2}$	Mean squared error.
[11.18]	$Se = \sqrt{MSE}$	The standard error of the estimate is the measure of the dispersion of the Y-values around their mean.
[11.19]	$SST = \Sigma(Y_i - \overline{Y})^2$	Total sum of squares.
[11.20]	$SSR = \Sigma(\hat{Y}_i - \overline{Y})^2$	Regression sum of squares.
[11.21]	$SSE = \Sigma(Y_i - \hat{Y}_i)^2$	Error sum of squares.
[11.22]	$r = \sqrt{\frac{SSR}{SST}}$	The correlation coefficient.

[11.23] $$r = \frac{SSxy}{\sqrt{(SSx)(SSy)}}$$ The computational form for the correlation coefficient.

[11.24] $$r^2 = \frac{SSR}{SST}$$ The coefficient of determination.

[11.25] $$r^2 = \frac{(SSxy)^2}{(SSx)(SSy)}$$ The computational form for the coefficient of determination.

[11.26] $$t_{\text{test}} = \frac{b_1 - \beta_1}{S_{b_1}}$$ The t-test for the population regression coefficient.

[11.27] $$S_{b_1} = \frac{Se}{\sqrt{SSx}}$$ Standard error of the regression coefficient.

[11.28] $$\text{C.I. for } \beta_1 = b_1 \pm t(s_{b_1})$$ Confidence interval for the population regression coefficient.

[11.29] $$t_{\text{test}} = \frac{r - \rho}{s_r}$$ A t-test for the population correlation coefficient.

[11.30] $$S_r = \sqrt{\frac{1 - r^2}{n - 2}}$$ The standard error of the correlation coefficient.

[11.31] $$S_Y = Se\sqrt{\frac{1}{n} + \frac{(X_i + \bar{X})^2}{SSx}}$$ Standard error of the conditional mean.

[11.32] $$\text{C.I. for } \mu_{y|x} = \hat{Y}_i \pm ts_Y$$ Confidence interval for the conditional mean.

[11.33] $$s_{Y_i} = Se\sqrt{1 = \frac{1}{n} + \frac{(X_i - \bar{X})^2}{SSx}}$$ Standard error of forecast.

[11.34] $$\text{C.I. for } Y_X = \hat{Y}_i \pm ts_{Y_i}$$ Confidence interval for the predictive interval.

[11.35] $$SSR = \frac{(SSxy)^2}{SSx}$$ Regression sum of squares.

Chapter Exercises

41. The residents of a small town are worried about a rise in housing costs in the area. The mayor thinks that home prices fluctuate with land values. Data on 10 recently sold homes and the cost of the land on which they were built are seen here in thousands of dollars. Treat cost of houses as the dependent variable. Construct and interpret the regression model. On this basis, does it appear that the mayor is correct?

Land Values	Cost of the House	Land Values	Cost of the House
7.0	67.0	3.8	36.0
6.9	63.0	8.9	76.0
5.5	60.0	9.6	87.0
3.7	54.0	9.9	89.0
5.9	58.0	10.0	92.0

42. Calculate and interpret the coefficient of determination for Exercise 41.

43. Test the hypothesis that Land values are significant at the 10 percent level in Exercise 41.

44. Calculate and interpret the 90 percent confidence interval for the regression coefficient in Exercise 41.

45. The student government at the local university is trying to determine whether the admission price to the game room in the student center has an impact on the number of students who use the facilities. The cost of admission and the number of students who enter the room are recorded for 12 successive Friday nights and shown here. Construct and interpret the regression model.

Price	Number of Tickets	Price	Number of Tickets
\$1.25	95	\$1.00	98
1.50	83	1.50	85
1.75	75	2.00	75
2.00	72	2.50	65
2.10	69	1.10	98
1.00	101	1.50	86

46. Calculate and interpret the 99 percent confidence interval for the regression coefficient in Exercise 45.

47. To reduce crimes, the president has budgeted more money to put more police on our city streets. What information does the regression model offer based on these data for the number of police on patrol and the daily number of reported crimes? Use the formulas that illustrate that the OLS model is indeed based on deviations from the mean by calculating

$$SSx = \Sigma(X - \overline{X})^2 \qquad SSy = \Sigma(Y - \overline{Y})^2$$

$$SSxy = \Sigma(X - \overline{X})(Y - \overline{Y})$$

Police	Number of Reported Crimes
13	8
15	9
23	12
25	18
15	8
10	6
9	5
20	10

48. Aunt Bea wants to get more yield from her Big Boy tomato plants this summer by increasing the number of times she uses fertilizer. Based on the data shown here, does the coefficient for the regression model suggest this is possible? Use the formulas that illustrate that the OLS model is indeed based on deviations from the mean by calculating

$$SSx = \Sigma(X - \overline{X})^2 \qquad SSy = \Sigma(Y - \overline{Y})^2$$

$$SSxy = \Sigma(X - \overline{X})(Y - \overline{Y})$$

Use of Fertilizer	Yield (pounds)
4.00	12.00
9.00	20.00
5.00	15.00
8.00	17.00
2.00	7.00

49. Twelve school districts in the Chicago area were interested in whether the rising property tax rates could be associated with the number of pupils in a classroom in the local schools. Does this seem to be the case based on the data shown here?

Tax Assessment Rates	Pupils per Class	Tax Assessment Rates	Pupils per Class
1.20	32	1.30	25
1.20	36	1.30	21
1.10	25	1.20	35
1.30	20	1.40	16
1.10	39	1.4Q	39
1.20	42	1.30	37

a. If it is thought that more pupils require higher taxes, which is the dependent variable? Calculate and interpret the regression model. Do larger classes seem to be associated with higher taxes?
b. Calculate and interpret the coefficient of determination and the correlation coefficient. Does it seem this model is useful?
c. Calculate and interpret the standard error of the estimate.

50. Test the significance for both the regression coefficient and the correlation coefficient at the 10 percent level for Exercise 49. What do the results tell you?

51. Calculate and interpret the 95 percent confidence interval for β_1 in Exercise 49.

52. Based on figures released by the Internal Revenue Service, a national group of citizens has expressed concern that the budget for the IRS has not been used effectively. The IRS argued that an increase in the number of taxpayers filing returns explains the budget problems. Relevant data are provided here.

Year	Tax Returns (in millions)	IRS Budget (in billions of dollars)
1	116	$6.7
2	116	6.2
3	118	5.4
4	118	5.9
5	120	3.7
6	117	5.9
7	118	4.7
8	121	4.2

a. Construct the regression model, Does the IRS argument seem plausible?
b. Calculate and interpret the coefficient of determination.
c. Calculate and interpret the standard error of the estimate.

53. What is the 95 percent confidence interval for the predictive interval in Exercise 52 if there are 119 returns filed?

54. A popular financial theory holds that there is a direct relationship between the risk of an investment and the return it promises. A stock's risk is measured by its β-value. Shown here are the returns and β-values for 12 fictitious stocks suggested by the investment firm of Guess & Pickum. Do these data seem to support this financial theory of a direct relationship?

Stock	Return (%)	β-Value	Stock	Return (%)	β-Value
1	5.4	1.5	7	5.3	1.3
2	8.9	1.9	8	0.5	−0.5
3	2.3	1.0	9	1.3	0.5
4	1.5	0.5	10	5.9	1.8
5	3.7	1.5	11	6.8	1.9
6	8.2	1.8	12	7.2	1.9

Investors typically view return as a function of risk. Use an interpretation of both the regression coefficient and the coefficient of correlation in your response.

55. Emergency service for certain rural areas of Ohio is often a problem, especially during the winter months. The chief of the Danville Township Fire Department is concerned about response time to emergency calls. He orders an investigation to determine whether distance to the call, measured in miles, can explain response time, measured in minutes. Based on 37 emergency runs, the following data were compiled.

$$\Sigma X = 234 \qquad \Sigma X^2 = 1{,}796$$
$$\Sigma Y = 831 \qquad \Sigma Y^2 = 20{,}037$$
$$\Sigma XY = 5{,}890$$

a. What is the average response time to a call eight miles from the fire station?
b. How dependable is that estimate, based on the extent of the dispersion of the data points around the regression line?

56. Referring to Exercise 55 at the 90 percent level of confidence, what can you say about the significance of the sample

a. Regression coefficient?
b. Correlation coefficient?

57. Referring to Exercise 55 with 90 percent confidence, what time interval would you predict for a call from Zeke Zipple, who lives 10 miles from the station?

58. In reference to Exercise 55 with 90 percent confidence, what is the average time interval that you would predict for many calls 10 miles from the station?

59. Using the data from Exercise 55, the fire chief is interested in a 95 percent confidence interval estimate of the population regression coefficient. Interpret your results for the chief.

Computer Exercise

You have just been hired by your new father-in-law, president of the Jesse James National Bank. Your first task is to estimate a simple regression model that will predict deposits. Your father-in-law has suggested several explanatory variables, including interest rates, an index for the general economic climate in the area, and the number of newly formed businesses. You also feel that population levels could be used as a predictor.

You have collected data for all these variables and must now decide which *one* can best be used as an explanatory variable since you wish to specify a *simple* regression model (actually, all variables might prove significant in a multiple regression mode like those examined in the next chapter). Access the file "BANK" on your data disk. it contains data for deposits (DEP) in millions of dollars, the interest rate (INT) the bank pays for deposits, an index of economic activity (IND), population (POP) in hundreds for different areas in which bank branches are located, and the number of new businesses (BUS) in those areas.

Compare the explanatory power of each variable in separate simple regression models. Provide a comparative analysis of each model with respect to all regression and correlation features you feel provide any useful information. Which model do you recommend be used? Prepare your final statistical report as described in Appendix I.

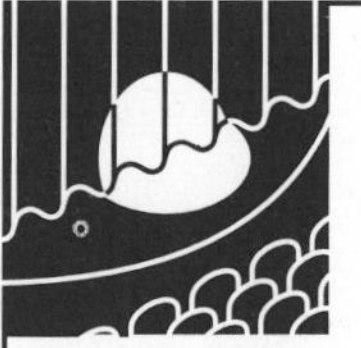

CURTAIN CALL

The "Cola War" between Coke and Pepsi, mentioned in Setting the Stage at the opening of this chapter, discussed efforts by the two companies to gain market share at one another's expense. Each has tried various strategies to achieve these goals. Neither company seems eager to engage in a prolonged price war to increase sales. Pepsi has relied heavily on celebrity names, using well-known personalities to promote its product, while Coke seems to prefer promotional schemes linked to popular movies and comic book heroes.

As an analyst for Coke, your job is to use the data provided here to learn whether price changes are effective in promoting sales. These data are from selected test markets across the nation for 12-packs of each soft drink. Sales are rounded to the nearest thousands of units.

Use all the tools of regression and correlation you learned in this chapter to fully analyze the impact of price changes on sales for both products. Develop and interpret the regression model for both companies by regressing sales on price. Construct and interpret all confidence intervals and test all pertinent hypotheses. Does it appear one company has been more successful in using price changes to promote sales? As an employee of Coke, what might you recommend?

Pepsi Sales	Pepsi Price	Coke Sales	Coke Price
25.00	$2.58	35.00	$2.10
21.00	3.10	25.00	3.52
18.00	3.25	21.00	2.10
35.00	2.10	19.00	2.55
29.00	2.90	23.00	3.50
24.00	2.85	31.00	2.00
18.00	4.21	24.00	3.50
16.00	5.26	31.00	2.99
18.00	5.85	20.00	2.99
32.00	2.50	19.00	2.25

From the Stage to Real Life

Where do you stand in the Coke and Pepsi war? What are your reasons? Do you know which product is winning the war and by how much? Visits to these companies' Web sites help to answer these questions. First visit the Coke site (*www.cocacola.com/sports*). Explore, and make list of, the feature areas on the Coke Home Page. Some areas are the About the Coca-Cola Company, a gift shop, and a games area. In the About the Coca-Cola Company area, click on each of the vending machine buttons to learn different facts about the company of interest to investors. Does any of this information mention Pepsi? Overall, is this site aimed more at the consumer or the investor? What non-price competitive marketing strategies are suggested at this site, for instance, collectibles and a gift shop?

Now visit the Pepsi site (*www.pepsico.com*). Make a list of the feature areas of this Home Page. Overall, is this site aimed at consumers or investors? What non-price competitive strategies are suggested at this site? Click on the Annual Report area. Then select "PepsiCo Facts" followed by "beverages." Read through the fact information. Are there graphs that display world and U.S. market shares? If so, what are the world and U.S. market shares for Coke and Pepsi? What reasons for the market share gaps are suggested by your visits to these two companies' Web sites?

CHAPTER 12

Multiple Regression and Correlation

Chapter Blueprint

By using more than one explanatory variable in a regression model it is possible to increase the explanatory power and the usefulness of the model in making many business decisions. This chapter discusses the construction of such multiple regression models and shows how they can be used to facilitate business decision making.

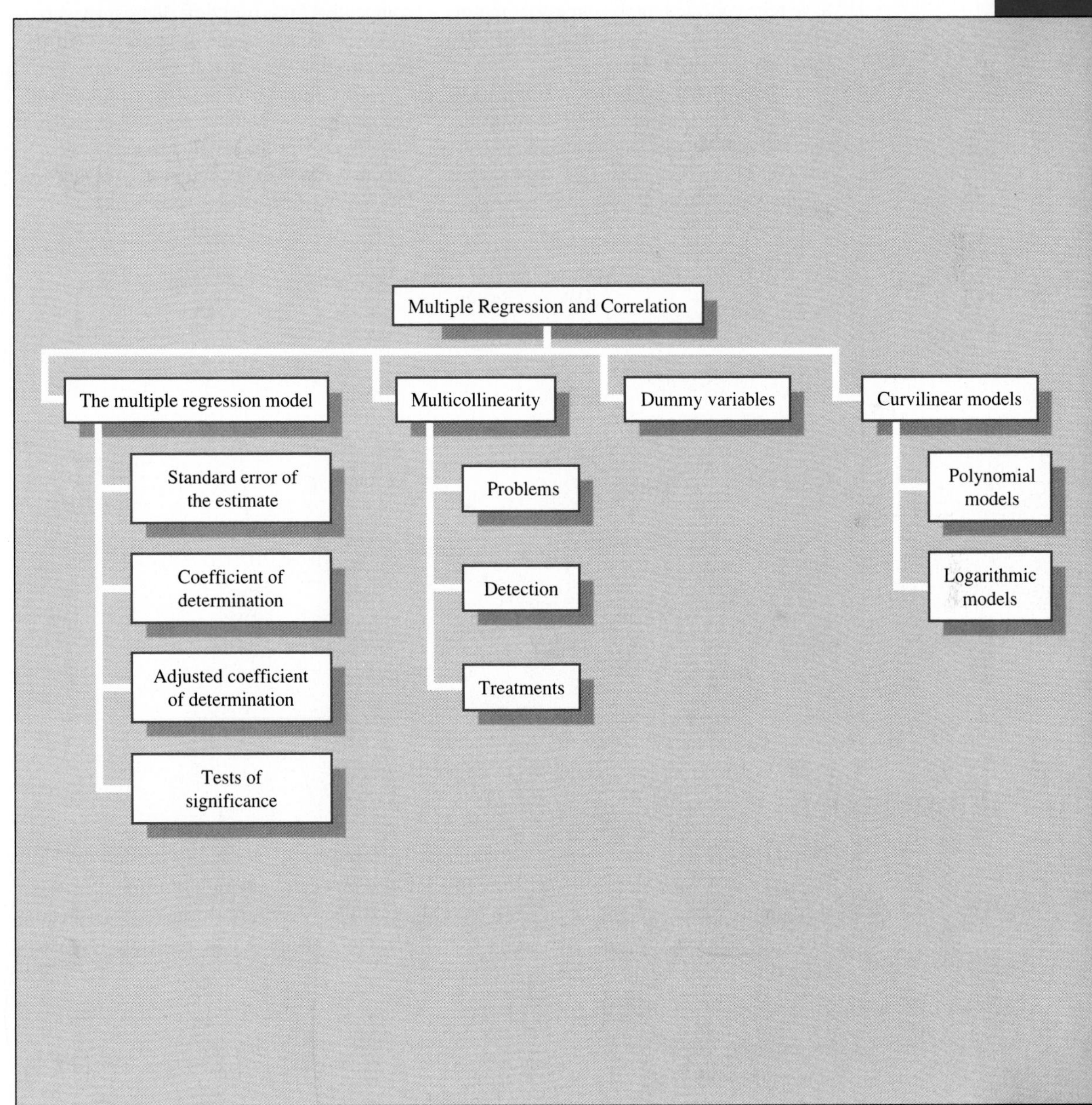

SETTING THE STAGE

In preparation for your graduation later this year, you have taken a position as an intern with Griffen Associates, an investment company in Chicago. As a measure of your financial skills, the company has given you the assignment of analyzing the market performance of mutual funds that operate as competitors of Griffen. Data have been collected for the three-year return (3YRET) and the one-year return (1YRET) for 15 competitive funds.

Mr. Griffen requests that you prepare a report on the performance of these competitors, based on several factors including their turnover rates (TOs), their total assets, and whether each fund has a sales load provision.

There is particular interest within Griffen Associates in whether there has been any change in the performance of these funds over the past three years. Griffen is considering significant changes in many of its operating procedures, and certain managers who have been with the firm for several years are worried about the outcomes of these changes. By analyzing the behavior of competitive firms over time, these managers feel they can gain some insight into the future direction of Griffen Associates.

This project will require you to set up and analyze a multiple regression model that can provide the insight needed to establish the important operational procedures that Griffen Associates is considering.

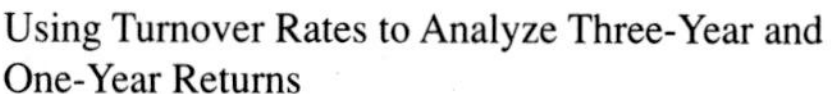
Using Turnover Rates to Analyze Three-Year and One-Year Returns

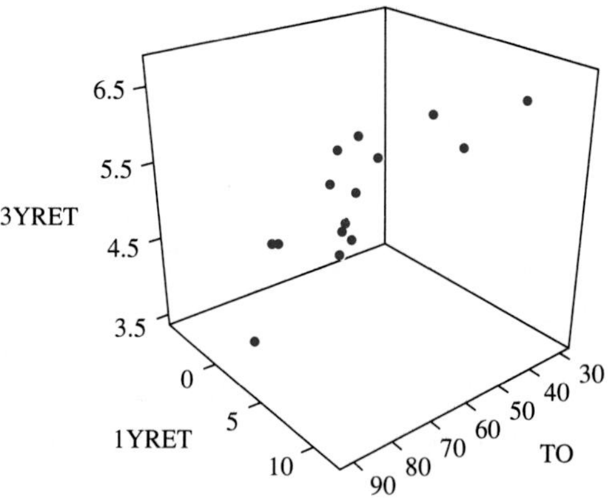

12.1 Introduction

In Chapter 11 we saw how a single explanatory variable could be used to predict the value of the dependent variable. Consider how much more powerful our model might become if we were to use more explanatory variables. This is precisely what multiple regression does, by allowing us to incorporate two or more independent variables. The multiple regression model with k independent variables is expressed as

The multiple regression model
$$Y = \beta_0 + \beta_1X_1 + \beta_2X_2 + \cdots + \beta_kX_k + \varepsilon \qquad [12.1]$$

where β_i are the regression coefficients and ε is the error term. The model is estimated using sample data as

The estimated multiple regression model	$\hat{Y} = b_0 + b_1X_1 + b_2X_2 + \cdots + b_kX_k$	[12.2]

where $\hat{Y}$ is the estimated value for the dependent variable and b_i are the estimates for the population coefficients β_i. The b_i are called the **partial (or net) regression coefficients** and carry the same interpretation as in simple regression. Thus, b_1 is the amount by which Y_i will change if X_1 changes by one unit, *assuming all other independent variables are held constant*. This assumption was not necessary under simple regression because there were no other independent variables to hold constant.

Multiple regression involves the same assumptions cited in the previous chapter for simple regression, plus two others. The first assumption requires that the number of observations, n, exceed the number of independent variables, k, by at least 2. In multiple regression there are $k + 1$ parameters to be estimated: coefficients for the k independent variables plus the intercept term. Therefore, the degrees of freedom associated with the model are d.f. $= n - (k + 1)$. If we are to retain even one degree of freedom, n must exceed k by at least 2, so that $n - (k + 1)$ is at least 1.

The second assumption involves the relationship between the independent variables. It requires that none of the independent variables be linearly related. For example, if $X_1 = X_2 + X_3$, or perhaps $X_1 = 0.5X_2$, then a linear relationship would exist between two or more independent variables and a serious problem would arise. This problem is **multicollinearity.**

Multicollinearity Multicollinearity exists if two or more of the independent variables are linearly related.

Multicollinearity may cause the algebraic signs of the coefficients to be the opposite of what logic may dictate, while greatly increasing the standard error of the coefficients. A more thorough discussion of multicollinearity follows later in this chapter.

12.2 The Multiple Regression Model for Hop Scotch Airlines

In Chapter 11, Hop Scotch Airlines used advertising in a simple regression model to explain and predict the number of passengers. The model carried a standard error of 0.907 and an r^2 of 94 percent. Suppose that Hop Scotch wishes to incorporate a second explanatory variable into its model to explain the number of passengers. Based on the economic principle that income is a primary determinant of demand, Hop Scotch chooses national income as that second variable. The model becomes

The multiple regression model for Hop Scotch	$\hat{Y} = b_0 + b_1X_1 + b_2X_2$	[12.3]

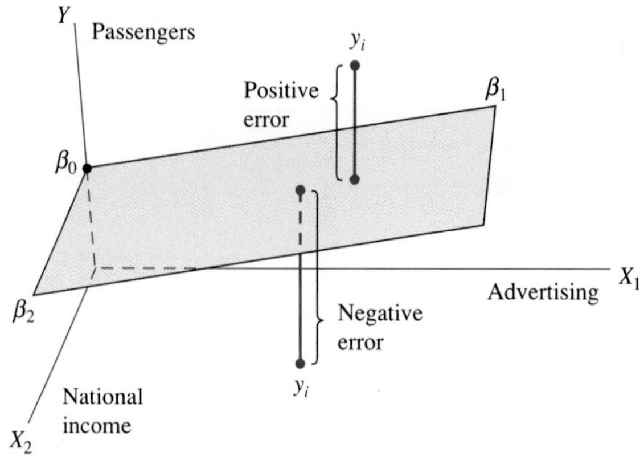

Figure 12.1
A Regression Plane for Hop Scotch Airline

where $\hat{Y}$ is the predicted value for passengers in thousands
X_1 is advertising in hundreds of dollars
X_2 is national income in trillions of dollars

With two explanatory variables, a scatter diagram can be plotted in a three-dimensional space forming a regression plane, as seen in Figure 12.1. The dependent variable is placed on the single vertical axis. A model with three of more independent variables requires a *hyperplane* and is difficult to depict graphically.

> **Regression Plane** The coefficients of the two independent variables are represented by the slopes of the regression plane.

The values for b_0, b_1, and b_2 in Formula (12.3) are found much as those in simple regression. We want estimates of the coefficients that minimize the sum of the squared errors: $\Sigma(Y_i - \hat{Y}_i)^2$. This will provide the least-squares model that best fits our data that are shown in Table 12.1. The last column represents the new variable *national income* in trillions of dollars.

Table 12.1
Multiple Regression Data for Hop Scotch Airlines

Observation (months)	Passengers (Y) (in 1,000's)	Advertising (X_1) (in \$1,000)	National Income X_2 (in trillions of \$)
1	15	10	2.40
2	17	12	2.72
3	13	8	2.08
4	23	17	3.68
5	16	10	2.56
6	21	15	3.36
7	14	10	2.24
8	20	14	3.20
9	24	19	3.84
10	17	10	2.72
11	16	11	2.07
12	18	13	2.33
13	23	16	2.98
14	15	10	1.94
15	16	12	2.17

Calculating a multiple regression model by hand is quite tedious and time consuming. The procedure requires $k + 1$ simultaneous equations with $k + 1$ unknowns, where k is the number of right-hand-side variables. We will therefore dispense with any effort to solve for the regression model by hand and rely sole on the computer for most of our calculations. Our attention will instead focus on the rationale necessary to understand and interpret the multiple regression model.

Display 12.1 is a partial Minitab printout for the data in Table 12.1. We can clearly see that, if we round the coefficients somewhat to facilitate discussion, the model is

$$Pass = 3.53 + 0.84Adv + 1.44NI$$

where *Pass*, *Adv*, and *NI* are passengers in thousands, advertising expenditures in thousands of dollars, and national income in trillions of dollars, respectively. Accordingly, the model predicts that if advertising is increased one unit ($1,000), passengers will go up 0.84 units (840 passengers) if national income does not change. Further, if national income rises by one unit ($1 trillion), passengers will increase by 1,440 if advertising is held constant.

Display 12.1

Regression Analysis

```
The regression equation is
PASS = 3.53 + 0.840 ADV + 1.44 NI

Predictor       Coef      Stdev     t-ratio       p
Constant      3.5284     0.9994        3.53   0.004
ADV           0.8397     0.1419        5.92   0.000
NI            1.4410     0.7360        1.96   0.074

s = 0.8217     R-sq = 95.3%      R-sq(adj) = 94.5%

Analysis of Variance

SOURCE         DF         SS          MS        F       p
Regression      2    163.632      81.816   121.18   0.000
Error          12      8.102       0.675
Total          14    171.733

SOURCE         DF     SEQ SS
ADV             1    161.044
NI              1      2.588
```

12.3 Evaluating the Model

After the model has been estimated, it is necessary to evaluate it to determine whether it provides a satisfactory fit and explanation for the data that have been collected. There are several tests that can be performed to make this determination. These tests are quite similar to those performed on our simple regression model. However, as noted above, we will emphasize the rationale behind these tests, leaving the actual computations to the computer. The mathematical calculations and required formulas will be presented only to demonstrate *conceptually* what each test is designed to do.

A. The Standard Error of the Estimate

As with simple regression, the standard error of the estimate *Se* can be used as a measure of goodness of fit. It carries the same interpretation as it did with simple regression. It measures the degree of dispersion of the Y_i-values around the regression plane, as seen in

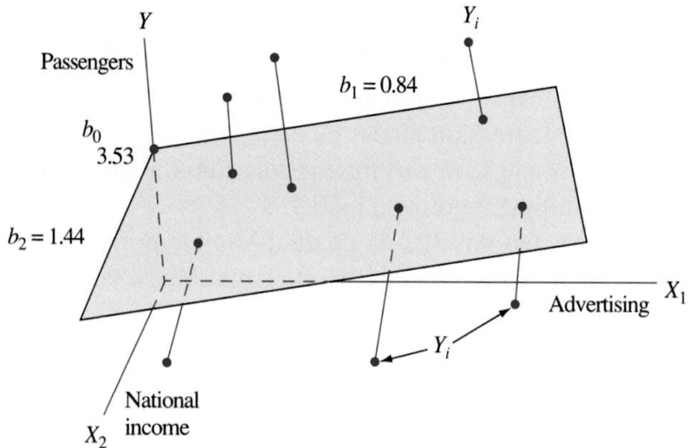

Figure 12.2
The Regression Plane for Hop Scotch

Figure 12.2. Of course, the less the dispersion, the smaller the *Se* and the more accurate the model in its prediction and forecasting.

The standard error is calculated in the same manner as with simple regression.

The standard error of the estimate	$Se = \sqrt{\dfrac{\Sigma(Y_i - \hat{Y}_i)^2}{n - k - 1}}$	[12.4]

where $n - k - 1$ is the number of degrees of freedom and k is the number of right-hand side variables. The numerator under the radical in Formula (12.4) is the sum of the squared errors and will be minimized in accord with the concept of ordinary least squares. Display 12.2 shows a Minitab printout of the actual values for passengers (Y_i), the predicted value for passengers, ($\hat{Y}_i$), the residual ($Y_i - \hat{Y}_i$), and the residual squared ($Y_i - \hat{Y}_i)^2$. The sum of this last column is the sum of squared errors and is found to be 8.1016. The standard error is then

$$Se = \sqrt{\frac{8.1016}{15 - 2 - 1}} = 0.8217$$

Display 12.2

Hop Scotch Data

Row	PASS Y_i	Y-HAT $\hat{Y}_i$	RESIDUAL $(Y_i - \hat{Y}_i)$	RESDSQ $(Y_i-\hat{Y}_i)^2$
1	15	15.3834	-0.38338	0.14698
2	17	17.5238	-0.52382	0.27438
3	13	13.2429	-0.24294	0.05902
4	23	23.1055	-0.10547	0.01112
5	16	15.6139	0.38607	0.14906
6	21	20.9650	0.03497	0.00122
7	14	15.1528	-1.15282	1.32900
8	20	19.8948	0.10519	0.01106
9	24	25.0154	-1.01536	1.03095
10	17	15.8445	1.15551	1.33521
11	16	15.7475	0.25248	0.06375
12	18	17.8015	0.19850	0.03940
13	23	21.2571	1.74287	3.03761
14	15	14.7205	0.27947	0.07810
15	16	16.7313	-0.73128	0.53477
MTB>				8.10160

The Minitab printout in Display 12.1 shows the standard error to be 0.8217. This represents an improvement over the standard error of the simple regression model in the previous chapter, which was reported to be 0.907.

B. Coefficient of Multiple Determination

As with simple regression, the coefficient of multiple determination is used as a measure of goodness of fit. For the sake of convenience, the term *multiple* is often asssumed given the context of the discussion, and the expression is shortened to coefficient of determination, the same for the simple model. Another similarity between the simple model and a model containing two or more explanatory variables is the interpretation of the coefficient of determination. In both instances it measures the portion of the change in Y explained by all the independent variables in the model.

> **Coefficient of Determination** The coefficient of determination measures the strength of the relationship between Y and the independent variables.

To measure that portion of the total change in Y explained by the regression model, we use the ratio of explained variation to total variation just as we did in the case of simple regression. As noted in Chapter 11, by *variation* we mean the variation in the observed Y-values (Y_i) from their mean ($\bar{Y}$). The variation in Y that is explained by our model is reflected by the regression sum of squares (SSR). The total variation in Y is, in turn, measured by the total sum of squares (SST). Thus,

Coefficient of multiple determination

$$R^2 = \frac{SSR}{SST} \qquad [12.5]$$

Since $SST = SSR + SSE$, we also have

$$R^2 = 1 - \frac{SSE}{SST} \qquad [12.6]$$

Notice that the coefficient is r^2 in the simple model and R^2 in our present discussion.

From the Minitab printout in Display 12.1, shown earlier, we see that

$$\begin{aligned} R^2 &= \frac{SSR}{SST} \\ &= \frac{163.632}{171.733} \\ &= 0.953 \end{aligned}$$

The R^2 can also be read directly from Display 12.1 as $R - \text{sq} = 95.3$ percent. Thus, 95.3 percent of the change in the number of passengers Hop Scotch transports is explained by changes in advertising and national income. This compares favorably to $r^2 = 0.93$ for the simple model in Chapter 11 containing only advertising. By incorporating NI as a second independent variable, we have increased the explanatory power of the model from

93 to 95.3 percent. As with the simple model, we always find $0 \leq R^2 \leq 1$. Of course, the higher the R^2, the more explanatory power the model has.

C. The Adjusted Coefficient of Determination

Because of its importance, R^2 is reported by most computer packages. It is a quick and easy way to evaluate the regression model and to determine how well the model fits the data. Outside of the regression coefficients themselves, R^2 is perhaps the most commonly observed and closely watched statistic in regression analysis.

However, it is possible for careless—or unscrupulous—statisticians to artificially inflate R^2. One can increase R^2 merely by adding another independent variable to the model. Even if some nonsensical variable with truly no explanatory power is incorporated into the model, R^2 will rise. Hop Scotch could "pump up" its R^2 by adding to the model, as an explanatory variable, the tonnage of sea trout caught by sport fishing off the Florida coast. Now, obviously, fishing has little or nothing to do with Hop Scotch's passenger list. Yet there is probably at least a tiny bit of totally coincidental correlation, either positive or negative, between fishing and air travel. Even a minute degree of correlation will inflate R^2. By adding several of these absurd "explanatory" variables, the R^2 could illegitimately be increased until it approached 100 percent. A model of this nature may appear to fit the data quite well, but would produce wretched results in any attempt to predict or forecast the value for the independent variable.

It is therefore a common practice in multiple regression and correlation to report the **adjusted coefficient of determination.** Symbolized as $\bar{R}^2$, and read "R bar squared," this statistic adjusts the measure of explanatory power for the number of degrees of freedom. Since the degree of freedom for SSE is $n - k - 1$, adding another explanatory variable results in the loss of another degree of freedom. $\bar{R}^2$ will *decrease* if a variable is added that does not offer sufficient explanatory power to justify this loss in the degrees of freedom. If it decreases too much, consideration should be given to its removal.

The adjusted coefficient of determination is obtained by dividing SSE and SST by their respective degrees of freedom.

Adjusted coefficient of multiple determination

$$\bar{R}^2 = 1 - \frac{SSE/(n - k - 1)}{SST/(n - 1)} \qquad [12.7]$$

A more computationally convenient formula for $\bar{R}^2$ is

Adjusted coefficient of multiple determination

$$\bar{R}^2 = 1 - (1 - R^2)\frac{n - 1}{n - k - 1} \qquad [12.8]$$

Since the numerator in Formula (12.7) is the MSE, it may be said the $\bar{R}^2$ is a combination of the two measures of the performance of a regression model: the mean squared error and the coefficient of determination.

The data for the Hop Scotch model yield

$$\begin{aligned}\bar{R}^2 &= 1 - (1 - 0.953)\frac{15 - 1}{15 - 2 - 1} \\ &= 0.945\end{aligned}$$

After adjusting for the degrees of freedom, we have $\bar{R}^2$ of 94.5 percent.

As you might expect, most computer programs also report the adjusted coefficient of determination. Display 12.1 reveals $R - s_q(\text{adj}) = 94.5\%$.

D. Evaluating the Model as a Whole

Given the regression model, one of the first questions to ask is, "Does it have any explanatory value?" This can perhaps best be answered by performing analysis of variance (ANOVA). The ANOVA procedure tests whether *any* of the independent variables has a relationship with the dependent variable. If an independent variable is not related to the Y-variable, its coefficient should be zero. That is, if X_i is not related to Y, then $\beta_i = 0$. The ANOVA procedure tests the null hypothesis that all the β-values are zero against the alternative that *at least one β is not zero.* That is,

$$H_0: \beta_1 = \beta_2 = \beta_3 = \cdots = \beta_k = 0$$
$$H_A: \text{At least one } \beta \text{ is not zero}$$

If the null is not rejected, then there is no linear relationship between Y and any of the independent variables. On the other hand, if the null is rejected, then at least one independent variable is linearly related to Y.

The ANOVA process necessary to test the hypothesis was presented in Chapter 10. An ANOVA table is set up, and the F-test is used. Table 12.2 provides the general format for an ANOVA table for multiple regression.

Table 12.2
A Generalized ANOVA Table

Source of Variation	Sum of Squares	Degrees of Freedom	Mean Square	F-value
Between samples (treatment)	SSR	k	$\frac{SSR}{k}$	$F = \frac{MSR}{MSE}$
Within samples (error)	SSE	$n - k - 1$	$\frac{SSE}{n - k - 1}$	
Total variation	SST	$n - 1$		

Table 12.3
ANOVA Table for Hop Scotch

Source of Variation	Sum of Squares	Degrees of Freedom	Mean Square	F-value
Between samples (treatment)	163.632	2	81.816	121.18
Within samples (error)	8.102	12	0.675	
Total variation	171.733	14		

Note the similarity of Table 12.2 to ANOVA tables you have already seen. Notice that the degree of freedom for the regression sum of squares is equal to k, the number of independent variables in the model, while the degree of freedom for the error sum of squares is $n - k - 1$. Each of the sums of squares is found exactly as it was for simple regression.

$$SST = \Sigma(Y_i - \bar{Y})^2 \qquad [12.9]$$

$$SSR = \Sigma(\hat{Y} - \bar{Y})^2 \qquad [12.10]$$

$$SSE = \Sigma(Y_i - \hat{Y}_i)^2 \qquad [12.11]$$

Table 12.3 provides the results in an ANOVA table for Hop Scotch Airlines. This information can also be seen in Display 12.1 (presented earlier) and in Display 12.3 (repeated here for your convenience).

Display 12.3

Analysis of Variance

SOURCE	DF	SS	MS	F	p
Regression	2	163.632	81.816	121.18	0.000
Error	12	8.102	0.675		
Total	14	171.733			

SOURCE	DF	SEQ SS
ADV	1	161.044
NI	1	2.588

Since the F-ratio is MSR/MSE, the degrees of freedom needed to perform an F-test seen from Table 12.3 are 2 and 12. To test the hypothesis, at say, the 5 percent level, we find from Table G (Appendix III) that $F_{0.05,2,12}$ is 3.89. The decision rule is: do not reject if $F \leq$ 389; reject if $F > 3.89$. This is displayed in Figure 12.3. Since $F = 121.18 > 3.89$, the null is rejected. We can conclude at the 5 percent level that a linear relationship exists between Y and at least one of the independent variables.

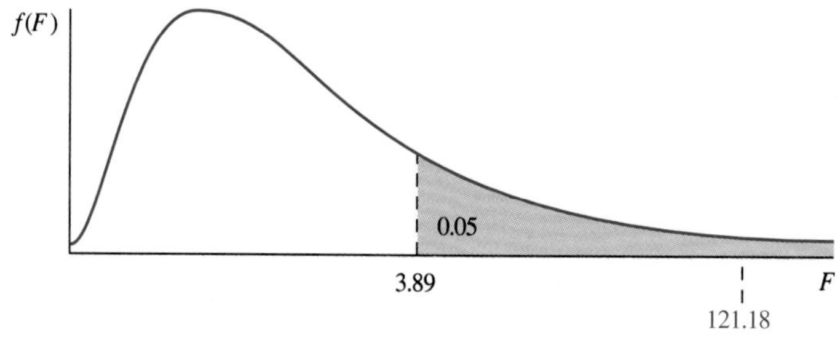

Figure 12.3
F-test for the Hop Scotch Regression Model

E. Testing Individual Partial Regression Coefficients

The next logical step is to test each coefficient individually to determine which one is (or ones are) significant. Let us test advertising first. The process is identical to simple regression:

$$H_0: \beta_1 = 0$$
$$H_A: \beta_1 \neq 0$$

where β_1 is the population regression coefficient for advertising. Failure to reject the null means that advertising does not contribute any additional explanatory power to the model, given that national income is already included.

The standard t-test with $n - k - 1$ degrees of freedom is used.

Hypothesis test for the significance of the partial regression coefficient

$$t = \frac{b_1 - \beta_1}{s_{b_1}} \qquad [12.12]$$

where s_{b_1} is the standard error of the regression coefficient. As with most statistics associated with multiple regression, s_{b_1} is difficult to calculate by hand. Luckily, most computer packages report this information. As seen in the Minitab printout in Display 12.4, the t-value for advertising is

$$t = \frac{0.8398 - 0}{0.1419} = 5.92$$

Display 12.4

Regression Analysis

```
The regression equation is
PASS = 3.53 + 0.840 ADV + 1.44 NI

Predictor      Coef      Stdev     t-ratio       p
Constant     3.5284     0.9994        3.53   0.004
ADV          0.8397     0.1419        5.92   0.000
NI           1.4410     0.7360        1.96   0.074
```

Figure 12.4
Test of Significance for Advertising

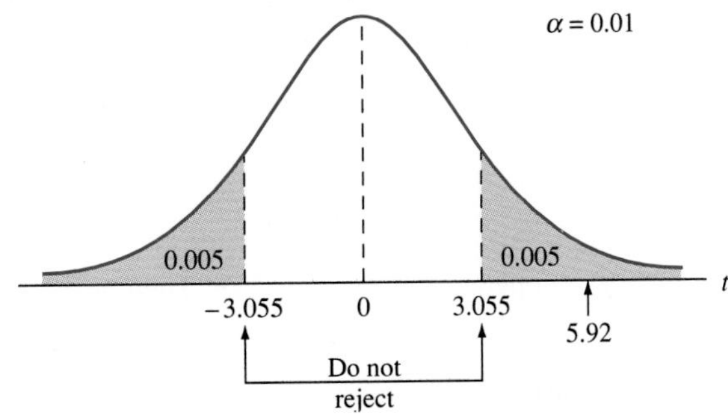

If an alpha value of 1 percent is selected, $t_{.01,12} = 3.055$. As seen in Figure 12.4, the decision rule is

Decision Rule Do not reject if t is between ± 3.055. Reject otherwise.

Since $t = 5.92 > 3.055$, the null is rejected. At the 1 percent level of significance, advertising contributes significantly to the explanatory power of the model even after national income has been added. This is confirmed by the p-value in Display 12.4 of 0.000. The p-value, you may remember, is the lowest alpha value you can set and still reject the null. Since the alpha value of 1 percent is greater than 0.000, we reject the null.

Recall from Chapter 11 that when advertising was the only explanatory variable it reported a t-value of 13.995. Why is it different now? The t-value of 5.92 in this model measures the additional contribution of advertising given that national income is already included. In rejecting the null, we have determined at the 1 percent level of significance that advertising contributes significantly to the model's explanatory power even after national income has been added.

The same test of significance is now performed on the second explanatory variable, national income.

$$H_0: \beta_2 = 0$$
$$H_A: \beta_2 \neq 0$$

Display 12.4 reveals that

$$t = \frac{1.441 - 0}{0.7360} = 1.96$$

Figure 12.5
Tests of Significance for National Income

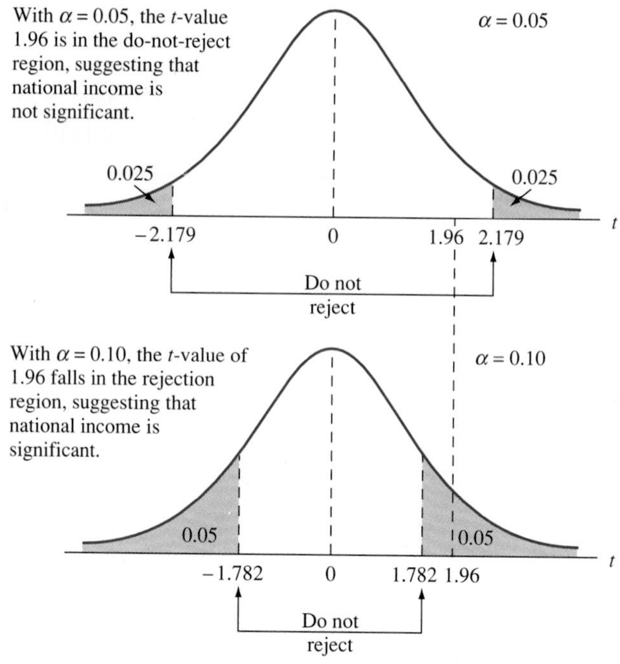
With $\alpha = 0.05$, the t-value 1.96 is in the do-not-reject region, suggesting that national income is not significant.
$\alpha = 0.05$
0.025
0.025
−2.179
0
1.96 2.179
t
Do not reject
With $\alpha = 0.10$, the t-value of 1.96 falls in the rejection region, suggesting that national income is significant.
$\alpha = 0.10$
0.05
0.05
−1.782
0
1.782 1.96
t
Do not reject

If $\alpha = 5$ percent, $t_{0.05,12} = 2.179$. Then, as Figure 12.5 shows,

Decision Rule Do not reject if t is between ± 2.179. Reject otherwise.

Clearly, the null $\beta_2 = 0$ is *not* rejected. We cannot conclude at the 5 percent level of significance that national income contributes to the explanatory power of the model if advertising is already included as an explanatory variable.

According to the p-value, we can lower the level of significance to only 7.4 percent and still reject the null. If the alpha value is set lower than 7.4 percent, such as 5 percent, we do not reject the null. In contrast, if alpha is instead set at 10 percent, $t_{0.10,12} = \pm 1.782$. and the decision rule is

Decision Rule Do not reject if t is between ± 1.782. Reject otherwise.

Since the t-value is 1.96, the null is rejected at the 10 percent level of significance. This too is reflected in Figure 12.5.

Section Exercises

1. Given regression model $\hat{Y} = 40 + 3X_1 - 4X_2$,
   a. Interpret the coefficients.
   b. Estimate Y if $X_1 = 5$ and $X_2 = 10$.
2. Given the regression equation, with t-values in parentheses,

$$\hat{Y} = 100 + \underset{(0.73)}{17X_1} + \underset{(6.21)}{80X_2}$$

   How might you improve this model?

3. For the equation

$$\hat{Y} = 100 - 20X_1 - 40X_2$$

a. What is the estimated impact of X_1 on Y?
b. What conditions regarding X_2 must be observed in answering part *a*?

4. A demand function is expressed as

$$\hat{Q} = 10 + 12P + 8I$$

where Q is quantity demanded, P is price, and I is consumer income. How would you respond to this equation?

5. A regression model with $n = 20$ observations and three independent variables reports an F-value of 3.89. Are any of the independent variables significant at the 1 percent level?

6. A regression of consumption on income and wealth, with t-values in parentheses, is shown here. Are the independent variables significant at the 5 percent level? There were 100 observations.

$$\hat{C} = 52 + \underset{(12.2)}{17.3I} + \underset{(0.87)}{4.6W}$$

7. A model regressing consumption (C) on income (I) and wealth (W) yielded the following results:

$$R^2 = 0.86$$
$$\bar{R}^2 = 0.79$$
$$F = 17.42$$
$$\hat{C} = \underset{(0.71)}{402} + \underset{(6.21)}{0.83I} + \underset{(5.47)}{0.71W}$$

where t-values are shown in parentheses. There were 25 observations in the data set.

a. What is the meaning of the intercept term?
b. Are the coefficients significant at the 5 percent level?
c. Is the model significant at the 10 percent level?

8. Batex Associates sells heating oil to residents in rural areas of Virginia. The director of the marketing department at Batex developed a model regressing the consumption of heating oil (in gallons) of their customers on the local temperature (TEMP), population (POP) by county, and the price of the oil. The results are given in the Minitab printout below.

a. What is the model?
b. Do the data suggest that all three variables are significant at the 5 percent level?
c. What is the lowest level of significance for each variable?
d. How might you suggest improving the model?
e. How strong is the relationship?

```
The regression equation is
OIL = 20.7 - 0.853 TEMP + 0.113 POP + 0.00193 PRICE

Predictor        Coef       Stdev    t-ratio       p
Constant       20.706       3.455       5.99   0.000
TEMP          -0.8530      0.6220      -1.37   0.085
POP           0.11287     0.02603       4.34   0.000
PRICE        0.001929    0.003570       0.54   0.595

s = 1.478        R-sq = 95.8%      R-sq(adj) = 95.2%
```

9. A field of economics referred to as human capital has often held that a person's income (I) could be determined on the basis of his or her (1) education level (E), (2) training (T), and (3) general level of health (H). Using 25 employees at a small textile firm in North Carolina,

a researcher regressed income on the other three variables and got the following results.

$$\hat{I} = 27.2 + 3.7E + 1.7T + 3.05H$$
$$(3.70) \quad (6.21) \quad (4.32) \quad (6.79)$$
$$R^2 = 0.67 \quad F = 5.97$$

I is measured in units of \$1,000, E and T are measured in years, and H is measured in terms of a scaled index of one's health: the higher the index, the better the level of health.

a. If one's education increases by two years, what happens to his or her income?

b. Is the model significant at the 5 percent level? State the hypothesis, the decision rule, and the conclusion.

c. Determine which variable(s) is (are) significant at the 10 percent level. State the hypotheses, the decision rule, and the conclusion.

d. What is the value of the adjusted coefficient of determination?

10. What does it mean if the null hypothesis in a test for a single β_i is not rejected?

11. In reference to the previous problem if H_0: $\beta_i = 0$ is not rejected, according to the model, what will happen to Y if X_i changes by one unit? by two units?

12. Consider the following model with $n = 30$.

$$\hat{Y} = 50 + 10X_1 + 80X_2$$
$$R^2 = 0.78 \qquad S_{b_1} = 2.73 \qquad S_{b_2} = 4.71$$

Which variable(s) is (are) significant at the 5 percent level? State the hypothesis and the decision rule, and draw a conclusion.

13. Economists have long held that a community's demand for money is affected by (1) level of income and (2) interest rate. As income goes up, people want to hold more money to facilitate their increased daily transactions. As the interest rate goes up, people choose to hold less money because of the opportunity to invest it at the higher interest rate.

An economist for the federal government regresses money demand (M) on income (I) and interest rates (r), where M is expressed in hundreds of dollars and I in thousands of dollars. The model is

$$\hat{M} = 0.44 + 5.49I + 6.4r$$

A partial ANOVA table is

Source	Sum of Squares	Degrees of Freedom
Between samples	93.59	2
Within samples	1.42	9

a. According to the theory of the demand for money, are the signs of the coefficients as expected? Explain.

b. Test the entire model at $\alpha = 0.01$.

14. Given the conditions in Exercise 13, if the standard error for the coefficient for I is 1.37 and that of r is 43.6, determine which variable is (or variables are) significant at the 1 percent level. State the hypothesis, the decision rule, and the conclusion.

15. An economic analyst for IBM wishes to forecast regional sales (S) in hundreds of dollars on the basis of the number of sales personnel (P), the number of new business starts in the region (B), and some measure of prices. As a proxy for the last variable, she uses changes in the Consumer Price Index (CPI). She then collects data for 10 sales regions and derives the following model and partial ANOVA table:

$$\hat{S} = -1.01 + 0.422P + 0.091B - 1.8\text{CPI}$$

Source	Sum of Squares	Degrees of Freedom
Between samples	391.57	3
Within samples	31.33	6

a. Test the significance of the entire model at 1 percent. State the hypothesis, the decision rule, and the conclusion.

b. If the standard errors of the coefficients for P, B, and CPI are 0.298, 0.138, and 2.15, respectively, test each coefficient at the 10 percent level. State the hypothesis, the decision rule, and the conclusion in each case.

c. How can you reconcile the findings from parts *a* and *b*?

12.4 The Presence of Multicollinearity

Earlier we noted the danger of multicollinearity. This problem arises when one of the independent variables is linearly related to one or more of the other independent variables. Such a situation violates one of the conditions for multiple regression. Specifically, multicollinearity occurs if there is a high correlation between two independent variables, X_i and X_j. In Chapter 11 we discussed the correlation coefficient r for the dependent variable and the single independent variable. If this same concept is applied to two independent variables, X_i and X_j, in multiple regression, we can calculate the correlation coefficient r_{ij}. If r_{ij} is high, multicollinearity exists.

What is *high?* Unfortunately, there is no answer to this critical question. There is no magic cutoff point at which the correlation is judged to be too high and multicollinearity exists. Multicollinearity is a problem of degree. Any time two or more independent variables are linearly related, some degree of multicollinearity exists. If its presence becomes too pronounced, the model is adversely affected. What is considered too high is largely a judgment call by the researcher. Some insight necessary to make that call is provided in this section.

Assume you are using regression techniques to estimate a demand curve (or demand function) for your product. Recognizing that the number of consumers is related to demand, you choose as explanatory variables.

$$X_1 = \text{All men in the market area}$$
$$X_2 = \text{All women in the market area}$$
$$X_3 = \text{Total population in the market area}$$

Obviously, X_3 is a linear combination of X_1 and X_2 ($X_3 = X_1 + X_2$). The correlation r_{13} between X_1 and X_3 and the correlation r_{23} between X_2 and X_3 are quite high. This ensures the presence of multicollinearity and creates many problems in the use of regression techniques. A discussion of some of the common problems follows.

A. The Problems of Multicollinearity

One of the more vexing problems of multicollinearity arises from our inability to separate the individual effects of each independent variable on Y. In the presence of multicollinearity, it is impossible to disentangle the effects of each X_i. Suppose in the model

$$\hat{Y} = 40 + 10X_1 + 8X_2$$

X_1 and X_2 showed a high degree of correlation. In this case, the coefficient of 10 for X_1 may not represent the true effect of X_1 on Y. The regression coefficients become unreliable and cannot be taken as estimates of the change in Y given a one-unit change in the independent variable.

Furthermore, the standard errors of the coefficients, s_{b_i}, become inflated. If two or more samples of the same size are taken, a large variation in the coefficients would be found. In the model specified above, instead of 10 as the coefficient of X_1, a second sample might yield a coefficient of 15 or 20. If b_1 varies that much from one sample to the next, we must question its accuracy.

Multicollinearity can even cause the sign of the coefficient to be opposite that which logic would dictate. For example, if you included price as a variable in the estimation of your demand curve, you might find it took on a positive sign. This implies that as the price of a good goes up, consumers buy more of it. This is an obvious violation of the logic behind demand theory.

B. Detecting Multicollinearity

Perhaps the most direct way of testing for multicollinearity is to produce a **correlation matrix** for all variables in the model, as shown in the Minitab printout in Display 12.5. The value of 0.870 for the correlation between the two independent variables indicates that NI and ADV are closely related. Although there is no predetermined value for r_{ij} which signals the onset of multicollinearity, a value of 0.870 is probably high enough to indicate a significant problem.

Display 12.5

Correlations (Pearson)

	ADV	PASS
PASS	0.968	
NI	0.870	0.903

Some of the guesswork can be eliminated by using a t-test to determine whether the level of correlation between two independent variables differs significantly from zero. Given the nonzero relationship between advertising and national income of $r = 0.870$ in our sample, we wish to test the hypothesis that the correlation is zero at the population level. We will test the hypothesis that

$$H_0: \rho_{12} = 0$$
$$H_A: \rho_{12} \neq 0$$

where ρ_{12} is the population correlation coefficient for X_1 (Pass) and X_2 (NI). We can do this using the techniques in Chapter 11. There we demonstrated that

$$t = \frac{r_{12}}{S_r}$$

where r_{12} is the sample correlation between advertising (X_1) and national income (X_2) and

$$S_r = \sqrt{\frac{1 - r_{12}^2}{n - 2}}$$

As an illustration, the hypothesis that $\rho_{12} = 0$, where ρ_{12} is the population correlation coefficient for the two independent variables, is conducted as

$$S_r = \sqrt{\frac{1 - (0.87)^2}{15 - 2}}$$
$$= 0.1367$$

Therefore,

$$t = \frac{0.870}{0.1367}$$
$$= 6.36$$

If α is set at 5 percent, the critical $t_{0.05,13} = 2.16$. There are $n - 2$ (not $n - k - 1$) degrees of freedom.

Decision Rule Do not reject if $-2.16 \leq t \leq 2.16$. Reject if $t < -2.26$ or $t > 2.16$.

Since $t = 6.36 > 2.16$, we can reject the null that there is no correlation between X_1 and X_2 ($\rho_{12} = 0$). Some multicollinearity does exist. This does not mean that the model is irrevocably defective. In fact, very few models are totally free of multicollinearity. How to handle this problem is discussed shortly.

Another way to detect multicollinearity is to compare the coefficients of determination between the dependent variable and each of the independent variables. From Display 12.5, we found the correlation between passengers and advertising to be $r^2 = (0.968)^2 = 0.937$, while that between passengers and national income is $r^2 = (0.903)^2 = 0.815$. Yet together the two independent variables revealed R^2 of only 0.953. If taken separately, the two independent variables explain 93.7 and 81.5 percent of the change in Y, respectively. But in combination they explain only 95.3 percent. Apparently there is some overlap in their explanatory power. Including the second variable of *NI* did little to increase the model's ability to explain the level of the passengers. Much of the information about passengers already provided by advertising is merely duplicated by *NI*. This is an indication that multicollinearity might be present.

A third way to detect multicollinearity is to use the **variance inflation factor** (VIF). The VIF associated with any X-variable is found by regressing it on all the other X-variables. The resulting R^2 is then used to calculate that variable's VIF. The VIF for any X_i represents that variable's influence on multicollinearity.

Variance Inflation Factor The VIF for any independent variable is a measure of the degree of multicollinearity contributed by that variable.

Since there are only two independent variables in Hop Scotch's model, regressing X_1 on all other independent variables (X_2) or regressing X_2 on all other independent variables (X_1) yields the same correlation coefficient ($r_{12} = 0.87$), as shown in Display 12.5. The VIF for any given independent variable X_i is

Variance inflation factor for X_i
$$\text{VIF}(X_i) = \frac{1}{1 - R_i^2} \qquad [12.13]$$

where R_i^2 is the coefficient of determination obtained by regressing X_i on all other independent variables. As noted, multicollinearity produces an increase in the variation, or standard error, of the regression coefficient. VIF measures the increase in the variance of the regression coefficient over that which would occur if multicollinearity were not present.

The VIF for advertising is

$$\text{VIF}(X_1) = \frac{1}{1 - (0.87)^2}$$
$$= 4.1$$

The same VIF for X_2 would be found since there are only two independent variables. This can be interpreted as the variance in b_1 and b_2 that is more than four times what it should be without multicollinearity in the model. However, in general, multicollinearity is not considered a significant problem unless the VIF of a single X_i measures at least 10, or the sum of the VIF's for all X_i is at least 10. Of course, computer packages will provide VIFs as shown in the Minitab printout in Display 12.6.

Display 12.6

Regression Analysis

```
The regression equation is
PASS = 3.53 + 0.840 ADV + 1.44 NI
```

Predictor	Coef	Stdev	t-ratio	p	VIF
Constant	3.5284	0.9994	3.53	0.004	
ADV	0.8397	0.1419	5.92	0.000	4.1
NI	1.4410	0.7360	1.96	0.074	4.1

With only two explanatory variables, both will have the same VIF.

Other indications of multicollinearity include large changes in coefficients or their sign when there is a small change in the number of observations. Furthermore, if the F-ratio is significant and the t-values are not, multicollinearity may be present. If the addition or deletion of a variable produces large changes in coefficients or their signs, multicollinearity may exist.

In summary, in the presence of multicollinearity we find

1. An inability to separate the net effect of individual independent variables upon Y.
2. An exaggerated standard error for the b-coefficients.
3. Algebraic signs of the coefficients that violate logic.
4. A high correlation between independent variables, and a high VIF.
5. Large changes in coefficients or their signs if the number of observations is changed by a single observation.
6. A significant F-ratio combined with insignificant t-ratios.
7. Large changes in coefficients or their signs when a variable is added or deleted.

C. Treating Multicollinearity

What can be done to eliminate or mitigate the influence of multicollinearity? Perhaps the most logical solution is to drop the offending variable. If X_i and X_j are closely related, one of them can simply be excluded from the model. After all, due to overlap, the inclusion of the second variable adds little to the further explanation of Y.

The question is, which one should be dropped? In reference to Hop Scotch's model, it might be advisable to drop NI since its correlation with Y is less than that of advertising. The t-tests performed earlier also suggested that NI was not significant at the 5 percent level.

However, simply dropping one of the variables can lead to **specification bias,** in which the form of the model is in disagreement with its theoretical foundation. Multicollinearity might be avoided, for example, if income were eliminated from a functional expression for consumer demand. However, economic theory, as well as plain common sense, tells us that income should be included in any attempt to explain consumption.

> **Specification Bias** A misspecification of a model due to the inclusion or exclusion of certain variables which results in a violation of theoretical principles is called specification bias.

If dropping a variable is precluded due to any resulting bias, we can often reduce multicollinearity by changing the form of the variable. Perhaps dividing the original values of the offending variable by population to obtain a per-capita figure would prove beneficial. Additionally, dividing certain monetary measures by a price index (such as the Consumer Price Index) and thereby obtaining a measure in "real" terms is also an effective method of eliminating multicollinearity. Both of these procedures could be applied to *NI*.

It is also possible to combine two or more variables. This could be done with the model for consumer demand, which employed X_1 = men, X_2 = women, and X_3 = total population. Variables X_1 and X_2 could be added to form X_3. The model would then consist of only one explanatory variable.

In any event, we should recognize that some degree of multicollinearity exists in most regression models containing two or more independent variables. The greater the number of independent variables, the greater the likelihood of multicollinearity. However, this will not necessarily detract from the model's usefulness because the problem of multicollinearity may not be severe. Multicollinearity will cause large errors in individual coefficients, yet the combined effect of these coefficients is not drastically altered. A predictive model designed to predict the value of Y on the basis of all X_i taken in combination will still possess considerable accuracy. Only explanatory models, created to explain the contribution to the value of Y by each X_i, tend to collapse in the face of multicollinearity.

Section Exercises

16. Define *multicollinearity.* Clearly explain all the problems it can cause in a regression model.

17. Why does multicollinearity increase the probability of a Type II error in testing a hypothesis about a single regression coefficient?

18. Describe the tests that can be used to detect multicollinearity.

19. How is a variance inflation factor calculated? Exactly what does it measure?

20. An economist for the Federal Research Board proposed to estimate the Dow Jones industrial average using, as explanatory variables, X_1, interest rate on AAA corporate bonds; X_2, interest rates on U.S. Treasury securities. Your advice is requested. How would you respond, and what statistical problem will likely by encountered?

12.5 Comparing Regression Coefficients

After developing the complete model, there is often a tendency to compare regression coefficients to determine which variable exerts more influence on Y. This dangerous temptation must be avoided. For the model

$$\hat{Y} = 40 + 10X_1 + 200X_2$$

where Y is tons of output, X_1 is units of labor input, and X_2 is units of capital input, one might conclude that capital is more important than labor in determining output, since it has the larger coefficient. After all, a 1-unit increase in capital, holding labor constant, results in a 200-unit increase in output. However, such a comparison is not possible. All variables are measured in totally dissimilar units; one in units of weight, another in number of people, and a third in machines.

Measuring all the variables in the same manner still does not allow us to judge the relative impact of independent variables based on the size of their coefficients. Suppose a model is stated in terms of monetary units, such as

$$\hat{Y} = 50 + 10{,}000X_1 + 20X_2$$

where Y is in dollars, X_1 is in units of \$1,000, and X_2 is in cents. Despite the large coefficient for X_1, it is not possible to conclude that it is of greater impact. A \$1,000 (1 unit) increase in X_1 increases Y by 10,000 units. A \$1,000 (100,000 units) increase in X_2 will increase Y by 2,000,000 units (100,000 $\times$ 20).

Even if we express Y, X_1, and X_2 in units of \$1, we cannot compare the relative impact of X_1 and X_2 on changes in Y. Factors other than a variable's coefficient determine its total impact on Y. For example, the variance in a variable is quite important in determining its influence on Y. The variance measures how often and how much a variable changes. Thus, a variable may have a large coefficient and every time it changes it affects Y noticeably. But if its variance is very small and it changes only once in a millennium, its overall impact on Y will be negligible.

To offset these shortcomings, we sometimes measure the response of Y to changes in the **standardized regression coefficients.** Standard regression coefficients, also called **beta coefficients** (not to be confused with the beta value β, which is the unknown coefficient at the population level), reflect the change in the mean response of Y, measured in the number of standard deviations of Y, to changes in X_i, measured in the number of standard deviations of X_i. The intended effect of calculating beta values is to make the coefficients "dimensionless."

The beta for an explanatory variable X_i is calculated as

The beta or standardized coefficient for X_i	$\text{Beta} = \dfrac{b_i}{s_Y/s_{X_i}}$	[12.14]

where s_Y and s_{X_i} are the standard deviations of the dependent variable Y and the independent variable X_i respectively. Given that these values are 3.502 for the dependent variable passengers and 0.605 for national income in our present example, the beta for national income becomes

$$\text{Beta} = \frac{1.441}{3.502/0.605} = 0.2436$$

Thus, a 1-standard-deviation change in national income results in a 0.2436-standard-deviation change in passengers. Similarly, the beta for advertising is 0.7519. This might suggest that advertising has a more pronounced impact on passengers. However, in the presence of multicollinearity, even these standardized coefficients suffer many of the same deficiencies as the normal coefficients. Hence, it is considered poor practice to measure the importance of a variable on the basis of its beta coefficient.

12.6 Stepwise Regression

Many modern computer packages offer a procedure that allows the statistician the option of permitting the computer to select the desired independent variables from a prescribed list of possibilities. The statistician provides the data for several potential explanatory variables and then, with certain commands, instructs the computer to determine which of those variables are best suited to formulate the complete model.

In this manner, the regression model is developed in stages; this is known as **stepwise regression.** It can take the form of (1) backward elimination or (2) forward selection. Let's take a look at each.

A. Backward Elimination

To execute backward elimination, we instruct the computer to calculate the entire model, using all independent variables. The t-values are then computed for all coefficients. If any prove to be insignificant, the computer eliminates the one with a t-value closest to zero and calculates the model again. This continues until all remaining b_i are significantly different from zero.

B. Forward Selection

As the name implies, forward selection is the opposite of backward elimination. First, the variable most highly correlated with Y is selected for inclusion in the model. The second step is the selection of a second variable based on its ability to explain Y, given that the first variable is already in the model. The selection of the second variable is based on its *partial coefficient of determination,* which is a variable's marginal contribution to the explanatory power of the model, given the presence of the first variable.

Assume, for example, that the first variable selected is X_5. Every possible two-variable model is computed in which one of those variables is X_5. That model which produces the highest R^2 is chosen. This process continues until all X-variables are in the model or until the addition of another variable does not result in a significant increase in R^2.

Although stepwise regression appears to be a convenient and effective method of model specification, certain precautions must be taken. The process will "mine" the data, prospecting for a statistically accurate model with the highest R^2. However, a computer cannot think or reason, and the resulting model may be statistically sound but contrary to all logical and theoretical principles, and thereby suffer from specification bias. Stepwise regression should therefore be used with extreme caution, and any model formulated in this manner should be closely scrutinized.

12.7 Dummy Variables

In your research efforts you may find many variables that are useful in explaining the value of the dependent variable. For example, years of education, training, and experience are instrumental in determining the level of a person's income. These variables can be easily measured numerically, and readily lend themselves to statistical analysis.

However, such is not the case with many other variables that are also useful in explaining income levels. Studies have shown that gender and geography also carry considerable explanatory power. A woman with the same number of years of education and training as a man will not have the same income. A worker in the Northeast may not earn the same as a worker in the South doing a similar job. Both gender and geography can prove to be highly useful explanatory variables in the effort to predict one's income. Because neither variable can readily be expressed numerically, they cannot be directly included in a regression model. We must therefore modify the form of these nonnumeric variables so we can include them in our model and thereby gain the additional explanatory power they offer.

Variables that are not expressed in a direct, quantitative fashion are called **qualitative variables** or **dummy variables.** As another illustration, the sales of a firm may depend on the season. Swimwear probably sells better in the spring than it does in the fall or winter. More snow shovels are sold in December than in July. This seasonal factor can only be captured by taking into account the time of year (fall, winter, spring, or summer), a variable that cannot be measured numerically. Whether a person is married, single, or divorced may affect his or her expenditures for recreational purposes, while place of residence (urban, suburban, or rural) will likely impact on a person's tax assessment. In all these cases, the variables we wish to measure cannot readily be expressed numerically. We must use dummy variables to obtain a more complete description of the impact of these nonnumeric measures.

Dummy Variable A variable that accounts for the qualitative nature of a variable and incorporates its explanatory power into the model is known as a dummy variable.

As the regional manager for a department store chain, you wish to study the relationship between the expenditures by your customers and those variables you feel might explain those expenditures. In addition to the logical choice of income as an explanatory variable, you feel that a customer's sex may also play a part in explaining expenditures. You therefore collect 15 observations for these three variables: expenditures in dollars, income in dollars, and sex.

But how do you encode the data for sex into the model? You cannot simply specify M or F for male and female, because these letters cannot be manipulated mathematically. The solution is found by assigning values of 0 or 1 to each observation based on sex. You might, for example, choose to record a 0 if the observation is male and 1 if the observation is female. The reverse is equally likely. You could just as well encode a 0 if female and a 1 if male. (We will examine the effects of this alternate coding scheme shortly.)

Suppose you chose to record a 0 if the observation is male and a 1 if it is female. The complete data set for $n = 15$ observations is shown in Table 12.4 with Y in dollars and X_1 in units of $1,000. Notice that X_2 contains only values of 0 for male and 1 for female.

Table 12.4
Data for Study of Customers' Expenditures

Observation	Expenditures (Y)	Income (X_1)	Sex (X_2)
1	51	40	1
2	30	25	0
3	32	27	0
4	45	32	1
5	51	45	1
6	31	29	0
7	50	42	1
8	47	38	1
9	45	30	0
10	39	29	1
11	50	41	1
12	35	23	1
13	40	36	0
14	45	42	0
15	50	48	0

Using the OLS procedures discussed in Chapter 11, the regression equation is

$$\begin{aligned}\hat{Y} &= b_0 + b_1X_1 + b_2X_2\\ &= 12.21 + 0.791X_1 + 5.11X_2\\ &\qquad\quad (0.000) \qquad (0.010)\end{aligned}$$

The *p*-values are shown in parentheses.

The use of a dummy variable for sex will actually produce two regression lines, one for males and one for females. These lines have the same slope but different intercepts. In other words, the equation gives two parallel regression lines that start at different points on the vertical axis. Since we encoded a 0 for males, the equation becomes

$$\begin{aligned}\hat{Y} &= b_0 + b_1X_1 + b_2X_2\\ &= 12.21 + 0.791X_1 + 5.11(0)\\ &= 12.21 + 0.791X_1\end{aligned}$$

for males. This line has an intercept of 12.21 and a slope of 0.791, and is shown in Figure 12.6.

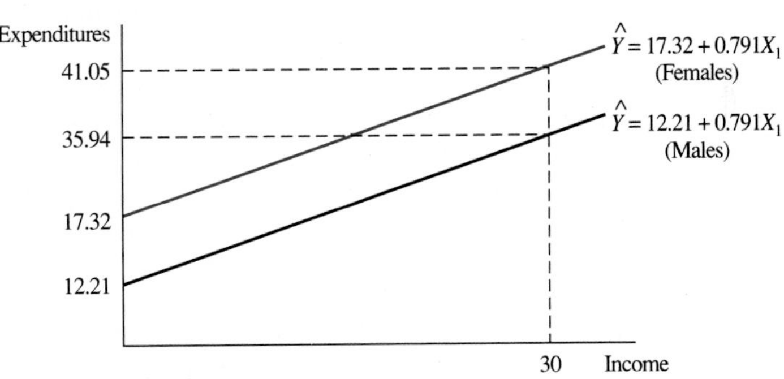

Figure 12.6
Regression Lines for Expenditures

For females, the encoded value of 1 produces

$$\begin{aligned}\hat{Y} &= 12.21 + 0.791X_1 + 5.11(1)\\ &= 17.32 + 0.791X_1\end{aligned}$$

This second line has the same slope as the line for males, but has an intercept of 17.32. Since $X_2 = 1$ for females, the intercept was determined as $b_0 + b_2 = 12.21 + 5.11 = 17.32$.

This means that for any given level of income, women customers spend $5.11 more on the average than do men. Let income equal 30 ($30,000). Then for women

$$\begin{aligned}\hat{Y} &= 12.21 + 0.791(30) + 5.11(1)\\ &= 41.05\end{aligned}$$

and for men

$$\begin{aligned}\hat{Y} &= 12.21 + 0.791(30) + 5.11(0)\\ &= 35.94\end{aligned}$$

The difference of $5.11 occurs because the encoded value of 0 for males cancels out the b_2 coefficient of 5.11, while the encoded value of 1 for females results in the addition of 5.11 to the equation.

If you had encoded the dummy variable by assigning a 1 for a male observation and a 0 for a female observation, the final results would be the same. A computer run shows the initial equation to be

$$\hat{Y} = 17.32 + 0.791X_1 - 5.11X_2$$

For females, we have

$$\hat{Y} = 17.32 + 0.791X_1 + 5.11(0)$$
$$= 17.32 + 0.791X_1$$

and for males

$$\hat{Y} = 17.32 + 0.791X_1 - 5.11(1)$$
$$= 12.21 + 0.791X_1$$

Encoding the dummy variable either way yields the same results.

If the data were put into a scatter diagram, they might appear as in Figure 12.7. In an extreme case, there could appear two almost totally separate diagrams, one for the male observations and one for the females. If the dummy variable was ignored and only one line was fitted, its slope would be much steeper than the other two, such as the line identified as Y^*. The effect attributed to income alone by the single regression line should be partially ascribed to sex.

Figure 12.7
Scatter Diagram for Expenditures

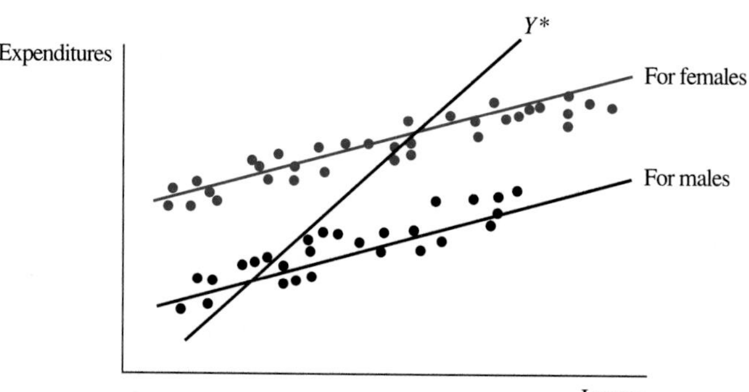

If a dummy variable has more than two possible responses, you cannot encode it as 0, 1, 2, 3, and so on. A variable with r possible responses will be expanded to encompass a total for $r - 1$ variables. For example, you might include a third variable in your model to study the effect of marital status on expenditures. Your possible responses might include married, single, divorced, and widowed. In addition to X_1 for income and X_2 for sex, these four possible responses require three additional variables, X_3, X_4, and X_5, to encode the data on marital status. This is done by entering only a 0 or a 1 for each variable in the following manner:

$$X_3 = 1 \quad \text{if married}$$
$$= 0 \quad \text{if not married}$$
$$X_4 = 1 \quad \text{if single}$$
$$= 0 \quad \text{if not single}$$
$$X_5 = 1 \quad \text{if divorced}$$
$$= 0 \quad \text{if not divorced}$$

No entry for widowed is necessary, because if $X_3 = X_4 = X_5 = 0$, the process of elimination reveals the observation to be widowed.

Assume 0 is encoded for male and 1 for female in X_2. The three observations (OBS) shown here are for a (1) married male with expenditures of 30 and income of 40, (2) a divorced female with expenditures of 35 and income of 38, and (3) a widowed male with expenditures of 20 and income of 45.

OBS	Y	X_1	X_2	X_3	X_4	X_5
1	30	40	0	1	0	0
2	35	38	1	0	0	1
3	20	45	0	0	0	0

For example, in the first observation, X_2 would be 0 since the observation is male, and X_3 is 1, while both X_4 and X_5 are 0 since the observation is married.

Section Exercises

21. A coal firm wants to set up a regression model to predict output (Y) that encompasses as explanatory variables hours of labor input (X_1) and whether a labor strike occurred during the time period under study (X_2). Devise the model and explain.
22. Given the model in the previous problem, should b_2 be positive or negative? Explain.
23. State what values you would assign to dummy variables to measure a person's race if the categories included (1) white, (2) black, (3) Asian, and (4) other.
24. Students at the Cosmopolitan School of Cosmetics are taught to encode data on hair color as 1 if blond, 2 if redhead, and 3 if other. Comment. What would you advise?
25. The manager of a local accounting firm created a regression model for the length of time it takes to complete an audit. The model was

$$\hat{Y} = 17 - 1.41X_1 + 1.73X_2$$

where $\hat{Y}$ is time in hours
X_1 is years of experience of auditor
X_2 whether auditor is a CPA: 0 if yes, 1 if no

    a. Interpret the coefficient for X_2.
    b. Would you expect b_2 to be positive? Explain.
    c. If the auditor has seven years of experience and is a CPA, how long would it take to complete the audit accordance to the model?
    d. If another auditor also has seven years' experience but is not a CPA, how long would it take to complete the audit according to the model?

26. If the dummy variable in Exercise 25 was 1 if CPA, 0 if not CPA, what would you expect the sign of b_2 to be? Explain.
27. A marketing representative establishes a regression equation for units sold based on the population in the sales district and whether the district has a home office to which sales personnel report. The model proves to be

$$\hat{Y} = 78.12 + 1.01X_1 - 17.2X_2$$

where $\hat{Y}$ is unit sold
X_1 is population in thousands
X_2 is 0 if district contains an office, 1 if it does not

    a. Interpret $b_2 = -17.2$
    b. How would you compare the slopes and the coefficients of the two regression lines provided by this model? Compute and compare the two regression formulas.
    c. Draw a graph to illustrate.

28. Considering the previous problem, if population is 17,000 in a district containing an office and 17,000 in a district without an office, what would the number of units sold in each one be? Draw a graph to illustrate.

29. Studies have shown that in states with more liberal regulations concerning the receipt of unemployment compensation, unemployment rates are higher. If a regression model for unemployment rates incorporates a dummy variable, coded 1 if regulations are liberal and 0 if otherwise, would its coefficient be greater than or less than zero according to these studies? Explain.

12.8 The Curvilinear Case

Throughout our discussion so far we have assumed that the relationship between X and Y can be expressed as a straight line. That is, the relationship is linear. However, this is not always the case. We may find that a curvilinear (nonlinear) model may provide a better fit. Presume that in an effort to predict tax revenues on the basis of population, Sam Jorden, mayor of Plattsburg, collects the data seen in Table 12.5. The data for both taxes and populations are in millions. A plot of these data in Figure 12.8 suggests that a curvilinear model is needed. It does not appear that a straight line would produce an adequate fit.

As noted in the previous chapter, in a simple regression model the change in Y is constant. As X changes, Y changes by a given amount. In a curvilinear model, as X changes, Y changes by a different amount. Figure 12.8 shows that as X goes up, Y increases at an *increasing* rate.

Such curvilinear models are often well-fitted using a polynomial function of the general form

A polynomial of degree k

$$Y = \beta_0 + \beta_1 X + \beta_2 X^2 + \cdots + \beta_k X^k + \varepsilon \qquad [12.15]$$

Table 12.5
Mayor Jorden's Data on Taxes and Population (in millions)

TAXES	POPULATION
85	2.68
118	2.98
164	3.50
228	3.79
31	1.57
43	2.01
61	2.15
611	4.90
316	4.16
444	4.50

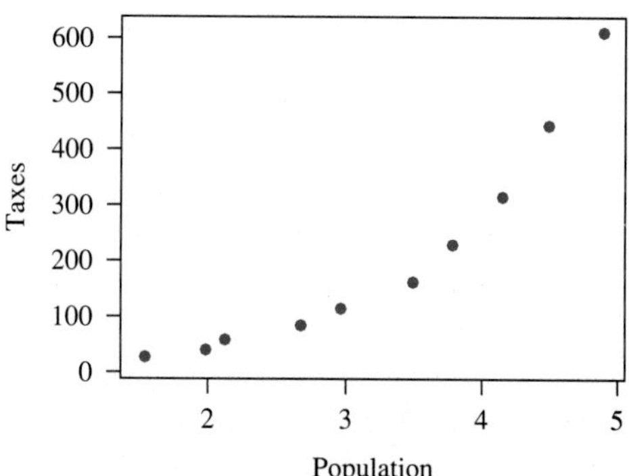

Figure 12.8
A Curvilinear Relationship for Tax Revenues and Population

Formula (12.15) is said to be a polynomial of degree *k* since that is the highest power of any explanatory variables. Mayor Jorden's model might best be fitted using a polynomial of degree 2, or a second-order polynomial, such as

The quadratic form of the polynomial	$\hat{Y} = b_0 + b_1X + b_2X^2$	[12.16]

which is the quadratic form of the model in which the second explanatory variable is merely the square of the first. In the mayor's case, it becomes

$$\hat{T} = b_0 + b_1POP + b_2(POP)^2$$

where *T* is taxes and *POP* is population.

Let us compare the results of this model to those obtained if a simple linear model is estimated. The Minitab printout for the simple model in which taxes are regressed on population is shown in Display 12.7. Notice that the R^2 value is a respectable 86.1 percent with $\bar{R}^2$ of 84.3 percent and a standard error of 76.38. The entire model is

$$\hat{T} = -302.39 + 158.96POP$$

Display 12.7 A Linear Model

```
Regression Analysis

The regression equation is
TAXES = -302 + 159 POP

Predictor       Coef      Stdev      t-ratio        p
Constant     -302.39      76.75        -3.94    0.004
POP           158.96      22.60         7.04    0.000

s = 76.38       R-sq = 86.1%      R-sq(adj) = 84.3%
```

If the quadratic model is used, as seen in the Minitab printout in Display 12.8, both the $\bar{R}^2$ and the standard error improve to 98.7 percent and 22.20 respectively. The model becomes

$$\hat{T} = 325.36 - 277.98POP + 67.692(POP)^2$$

Obviously, the quadratic model provides the better fit.

Display 12.8 A Quadratic Fit

```
Regression Analysis

The regression equation is
TAXES = 325 - 278 POP + 67.7 POPSQ

Predictor        Coef        Stdev     t-ratio        p
Constant       325.36        70.63        4.61    0.000
POP           -277.98        47.10       -5.90    0.000
POPSQ          67.692        7.226        9.37    0.000

s = 22.20        R-sq = 99.0%      R-sq(adj) = 98.7%
```

An alternative approach to curvilinear models can be achieved by transforming the data in some manner. A common method of transformation involves the use of logarithms. This logarithmic transformation may make the data *linear in the log*. Table 12.6 shows Mayor Jorden's original data in the first two columns and their natural logarithms in the last two columns. The mayor then simply regresses the log of taxes on the log of population, as

Table 12.6
Logrithmic Transformation

Taxes	*POP*	*LOGTX*	*LOGPOP*
85	2.68	4.44265	0.98582
118	2.98	4.77068	1.09192
164	3.50	5.09987	1.25276
228	3.79	5.42935	1.33237
31	1.57	3.43399	0.45108
43	2.01	3.76120	0.69813
61	2.15	4.11087	0.76547
611	4.90	6.41510	1.58924
316	4.16	5.75574	1.42552
444	4.50	6.09582	1.50408

seen in the Minitab printout in Display 12.9. Note the further improvement in the standard error and the $\bar{R}^2$ of only 0.1680 and 97.2 percent, respectively. The model is

$$LOGTX = 2.0302 + 2.6147(LOGPOP)$$

Display 12.9 A Logarithmic Transformation

```
Regression Analysis

The regression equation is
LOGTX = 2.03 + 2.61 LOGPOP

Predictor        Coef       Stdev     t-ratio        p
Constant       2.0302      0.1724       11.78    0.000
LOGPOP         2.6147      0.1478       17.69    0.000

s = 0.1680        R-sq = 97.5%        R-sq(adj) = 82.2%
```

Then, if population is 3.2, log POP = 1.163 and

$$\begin{aligned} logTX &= 2.0302 + 2.6147(1.163) \\ &= 5.071 \end{aligned}$$

Taking the antilog of 5.071 yields 159.33; or, since the data were originally in millions, the mayor's tax receipts would be estimated at $159,330,000.

It may be necessary to experiment with different functional forms in order to determine which provides the best fit. In search of the optimal model, the results from different logarithmic models may be compared with those obtained using polynomial functions. The use of computers makes this comparison practical.

The results of such comparisons may, however, prove inconsistent. One model may report a higher coefficient of determination than another (that's good) while carrying a higher standard error of the estimate (that's bad). The question then becomes, which model do you use?

The answer depends, at least in part, on the purpose for which the model is intended. If you wish to use the model to explain present values of Y and to understand why it behaves as it does, use the model with the higher coefficient of determination. That is, if the intent is to explain, then the model with the higher explanatory value should be used.

If, on the other hand, the purpose of the model is to predict future values of Y, use the model with the lower standard error of the estimate. If you want to predict, you will enjoy greater success with the model that generates the lower prediction error.

However, such experimentation should be kept to a minimum. It is considered questionable, even unethical, to experiment wildly with first one model and then another. You should know from the outset, given the nature of your research study, what procedure should be followed. The analogy is often made that to search blindly for the best model is similar to shooting the arrow at the target and then drawing the bull's-eye at the spot where the arrow landed.

Section Exercises

30. Plot the data below. Compare a linear model to the quadratic form and provide a comparative evaluation of each. Using the better model, predict Y if $X = 22$.

Y	X	Y	X
2170	31	731	18
2312	32	730	18
2877	36	815	19
7641	48	1408	25
2929	36	2768	35
		1297	24

31. Using the data from Exercise 30, perform a logarithmic transformation and test the regression results. What are your observations?

32. Mayor Jorden wants to estimate tax revenues on the basis of new business formations. He collects the data displayed below from 22 cities he feels are similar to his.

a. Plot the scatter diagram

b. Compare a linear model to a quadratic form. Which seems to give the best fit?

c. Predict tax revenues if there are 68 new businesses.

City	New Business	Tax Revenues	City	New Business	Tax Revenues
1	47	$10,154,589	12	68	$26,272,898
2	51	18,215,568	13	47	6,074,615
3	57	27,171,076	14	58	18,215,568
4	68	26,272,898	15	51	13,546,448
5	57	6,074,615	16	48	17,500,544
6	45	5,693,092	17	65	14,801,029
7	85	43,918,912	18	68	18,215,568
8	87	46,334,860	19	85	43,918,912
9	48	11,781,520	20	68	42,738,224
10	57	17,500,544	21	86	45,117,748
11	68	26,272,898	22	58	25,391,750

33. Using the data from Exercise 32, compute the logarithmic regression model. How does it compare to the one developed in the previous problem? Estimate taxes if there are 68 new businesses formed.

List of Formulas

[12.1] $$Y = \beta_0 + \beta_1 X_1 + \beta_2 X_2 + \cdots + \beta_k X_k + \varepsilon$$ The multiple regression model

[12.4] $$Se = \sqrt{\frac{\Sigma(Y_i - \hat{Y}_i)^2}{n - k - 1}}$$ Standard error of the estimate

[12.5] $$R^2 = \frac{SSR}{SST}$$ Coefficient of multiple determination

[12.8] $$\bar{R}^2 = 1 - (1 - R^2)\frac{n - 1}{n - k - 1}$$ Adjusted coefficient of multiple determination

[12.12] $$t = \frac{b_i - \beta_i}{s_{b_i}}$$ t-test for significance of β_i

[12.13]	$\text{VIF}(X_i) = \dfrac{1}{1 - R_i^2}$	Variance inflation factor for X_i
[12.14]	$\text{Beta} = \dfrac{b_i}{s_Y/s_{X_i}}$	The beta or standardized coefficient for X_i
[12.15]	$Y = \beta_0 + \beta_1 X + \beta_2 X^2 + \cdots + \beta_k X^k + \varepsilon$	A polynomial of degree k
[12.16]	$\hat{Y} = b_0 + b_1 X + b_2 X^2$	The quadratic form of the polynomial

Chapter Exercises

Note: Most of these problems require a computer.

34. A management director is attempting to develop a system designed to identify what personal attributes are essential for managerial advancement. Fifteen employees who have recently been promoted are given a series of tests to determine their communication skills (X_1), ability to relate to others (X_2), and decision-making ability (X_3). Each employee's job rating (Y) is regressed on these three variables. The original raw data are as follows:

Y	X_1	X_2	X_3	Y	X_1	X_2	X_3
80	50	72	18	69	39	73	19
75	51	74	19	68	40	71	20
84	42	79	22	87	55	80	30
62	42	71	17	92	48	83	33
92	59	85	25	82	45	80	20
75	45	73	17	74	45	75	18
63	48	75	16	80	61	75	20
				62	59	70	15

a. Develop the regression model. Evaluate it by determining whether it shows a significant relationship among the dependent variable and the three independent variables.

b. What can be said about the significance of each X_i?

35. To what cause might you attribute the insignificance of X_1 and X_3 in Exercise 34? Obtain the correlation matrix for these variables and test each pair for multicollinearity. Set $\alpha = 5$ percent.

36. Compare your results in Exercise 35 to those obtained based on VIF.

37. Should the management director in Exercise 36 use this model to identify characteristics that made an employee eligible for advancement?

38. As a class project, a team of marketing students devises a model that explains rent for student housing near their university. Rent is in dollars, SQFT is the square footage of the apartment or house, and DIST is distance in miles from house to campus.

Rent	SQFT	DIST	Rent	SQFT	DIST
220	900	3.2	400	1,290	1.5
250	1,100	2.2	450	1,370	0.5
310	1,250	1.0	500	1,400	0.5
420	1,300	0.5	550	1,550	0.3
350	1,275	1.5	450	1,200	0.5
510	1,500	0.5	320	1,275	1.5

a. Devise the model. Is it significant at the 1 percent level?

b. Evaluate the significance of both coefficients.

c. Are the signs appropriate? Explain.

39. Evaluate the model from the previous problems. Does it appear useful in predicting rent? Explain.

40. Is there evidence of multicollinearity in the model from the previous problem? Does it invalidate the model for predicting rent? Why or why not?

41. From the model developed above for student rents, can you conclude distance from campus is a stronger determinant of rent than is square footage? Why or why not?

42. If two apartments have the same space, but one is 2 miles closer to campus, how will its rent differ from that of the more distant dwelling?

43. In order to expand their model on students' rents, the marketing majors from the problems above devise a luxury index in which students rate the amenities of an apartment based on available comforts, such as swimming pools, tennis courts, maid service, and other luxuries to which students are traditionally accustomed. For the 12 observations above, this index measured 22, 23, 35, 40, 32, 55, 36, 41, 51, 50, 48, and 29. Incorporate the variable in your model to explain rents. Analyze and explain why you got these results. Is your model better with this additional variable? What problem are you likely encountering, and what change would you make to correct it?

44. Make the change you suggested in the previous problem and discuss your results.

45. In the past, many economists have studied the spending patterns of consumers in the economy. A famous study by Milton Friedman concludes that consumption is a function of *permanent income,* which is defined as the average level of income the consumer expects to receive well into the future. The *habit-persistence* theory of T. M. Brown argues that consumption is shaped by a consumer's most recent peak income—the highest income received in the recent past.

To combine these two theories, an economist collected data on consumption (CONS), permanent income (PERM), and peak income (PEAK), and performed OLS to devise a model. Given these data, what did that model look like? (All values are in thousands of dollars.)

CONS	PERM	PEAK	CONS	PERM	PEAK
12	15	17	14	17	20
22	28	31	20	25	29
15	19	21	17	21	25
17	19	24	15	19	22
19	24	27	16	20	26

a. Evaluate the model.

b. Would multicollinearity explain the insignificance of PEAK? How can you tell?

46. The data shown here were collected to explain salary levels for workers at a local plant.

Salary ($1,000's)	Years of Education	Sex
42.2	8	M
58.9	12	M
98.8	16	M
23.5	6	F
12.5	5	M
67.8	12	M
51.9	10	F
81.6	14	F
61.0	12	F

a. Compute the regression model, using a computer.

b. Is there evidence of sex discrimination in salary levels?

c. Is education useful in explaining salary?

d. Are autocorrelation and heteroscedasticity problems?

47. You have just run a model regressing employee retention (in years) on age at hiring and gender, encoding the dummy variable for gender as 1 if male and 0 if female. The results were

$$\hat{Y} = 3.2 + 0.65AGE - 1.3GENDER$$

a. What is the formula for male? For female?
b. You then realize that you meant to encode 1 if female and 0 if male. What will the equation become?
c. Now what is the formula for male? For female?
d. Using the formula seen above, what is the estimate of years of retention if a male is hired at age 23? What is it using your revised formula?

Computer Exercise

Studies in finance have shown that the price of a share of stock is directly related to the issuing company's level of debt and to the dividend rate, but is inversely related to the number of shares outstanding. Access the computer file STOCK from your data disk. PRICE and the dividend rate, DIVRATE, are in dollars, DEBT is in millions of dollars and the number of shares outstanding, OUTSTD, is in millions of shares. Using PRICE as the dependent variable, evaluate the model. Provide all relevant statistical interpretations and conclusions. Prepare your final statistical report as described in Appendix I.

CURTAIN CALL

Your assignment as an intern for Griffen Associates, described in Setting the Stage at the opening of the chapter, briefly illustrated the need to analyze the performance of several competitive mutual funds. You are to develop models that will examine three-year returns and compare them to the one-year returns of these funds, using as explanatory variables the turnover rates (the percentage of the funds bought and sold over each time period in question), initial total assets in billions of dollars at the time the fund was opened, and whether the fund carries a sales load. This last variable is encoded as 1 if it has a load, and no-load funds are encoded as 0.

Your supervisor at Griffen wants you to prepare a full report, including all statistical analysis presented in this chapter. You must specify the models for both one-year and three-year returns for both load and no-load funds. Tests for multicollinearity must be conducted along with all relevant statistical analysis. Using the data provided here, prepare your statistical report as described in Appendix I.

Three-year Return	One-year Return	Load	Three-year Turnover	One-year Turnover	Assets
5.6	0.1	0	112	58	220.00
4.7	1.9	1	95	62	158.00
4.5	2.6	1	241	65	227.25
4.8	2.0	1	87	61	242.40
5.7	3.5	0	98	57	287.85
4.1	−4.3	1	102	66	207.05
4.7	3.2	1	72	63	237.35
4.1	−4.1	1	96	65	207.05
5.2	2.2	0	78	59	262.60
3.7	2.1	1	118	87	186.85
6.2	5.3	0	98	47	313.10
6.6	11.0	0	87	41	333.30
5.2	0.3	0	117	61	262.60
5.5	−2.1	0	87	46	277.75
5.6	4.7	0	85	35	282.80

From the Stage to Real Life

In the Chapter 3 From the Stage to Real Life exercise, we became familiar with some mutual funds investor information sites and with the Vanguard Group of Funds in particular. Here we will look at more detailed information that is routinely reported about the funds and their performance. This chapter's Curtain Call analysis required information about loads (fees), assets, and 1- and 3-year returns. Is this information available at mutual funds company web sites? Let's look at three major mutual funds companies.

At the Vanguard Group (*www.vanguard.com*) Home Page, select the "mutual funds" icon. Next, clock on "Funds by Category." In the Growth funds, select the "U.S. Growth Portfolio." Click through the tabs on the folders and make notes on where to obtain data on loads, assets, and 1- and 3-year returns.

Do the same for Fidelity Funds (*www.fidelity.com*). At the Home Page, go to "Fund Information." In the search area, type in "Emerging Growth" and click the "go." Note the available data.

Repeat this again for the Dreyfus Funds (*www.dreyfus.com*). At the Home Page, select "Mutual Funds" under the Products heading, and then click on "Growth" funds. Look at the Emerging Leaders Fund information for the availability of this same data.

CHAPTER 13

Time Series and Index Numbers

Chapter Blueprint

This chapter examines the use of time-series data and their application to common business situations. The manner in which index numbers are used to make time series data more comparable over time is also demonstrated.

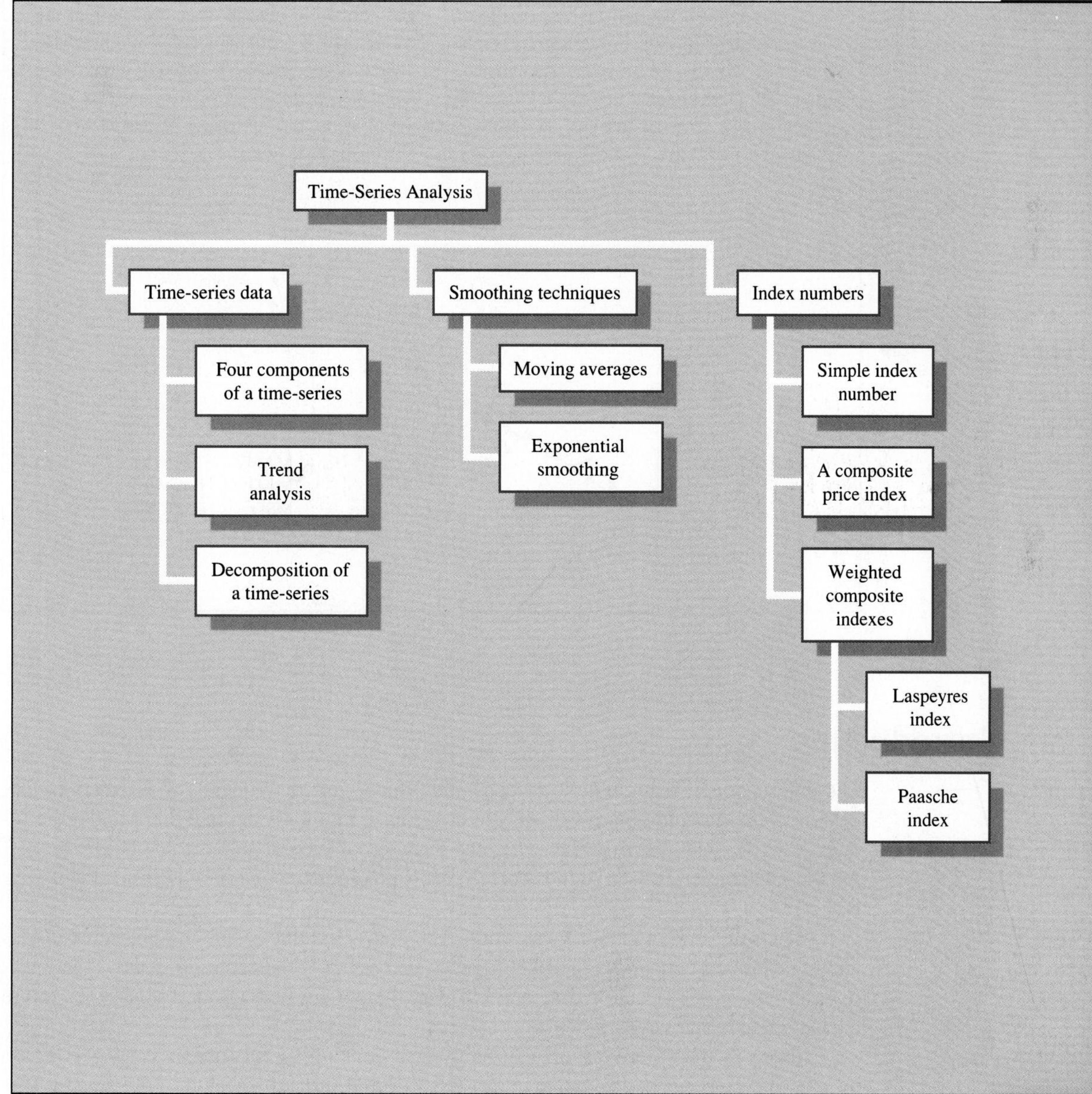

SETTING THE STAGE

Over the past few years Dickson Industries has enjoyed considerable growth in sales revenues and profits. Much of this success is due to hard work by Jeremy Dickson, owner and chief executive officer of the business, as well as that of his close and trusted staff. Mr. Dickson has always relied heavily on careful planning based on a thorough analysis of market conditions.

This analysis is often designed to detect future movements in business activity and to determine whether the present trend will continue. Mr. Dickson also insists that his staff examine any cyclical activity in business fluctuations over the course of several years.

Furthermore, Mr. Dickson observes any detectable patterns regularly occurring at specific times within the year or during certain seasons in planning his operations. He has noticed that his business is quite seasonal, in that his profits are usually higher at certain times of the year.

However, Mr. Dickson realizes that the upward trend in sales he has experienced is not as favorable as it may seem. Changes in the economic climate over time affect the values of his profits and sales revenues. He therefore recognizes the need to index these measures of business performance to get a more accurate impression of just how well his business is doing.

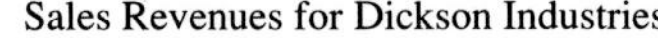

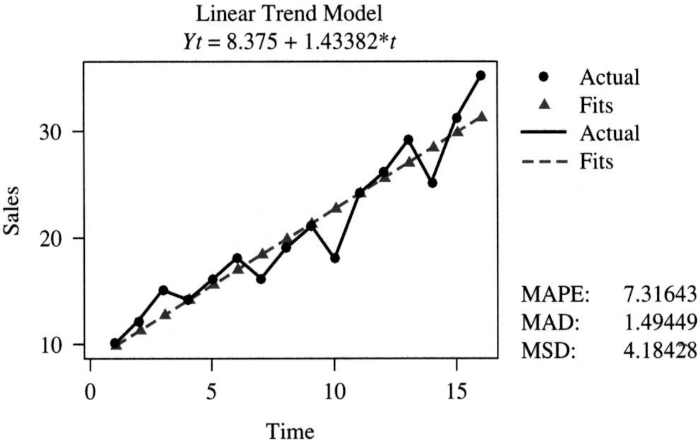

13.1 Introduction

The importance of being able to forecast the future with some degree of accuracy cannot be overstated. Imagine the results if you could gaze into a crystal ball and predict the future on the first Saturday in May when the Kentucky Derby is held, or just before kickoff for the next Super Bowl. Your success rate in predicting winners would no doubt skyrocket!

Such is the case in the business world. The ability to forecast and predict future events and trends greatly enhances the likelihood of success. It is therefore no wonder that businesses spend a good deal of time and effort in the pursuit of accurate forecasts of future business trends and developments.

Numerous quantitative tools can be used to develop useful forecasts. By relying on these tools, you can build your own crystal ball and use it to peer into the future. This chapter examines ways in which time-series data can be used to make forecasts, and how those forecasts can be used to make informed decisions.

13.2 Time Series and Their Components

The process of developing a forecast starts with the collection of past data for several time periods. The resulting data set is called a **time series** because it contains observations for some variable over time. The time periods can vary in length. They can be yearly, quarterly, monthly, or even daily. Time periods of only one hour may be used for highly volatile variables such as the price of a heavily traded stock on one of the organized exchanges.

> **Time Series** A collection of data for some variable or set of variables over several time periods.

Table 13.1 contains quarterly sales data for Rampart Industries in millions of dollars where, for example, 1998-III is the third quarter of the year 1998.

Table 13.1
Quarterly Sales Figures for Rampart Industries

Time period	Sales (in millions)	Time period	Sales (in millions)
1995-IV	31.1	1997-II	61.8
1996-I	35.6	III	75.9
II	42.8	IV	74.1
III	50.3	1998-I	88.7
IV	49.2	II	79.1
1997-I	62.0	III	92.5

The purpose of time-series analysis is to predict or forecast future values of the variable from past observations. One direct approach is the **naive method of forecasting,** which presumes that the best predictor of the value of the variable in the next time period is its value in the current time period. In its simplest form it can be expressed as

The naive forecasting model $$\hat{Y}_{t+1} = Y_t \qquad [13.1]$$

where $\hat{Y}_{t+1}$ is the estimate of the value of the time series in the next time period $t + 1$ and Y_t is the actual value in the current time period t. This approach is often used when the data exhibit a **random walk.** Random walk movements exhibit no trend upward or downward and typically shift direction suddenly. Such movements are analogous to an individual out for a evening stroll to nowhere in particular. When he comes to an intersection he randomly decides, perhaps by flipping a coin, which way to turn. Such randomness cannot be predicted, and the best we can do is use the most recent observation as our prediction for the next value. This method of forecasting is most successful for data that are collected for short time intervals such as on a daily or a weekly basis.

However, most time series are more complex than that. All times series contain at least one of the following four components: (1) secular trend; (2) seasonal variation; (3) cyclical variation; or (4) irregular, or random, variation. The remainder of this section examines each of these time-series components.

A. Secular Trend

The **secular trend,** or merely the trend, is the long-run behavior of the variable over an extended length of time. It reflects the general direction of the time series as upward or downward. Examples include the rising number of foreign cars sold in the United States, the increase in the volume of credit transactions over the past few years, and the downward movement in the number of people living in rural areas in the last two decades.

> **Secular Trend** The continuous long-term movement in a variable over an extended period of time.

Figure 13.1 shows the trend in output for Rampart Industries for the past decade. Although the data show considerable variation above and below the trend line drawn through the middle of the data, the secular trend is unmistakably upward.

Figure 13.1
Trend Line for Rampart Industries (annual output)

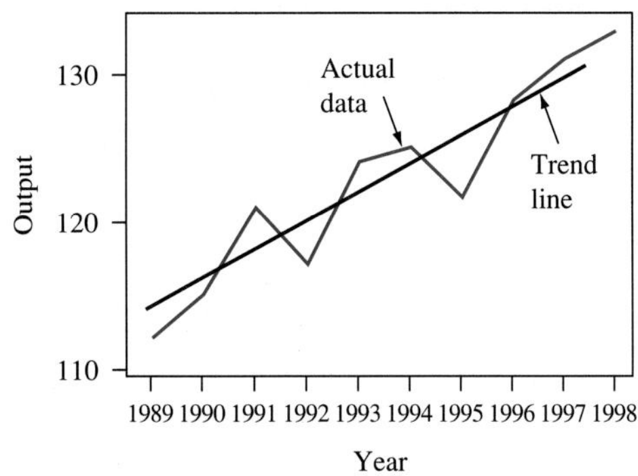

B. The Seasonal Component

A lot of business activity is influenced by changing seasons of the year. For example, sales of certain seasonal goods such as Honda snowmobiles, Jantzen swimwear, and Hallmark Valentine cards would likely display a strong seasonal component. **Seasonal fluctuations** are patterns that tend to reoccur regularly during the time period. Although we often think of seasonal variations as occurring regularly each year, such as the annual sales of Christmas hams, the time period in question can be much shorter. The daily influx of customers at the lunch counter each noon is an example. If the seasonal variation does occur on a yearly basis, annual data will not capture or reflect these changes. The data must be collected on a quarterly, monthly, or even weekly basis.

> **Seasonal Fluctuations** Movements in the time series that reoccur each year about the same time.

Figure 13.2 shows that each year the unemployment rate tends to go up in May when high school students enter the summer job market, and that it goes down in November when retail stores hire temporary help to handle the Christmas rush. Notice that no apparent trend exists in the unemployment rate.

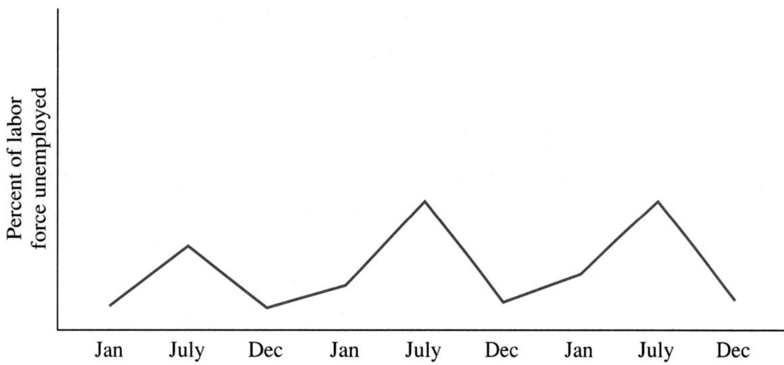

Figure 13.2 Seasonal Fluctuations in Unemployment

C. Cyclical Variations

Many variables exhibit a tendency to fluctuate above and below the long-term trend over a long period of time. These fluctuations are called **cyclical fluctuations** or **business cycles.** They cover much longer time periods than do seasonal variations, often encompassing three or more years in duration.

> **Cyclical Fluctuations** Wavelike variations in the general level of business activity over a relatively long time period.

A cycle contains four phases: (1) the upswing or expansion, during which the level of business activity is accelerated, unemployment is low, and production is brisk; (2) the peak, at which point the rate of economic activity has "topped out"; (3) the downturn, or contraction, when unemployment rises and activity wanes; and (4) the trough, where activity is at the lowest point. A cycle runs from one phase to the next like phase and, as shown in Figure 13.3, fluctuates above and below the long-term trend in a wavelike manner.

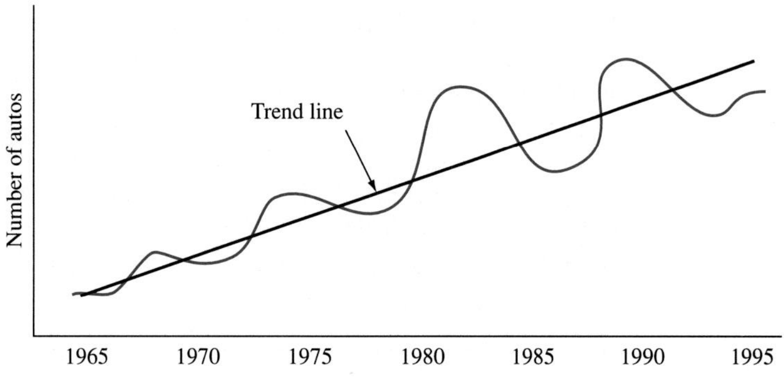

Figure 13.3 Cyclical Fluctuations of Foreign Auto Imports

D. Irregular Fluctuations

Time series also contain **irregular,** or **random, fluctuations** caused by unusual occurrences producing movements that have no discernible pattern. These movements are, like fingerprints and snowflakes, unique, and unlikely to reoccur in similar fashion. They can be caused by events such as wars, floods, earthquakes, political elections, or oil embargoes.

13.3 Time-Series Models

A time-series model can be expressed as some combination of these four components. The model is simply a mathematical statement of the relationship among the four components. Two types of models are commonly associated with time series: (1) the additive model and (2) the multiplicative model. The additive model is expressed as

$$Y_t = T_t + S_t + C_t + I_t$$

where Y_t is the value of the time series for time period t, and the right-hand side values are the trend, the seasonal variation, the cyclical variation, and the random or irregular variation, respectively, for the same time period. In the additive model, all values are expressed in original units, and S, C, and I are deviations around T. If we were to develop a time-series model for sales in dollars for a local retail store, we might find that $T = \$500$, $S = \$100$, $C = -\$25$, and $I = -\$10$. Sales would be

$$\begin{aligned} Y &= \$500 + \$100 - \$25 - \$10 \\ &= \$565 \end{aligned}$$

Notice that the positive value for S indicates that existing seasonal influences have had a positive impact on sales. The negative cyclical value suggests that the business cycle is currently in a downswing. There was apparently some random event that had a negative impact on sales.

The additive model suffers from the somewhat unrealistic assumption that the components are independent of each other. This is seldom the case in the real world. In most instances, movements in one component will have an impact on other components, thereby negating the assumption of independence. Or, perhaps even more commonly, we often find that certain forces at work in the economy simultaneously affect two or more components. Again, the assumption of independence is violated.

As a result, the multiplicative model is often preferred. It assumes that the components interact with each other and do not move independently. The multiplicative model is expressed as

$$Y_t = T_t \times S_t \times C_t \times I_t$$

In the multiplicative model, only T is expressed in the original units, and S, C, and I are stated in terms of percentages. For example, values for bad debts at a commercial bank might be recorded as $T = \$10$ million, $S = 1.7$, $C = 0.91$ and $I = 0.87$. Bad debts could then be computed as

$$Y = (10)(1.7)(0.91)(0.87) = \$13.46 \text{ million}$$

Since seasonal fluctuations occur within time periods of less than one year, they would not be reflected in annual data. A time series for annual data would be expressed as

$$Y_t = T_t \times C_t \times I_t$$

13.4 Smoothing Techniques

The general behavior of the variable can often be best discussed by examining its long-term trend. However, if the time series contains too many random fluctuations or short-term seasonal changes, the trend may be somewhat obscured and difficult to observe. It is possible to eliminate many of these confounding factors by averaging the data over several time periods. This is accomplished by using certain smoothing techniques that remove random fluctuations in the series, thereby providing a less obstructed view of the true behavior of the series. We examine two common methods of smoothing time-series data: a moving average and exponential smoothing.

A. Moving Averages

A **moving average** (MA) will have the effect of "smoothing out" the data, producing a movement with fewer peaks and valleys. It is computed by averaging the values in the time series over a set number of time periods. The same number of time periods is retained for each average by dropping the oldest observation and picking up the newest. Assume that the closing prices for a stock on the New York Stock Exchange for Monday through Wednesday were \$20, \$22, and \$18, respectively. We can compute a three-period (day) moving average as

$$(20 + 22 + 18)/3 = 20$$

This value of 20 then serves as our forecast or estimate of what the closing price might be at any time in the future. If the closing on Thursday is, say, 19, the next moving average is calculated by dropping Monday's value of 20 and using Thursday's closing price of 19. Thus, the forecast becomes

$$(22 + 18 + 19)/3 = 19.67$$

The estimate figured in this manner is seen as the long-run average of the series. It is taken as the forecast for the closing price on any given day in the future.

> **Moving Average (MA)** A series of arithmetic averages over a given number of time periods; the estimate of the long-run average of the variable.

Consider the sales for Arthur Momitor's Snowmobiles, Inc., over the past 12 months as shown in Table 13.2. Both a three-month MA and a five-month MA are calculated. We obtain the first entry in the three-month MA by averaging the sales of snowmobiles in January, February, and March. The resulting value of $(52 + 81 + 47)/3 = 60$ is centered on the middle time period of February. We determine the next entry by averaging February, March, and April, and centering the value of 64.33 in the middle of those three periods, which is March. The remaining entries are determined similarly.

The first entry in the five-month MA series uses values for months January through May. The average of $(52 + 51 + 47 + 65 + 50)/5 = 59$ is centered in the middle of those five time periods at March.

Table 13.2
Snowmobile Sales for Arthur Momitor

Month	Sales ($100)	Three-Month MA	Five-Month MA
January	52		
February	81	60.00	
March	47	64.33	59.00
April	65	54.00	63.20
May	50	62.67	56.00
June	73	56.00	58.60
July	45	59.33	55.60
August	60	51.67	61.40
September	50	63.00	55.80
October	79	58.00	59.20
November	45	62.00	
December	62		

Moving averages have the effect of smoothing out large variations in the data. This smoothing effect occurs because unusually large or unusually small observations are averaged in with other values, and their impact is thereby restrained. The larger the number of time periods in a moving average, the more pronounced the smoothing effect will be. Notice that the range of values in the three-month MA is less than that in the original data and greater than the range found in the five-month MA. Figure 13.4 illustrates this tendency for the smoothing effect to increase with the number of time periods in the moving average.

Notice that when an odd number of time periods is used in the moving average, the results can be automatically centered at the middle time period. When Arthur Momitor calculated his three-period moving average for snowmobiles, the first value, for example, could be readily centered at the middle time period of February.

Figure 13.4
Comparing Moving Averages

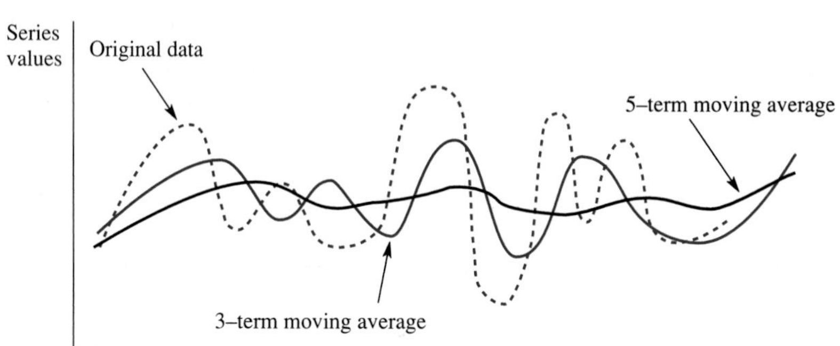

Table 13.3
Sales for Sun Shine Cards ($1,000)

Time Period	Sales	Four-Quarter MA	Centered Four-Quarter MA
1996-I	40		
II	45		
		42.50	
III	38		44.13
		45.75	
IV	47		45.00
		44.25	
1997-I	53		45.38
		46.50	
II	39		44.63
		42.75	
III	47		42.50
		42.25	
IV	32		43.00
		43.75	
1998-I	51		42.50
		41.25	
II	45		44.00
		46.75	
III	37		
IV	54		

However, if there is an even number of time periods in the moving average, an adjustment must be made because there is no middle observation at which the value is automatically centered. Consider the quarterly sales data for Sun Shine Greetings Cards in Table 13.3. The data run from the first quarter of 1996 to the last quarter of 1998. If a four-period (quarter) moving average is to be calculated, the first entry of 42.50 is obtained by averaging the data for all four quarters of 1996. This value, however, does not correspond to any specific time period in the original data series, but is set *between* the second and third quarters of 1996. The remaining entries are similarly off center.

It is necessary to center the moving average by taking the mean of each successive *pair* of moving averages. Thus, the average of the first and second values yields

$$(42.50 + 45.75)/2 = 44.13$$

which is then centered at the third quarter. The next entry of 45.00 is obtained by averaging the second and third values, yielding

$$(45.75 + 44.25)/2 = 45.00$$

which is centered at the fourth quarter of 1996. The remaining values are likewise centered at their respective time periods.

Moving averages can be used to remove irregular and seasonal fluctuations. Each entry in the moving average is derived from four observations of quarterly data—that is, one full year's worth. Thus, the moving average "averages out" any seasonal variations that might occur within the year, effectively eliminating them and leaving only trend and cyclical variations.

In general, if the number of time periods in a moving average is sufficient to encompass a full year (12 if monthly data are used; 52 if weekly data are used), seasonal variations are averaged out and removed from the series. The data are then said to be **deseasonalized.**

As noted, the use of a larger number of time periods results in a smoother averaged series. Therefore, if the data are quite volatile, a small number of periods should be used in the forecast to avoid placing the forecast too close to the long-run average. If the data do not vary greatly from the long-run mean, a larger number of time periods should be used in forming the moving average.

Minitab Display 13.1 shows the Minitab printout for the Sun Shine cards illustration. Example 13.1 further demonstrates the moving average principle.

Minitab Display 13.1

Four-Period Moving Average for Sun Shine Cards

Row	Period	C1	. MA	Predict	Error
1	1	40	*	*	*
2	2	45	*	*	*
3	3	38	44.125	*	*
4	4	47	45.000	*	*
5	5	53	45.375	*	*
6	6	39	44.625	44.125	-5.125
7	7	47	42.500	45.000	2.000
8	8	32	43.000	45.375	-13.375
9	9	51	42.500	44.625	6.375
10	10	45	44.000	42.500	2.500
11	11	37	*	43.000	-6.000
12	12	54	*	42.500	11.500

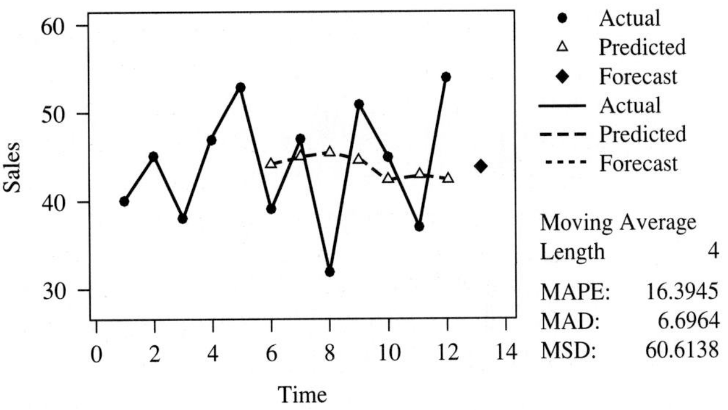

Example 13.1 TransAmerica Trucking has collected data for the last 10 months on the tonnage of shipments. Assist their research department by computing the three-term moving average. What is your forecast for shipments in the future?

Solution:

Month	Shipments	Three-Period MA	Month	Shipments	Three-Period MA
1	70		6	81	76.67
2	68	71.00	7	82	77.33
3	75	74.00	8	69	74.33
4	79	73.67	9	72	69.67
5	67	75.67	10	68	

The first three values of 70, 68, and 75 average to 71. The values for periods two through four of 68, 75, and 79 average to 74. The process continues until the last observation is encountered. The forecast for any future month is 69.67 tons.

Interpretation: Since the data do not exhibit any trend up or down, the moving average technique is suited to forecast future shipments. The forecast of 69.67 will of course change when the shipment for the eleventh month is reported and the moving average for month 10 is computed.

B. Exponential Smoothing

As the name implies, exponential smoothing has the effect of smoothing out a series. It also provides an effective means of prediction. **First-order exponential smoothing** is used when the data do not exhibit any trend pattern. The model contains a self-correcting mechanism that adjusts forecasts in the opposite direction of past errors. The equation is

Exponential smoothing $$F_{t+1} = \alpha A_t + (1 - \alpha)F_t \qquad [13.2]$$

where F_{t+1} is the forecast for the next time period
A_t is the actual, observed value for the current time period
F_t is the forecast previously made for the current time period

The α is a "smoothing constant" which is given a value between 0 and 1. Since the data do not trend up or down but fluctuate around some long-run average, we take the value F_{t+1} as the forecast for any future time period.

Exponential Smoothing A forecasting tool in which the forecast is based on a weighted average of current and past values.

As an illustration, suppose it is currently the last business day of February. Sales for Uncle Vito's Used Cars for the month total \$110 thousand. Uncle Vito has decided to forecast sales for March. According to Formula [13.2], the March forecast, F_{t+1}, requires

1. February's actual sales, A_t.
2. The forecast for February, F_t.

However, since March is the first month in which Uncle Vito is developing his forecast, there was no forecast made for February and F_t is unknown. The general practice is to simply use the actual value of the previous time period, January in this case, for the first forecast. Uncle Vito's records show that January sales were $105 thousand. Assuming a value of 0.3 for α, the forecast for March is

$$\begin{aligned} F_{t+1} &= \alpha A_t + (1 - \alpha)F_t \\ &= \alpha A_{\text{Feb}} + (1 - \alpha)F_{\text{Feb}} \\ &= (0.3)(110) + (0.7)(105) \\ &= \$106.5 \text{ thousand as the forecast for sales in March} \end{aligned}$$

As Table 13.4 reveals, Uncle Vito can plan for sales of $106.5 thousand. If actual sales in March are $107 thousand, the error is computed as $F_t - A_t = 106.5 - 107 = -0.5$. Also, $F_{\text{Apr}} = (0.3)(107) + (0.7)(106.5) = 106.65$.

Table 13.4
Uncle Vito's Auto Sales ($1,000)

Month	Forecast	Actual	Error ($F_t - A_t$)
January	–	105	
February	105	110	−5.0
March	106.5	107	−0.5
April	106.65	112	−5.35

Assume sales in April prove to be $112 thousand. The error is then −$5.35 thousand. Uncle Vito can also predict sales for May:

$$\begin{aligned} F_{t+1} &= \alpha A_t + (1 - \alpha)F_t \\ F_{\text{May}} &= \alpha A_{\text{Apr}} + (1 - \alpha)F_{\text{Apr}} \\ &= (0.3)(112) + (0.7)(106.65) \\ &= \$108.26 \text{ thousand} \end{aligned}$$

Of course, the value selected for α is crucial. Since we desire to produce a forecast with the smallest possible error, the α-value that minimizes the mean square error (MSE) is optimal. Trial and error often serves as the best method to determine the proper α-value. Table 13.5 contains Uncle Vito's actual sales data for the first seven months. Errors are based on forecasts calculated using α-values of 0.3 and 0.8. The *MSE* is

Mean square error $$MSE = \frac{\Sigma(F_t - A_t)^2}{n - 1} \quad [13.3]$$

Table 13.5
Sales Data for Uncle Vito

Month	Actual	Forecast ($\alpha = 0.3$)	Error	Forecast ($\alpha = 0.8$)	Error
January	105				
February	110	105.00	−5.00	105.00	−5.00
March	107	106.50	−0.50	109.00	2.00
April	112	106.65	−5.35	107.40	−4.60
May	117	108.26	−8.74	111.08	−5.92
June	109	110.88	1.88	115.82	6.82
July	108	110.32	2.32	110.36	2.36
August		109.62		108.47	

For = 0.3, the *MSE* is

$$MSE = \frac{(-5)^2 + (-0.5)^2 + (-5.35)^2 + (-8.74)^2 + (1.88)^2 + (2.32)^2}{7 - 1}$$

$$= 23.20$$

An α of 0.8 yields

$$MSE = \frac{(-5)^2 + (2)^2 + (-4.6)^2 + (-5.92)^2 + (6.82)^2 + (2.36)^2}{7 - 1}$$

$$= 22.88$$

An α of 0.8 produces better forecasting results since it generates a smaller error factor. Other values of α may be tried to determine their impact on MSE and the accuracy of the resulting forecasts. Generally speaking, if the data are rather volatile, a lower α-value is called for. This is because smaller values for α assign less weight to more recent observations. If the data show considerable movement, the last observation may not be representative of the long-run average.

Remember, first-order exponential smoothing in the manner described here is appropriate if the data show no trend, but move around some average value over the long run. If a downward or an upward trend can be detected by plotting the data, second-order exponential smoothing, the mechanics of which will not be examined here, should be used.

Example 13.2 **Predicting Unemployment Rates**

Monthly unemployment rates for 1997 are shown here. As an analyst for the U.S. Department of Labor, you are to (1) smooth out the fluctuations using a moving average with four time periods, and (2) use an exponential smoothing model with α set at 0.4 to forecast unemployment for some future month. The data do not show any pronounced trend up or down.

January	5.4	July	5.4
February	5.1	August	5.5
March	5.0	September	5.2
April	5.2	October	5.5
May	5.3	November	5.1
June	5.3	December	5.4

Solution:

Month	Rate	MA	Centered MA	F_t
1997 January	5.4			
February	5.1	5.175		5.4
March	5.0	5.150	5.163	5.28
April	5.2	5.200	5.175	5.17
May	5.3	5.300	5.250	5.18
June	5.3	5.375	5.338	5.23
July	5.4	5.350	5.363	5.26
August	5.5	5.400	5.375	5.31
September	5.2	5.325	5.363	5.39
October	5.5	5.300	5.313	5.31
November	5.1			5.39
December	5.4			5.27
1998 January				5.32

The table shows the first moving average of 5.175, calculated by averaging rates for January through April. It is situated in the middle of those four months between February and March. The second entry of 5.150 is the average of the months February through May and is placed between March and April. The remaining values for MA are figured similarly. These values are then centered by averaging successive pairs of moving averages.

To forecast using exponential smoothing, you must compute all forecasted figures for February through December in order to obtain $F_{\text{Dec}} = 5.27$, which you then use in the January 1998 forecast:

$$\begin{aligned} F_{\text{Jan}} &= \alpha(A_{\text{Dec}}) + (1 - \alpha)(F_{\text{Dec}}) \\ &= (0.4)(5.4) + (0.6)(5.27) \\ &= 5.32\% \end{aligned}$$

Interpretation: The moving average method forecasts a rate of 5.313 percent. Exponential smoothing provides a forecast of 5.32 percent. This value (of 5.313 percent or 5.32 percent) is the forecast for January, or for any future time period, since the data do not exhibit a trend but are thought to fluctuate around this long-term average.

Unlike moving averages, which use only a set number of time periods of data, exponential smoothing uses all past values of the time series. This is because F_{t+1} depends on A_t and F_t. Yet, F_t used A_{t-1} and F_{t-1} in its calculation, and F_{t-1} used A_{t-2} and F_{t-2}. Thus, each forecast depends on previous actual values of A_{t-n} all the way back to where the forecasts first began. The further back in time you go, the less impact a value of A has on the current forecast.

Section Exercises

1. If the data in a time series have a large variance, should a moving average with a large number of time periods or one with a small number of time periods be used? Why?
2. Why should a moving average be used only when the data exhibit no upward or downward trend?
3. The number of daily telephone calls coming into a switchboard at a busy office are shown below. Calculate the 3-period moving average.

Day	1	2	3	4	5	6	7	8	9	10	11
Calls	40	37	45	32	42	47	39	47	41	36	38

4. The daily numbers of employees absent from their jobs at a large factory are shown here. Calculate the four-period moving average associated with these data. Center the averages.

Day	1	2	3	4	5	6	7	8	9	10	11	12
Employees	45	54	63	39	42	31	48	54	64	36	41	52

5. Excess inventories for Mom's Apple Pies, Inc., over the past 10 weeks have been 101, 122, 109, 111, 120, 117, 115, 118, 112, and 117. Using exponential smoothing, set alpha at 0.20 and forecast inventories for the eleventh week.
6. Monthly loans at the local bank in thousands of dollars are 211, 234, 209, 217, 215, 232, 221, 211 and 203. Use exponential smoothing to forecast loans for the next time period using an alpha value of 0.10. Calculate the mean square error and compare it to the mean square error if alpha is 0.80. Which alpha value provides the best forecast?

13.5 Trend Analysis

If a time series has a long-term trend upward or downward (like Figure 13.1 for example), trend analysis can be useful in developing forecasts. That is, if a trend is present in that the data do not fluctuate around some long-run average like those for Sun Shine Cards discussed above, smoothing methods such as moving averages and exponential smoothing are not appropriate. Instead, a trend line can be estimated using the techniques of simple regression discussed in Chapter 11. The dependent variable is the time series we wish to forecast, and time is used as the independent variable. The model to be estimated is then simply

Trend line using simple regression

$$\hat{Y}_t = b_0 + b_1 t \qquad [13.4]$$

Consider the data for the number of housing starts (in hundreds) in Happy Valley, California, seen in Table 13.6. Mayfield Construction wants to fit this time series using OLS to develop a model to predict future housing starts.

Table 13.6
Housing Starts in Happy Valley (in 100's)

Year	t(X)	Housing Starts (Y)	XY	X^2
1983	1	7.0	7.0	1
1984	2	7.1	14.2	4
1985	3	7.9	23.7	9
1986	4	7.3	29.2	16
1987	5	8.2	41.0	25
1988	6	8.3	49.8	36
1989	7	8.1	56.7	49
1990	8	8.6	68.8	64
1991	9	8.8	79.2	81
1992	10	8.9	89.0	100
1993	11	8.7	95.7	121
1994	12	9.1	109.2	144
1995	13	9.4	122.2	169
1996	14	9.1	127.4	196
1997	15	9.5	142.5	225
1998	16	9.9	158.4	256
	136	135.9	1,214.0	1,496.0

The values for t are obtained by coding each time period starting with 1 for the first time period, 2 for the second, and so on. As we learned in Chapter 11, the sums of squares and cross-products, used to calculate the regression line, are

Sum of the squares of X

$$SSx = \Sigma X^2 - \frac{(\Sigma X)^2}{n} \qquad [13.5]$$

$$= 1{,}496 - \frac{(136)^2}{16}$$

$$= 340$$

Sum of the squares of cross-products	$SSxy = \Sigma XY - \dfrac{(\Sigma X)(\Sigma Y)}{n}$	[13.6]

$$= 1{,}214 - \frac{(136)(135.9)}{16}$$

$$= 58.85$$

The formulas for b_1 and b_0 are

Slope of the trend line	$b_1 = \dfrac{SSxy}{SSx}$	[13.7]

$$= \frac{58.85}{340}$$

$$= 0.173$$

Intercept of trend line	$b_0 = \overline{Y} - b_1\overline{X}$	[13.8]

$$= 7.02$$

The equation for the trend line is

$$\hat{Y}_t = 7.02 + 0.173t$$

Figure 13.5 displays the raw data and the trend line they produce.

Figure 13.5

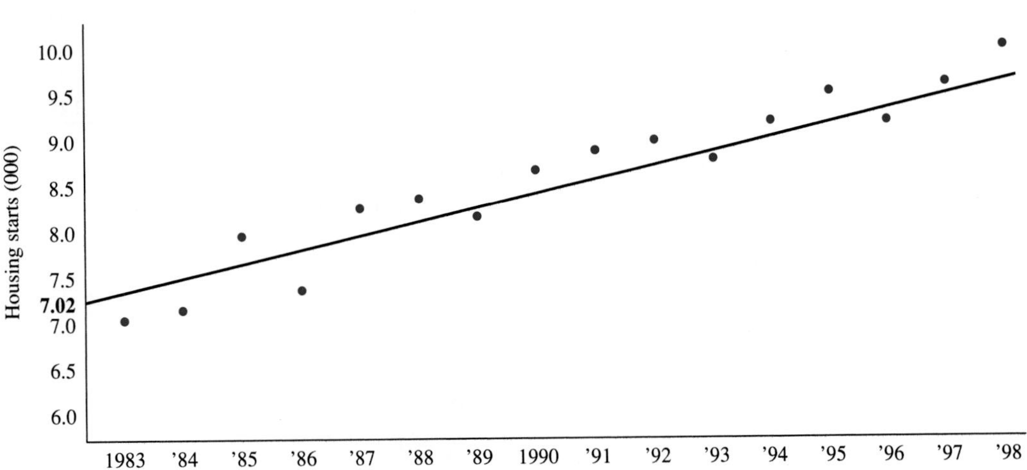

Given this equation, it is possible to predict the number of housing starts for future time periods merely by substituting the appropriate value for t. Suppose Mayfield Construction wants to forecast the housing starts for 1999. Since the value of t would be 17 in

1999, the forecast becomes

$$\begin{aligned}\hat{Y} &= 7.02 + 0.173(17)\\ &= 9.96\end{aligned}$$

or 9,960 starts, since the data were expressed in units of 1,000.

Similarly, since 2001 would carry a t value of 19, the forecast for 2001 would be

$$\begin{aligned}\hat{Y} &= 7.02 + 0.173(19)\\ &= 10.31\end{aligned}$$

It is estimated that there will be 1,031 housing starts in 2001.

Of course, the further into the future a forecast is made, the less confidence you can place in its precision. Additionally, its accuracy is based on the condition that the past provides a representative picture of future trends.

Example 13.3 Larry's Lawn Service advertises a new chemical to kill weeds. To determine the trend in the number of customers, Larry consults company records and finds the data shown here. He wishes to forecast customers for future time periods.

Time Period	$t(X)$	Customers (Y)	XY	X^2
1997 January	1	41	41	1
February	2	43	86	4
March	3	39	117	9
April	4	37	148	16
May	5	42	210	25
June	6	35	210	36
July	7	30	210	49
August	8	31	248	64
September	9	32	288	81
October	10	30	300	100
November	11	28	308	121
December	12	28	336	144
1998 January	13	29	377	169
February	14	26	364	196
	105	471	3,243	1,015

Solution:

$$\begin{aligned}SSx &= 1{,}015 - \frac{(105)^2}{14}\\ &= 227.5\end{aligned}$$

$$\begin{aligned}SSxy &= 3{,}243 - \frac{(105)(471)}{14}\\ &= -289.5\\ b_1 &= -1.27\\ b_0 &= \overline{Y} - b_1\overline{X}\\ &= 33.64 - (-1.27)(7.5)\\ &= 43.2\end{aligned}$$

The equation for the trend line is

$$\hat{Y}_t = 43.2 - 1.27t$$

If Larry wished to forecast the number of customers his firm might get in March 1998, which would be time period 15, he would have

$$\hat{Y}_{\text{Mar}} = 43.2 - 1.27(15)$$
$$= 24.15, \text{ or } 24 \text{ customers}$$

The forecast for August is

$$\hat{Y}_{\text{Aug}} = 43.2 - 1.27(21)$$
$$= 16.53 \text{ customers}$$

Interpretation: The negative coefficient for t of -1.27 tells Larry that business is trending downward at the rate of 1.27 customers each time period (month).

Section Exercises

7. Below are annual national test scores for high school seniors applying to colleges. Develop a trend line and forecast the test score for 1998.

	1989	1990	1991	1992	1993	1994	1995	1996	1997
Score	412	423	453	432	541	539	587	591	602

8. The research department for National Industries has recorded the level of output in thousands of units produced over the past several months. Using the data shown here, develop a trend line and forecast output for November and December.

	January	February	March	April	May	June	July	August
Output	89	78	71	75	68	61	65	54

9. City Utilities has undergone rapid expansion over the past several years. This growth has required additions to its labor force each year. Use trend analysis to predict the size of the labor force (in hundreds) in the year 2000.

	1990	1991	1992	1993	1994	1995	1996	1997	1998
Employees	3.5	4.8	5.2	4.9	5.6	5.2	6.5	7.8	8.5

13.6 Time-Series Decomposition

It often proves useful to *decompose* a time series by "breaking-out" each of its four components. Thus, we can examine each component individually. The historic trend can reflect past patterns of behavior, allowing us to gain insight into the long-run movements of the variables we wish to examine. This permits the development of trend models useful in prediction and forecasting, as we saw in the previous section dealing with trend analysis. By examining the seasonal factor we can determine whether business activity exhibits any seasonal variation that must be considered in formulating future plans. For example, if we market swimwear or some other seasonal product we may find that sales are much higher in the spring than in the fall or winter. In addition, the cyclical performance of our business may also influence the direction of business planning.

A. Isolating the Seasonal Component

The first step in decomposition is to obtain a seasonal index. Consider the data in Table 13.7 for Vinnie's Video Village. A superficial examination reveals that profits seem to be higher during the summer months when school is out, and lower at other times of the year. This suggests the presence of seasonal factors.

Table 13.7
Seasonal Fluctuations in Vinnie's Profits

Time Period	(Y) Profits ($100's)	12-Month MA ($T \cdot C$)	Centered MA	Ratio to MA $Y/CMA = S \cdot I$
1996				
January	10			
February	9			
March	11			
April	12			
May	18			
June	23	15.5833		
July	27	15.5000	15.5417	1.7373
August	26	15.6667	15.5833	1.6685
September	18	15.5833	15.6250	1.1520
October	13	15.5833	15.5833	0.8342
November	10	15.6667	15.6250	0.6400
December	10	15.8333	15.7500	0.6349
1997				
January	9	15.9167	15.8750	0.5669
February	11	16.3333	16.1250	0.6822
March	10	16.6667	16.5000	0.6061
April	12	16.8333	16.7500	0.7164
May	19	16.9167	16.8750	1.1259
June	25	17.0833	17.0000	1.4706
July	28	17.1667	17.1250	1.6350
August	31	16.9167	17.0417	1.8191
September	22	16.9167	16.9167	1.3005
October	15	16.9167	16.9167	0.8867
November	11	16.9167	16.9167	0.6502
December	12	16.9167	16.9167	0.7094
1998				
January	10	17.0000	16.9583	0.5897
February	8	17.0000	17.0000	0.4706
March	10	16.9167	16.9583	0.5897
April	12	17.0000	16.9583	0.7076
May	19	17.5833	17.2916	1.0988
June	25	18.1667	17.8750	1.3986
July	29			
August	31			
September	21			
October	16			
November	18			
December	19			

The first step in developing a seasonal index is to calculate a centered moving average. Since Vinnie's profits tend to fluctuate over the course of the year, and monthly data are used, we calculate a 12-period (month) moving average. If we were to analyze activity on organized stock exchanges, we might want to use daily data and employ a five-period (for the five business days) moving average since, as noted, activity on the exchanges seems to depend on the day of the week.

Table 13.7 shows the 12-month moving average and the centered moving average (CMA). As noted, the year-long moving average eliminates recurring seasonal movements (because seasonal variations occur *within* a year), as well as any random effects over the course of the year. Thus, given a multiplicative model $Y = T \cdot C \cdot S \cdot I$, the moving average eliminates S and I and contains only T and C. That is, $MA = T \cdot C$.

It is now possible to calculate the **ratio to moving average.** To do this, divide the original series value Y by the moving average. The result produces the S and I components of the time series.

$$\frac{Y}{MA} = \frac{T \times C \times S \times I}{T \times C} = S \times I \qquad \text{Ratio to moving average}$$

By dividing the time-series values by the moving average, we arrive at the ratio to moving average, which contains only S and I components. The I component will be removed shortly.

To summarize, we seek to isolate and analyze the seasonal component. Strangely, we begin by eliminating S (and I) by calculating the moving average. We then restore the seasonal component by calculating the ratio to moving average. These values also appear in the last column of Table 13.7.

Ratio to Moving Average By dividing the original time-series data by the moving average, we obtain the ratio to moving average, which contains the *S* and *I* components.

We must now calculate a **mean ratio to moving average** for all twelve months. This is done by averaging the ratio to moving average for each month as shown in Table 13.8. For example, notice from Table 13.7 that January has two ratios to moving average: 0.5669 for 1997 and 0.5897 for 1998. Table 13.8 shows that these average to $0.5669 + 0.5897/2 = 0.5783$. The mean ratios for the remaining months are similarly calculated. These twelve mean ratios are then summed. Ideally, they would sum to 12. But due to rounding and averaging, this is rarely the case. As Table 13.8 shows, the sum is actually 11.8454.

Table 13.8
Seasonal Indexes for Vinnie's Profits

(1) Month	(2) 1996	(3) 1997	(4) 1998	(5) Mean Ratio to MA	(6) Seasonal Index (Column 5 × 1.01305)
January		0.5669	0.5897	0.5783	0.5858
February		0.6822	0.4706	0.5764	0.5839
March		0.6061	0.5897	0.5979	0.6057
April		0.7164	0.7076	0.7120	0.7213
May		1.1259	1.0988	1.1124	1.1269
June		1.4706	1.3986	1.4346	1.4533
July	1.7373	1.6350		1.6861	1.7082
August	1.6685	1.8191		1.7438	1.7665
September	1.1520	1.3005		1.2262	1.2422
October	0.8342	0.8867		0.8605	0.8717
November	0.6400	0.6502		0.6451	0.6535
December	0.6349	0.7094		0.6721	0.6809
				11.8454	11.9999 ≈ 12

We must therefore *normalize* these mean ratios to get a seasonal index. This is done by dividing 12 (since there are twelve-periods) by the sum of the mean ratios to moving average 11.8454. The result of

$$\frac{12}{11.8454} = 1.01305$$

is the **normalization ratio.** This normalization ratio is then multiplied by each of the mean ratios to get the seasonal index for each time period as shown in Table 13.8. This normalization process has removed any remaining irregular activity leaving only the seasonal factor.

The uses of the seasonal index are as follows

1. After going to all the trouble to calculate these seasonal indexes, you will be glad to learn that they can be put to vital use. For example, the seasonal index for a particular month indicates how that month performs relative to the year as a whole. The index of 0.5858 for January tells Vinnie that profits in January are only 58.58 percent of the average for the full year. Profits are 41.42 percent (1.000 − 0.5858) below the year's monthly average.
2. Perhaps more important, the indexes can be used to *deseasonalize data.* This has the effect of removing seasonal variation from a series to determine what the values would be in the absence of seasonal variations. It yields the average value per month that would occur if there were no seasonal changes. The deseasonalized value is found by dividing the actual value during the month by the seasonal index in that month. For example, in January 1996, the deseasonalized value is

$$\frac{10}{0.5858} = 17.07$$

In other words, if Vannie's business was not subject to seasonal variation, profits in January 1996 would have been $1,707.

Deseasonalized values are also called **seasonally adjusted** because they tell us what the values would be if we adjusted for seasonal influences. The classic example involves unemployment rates. Since unemployment is usually higher in May than in most other months due to school dismissals and the influx of many teenagers into the job market, the seasonal index for May will be greater than 1. If actual unemployment in May is 7.2 percent and the index is, say, 1.103, the deseasonalized, or seasonally adjusted, rate of unemployment is 7.2/1.103 = 6.53 percent. This is not to say that unemployment was 6.53 percent. (It was actually 7.2 percent.) But when we adjust for seasonal forces, which typically inflate the rate of unemployment in May, the deseasonalized rate is lower. In this manner a measure or index of seasonal variation can be used to determine whether the change in some series is more or less than what might be expected given the typical seasonal behavior.

Deseasonalized Values Values obtained by dividing the actual values by their respective seasonal indexes. They reflect what the variable would be if we adjusted for seasonal influence.

3. The reverse is possible, in that the seasonal index can be used to *seasonalize data* to get a better picture of what any one month might generate in profits. Assume Vinnie felt that profits might total 190 during the year. Without any seasonalization it might be argued that each month would generate 190/12 = 15.83, or $1,583 in profits. However, Vinnie knows that monthly variations will occur. He could seasonalize the data to determine the extent of that monthly variation by multiplying 15.83 by the seasonal index. He knows that in January profits tend to be 58.58 percent of the yearly total. His estimate of profits for January is (15.83)(0.5858) = 9.27, or $927.

Or perhaps Vinnie is working with the trend equation which, given the data, is

$$Y_t = 13.85 + 0.167t$$

The forecast for January 1999, the 37th time period, is

$$\hat{Y} = 13.85 + 0.167(37)$$
$$= 20.03$$

However, this does not account for the seasonal lows that occur in January. The value can be seasonalized by multiplying by the seasonal index for January, yielding (20.03)(0.5858) = 11.73, which probably more accurately reflects profits during that month.

Minitab Display 13.2 shows the Minitab printout for Vinnie's profits. The trend line (which we didn't calculate here) is given along with the seasonal indexes. These differ somewhat from our hand calculations in Table 13.8 due to rounding. However, notice that the indexes are greater than 1 for periods May through September, just as they were in our calculations.

Minitab Display 13.2

Time Series Decomposition for Vinnie's Profits

```
Data       profits
Length     36.0000
NMissing   0

Trend Line Equation

Yt = 13.8540 + 0.167053*t

Seasonal Indices

Period     Index
   1       0.584635
   2       0.587189
   3       0.612000
   4       0.729246
   5        1.13705
   6        1.46259
   7        1.70946
   8        1.76051
   9        1.23313
  10       0.862486
  11       0.646247
  12       0.675462
```

Minitab Display 13.3

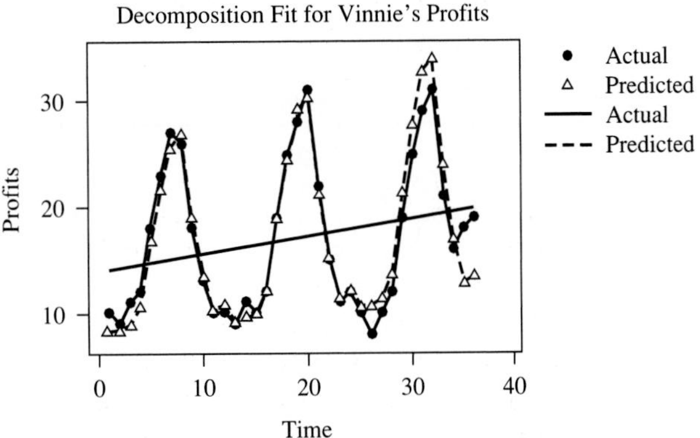

Minitab Display 13.3 plots the actual values for profits against the predicted values based on the trend line. Finally, Minitab Display 13.4 provides several plots. The detrended

Minitab Display 13.4

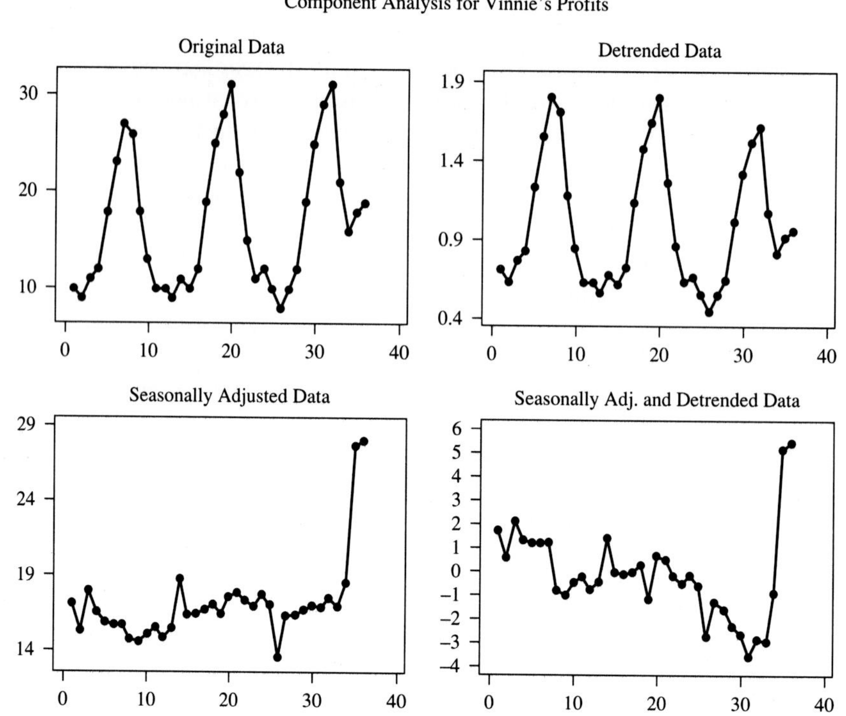

data reflect the movements in profits if the trend is removed. Notice that profits seem to move above and below a long-run average somewhere between 0.9 and 1.4. The seasonally adjusted data are obtained when the actual data are divided by the seasonal indexes in Minitab Display 13.2 just as we discussed in this section.

Example 13.4 Marge Spaniel has owned and managed a successful breeding kennel for several years. She wishes to determine seasonal indexes for the quarterly data on revenue shown here in thousands of dollars in the first two columns of the table.

Solution: Since quarterly data are used, a four-period moving average will remove the seasonal variations.

Year-Quarter	Revenue	MA	Centered MA	Ratio to MA $Y/CMA = S \cdot I$
1996-I	24			
II	31			
III	21	29.50	29.8750	0.7029
IV	42	30.25	30.3750	1.3827
1997-I	27	30.50	31.0000	0.8710
II	32	31.50	31.3750	1.0199
III	25	31.25	30.3750	0.8230
IV	41	29.50	28.8750	1.4200
1998-I	20	28.25	27.3750	0.7306
II	27	26.50	26.2500	1.0286
III	18	26.00		
IV	39			

The sum of the mean ratio to moving averages is 3.9895 as seen in the next table. The normalization ratio is $4/3.9895 = 1.0026$.

	Ratios to Moving Average			Mean Ratio to MA	Seasonal Index
	1996	1997	1998		
I		0.8710	0.7306	0.8008	0.8029
II		1.0199	1.0286	1.0243	1.0270
III	0.7029	0.8230		0.7630	0.7650
IV	1.3827	1.4200		1.4014	1.4050
				3.9895	$3.99 \approx 4$

Each seasonal index is then calculated by multiplying the mean ratio by the normalization ratio. For Quarter I it is $0.8008 \times 1.0026 = 0.8029$.

Interpretation: Sales in the fourth quarter, for example, are 40.5 percent greater than the yearly average. The deseasonalized value for the fourth quarter of 1996 is $42/1.4050 = 29.89$.

B. Isolating the Cyclical Variation

Many businesses are affected by swings in the business cycle. When the economy in general turns up, their business activity may accelerate, while an economic downturn brings on a drop in business. Some industries often exhibit movements in the opposite direction of the cycle. The entertainment industry, for example, has been known to experience countercyclical movements. Presumably, when economic conditions worsen, many people seek relief from harsh reality by escaping to the movies.

The cyclical component can be identified by first obtaining the trend and seasonal components as described earlier. The data from Example 13.4 for Ms. Spaniel will illustrate. The trend line is

$$\hat{Y}_t = 28.58 + 0.0524t$$

The original data of the time series, the values predicted on the basis of this trend model, and the seasonal indexes as determined in Example 13.4 are shown in columns (2), (3), and (4) in Table 13.9. For example, the trend value for the second time period, 1996-II, is

$$\hat{Y} = 28.58 + 0.0524(2) = 28.68$$

Table 13.9
Isolating the Cyclical Component

(1) Time	(2) Revenue	(3) Trend Projection	(4) Seasonal Index	(5) Statistical Norm (3) × (4)	(6) Cyclical-Irregular [(2)/(5)](100)	(7) Cyclical Component
1996-I	24	28.63	0.8029	22.99	104.39	
II	31	28.68	1.0270	29.45	105.26	
III	21	28.73	0.7650	21.98	95.54	103.78
IV	42	28.79	1.4050	40.45	103.83	105.63
1997-I	27	28.84	0.8029	23.16	116.58	108.13
II	32	28.89	1.0270	29.67	107.85	109.90
III	25	28.94	0.7650	22.14	112.92	105.64
IV	41	29.00	1.4050	40.75	100.61	99.60
1998-I	20	29.05	0.8029	23.32	85.76	93.38
II	27	29.10	1.0270	29.89	90.33	88.65
III	18	29.15	0.7650	22.30	80.72	
IV	39	29.21	1.4050	41.04	95.03	

The *statistical norm* is then calculated by multiplying the trend projection by the seasonal index. This is called the *norm* because it represents the values that would occur if only the trend and seasonal variations were present.

The cyclic and irregular components are obtained next by dividing the original data by the statistical norm, which contains T and S. That is, since $Y = T \times S \times C \times I$,

$$\frac{Y}{T \times S} = \frac{T \times S \times C \times I}{T \times S} = C \times I$$

The results are then multiplied by 100 to express the answer in percentage form as shown in column (6) of Table 13.9. The values in column (6) contain both cyclical and irregular components. The latter is eliminated by taking a four-period moving average, leaving only the cyclical factor. This is done in column (7). The final measures in column (7) represent the actual levels in Ms. Spaniel's revenue in those time periods as a percentage of the trend.

Note that if annual data are used, they will, by definition, contain no seasonal variations. The seasonal index (as found in column (4) of Table 13.9, for example) would be unnecessary. The values of the time series would consist only of

$$Y = T \times C \times I$$

The components C and I could be found directly by dividing only by the trend values:

$$\frac{Y}{T} = \frac{T \times C \times I}{T} = C \times I$$

C. Irregular Variation

Having isolated the other three components of a time series, we need say little more about irregular variations. Suffice it to say that it is often possible to smooth out and effectively eliminate them by using a moving average as we did for column (7) of Table 13.9.

Section Exercises

10. Quarterly exports of pipe fittings in thousands of dollars to Pacific Rim countries by International Metals, Inc., are shown here. Calculate and interpret the seasonal indexes for each quarter.

1995		1997	
I	12	I	10
II	15	II	15
III	18	III	14
IV	26	IV	25
1996		**1998**	
I	15	I	12
II	18	II	14
III	21	III	15
IV	36	IV	25

11. Quarterly data for the number of customers for Eastern Electronics are shown here. Compute the trend line and the indexes for each quarter.

1995		1996		1997		1998	
I	215	I	366	I	587	I	621
II	253	II	471	II	571	II	655
III	351	III	451	III	569	III	687
IV	398	IV	652	IV	588	IV	699

12. The costs in hundreds of dollars of international telephone calls by USA Investment Funds are given below. Compute and interpret the quarterly indexes.

1995		1996		1997		1998	
I	14	I	21	I	21	I	26
II	18	II	24	II	23	II	28
III	26	III	29	III	38	III	48
IV	15	IV	18	IV	21	IV	31

13. Deseasonalize the data for USA Investment Funds in the preceding exercise.

13.7 The Use of Index Numbers

In the study of time series we often compare data in one time period with data from a different time period. Such comparisons must be made with care because economic conditions change over time. These changes make it difficult to analyze business data or interpret economic variables. Direct comparisons from one time period to the next often become misleading.

The use of index numbers can provide decision makers with a more accurate picture of the behavior of economic variables over time and make comparisons across time periods more meaningful. An index number relates a value in one time period, called the **base period,** to a value in another time period, called the **reference (or current) period.**

A. A Simple Price Index

A **simple price index** characterizes the relationship between the price of a good or service in the *base period,* to the price of that same good or service in the *reference period.*

Simple Price Index Measures the relative change in the price of a single good or service from the base period to the reference period.

To calculate a simple index, you merely divide the price of the commodity in the reference period by its price in the base period and multiply by 100.

Simple price index $$PI_R = \frac{P_R}{P_B} \times 100 \qquad [13.9]$$

For example, if you wished to determine the price index for the reference period 1995 and chose 1990 as the base period, you would have

$$PI_{1995} = \frac{P_{1995}}{P_{1990}} \times 100$$

where PI is the price index and P is the price in the respective years.

Jack Nipp and his partner, Harry Tuck, own a meat packing plant in Duluth. Data for their three most popular items are shown in Table 13.10. Nipp tells Tuck to compute a simple price index for each product with 1995 as the base period. Using Formula [13.9], Tuck

Table 13.10
Data for Nipp and Tuck, Inc.

Item	Unit	Price/Unit 1995	1996	1997
Beef	1 pound	3.00	3.30	4.50
Pork	1 pound	2.00	2.20	2.10
Veal	1 pound	4.00	4.50	3.64

finds that the price indexes for beef in each of the three years are

$$\begin{aligned} PI_{1995} &= \frac{P_{1995}}{P_{1995}} \times 100 = \frac{3.00}{3.00} \times 100 \\ &= 100 \end{aligned}$$

$$\begin{aligned} PI_{1996} &= \frac{P_{1996}}{P_{1995}} \times 100 = \frac{3.00}{3.00} \times 100 \\ &= 110 \end{aligned}$$

$$\begin{aligned} PI_{1997} &= \frac{P_{1997}}{P_{1995}} \times 100 = \frac{3.00}{3.00} \times 100 \\ &= 150 \end{aligned}$$

From the base year of 1995 to 1996, the price index rose from 100 to 110. Tuck can therefore conclude that the price of beef increased by 10 percent. This is calculated as the difference between the two index numbers divided by the base number. That is,

$$\begin{aligned} \frac{PI_{1996} - PI_{1995}}{PI_{1995}} &= \frac{110 - 100}{100} \\ &= 10\% \end{aligned}$$

Similarly, it can be concluded that a 50 percent increase occurred from 1995 to 1997:

$$\begin{aligned} \frac{PI_{1997} - PI_{1995}}{PI_{1995}} &= \frac{150 - 100}{100} \\ &= 50\% \end{aligned}$$

You might want to conclude that a 40 percent increase in price occurred from 1996 to 1997 since the price index increased by 40. However, this is *not* the case. The percentage increase from 1996 to 1997 is

$$\begin{aligned} \frac{PI_{1997} - PI_{1996}}{PI_{1996}} &= \frac{150 - 110}{100} \\ &= 36.4\% \end{aligned}$$

The 40 percent difference between the index numbers in 1996 and 1997 is called the *percentage point* increase, not the percentage increase.

Notice that the price index in the base year is always 100. This will always be the case since the price in the base year is, of course, 100 percent of itself.

The indexes for pork and veal are calculated in similar fashion and are shown in Table 13.11. Notice that the 1997 index for veal is less than 100. This reflects the fact that veal prices in 1997 were lower than they were in the base year of 1995. Specifically, prices for veal went down by $(100 - 91)/100 = 9$ percent from 1995 to 1997.

Table 13.11
Price Indexes for Nipp and Tuck, Inc. (1995 = 100)

Item	1995	1996	1997
Beef	$\frac{3.00}{3.00} \times 100 = 100$	$\frac{3.30}{3.00} \times 100 = 110$	$\frac{4.50}{3.00} \times 100 = 150$
Pork	$\frac{2.00}{2.00} \times 100 = 100$	$\frac{2.20}{2.00} \times 100 = 110$	$\frac{2.10}{2.00} \times 100 = 105$
Veal	$\frac{4.00}{4.00} \times 100 = 100$	$\frac{4.50}{4.00} \times 100 = 112$	$\frac{3.64}{4.00} \times 100 = 91$

Example 13.5 Monthly prices for a gallon of gasoline are shown here. Using March as the base period, calculate the price indexes. What were the percentage increases, from March to May, and from May to June? What is the percentage point increase from May to June?

Jan	Feb	Mar	Apr	May	June	July
1.79	1.82	1.96	2.01	2.10	2.25	2.15

Solution:

Price Indexes (March = 100)			
Month	**Index**	**Month**	**Index**
Jan	$\frac{1.79}{1.96}(100) = 91.3$	May	$\frac{2.10}{1.96}(100) = 107.1$
Feb	$\frac{1.82}{1.96}(100) = 92.9$	June	$\frac{2.25}{1.96}(100) = 114.8$
March	$\frac{1.96}{1.96}(100) = 100$	July	$\frac{2.15}{1.96}(100) = 109.7$
Apr	$\frac{2.01}{1.96}(100) = 102.6$		

The percentage increase from March to May is

$$\frac{107.1 - 100.0}{100.0} = 7.1\%$$

From May to June, the percentage increase is

$$\frac{114.8 - 107.1}{107.1} = 7.2\%$$

and the percentage point increase is $114.8 - 107.1 = 7.7\%$

Interpretation: The base period will always report an index of 100. Periods in which the values are less than the base year will have an index less than 100, and periods with values in excess of that in the base year will have an index above 100.

B. Composite Price Indexes

Often we want to calculate a price index for several goods. This is called a **composite price index.** Firms that produce two or more products are usually interested in a composite index. So are many government agencies that chart consumer behavior. The U.S.

Department of Labor compiles the Consumer Price Index, which measures relative prices for a typcal "market basket" of goods and services consumed by the general public.

The composite index is computed by adding the price of the individual commodities in the reference year and dividing by the summation of those prices in the base year. The result is then multiplied by 100.

Composite price index	$PI_R = \dfrac{\Sigma P_R}{\Sigma P_B} \times 100$	[13.10]

Using the data for Nipp and Tuck, we find that the 1995 composite index for all three products, retaining 1995 as the base period, is

$$PI_{1995} = \frac{3.00 + 2.00 + 4.00}{3.00 + 2.00 + 4.00}(100) = 100.0$$

The index for 1996 is

$$PI_{1996} = \frac{3.30 + 2.20 + 4.50}{3.00 + 2.00 + 4.00}(100) = 111.1$$

And 1997 produces

$$PI_{1997} = \frac{4.50 + 2.10 + 3.64}{3.00 + 2.00 + 4.00}(100) = 113.8$$

This means that in 1997 it would take $113.80 to buy what $100 would buy in 1995.

C. Weighted Composite Price Indexes

At least two problems arise with the use of composite price indexes. The first concerns the arbitrary way in which the units are expressed. Had Nipp and Tuck priced beef at $1.50 per half-pound instead of $3.00 per pound, the price index would have been entirely different. Second, the composite indexes as computed do not take into account the fact that some goods sell in larger quantities than do other, less popular, products. No consideration is given to the respective amounts of each product that are sold.

For example, the composite index calculated for Nipp and Tuck gives the same importance, or weight, to beef as to pork, even though twice as much of the former may have been purchased by the consumers. It is for these reasons that we may want to compute a **weighted price index.** Such a calculation assigns different weights to individual prices. These weights are established so as to measure the amounts sold of each product. This provides a more accurate reflection of the true cost of the consumer's market basket of goods.

The quantities selected as weights can be taken from the number of units sold in (1) the base period or (2) the reference period. Two common indexes are the Laspeyres index and the Paasche index. The Laspeyres index uses quantities sold in the base year as weights; the Paasche index relies on quantities sold in the reference year as weights. Each procedure has its own advantages and disadvantages.

The **Laspeyres index** uses **base period** weights (quantities) in its calculation. The rationale is that these quantities will not change from one calculation to the next, thereby permitting more meaningful comparisons over time.

Laspeyres Index A weighted composite price index that uses quantities sold in the base period as the weight factor.

To illustrate, consider the data for Nipp and Tuck in Table 13.12, which also includes the amounts sold for each product. The Laspeyres index is

Laspeyres index $$L = \frac{\Sigma(P_R \times Q_B)}{\Sigma(P_B \times Q_B)} \times 100 \qquad [13.11]$$

where P_R is the price in the reference period, and P_B and Q_B are the price and quantities sold in the period selected as the base period.

Table 13.12
Nipp and Tuck, Inc.

Item	Unit	Price/Unit			Quantity Sold (100's lb)		
		1995	1996	1997	1995	1996	1997
Beef	1 pound	3.00	3.30	4.50	250	320	350
Pork	1 pound	2.00	2.20	2.10	150	200	225
Veal	1 pound	4.00	4.50	3.64	80	90	70

Table 13.13
The Laspeyres Index for Nipp and Tuck (1995 = 100)

Item	Price			Quantities in 1995	$P_R \times Q_B$		
	1995	1996	1997		$P_{95}Q_{95}$	$P_{96}Q_{95}$	$P_{97}Q_{95}$
Beef	3.00	3.30	4.50	250	750	825	1,125.0
Pork	2.00	2.20	2.10	150	300	330	315.0
Veal	4.00	4.50	3.64	80	320	360	291.2
					1,370	1,515	1,731.2

The numerator uses Q_B, the quantities of each item in the base year. Table 13.13 shows the computations necessary for the Laspeyres index using 1995 as the base year. The numerator for L is figured by first multiplying each price by the quantities sold in the base period of 1995. The denominator is then determined by multiplying the price in the base year by the quantity in the base year. The index for 1995

$$L_{1995} = \frac{\Sigma(P_{1995} \times Q_{1995})}{\Sigma(P_{1995} \times Q_{1995})}(100)$$
$$= \frac{1{,}370}{1{,}370}(100) = 100$$

The index for 1996 uses the prices in the reference year (1996) and the quantities in the base year (1995) for the numerator:

$$L_{1996} = \frac{\Sigma(P_{1996} \times Q_{1995})}{\Sigma(P_{1995} \times Q_{1995})}(100)$$
$$= \frac{1{,}515}{1{,}370}(100)$$
$$= 110.58$$

The numerator for 1997 uses prices in 1997 and quantities in 1995:

$$L_{1997} = \frac{\Sigma(P_{1997} \times Q_{1995})}{\Sigma(P_{1995} \times Q_{1995})}(100)$$

$$= \frac{1{,}731.2}{1{,}370}(100)$$

$$= 126.36$$

The interpretation of the Laspeyres index is like that for our earlier indexes. From 1995 to 1997, the price of the market basket for these three meat items increased by 26.36 percent. It would take \$126.36 in 1997 to buy what \$100 did in 1995. Or, alternatively, it would require \$1.26 in 1997 to buy what \$1.00 did in 1995.

Notice that the denominator is the same in all three years: the Laspeyres index always uses quantities from the base period.

The **Paasche index,** on the other hand, uses as weights the quantities sold in each of the various reference years. This has the advantage of basing the index on current consumer behavior patterns. As consumers change their buying habits, these changes in consumer tastes are reflected by the index. Commodities that no longer attract consumers' interest, such as buggy whips and top hats, do not receive as much consideration. However, using different quantity measures makes it impossible to attribute any differences in the index to changes in prices alone.

Paasche Index A weighted composite price index that uses quantities sold in the reference period as the weight factor.

Its calculation is a bit more involved than the Laspeyres:

Paasche index
$$P = \frac{\Sigma(P_R \times Q_R)}{\Sigma(P_B \times Q_R)} \times 100 \qquad [13.12]$$

The quantities for the reference years appear in both the numerator and the denominator. Table 13.14 provides the computation necessary for the Paasche, using the Nipp and Tuck data with 1995 as the base. We must first multiply prices and quantities for all three years to get $P_R \times Q_R$, which is used in the numerator. We also need the value for price in the base year, 1995, times the quantity for each reference year to get $P_B \times Q_R$, which is used in the

Table 13.14
Paasche Index for Nipp and Tuck (1995 = 100)

	1995		1996		1997	
Item	*P*	*Q*	*P*	*Q*	*P*	*Q*
Beef	3.00	250	3.30	320	4.50	350
Pork	2.00	150	2.20	200	2.10	225
Veal	4.00	80	4.50	90	3.64	70
	$P_{95}Q_{95}$	$P_{96}Q_{96}$	$P_{97}Q_{97}$	$P_{95}Q_{96}$	$P_{95}Q_{97}$	
	750	1,056	1,575.0	960	1,050	
	300	440	472.5	400	450	
	320	405	254.8	360	280	
	1,370	1,901	2,302.3	1,720	1,780	

denominator. The Paasche index for 1995 is

$$P_{1995} = \frac{\Sigma(P_{95} \times Q_{95})}{\Sigma(P_{95} \times Q_{95})}(100)$$
$$= \frac{1{,}370}{1{,}370}(100) = 100$$

For 1996, it is

$$P_{1996} = \frac{\Sigma(P_{96} \times Q_{96})}{\Sigma(P_{95} \times Q_{96})}(100)$$
$$= \frac{1{,}901}{1{,}720}(100) = 110.5$$

For 1997, it is

$$P_{1995} = \frac{\Sigma(P_{97} \times Q_{97})}{\Sigma(P_{95} \times Q_{97})}(100)$$
$$= \frac{2{,}302.3}{1{,}780}(100) = 129.3$$

The usual interpretation applies.

The Laspeyres index requires quantity data for only one year and is easier to compute. Therefore, it is used more frequently than the Paasche. Since the base period quantities are always used, more meaningful comparisons over time are permitted.

However, the Laspeyres tends to overweigh goods whose prices increase. This occurs because the increase in price will decrease quantities sold, but the lower quantity will not be reflected by the Laspeyres index because it uses quantities from the base year.

Example 13.6 The Dippy Doo Hair Salon is considering price adjustments in its services. Harriet Follicle, manager of Dippy Doo, wants to calculate Laspeyres and Paasche indexes, using these data for prices and the number of services rendered. January is taken as the base period.

	Price			Quantity		
	Jan	Feb	Mar	Jan	Feb	Mar
Shampoo	$10	$12.00	$16.50	20	22	25
Trim	8	10.50	9.50	25	20	25
Style	12	13.50	14.00	30	31	33

Solution: The Laspeyres is based on the following table:

	Price			Quantity in Jan	$P_R \times Q_{Jan}$		
	Jan	Feb	Mar		Jan	Feb	Mar
Shampoo	$10	$12.00	$16.50	20	200	240.0	330.0
Trim	8	10.50	9.50	25	200	262.5	237.5
Style	12	13.50	14.00	30	360	405.0	420.0
					760	907.5	987.5

$$L_{Jan} = \frac{\Sigma(P_{Jan} \times Q_{Jan})}{\Sigma(P_{Jan} \times Q_{Jan})}(100)$$
$$= \frac{760}{760}(100)$$
$$= 100$$

$$L_{Feb} = \frac{\Sigma(P_{Feb} \times Q_{Jan})}{\Sigma(P_{Jan} \times Q_{Jan})}(100)$$
$$= \frac{907.5}{760}(100)$$
$$= 119.4$$

$$L_{Mar} = \frac{\Sigma(P_{Mar} \times Q_{Jan})}{\Sigma(P_{Jan} \times Q_{Jan})}(100)$$
$$= \frac{987.5}{760}(100)$$
$$= 129.9$$

The Paasche index requires another set of calculations.

	Jan		Feb		Mar	
	P	Q	P	Q	P	Q
Shampoo	10	20	12.00	22	16.50	25
Trim	8	25	10.50	20	9.50	25
Style	12	30	13.50	31	14.00	33

Price × Quantity				
$P_{Jan}Q_{Jan}$	$P_{Feb}Q_{Feb}$	$P_{Mar}Q_{Mar}$	$P_{Jan}Q_{Feb}$	$P_{Jan}Q_{Mar}$
200	264.0	412.5	220	250
200	210.0	237.5	160	200
360	418.5	462.0	372	396
760	892.5	1,112.0	752	846

$$P_{Jan} = \frac{\Sigma(P_{Jan} \times Q_{Jan})}{\Sigma(P_{Jan} \times Q_{Jan})}(100)$$
$$= \frac{760}{760}(100)$$
$$= 100$$

$$P_{Feb} = \frac{\Sigma(P_{Feb} \times Q_{Feb})}{\Sigma(P_{Jan} \times Q_{Feb})}(100)$$
$$= \frac{892.5}{752}(100)$$
$$= 118.7$$

$$P_{Mar} = \frac{\Sigma(P_{Mar} \times Q_{Mar})}{\Sigma(P_{Jan} \times Q_{Mar})}(100)$$
$$= \frac{1{,}112}{846}(100) = 131.4$$

Interpretation: The two indexes produce different results. They are based on different weighting systems. However, it is clear that an increase in prices by Dippy Doo is unwise. Prices have risen by 29.9 percent according to the Laspeyres index and 31.4 percent according to the Paasche index in only three months.

As noted, the Laspeyres tends to overweigh goods whose prices rise, since this price increase is accompanied by a reduction in quantity that is not reflected in the Laspeyres, which uses fixed-base quantities as the weight. The Paasche, on the other hand, tends to overweigh goods whose prices go down. In an effort to offset these shortcomings, **Fisher's ideal index** is sometimes suggested. This index combines the Laspeyres and the Paasche by finding the square root of their products:

$$F = \sqrt{L \times P}$$

The interpretation of the Fisher index is subject to some dispute. For this reason, it is not widely used.

Table 13.15 provides a brief comparison of the advantages and disadvantages of the Laspeyres and Paasche indexes.

Table 13.15 Relative Advantages and Disadvantages of the Laspeyres and Paasche Indexes

	Advantages	Disadvantages
Laspeyres	Requires quantity data for only one time period. Thus: (1) data are obtained more easily, and (2) a more meaningful comparison over time can be made since any changes can be attributed to price movements.	Overweighs goods whose prices increase. Does not reflect changes in buying patterns over time.
Paasche	Reflects changes in buying habits since it uses quantity data for each reference period.	Requires quantity data for each year; these data are often difficult to obtain. Since different quantities are used, it is impossible to attribute differences in the index to price changes alone. Overweighs goods whose prices decrease.

13.8 Specific Indexes

Numerous government agencies as well as the Federal Reserve System (which is not part of the federal government) and private businesses compile different indexes for a variety of purposes. The use for a specific index depends on who is compiling it and what factors go into its formulation. Perhaps the best-known index series is the **consumer price index.**

A. Consumer Price Index

The consumer price index (CPI) is reported monthly by the Bureau of Labor Statistics (BLS) of the U.S. Department of Labor. It was first reported in 1914 as a means to determine whether the wages of industrial workers were keeping pace with the inflation pressures brought on by World War I. Prior to 1978, there was only one CPI. This traditional measure reflected changes in prices of a fixed market basket of about 400 goods and services commonly purchased by "typical" urban and clerical workers. It encompassed about 40 percent of the nation's total population.

In January 1978, the BLS began reporting a more comprehensive index, the consumer price index for all urban consumers. It is called CPI-U, while the older index is CPI-W. The newer CPI-U covers about 80 percent of the population and includes around 3,000 consumer products ranging from basic necessities, such as food, clothing, and housing, to allowances for educational and entertainment expenses. In 1988 both CPI series were rebased from 1967 to 1982–1984.

Both the CPI-W and the CPI-U employ a weighting system for the types of goods and services purchased by consumers. Food, for example, is assigned a weight, or measure of relative importance, of about 18, while housing is given a weight of about 43. Medical care and entertainment each receive a weight of 5. The total weights for all commodities sum to 100. The weights on these products are adjusted about every 10 years. In this manner, the CPI-W and the CPI-U are similar to the Laspeyres index. Technically, the CPI differs slightly from a true Laspeyres because the weighting system used by the CPI is not revised at the same time that the index is rebased. The CPI is therefore sometimes referred to as a *fixed-weight aggregate price index.*

The CPI is highly useful in gauging inflation, measuring "real" changes in monetary values by removing the impact of price changes, and to a limited extent, serving as a cost-of-living index. It is even instrumental in determining raises in Social Security benefits and negotiated wage settlements in labor contracts. Its many uses will be more fully examined in the next section.

B. Other Indexes

The **producer price index** (formerly, the wholesale price index) is also published monthly by the BLS. It measures changes in the prices of goods in primary markets for raw materials used in manufacturing. It, too, is similar to the Laspeyres index and covers almost 3,000 producer goods.

The **industrial production index** is reported by the Federal Reserve System. It is not a monetary measurement, but tracks changes in the volume of industrial output in the nation. The base period is currently 1977.

There are numerous stock market indexes. Perhaps the most well-known is the **Dow Jones industrial average.** This index covers 30 selected industrial stocks to represent the almost 1,800 stocks traded in the New York Stock Exchange. **Standard & Poor's composite index** of 500 industrial stocks is also highly watched.

13.9 Uses for the CPI

Movements in the CPI have a major impact on many business conditions and economic considerations. As noted, the CPI is often viewed as a measure of inflation in the economy. Annual rates of inflation are measured by the percentage change in the CPI from one year to the next. The inflation rate from year to year is

$$\frac{\text{CPI}_t - \text{CPI}_{t-1}}{\text{CPI}_{t-1}} \times 100$$

where CPI_t is the CPI in time period t, and CPI_{t-1} is the CPI in the previous time period.

Table 13.16
CPI and Inflation Rates

Year	CPI	Inflation Rate (%)	Year	CPI	Inflation Rate (%)
1986	109.6		1992	140.3	3.0
1987	113.6	3.6	1993	145.3	3.6
1988	118.3	4.1	1994	148.2	1.9
1989	124.3	5.1	1995	152.4	2.8
1990	127.2	2.3	1996	156.9	3.0
1991	136.2	7.1	1997	158.6	1.1

Table 13.16 shows the CPI for 1986 to 1997 using 1982–1984 as the base. The figures were taken from the *Federal Reserve Bulletin,* published monthly by the Board of

Governors of the Federal Reserve System. The inflation rate for 1987, for example, is

$$\frac{113.6 - 109.6}{109.6}(100) = 3.6\%$$

Changes in the CPI are also often taken as a measure of the cost of living. It is argued, however, that such a practice is questionable. The CPI does not reflect certain costs or expenditures such as taxes, nor does it account for changes in the quality of goods available. Further, the CPI fails to measure other valued items in our economic structure, such as increased leisure time by the average worker or improvements in the variety of commodities from which consumers can choose. Nevertheless, the CPI is often cited in the popular press as a measure of the cost of living.

The CPI is often the basis for adjustments in wage rates, Social Security payments, and even rental and lease agreements. Many labor contracts contain cost-of-living adjustments (COLAs) which stipulate that an increase in the CPI of an agreed-upon amount will automatically trigger a rise in the workers' wage levels.

The CPI can also be used to **deflate** a time series. Deflating a series removes the effect of price changes and expresses the series in *constant* dollars. Economists often distinguish between nominal (or current) dollars and real (or constant) dollars. If a time series, such as your annual income over several years, is expressed in terms of 1982 dollars, that income is said to be real income. Assume your money (nominal) income was as shown in Table 13.17. In 1994, for example, you actually earned $42,110. It would seem that you are doing quite well financially. Your income increased from $42,110 to $53,500 over that time period. However, prices have been going up also. To obtain a measure of how much your income has really increased, in real terms, you must deflate your income stream. This is done by dividing your money income by the CPI and multiplying by 100. The result is your real income expressed in constant (real) dollars of a given base year.

Table 13.17
Money and Real Incomes for Selected Years

Year	Money Income	CPI (1982–84 = 100)	Real Income
1994	$42,110	148.2	28,414
1995	46,000	152.4	30,183
1996	49,800	156.9	31,739
1997	53,500	158.6	33,732

Real Income The purchasing power of money income.

$$\text{Real income} = \frac{\text{Money income}}{\text{CPI}} \times 100$$

You earned $42,110 in 1994, but, as seen in Table 13.17, it was worth only $28,414 in 1982–1984 prices. That is, keeping prices constant at the 1982–1984 level, you are earning an equivalent of only $28,414.

Economists commonly deflate gross national product (GNP) to obtain a measurement of the increase in our nation's real output. **Gross national product** is the monetary value of all final goods and services produced in our economy. By deflating GNP over time, economists eliminate any increase due to price inflation, and arrive at a measure of the actual increase in the production of goods and services available for consumption.

> **Real GNP** A measure of the value of our nation's output in constant dollars in some base period; omits any fluctuation due to changing prices..
>
> $$\text{Real GNP} = \frac{\text{National GNP}}{\text{CPI}} \times 100$$

Section Exercises

14. The costs of ingredients used by Hobson Industries to manufacture candy are shown here for selected months. Develop and explain a simple price index for each ingredient, using May as the base period.

	March	April	May	Jun	July
Sugar	$5.12	$5.89	$6.12	$6.03	$6.29
Gum base	1.15	1.20	2.03	1.96	1.84
Corn oil	0.97	1.04	1.09	1.15	1.25

15. Retail prices for soup and nuts are given here. Calculate a composite price index for both goods, using 1995 as the base. Interpret the results.

	1993	1994	1995	1996	1997
Soup	$2.03	$2.12	$2.35	$2.45	$2.50
Nuts	0.79	0.83	0.94	1.02	1.15

16. During his last three years at State University, Sammy Student's diet has remained unchanged. The prices and quantities for the three commodities that constitute Sammy's main staples are given here. Compute and compare a Laspeyres index and a Paasche index with 1997 as the base.

	Prices			Quantities		
	1996	1997	1998	1996	1997	1998
Pizza	$3.00	$4.50	$5.00	500	700	850
Drink	4.00	4.50	4.50	300	350	400
Pretzels	1.50	2.50	3.00	100	100	90

Solved Problems

1. *a.* Ralph Rhodes wishes to use smoothing techniques to average out and forecast levels of capital investments his firm has made over the past several years. He calculated both three-year and four-year moving averages. The four-year MA, since it contains an even number of terms, must subsequently be centered.

Year	Investment ($1,000)($Y$)	Three-Term MA	Four-Term MA	Centered Four-Term MA
1985	73.2			
1986	68.1	71.37	72.50	
1987	72.8	72.27	72.15	72.33
1988	75.9	73.50	72.45	72.30
1989	71.8	72.33	71.25	71.85
1990	69.3	69.70	69.15	70.20
1991	68.0	68.27	68.68	68.91
1992	67.5	68.47	69.65	69.16
1993	69.9	70.20	71.48	70.56
1994	73.2	72.80	72.83	72.15
1995	75.3	73.80		
1996	72.9			

Using the three-term MA, 73.8 is the estimate of the long-run average around which all observations tend to fall and, as such, is the forecast for any future time period. The four-term MA produces an estimate of 72.15.

2. For the past several years, business conditions for Rainbow Enterprises have been rather black. The CEO has collected quarterly totals of the number of employees who have been laid off over the past four years.

a. The CEO would like to forecast the number of layoffs for the first and second quarters of 1998, using linear trend analysis.

Time	Layoffs (Y)	$t(X)$	XY	X^2
1994-I	25	1	25	1
II	27	2	54	4
III	32	3	96	9
IV	29	4	116	16
1995-I	28	5	140	25
II	32	6	192	36
III	34	7	238	49
IV	38	8	304	64
1996-I	35	9	315	81
II	37	10	370	100
III	37	11	407	121
IV	39	12	468	114
1997-I	38	13	494	169
II	42	14	588	196
III	44	15	660	225
IV	45	16	720	256
	562	136	5,187	1,496

$$SSx = \Sigma X^2 - \frac{(\Sigma X)^2}{n}$$

$$= 1{,}496 - \frac{(136)^2}{16}$$

$$= 340$$

$$SSxy = \Sigma XY - \frac{(\Sigma X)(\Sigma Y)}{n}$$

$$= 5{,}187 - \frac{(136)(562)}{16}$$

$$= 410$$

$$b_1 = \frac{410}{340}$$

$$= 1.206$$

$$b_0 = \overline{Y} - b_1\overline{X}$$

$$= 35.13 - 1.206(8.5)$$

$$= 24.88$$

For the first quarter of 1998,

$$\hat{Y}_t = 24.88 = 1.206(17)$$

$$= 45.38$$

for the second quarter of 1998,

$$\hat{Y}_t = 24.88 = 1.206(18)$$
$$= 46.59$$

b. The CEO now wants to develop the seasonal indexes for the number of layoffs.

Time	Layoffs	Centered MA	Ratio to MA
1994-I	25		
II	27		
III	32	28.625	1.1179
IV	29	29.625	0.9789
1995-I	28	30.500	0.9180
II	32	31.875	1.0039
III	34	33.875	1.0037
IV	38	35.375	1.0742
1996-I	35	36.375	0.9622
II	37	36.875	1.0034
III	37	37.375	0.9900
IV	39	38.375	1.0163
1997-I	38	39.875	0.9530
II	42	41.500	1.0120
III	44		
IV	45		

The four-term (since quarterly data are used) MA is calculated and centered, followed by the ratio to MA. The mean ratio to MA is then determined for each quarter. Since the means sum to 4.0111, the normalization ratio is $4/4.011 = 0.999$. The seasonal indexes are obtained by multiplying each mean ratio to MA by 0.997.

	1994	1995	1996	1997	Mean	Seasonal Indexes
I		0.9180	0.9622	0.9530	0.9444	0.9416
II		1.0039	1.0034	1.0120	1.0064	1.0034
III	1.1179	1.0037	0.9900		1.0372	1.0341
IV	0.9789	1.0742	1.0163		1.0231	1.0200
					4.0111	3.9991 ≈ 4

c. The CEO for Rainbow wants to determine layoffs if the seasonal factors are eliminated. Deseasonalized levels of layoffs for 1994-I and 1994-II are, respectively,

$$\frac{25}{0.9416} = 26.55 \text{ employees}$$

and

$$\frac{27}{1.0034} = 26.91 \text{ employees}$$

d. Rainbow executives think that general movements in the business cycle influence their need to lay off employees. They decide to calculate the cyclical components for each time period.

(1) Time Period	(2) Layoffs	(3) Trend Projection	(4) Seasonal Index	(5) Statistical Norm	(6) Cyclical-Irregular	(7) Cyclical Component
1994-I	25	26.08	0.9416	24.56	101.80	
II	27	27.29	1.0034	27.38	98.61	
III	32	28.49	1.0341	29.46	108.62	100.5
IV	29	29.70	1.0200	30.29	95.73	99.61
1995-I	28	30.90	0.9416	29.10	96.24	98.73
II	32	32.11	1.0034	32.22	99.32	99.01
III	34	33.32	1.0341	34.46	98.68	101.51
IV	38	34.52	1.0200	35.21	107.92	102.55
1996-I	35	35.73	0.9416	33.64	104.03	102.01
II	37	36.93	1.0034	37.06	99.85	100.06
III	37	38.14	1.0341	39.44	93.81	98.15
IV	39	39.35	1.0200	40.14	97.17	97.64
1997-I	38	40.55	0.9416	38.18	99.52	98.34
II	42	41.76	1.0034	41.90	100.23	99.33
III	44	42.96	1.0341	44.42	99.04	
IV	45	44.17	1.0200	45.05	99.88	

They take a four-term MA of the cyclical-irregular values to produce just the cyclical component in column (7). For 1994-III, the layoff of 32 employees represents 100.5 percent of the trend.

e. If layoffs in 1998-I are 46, what might Rainbow expect total layoffs for 1998 to be? Since the first quarter typically repreents a period in which layoffs are only 94.16 percent of the average for the full year, quarterly layoffs based on 46 for 1998-I would be

$$\frac{46}{0.9416} = 48.85$$

For the whole year, layoffs would total (48.85)(4) = 195 employees.

f. In a final effort to control the number of necessary layoffs, Rainbow executives wish to obtain deseasonalized figures for each time period. They obtain these by dividing the actual number of layoffs by the appropriate seasonal (quarterly) index. A partial listing of the results is shown.

Year-Quarter	Layoffs	Seasonal Index	Deseasonalized Layoffs
1994-IV	25	0.9416	26.55
II	27	1.0034	26.91
III	32	1.0341	30.94
IV	29	1.0200	28.43
1995-I	28	0.9416	29.74

3. **The Laspeyres and Paasche Indexes** Your firm manufactures three grades of lubricant. The prices and quantities sold for each are as follows:

	Prices			Quantities		
Grade	Oct	Nov	Dec	Oct	Nov	Dec
A	$3.00	$3.30	$4.00	250	320	350
B	2.00	2.10	2.10	150	200	225
C	4.00	4.50	3.64	80	90	70

a. Calculate the Laspeyres index with October as the base.

$P_{Oct}Q_{Oct}$	$P_{Nov}Q_{Oct}$	$P_{Dec}Q_{Oct}$
750	825	1,125.0
300	330	315.0
320	360	291.2
1,370	1,515	1,731.2

$$L = \frac{\Sigma(P_R \times Q_B)}{\Sigma(P_B \times Q_B)}(100)$$

October:

$$L_{\text{Oct}} = \frac{1,370}{1,370}(100) = 100$$

November:

$$L_{\text{Nov}} = \frac{1,515}{1,370}(100) = 110.58$$

December:

$$L_{\text{Dec}} = \frac{1,731.2}{1,370}(100) = 126.4$$

b. Calculate the Paasche index with October as the base.

$P_{Oct} \times Q_{Oct}$	$P_{Nov} \times Q_{Nov}$	$P_{Dec} \times Q_{Dec}$	$P_{Oct} \times Q_{Nov}$	$P_{Oct} \times Q_{Dec}$
750	1,056	1,575.0	960	1,050
300	440	472.5	400	450
320	405	254.8	360	280
1,370	1,901	2,302.3	1,720	1,780

$$P = \frac{\Sigma(P_R \times Q_R)}{\Sigma(P_B \times Q_R)}(100)$$

October:

$$P_{\text{Oct}} = \frac{1,370}{1,370}(100) = 100$$

November:

$$P_{\text{Nov}} = \frac{1,901}{1,720}(100) = 110.52$$

December:

$$P_{\text{Dec}} = \frac{2,302.3}{1,780}(100) = 129.34.$$

List of Formulas

[13.1]	$Y_{t+1} = Y_t$	The naive forecasting model.
[13.2]	$F_{t+1} = \alpha A_t + (1 - \alpha)F_t$	Forecasts the value in a time series using exponential smoothing.

[13.3]	$$MSE = \frac{\Sigma(F_t - A_t)^2}{n - 1}$$	Calculates the mean square error.
[13.4]	$$\hat{Y}_t = b_0 + b_1 t$$	Estimate for the trend line.
[13.5]	$$SSx = \Sigma X^2 - \frac{(\Sigma X)^2}{n}$$	Sums of squares of X used to compute the trend line.
[13.6]	$$SSxy = \Sigma XY - \frac{(\Sigma X)(\Sigma Y)}{n}$$	Sums of the cross-products of X and Y used to compute the trend line.
[13.7]	$$b_1 = \frac{SSxy}{SSx}$$	Computes the slope of the trend line.
[13.8]	$$b_0 = \overline{Y} - b_1\overline{X}$$	Computes the intercept of the trend line.
[13.9]	$$PI_R = \frac{P_R}{P_B} \times 100$$	A simple price index; measures the relative change in the price of a single good or service from the base period to the reference period.
[13.10]	$$PI_R = \frac{\Sigma P_R}{\Sigma P_B}(100)$$	A composite price index; calculates the index for several goods or services.
[13.11]	$$L = \frac{\Sigma(P_R \times Q_B)}{\Sigma(P_B \times Q_B)}(100)$$	The Laspeyres index uses the quantities in the base year as weights.
[13.12]	$$P = \frac{\Sigma(P_R \times Q_R)}{\Sigma(P_B \times Q_R)}(100)$$	The Paasche index uses quantities in the reference year as weights.

Chapter Exercises

17. Cars-R-Us has recorded sales (in $1,000s) over the last three years of

Month	1996	1997	1998	Month	1996	1997	1998
Jan	17.2	18.1	16.3	July	24.2	23.9	22.7
Feb	18.7	19.2	17.3	Aug	25.7	26.2	25.0
March	19.7	20.3	18.5	Sep	21.2	22.0	21.9
April	20.2	21.5	20.3	Oct	19.3	18.0	17.3
May	21.7	22.0	21.0	Nov	22.7	19.7	21.2
June	23.1	24.7	25.0	Dec	19.3	17.3	16.2

a. Plot the data. Does there appear to be any trend in the data? Any cyclical or seasonal variation?

b. Compute a 12-month moving average. Which component or components do these values reflect?

18. Calculate the seasonal indexes for each month using the data for Cars-R-Us from the previous exercise.

19. In Exercise 17, what are the seasonally adjusted sales figures for the last six months of 1998? How do you interpret them?

20. In Exercise 17, what are the deseasonalized values for the last six months of 1998? How would you interpret them?

21. *Business Monthly* recently reported the dollar value of "perks" received by business executives over the past several years. These data do not include that portion of the executives' health care paid by the employer, and are adjusted for inflation. Use linear trend analysis to predict the value for the year 2000. How well does the model explain the trend in perk levels?

Year	Perk	Year	Perk
1980	$3,200	1989	$4,280
1981	3,640	1990	4,450
1982	3,850	1991	4,500
1983	3,700	1992	4,490
1984	3,920	1993	4,560
1985	3,880	1994	4,680
1986	3,950	1995	4,790
1987	4,100		
1988	4,150		

22. Inventories for Bake-O-Donuts for the past two years were

Month	1995	1996	Month	1995	1996
Jan	$ 87	$ 95	July	$ 80	$83
Feb	93	102	Aug	73	79
March	102	112	Sep	93	84
April	112	115	Oct	102	89
May	93	99	Nov	115	92
June	82	90	Dec	112	91

a. Use a 12-period moving average to remove seasonal variations.
b. Calculate the seasonal indexes.
c. What are the seasonally adjusted inventory levels?

23. Mopeds, Inc., is concerned about slumping sales. If monthly sales fall below $9,000 the Northeast regional office must be closed down. According to the figures shown here, is that likely to occur within the next five months? Figures are in thousands.

					1996						
J	F	M	A	M	J	J	A	S	O	N	D
18	17.3	16.9	18.1	16.8	16.3	15.1	14.5	14	14.5	14	13.1
					1997						
13.9	13.1	12.8	12.4	11.8	11.9	11.7	11.5	11.1	11.2	11.2	11.1

24. Using the data from the previous exercise, calculate the seasonal indexes.

25. Using the data for Mopeds, Inc., what is the strength of the relationship between sales and time? Plot the trend line against the actual data.

26. From the regression model you calculated in the exercise for Mopeds, Inc., what is the average monthly change in sales?

27. John Wolf feels that exponential smoothing with an α-value of 0.8 can best forecast September inventories of his medical supply firm. His brother and business partner thinks an α of 0.4 should be used. What is the forecast in each case? Who is correct, based on the values shown

below for inventories per month?

Inventories	J	F	M	A	M	J	J	A
($100)	41	48	37	32	45	43	49	38

28. Three Finger Louis, the town's only butcher, is concerned about the volume of customers' bad debt he must write off as uncollectable each month. Dollar amounts in hundreds are shown here for the past three years.

					1995						
14.1	13.7	12.1	13.1	13.5	9.1	7.2	6.1	8.7	10.1	11.8	12.2
					1996						
15.2	14.1	13.2	13.9	14.0	9.5	7.2	6.5	9.1	11.5	12.2	13.4
					1997						
13.7	12.5	11.8	12.0	13.0	8.7	6.3	6.0	8.2	9.8	10.9	11.8

a. Plot the data. Does a seasonal factor seem to exist? (Consider a "season" to be one month.)
b. Use a 12-month moving average to smooth out the seasonal variation.
c. Calculate seasonal indexes.
d. Deseasonalize the data.
e. Plot the original data and the deseasonalized data.

29. Packer Industries is concerned that sales may fall below $100,000 in December. Using the data shown below in thousands of dollars, what is your projection? Plot the data first.

Jan	Feb	Mar	Apr	May	June	July	Aug
42.7	57.3	68.3	76.8	84	88.1	90	90.1

30. *U.S. News & World Report* stated that projections by the U.S. Department of Commerce for median earnings of full-time workers were

Year	Earnings ($1,000)	Year	Earnings ($1,000)
1990	24.28	2020	90.94
1995	30.26	2025	113.33
2000	37.71	2030	171.23
2005	47.00	2035	176.00
2010	58.56	2040	219.33
2015	73.00		

a. Plot the data.
b. Compute the trend model.
c. What is the projection for the year 2050?

31. Milles Products recorded the profits shown in the table.

a. Use exponential smoothing to forecast future profits. First, set $\alpha = 0.2$, then 0.9.
b. Which α-value produces a more reliable estimate?

c. How could you have known this beforehand?

Week	1	2	3	4	5	6	7
Profits ($1,000)	10	25	3	15	2	27	5

32. Consumer data supplied by the U.S. Department of Commerce for the summer of 1998 revealed the following:

	Unit	Prices 1996	Prices 1997	Prices 1998
Beef	1 pound	$3.12	$3.89	$3.92
Milk	1 gallon	2.10	2.42	2.51
Chicken	1 pound	1.95	2.10	2.12
Bread	1 loaf	0.99	0.89	1.12

Compute and interpret the simple index for each commodity using 1996 as the base period.

33. Given the data from the previous problem, compute

a. The percentage increase in the price of each product for
1996 to 1997.
1996 to 1998.
1997 to 1998.

b. The percentage point increase for each product for
1996 to 1997.
1996 to 1998.
1997 to 1998.

34. Below are costs for a one-day stay in the hospital. Use 1993 as the base year and compute the simple index. Interpret the index obtained for 1990.

1990	1991	1992	1993	1994	1995
$356	$408	$512	$589	$656	$689

35. Sammy Studd wants to purchase an entire new wardrobe of athletic wear for the summer. He has collected the data shown below and wonders how prices have changed over the past three years. Compute and interpret the composite price index for all four goods, using 1996 as the base year.

	1996	1997	1998
Shoes	$89.90	$115.12	$125.00
Sweats	52.50	65.50	75.50
Shorts	25.75	35.95	45.90
Socks	12.10	10.00	9.50

36. Prices for a new line of toy dolls by The Krazy Kid Kollection are shown below. Using 1994–1995 as the base period, calculate a simple price index for all three toys.

	1994	1995	1996
Killer Joe	$17.90	$21.50	$25.00
Pyro Phil	15.00	25.00	29.95
Maniac Mark	10.00	11.00	12.00

37. Bell electronic wishes to analyze price changes for three of its products over the past three years. The necessary data are given here.

	Prices			Quantities		
Product	1996	1997	1998	1996	1997	1998
A	$10.00	$15.50	$20.00	150	170	160
B	3.00	5.00	7.50	55	68	120
C	69.00	75.00	75.00	100	90	85

38. Compute and interpret the Laspeyres and Paasche indexes using 1996 as the base period. Using the data from the previous exercise, compute the Fisher index.

39. Pam McGuire, the director of operations for Columbia Records, compiled the following data on recording costs and the number of times each item was used over the last three years for three items commonly used in the recording business.

	Cost per Usage			Usage Frequency		
	1996	1997	1998	1996	1997	1998
Studio costs	$120	$145	$165	30	35	37
Recording equipment	420	530	620	40	43	46
Backup singers	300	250	250	50	63	72

Sam O'Donnell, the director of statistical procedures, must calculate a Laspeyres index and a Paasche index, using 1996 as the base, and must then determine the rate at which costs have risen each year under both indexes, as well as the rate of inflation over all three years.

40. From Exercise 39, which index is probably a better measure of Columbia's rise in costs? Why? Support your choice.

41. Just Pizza bought the amounts of ingredients at the prices shown in the table below. Janet Jackson, manager of Just Pizza, is worried about rising prices. Develop Laspeyres and Paasche indexes for her, using January as the base.

	Price/Pound				Pounds Used (100's)			
	Jan	Feb	Mar	Apr	Jan	Feb	Mar	Apr
Cheese	2.10	2.15	2.20	2.25	10	12	15	12
Pepperoni	1.18	1.20	1.25	1.31	8	10	8	10
Sausage	1.25	1.31	1.35	1.42	7	6	7	7

42. Using Janet's data from the previous exercise, does the Paasche index show that the rate at which prices are going up is increasing or decreasing?

Computer Exercise

Spark Industries has been suffering a noticeable drop in profits over the past several years. While the price of its product has remained fairly stable, the number of employees necessary to maintain production has shown a pronounced upward trend, causing labor costs to rise dramatically.

To curb this undesirable trend, you have been charged with the responsibility of analyzing Spark's price levels and number of employees. Access the file SPARK on your data disk. It contains

50 observations of quarterly data for the retail price of their product (PRICE) and for the number of employees (EMPL).

You must use smoothing techniques to forecast future prices and provide a complete decomposition of the time series data for employees. Prepare your findings in a statistical report as described in Appendix I.

CURTAIN CALL

In Setting the Stage at the opening of this chapter, we noted how Mr. Dickson uses statistical analysis in making business decisions. As owner and chief executive officer, he places considerable importance on careful planning and the timing of his operations.

Mr. Dickson has hired you as an outside statistical consultant to provide him with valuable information about his business that he feels will prove highly useful in formulating future plans. Specifically, your task is to predict profits using a four-period moving average based on the data below. Further, you are to compare this projection to that obtained through exponential smoothing. Mr. Dickson has not specified an alpha value for the smoothing constant and expects you to determine what value is optimal.

Finally, the sales of the firm are also of concern to Mr. Dickson. Given the data provided here, you must develop and interpret a trend line as well as decompose the time series by breaking out each component individually. Present your final report to Mr. Dickson in the form of a statistical report as described in Appendix I. Include all relevant results as well as your interpretation.

Time Period	Profits ($00)	Revenues ($000)	Time Period	Profits ($00)	Revenues ($000)
1995-I	25	10	1997-I	32	25
II	29	12	II	28	20
III	24	15	III	33	26
IV	28	14	IV	31	32
1996-I	31	17	1998-I	24	34
II	27	19	II	35	38
III	24	17	III	28	41
IV	28	21	IV	25	45

From the Stage to Real Life

Mr. Dickson, the industrial business owner of the Setting the Stage chapter opening, believes that changes in the overall economic climate affect the values of his profits and sales revenues. In fact, he would be able to investigate the extent that the general economy affects the value of his profits by adjusting them for changes in the overall price level, using the CPI (consumer price index) published by the U.S. Department of Labor. He also is able to compare his sales levels to both the GDP (gross domestic product) and the final sales of all U.S. finished goods, using indexes published by the U.S. Department of Commerce.

These indexes are available on the Internet. To locate the CPI data, go to the statistics location of the Department of Labor (*http://stats.bls.gov:80/*). Once there, choose the "Data" area. Then click on "Most Requested Series." At the next page, click on "Overall Most Requested Series." The following page allows you to select the index, the years covered, and the data delivery format you desire. Scroll down to the heading "Price Indexes" and choose CPI for All Urban Consumers 1982–1984 = 100. Further down this page, choose the years for your analysis, say 1987–1997. Last, on this same page, select the Table of your choice under the "Format" heading. This completes your request for data. Clicking on "Retrieve" produces the CPI data of interest to you.

GDP and Final sales of goods are found at the Department of Commerce site (*http://www.doc.gov/*). At the home page, click on "Commerce Web Sites (arranged by bureau)." Next, click on the "Bureau of Economic Analysis" (BEA). Then choose the BEA data area. Click on "National." Scroll down to the heading "Historical time series" and click on "Tables." Here you can choose to click on either "GDP and final sales, Annually" or "GDP and final sales, Quarterly" for the data of your interest.

CHAPTER 14

Chi-Square and Other Nonparametric Tests

Chapter Blueprint

Many of the tests we performed in previous chapters required certain basic assumptions before the test could be carried out. We assumed that the population was normally distributed or that variances fit particular patterns. When those assumptions cannot be made, or essential knowledge about the population is not attainable, we have to rely on the nonparametric tests contained in this chapter.

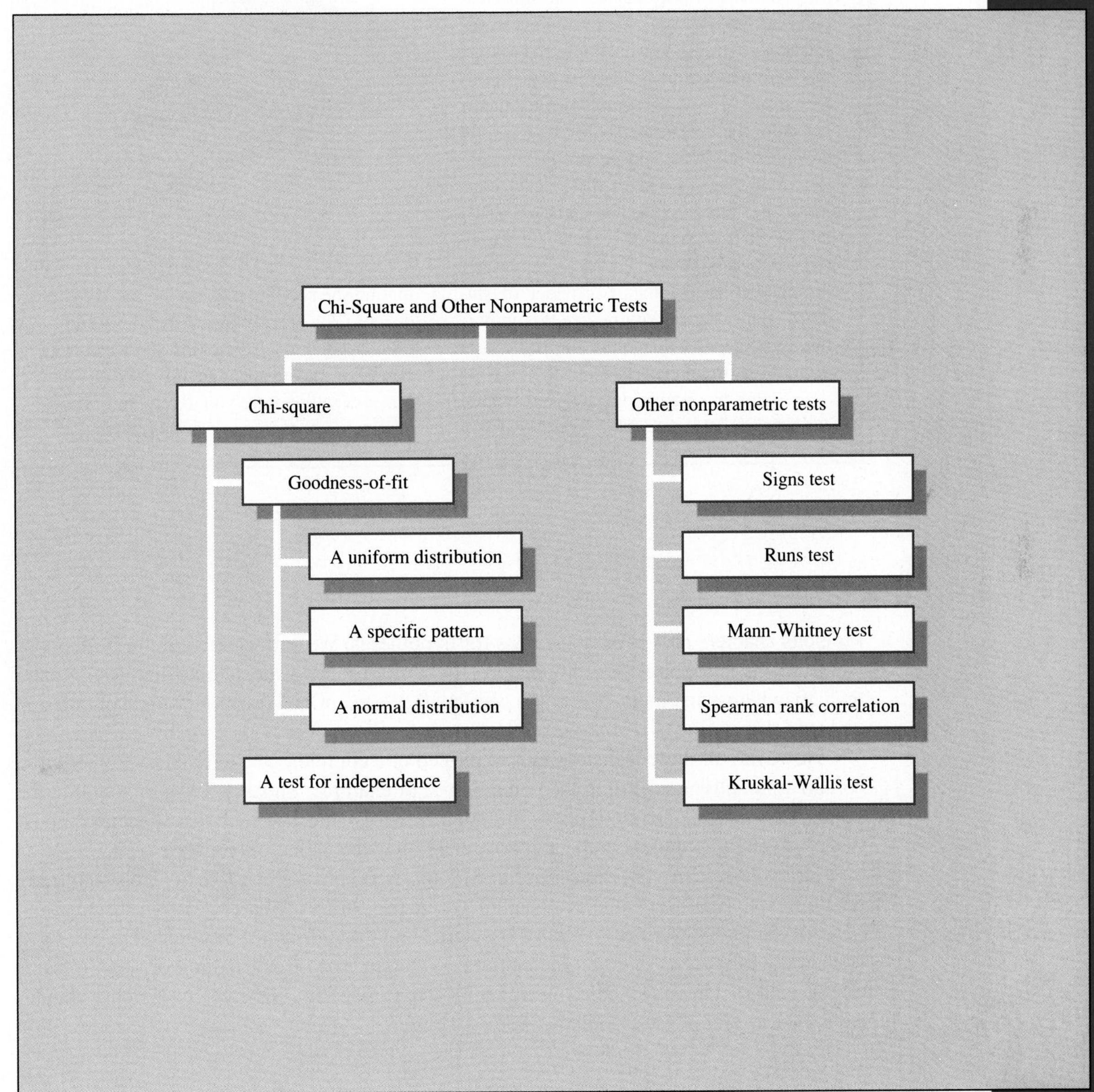

SETTING THE STAGE

For many years Mama's Pizzeria has been a popular hangout for students at the nearby university. This year, however, Mama has faced vigorous competition from Dante's, a new business that opened on the other side of the campus. Dante's offers an extensive menu that attracts many students eager to sample the new fare.

Mama has decided that she must expand her selection or lose customers to the interloper who has intruded into the market that before had been exclusively hers. Mama recognizes this will require many delicate decisions that can be made only after careful consideration of the consequences.

In order to make these decisions, Mama has hired you as her statistical assistant to analyze the market, evaluate the alternatives, and devise a plan to regain her prominence as the major provider of students' staple needs. You realize this important assignment will require the full extent of your statistical expertise.

Mama has agreed to pay you in food and drink for the rest of the semester if you can help her. Spurred by this generous offer, you are determined to provide Mama with the best possible advice.

After careful thought, you determine what data you must collect, how they must be organized, and precisely what tests you must run to provide Mama with the information she needs to make some pressing decisions. You are also aware that the assumptions needed to carry out the statistical tests you have studied so far are not valid and that this task will require you to rely on the nonparametric tests covered in this chapter.

14.1 Introduction

Previous chapters presented many tests for hypotheses. We performed tests for both population means and population proportions. In some instances the sample size was greater than 30, whereas in others the sample was small. We examined tests for a single population and tests comparing two or more populations.

However, all these test situations exhibited one common characteristic: they required certain assumptions regarding the population. For example, t-tests and F-tests required the assumption that the population was normally distributed. Since such tests depend on postulates about the population and its parameters, they are called **parametric tests.**

In practice, many situations arise in which it is simply not possible to safely make any assumptions about the value of a parameter or the shape of the population distribution. Most of the tests described in earlier chapters would therefore not be applicable. We must instead use other tests that do not depend on a single type of distribution or specific parametric values. These are called **nonparametric** (or distribution-free) **tests.** This chapter examines several of these statistical tools.

Nonparametric Tests Statistical procedures that can be used to test hypotheses when no assumptions regarding parameters or population distributions are possible.

14.2 Chi-Square Distribution (χ^2)

One of the more useful nonparametric tools is the chi-square (χ^2) test. Like the t-distribution, the chi-square distribution is an entire family of distributions. There is a different chi-square distribution for each degree of freedom. Figure 14.1 shows that as the number of degrees of freedom increases, the chi-square distribution becomes less skewed. The two most common applications of chi-square are (1) goodness-of-fit tests and (2) tests for independence. We will examine each in turn.

Figure 14.1
The Chi-Square Distribution

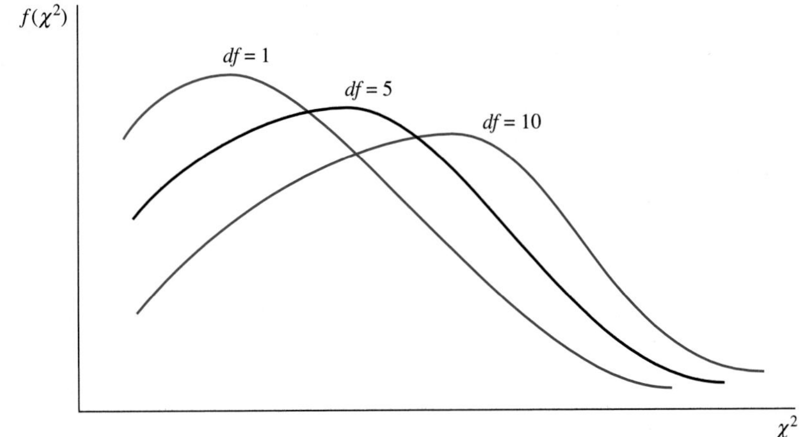

A. Goodness-of-Fit Tests

Business decisions often require that we test some hypothesis about the unknown population distribution. We might, for instance, hypothesize that the population distribution is uniform and that all possible values have the same probability of occurring. The hypotheses that we would test are

H_0: The population distribution is uniform.

H_A: The population distribution is not uniform.

The goodness-of-fit test is then used to determine whether the distribution of values in the population fits a particular hypothesized shape—in this case, a uniform distribution. As with all the statistical tests of this nature, sample data are taken from the population and these form the foundation for our findings.

Goodness-of-Fit Tests Measures of how closely observed sample data fit a particular hypothesized distribution. If the fit is reasonably close, it may be concluded that the hypothesized distribution exists.

If there is a large difference between what is actually observed in the sample and what you would expect to observe if the null hypothesis were correct, then it is less likely that the null is true. That is, the null hypothesis must be rejected when the observations obtained in the sample differ significantly from the pattern that is expected to occur if the hypothesized distribution does exist.

For example, if a fair die is rolled, it is reasonable to hypothesize a pattern in the outcomes such that each outcome (numbers 1 through 6) occurs approximately one-sixth of the time. However, if a significantly large or significantly small percentage of even numbers occurs, it may be concluded that the die is not properly balanced and that the hypothesis is false. That is, if the difference between the pattern of events actually observed and the pattern of events expected to occur if the null is correct proves too great to attribute to sampling error, it must be concluded that the population exhibits a distribution other than that specified in the null hypothesis.

To test the hypothesis regarding a population distribution, we must analyze the difference between our expectations based on the hypothesized distribution and the actual data occurring in the sample. This is precisely what the chi-square goodness-of-fit test does. It determines if the sample observations "fit" our expectations. The test takes the form

Chi-square test

$$\chi^2 = \sum_{i=1}^{K} \frac{(O_i - E_i)^2}{E_i} \qquad [14.1]$$

where O_i is the frequency of observed events in the sample data
E_i is the frequency of expected events if the null is correct
K is the number of categories or classes

The test carries $K - m - 1$ degrees of freedom, where m is the number of parameters to be estimated. The exact impact of m will become more apparent as our discussion progresses.

Notice that the numerator of Formula [14.1] measures the difference between the frequencies of the observed events and the frequencies of the expected events. When these differences are large, causing χ^2 to rise, the null should be rejected.

1. A test for a Uniform Fit Chris Columbus, marketing director for Seven Seas, Inc., has the responsibility of controlling the inventory level for four types of sailboats sold by his firm. In the past he has ordered new boats on the premise that all four types are equally popular and the demand for each type is the same. Recently, however, inventories have become more difficult to control, and Chris feels that he should test his hypothesis regarding a uniform demand. His hypotheses are

H_0: Demand is uniform for all four types of boats.

H_A: Demand is not uniform for all four types of boats.

By assuming uniformity in demand, the null hypothesis presumes that out of a random sample of sailboats, weekend sailors would purchase an equal number of each type. To test this hypothesis, Chris selects a sample of $n = 48$ boats sold over the past several months. If demand is uniform, he can expect that $48/4 = 12$ boats of each type were sold. Table 14.1 shows this expectation, along with the number of each type that actually was sold. Notice that $\Sigma(O_i) = \Sigma(E_i)$. Chris must now determine whether the numbers actually sold in each

Table 14.1
Seven Seas Sales Record

Type of Boat	Observed Sales (O_i)	Expected Sales (E_i)
Pirates' Revenge	15	12
Jolly Roger	11	12
Bluebeard's Treasure	10	12
Ahab's Quest	12	12
	48	48

Figure 14.2
A Chi-Square Test for Seven Seas

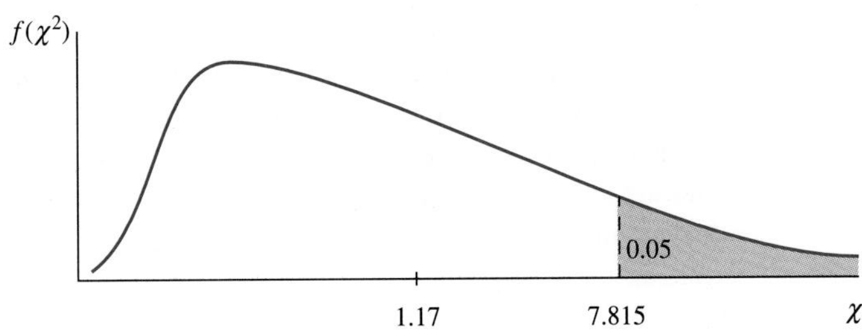

of the $K = 4$ categories are close enough to what he would expect if demand was uniform. Formula [14.1] gives

$$\chi^2 = \frac{(15-12)^2}{12} + \frac{(11-12)^2}{12} + \frac{(10-12)^2}{12} + \frac{(12-12)^2}{12}$$
$$= 1.17$$

The value 1.17 is then compared with a critical χ^2-value taken from Table H in Appendix III. Since there were no parameters that had to be estimated, $m = 0$ and there are $K - 1 = 3$ degrees of freedom. If Chris wanted to test at the 5 percent level, he would find, as shown in Figure 14.2, that $\chi^2_{0.05,3} = 7.815$.

Decision Rule Do not reject if $\chi^2 \leq 7.815$. Reject if $\chi^2 > 7.815$.

Since $1.17 < 7.815$, the null hypothesis that demand is uniform is not rejected. The differences between what was actually observed, O_i, and what Chris would expect to observe if demand was the same for all four types of sailboats, E_i, are not large enough to refute the null. The differences are not significant and can be attributed merely to sampling error.

Minitab can be used to perform the calculations. Merely input the data for the observed frequencies in the first column and the data for the expected frequencies in the second column. In the session window, type

```
MTB> LET K1 = SUM((C1 - C2)**2/C2)
MTB> PRINT K1.
```

The first line tells Minitab to calculate Formula [14.1]. The second line tells Minitab to report back the chi-square statistic. Using the data for Chris' boats, the value of 1.16667 is returned.

The p-value for the test is the area to the right of our sample findings of 1.17 as seen in Figure 14.2. We can see only that it is greater than 5 percent. Minitab will also compute the p-value by

```
MTB> CDF K1 K2;
SUBC> CHISQUARE 1.
MTB> LET K3 = 1 - K2
MTB> PRINT K3.
```

Minitab will return the p-value of 0.280087.

2. A Test for a Fit to a Specific Pattern In our example regarding the sailboats, Chris assumed that the demand for all four types of sailboats was the same. The values for the expected frequencies were therefore all the same. However, many instances arise in which frequencies are tested against a certain pattern in which expected frequencies are not all the same. Instead, they must be determined as

Expected frequencies $$E_i = np_i \qquad [14.2]$$

where n is the sample size

p_i is the probability of each category as specified in the null hypothesis

Example 14.1 demonstrates.

Example 14.1 The John Dillinger First National Bank in New York City tries to follow a policy of extending 60 percent of its loans to business firms, 10 percent to individuals, and 30 percent to foreign borrowers.

To determine whether this policy is being followed, Jay Hoover, vice-president of marketing, randomly selects 85 loans that were recently approved. He finds that 62 of those loans were extended to businesses, 10 to individuals, and 13 to foreign borrowers. At the 10 percent level, does it appear the bank's desired portfolio pattern is being preserved? Test the hypothesis that

H_0: The desired pattern is maintained: 60 percent are business loans, 10 percent are individual loans, and 30 percent are foreign loans.

H_A: The desired pattern is not maintained.

Solution: If the null hypothesis is correct, Mr. Hoover would expect 60 percent of the 85 loans in the sample to be business loans. So, for the first category, $E_i = np_i = (85)(0.60) = 51$ loans to businesses. In addition, he would expect that $(85)(0.10) = 8.5$ of the loans would be to individuals, and $(85)(0.30) = 25.5$ loans to foreign customers. The data are summarized in the table.

Type of Loan	Observed Frequencies (O_i)	Expected Frequencies (E_i)
Business	62	51.0
Private	10	8.5
Foreign	13	25.5
	85	85.0

The χ^2-value is

$$\chi^2 = \frac{(62 - 51)^2}{51} + \frac{(10 - 8.5)^2}{8.5} + \frac{(13 - 25.5)^2}{25.5}$$

$$= 8.76$$

Again, no parameters were estimated and $m = 0$. With α set at 10 percent and $K = 3$ categories of loans (business, private, and foreign), there are $K - m - 1$ or $3 - 0 - 1 = 2$ degrees of freedom. Mr. Hoover finds from Table H in Appendix III that the critical $\chi^2_{0.10,2} = 4.605$.

Decision Rule Do not reject the null if $\chi^2 \leq 4.605$. Reject the null if $\chi^2 > 4.605$.

As shown by the figure, the null should be rejected since $8.76 > 4.605$.

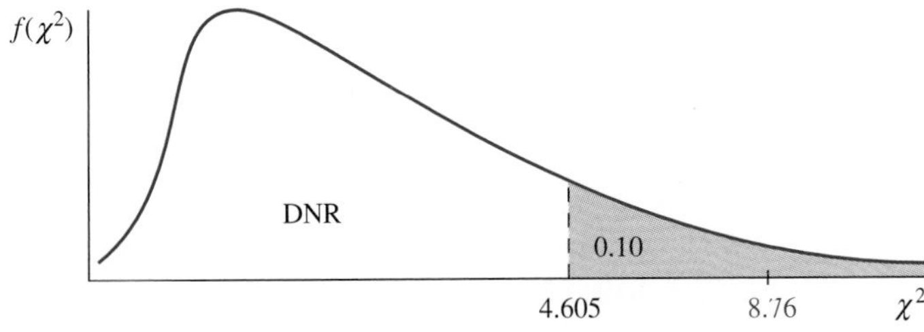

Interpretation: The differences between what Mr. Hoover observed and what he would expect to observe if the desired loan pattern was achieved is too great to occur by chance. There is only a 10 percent probability that a sample of 85 randomly selected loans could produce the observed frequencies shown here if the desired pattern in the bank's loan portfolio was being maintained.

---

3. A Test for Normality Specifications for the production of air tanks used in scuba diving require that the tanks be filled to a mean pressure of 600 pounds per square inch (psi). A standard deviation of 10 psi is allowed. Safety allowances permit a normal distribution in fill levels. You have just been hired by Aqua Lung, a major manufacturer of scuba equipment. Your first assignment is to determine whether fill levels fit a normal distribution. Aqua Lung is certain that the mean of 600 psi and the standard deviation of 10 psi prevail. Only the nature of the distribution remains to be tested. In this effort, you measure $n =$ 1,000 tanks and find the distribution shown in Table 14.2. Your hypotheses are

H_0: Fill levels are normally distributed.

H_A: Fill levels are not normally distributed.

As before, the test requires that you compare these actual observations with those you would expect to find if normality prevailed. To determine these expected frequencies, you must calculate the probabilities that tanks selected at random would have fill levels in the intervals shown in Table 14.2. The probability that a tank would fall in the first interval is

Table 14.2
Fill Levels for Scuba Tanks

PSI	Actual Frequency
0 and under 580	20
580 and under 590	142
590 and under 600	310
600 and under 610	370
610 and under 620	128
620 and above	30
	1,000

$P(0 < X < 580)$. The problem facing you is depicted in Figure 14.3(a). You must determine the shaded area under the curve. Thus,

$$Z = \frac{X - \mu}{\sigma}$$

$$Z = \frac{580 - 600}{10}$$

$$= -2, \text{ or an area of } 0.4772$$

Then

$$P(0 < X < 580) = 0.5000 - 0.4772 = 0.0228$$

There is slightly more than a 2 percent chance that any tank selected at random would have a fill level less than 580 psi if the mean fills are 600 psi with a standard deviation of 10 psi and are distributed normally. For the second interval, the probability that a tank selected at random would have a fill level between 580 and 590 is $P(580 < X < 590)$, and is shown in Figure 14.3(b).

$$Z_1 = \frac{580 - 600}{10}$$

$$= -2, \text{ or an area of } 0.4772$$

$$Z_2 = \frac{590 - 600}{10}$$

$$= -1, \text{ or an area of } 0.3413$$

Then

$$P(580 < X < 590) = 0.4772 - 0.3413 = 0.1359$$

Figure 14.3 Probabilities of Tank Fills

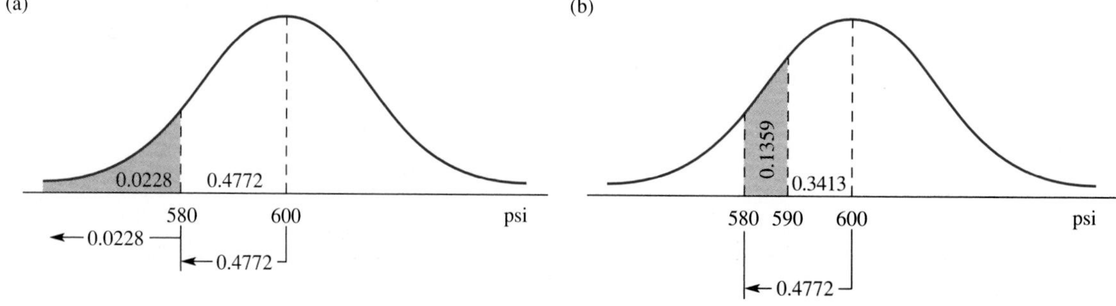

The probabilities for the remaining intervals are calculated in like fashion and are shown in Table 14.3, along with the expected frequencies. The expected frequencies, as before, are $E_i = np_i$. For the first interval this becomes (1,000)(0.0228) = 22.8. You wish to test the hypothesis at the 5 percent level. Since both the population mean and the standard deviation were given and do not have to be estimated, $m = 0$. There are $K = 6$ classes in the frequency table, so the degrees of freedom are $K - 1 = 5$. You find the critical χ^2 to be $\chi^2_{0.05,5} = 11.07$.

Table 14.3
Probabilities of Fill Levels

PSI	Actual Frequency (O_i)	Probabilities (p_i)	Expected Frequency (E_i)
0 and under 580	20	0.0228	22.8
580 and under 590	142	0.1359	135.9
590 and under 600	310	0.3413	341.3
600 and under 610	370	0.3413	341.3
610 and under 620	128	0.1359	135.9
620 and above	30	0.0228	22.8
	1,000	1.0000	1000.0

Decision Rule Do not reject the null if χ^2 is less than 11.07. Reject the null if χ^2 is greater than 11.07.

Using Formula [14.1], you find

$$\chi^2 = \frac{(20 - 22.8)^2}{21.5} + \frac{(142 - 135.9)^2}{135.9} + \cdots + \frac{(30 - 22.8)^2}{21.5}$$
$$= 8.63$$

As shown in Figure 14.4, the null should not be rejected. The differences between what were observed and what you would expect to observe if the fills were normally distributed with a mean of 600 and a standard deviation of 10 can be attributed to sampling error.

Had the population mean and standard deviation not been known, we would have had to estimate them from the sample data in Table 14.2. Then m would be 2, and the degrees of freedom would be $K - 2 - 1$ or $6 - 2 - 1 = 3$.

Caution: The chi-square test for goodness-of-fit is reliable only if all E_i are at least 5. If a class has an $E_i < 5$, it must be combined with adjacent classes to ensure that all $E_i \geq 5$. Had you selected a sample of only $n = 100$ instead of 1,000 scuba tanks, the E_i for the first class would have been $E_i = np_i = (100)(0.0228) = 2.28$ instead of 22.8. This first class would be combined with the second class so that $E_i \geq 5$. Similarly, class 6 would

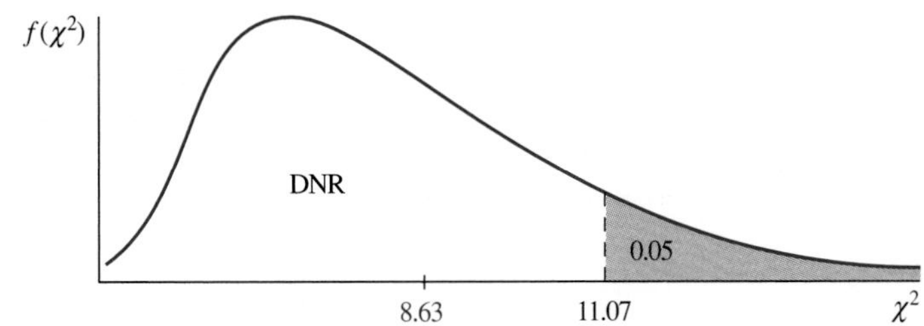

Figure 14.4
Chi-Square Test for Normality

have an $E_i = 2.28$ and would be combined with class 5. Of course, the degrees of freedom are reduced accordingly.

What would happen if you set the first class at "570 and under 580" and the last one at "620 and under 630" to keep all intervals equal? Very little. The $P(X_i)$ would not quite equal 1, and $\Sigma(E_i)$ would not quite equal $\Sigma(O_i)$. However, it would be entirely possible to do so.

Again, Minitab will produce the desired results. Minitab Display 14.1 contains the input commands and the resulting output. The p-value is $0.00329876 < 0.05$, leading to the rejection of the null.

Minitab Display 14.1

```
MTB > let k1 = sum((c1 - c2)**2/c2)   [Calculates the chi-square value]
MTB > print k1

Data Display

K1        8.63444        [The chi-square value]
MTB > cdf k1 k2;
SUBC> chisquare 1.                    [Calculates the p-value]
MTB > let k3 = 1 - k2
MTB > print k3

Data Display

K3        0.00329876     [The p-value]
MTB >
```

B. Contingency Tables—A Test for Independence

Notice that in all the problems so far, there was one and only one factor that captured our interest. However, chi-square will also permit the comparison of two attributes to determine whether there is a relationship between them. A retailer may want to discover whether there is a connection between consumers' income levels and their preference for his product. Production managers are always concerned about any relationship that might exist between the productivity of their employees and the type or degree of training they received.

Wilma Keeto is the director of product research at Dow Chemical. In her current project Ms. Keeto must determine whether there is any relationship between the effectiveness rating consumers assign to a new insecticide and the location (urban or rural) in which it is used. Of the 100 consumers surveyed, 75 lived in urban areas and 25 in rural areas. Table 14.4 summarizes the ratings by each consumer in a contingency table like those discussed in Chapter 4.

The table has $r = 3$ rows and $c = 2$ columns. There are $rc = 6$ cells in the table. Notice, for example, that 31 customers rated the product "above average"; 20 of those were in urban areas.

Table 14.4
Contingency Table for Dow Chemical

	Attribute B—Location		
Attribute A—Rating	**Urban**	**Rural**	**Total**
Above average	20	11	31
Average	40	8	48
Below average	15	6	21
Total	75	25	100

Ms. Keeto wants to compare attribute B (location) to attribute A (the product's rating). Her hypotheses are

H_0: Rating and location are independent.

H_A: Rating and location are not independent.

If location has no impact on effectiveness rating, then the percentage of urban residents who rated the product "above average" should equal the percentage of rural residents who rated the product "above average." This percentage in turn should equal that of all users who rated the product "above average."

As shown in Table 14.4 above, 31 percent of all 100 users rated the product "above average." Then 31 percent of the 75 urban residents and 31 percent of the 25 rural residents should also give this rating if rating and location are independent. These values of $(75)(0.31) = 23.3$ and $(25)(0.31) = 7.75$ give the expected frequencies E_i for each cell, as shown in Table 14.5.

Table 14.5
Rating Frequencies

	Attribute B		
Attribute A	Urban	Rural	Totals
Above average	$O_i = 20$ $E_i = 23.3$	$O_i = 11$ $E_i = 7.75$	31
Average	$O_i = 40$ $E_i = 36$	$O_i = 8$ $E_i = 12$	48
Below average	$O_i = 15$ $E_i = 15.8$	$O_i = 6$ $E_i = 5.25$	21
Total	75	25	100

The remaining E_i are calculated in similar fashion and displayed in Table 14.5. For example, 48 percent of the 100 users rated the product as "average." Therefore, if the null is correct, 48 percent of the 75 urban customers should also rate the product "average," and 48 percent of the 25 rural consumers should record a rating of "average." The E_i are calculated as $(75)(0.48) = 36$ and $(25)(0.48) = 12$. Similarly, since 21 of the 100 users, or 21 percent, rated the product "below average," then 21 percent of the 75 people living in urban centers ($E_i = 15.8$) and 21 percent of the 25 living in rural areas ($E_i = 5.25$) should provide a "below average" rating.

Testing the hypothesis requires a comparison of O_i and E_i over the $rc = 6$ cells, using the equation

Chi-square test

$$\chi^2 = \sum_{i=1}^{rc} \frac{(O_i - E_i)^2}{E_i} \qquad [14.3]$$

For the current problem, Wilma finds

$$\begin{aligned} \chi^2 &= \frac{(20 - 23.3)^2}{23.3} + \frac{(11 - 7.75)^2}{7.75} + \frac{(40 - 36)^2}{36} \\ &\quad + \frac{(8 - 12)^2}{12} + \frac{(15 - 15.8)^2}{15.8} + \frac{(6 - 5.25)^2}{5.25} \\ &= 3.76 \end{aligned}$$

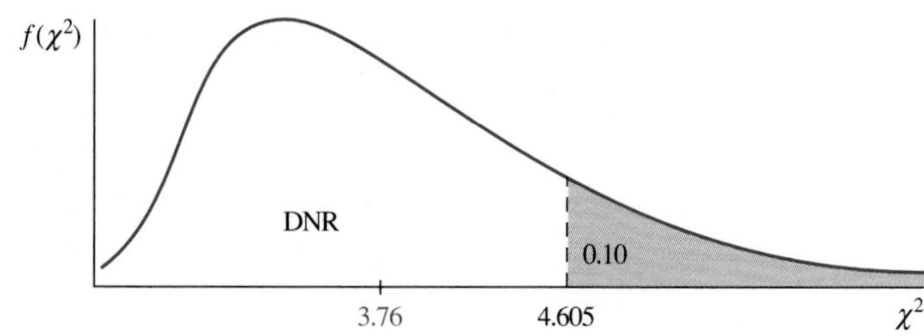

Figure 14.5
Chi-Square Test of Independence

The test carries $(r - 1)(c - 1) = (3 - 1)(2 - 1) = 2$ degrees of freedom. If Wilma set $\alpha = 10$ percent, $\chi^2_{0.10,2} = 4.605$. As Figure 14.5 shows, the null is not rejected according to the decision rule:

Decision Rule Do not reject the null if $\chi^2 \leq 4.605$. Reject if $\chi^2 > 4.605$.

Minitab Display 14.2 is obtained by placing the data for urban customers in column 1 and those for rural residents in column 2 and then clicking on **STAT > TABLES > CHISQUARE TEST.**

Minitab Display 14.2

```
Chi-Square Test

Expected counts are printed below observed counts

            C1        C2     Total
1           20        11        31   — The top number in each cell is Oi.
         23.25      7.75             — The bottom number is Ei.

2           40         8        48
         36.00     12.00

3           15         6        21
         15.75      5.25

Total       75        25       100

Chisq =  0.454 +  1.363 +
         0.444 +  1.333 +
         0.036 +  0.107 = 3.738
df = 2, p = 0.155
```

Notice that the chi-square value of 3.738 and the p-value of 0.155 are reported.

Example 14.2 provides further illustration.

Example 14.2 Hedonistic Auto Sales sets out to determine whether there is any relationship between income of customers and the importance they attach to the price of luxury automobiles. The company's managers want to test the hypotheses that

H_0: Income and importance of price are independent.

H_A: Income and importance of price are not independent.

Solution: Customers are grouped into three income levels and asked to assign a level of significance to price in the purchase decision. Results are shown in the contingency table. Since $182/538 = 33.83$ percent of all respondents attach a "great" level of importance to price, then, if income and price are not related, we would expect 33.83 percent of those in each income bracket to respond that price was of "great" importance. Thus, the E_i for a "low" level of importance are (198) (0.3383) = 66.98, (191)(0.3383) = 64.62, and (149)(0.3383) = 50.41.

Attribute A: Importance Level	Attribute B: Income Low	Medium	High	Total
Great	$O_i = 83$ $E_i = 66.98$	$O_i = 62$ $E_i = 64.62$	$O_i = 37$ $E_i = 50.41$	182
Moderate	$O_i = 52$ $E_i = 63.32$	$O_i = 71$ $E_i = 61.06$	$O_i = 49$ $E_i = 47.64$	172
Little	$O_i = 63$ $E_i = 67.72$	$O_i = 58$ $E_i = 65.32$	$O_i = 63$ $E_i = 50.96$	184
Totals	198	191	149	538

In like fashion, $172/538 = 31.97$ of all respondents rated price moderately important. Thus, the E_i for the "moderate" category are 198(0.3197) = 63.32, 191(0.3197) = 61.06, and 149(0.3197) = 47.64.

For the "little" category, the data show $184/538 = 34.20$ percent of all customers attached little limportance to the price. Therefore, the E_i are (198)(0.342) = 67.72, (191) (0.342) = 65.32, and (149)(0.342) = 50.96.

The chi-square is

$$\chi^2 = \frac{(83 - 66.98)^2}{66.98} + \frac{(62 - 64.62)^2}{64.62} + \frac{(37 - 50.41)^2}{50.41} + \frac{(52 - 63.32)^2}{63.32} + \cdots + \frac{(63 - 50.96)^2}{50.96}$$

$$= 15.17$$

If α is set at 1 percent, and with $(r - 1)(c - 1) = (3 - 1)(3 - 1) = 4$ degrees of freedom. $\chi^2_{0.01,4} = 13.277$. As seen in the figure, the decision rule is

Decision Rule Do not reject the null if $\chi^2 \leq 13.277$. Reject if $\chi^2 > 13.277$.

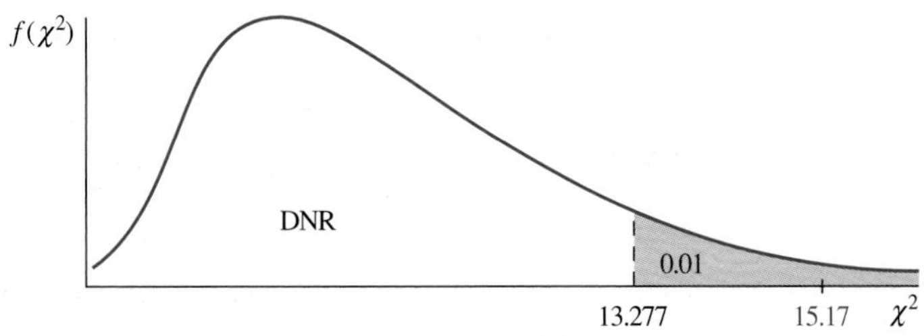

Interpretation: The null hypothesis is rejected. There is only a 1 percent chance that if there were no relationship between income and price significance, the differences between Q_i and E_i would be great enough to produce a chi-square larger than 13.277. There is evidence of a

relationship between customers' income and the importance attached to the price of a luxury automobile.

The remainder of the chapter is devoted to different nonparametric tests. Several tests are examined to illustrate (1) when the test should be used, (2) the primary purpose and application of the test, and (3) the interpretation of the test. We explore the

Sign test.

Runs test.

Mann-Whitney U test.

Spearman rank correlation test.

Kruskal-Wallis test.

We begin with the sign test.

Section Exercises

1. The vice-president of operations at First National Bank argues that the three types of loans—auto loans, student loans, and general-purpose loans—are granted to customers in the same proportions. To test his hypothesis, you collect data on 200 recent loans and find 55 were auto loans, 47 were student loans, and the rest were for general purposes. At the 5 percent level, what do you tell the vice-president?

2. Given the results of the previous exercise, you attest that the loans extended to customers fit a pattern such that one-half are for general purposes and the rest are evenly divided between the two remaining types. Using the sample for the previous problem, what do you conclude at the 5 percent level?

3. Shoppers at the local mall are asked to rate a new product on a continuous scale starting at zero. Based on the grouped data below, can you conclude at the 5 percent level that the data are normally distributed, with a mean of 100 and a standard deviation of 25?

Rating	Frequency
Less than 50	1
50–70	51
70–90	112
90–110	151
110–130	119
130–150	43
150–170	21
Over 170	2

4. Analysts at Federated Stores hypothesize that the incomes of their customers are normally distributed. Based on the data provided here, what conclusion do you reach at the 1 percent level?

Income ($1,000)	Frequency
Less than 35	1
35–40	4
40–45	26
45–50	97
50–55	96
55–60	65
60–65	8
65–70	2
Above 70	1

5. TransWorld AirWays wants to determine whether there is any relationship between the number of flights people take and their income. What conclusion do you reach at the 1 percent level based on the data for 100 travelers in the contingency table?

	Frequency of Flights		
Income	Never	Seldom	Often
Less than $30,000	20	15	2
$30,000–50,000	8	5	1
$50,000–70,000	7	8	12
Over $70,000	2	5	15

14.3 Sign Test

A nonparametric test commonly used to make business decisions is the **sign test.** It is most often used to test the hypothesis comparing two population distributions, and often involves the use of matched pairs. Suppose we have before-and-after data for a sample and wish to compare these matched sets of data. We do it by subtracting the paired observations in one data set from those in the second, and noting the algebraic sign that results. We have no interest in the magnitude of the difference, only whether a plus sign or a minus sign results.

The sign test is the nonparametric counterpart to the t-test for matched pairs. The t-test required the assumption that the populations were normally distributed. In many instances, this assumption is not possible. The sign test is useful in these cases.

The null hypothesis states that there is no difference in the data sets. If this is true, then a plus sign and a minus sign are equally likely. The probability that either would occur is 0.50. A two-tailed test is

$$H_0: m = p$$
$$H_A: m \neq p$$

where m and p are the numbers of minus signs and plus signs, respectively. A one-tailed test is

$$H_0: m \leq p$$
$$H_A: m > p$$

or

$$H_0: m \geq p$$
$$H_A: m < p$$

Sign Test A test designed to test the hypothesis comparing the distributions of two populations.

Since there are only two possible outcomes, a minus sign and a plus sign, and the probability of each remains constant from trial to trial, we can use the binomial distribution.

Assume you are working as a market analyst and wish to measure the effectiveness of a promotional game on your firm's product. Prior to the promotional game, you select 12 retail outlets and record sales for the month, rounded to the nearest $100. During the

Table 14.6
Sales for Twelve Retail Stores

Store	Before the Game	During the Game	Sign
1	$42	$40	+
2	57	60	–
3	38	38	0
4	49	47	+
5	63	65	–
6	36	39	–
7	48	49	–
8	58	50	+
9	47	47	0
10	51	52	–
11	83	72	+
12	27	33	–

second month, the promotional game is implemented and you again record sales. Table 14.6 displays these sales levels, along with the algebraic sign that results when sales in the second month are subtracted from those in the first month. A plus sign recorded in the last column means that sales went down during the second month.

Assume further that you want to test at the 5 percent level the hypothesis that the promotion increased sales. If sales went up in the second month when the promotion was in effect, then subtracting those sales from sales in the first month would produce minus signs. You would then expect the number of minus signs, m, to exceed the number of plus signs, p. That is, $m > p$. This statement does not contain an equal sign and is, therefore, the alternative hypothesis, producing a right-tailed test:

$$H_0: m \leq p$$
$$H_A: m > p$$

You must now ask, "What would cause the null to be rejected?" Since the null states that $m \leq p$, then either (1) a significantly large number of minus signs or (2) a significantly small number of plus signs would result in the rejection of the null. That is, the null is rejected if m is too large or if p is too small.

Table 14.6 shows 6 minus signs and 4 plus signs for a total of $n = 10$ signs. Values resulting in a zero difference are ignored. Observations 3 and 9 are therefore dropped from consideration. You must then determine the probability of six or more minus signs or four or fewer plus signs if the probabilities of both are $\pi = 0.50$. If this probability is less than the chosen α-value, the sample results are significant and the null hypothesis is rejected. However, if the probability of the sample results is greater then α, the results can be attributed to sampling error; do not reject the null. That is, if the sample results actually observed are likely to occur, they are not interpreted as being a significant finding and the null cannot be rejected.

From Table C in Appendix III, the probability of six or more minus signs is

$$\begin{aligned} P(m \geq 6 \mid n = 10, \pi = 0.5) &= 1 - P(X \leq 5) \\ &= 1 - 0.6230 \\ &= 0.3770 \end{aligned}$$

Of course, if you obtained six or more minus signs, you must have obtained four or fewer plus signs. Therefore, the probability of four or fewer plus signs is also 0.3770:

$$P(p \leq 4 \mid n = 10, \pi = 0.5) = 0.3770$$

This value of 0.3770 is the probability of obtaining six or more minus signs (or four or fewer plus signs) if π, the probability of the occurrence of either sign on any trial, is 0.50. We noted that if the number of minus signs was unusually large, it would refute the null. However, 6 is not an unusually large number. The probability of getting six or more signs is quite high at 37.7 percent. Since the probability of their occurrence is greater than an α of 5 percent, the event of six minus signs is not considered large, and the null that H_0: $m \geq p$ is not rejected.

If the promotion were effective, there would be a large number of minus signs, and the null that $m \leq p$ would be rejected. But as we have seen, six minus signs is not an unusually large number, and you cannot consider the promotion successful.

If a test were based on the left-tailed test, the hypothesis would be

$$H_0: m \geq p$$
$$H_A: m < p$$

If m is unusually small, or p is unusually large, the null would be rejected. Assume that an experiment with $n = 12$ trials yields five minus signs and seven plus signs. You would then find the probability of obtaining five or less minus signs, or the probability of seven or more plus signs. If this probability is less than the chosen α, reject the null.

Example 14.3 illustrates a two-tailed test. The only adjustment is that α must be divided by 2. The hypotheses are

$$H_0: m = p$$
$$H_A: m \neq p$$

The hypotheses are tested by comparing $\alpha/2$ to either (1) the probability that the sign that occurred less often could occur that many times or less, or (2) the probability that the sign that occurred more often could occur that many times or more.

Example 14.3 Honda tested the wear resistance of two types of tire tread on its Nighthawk motorbike. Ten bikes were randomly chosen. Mechanics mounted tires with one type of tread on the front, and the other tread on the rear. After driving the bikes a specified number of miles under set conditions, they gave a wear rating between 0 and 40 to each tire. A higher rating indicated a better tire. The results are shown here. Honda's research analysts want to test the hypothesis that there is no difference in wear ratings at the 10 percent level. The hypotheses are

$$H_0: m = p$$
$$H_A: m \neq p$$

	Wear Rating		
Tires	**Tread Type I**	**Tread Type II**	**Sign**
1	32	37	–
2	27	25	+
3	21	21	0
4	13	17	–
5	25	29	–
6	38	39	–
7	17	23	–
8	29	33	–
9	32	34	–
10	34	37	–

Solution: Observation 3 is ignored because the difference is zero. There is one plus sign and eight minus signs. Honda can calculate the probability that one or fewer plus signs could occur or the probability that eight or more minus signs could occur. Focusing on the number of plus signs, we have, from Table C (Appendix III),

$$P(p \leq 1 \mid n = 9, \pi = 0.5) = 0.0195$$

Of course, we get the same answer if we use the number of minus signs is the test:

$$P(m \geq 8 \mid n = 9, \pi = 0.5) = 1 - P(m \leq 7) = 1 - 0.9805 = 0.0195$$

Since $\alpha/2 = 0.10/2 = 0.05 > 0.0195$, the null is rejected.

Interpretation: If the null is true, and $m = p$, there is only a 1.95 percent chance of getting one or fewer plus signs (or eight or more minus signs). There is a less than $\alpha/2 = 0.05$ percent chance that the null is true. We can conclude that there is a difference in wear ratings. Tread type II is superior since there was a significant number of minus signs.

If $n \geq 30$, it is permissible to use the normal approximation to the binomial. Assume that in the preceding example, Honda had sampled 40 motorbikes and obtained 8 plus signs, 28 minus signs, and 4 zero differences. The company would have $n = 36$ useful observations.

As we learned in Chapter 8, if the test is two-tailed with $\alpha = 0.10$, the critical Z-value is 1.65.

Decision Rule Do not reject if $-1.65 \leq Z_{\text{test}} \leq 1.65$. Reject if $Z_{\text{test}} < -1.65$ or $Z_{\text{test}} > 1.65$.

The value for Z_{test} is

Z-value for large sample sign test

$$Z_{\text{test}} = \frac{k \pm 0.5 - 0.5n}{0.5\sqrt{n}} \qquad [14.4]$$

where k is the appropriate number of plus or minus signs and n is the sample size. If $k < n/2$, $k + 0.5$ is used. If $k > n/2$, $k - 0.5$ is used. It is necessary to adjust k by 0.5 because the binomial distribution represents discrete data, while the normal distribution applies to continuous data.

Since the Honda example is a two-tailed test, we can test either the number of plus signs or the number of minus signs. Testing the number of plus signs, we have

$$Z_{\text{test}} = \frac{8 + 0.5 - (0.5)(36)}{0.5\sqrt{36}}$$

$$= -3.17$$

Testing the number of minus signs, we find

$$Z_{\text{test}} = \frac{28 - 0.5 - (0.5)(36)}{0.5\sqrt{36}}$$

$$= 3.17$$

Since $-3.17 < -1.65$, or $3.17 > 1.65$, the null is rejected. There is a difference in the two types of tires. Trend type II is superior.

Section Exercises

6. Two advertisements for computers are rated by 15 potential customers to determine whether a preference exists. The results are shown here. At the 10 percent level, what are the results?

Consumer	1	2	3	4	5	6	7	8	9	10	11	12	13	14	15
Ad 1	8	9	5	7	9	4	3	8	9	5	7	8	8	7	9
Ad 2	7	3	2	8	5	5	7	2	1	3	7	2	2	3	8

7. The manufacturer of 10 snack foods hypothesizes that the sales of each product with a high fat content will be less than those of the same product with reduced fat. Sales in thousands of units are given below. At the 10 percent level, what is your conclusion?

Food	1	2	3	4	5	6	7	8	9	10
With fat	10	12	14	18	17	18	5	21	6	8
Without fat	15	13	12	9	17	19	3	27	12	14

8. The brilliance of glassware is measured on a scale from 1 to 100. Twenty glasses are tested before and after being treated by a new process. If subtracting the brilliance factor after treatment from that before treatment results in 5 plus signs and 3 negative signs, is there any difference at the 5 percent level? How do you interpret the results of the test?

9. Fifty employees who have received special training are matched with 50 others who are similar in every aspect but did not receive the training. The productivity of those who were trained is subtracted from that of those who were not trained, resulting in 15 plus signs and 17 negative signs. At the 5 percent level, did the training make a difference?

14.4 Runs Test

The importance of randomness in the sampling process has been repeatedly stressed. In the absence of randomness, many of the statistical tools upon which we rely are of little or no use. It is therefore often necessary to test for randomness in our samples. We can accomplish this using a **runs test.**

> **Runs Test** A nonparametric test for randomness in the sampling process.

To complete a runs test, we assign all observations in the sample one of two symbols. A **run** consists of a sequence of one or more like symbols. If the observations are grouped into categories of, say, A and B, we might find the following sequences:

AA	BBB	A	BB	AAA	B
1	2	3	4	5	6

There are six runs, each consisting of one or more like observations.

> **Run** An unbroken series of one or more like symbols.

Suppose employees are selected for a training program. If selection does not depend on whether the employee is male (m) or female (f), we would expect gender to be a random event. However, if some pattern in gender is detected, we might assume randomness is absent and selection was made at least in part on the basis of a worker's gender. If there is an unusually large or an unusually small number of runs, a pattern is suggested.

Assume that the gender of each employee is recorded in order of selection and proves to be

mmm	ffffff	mmm
1	2	3

Three runs occur in this sample. There are three males, followed by six females, and then three males. It would seem that the selections are not sufficiently mixed, causing a systematic pattern which implies an absence of randomness. Assume instead that the order of selection is

m	f	m	f	m	f	m	f	m	f	m	f
1	2	3	4	5	6	7	8	9	10	11	12

Again, there appears to be a pattern producing an unusually large number of 12 separate runs.

Detection of a Pattern If too few or too many runs occur, randomness may be absent.

The set of hypotheses to be tested is

H_0: Randomness exists in the sample.

H_A: Randomness does not exist in the sample.

To test the hypothesis, we must determine whether the number of runs (r) is either too large or too small. Table M1 and M2 (Appendix III), show critical values for the number of runs if α is 5 percent. Since on the surface both of our examples appear nonrandom, let's take a less obvious set of selections. Suppose the selections were

m	fff	mmm	ff	mmm
1	2	3	4	5

The selections seem more random than the other two examples in that no pattern is obvious. Notice that $n_1 = 7$ is the number of males and $n_2 = 5$ is the number of females.

Table M1 shows the minimum critical number of runs for an α-value of 5 percent. If the number of runs is equal to or less than the value shown in Table M1, it suggests that, at the 5 percent level, there are too few runs to support the null hypothesis of randomness. Given that $n_1 = 7$ and $n_2 = 5$, we find the critically low value to be 3. Since the number of runs exceeds this minimum, there is not a significantly low number of runs to warrant rejection of the null. Table M2 provides critically high values for r. If the number of runs in a sample is equal to or greater than those values, we may conclude that there is an extremely large number of runs, suggesting the absence of randomness. For

$n_1 = 7$ and $n_2 = 5$, Table M2 reveals that the maximum number of runs is 11. If the number of runs exceeds 11, there are too many to support the hypothesis of randomness. Since the number of runs is less than 11, it is not significantly high and the null is not rejected at the 5 percent level. It would seem that our sample selection is the result of randomness.

When the sample data do not naturally fall into one of two possible categories, it is possible to use the median as a measure to bifurcate the data. Assume levels of daily output at a coal mine selected for a statistical study are, in order of selection, 31, 57, 52, 22, 24, 59, 25, 29, 27, 44, 43, 32, 40, 37, 60 tons. The median of 37 can be used as a benchmark value. Observations fall either above (A) or below (B) 37, yielding eight runs of

31	57 52	22 24	59	25 29 27	44 43	32	40 60
B	AA	BB	A	BBB	AA	B	AA
1	2	3	4	5	6	7	8

With $n_1 = 7$ for B and $n_2 = 7$ for A, Table M reveals critical values of 3 and 13 runs. Since there were eight runs, randomness is assumed and the null is not rejected.

Another application of the runs test is found in a test of randomness in the ordinary least squares (OLS) method of regression analysis. A basic property of the OLS regression model is that the errors are random. No pattern should exist in the signs of these errors. Example 14.4, illustrates how the runs test can be used to test this condition.

Example 14.4 A marketing research firm developed a model to predict monthly sales for a new product. After 17 months, the errors were calculated and proved to have the following signs:

+ + + + + +	− − − − −	+ + + +	− −
1	2	3	4

At the 5 percent level, does there appear to be randomness in the error terms?

Solution: There are $n_1 = 10$ plus signs, $n_2 = 7$ minus signs, and $r = 4$ runs. Tables M1 and M2 reveal the critical minimum and maximum numbers of runs, respectively, to be 5 and 14. The hypotheses are

H_0: Randomness prevails.

H_A: Randomness does not prevail.

Decision Rule Do not reject the null if $5 < r < 14$. Reject if $r \leq 5$ or $r \geq 14$.

Since $r = 4$, the null should be rejected at the 5 percent level.

Interpretation: The number of runs is significantly small. There are too few runs to support the hypothesis of randomness. The validity of the regression model is questionable, and the firm should examine alternatives. The low number of runs results from the fact that errors of one sign are followed by errors of like signs, an indication of positive autocorrelation.

If both n_1 and n_2 are greater than 20, the sampling distribution for r approximates normality. The distribution has a mean of

Mean of the sampling distribution of the number of runs	$\mu_r = \dfrac{2n_1n_2}{n_1 + n_2} + 1$	[14.5]

and a standard deviation of

Standard deviation for runs test	$\sigma_r = \sqrt{\dfrac{2n_1n_2(2n_1n_2 - n_1 - n_2)}{(n_1 + n_2)^2(n_1 + n_2 - 1)}}$	[14.6]

Standardizing the distribution of runs can be accomplished by using the normal deviate:

Normal deviate for distribution of runs	$Z = \dfrac{r - \mu_r}{\sigma_r}$	[14.7]

A sales presentation made to a group of 52 potential buyers resulted in 27 sales, 25 no-sales, and 18 runs. At the 1 percent level of significance, is the sample random?

H_0: The sample is random.

H_A: The sample is not random.

At 1 percent, the critical Z for the two-tailed test is 2.58. As shown in Figure 14.6, the decision rule is

Figure 14.6 Testing for Randomness in Sales

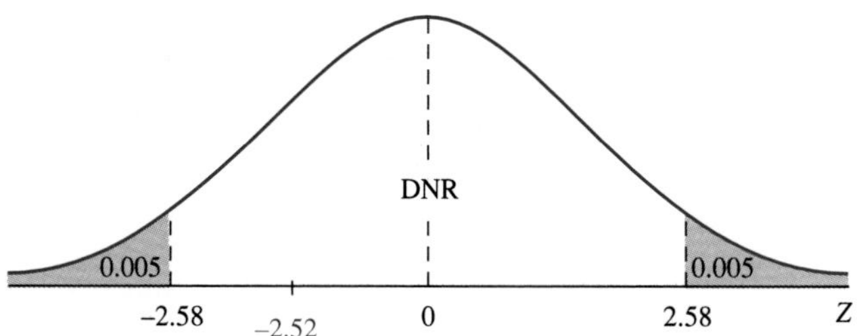

Decision Rule Do not reject the null if $-2.58 \leq Z \leq 2.58$. Reject the null if $Z < -2.58$ or $Z > 2.58$.

Then, by Formula [14.5],

$$\begin{aligned}\mu_r &= \frac{2n_1n_2}{n_1 + n_2} + 1\\ &= \frac{2(27)(25)}{27 + 25} + 1\\ &= 26.96\end{aligned}$$

and, by Formula [14.6],

$$\sigma_r = \sqrt{\frac{2n_1n_2(2n_1n_2 - n_1 - n_2)}{(n_1 + n_2)^2(n_1 + n_2 - 1)}}$$

$$= \sqrt{\frac{[2(27)(25)][2(27)(25) - 27 - 25]}{(27 + 25)^2(27 + 25 - 1)}}$$

$$= 3.56$$

The normal deviate is

$$Z = \frac{r - \mu_r}{\sigma_r}$$

$$= \frac{18 - 26.96}{3.56}$$

$$= -2.52$$

There is insufficient evidence to reject the null. It would appear that the sample is random. There is a 99 percent probability that a random sampling process with 27 and 25 observations in the two categories, and with 18 runs, would lead to a Z between ± 2.58.

Example 14.4 can be used to illustrate how Minitab can perform a runs test. In column 1 of the data window, enter six 1's for the 6 plus signs, five 2's for the 5 minus signs, four 1's for the next four plus signs, and then two 2's for the last two minus signs. Click on **STAT > NONPARAMETRICS > RUNS TEST.** Select **Above** and **Below** and enter 1.5. Click **OK**. The printout is shown as Minitab Display 14.3. The p-value tells us that the null is rejected at any alpha value above 0.0068.

Minitab Display 14.3

Runs Test

```
   C1

   K =      1.5000


   The observed no. of runs =   4
   The expected no. of runs =   9.2353
    7 Observations above K   10 below
 * N Small -- Following approx. may be invalid
            The test is significant at   0.0068
```

14.5 Mann-Whitney U Test

The **Mann-Whitney *U* test** (or simply the ***U* test**) tests the equality of two population distributions. It is based on the assumption that two random samples are independently drawn from continuous variables. In its broadest sense, the null hypothesis states that the distributions of two populations are identical. However, the test can be tailored to examine the equality of two population means or medians. To test the equality of means, we must assume that the populations are symmetrical and have the same variance. Under these conditions the Mann-Whitney U test serves as the nonparametric alternative to the t-test, except it does not require the assumption of normality. If the assumption of symmetry is dropped, the median replaces the mean as the test statistic.

Mann-Whitney *U* Test The nonparametric counterpart to the *t*-test for independent samples. It does not require the assumption that the differences between the two samples are normally distributed.

The data are ordered or ranked from lowest to highest. There is no effort to match pairs, as we have often done when two samples were taken. (Note that the Mann-Whitney *U* test is the same as the Wilcoxon rank sum test, but differs from the Wilcoxon signed-rank test. The similarity in names can be confusing.)

To illustrate the *U* test, suppose a pottery factory wants to compare the time it takes for clay pieces to cool after being "fired" in the oven by two different firing methods.

Potters fire 12 pieces using method 1, and 10 using method 2. The number of minutes required for each piece to cool is as follows:

Method 1:	27*	31	28	29	39	40	35	33	32	36	37	43
Method 2:	34	24*	38	28	30	34	37	42	41	44		

The observations are then ordered and ranked from lowest to highest as shown in Table 14.7. The value 24 in method 2 is the lowest of all 22 observations and is given the rank of 1, and 27 in method 1 has a rank of 2. Ties, such as 28, are averaged over the appropriate ranks. The value 28 is the third lowest observation, and both values of 28 receive a ranking of 3.5. There is no rank of 4, since two observations have the rank of 3.5. The rankings are then summed, yielding ΣR_1 and ΣR_2.

Table 14.7
Ranking Cooling Times

Method 1	Rank	Method 2	Rank
		24	1
27	2		
28	3.5	28	3.5
29	5		
		30	6
31	7		
32	8		
33	9		
		34	10.5
		34	10.5
35	12		
36	13		
37	14.5	37	14.5
		38	16
39	17		
40	18		
		41	19
		42	20
43	21		
		44	22
	$\Sigma R_1 = 130$		$\Sigma R_2 = 123$

We calculate the Mann-Whitney U-statistic for each sample from the equations as

Mann-Whitney U-statistic for first sample	$U_1 = n_1 n_2 + \frac{n_1(n_1 + 1)}{2} - \Sigma R_1$	[14.8]

and

Mann-Whitney U-statistic for second sample	$U_2 = n_1 n_2 + \frac{n_2(n_2 + 1)}{2} - \Sigma R_2$	[14.9]

The data in Table 14.7 yield

$$U_1 = (12)(10) + \frac{12(12 + 1)}{2} - 130$$
$$= 68$$

and

$$U_2 = (12)(10) + \frac{10(10 + 1)}{2} - 123$$
$$= 52$$

Notice that $U_1 + U_2 = n_1 n_2$ provides a quick check of your arithmetic.

If n_1 and n_2 are both at least 10, the mean and standard deviation of the sampling distribution for the U-statistic are

Mean of the sampling distribution for Mann-Whitney U test	$\mu_u = \frac{n_1 n_2}{2}$	[14.10]

and

Standard deviation of the sampling distribution for the Mann-Whitney U test	$\sigma_u = \sqrt{\frac{n_1 n_2 (n_1 + n_2 + 1)}{12}}$	[14.11]

In the present case, we find

$$\mu_u = \frac{(12)(10)}{2}$$
$$= 60$$

and

$$\sigma_u = \sqrt{\frac{(12)(10)(12 + 10 + 1)}{12}}$$
$$= 15.17$$

The distribution of the U-statistic can then be normalized by the formula

Z-value to normalize the Mann-Whitney U test	$Z = \dfrac{U_i - \mu_u}{\sigma_u}$	[14.12]

where U_i is the appropriate U-value, either U_1 or U_2, depending on the nature of the test. Let's now determine which U-value is appropriate.

A. Two-Tailed Test

In our example of the firing ovens, the pottery factory may want to test the hypothesis that the mean cooling times of method 1 and method 2 are the same. This requires a two-tailed test with hypotheses

$$H_0: \mu_1 = \mu_2$$
$$H_A: \mu_1 \neq \mu_2$$

In a two-tailed test, either U_1 or U_2 can be used in Formula [14.12]. Thus, arbitrarily using U_2, we find

$$Z = \frac{52 - 60}{15.17}$$
$$= -0.53$$

If $\alpha = 10$ percent, the decision rule, as reflected in Figure 14.7, is

Figure 14.7
A Two-Tailed Test of Mean Cooling Times

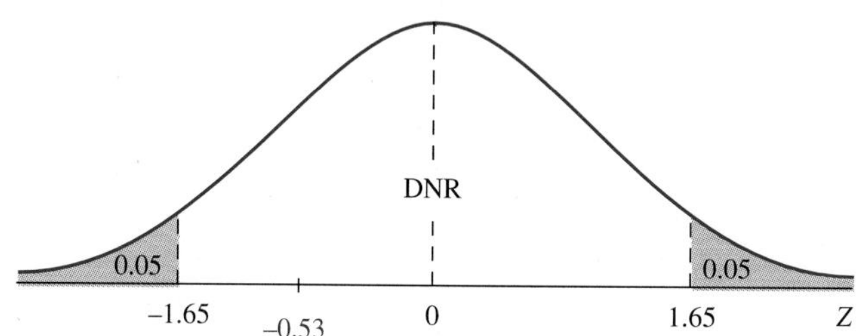

Decision Rule Do not reject if $-1.65 \leq Z \leq 1.65$. Reject if $Z < -1.65$ or $Z > 1.65$.

Since $Z = -0.53$ is in the DNR region, the pottery factory can conclude at the 10 percent level of significance that the mean cooling times are the same for both firing methods.

B. One-Tailed Test

Suppose the factory felt that method 1 would result in a longer mean cooling time: $\mu_1 > \mu_2$. Then the hypotheses

$$H_0: \mu_1 \leq \mu_2$$
$$H_A: \mu_1 > \mu_2$$

call for a right-tailed test. If a right-tailed test is to be conducted, then the U-value in Formula [14.12] must be the higher of the two U-values. Since $U_1 = 68 > U_2 = 52$, U_1 is used to calculate the Z-value. If this were a left-tailed test, the lower U-value would be used to compute Z.

Given our right-tailed test, we have

$$Z = \frac{68 - 60}{15.17}$$
$$= 0.53$$

If a = 0.10 is retained for this one-tailed test, the decision rule, as shown in Figure 14.8, is

Figure 14.8
A One-Tailed Test for Mean Cooling Times

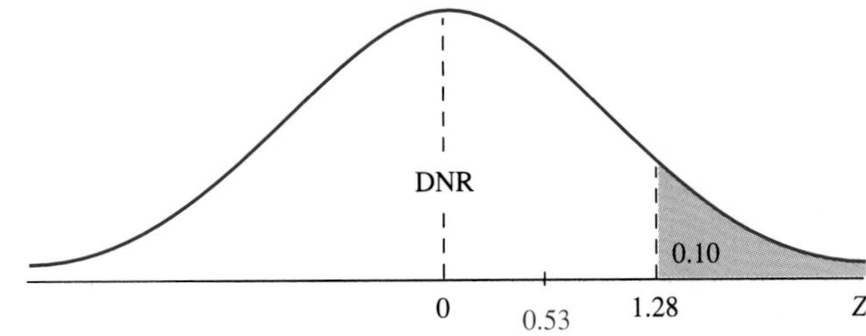

Decision Rule Do not reject if $Z \leq 1.28$. Reject if $Z > 1.28$.

The Z-value of 0.53 is clearly in the DNR region. The pottery factory does not reject the null hypothesis that $\mu_1 \leq \mu_2$ and cannot conclude that method 2 leads to faster cooling times.

Minitab Display 14.4 shows the results of the test for the pottery factory discussed above. Point and interval estimates for the difference in population medians are given. The value of $W = 130.0$ is the sum of the ranks of the variable stored in the first column and can be used to calculate U_1 and U_2. The p-value of 0.4057 is greater than our selected alpha value of 10 percent and therefore tells us that we cannot reject the null.

Minitab Display 14.4

```
Mann-Whitney Confidence Interval and Test

C1          N =  12     Median =        34.00
C2          N =  11     Median =        37.00
Point estimate for ETA1-ETA2 is        -2.00
90.9 Percent C.I. for ETA1-ETA2 is (-7.00,3.00)
W = 130.0
Test of ETA1 = ETA2 vs.  ETA1 ~= ETA2 is significant at 0.4060
The test is significant at 0.4057 (adjusted for ties)
```

Section Exercises

10. The proprietor of a local pub popular with students at a nearby university was overheard to say that female customers tended to spend less than males. Challenged to support his claim by the statistics professor occupying his usual space at the end of the bar, the pub keeper

recorded the expenditures of 10 female and 10 male customers. The results in dollars are provided here. Is his claim supported at the 10 percent level?

Females	5.12	3.15	8.17	3.42	3.02	4.42	3.72	2.12	5.72	4.87
Males	5.83	6.49	4.45	5.12	9.02	9.73	5.42	6.43	8.79	8.89

11. Rapid Roy tested two types of fuel in his classic roadster, noting the top speed each fuel permitted. Based on the results shown here in miles per hour, is there a difference in the mean speed of each fuel at the 1 percent level?

Fuel 1	45	67	54	41	38	59	48	31	59	31	
Fuel 2	79	82	69	84	76	77	81	65	73	70	69

12. Housing costs of 42 residents in Topeka, Kansas, were compared to those of 35 residents in Erie, Pennsylvania. The observations were ranked, yielding ΣR_T = 1,833.5 and ΣR_E = 1,169.5. At the 5 percent level, does there appear to be a difference in mean housing costs in the two cities?

13. Petroleum Transport ships crude oil via two shipping lines, FreightWays and OverSeas. Lately, it has become obvious that some of the shipments are arriving with less oil than is listed on the manifest. Shortages measured in thousands of barrels are discovered for 50 shipments from FreightWays and 45 shipments from OverSeas. The results are ranked yielding ΣR_F = 1,434.5 and ΣR_O = 1,258.5. Is there evidence to suggest that FreightWays has a larger shortage? Set alpha at 10 percent.

14.6 Spearman Rank Correlation

Our earlier discussion of regression and correlation provided us with a means to measure the relationship between two variables. We learned how to calculate and interpret the Pearsonian correlation coefficient and thereby measure the strength of the relationship between two variables.

However, this approach required precise numerical values and the assumption of normality in the distribution of those values. In many instances, such numerical measurement may not be possible, and there may be no support for the assumption of normality. In such cases, the Pearsonian method cannot be used.

Nevertheless, we may still be able to systematically rank or order the observations. This ordinal ranking permits us to measure the degrees of correlation between two variables by using the **Spearman rank correlation coefficient.**

> **Spearman Rank Correlation** A measure of the relationship between two variables that have been ordinally ranked from lowest to highest (or highest to lowest).

Last year, Amco Tech, a U.S. manufacturer of computer microchips, hired seven computer technicians. The technicians were given a test designed to measure their basic knowledge. After a year of service, their supervisor was asked to rank each technician's job performance. Test scores and performance rankings for all seven employees are shown in Table 14.8.

Notice that although the test score is a quantitative measure of the technician's knowledge, the performance ranking is merely an ordered list by the supervisor of which

Table 14.8
Data on Amco Tech Technicians

Technician	Test Score	Performance Ranking
J. Smith	82	4
A. Jones	73	7
D. Boone	60	6
M. Lewis	80	3
G. Clark	67	5
A. Lincoln	94	1
G. Washington	89	2

Table 14.9
Rankings of Amco Tech Technicians

Technician	Test Score	Test Rank (X)	Performance Rank (Y)	$X - Y = d_i$	$(X - Y)^2 = d_i^2$
J. Smith	82	3	4	−1	1
A. Jones	73	5	7	−2	4
D. Boone	60	7	6	1	1
M. Lewis	80	4	3	1	1
G. Clark	67	6	5	1	1
A. Lincoln	94	1	1	0	0
G. Washington	89	2	2	0	0
					$8 = \Sigma d_i^2$

technicians he feels are doing a better job. The director of management operations therefore decides to use the Spearman rank correlation to determine whether there is any relationship between test scores and job performance. The director must first develop the ranking for test scores. These rankings, along with some necessary calculations, are displayed in Table 14.9.

The director may then calculate the Spearman rank correlation coefficient, r_S, using Formula [14.13].

Spearman rank correlation coefficient
$$r_S = 1 - \frac{6\Sigma d_i^2}{n(n^2 - 1)} \qquad [14.13]$$

where d_i is the difference between the rankings for each observation
n is the sample size

Then

$$r_S = 1 - \frac{(6)(8)}{7(7^2 - 1)}$$
$$= 0.857$$

Recalling that a correlation coefficient falls between −1 and 1, our sample suggests a rather strong, positive relationship between a technician's test score and his or her job performance rating.

We often want to test the hypothesis that the population correlation coefficient, ρ_s, is zero. That is, we want to determine the likelihood that, despite our sample findings suggesting a relationship between score and rating, there actually is no such relationship and $\rho_s = 0$.

For small samples ($n < 30$), the distribution of r_S is not normal, nor is the t-test appropriate. Instead, Table N in Appendix III must be used. Critical values taken from Table N are compared with r_S to test the hypotheses

$$H_0\text{: } \rho_s = 0\text{; there is no relationship between the two variables.}$$

$$H_A\text{: } \rho_s \neq 0\text{; there is a relationship between the two variables.}$$

With the aid of Figure 14.9, Table N reveals that if we test the hypotheses at $\alpha = 0.10$, a sample of size $n = 7$ carries critical values of ± 0.6786.

Figure 14.9
A Hypothesis Test for Amco Tech

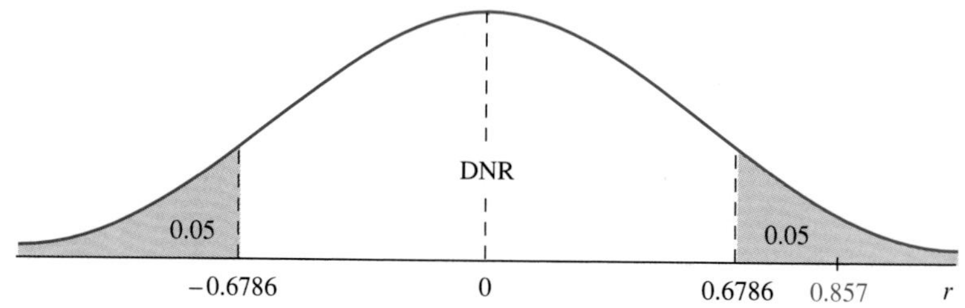

Decision Rule Do not reject the null if $-0.6786 \leq r_S \leq 0.6786$. Reject the null if $r_S < -0.6786$ or $r_S > 0.6786$.

The value $r_S = 0.857$ is in the right-hand rejection region. We can therefore reject the null of $\rho_s = 0$ and conclude at the 10 percent level of significance that a relationship exists between test scores and job performance rankings.

If $n > 30$, the distribution of r_S approximates normality with a mean of zero and a standard deviation of $1/\sqrt{n-1}$. The Z-test is

Normal deviate for Spearman rank test

$$Z = \frac{r_S - 0}{1/\sqrt{n-1}} = r_S\sqrt{n-1} \qquad [14.14]$$

Example 14.5 demonstrates.

Example 14.5 Amco Tech is considering whether to market a hard drive for desktop computers. An experiment is conducted on 32 randomly selected drives to determine whether a relationship exists between the number of hours a drive is tested prior to sale and the number of times the drive fails in the process of completing a computer run. The manager of the quality control division reasonably expects the failure rate to decrease as the number of hours a drive is tested increases. The test hours and the number of failures for all 32 drives, along with the rankings for each variable, are shown here. For both variables, the highest observation received the first ranking, and the lowest observation was given the thirty-second ranking.

Drive	Hours	Hours Ranking (X)	Failures	Failures Ranking (Y)	$X-Y$	$(X-Y)^2$
1	100	1.0	2	32.0	−31.0	961.00
2	99	2.5	3	30.5	−28.0	784.00
3	99	2.5	3	30.5	−28.0	784.00
4	97	4.0	4	28.5	−24.5	600.25
5	96	5.5	4	28.5	−23.0	529.00
6	96	5.5	5	27.0	−21.5	462.25
7	95	7.0	8	21.5	−14.5	210.25
8	91	8.0	6	25.5	−17.5	306.25
9	89	9.0	7	23.5	−14.5	210.25
10	88	10.5	10	17.5	−7.0	49.00
11	88	10.5	8	21.5	−11.0	121.00
12	80	12.0	9	19.5	−7.5	56.25
13	79	13.0	9	19.5	−6.5	42.25
14	78	14.5	10	17.5	−3.0	9.00
15	78	14.5	11	15.5	−1.0	1.00
16	77	16.0	7	23.5	−7.5	56.25
17	75	17.5	12	13.5	4.0	16.00
18	75	17.5	13	12.0	5.5	30.25
19	71	19.0	11	15.5	3.5	12.25
20	70	20.5	14	11.0	9.5	90.25
21	70	20.5	12	13.5	7.0	49.00
22	68	22.5	6	25.5	−3.0	9.00
23	68	22.5	16	7.5	15.0	225.00
24	65	24.0	15	9.5	14.5	210.25
25	64	25.0	15	9.5	15.5	240.25
26	60	26.5	16	7.5	19.0	361.00
27	60	26.5	18	3.5	23.0	529.00
28	58	28.0	19	2.0	26.0	676.00
29	56	29.0	17	5.5	23.5	552.25
30	55	30.5	20	1.0	29.5	870.25
31	55	30.5	18	3.5	27.0	729.00
32	50	32.0	17	5.5	26.5	702.25
						10,484.00

Solution:

$$r_S = 1 - \frac{6(10{,}484)}{32(32^2 - 1)}$$
$$= -0.922$$

Set $\alpha = 0.01$. A test of the hypothesis regarding the population correlation coefficient follows:

$$H_0: \rho_s = 0$$
$$H_A: \rho_s \neq 0$$

The critical Z-value is ± 2.58. Then

$$Z = (-0.922)\sqrt{32 - 1}$$
$$= -5.14$$

As shown in the figure, the null should be rejected.

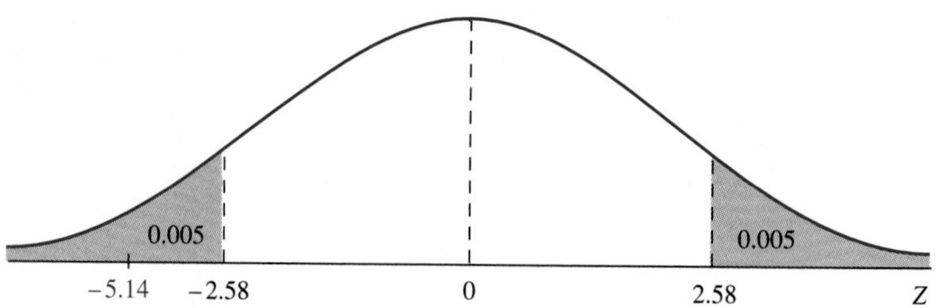

Interpretation: The r_S-value of -0.922 indicates a strong negative relationship between hours and failures. The longer a drive is tested before it is used, the fewer failures it experiences in completing the run.

To use Minitab, enter the data for each variable in separate columns. Rank each with MANIP > Rank. Then click on **STAT > BASIC STATISTICS > CORRELATION.** Minitab will report r_S.

Section Exercises

14. Economists at the Mid-West Research Institute are conducting a study to analyze the relationship between people's incomes and their consumption levels. Eleven consumers report the figures below in thousands of dollars. At the 5 percent level of significance, does the Spearman rank correlation coefficient suggest a relationship?

Income	97	58	69	47	58	38	91	67	68	47	48
Consumption	55	63	54	37	45	38	71	52	53	37	37

15. At the 10 percent level, is there a relationship between study time in hours and grades on a test, according to these data?

Time	21	18	15	17	18	25	18	4	6	5
Grade	67	58	59	54	58	80	14	15	19	21

16. The rankings of the rates of return on 50 stocks are compared to the rankings on their price-earnings ratio yielding $\Sigma d_i^2 = 19{,}412.5$. At the 5 percent level, what can you conclude about a relationship between the two stock variables?

17. Eighty-five men and 85 women rate a product yielding $\Sigma d_i^2 = 10{,}010.25$. At the 1 percent level of significance, is there any correlation between the ratings based on gender?

14.7 Kruskal-Wallis Test

The Mann-Whitney U test serves as the nonparametric counterpart to the t-test for two independent samples; we use it to compare two populations. If we need to compare more than two populations, the **Kruskal-Wallis test** then applies as a logical extension of the Mann-Whitney test, and we use it to test hypotheses regarding the distribution of three or more populations. In this capacity, the Kruskal-Wallis test functions as the nonparametric counterpart to the completely randomized design used in ANOVA tests. While the ANOVA tests depend on the assumption that all populations under comparison are normally distributed, the Kruskal-Wallis test places no such restriction on the comparison.

Kruskal-Wallis Test A test that compares three or more populations to determine whether a difference exists in the distribution of the populations. It is the analogue to the *F*-test used in ANOVA tests.

The null hypothesis states that no difference exists in the distribution of the k populations under comparison. The hypotheses are thus

H_0: All k populations have the same distribution.

H_A: Not all k populations have the same distribution.

The test requires that the observations be ranked, just as in the Mann-Whitney test.

To illustrate, assume that, as the new accounts manager for Pox Skin Ointment, you must compare the time it takes for three customers to pay for shipments of No-Flaw Face Cream, a new product offered by Pox. You randomly select several purchases for each customer, along with the number of days each took to settle its account. The results are shown in Table 14.10. Notice that number of observations in all samples do not have to be equal.

Table 14.10
Number of Days to Pay Pox for Delivery

	Customer		
Purchase	1	2	3
1	28	26	37
2	19	20	28
3	13	11	26
4	28	14	35
5	29	22	31
6	22	21	
7	21		

Each observation must then be ranked from lowest to highest. As with the Mann-Whitney, ties are assigned a rank equal to the mean ranking for those observations. The rankings are then summed for all $k = 3$ samples. Table 14.11 contains the results. The Kruskal-Wallis statistic is

Kruskal-Wallis test $$K = \frac{12}{n(n+1)}\left[\Sigma\frac{R_i^2}{n_i}\right] - 3(n+1) \qquad [14.15]$$

where n_i is the number of observations in the ith sample
n is the total number of observations in all samples
R_i is the sum of the ranks of the ith sample

Table 14.11
The Rankings for Pox

Customer 1		Customer 2		Customer 3	
Days	Rank	Days	Rank	Days	Rank
		11	1		
13	2				
		14	3		
19	4				
		20	5		
21	6.5	21	6.5		
22	8.5	22	8.5		
		26	10.5	26	10.5
28	13				
28	13			28	13
29	15				
				31	16
				35	17
				37	18
	$\Sigma R_1 = 62$		$\Sigma R_2 = 34.5$		$\Sigma R_3 = 74.5$

Figure 14.10
A Chi-Square Test for Pox

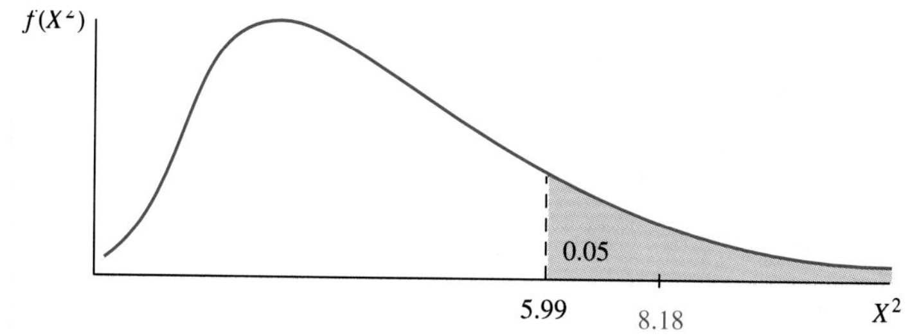

K is then found, using Formula [14.15], as

$$K = \frac{12}{18(18+1)}\left[\frac{(62)^2}{7} + \frac{(34.5)^2}{6} + \frac{(74.5)^2}{5}\right] - 3(18+1)$$
$$= 8.18$$

It is now left to compare K with a critical value. The distribution of K is approximated by a chi-square distribution with $k - 1$ degrees of freedom. If K exceeds the critical value for chi-square, the null is rejected. Figure 14.10 illustrates. Should you choose an α-value of 5 percent in your test for Pox, the critical chi-square value, given $3 - 1 = 2$ degrees of freedom, becomes $\chi^2_{0.05,2} = 5.99$.

Decision Rule Do not reject if $k \leq 5.99$. Reject if $k > 5.99$.

Since $k = 8.18 > 5.99$, we reject the null that there is no difference in the time it takes these three customers to settle their accounts with Pox.

In the event that the null hypothesis is rejected, the next logical step is to determine which differences are statistically significant and which are due to sampling error. That is, once we have determined that not all populations have the same distribution, we must identify those populations that are significantly different. This is much like the process in which we used the Tukey methods to detect significant differences in our study of ANOVA. As with the Tukey approach, this involves a pair-wise comparison of all possible pairs.

We must first compute the average rank for each sample $\bar{R}_i$ by dividing the sum of the sample's rank by the number of observations in that sample. For the first sample this is

$$\bar{R}_1 = \frac{62}{7} = 8.86$$

Similarly, $\bar{R}_2 = \dfrac{34.5}{6} = 5.75$ and $\bar{R}_3 = \dfrac{74.5}{5} = 14.9$. The absolute differences are found as

$$\begin{aligned}
|\bar{R}_1 - \bar{R}_2| &= |8.86 - 5.75| = 3.11 \\
|\bar{R}_1 - \bar{R}_3| &= |8.86 - 14.9| = 6.04 \\
|\bar{R}_2 - \bar{R}_3| &= |5.75 - 14.9| = 9.15
\end{aligned}$$

These absolute values are then compared to a critical value to determine whether they differ significantly. This critical value C_k is calculated as

Critical value for the Kruskal-Wallis test

$$C_k = \sqrt{\chi^2_{\alpha,k-1}\left[\frac{n(n+1)}{12}\right]\left[\frac{1}{n_i} + \frac{1}{n_j}\right]} \qquad [14.16]$$

where $\chi^2_{\alpha,k-1}$ is the chi-square value used to test the original hypothesis, 5.99 in this case

n_i and n_j are the sizes of the two samples under comparison

If the actual difference between the average ranks of the two samples is greater than the critical difference, it is considered a significant difference and the two populations are found to be different.

If we have a balanced design with equal size samples, C_k will be the same for all pair-wise comparisons. If the design is unbalanced as in this case, a different value for C_k must be computed for each comparison. To compare customer 1 and customer 2 for Pox, C_k is

$$\begin{aligned}
C_k &= \sqrt{5.99\left[\frac{(18)(19)}{12}\right]\left[\frac{1}{7} + \frac{1}{6}\right]} \\
&= 7.27
\end{aligned}$$

Since $|\bar{R}_1 - \bar{R}_2| = |8.86 - 5.75| = 3.11$ is less than 7.27, populations 1 and 2 do not differ. In a similar manner, C_k for populations 1 and 3 is 7.65. Since the observed absolute difference between 1 and 3 is 6.04 < 7.65, these two populations are not different. Finally, C_k for populations 2 and 3 is 7.91. The actual difference between 2 and 3 is 9.15 > 7.91, and populations 2 and 3 are said to be different.

Common underscoring can be used to summarize based on the average ranks.

$\bar{R}_2$	$\bar{R}_1$	$\bar{R}_3$
5.75	8.86	14.9

Minitab Display 14.5 provides the results for the Pox test. The $H = 8.18$ is the k-value we calculated above. The p-value of 0.017 is also given.

Minitab Display 14.5

```
Kruskal-Wallis Test

LEVEL      NOBS     MEDIAN   AVE. RANK    Z VALUE
    1         7      22.00         8.9      -0.41
    2         6      20.50         5.7      -2.11
    3         5      31.00        14.9       2.66
OVERALL      18                    9.5

H = 8.18  d.f. = 2  P = 0.017
H = 8.24  d.f. = 2  p = 0.017 (adjusted for ties)
```

It should be apparent by now that it is possible to substitute certain nonparametric tests when essential assumptions required for those statistical procedures studied in earlier chapters may not hold. In the absence of specific conditions such as a normally distributed population, these nonparametric tests may be the only appropriate course of action.

Table 14.12 compares nonparametric tests with their parametric counterparts. Where appropriate, the parametric analogue for each nonparametric test is shown. The table also indicates the assumptions required by the parametric tests that are not necessary to conduct the nonparametric counterpart.

Table 14.12
A Comparison of Parametric and Nonparametric Tests

Nonparametric Test	Purpose	Assumption Not Required	Parametric Counterpart
Sign	Test for location of population distribution	Normal distribution of populations	*t*-test for matched pairs
Runs	Test for randomness		None
Mann-Whitney *U*	Compare two independent samples	Difference between samples is normal	*t*-test for independent samples
Kruskal-Wallis	Compare three or more samples	Sample means normally distributed	*F*-test with ANOVA
Spearman rank	Test for relationship between two ordinally ranked variables	Distribution of both variables is normal	Pearsonian correlation coefficient

Section Exercises

18. Recently, Bytec, Inc., has had a problem with employee absenteeism at its three production plants. Based on the data below, taken over a six-day period for the number of employees who are absent, does it seem at the 5 percent level of significance that there is a difference in the number of employees who fail to show for work? If you reject the null, perform a pair-wise comparison complete with common underscoring.

	Number of Absent Employees
Plant 1	25, 36, 38, 31, 29, 33
Plant 2	31, 28, 39, 41, 21, 20
Plant 3	29, 28, 22, 26, 24, 20

19. To test a new pet food, Puppy Love feeds four groups of 10-week old puppies different meal mixes. After three weeks the increase in weights are recorded. Is there a significant difference in the weight increases at the 5 percent level? If you reject the null, perform a pair-wise comparison complete with common underscoring.

	Increase in Weights (pounds)
Mix 1	3, 6, 9, 5, 6
Mix 2	3, 4, 8, 9, 7
Mix 3	10, 8, 9, 8, 7
Mix 4	8, 10, 11, 8, 8

20. Security Investments uses three methods to select stocks for their portfolio. At the 5 percent level, is there a difference in the rates of return for each method based on these data? If you reject the null, perform a pair-wise comparison complete with common underscoring.

	Rates of Return (percentages)
Portfolio 1	14, 12, 10, 15, 13
Portfolio 2	9, 6, 8, 5, 5
Portfolio 3	6, 8, 5, 9, 7

Solved Problems

1. 2B or not 2B—A Quality Control Problem According to *U.S. News & World Report,* a laboratory in Atlanta is processing snake venom for use in medical research. Five processing methods are being tested to determine which is least likely to contaminate the processed venom. If a venom solution is tested as contaminated, it is marked with the symbol "2B." Each method produces 25 vials of venom each day. The vials from each processing method are then boxed for shipment to medical research facilities.

Assume for our purposes that scientists in the laboratory feel that the contamination is uniformly distributed, but others argue that it is binomially distributed. A statistical consultant is retained to examine defect patterns.

a. Is Contamination Uniform? Output over a 100-day period is selected for each processing method, and notation is made as to which method produced the fewer contaminated vials that day. If contamination rates were uniform, the scientists would expect each method to produce the fewest contaminated vials on an equal number of days. Thus, $E_i = n/k = 100/5 = 20$. Both observed and expected frequencies are shown in the accompanying table. For example, on 34 of the 100 days, method 1 produced the fewest contaminated vials of snake venom. The hypotheses are

H_0: Contamination rates are uniform.

H_A: Contamination rates are not uniform.

Processing Method	E_i	O_i	$(O_i - E_i)^2$	$(O_i - E_i)^2/E_i$
1	20	34	196	9.80
2	20	17	9	0.45
3	20	14	36	1.80
4	20	12	64	3.20
5	20	23	49	0.45
	100	100		15.70

With $K - 1 = 4$ degrees of freedom, Table H (Appendix III) shows that a 1 percent test reveals a critical χ^2-value of $\chi^2_{0.01,4} = 13.277$. As shown in the figure, the decision rule is

Decision Rule Do not reject if $\chi^2 \leq 13.277$. Reject if $\chi^2 > 13.277$.

$$\chi^2 = \sum \frac{(O_i - E_i)^2}{E_i}$$
$$= 15.7$$

Since 15.7 > 13.277, we reject the null. The contamination rates do not appear to be uniform.

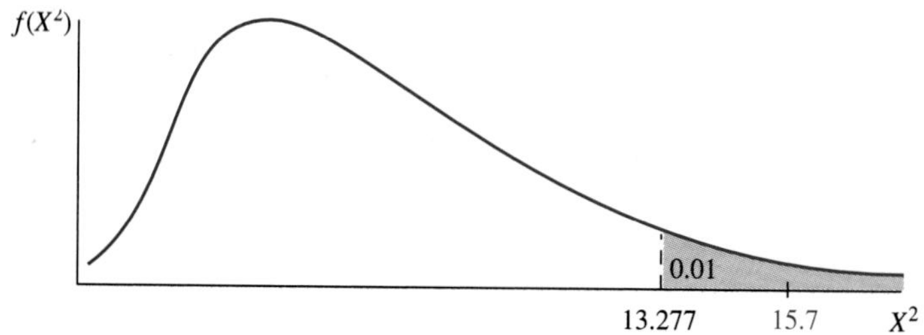

b. *Is Contamination Binomial?* Those scientists in the laboratory who support the idea of a binomial contamination pattern argue that 5 percent of the vials produced are contaminated. Given the 5 percent rate, the statistical consultant is to test the following hypotheses:

H_0: Contamination rates are binomial.

H_A: Contamination rates are not binomial.

The test is first applied to method 1. Each box contains $n = 25$ vials. If a binomial distribution exists in contamination rates with $\pi = 0.05$ as the scientists argued, the probability that any box contains a given number of contaminated vials, X, is found in the binomial table. For example, if $n = 25$ and $\pi = 0.05$, the probability that a box contains zero contaminated vials can be found from Table C (Appendix III) as $P(X = 0 \mid n = 25, \pi = 0.05) = 0.2744$. The probability that only 1 of the 25 vials is contaminated can be found from Table C as $P(X \leq 1) - P(X \leq 0) = 0.6424 - 0.2740 = 0.3650$, and so on. Thus, the expected number of boxes out of the 100 samples that contain zero contaminated vials is $nP_i = (100)(0.2774) = 27.74$ boxes. Notice that for purposes of determining the $P(x)$ from the binomial table, $n = 25$ because there are 25 vials in each box. For determining the number of boxes with x contaminated vials, $n = 100$ because there are 100 boxes.

The values of E_i and O_i are shown in the tables below. The first table shows that 31 of the 100 boxes from method 1 had zero contaminated vials.

Number of Contaminated Vials	O_i	$P(X)$	E_i
0	31	0.2774	27.74
1	32	0.3650	36.50
2	24	0.2305	23.05
3	10	0.0930	9.30
4	2	0.0269	2.69
5 or more	1	0.0072	0.72
	100		

However, some of the values for E_i are less than 5. The last three classes must be combined to correct for this. The second table is the result.

Number of Contaminated Vials	O_i	$P(X)$	E_i	$(O_i - E_i)^2/E_i$
0	31	0.2774	27.74	0.3831
1	32	0.3650	36.50	0.5548
2	24	0.2350	23.50	0.0106
3 or more	13	0.1226	12.26	0.0447
	100			0.9932

If $\alpha = 0.05$, $\chi^2_{0.05,3} = 7.815$.

Decision Rule Do not reject if $\chi^2 \leq 7.815$. Reject if $\chi^2 > 7.815$.

Since $\chi^2 = 0.9932$, we do not reject the null. Contamination rates appear to be binomially distributed.

2. **The Sign Test—A Case of Quality Control** In an effort to improve its product, a firm selling bakery products asks 15 taste testers to rate its whole wheat bread between 0 and 10 before and after a slight change in the ingredients. The results are partially shown in the table.

Tester	Rating Before	Rating After	Sign
1	7	8	–
2	6	6	0
3	9	8	+
4	5	7	–
⋮	⋮	⋮	⋮
15	8	7	+

In total, eight plus signs, five minus signs, and two zero differences were recorded. The firm wants to test at the 5 percent level whether there is any difference. Thus,

$$H_0: m = p$$
$$H_A: m \neq p$$

Then

$$P(m \leq 5 \mid n = 13, \pi = 0.50) = 0.2905$$

The probability of getting at most five minus signs given $m = p$ is greater than $0.05/2 = 0.025$. The firm does not reject the null.

If the sample size had exceeded 30, the Z-test Formula [14.4] would have been used.

3. **A Mann-Whitney *U* Test of Means** Two advertising displays are used to aid the sales of a product. The first display resulted in daily sales of 110, 117, 82, 95, 123, 79, 92, 102, 108, and 113. The second display produced sales of 111, 85, 97, 117, 111, 89, 118, 121, and 109. Would it appear that at the 5 percent level, $\mu_1 = \mu_2$?

Display 1	Rank	Display 2	Rank
79	1	85	3
82	2	89	4
92	5	97	7
95	6	109	10
102	8	111	12.5
108	9	111	12.5
110	11	117	15.5
113	14	118	17
117	15.5	121	18
123	19		
	$90.5 = \Sigma R_1$		$99.5 = \Sigma R_2$

If α is set at 5 percent, the critical Z-value is ± 1.96.

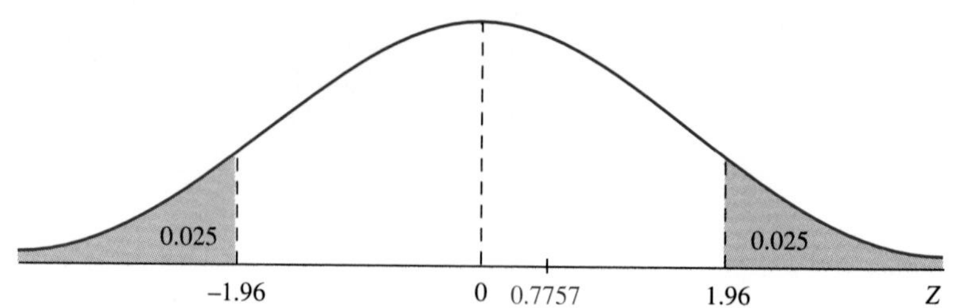

$$H_0\colon \mu_1 = \mu_2$$

$$H_A\colon \mu_1 \neq \mu_2$$

$$\begin{aligned}
U_1 &= n_1 n_2 + \frac{n_1(n_1 + 1)}{2} - \Sigma R_1 \\
&= (10)(9) + \frac{10(10 + 1)}{2} - 90.5 \\
&= 54.5
\end{aligned}$$

$$\begin{aligned}
U_2 &= n_1 n_2 + \frac{n_2(n_2 + 1)}{2} - \Sigma R_2 \\
&= (10)(9) + \frac{9(9 + 1)}{2} - 99.5 \\
&= 35.5
\end{aligned}$$

$$\begin{aligned}
\mu_u &= \frac{n_1 n_2}{2} \\
&= 45
\end{aligned}$$

$$\begin{aligned}
\sigma_u &= \sqrt{\frac{n_1 n_2(n_1 + n_2 + 1)}{12}} \\
&= 12.247
\end{aligned}$$

$$\begin{aligned}
Z &= \frac{U_i - \mu_u}{\sigma_u} \\
&= \frac{54.5 - 45}{12.247} \\
&= 0.7757
\end{aligned}$$

The sample suggests that the null is not to be rejected, and that both displays have the same effect on sales.

4. **Spearman Rank Correlation** A financial consultant is asked to evaluate the investment qualities of eight stocks. She uses the stock's dividend rate as reported in *The Wall Street Journal* and an index potential for growth assigned to each stock by a New York investment firm. The data are shown here and are used to determine whether a relationship might exist between dividends and growth potential.

Stock	Dividend Rate (%)	Dividend Ranking (*X*)	Growth Index	Growth Ranking (*Y*)	*X* − *Y*	$(X - Y)^2$
1	4.20	7	40	6	1	1
2	8.12	2	20	8	−6	36
3	7.20	5	60	4	1	1
4	3.20	8	35	7	1	1
5	8.00	3	85	1	2	4
6	12.73	1	70	2	−1	1
7	7.90	4	50	5	−1	1
8	6.20	6	65	3	3	9
						54

$$r_S = 1 - \frac{6\Sigma d_i^2}{n(n^2 - 1)}$$

$$= 1 - \frac{6(54)}{8(8^2 - 1)}$$

$$= 0.357$$

If $\alpha = 0.10$, test

$$H_0: P_S = 0$$
$$H_A: P_S \neq 0$$

Table N (Appendix III) reveals a critical value of 0.6190. Therefore, do not reject the null.

List of Formulas

[14.1]	$\chi^2 = \sum_{i=1}^{K} \frac{(O_i - E_i)^2}{E_i}$	The chi-square is used to compare observed frequencies with those frequencies we would expect if the null is correct.
[14.2]	$E_i = np_i$	The expected frequencies are those we would expect to happen if the null is correct.
[14.4]	$Z_{\text{test}} = \frac{k \pm 0.5 - 0.5n}{0.5\sqrt{n}}$	Z-value for a large-sample sign test.
[14.5]	$\mu_r = \frac{2n_1n_2}{n_1 + n_2} + 1$	Mean of the sampling distribution of the number of runs.
[14.6]	$\sigma_r = \sqrt{\frac{2n_1n_2(2n_1n_2 - n_1 - n_2)}{(n_1 + n_2)^2(n_1 + n_2 - 1)}}$	Standard deviation for the runs test.
[14.7]	$Z = \frac{r - \mu_r}{\sigma_r}$	Normal deviate for the distribution of runs.
[14.8]	$U_1 = n_1n_2 + \frac{n_1(n_1 + 1)}{2} - \Sigma R_1$	The Mann-Whitney *U* statistic tests the equality of two populations.
[14.10]	$\mu_u = \frac{n_1n_2}{2}$	Mean of the sampling distribution of the Mann-Whitney *U* statistic.
[14.11]	$\sigma_u = \sqrt{\frac{n_1n_2(n_1 + n_2 + 1)}{12}}$	Standard deviation of the Mann-Whitney *U* statistic.
[14.12]	$Z = \frac{U_i - \mu_u}{\sigma_u}$	Normalization of the Mann-Whitney *U* statistic.

[14.13]	$r_S = 1 - \dfrac{6\Sigma d_i^2}{n(n^2 - 1)}$	The Spearman rank correlation coefficient tests for any relationship between ordinally ranked variables.
[14.14]	$Z = r_s\sqrt{n - 1}$	Normal deviate for the Spearman rank test with large samples.
[14.15]	$K = \dfrac{12}{n(n+1)}\left[\Sigma\dfrac{R_i^2}{n_i}\right] - 3(n+1)$	The Kruskal-Wallis test is used to compare three or more populations.
[14.16]	$C_k = \sqrt{\chi^2_{\alpha,k-1}\dfrac{n(n+1)}{12}\left[\dfrac{1}{n_i} = \dfrac{1}{n_j}\right]}$	Determines the critical value in a Kruskal-Wallis Test for pair-wise comparisons.

Chapter Exercises

21. You have been asked by your supervisor to determine whether there is a relationship between the type of capital budgeting technique a firm uses and its net income after taxes. The data you collect relate three techniques—net present value, internal rate of return, and profitability index—to four income levels: 0 to \$3 million, \$3 million to \$6 million, \$6 million to \$9 million, and above \$9 million. The number of firms falling in the joint categories has been tabulated. What statistical tool would you use to detect any relationship?

22. You are to compare the mean spending levels of three groups of consumers, but you cannot assume that the populations are normally distributed or that their variances are equal. What tool should you use?

23. As regional manager for a retail firm, you want to determine whether people's income levels and their consumption patterns are related. What tool should you use?

24. An economist for an international bank holding company collected data on the consumption levels of 25 people before and after the federal government announced a large tax increase. What tool will allow the economist to determine whether the tax affected mean consumption?

25. You are to select a sample of your firm's customers based on gender. How can you determine whether the sampling procedure is random?

26. Your statistical assistant has obtained data on two independent samples taken to compare people's ages. If it cannot be assumed that the populations are normal, what test should he use?

27. Why do we use nonparametric tests? Why not always rely on parametric tests, since they are stronger?

28. What is being measured by a sign test?

29. What is measured by a runs test?

30. Cite your own example in which the Spearman test would be required, and describe exactly what it is you are measuring in this example.

31. A bank in Des Moines wants to determine whether the distribution of customers is uniform throughout the week. A survey finds that the numbers of customers Monday through Friday are 150, 179, 209, 79, and 252. At the 5 percent level, does it appear that a uniform distribution exists?

a. State the hypotheses.
b. State the decision rule.
c. Conduct the test and make your determination.

32. Professor Showers argues that his grade distribution is 5 percent A's, 20 percent B's, 30 percent C's, 40 percent D's, and the rest F's. If this is the case, his dean has promised him a 15 percent raise. At the 1 percent level, does the kind professor get his raise if 100 randomly selected grades provide this breakdown: 7 A's, 20 B's, 27 C's, 36 D's, and 10 F's?

33. Creative Floorings has decided to order its supplies in bulk if the size of carpet placed in homes is normally distributed. Help the company managers make this decision based on the following sample data. Set alpha at 1 percent.

Square Yards (100's)	Number of Houses of This Size
Up to 5	97
5 to 10	137
10 to 15	245
15 to 20	256
20 to 25	154
25 and above	111

34. The frequency table shown records daily sales for 200 days. At $\alpha = 0.05$, do sales appear to be normally distributed?

Sales	Frequency
40 up to 60	7
60 up to 80	22
80 up to 100	46
100 up to 120	42
120 up to 140	42
140 up to 160	18
160 up to 180	11
180 up to 200	12

35. Citizens for a Nonviolent Media provided data that were subsequently published in a recent issue of *U.S. News & World Report* on the number of acts of violence seen in types to television programs. The organization claimed that such acts occur with equal frequency across all program types. Test this claim at the 10 percent level.

Type of Program	Acts of Violence
Drama	42
Old movies	57
Cartoons	83
Police/detective	92
Comedy	38
News	81

36. Greenpeace, the worldwide conservation group, recently called for a United Nations sanction on the killing of baby harp seals in what it called "high mortality months." Finland, which still permits these "harvests," stated that the activity was consistent throughout the year and did not vary by month. Given the data for 1997 provided by Greenpeace, what conclusion can you reach? Set alpha at 1 percent.

Month	Number of Kills
January	112
February	89
March	156
April	104
May	165

37. The production manager of AAA, Inc., must ensure that his product mix fits a particular quota system. He is instructed to adjust to a pattern that produces 30 percent silk goods, 20 percent wool, 10 percent cotton, and 40 percent leather. Of the last 200 units produced, 65 were silk, 45 were wool, 25 were cotton, and 65 were leather. At the 5 percent level, should he adjust the current production pattern? State the hypotheses.

38. A retail chain has six outlets. It has been spending heavily to produce similar sales levels at all six stores. The advertising firm handling the promotional efforts claims that now each store should report equal sales. If sales are not the same, the retail chain has decided to discontinue its association with the ad agency. What decision should be made based on the data shown here? State your hypotheses. Set $\alpha = 0.01$.

Store	Sales ($100's)
1	42
2	37
3	53
4	51
5	45
6	47

39. Macy's department store in New York recently did a study to determine whether there was any relationship between a customer's marital status and his or her dollar volume of purchases. The results are shown in the table. What is your conclusion at the 5 percent level of significance?

	Dollar Volume				
	<10	10–19	20–29	30–39	40–49
Married	32	23	15	12	14
Divorced	51	17	10	15	13
Single	21	19	29	35	39
Widowed	18	15	19	10	9

40. The U.S. Treasury Department has estimated that the "increase in the typical taxpayer's fee necessary to balance the budget is uniformly distributed across states." The February 28, 1994, issue of *U.S. News & World Report* published the following statistics:

State	Average Taxpayer's Hike (Top 10 States)
Connecticut	$1,100
New Jersey	952
New York	877
Massachusetts	852
DC	851
Maryland	840
Nevada	828
Illinois	822
Washington	809
California	789

At the 5 percent level, can the Treasury Department be supported?

41. The General Store will determine sales dates based on the distribution of revenues. Given the data below, does it appear at the 5 percent level that revenues are normal? The mean is known to be 25.6, and σ is 10.1.

Revenue/Month ($100's)	Number of Months
Up to 10	10
10 to 20	23
20 to 30	30
30 to 40	25
40 and above	12

42. Consider the data below for job completion times, which were taken from a population with a mean of 18 and a standard deviation of 4.

Times (Hours)	Number of Jobs
Up to 10	10
10 to 15	101
15 to 20	223
20 to 25	146
25 and above	20

a. At the 5 percent level, can it be concluded that times are normally distributed?

b. How do the results differ if the first inteval is "5 to 10" and the last is "25 to 30"?

43. The chief economist at the state revenue office is debating with his supervisor who argues that tax payments are normally distributed. Data on 2,000 taxpayers provided the results seen here. At the 1 percent level, is the supervisor correct?

Tax Payment ($10's)	Taxpayers
Up to 15	248
15 to 30	232
30 to 45	489
45 to 60	512
60 to 75	263
75 and above	256

44. *Runner's World* reported that a survey by Converse of people who regularly run for exercise resulted in the data shown here. The intent of the survey was to determine whether the distances were independent of runners' preference for a gel-like product built into the heels of their jogging shoes. At the 1 percent level, does there appear to be any relationship? State the hypotheses.

Distance/Week (miles)	Prefer Gel	Do Not Prefer Gel	No Opinion
<3	14	5	27
3–6	18	5	17
7–10	12	8	8
10–13	17	12	5
>13	19	8	2

45. Data on years of experience and efficiency ratings for 431 employees at XYZ, Inc. are shown in the table. Can you conclude that these attributes are independent of each other? Set $\alpha = 5$ percent.

	Efficiency			
Experience in Years	Poor	Good	Excellent	Superior
<5	14	18	12	17
5–10	18	13	27	42
11–16	16	32	24	37
17–22	24	28	21	32
>22	17	15	14	10

46. The results of a study by the American Marketing Association to determine the relationship between the importance store owners attach to advertising and the size of store they own are shown in the table. Would it seem that all store owners place the same emphasis on advertising? Set $\alpha = 0.10$. State the hypotheses.

	Advertising		
Size	Important	Not Important	No Opinion
Small	20	52	32
Medium	53	47	28
Large	67	32	25

47. A bottling company in Atlanta is interested in the effects of three methods used to sanitize glass containers. It grades containers to determine whether sanitation is independent of the method. At the 10 percent level of significance, what is your conclusion based on the data in the table?

	Sanitation Grade		
Method	Acceptable	Marginal	Unacceptable
A	140	132	63
B	89	74	44
C	104	98	50

48. Eight test subjects are asked to rate a product before and after viewing a commercial for it. The ratings are shown in the table, where a rating of 10 is best. Set $\alpha = 0.10$ and use a sign test for the hypothesis that the commercial improved the product's rating. State the hypotheses.

	Ratings	
Test Subject	Before Commercial	After Commercial
1	8	9
2	7	6
3	5	6
4	5	5
5	5	4
6	7	8
7	6	7
8	6	8

49. A chemical compound is added to an oil base solution in hopes of increasing its lubricating qualities. Twenty solutions, 10 with the compound and 10 without, are compared with respect to their ability to lubricate machinery. Each is graded on a scale from 0 to 10, with 10 being the best. Based on the data in the table, does it appear that addition of the compound increases lubrication? Set $\alpha = 0.10$. State the hypotheses. What is your conclusion regarding the value of the chemical compound?

	Lubrication Grade	
Solution	Without Compound	With Compound
1	8	4
2	7	8
3	5	2
4	6	9
5	9	5
6	4	4
7	9	2
8	8	6
9	7	6
10	6	7

50. Shytel, Inc. offers communication services anywhere in the world with two satellites, the *Falcon* and the *Eagle*. Shytel's CEO thinks that the *Eagle* results in longer delays in transmission. Transmission times are shown in minutes in the table. At the 5 percent level, does it appear that the CEO is correct? State your hypotheses.

Transmission Times (minutes)		
Falcon	Eagle	Sign
5.2	4.7	+
8.6	7.9	+
9.0	9.7	−
4.3	8.4	−
6.2	3.7	+
7.9	7.3	+

51. Clyde Bloomquist has proposed a change in corporate policy concerning collection of accounts receivable. He feels it will speed the time required to obtain outstanding debts from creditors. Company records show that eight creditors took the number of days shown in the table before and after the policy change to remit funds due. Is Clyde correct? Should the policy change be retained? Set $\alpha = 0.10$. State the hypotheses.

Creditor	Before	After
1	18	12
2	27	22
3	32	31
4	23	24
5	31	28
6	36	24
7	18	16
8	35	25

52. Shoppers in a large mall in Dayton were randomly asked which of two brands of yogurt they preferred. Forty-two said Swedish Heaven, 31 chose Merry Melody, and 12 expressed no preference. If the local yogurt shop is to carry only one brand, which should it be? Set $\alpha = 0.10$. State the hypotheses.

53. A manufacturer uses parts from either supplier A or supplier B to make his product. A check of yesterday's output reveals that the order in which these suppliers' parts were used was

AA	BBB	AAA	B	A	BB	AA	BB

Does it appear that the parts are being used randomly? Set $\alpha = 0.05$. State your hypotheses and conclusion.

54. Smile Bright sells toothpaste in 17-ounce containers. Management expects overfills and underfills to be random. If they are not, management assumes something is wrong with the fill system, and shuts down the production line. Should the line be shut down if containers measure 16.8, 18.2, 17.3, 17.5, 16.3, 17.4, 16.1, 16.9, 17, 18.1, 17.3, 16.2, 17.3, and 16.8 ounces? Let $\alpha = 0.05$

55. Sales receipts are recorded for the past 37 days. You denote those values below the median with a "B" and those above it with an "A." Counting the results, you find 18 A's and 19 B's with 10 runs. Your policy is to increase advertising if receipts are not randomly distributed. Should you increase advertising? State the hypotheses. Let $\alpha = 0.05$.

56. Acme Plumbing bids on construction jobs for city buildings. If contracts are granted by the city without regard to political consideration, Acme should witness no pattern in whether its bid is accepted or rejected. For the last 63 bids, Acme has had 32 accepted and the rest rejected, with 27 runs. At the 5 percent level, would it appear that bids are let on the basis of politics? State the hypotheses, the decision rule, and your conclusion.

57. Gladys Glucose offers vanilla- and chocolate-flavored ice cream to visitors in the park. The last 73 sales consisted of 40 vanilla and 33 chocolate, with 16 runs. If sales are not random, Gladys will move her ice cream truck to the local zoo. Where should she set up business? Let $\alpha = 0.05$.

58. A large company hired 52 men and 41 women, resulting in 32 runs. If absence of randomness in the hiring process indicates discrimination, can it be alleged that the company practices sex discrimination in its hiring practices? Set $\alpha = 0.10$.

59. Over a 12-day period, Gladys Glucose sold 4, 11, 5, 7, 10, 13, 12, 5, 9, 6, 2, and 1 gallons of vanilla, and 19, 4, 6, 8, 18, 17, 17, 15, 3, 16, 14, and 0 gallons of chocolate. Using the Mann-Whitney *U* test, can she conclude that she sells the same amount of both flavors on the average? Set $\alpha = 0.01$.

60. The marketing director for Software, Inc., treated 15 computer disks with a solution designed to reduce wear. A second solution was used to treat 15 other disks, and all were graded on the basis of wear. Those treated with the first solution showed improved wear, measured in hours of use of 65, 73, 82, 52, 47, 51, 85, 92, 69, 77, 84, 68, 75, 74, and 89 hours. Those subjected to the second solution reported increased wear times of 73, 84, 91, 87, 90, 71, 72, 93, 99, 98, 89, 88, 79, 88, and 98 hours. At the 10 percent level, can the director conclude that there is any difference in the improved wear factors?

61. The quality control manager for a large plant in Denver gives two operations manuals to two groups of employees. Each group is then tested on operations procedures. The scores are shown in the table. The manager has always felt that manual 1 provides a better base of knowledge for new employees. Compare the mean test scores of the employees shown here and report your conclusion. State the hypotheses. Set $\alpha = 0.05$.

	Employee Test Scores													
Manual 1	87	97	82	97	92	90	81	89	90	88	87	89	93	
Manual 2	92	79	80	73	84	93	86	88	91	82	81	84	72	74

62. Two manufacturing processes are used to make I-beams for construction of large buildings. Each I-beam is tested, and its tensile strength is recorded. Twenty-three beams made with the first process result in $\Sigma R_1 = 690$, and 27 beams made via the second process produce $\Sigma R_2 = 585$. A construction engineer argues that the first process results in beams that have at least the tensile strength demonstrated by beams made by the second process. At the 5 percent level, is she right?

63. An agricultural economist treats 50 acres of land with the chemical docide to increase crop yield. Fifty other acres are treated with mildolmine, and yields are measured. $\Sigma R_D = 2{,}125$ and $\Sigma R_M = 2{,}925$. The economist tells farmers that docide, which is a cheaper chemical, will produce a yield higher than mildolmine. At the 10 percent level, is he correct? State the hypotheses.

64. *Personnel Management* carried an article describing efforts by a manufacturing firm in Toledo to evaluate its supervisors. Employees were asked to rate their supervisors on a scale of 10 to 100. A subset of the results is shown here for three of the work areas. Determine whether a difference exists in the ratings received by the supervisors. State the hypotheses, the decision rule, and your conclusion. Set α at 5 percent.

Shop	Office	Loading Dock
40	63	50
52	59	52
63	55	63
81	61	55
72	48	71
72	53	45
	49	

65. A total of 48 service calls are sampled by a local plumbing contractor to determine which of four types of plumbing fixtures produce the most problems. The results are shown here.

Fixture Model	Number of Failures
1	15
2	11
3	10
4	12

At the 1 percent level of significance, does the failure of the fixtures appear to be uniformly distributed? State your hypotheses, decision rule, and conclusion.

66. Four methods of treating steel rods are analyzed to determine whether there is any difference in analyzed the pressure the rods can bear before breaking. The results of tests measuring the pressure in pounds before the rods bent are shown. Conduct the test, complete with the hypotheses, decision rule, and conclusion. Set $\alpha = 1$ percent.

Method 1	Method 2	Method 3	Method 4
50	10	72	54
62	12	63	59
73	10	73	64
48	14	82	82
63	10	79	79

67. The World's-Second-Best-Yogurt asks 60 people which of four new yogurt flavors they preferred. Twenty-one chose coconut-pickle, 13 chose prune with ketchup topping, 10 selected mustard á la peanut butter, and 16 expressed a partiality for essence of tuna. Does there appear to be a preference among the flavors by the customers? Set α at 10 percent. State the hypotheses and your conclusion.

68. For extra credit in her statistics course, Barbara must determine whether there is a difference in the average number of hours spent studying by freshmen, sophomores, juniors, and seniors at her university. Her research revealed the following:

Freshmen	Sophomores	Juniors	Seniors
20	18	22	29
29	9	19	31
10	12	21	27
17	15	31	22
15	14	42	18
23	22	22	31
27			

Help Barbara earn her extra credit in statistics by stating her hypotheses and conclusion. Set $\alpha = 10$ percent.

69. As product manager of Sports Wear, Inc., Beverlee Hills must ensure that the sizes of its new line of active wear are produced according to a certain predetermined pattern. The market research indicates that customers prefer 20 percent extra large, 30 percent large, 25 percent medium, and 25 percent small. A random sample of 145 garments reveals 32 extra large, 40 large, 41 medium, and 32 small. At the 5 percent level, does it appear that the desired proportion of sizes is being observed?

70. Ms. Hills, from the previous exercise, must determine whether the spending habits of various demographic groups are the same. She examines the size of typical purchases, measured in dollars, of four groups: married males (MM), married females (MF), single males (SM), and single females (SF). She finds the following information.

MM	MF	SM	SF
$50	$20	$19	$87
17	23	32	20
23	82	66	95
48	46	72	34
63	13	41	11

At the 1 percent level of significance, does it appear that a difference exists in spending habits of these four groups?

71. Seven corporate bond issues are ranked as to their investment worth by two financial analysts. The results are shown here. Using these rankings as a sample, calculate the Spearman rank correlation test to determine whether there is any correlation between the rating practices of these two analysts at the 10 percent level.

Corporation	Rating of First Analyst	Rating of Second Analyst
1	4	3
2	3	4
3	1	2
4	2	5
5	7	6
6	6	1
7	5	7

72. Six truck models are rated on a scale of 1 to 10 by two companies that purchase entire fleets of trucks for industrial use. Calculate the Spearman rank coefficient to determine at the 1 percent level whether the rankings are independent.

Model	Rating by First Company	Rating by Second Company
1	8	9
2	7	6
3	5	8
4	7	5
5	3	7
6	2	8

73. All 50 states are ranked by two travel agencies as to their desirability as a vacation spots. The results reveal $\Sigma d^2 = 22{,}712$. Test for independence in ratings at the 10 percent level.

74. The top 10 firms on Fortune's 500 list were ranked by the AFL-CIO and by a management group on the basis of the quality of the health care system each company provides its employees. Using the results shown here, determine at the 5 percent level whether there is any correlation in the rating practices of unions and management.

Firm	Union Ranking	Management Ranking	Firm	Union Ranking	Management Ranking
1	5	6	6	6	4
2	8	10	7	1	8
3	2	3	8	9	1
4	7	9	9	3	2
5	4	7	10	10	5

75. Seventy-three employees are ranked by two managers on the basis of their productivity levels. Calculate the Spearman rank coefficient to determine whether the rankings are independent at the 1 percent level of $\Sigma d^2 = 78{,}815$.

CURTAIN CALL

In order to help Mama resolve her problems with Dante's, as described in Setting the Stage, you must first determine students' preferences for pizza toppings. Surveying 135 students, you find that 47 prefer pepperoni, 63 sausage, and 21 cheese, whereas 4 want veggie pizza. Mama feels these preferences are uniformly distributed, while you think they are more likely to fit a pattern described as 35 percent, 45 percent, 15 percent, and 5 percent, respectively.

You try to fit a normal distribution to students' expenditures based on your survey, which yielded the pattern described in the following frequency table. What are your findings?

Expenditure	Frequency
$0 and under $5	4
$5 and under $10	11
$10 and under $15	45
$15 and under $20	47
$20 and under $25	25
$25 and above	3

You also want to determine whether there is any relationship between the students' preferences for large (L), medium (M), and small (S) pizzas and their status as either graduate students (G) or undergraduates students (U). Your data show the following outcome:

	L	M	S
U	51	19	9
G	22	15	19

Mama is interested in whether there is a difference in the mean number of times per week undergraduates eat out as compared to graduate students. Taking a subset of 10 graduates and 10 undergraduates from your sample of 135 students, you find these numbers to be

Student	1	2	3	4	5	6	7	8	9	10
Undergraduate	6	9	11	8	6	12	15	5	7	9
Graduate	3	0	8	4	2	2	5	4	1	0

What do you report to Mama?

Finally, you are to determine whether there is any relationship for undergraduates between the number of times per week a student eats at Mama's and his or her income. The ten undergraduates report incomes per week of $50, $60, $80, $55, $45, $90, $100, $50, $55, and $60 respectively.

Prepare your report to Mama in the form of a statistical report, as described in Appendix I.

From the Stage to Real Life

As the market analyst in the Setting the Stage chapter opener, you will likely want to gather menu information from franchise companies such as Pizza Hut and Dominos. Their offerings in your own area or in similar college towns in other parts of the county can provide new ideas for you to test as well as to gain collaboration the results of your survey.

You can check out Pizza Hut menus at (*http://www.pizzahut.com.hk*). At the home page, click on the animated pizza box. Then click on "Full Menu." Here you can link to different areas to see the variety of their pizza offerings as well as their pasta and appetizer and beverage menus. Explore these areas. Do you see any pizza combination specials of potential interest in your local market? Have you already included those in the survey you are doing for Mama's Pizzeria? Are some of the appetizers appealing in your local market as well as reasonable for offering within Mama's operation? How might an extended menu help the business?

You can check out Domino's offerings at (*http://www.dominos.com*). At the home page, click on "Explore." At the next page, click on "Pizza Fest." Scroll down to the "To 10!" link and click on it. After viewing this information, scroll to the bottom of the page and click on "Pizza Oven." The left column provides more extensive menu information than the Top 10! location. Answer the same questions that were posed for Pizza Hut.

Which of these sites is more helpful to you and why?

CHAPTER 15

Quality Control Techniques

Chapter Blueprint

As competition for consumer dollars intensifies worldwide, the importance that a firm attaches to improving the quality of its product grows proportionately. This chapter explores the tests that a firm may conduct to implement a quality control program designed to promote reliability and expand its competitive position in the market.

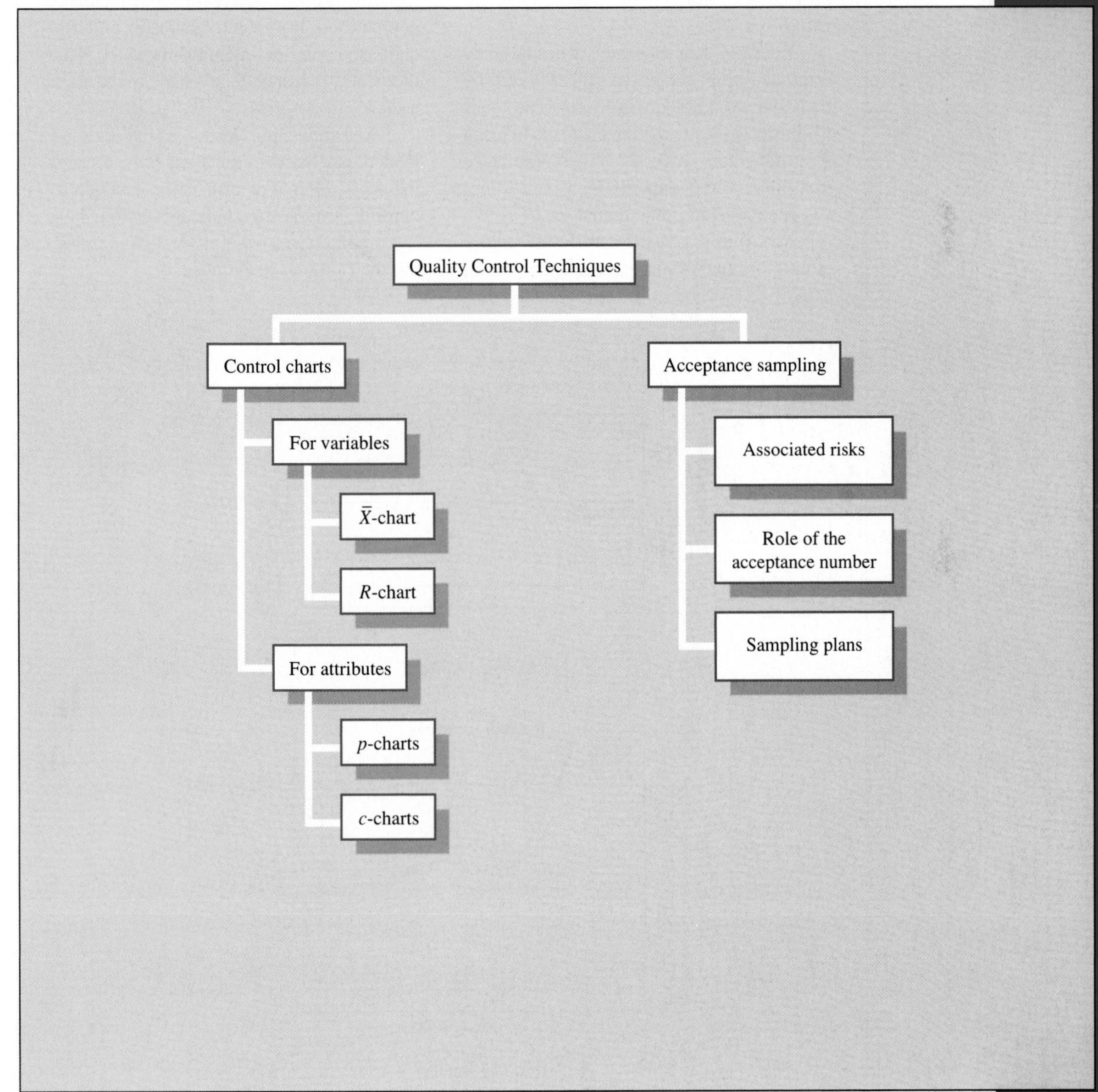

SETTING THE STAGE

Last year Minot Industries, a major manufacturer of glassware, was forced to modernize its plant in Toledo to stay current with the level of technology many of its competitors had adopted earlier. Since the plant was redesigned, Minot has experienced numerous problems with cost overruns, defective production, employee morale, and other troublesome developments.

Recently, Ray Murdock was appointed as the new chief executive officer (CEO) by the major stockholders in Minot. The focus of Murdock's rejuvenation efforts is to bring all production processes into compliance with the quality standards for which Minot was once revered in the industry.

Mr. Murdock realizes this will require an extraordinary team effort on the part of all his executive officers, as well as the line personnel who in the past have been faithfully committed to the goals and aspirations of Minot Industries.

In the past, Minot was able to maintain its production standards with little effort and with little concern for quality. The raw materials used by its capable labor force ensured that Minot would produce a superior product. However, with increased competition from both domestic and foreign sources, maintaining product standards at a reasonable cost has proved to be a more elusive goal.

Reestablishing Minot as an industry leader can be accomplished only through the application of precise methods of quality control. This is the challenge facing those loyal employees, who are willing to carry out their professional duties.

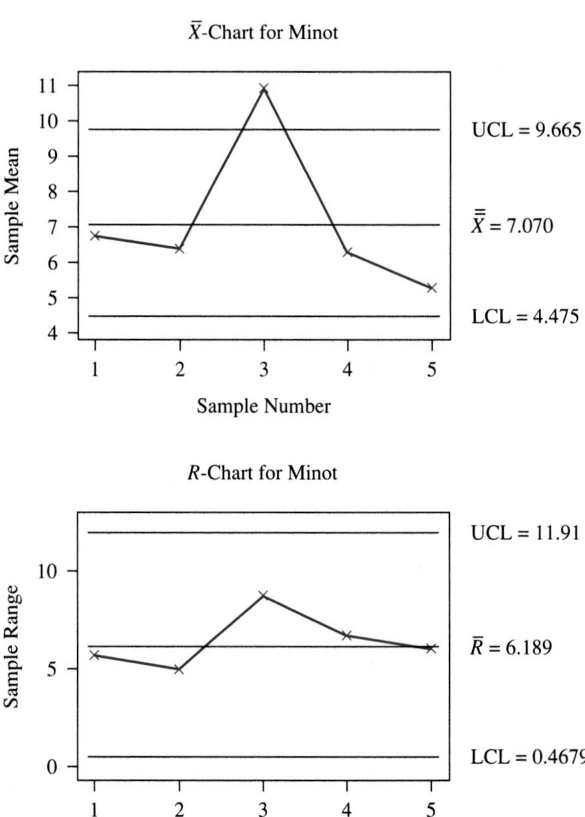

15.1 Introduction

Over the past several years the level of domestic and foreign competition has intensified considerably. This increased level of rivalry among business firms has created an ever-pressing need to monitor and maintain the quality of products. As competition stiffens, it becomes increasingly difficult to acquire and retain a share of the market sufficient to permit economic survival. Without careful measures to ensure that its product meets certain minimum specifications, a business is even less likely to survive the harsh competitive conditions of today's marketplace.

This chapter examines the numerous statistical tools that firms can use to administer an effective program to regulate the overall quality of their products, thereby making them more competitive. A quality control program of this nature usually relies quite heavily on techniques such as:

- Control charts for variables:
  - $\bar{X}$-charts.
  - R-charts.
- Control charts for attributes:
  - p-charts.
  - c-charts.
- Operating characteristic curves.
- Acceptance sampling.

15.2 A Brief History of the World Development of Quality Control

Prior to the Industrial Revolution, production was carried out primarily by skilled artisans. So strong was the pride they took in their work that they often signed each finished piece. With the advent of the Industrial Revolution and the growth of the factory system, production became fragmented, with sole culpability for the product resting on no one in particular. All too often, this shift in production methods minimized the worker's identification with the product, and the care he or she took in completing a job. Production quality and care for consumer needs dwindled as a result.

In the mid-1920s, Walter Shewhart, a researcher at Bell Laboratories, made an early and significant breakthrough in the area of product improvement. He recognized that, although variation in manufactured products was inevitable, this variation could be monitored and controlled using certain statistical processes. He developed a simple graphical tool, called a control chart, to determine when this variation exceeded acceptable limits.

During World War II, the nation's need for large quantities of high-quality war materials spurred further interest in control charts and related statistical tools, and promoted a general concern for quality control. However, it was not until the late 1970s, when U.S. manufacturers faced relentless competition from a flood of superior Japanese imports, that U.S. interest in quality control became widespread.

W. Edwards Deming studied with Shewhart, and then took a position with the Department of Agriculture and later with the Census Bureau. Although he is now recognized worldwide as one of the leading pioneers in the field of quality control, early on, only the Japanese studied his ideas seriously. Deming developed an entire philosophy of quality management based on his "14 points," which state, among other things, that with the proper organizational climate, statistical methods of process improvement can reduce the variation referred to by Shewhart, decrease cost dramatically, and improve an organization's image as well as its financial position. Deming argued that quality development was an ongoing and never-ending process that required close and continual monitoring of the production process.

In 1951, Deming was invited to speak before the Japanese Union of Scientists and Engineers. The Japanese were concerned about the reputation they had developed for producing and exporting inferior, cheaply made products. In a lengthy series of lectures and meetings with Japanese leaders in both industry and government, Deming convinced the Japanese that, by listening to the consumer and by applying statistical methods of quality control, they could expand their production and export products of high quality throughout the world. Deming's ideas and teachings were instrumental in placing the Japanese in the enviable position they now enjoy as a world economic power. In his honor, the Japanese established the Deming prize, which is given to companies recognized for outstanding quality improvement.

Table 15.1
The Malcolm Baldrige National Quality Award Criteria

Examination Categories/Items		Point Values
1 Leadership		**110**
1.1 Leadership System	80	
1.2 Company Responsibility and Citizenship	30	
2 Strategic Planning		**80**
2.1 Strategy Development Process	40	
2.2 Company Strategy	40	
3 Customer and Market Focus		**80**
3.1 Customer and Market Knowledge	40	
3.2 Customer Satisfaction and Relationship Enhancement	40	
4 Information and Analysis		**80**
4.1 Selection and Use of Information and Data	25	
4.2 Selection and Use of Comparative Information and Data	15	
4.3 Analysis and Review of Company Performance	40	
5 Human Resource Development and Management		**100**
5.1 Work Systems	40	
5.2 Employee Education, Training, and Development	30	
5.3 Employee Well-Being and Satisfaction	30	
6 Process Management		**100**
6.1 Management of Product and Service Processes	60	
6.2 Management of Support Processes	20	
6.3 Management of Supplier and Partnering Processes	20	
7 Business Results		**450**
7.1 Customer Satisfaction Results	130	
7.2 Financial and Market Results	130	
7.3 Human Resource Results	35	
7.4 Supplier and Partner Results	25	
7.5 Company Specific Results	130	
TOTAL POINTS		**1,000**

Source: 1997 Award Criteria, The Malcolm Baldrige National Quality Award, United States Department of Commerce.

Joseph Juran was noted for preaching the benefits of quality control to the Japanese. As did Deming, Juran argued that a commitment by top management to quality control was essential. He stated that quality was the responsibility of managers, and that they should attend to it as they would to any other functional area such as finance or marketing.

Many awards have been developed to recognize achievement in American industry. Perhaps most notable is the Malcolm Baldrige National Quality Award. Established in 1988 and named after the U.S. Secretary of Commerce from 1981 until his death in 1987, this award is designed to recognize those firms that exhibit a commitment to product excellence. Past winners include Motorola (1988): Xerox (1989); and IBM, Federal Express, and Cadillac (1990). Table 15.1 shows the specific criteria used to determine the winners. Based on these criteria, the winners of the award in 1997 were 3M Dental Products Division; Merrill Lynch Credit Corporation; Xerox Business Services; and Solectron Corporation, a designer and manufacturer of high-tech equipment.

In the rest of this chapter we will examine many of the tools useful to quality management. We begin with the control charts first developed by Walter Shewhart.

15.3 Control Charts for Variables

Control charts are commonly used to monitor the quality of a product in an ongoing manufacturing process. They allow the quality control expert to closely observe any variation in the process, and alert the manufacturer to changes in the nature of the product. This aids in the assurance that the product meets certain manufacturing specifications and quality standards.

Almost all manufacturing firms pursue quality control programs. The purpose is to detect as soon as possible any variation in an important characteristic of a product, such as its size, weight, color tone, or, in the case of containers, fill level. Such variation has two sources: (1) chance (or common) variation, and (2) assignable cause variation. **Chance variation** occurs simply because, like snowflakes, no two items are identical. Natural differences are to be expected, and cause no real problems in terms of controlling a product's quality level. Every product contains some slight inherent variation.

> **Chance Variation** Small variations in the product or production process are to be expected, due to the inherent dissimilarity in productive inputs used in the production process.

An **assignable cause variation,** however, is a variation in excess of any natural difference. It is due to some specific cause that can (and must) be identified and corrected. An assignable cause variation results in defective products and suggests that the production process is "out of control." It is caused by human error, a faulty mechanical device used in the production process, or other improper procedure.

> **Assignable Cause Variation** Assignable cause variation in the product or production process signals that the process is out of control and corrective efforts are required.

In collecting data for a quality control study, it is common to take a series of samples over time during the production process. It is suggested that the number of samples collected,

k, should be at least 20, and the size of each sample, n, should be between 5 and 15. Each sample is called a **subgroup.**

In selecting each sample it is often necessary to observe **rational subgrouping.** This requires that each sample be selected in such a way as to ensure that the force causing variation occurs *between* samples, not *within* samples. Thus, none of the observations in the sample prior to the onset of the causal force are affected, while all the observations in the sample taken after onset are subject to the variation caused by the force.

For example, FCI Telemarketing uses a "hot room" to market its clients' products and services. A hot room contains a large telephone bank from which operators call as many potential customers as possible, and deliver a sales pitch hoping to get an order. Operators are graded in part on the speed with which they complete calls. To avoid boredom, the operators work for only one hour at a time; then a new shift of workers is rotated through. To detect any differences in operator performance, samples should be selected within a given hour. No sample should span across two or more shifts of workers. Thus, any differences in means beyond chance variation can be assigned to the suspected force—in this case, a change in personnel.

Eastman-Kodak manufactures a shutter release for its cameras which must meet precise production specifications. The device must measure 0.94 centimeters (cm), with an allowable tolerance of 0.03 cm. That is, its acceptable range is from 0.91 to 0.97 cm. Measurements are taken periodically and the results are recorded in a control chart. In this manner it can be quickly determined whether the release mechanism is meeting production specifications.

Figure 15.1
Result of a Change in the Mean

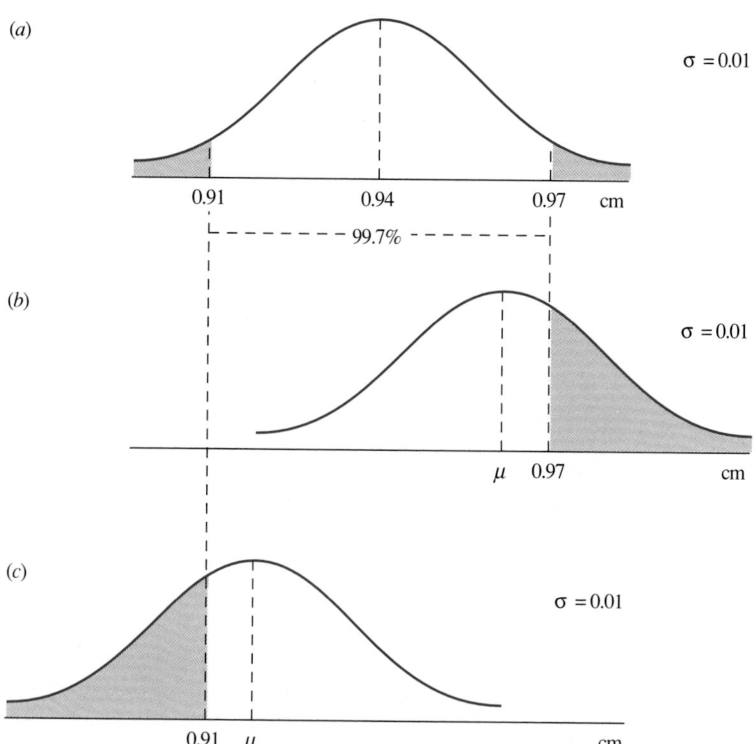

Assume for the moment that the process is in perfect control, producing a mean of 0.94 cm with a standard deviation of 0.01 cm. Figure 15.1(a) illustrates this condition. We see that 99.7 percent of all the mechanisms are within production specifications. The remaining 0.03 percent are defective due only to chance variation.

Figure 15.1(b) displays the result of a process that is out of control and is producing a mean greater than 0.94 cm (assume that the standard deviation remains 0.01). This might occur if, to cite one example, the machine used in the production process experienced unusual wear. The area in Figure 15.1(b) above 0.97 cm represents the percentage of defects due to assignable cause variation—in this case machine wear.

Machine wear might be just as likely to cause the process to go out of control by producing a mean *less* than 0.94 cm, as we see in Figure 15.1(c). Again, the area below 0.91 cm represents the proportion of output unacceptable due to assignable cause.

Figure 15.2 illustrates the impact of a change in dispersion. Figure 15.2(a) depicts a process in control, with a mean of 0.94 cm and an acceptable standard deviation. However, worker fatigue over time, for example, might result in production that varies considerably from unit to unit. The results of this increased deviation are shown in Figure 15.2(b). Assuming the mean has not changed, the process is nevertheless out of control due to excessive variation in dispersion. The units above 0.97 cm and below 0.91 cm are defective. Of course, it is possible for both the location and the dispersion to go out of control at the same time.

Figure 15.2
Result of Change in Dispersion

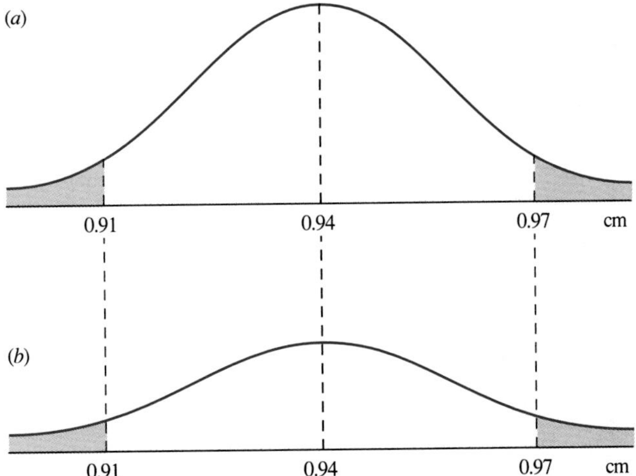

In contrast to Figure 15.2, showing the condition of the production process at a point in time, control charts more often plot measures over time. Figure 15.3 illustrates four different ways a process may go out of control over time. Figure 15.3(a) is said to result from a "shock" effect in that the sudden change in location can likely be attributed to some occurrence that happened abruptly. A shift change in which an inexperienced worker came on duty, or the abrupt introduction of inferior raw materials, might cause such an occurrence. In any event, assignable cause variation (in the mean) has been identified and action must be taken to locate and correct the cause of this varaition.

Both Figure 15.3(b) and 15.3(c) suggest a much more gradual loss of control. The cause might be progressive wear on the machine. In the first instance, the variation in dispersion causes the process to lose control; in the second, control is lost due to an upward trend in the mean. Again, corrective steps must be taken. Finally, Figure 15.3(d) indicates a loss of control as a result of assignable cause variation in both the mean (location) and the dispersion.

Figure 15.3 Patterns in Means and Dispersion Indicating Loss of Control

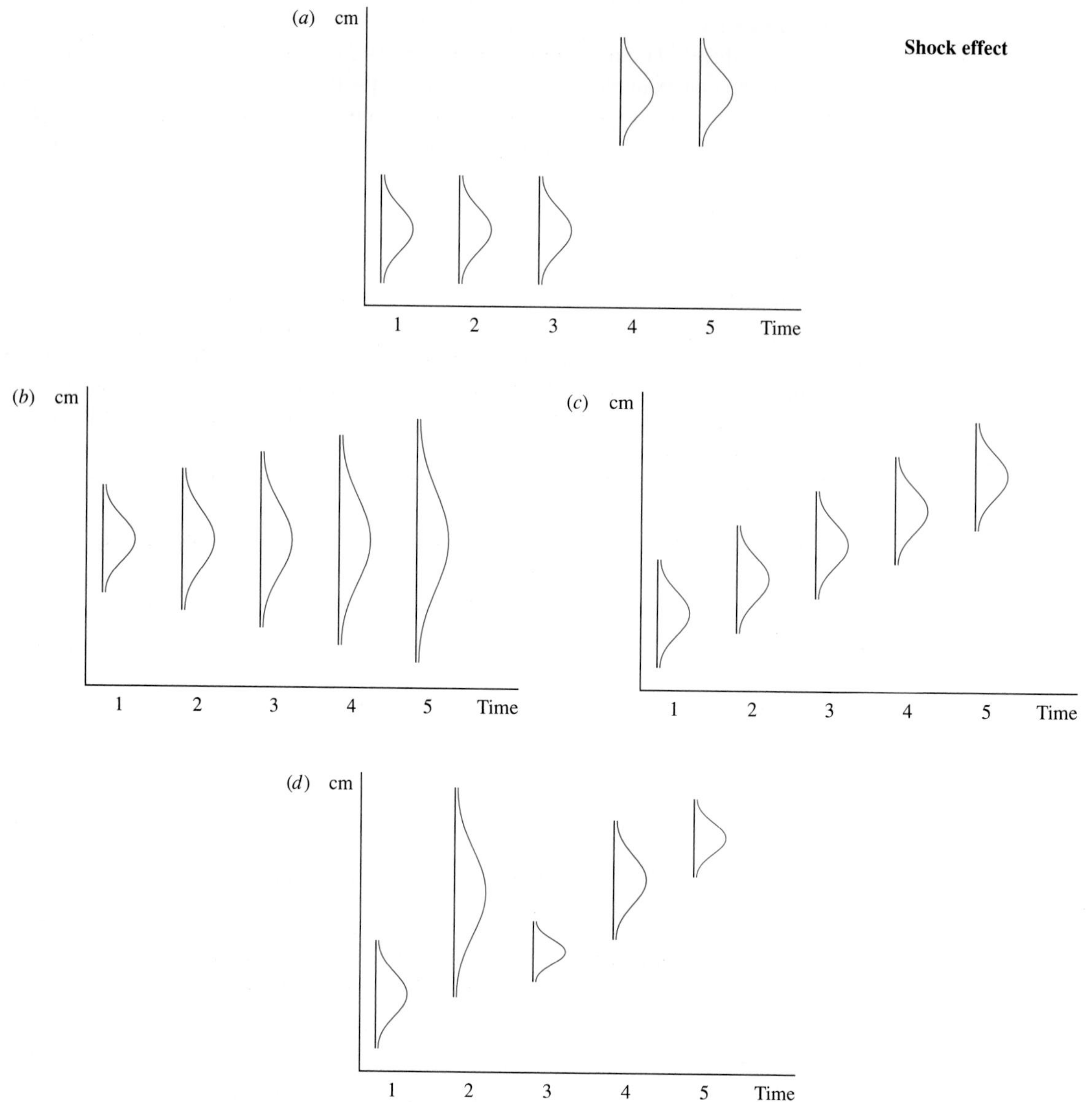

15.4 Control Charts for the Mean and Dispersion

Control charts aid in the detection of assignable cause variation. Different types of control charts are formed for at least two variables. The first type, often called an $\bar{X}$-chart, is designed to measure the variation in sample means. The second type measures variation in the range of samples. Logically, it is called an R-chart. A discussion of both types follows.

A. The $\bar{X}$-Chart

The typical $\bar{X}$-chart is used to measure the variation of sample means around some generally accepted level. As Figure 15.4 shows, an upper control limit ($UCL_{\bar{X}}$) and a lower control

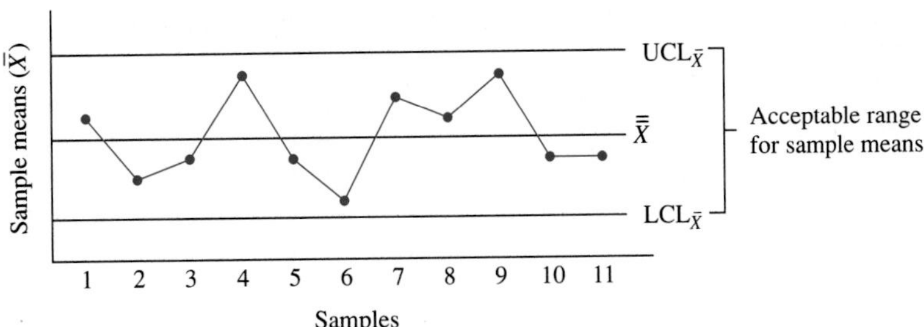

Figure 15.4
An $\bar{X}$-Chart

limit ($LCL_{\bar{X}}$) are established around an acceptable measure, which is determined as the grand mean, $\bar{\bar{X}}$, of several sample means. The value $\bar{\bar{X}}$ serves as our estimate of μ.

If the sample means fall within the acceptable range, as shown in Figure 15.4, only chance variation is said to occur. However, if the sample means exceed the $UCL_{\bar{X}}$ or fall below the $LCL_{\bar{X}}$, the quality control process has detected an assignable cause variation, and the production process is out of control. The cause for this excessive variation must be determined and corrected.

It is customary in quality control procedures to set the $UCL_{\bar{X}}$ and the $LCL_{\bar{X}}$ three standard errors above and below $\bar{\bar{X}}$. This custom results from the empirical rule stating that 99.7 percent of all observations in a normal distribution will be within that range.

Thus,

Upper control limit for means	$UCL_{\bar{X}} = \bar{\bar{X}} + 3\sigma_{\bar{x}}$	[15.1]

and

Lower control limit for means	$LCL_{\bar{X}} = \bar{\bar{X}} - 3\sigma_{\bar{x}}$	[15.2]

However, in practice, $3\sigma_{\bar{X}}$ is estimated as $A_2\bar{R}$, where $\bar{R}$ is the range of several samples means, and A_2 is a constant based on the sample size. Values for A_2 can be found in Appendix III, Table O. Using $A_2\bar{R}$ instead of $3\sigma_{\bar{X}}$ produces similar results and is considerably easier to compute. We then find

Upper control limit for means	$UCL_{\bar{X}} = \bar{\bar{X}} + A_2\bar{R}$	[15.3]

and

Lower control limit for means	$LCL_{\bar{X}} = \bar{\bar{X}} - A_2\bar{R}$	[15.4]

Consider the problem faced by Janet Lugg, director of quality control measures for AT&T. Her plant produces frames for desktop computers which must meet certain size specifications. To ensure these standards are met, Janet collects $K = 24$ samples (subgroups), each of size $n = 6$, and measures their width. The results are reported in Table 15.2.

Table 15.2
Measurements in Centimeters of AT&T Desktop Computers ($K = 24$, $n = 6$)

Sample	Sample Measurements						$\bar{X}$	R
1	15.2	14.5	15.4	16.5	15.9	16.2	15.6170	2.0
2	16.2	15.4	15.9	15.2	15.2	14.5	15.4000	1.7
3	15.6	16.5	15.9	16.2	15.9	16.2	16.0500	0.9
4	18.5	14.8	15.7	15.2	16.8	14.2	15.8667	4.3
5	17.5	15.7	14.5	14.2	14.5	15.2	15.2667	3.3
6	14.3	15.9	16.5	14.8	15.4	14.8	15.2833	2.2
7	15.4	15.2	15.4	15.8	14.2	15.7	15.2833	1.6
8	18.0	14.5	14.4	16.2	14.8	16.8	15.7833	3.6
9	14.2	15.6	14.5	16.1	15.7	15.9	15.3333	1.9
10	15.7	16.5	14.5	14.8	16.8	16.1	15.7333	2.3
11	14.8	14.5	16.5	14.9	15.8	16.3	15.4667	2.0
12	16.8	15.8	15.2	15.8	15.7	16.2	15.9167	1.6
13	15.2	15.9	14.5	15.1	15.9	14.7	15.2167	1.4
14	15.4	15.7	16.8	15.3	14.8	14.9	15.4833	2.0
15	18.4	15.7	15.9	14.8	15.5	14.8	15.8500	3.6
16	16.5	16.8	15.0	15.7	16.9	14.7	15.9333	2.2
17	15.2	16.9	16.8	17.0	17.1	15.4	16.4000	1.9
18	16.8	17.2	18.9	18.5	18.5	18.9	18.1333	2.1
19	13.5	17.6	18.7	21.1	17.2	16.0	17.3500	7.6
20	19.8	14.5	20.8	19.2	19.2	18.7	18.7000	6.3
21	18.7	17.9	18.7	20.8	18.4	17.5	18.6667	3.3
22	17.5	18.0	18.2	20.2	14.2	17.8	17.6500	6.0
23	14.9	18.9	20.0	16.8	16.2	18.5	17.5500	5.1
24	18.7	17.9	17.4	18.7	17.2	16.5	17.7333	2.2

$$\bar{\bar{X}} = \frac{\Sigma \bar{X}}{K} = \frac{15.6170 + 15.4000 + \cdots + 17.7333}{24}$$
$$= 16.3194$$

$$\bar{R} = \frac{\Sigma R}{K} = \frac{2.0 + 1.7 + \cdots + 2.2}{24}$$
$$= 2.9625$$

The mean and range for each sample are shown in the last two columns of the table. The grand mean and the mean range are computed. With this information, the UCL and LCL for $\bar{X}$ can be determined. Since each sample size is $n = 6$, Table O in Appendix III reveals A_2 to be 0.483. Then

$$\begin{aligned}
\text{UCL}_{\bar{X}} &= \bar{\bar{X}} + A_2\bar{R} \\
&= 16.3194 + (0.483)(2.9625) \\
&= 17.75 \\
\text{LCL}_{\bar{X}} &= \bar{\bar{X}} + A_2\bar{R} \\
&= 14.89
\end{aligned}$$

Figure 15.5, which was produced by Minitab, is the control chart for Janet Lugg. Notice that the means for subgroups 18, 20, and 21 reveal that the process is out of control: The means have increased to levels exceeding the UCL, indicating the presence of assignable cause variation. Perhaps over time the machines producing the computer parts have suffered unusual wear, resulting in improper performance. Or the variation might have been caused by the introduction of inferior raw materials obtained from a new

Figure 15.5
$\bar{X}$-Chart for Janet Lugg

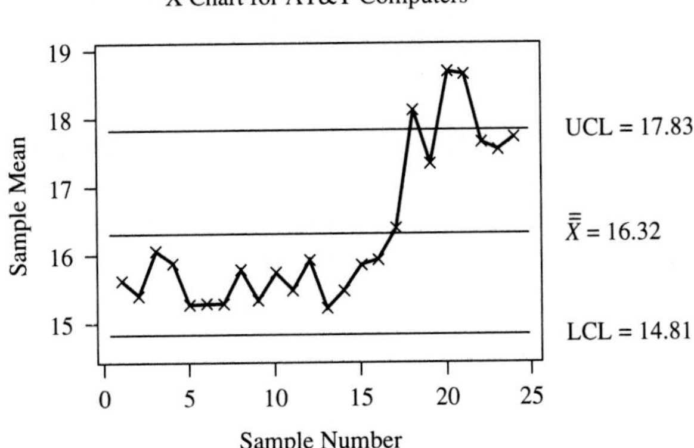

supplier around the time sample 18 was taken. In any event. Ms. Lugg must locate and correct the cause for the unacceptable variation.

B. The R-Chart

In addition to monitoring changes in the mean, it is useful to closely scrutinize variation in the process. Although the standard deviation is a dependable measure of dispersion, quality control techniques usually rely on the range as an indication in the variability of the process. The range is easier to compute, and more readily understood by those without a sufficient statistical background.

A lower control limit (LCL_R) and upper control limit (UCL_R) for the range are calculated; like those for the $\bar{X}$-chart, they are three standard errors above and below the mean. In principle, they are determined as follows:

Upper control limit for the range

$$UCL_R = \bar{R} + 3s_R \qquad [15.5]$$

and

Lower control limit for the range

$$LCL_R = \bar{R} - 3s_R \qquad [15.6]$$

where s_R is the standard deviation in the sample ranges. However, in practice, it is simpler to use

Upper control limit for the range

$$UCL_R = D_4\bar{R} \qquad [15.7]$$

and

Lower control limit for the range

$$LCL_R = D_3\bar{R} \qquad [15.8]$$

Values for D_4 and D_3 are taken from Appendix III, Table O.

Using Lugg's data from Table 15.2, we find

$$\text{UCL}_R = (2.004)(2.9625) = 5.936$$
$$\text{LCL}_R = (0)(2.9625) = 0$$

The R-chart shown in Figure 15.6 was generated using Minitab. Notice again that the later samples indicate the process is out of control: The R-values for samples 19, 20, and 22 exceed the UCL. Action must be taken to identify and correct the source of the assignable cause variation.

Figure 15.6
R-Chart for Janet Lugg

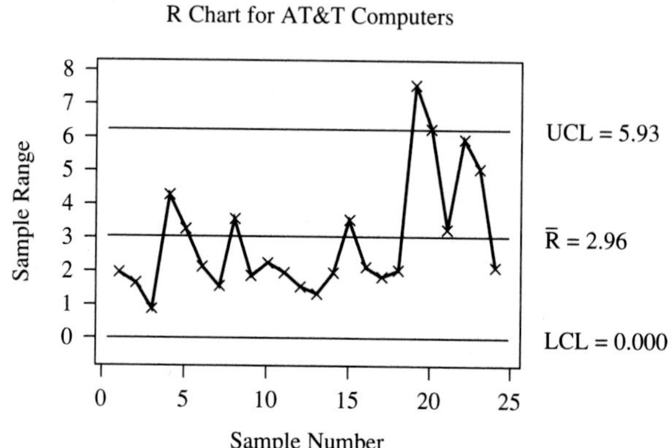

By examining the $\bar{X}$- and R-charts, Ms. Lugg determines that the process is out of control. It is common to use both charts jointly in the effort to detect control problems. A process may exhibit a stable mean that stays within statistical control, but the variation around that mean, as measured by the standard deviation or the range, is so large that most units are defective. For example, a process may be designed to produce units 10 feet in length. If one-half of them are 5 feet and the other one-half are 15 feet, the desired mean of 10 feet is maintained, but none of the units are acceptable—they are all either too long or too short. Processes should operate so as to produce both a stable mean and a stable variation. Thus, R-charts and $\bar{X}$-charts are best used in conjunction.

In fact, it is often suggested that the R-chart should be constructed and interpreted first. Recall that the $\bar{X}$-chart depends on the range (see Formulas [15.3] and [15.4]). Therefore, if the process variation in dispersion is out of control, the control limits on the $\bar{X}$-chart have little meaning. If the R-chart indicates the process variation is in control, only then does it make sense to construct and interpret the means chart. Example 15.1 illustrates this practice.

Example 15.1 In December 1997, GTW Electronics, a small manufacturing firm in New Jersey, announced its intention to compete directly with General Electric in the manufacturing of certain electrical components. The CEO for GTW called for quality control checks designed to measure the variation in the weight of one of the components. Samples of size $n = 6$ were taken each hour for $K = 5$ hours. The results, in ounces, are tabulated here. If the control study suggests unacceptable variation, the CEO has issued a standing order that the production process be interrupted until the assignable cause is identified and corrected.

	Hour (A.M.)	1	2	3	4	5	6	$\bar{X}$	R
Samples	8:00	4.9	4.8	4.8	5.1	6.6	5.2	5.23	1.8
	9:00	6.8	5.1	5.2	7.1	5.3	5.2	5.78	2.0
	10:00	7.1	6.9	5.9	6.2	6.9	6.9	6.65	1.2
	11:00	6.8	6.2	6.5	7.1	7.6	6.8	6.83	1.4
	12:00	6.0	4.6	4.5	4.5	4.3	5.2	4.85	1.7
								29.34	8.1

$\bar{\bar{X}} = 5.87$
$\bar{R} = 1.61$

Although $K = 5$ is likely insufficient (recall, it is suggested that $K \geq 20$), its use will simplify the arithmetic in the illustration.

Solution:

$$\begin{aligned} \text{UCL}_R &= D_4\bar{R} \\ &= (2.004)(1.62) \\ &= 3.25 \\ \text{LCL}_R &= D_3\bar{R} \\ &= (0)(1.62) \\ &= 0 \end{aligned}$$

Thus, the R-chart appears as

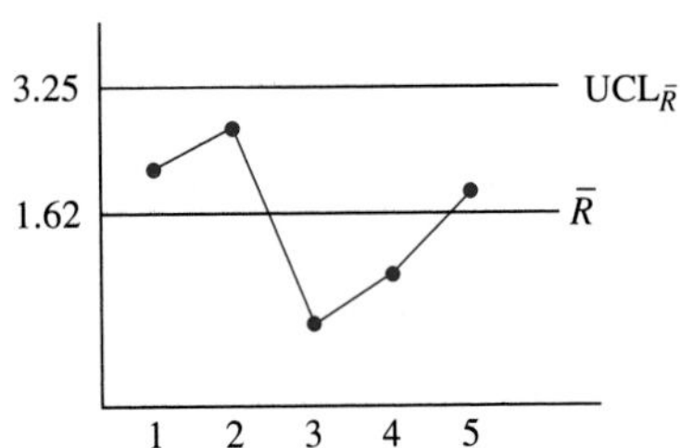

Since the R-chart suggests the variation in R is in control, the $\bar{X}$-chart can be constructed to test for variation in means.

$$\begin{aligned} \text{UCL}_{\bar{X}} &= \bar{\bar{X}} + A_2\bar{R} \\ &= 5.87 + (0.483)(1.62) \\ &= 6.65 \\ \text{LCL}_{\bar{X}} &= \bar{\bar{X}} - A_2\bar{R} \\ &= 5.09 \end{aligned}$$

The $\bar{X}$-chart becomes

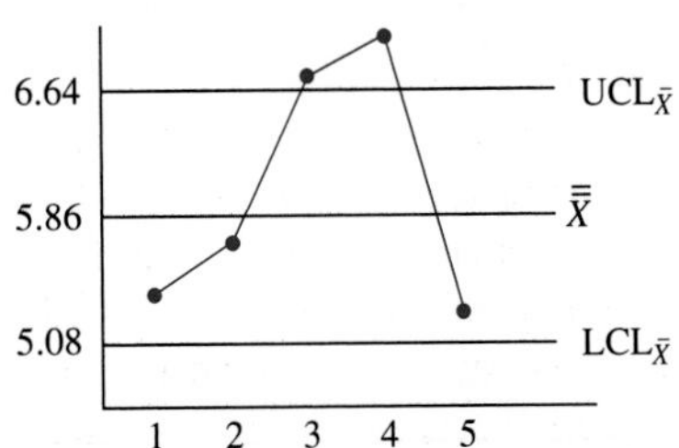

Interpretation: It can be seen that the process is out of control. The means for samples 3 and 4 exceed the UCL. The production process should be interrupted and the assignable cause identified and corrected.

Section Exercises

1. Seven samples of size 5 each were taken for the pounds per square inch contained in pressurized containers. Does it appear that the system is out of control based on $\bar{X}$-charts and R-charts?

Sample						
1	2	3	4	5	6	7
25.00	35.00	22.00	24.00	27.00	21.00	31.00
29.00	31.00	29.00	30.00	19.00	23.00	30.00
27.00	29.00	27.00	31.00	18.00	22.00	21.00
31.00	27.00	24.00	21.00	27.00	25.00	22.00
27.00	25.00	20.00	26.00	20.00	35.00	31.00

2. The tensile strength for wire is measured in pounds by taking 10 samples of size 4 each. Test for statistical control using an $\bar{X}$-chart and an R-chart.

Sample									
1	2	3	4	5	6	7	8	9	10
10	19	14	18	8	15	23	18	21	19
2	18	12	19	9	17	15	17	18	21
15	21	10	14	6	18	14	15	15	22
13	23	9	15	6	14	16	15	14	14

3. Five samples of size 7 are chosen, yielding

$$\bar{X}_1 = 6.2 \quad \bar{X}_2 = 7.3 \quad \bar{X}_3 = 8.1 \quad \bar{X}_4 = 7.2 \quad \bar{X}_5 = 6.3$$

and

$$R_1 = 1.5 \quad R_2 = 1.7 \quad R_3 = 1.9 \quad R_4 = 1.2 \quad R_5 = 1.1$$

Determine the upper and lower limits for an $\bar{X}$-chart and an R-chart. Is the process in control?

4. Rector Public Accounting concluded that completion times for audits should be fairly standard. Ten audits are selected for all five of Rector's storefront offices. Based on the results shown here, construct and interpret the appropriate control charts to determine whether completion times are in control.

Sample				
1	2	3	4	5
4.10	10.50	9.70	7.80	15.70
3.20	15.00	11.90	9.50	8.90
3.60	6.00	12.00	6.90	7.80
5.60	9.00	5.80	5.80	7.60
6.30	8.00	6.90	4.80	6.80
5.20	5.60	14.80	7.20	5.90
6.70	3.90	21.80	15.30	3.60
9.90	7.20	10.90	14.20	5.80
8.70	5.50	10.80	15.90	4.10
8.80	6.80	12.80	13.60	5.60

15.5 Control Charts for Attributes

The control charts for $\overline{X}$ and R are designed to monitor quantitative data in a process. In many cases it is necessary or desirable to measure the *quality* of a process, or the output of that process, based on the attribute of acceptability. This statistical procedure determines whether a process is acceptable based on the proportion and number of defects. Two common types of control charts focus on acceptability: **p-charts** measure the proportion of defects, and **c-charts** record the number of defects per item.

A. p-Charts

In constructing *p*-charts, we simply take note of the proportion of defective items in a sample. This proportion, p, is

$$p = \frac{\text{Number of defects in a sample}}{\text{Sample size}}$$

As with control charts for variables, we take several samples, yielding several values for p. The mean proportion of defects for these several samples, $\overline{p}$, is then calculated as

$$\overline{p} = \frac{\text{Total number of defects in all samples}}{\text{Total number of all items inspected}}$$

The value $\overline{p}$ serves as our estimate of π, the population proportion of defects, in the event π is unknown.

The standard deviation of the proportion of defects is

Standard deviation for proportion of defects	$\sigma_p = \sqrt{\frac{\pi(1-\pi)}{n}}$	[15.9]

In the likely event that π is unknown, σ_p is estimated by s_p, where

Standard deviation for proportion of defects when σ is unknown	$s_p = \sqrt{\frac{\overline{p}(1-\overline{p})}{n}}$	[15.10]

Recall from our discussion of the binomial distribution that the detection of defects is based on the Bernoulli processes.

Upper control limits (UCL_p) and lower control limits (LCL_p) are formed three standard deviations above and below the population of defects. If π is known,

Upper control limit for proportions	$\text{UCL}_p = \pi + 3\sigma_p = \pi + 3\sqrt{\frac{\pi(1-\pi)}{n}}$	[15.11]

and

Lower control limit for proportions	$$\begin{aligned}\text{LCL}_p &= \pi - 3\sigma_p \\ &= \pi - 3\sqrt{\frac{\pi(1-\pi)}{n}}\end{aligned}$$	[15.12]

If π is unknown,

Upper control limit for proportions	$$\begin{aligned}\text{UCL}_p &= \bar{p} + 3s_p \\ &= \bar{p} + 3\sqrt{\frac{\bar{p}(1-\bar{p})}{n}}\end{aligned}$$	[15.13]

and

Lower control limit for proportions	$$\begin{aligned}\text{LCL}_p &= \bar{p} - 3s_p \\ &= \bar{p} - 3\sqrt{\frac{\bar{p}(1-\bar{p})}{n}}\end{aligned}$$	[15.14]

Opus, Inc. makes electric guitars and other musical instruments. A quality control procedure to detect defects in the company'sAuditory Annihilator model 1000 guitar entailed the selection of $K = 15$ different samples of size $n = 40$. The number of defects in each sample is shown in Table 15.3. A total of $(15)(40) = 600$ guitars is inspected.

Table 15.3
Defects in $K = 15$ Samples of Size $n = 40$

Sample	Number of Defects	p	Sample	Number of Defects	p
1	10	0.250	9	13	0.325
2	12	0.300	10	15	0.375
3	9	0.225	11	17	0.425
4	15	0.375	12	3	0.075
5	27	0.675	13	25	0.625
6	8	0.200	14	18	0.450
7	11	0.275	15	17	0.425
8	11	0.275			
				211	

With these data, a quality control specialist for Opus finds

$$\begin{aligned}\bar{p} &= \frac{211}{600} \\ &= 0.3517\end{aligned}$$

Then

$$UCL_p = \bar{p} + 3\sqrt{\frac{\bar{p}(1-\bar{p})}{n}}$$

$$= 0.3517 + 3\sqrt{\frac{(0.3517)(0.6483)}{40}}$$

$$= 0.5782$$

$$LCL_p = \bar{p} - 3\sqrt{\frac{\bar{p}(1-\bar{p})}{n}}$$

$$= 0.1252$$

A **preliminary** control chart is formed from these findings, as in Figure 15.7, which was produced using Minitab.

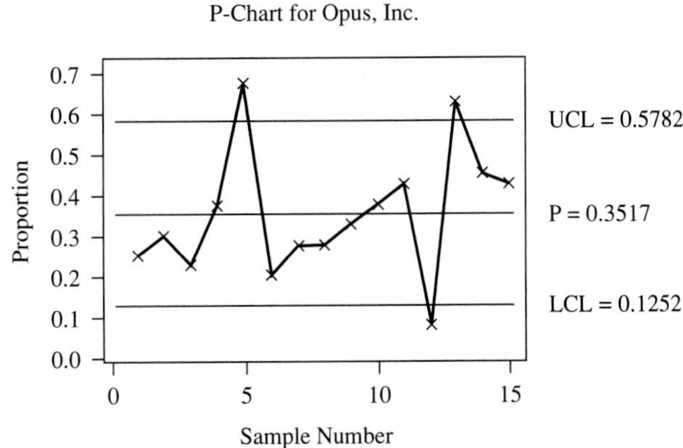

Figure 15.7
p-Chart for Opus, Inc.

Samples 5 ($p = 0.675$), 12 ($p = 0.075$), and 13 ($p = 0.625$) are clearly out of control. The search for the assignable causes revealed that sample 5 was taken during a time when certain key personnel were on vacation, and less skilled employees were forced to fill in. The unusually low proportion of defects for sample 12 resulted from a one-time use of superior raw materials when the regular supplier was unable to provide Opus with the usual materials. Sample 13 was taken when new construction at the plant temporarily interrupted electric power, thus disallowing the use of computerized production methods.

The assignable cause has been identified for each anomaly. If desired, action can be taken to prevent their reoccurrence. Opus may, for example, ensure that in the future key personnel stagger their vacations to prevent a repeat of sample 5.

You might presume that an LCL_p would not be a concern, since low rates of defects are desirable. However, unusually low values for p might aid in identifying ways in which defects can be minimized. For example, Opus may want to consider regular use of the superior raw materials obtained in sample 12 if they are not cost-prohibitive. Perhaps a study should be done to compare the effect on profits of using the higher-grade raw materials. Furthermore, exceptionally low p-values can indicate a problem in that the quality control program is simply not effectively detecting defects.

Example 15.2 The Home Mortgage Company processes home loans for central Illinois residents. Mr. Mooney, president of the company, has been alerted by a new loan officer that several mistakes in loan applications have not been detected by the employees who must provide final approval of the loan. Since such carelessness could prove very costly, Mr. Mooney selects 25 samples of appplications that have received approval. Each sample has 50 applications. Upon personally reviewing each application, Mr. Mooney finds that each sample contains applications that should not have been accepted. He records the number of these applications for each sample. Based on his findings, Mr. Mooney asks you to construct a p-chart and to comment on the results.

Sample	Number of Applications with Errors	Proportion	Sample	Number of Applications with Errors	Proportion
1	8	0.16	14	5	0.10
2	12	0.24	15	6	0.12
3	2	0.04	16	8	0.16
4	5	0.10	17	7	0.14
5	6	0.12	18	7	0.14
6	6	0.12	19	6	0.12
7	15	0.30	20	9	0.18
8	8	0.16	21	8	0.16
9	7	0.14	22	15	0.30
10	7	0.14	23	6	0.12
11	5	0.10	24	6	0.12
12	21	0.42	25	8	0.16
13	23	0.46		216	

Solution: The total number of applications that were in error is 216, and the total number of applications that were reviewed is $25 \times 50 = 1{,}250$. Therefore, $\bar{p} = 216/1{,}250 = 0.1728$. The upper limit is found as

$$\begin{aligned} UCL_p &= 0.1728 + 3\sqrt{\frac{(0.1728)(0.8272)}{50}} \\ &= 0.3332 \end{aligned}$$

The lower limit is

$$\begin{aligned} LCL_p &= 0.1728 - 3\sqrt{\frac{(0.1728)(0.8272)}{50}} \\ &= 0.0124 \end{aligned}$$

This is shown in the accompanying p-chart

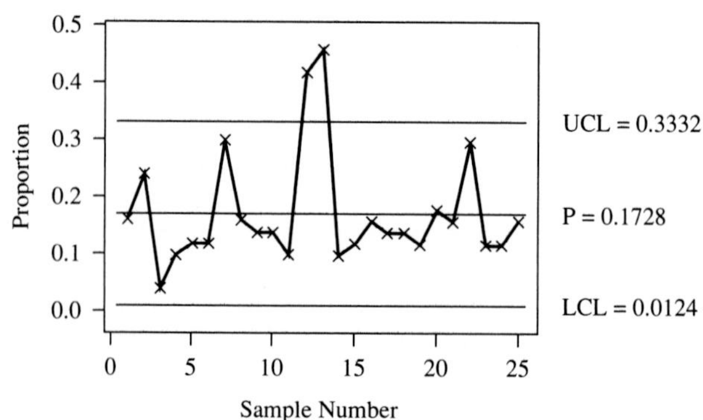

Any of the samples with more than 33.32 percent of the applications or less than 1.24 percent of the applications in error indicate that the approval process is out of control.

Interpretation: Samples 12 and 13 reveal that the process is out of control. Mr. Mooney should consider actions to improve the way in which loans are reviewed for approval.

B. c-Charts

A second type of attribute control chart is the *c*-chart, designed to detect the number of defects in a single unit. In developing a *p*-chart, an entire unit was deemed either defective or not defective. In many instances, however, the presence of one or more defects may not render the unit unacceptable. A manufacturer of furniture may find several minor defects in a sofa and yet not consider it unacceptable. If the defects per 100 square yards of floor covering were few and minor, the manufacturer may decide to sell it despite the flaws. A *c*-chart is used to analyze the number of flaws per unit of output.

The *c*-chart is concerned with the number of occurrences (defects) per unit (per sofa or per 100 square yards). This consideration fits a Poisson distribution.

Control limits are established around the number of defects in the population, c. In the likely event c is unknown, it is estimated by $\bar{c}$, the mean number of defects in the units.

A unit may consist of a single item, such as a sofa or a 100-square-yard piece of carpet, or it might contain, for example, a shipment of 50 printed pages in which typos are detected. The unit must be consistent in size, number, or area. Earlier we defined the standard deviation of the number of occurrences as the square root of the mean number of occurrences. Thus,

Standard deviation for the number of defects	$s_{\bar{c}} = \sqrt{\bar{c}}$	[15.15]

The control limits are three standard deviations above and below $\bar{c}$.

Upper control limit for the number of defects	$UCL_c = \bar{c} + 3s_{\bar{c}}$	[15.16]

and

Lower control limit for the number of defects	$LCL_c = \bar{c} - 3s_{\bar{c}}$	[15.17]

International Paper inspected 20 sheets of a new type of gift wrap for defects. The results are shown in Table 15.4. A *c*-chart is to be constructed.

$$\bar{c} = \frac{152}{20}$$

$$= 7.6$$

$$s_{\bar{c}} = \sqrt{7.6}$$

$$= 2.757$$

$$\begin{aligned}\text{UCL}_c &= \bar{c} + 3s_{\bar{c}} \\ &= 7.6 + 3(2.757) \\ &= 15.87 \\ \text{LCL}_c &= \bar{c} - 3s_{\bar{c}} \\ &= -0.67\end{aligned}$$

Figure 15.8 containing the *c*-chart, was produced using Minitab.

Units 5 and 20 indicate the process is out of control, and the assignable cause or causes should be determined. If $\text{LCL}_c < 0$, it is set equal to zero since a negative number of defects is impossible.

Example 15.3 further illustrates the use of a *c*-chart.

Table 15.4
Number of Defects in 20 Pieces of Gift Wrap

Sheet	Number of Defects	Sheet	Number of Defects
1	5	11	3
2	4	12	15
3	3	13	10
4	5	14	8
5	16	15	4
6	1	16	2
7	8	17	10
8	9	18	12
9	9	19	7
10	4	20	17
			152

Figure 15.8
c-Chart for International Paper

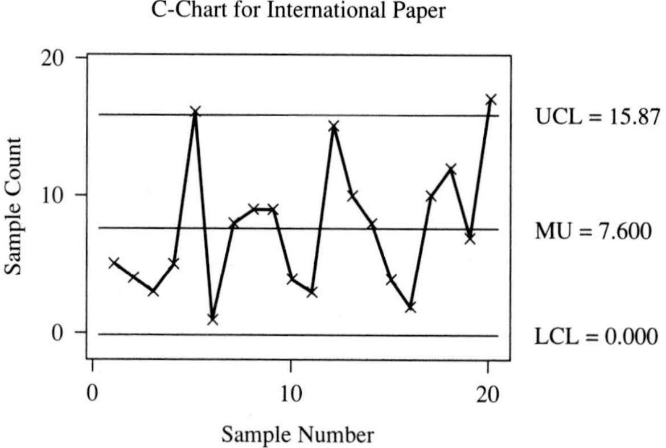

Example 15.3 Sammy Bates, the new personnel director at Bates Electronics, has recently introduced a strategy to control the number of employees who fail to report to work each day. To test the effectiveness of the procedure, 20 days are randomly selected and the numbers of absent workers are recorded:

Day	Number of Absences	Day	Number of Absences
1	6	11	5
2	3	12	6
3	3	13	5
4	5	14	8
5	2	15	7
6	0	16	5
7	5	17	6
8	12	18	3
9	0	19	5
10	0	20	6
			92

Mr. Bates must construct a c-chart to evaluate the new system.

Solution: Since a total of 92 employees were absent over the 20-day period, $\bar{c} = 92/90 = 1.02$. Then,

$$\text{UCL}_c = 1.02 + 3\sqrt{1.02}$$
$$= 4.05$$

and

$$\text{LCL}_c = 1.02 - 3\sqrt{1.02}$$
$$= -2.01$$

Since the number of employees who fail to report cannot be a negative value, the UCL_c becomes 0. The occurrence of any days with more than 4 employees absent indicates the system is out of control. The c-chart shown here summarizes the results of the test.

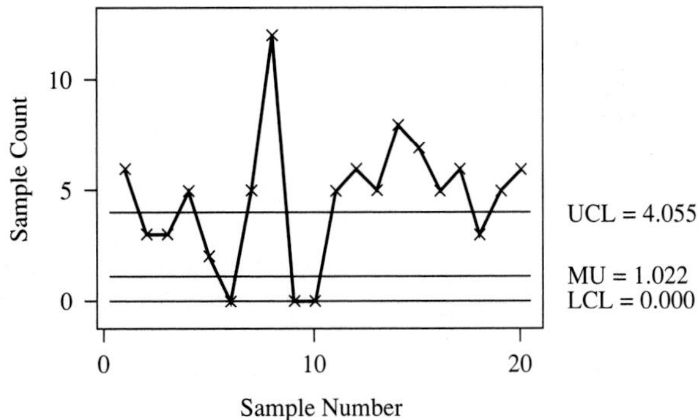

Interpretation: On 13 of the 20 days the number of absent employees was excessive. Action must be taken.

Section Exercises

5. A manufacturer takes 16 samples of size 25 each and finds the number of defects to be 5, 8, 9, 6, 5, 4, 7, 5, 8, 2, 5, 8, 9, 8, 7, and 5. Construct a p-chart and comment on whether the production process is out of control.
6. MedTec produces aspirin and other over-the-counter drugs. The company's bottling requirements certify that between 98 and 104 aspirin tablets must be in each bottle. Twelve samples

of 200 bottles each are selected. The number of bottles in each sample that do not meet production specifications is given below. Is MedTec's bottling process in control?

Number of bottles in each sample that does not contain the proper number of pills:

35, 36, 21, 10, 49, 52, 36, 36, 25, 24, 26, 15

7. The sample proportions of cellular telephones produced by ComWorld that do not meet government regulations were found to be, in percentages, 44, 24, 30, 40, 38, 36, 26, 34, 30, 18, 24, 34, and 36. Each sample contained 50 cell phones. Construct and interpret the proper control chart. Should ComWorld take action to place its production process back in control?

8. Moroccan Export in Casablanca selects 25 Persian rugs and finds the number of defects per rug shown below. Construct the proper control chart and comment.

Number of Defects per Rug				
2	6	3	5	8
10	3	6	6	4
5	8	6	9	4
5	2	5	6	6
6	5	9	4	5

9. Green Leaf Nurseries sells trees to suburbanites who like to rake leaves out of their lawns every fall. After spraying a chemical treatment to kill parasites, Green Leaf selects 20 trees and finds the following number of bugs and other undesirable critters on each tree. Based on the proper control chart, is the spraying process out of control? Comment.

Number of Parasites per Tree						
23	10	9	5	8	9	25
14	10	9	6	8	9	15
20	6	5	8	6	12	

10. Ole Town Press publishes a small newpaper every week in upstate Maine. The editor of the paper, Kent Clark, is concerned about what he fears is a growing number of typographical errors. Mr. Clark randomly selects 15 newspapers over the last several months and finds the number of "typos" per paper to be:

2	6	3	5	9
1	0	5	6	8
3	2	4	5	6

Does Mr. Clark have to worry that the printing process is out of control?

15.6 Interpreting Control Charts

How can control charts be used to monitor a process? How can we tell if a system is not in compliance with production specifications? Does the occurrence of only one or two points outside the upper or the lower control limit suggest the process is out of control? Several factors must be considered in answering these questions.

Of course, the first and most basic consideration in reading a control chart is whether any data points fall outside the upper or lower control limits. If even a single point falls outside the limits, there is statistical evidence that the process is out of control. However, this is not necessarily cause for great alarm. This one occurrence may simply be due to chance variation. As much information as possible should be gathered about the possible cause or causes of this anomaly, and a determination should be made whether a problem really does exist in that an assignable cause variation can be identified.

In addition, even if all points are *within* the control limits, the detection of certain patterns may signal a serious problem. If, for example, a large number of points are on only one side of the center line, the analyst should consider the cause for such a configuration. If the shift to one particular side of the center line appears to have happened abruptly, the cause might be assigned to a sudden change in the use of raw materials or to the introduction of a new training system for incoming employees. If the shift seems to be occurring gradually, evidencing a trend over time, this might indicate that the machinery used in the production process is becoming continuously worn and not performing to specifications. If an assignable cause can be identified, corrective action can be taken. In general, even if all points are within the control limits, there should still be a random fluctuation above and below the center line.

Keep in mind that the control limits are established at three standard deviations above and below the center line. According to the empirical rule, 99.7 percent of all the observations should be within these limits. Thus, less than 0.5 percent should fall outside the UCL and the LCL by mere chance. If the system is in control, very few, if any, of the points should be out of the established limits.

Furthermore, the empirical rule points out that 95.5 percent of all the observations should be within two standard deviations of the center line. That is, 95.5 percent of the data points should fall within the first two-thirds of the area around the center line. Only about 4.5 percent should deviate from the center line by more than two standard deviations. Thus, even if all the data points are within the control limits of three deviations, but an inordinate number are more than two standard deviations from the centerline, action should be taken to explain this departure from what the empirical rule states.

This is shown in Figure 15.9. The UCL and the LCL are within 3σ of the centerline. This area should contain 99.7 percent of the data points. The first two-thirds of that area above and below the center line is within 2σ of the center line and should encompass 95.5 percent of the data points. In Figure 15.9, for example, although no data points fall outside the control limits, a problem may still exist, since so many points are in the area beyond two standard deviations from the center line.

Figure 15.9
A Control Chart Evidencing Lack of Compliance

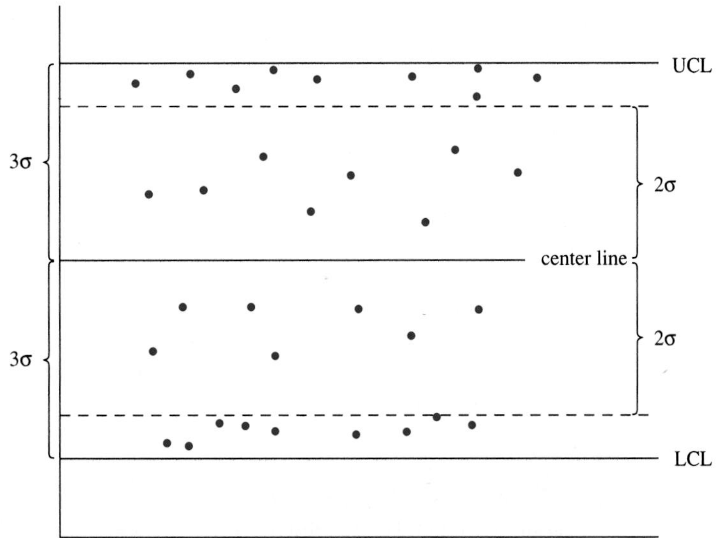

15.7 Acceptance Sampling

Decisions must often be made regarding the acceptability of an entire lot or shipment of goods. A firm may purchase raw materials from its supplier without complete knowledge of the quality of those materials. It must then test the shipment to determine whether the materials meet certain minimum specifications. Rarely does a firm examine every item in a shipment. Such a process would be too time-consuming and costly. Instead, a sample is selected to determine whether the entire shipment should be accepted or returned to the supplier.

During production a manufacturing firm often inspects several unfinished units to determine whether production should continue, or whether the semifinished units should be scrapped and procedures reviewed to determine the cause for excessive defects. This decision also involves the use of samples in deciding whether minimum standards are being met. This practice is called **acceptance sampling.**

> **Acceptance Sampling** A sample of a shipment or production lot is examined to determine whether it meets certain minimum quality specifications and is therefore acceptable.

Acceptance sampling is an important and integral part of quality control measures. Decisions regarding the acceptability of materials have a significant bearing on the firm's revenue and cost structure.

Ensuring that a part fits production standards is crucial to the overall manufacturing process. Whether the manufacturing firm produces the part or obtains it from a supplier, specific production standards must be met. If a manufacturer of compact disk systems uses a part that is too small, the entire system may not function properly. If an aircraft assemblage company relies on a metal that is too heavy or unable to withstand minimum stress, a serious consequence is likely. Obviously, quality control decisions concerning production specifications are critical.

Consider a firm making cellular telephones. It obtains a critical part for each phone from a supplier in Chicago. The parts are shipped in lots of several hundred. The firm cannot test each part received, so acceptance sampling is necessary. The firm is willing to accept a maximum of 5 percent defective parts in each shipment. This number is called the **acceptance quality level** (AQL). The firm also limits to 1 percent those shipments that meet the AQL but are mistakenly rejected. This has the effect of constraining the number of nondefective shipments that are discarded.

In common practice, decisions regarding these percentages are most often determined on the basis of company policy, often in agreement with the supplier. If a less judgmental approach is desired in arriving at proper percentages, the *Military Standard Sampling Procedures and Tables for Inspection by Attributes* (MIL-STD-105D) can be used. These tables specify the proper sample size and number of defects necessary to reject the shipment.

Since sampling is involved, it is possible to make an error in deciding whether to accept or reject a shipment. A shipment that meets the minimum specifications might be rejected. This is a Type I error, and is called **producer risk,** because producers run the risk of having a good shipment returned to them.

> **Producer Risk** The probability that sampling error will cause a buyer to mistakenly reject a shipment and return it to the seller is a producer risk. This is called a Type I error.

A Type II error occurs when a bad shipment is accepted. Accepting a bad shipment is called **consumer risk,** since the buyer would unknowingly retain a shipment with an excessive number of defects.

> **Consumer Risk** The probability that sampling error will lead the buyer to retain a shipment that contains a disproportionate number of defects is a consumer risk. This is called a Type II error.

A Type I error is called the α-level, and the probability of a Type II error is called β.

Consider again the cellular phone company. It was stated that a shipment containing more than 5 percent defects should be rejected (AQL = 5 percent), and only 1 percent of the good shipments would be erroneously returned (α = 1 percent). This 1 percent is the value of the producer's risk. Its purpose is to protect the firm's suppliers from unwarranted rejection of a good lot or shipment.

Recall from our earlier discussion of probability distributions that a hypergeometric distribution could be used to determine the probability that a certain number of defects would be found in a shipment. In practice, the binomial distribution, due to its simplicity, is more often used to provide an accurate approximation.

Assume that from several hundred parts received by the cellular phone company, a sample of $n = 50$ is taken. Given that the firm agrees to an AQL of 5 percent, π is set at 0.05. It is then necessary to determine what number of defects ensure that no more than 1 percent of the good shipments are rejected. That is, what number of defects will ensure that at least 99 percent of the good shipments containing 95 percent (1.00 − AQL) nondefects are accepted? This number of defects which determines whether to accept the shipment is called the **acceptance number.**

> **Acceptance Number** The acceptance number is the maximum number of defects out of a sample that can occur without rejection of the shipment. It ensures that the AQL is maintained without rejecting more than some prescribed percentage of good shipments.

The maximum number of defects, C, can then be found in the extension to Table C (Appendix III). For $n = 50$, move down the column headed by $\pi = 0.05$ until you find the first value that exceeds 1.00 − producer's risk, here $1.00 - 0.01 = 0.99$. This value is 0.9968, which is associated with $C = 7$. The closest probability not exceeding 1 percent defects is $1.00 - 0.9968 = 0.0032 < 0.01$. If there are more than $C = 7$ defects out of a sample of $n = 50$, the entire lot should be returned.

Example 15.4 **Claude and Carol's Dilemma**

Claude Vaughan is director of quality control at the PepsiCo bottling plant in Cincinnati. Data on production levels show that an inordinate number of bottles are underfilled. Fearing that shipment of the bottles could drive away customers, Claude proposes an acceptance sampling plan to minimize underfill shipments without causing too many bottles that are properly filled to be discarded.

He agrees with the production supervisor, Carol Henning, that they can ship a maximum of 1 percent underfills. This represents the acceptable level of defects, so AQL = 1 percent. Carol insists that not more than 10 percent of the acceptable production lots should be rejected. That is, the producer's risk should be limited to 10 precent. If samples of 100 are taken from a production run, what is the acceptance number of underfills Claude and Carol can tolerate before the entire run must be rejected?

Solution: Using the extension of the cumulative binomial table, π is set equal to the AQL of 1 percent. Claude and Carol must find the number of underfills that would not result in the rejection of more than 10 percent of the good production runs. They select a sample of 100 bottles from the most recent run. Given $\pi = 0.01$, the number of underfills that ensures that no more than 10 percent of the good runs are rejected is that value of C with a probability that exceeds 1.00 − producer's risk, or $1.00 - 0.10 = 0.90$. In the table under $n = 100$, find the column headed $\pi = 0.01$. Travel down the column until you find a probability in excess of 0.90. This value is 0.9206, which carries an acceptance number of $C = 2$.

Interpretation: By rejecting all production runs from which samples of $n = 100$ were taken that contain more than two underfills, Claude and Carol will ensure that, over the long run, production runs will not contain more than 1 percent underfills and that runs with less than 1 percent underfills will be rejected no more than 10 percent of the time.

A. Different Sampling Plans

Acceptance sampling assumes that only one sample is taken. This, logically, is referred to as a single-sample plan. However, two or more samples can be taken. Such plans are termed **multiple,** or **sequential,** sampling plans.

A **double-sampling** plan involves selection of a primary sample. On the basis of the results of this first sample, the plan then calls for one of three actions: (1) the lot may be rejected: (2) the lot may be accepted: or (3) a second sample may be taken. Two values of C are specified, where C_1 is the acceptance number for the first sample, and C_2 is the acceptance number for both samples.

To illustrate, assume a double-sampling plan stipulates $n_1 = 100$, $n_2 = 100$, $C_1 = 3$, $C_2 = 8$. A preliminary sample of 100 is selected. If three or fewer defects are found, the lot is accepted. If $3 + 8 = 11$ or more are found, the lot is rejected. If the first sample contains 4 to 10 defects, a second sample of $n_2 = 100$ is taken. If the total defects in both samples exceed 11, the lot is rejected.

Sequential plans tend to be more efficient than single-sampling plans in that fewer observations are needed to ensure the same degree of accuracy. Sequential plans are often used when testing requires the destruction of each unit.

As competition stiffens in the world market, a firm must ensure that its product or service meets minimum standards if it expects to stay in business. Hence, quality control mesures are vital.

B. Operating Characteristic Curves

Those involved with quality control plans often find it convenient to construct operating characteristic (OC) curves. These curves display the probability of acceptance under a variety of conditions. Specifically, an OC curve can allow the quality control specialist to ascertain, given different values for the proportion of defects π, the likelihood of accepting a lot given (1) the size of the sample n, and (2) the maximum number of allowable defects, C.

To illustrate, a sampling plan may be devised in which $n = 10$ units are routinely chosen from each shipment on a random basis. It is determined that if $C = 3$ or fewer units, the entire lot will be accepted. Under this scheme, it is possible to calculate the probability of acceptance for different values of π. For example, if, typically, $\pi = 5$ percent of the units are defective, what is the probability that a given lot will be accepted? This question can, of course, be answered with the use of the cumulative binomial distribution. From the cumulative binomial table, it can be seen that the probability of acceptance $= P(C \leq 3 \mid n = 10, \pi = 0.05) = 0.9990$. If, on the other hand, the proportion of defects in the past has proved to be 10 percent, the probability of acceptance becomes $P(C \leq 3 \mid n = 10, \pi = 0.10) = 0.9872$. Notice, logically, that the higher the value for π, the less likely it is that the shipment will be accepted. If other possible values for π are selected, the relationship between π and the probability of acceptance can be determined and depicted by an OC curve as shown in Figure 15.10.

Figure 15.10
An Operating Characteristic Curve for $n = 10$, $C = 3$

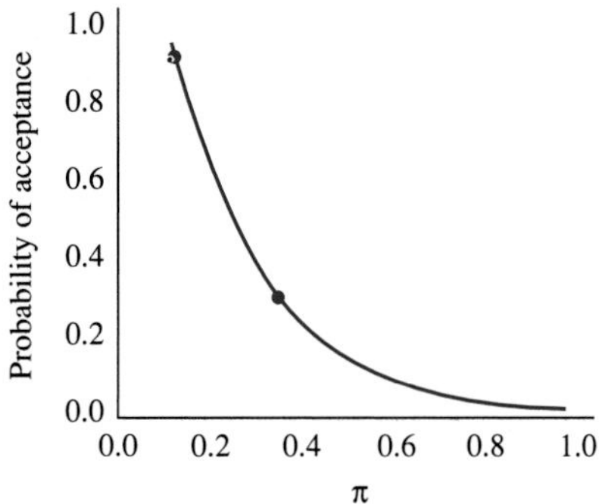

The shape of the OC is determined by the π-value, but other factors also affect it. If, for example, C is increased, the probability of acceptance goes up for any value of π. Thus, the entire OC curve would shift upward.

If the sample size n were increased, the entire curve would shift downward. We have $P(C \leq 3 \mid n = 10, \pi = 0.10) = 0.9872$, and $P(C \leq 3 \mid n = 15, \pi - 0.10) = 0.9444$. The likelihood that a larger sample will result in acceptance, given values for C and π, is smaller than that for a smaller sample with corresponding values for C and π. In this manner an OC curve can be used to tailor a quality control plan to the specific needs of any business operation.

Solved Problems

1. **Finding the Fault for Defaults** *Business Week* described the problem a major bank in Chicago had with load defaults. Assume that samples of size 5 for seven officials were selected, and the results tabulated. Develop an $\bar{X}$-chart and an R-chart for the bank.

	Loan Amount (in $1,000's)						
Official	**1**	**2**	**3**	**4**	**5**	$\bar{X}$	R
1	14.2	9.2	7.1	6.8	6.0	8.7	8.2
2	45.5	65.5	45.2	55.2	55.1	53.3	20.3
3	23.4	31.2	36.3	31.5	32.6	31.0	12.9
4	32.3	31.2	29.1	27.8	28.1	29.7	4.5
5	56.7	65.3	45.2	55.5	58.2	56.2	20.1
6	89.7	90.2	84.2	85.5	89.2	87.8	6.0
7	112.0	99.2	115.3	98.5	153.2	115.6	54.7
						382.3	126.7

$\bar{\bar{X}} = 54.6$
$\bar{R} = 18.1$

Solution:

$$\begin{aligned}\text{UCL}_{\overline{X}} &= \overline{\overline{X}} + A_2\overline{R}\\ &= 54.6 + (0.577)(18.1)\\ &= 65.04\\ \text{LCL}_{\overline{X}} &= \overline{\overline{X}} + A_2\overline{R}\\ &= 44.16\end{aligned}$$

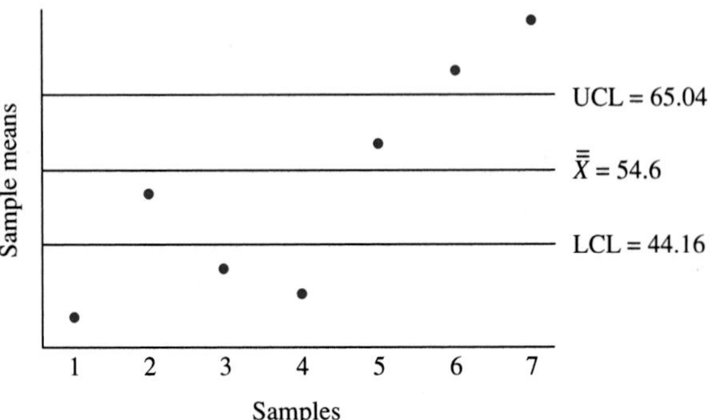

There is apparent inconsistency in the size of loans granted by the seven bank officers. Perhaps some effort should be made to find an explanation for the disparity in the officers' practices. The first, third, and fourth officers are granting unusually small loans, and the last officer seems to extend exceedingly large loans.

The R-chart is found as

$$\begin{aligned}\text{UCL}_R &= D_4\overline{R}\\ &= (2.115)(18.1)\\ &= 38.3\\ \text{LCL}_R &= D_3\overline{R}\\ &= (0)(18.1)\\ &= 0\end{aligned}$$

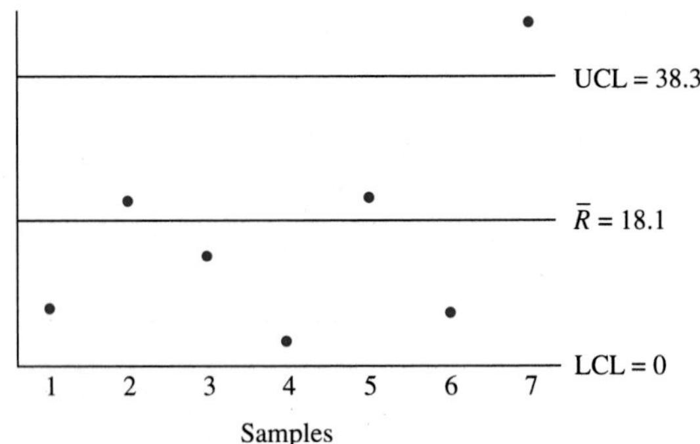

Only one officer seems to violate the control limits for the range. Again, the pattern of the seventh officer stands out from the rest, suggesting that his or her practices should be reviewed.

2. **A Comparison of the Officers** Considering the disparity in the officers' performances, it might be wise to use a p-chart to compare each officer. Samples of 10 loans by each officer are selected, and the proportion of loan defaults for each is recorded.

Officer	Number of Defects (defaults), c	Proportion of Defects, p
1	4	0.4
2	3	0.3
3	3	0.3
4	2	0.2
5	0	0.0
6	3	0.3
7	8	0.8
	23	

$\bar{p} = \frac{23}{70} = 0.33$

Solution:

$$\text{UCL}_p = \bar{p} + 3\sqrt{\frac{\bar{p}(1-\bar{p})}{n}}$$

$$= 0.33 + 3(0.056)$$

$$= 0.498$$

$$\text{LCL}_p = \bar{p} - 3\sqrt{\frac{\bar{p}(1-\bar{p})}{n}}$$

$$= 0.162$$

We find that 0.498 and 0.162 are the preliminary limits for p and are shown on the p-chart. The last officer is again differentiated from the rest. His or her rate of default is excessive. Further, the fact that the fifth officer had no defaults might also indicate a trouble spot. He or she is perhaps being too conservative in extending loans, and a greater degree of aggressiveness might be called for.

By eliminating the fifth and seventh samples, we can determine final limits. These are $\text{UCL}_p = 0.495$ and $\text{LCL}_p = 0.105$.

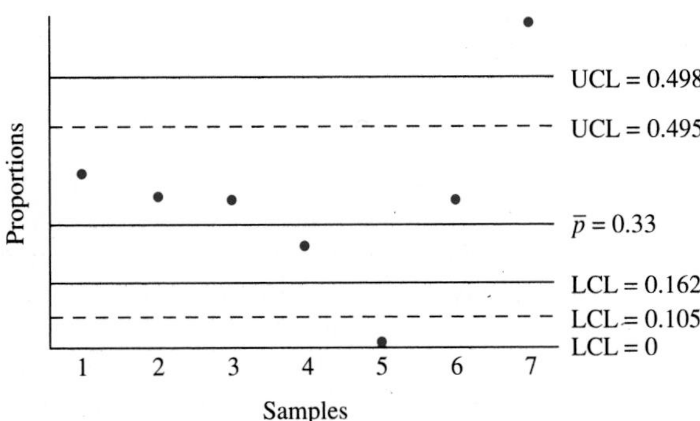

A further examination of the loan process might involve the use of c-charts to control for the number of errors (defects) made in each loan application (unit). In this effort, $n = 12$ loans are randomly selected, and the number of violations of bank policy for each loan application is tallied.

Loan	Violations (defects), c	Loan	Violations (defects), c
1	3	7	2
2	4	8	0
3	2	9	3
4	3	10	4
5	10	11	2
6	1	12	3
			37

In 37 instances bank policy was not followed in extending the 12 loans. Thus,

$$\bar{c} = \frac{37}{12} = 3.08$$

$$s_{\bar{c}} = \sqrt{3.08}$$

$$= 1.75$$

Then

$$\text{UCL}_c = \bar{c} + 3s_{\bar{c}}$$

$$= 8.33$$

$$\text{LCL}_c = c - 3s_{\bar{c}}$$

$$= -2.3\text{, and is set equal to 0}$$

Only the fifth loan in the sample suggests a problem. Management should determine who approved that loan: action can then be taken to reduce the number of loan defaults.

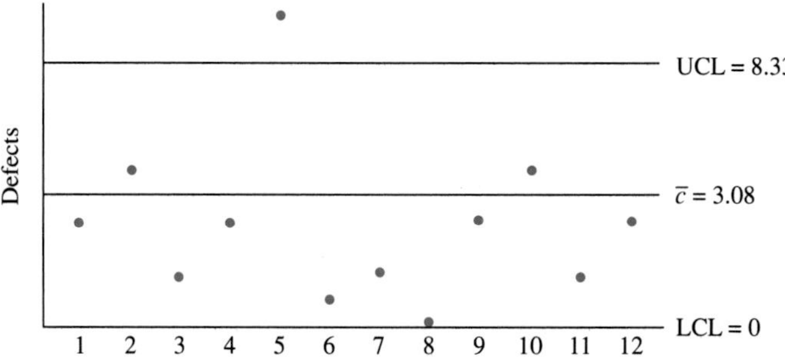

3. **These Scoops or You're Out** Crisp-O Raisin Bran, a major cereal manufacturer, promises three scoops of raisins in every box. A box with fewer raisins is considered defective. A customer of Crisp-O will accept a maximum of only 1 percent defective boxes. Crisp-O agrees to this quality check, but insists on limiting its producer's risk to 5 percent. That is, no more than 5 percent of the shipments that meet this restriction of containing at least 99 percent of boxes with three scoops must be rejected. Thus, at least 95 percent of the good shipments must be accepted. From a sample of 100 boxes selected from a large shipment, what is the acceptance number of defects that will result in rejection of that shipment?

Since the customer will accept no more than 1 percent defects, the AQL is set at 1 percent. From the extension to the binomial table, we must find a number C that will not cause the rejection of more than 5 percent of the good shipments. (A good shipment is one that contains at least 99 percent of the boxes with three scoops.) The value of π is set equal to 1 percent. Moving down the column headed by $\pi = 0.01$ with $n = 100$, we find the first number to exceed 1.00 − producer's risk, or 1.00 − 0.05 = 0.95, is 0.9816, which is associated with $C = 3$. Thus, if a sample of $n = 100$ is taken from a large shipment, and more than three boxes out of the 100 examined contain less than three scoops, the entire shipment should be returned to Crisp-O.

List of Formulas

[15.3] $$\text{UCL}_{\bar{X}} = \bar{\bar{X}} + A_2\bar{R}$$ The upper control limit is the maximum value a sample mean can take without indicating the process is out of control.

[15.4] $$\text{LCL}_{\bar{X}} = \bar{\bar{X}} - A_2\bar{R}$$ The lower control limit is the minimum value a sample mean can take without indicating the process is out of control.

[15.7] $$\text{UCL}_R = D_4\bar{R}$$ The upper control limit is the maximum value a sample range can take without indicating the process is out of control.

[15.8] $$\text{LCL}_R = D_3\bar{R}$$ The lower control limit is the minimum value a sample range can take without indicating the process is out of control.

[15.10] $$s_p = \sqrt{\frac{\bar{p}(1-\bar{p})}{n}}$$ The standard deviation of the number of defects.

[15.13] $$\text{UCL}_p = \bar{p} + 3\sqrt{\frac{\bar{p}(1-\bar{p})}{n}}$$ The upper control limit is the maximum value a sample proportion can take without indicating the process is out of control.

[15.14] $$\text{LCL}_p = \bar{p} - 3\sqrt{\frac{\bar{p}(1-\bar{p})}{n}}$$ The lower control limit is the minimum value a sample proportion can take without indicating the process is out of control.

[15.15] $$s_{\bar{c}} = \sqrt{\bar{c}}$$ The standard deviation of the number of defects in a c-chart.

[15.16] $$\text{UCL}_c = \bar{c} + 3s_{\bar{c}}$$ The upper control limit is the maximum number of defects that can occur without indicating the process is out of control.

[15.17] $$\text{LCL}_c = \bar{c} - 3s_{\bar{c}}$$ The lower control limit is the minimum number of defects that can occur without indicating the process is out of control.

Chapter Exercises

11. The director of your division at your firm happens by your desk and notices that you are working with something called a control chart. Since he got his job because he is the boss's son-in-law, and he knows nothing about control charts or quality control, he wants you to describe what you are doing and why you are doing it. Describe in your own words the purpose and function of $\bar{X}$-, R-, c-, and p-control charts.

12. Define the acceptance number and the acceptance quality level as used in acceptance sampling. If AQL is 5 percent and producer's risk is 1 percent, how would you describe the acceptance number in terms of these two percentages?

13. Acme Salt Mine, where you work as a gofer trainee, has asked you to record the number of miles the sales staff drives in making sales calls. Using these data, samples are taken over five consecutive days. From the results shown, construct $\overline{X}$- and R-charts. Does the system appear out of control?

Sample	Miles Driven					
1	112	132	145	117	125	189
2	214	252	274	189	236	203
3	198	205	185	214	236	199
4	236	250	245	210	210	259
5	109	111	125	132	145	152

14. Over a period of several days, Tolbart Manufacturing collects seven samples of size 5 on the weight of a new product. Construct an R-chart to determine whether the production process is in control. The weights in ounces are shown here.

Samples	Observations				
1	42	48	28	43	52
2	52	57	24	41	21
3	48	65	54	35	45
4	59	35	53	63	56
5	68	65	62	35	56
6	57	54	42	32	35
7	51	51	51	34	35

15. What does an $\overline{X}$-chart reveal about the process in the previous problem?

16. A producer of snowmobiles samples daily output by taking 10 samples, each of five days' output. The data are shown here. Construct an R-chart and draw a conclusion regarding the control of the process.

Samples	Observations				
1	5	3	5	5	5
2	2	6	1	3	1
3	6	9	5	6	2
4	4	8	8	5	12
5	2	5	9	8	10
6	5	7	6	9	11
7	6	4	5	5	16
8	8	5	4	4	8
9	9	9	7	7	9
10	5	6	8	8	8

17. Using the data from Exercise 16, construct and interpret an $\overline{X}$-chart.

18. The lengths of rope measured in feet that are produced by a new technology are shown here. Construct an R-chart and form a conclusion regarding the benefit of this new method of production.

Sample	Observations					
1	12.5	14.8	21.5	15.8	23.6	12.5
2	13.6	15.9	23.6	14.6	25.4	21.5
3	15.8	26.0	15.6	21.5	21.5	14.2
4	15.6	8.0	25.7	23.5	19.2	15.6
5	12.5	26.0	32.8	15.4	19.7	15.5
6	14.8	15.8	32.5	18.2	18.2	12.5
7	22.5	16.9	12.8	14.7	14.5	18.2
8	32.6	14.5	14.9	12.0	15.6	14.5
9	15.5	14.2	15.8	14.5	21.5	12.2

19. Using the data from Exercise 18, construct and interpret an $\overline{X}$-chart.

20. Twenty samples of size 7 for the weights (in ounces) of filled cola cans produced the results shown here. Must the producer search for assignable causes based on an R-chart or on an $\overline{X}$-chart?

Sample	Mean	Range	Sample	Mean	Range
1	27	6	11	32	7
2	32	8	12	45	9
3	21	4	13	34	5
4	24	8	14	23	7
5	43	6	15	32	8
6	31	7	16	21	4
7	23	5	17	34	4
8	12	6	18	21	7
9	21	5	19	27	5
10	32	9	20	34	6

21. The results of ten samples of size 6 each for the length (in inches) of electrical cord are shown here. As measured by an R-chart and an $\overline{X}$-chart, is the system out of control?

Sample	Mean	Range	Sample	Mean	Range
1	20	7	6	34	4
2	18	9	7	21	3
3	17	8	8	12	2
4	23	2	9	18	6
5	19	5	10	13	5

22. The AllRight Insurance Company of Buffalo, New York, collects five samples of size 12 each of claims filed against them for auto damage. The means and ranges are given here. Construct $\overline{X}$- and R-charts, and comment.

Sample	Mean	Range
Jan	$812	$54
Feb	234	23
Mar	321	27
Apr	250	29
May	276	20

23. In Exercise 22, what would a heavy snowstorm in January constitute?

24. A large auto parts store in Little Rock refuses to accept a shipment of distributor caps if more than 5 percent are defective. The store managers agree, to protect their suppliers, that in sampling shipments they will not return more than 20 percent of all shipments that meet the 5 percent requirement. If samples of 50 are taken, what is the acceptance number?

25. For Exercise 24, what is the acceptance number if samples of 20 are taken?

26. In Exercise 24, if the actual percentage of defective caps is 10 percent, what is the probability a shipment will be accepted if a sample of 50 caps is taken?

27. From Exercises 24 and 26, if the true percentage of defects is 1 percent, what is the probability that the shipment will be accepted? Comment on the difference in your answers in this problem and in Exercise 26.

28. Kmart sells radar detector units used by motorists. Company policy is to accept a maximum of 5 percent defective units. Only 10 percent of those shipments that contain fewer than 5 percent defects will be sent back to the supplier. What is the maximum number of defective detectors that can occur in a sample of 50?

29. If producer risk is reduced to 1 percent in Exercise 28, what is the acceptance number? Comment on the difference in your answer from Exercise 28.

30. A recent graduate of the MBA program at a small private university is now in business for himself. He wishes to test his production method by taking 10 samples of size 8 each. He finds $\overline{\overline{X}} = 42$ and $\overline{R} = 17$. Determine his control limits for both R-charts and $\overline{X}$-charts.

31. To further test his product, the graduate from Exercise 30 takes 15 samples of size 100, and finds the number of defects in each sample to be

Sample	Defects	Sample	Defects
1	4	8	8
2	8	9	7
3	8	10	9
4	3	11	3
5	8	12	9
6	5	13	6
7	6	14	8
		15	7

If his p-chart reveals his production process to be in control, he plans to "go global" with his product. Should he do so?

32. TCBY Yogurt tested the stability of its franchise operation by taking samples of 25 each in six states. The numbers of failed franchises were 4, 7, 2, 6, 8, and 12. Develop a p-chart to help TCBY monitor its outlets.

33. Bradley University uses two word processing packages: Professional Write and WordPerfect. In a comparison of their relative merits, samples of size 18 are taken for the time required for faculty and staff to master each package. The results are shown here. Prepare $\overline{X}$- and R-charts for use in evaluating each package. What are your conclusions?

Professional Write v.2.0		
Sample	Mean (hours)	Range (hours)
1	3.2	1.2
2	3.9	0.9
3	3.9	1.5
4	3.7	1.5

(Continued)

Professional Write v.2.0		
Sample	Mean (hours)	Range (hours)
5	3.6	1.1
6	3.3	1.9
7	2.5	1.8
8	3.6	1.7

WordPerfect v.5.1		
Sample	Mean (hours)	Range (hours)
1	78.5	10.2
2	79.5	8.7
3	55.6	6.8
4	78.6	7.8
5	58.9	11.3
6	72.8	10.6
7	86.9	12.3

34. In a continued review (see Exercise 33) of the word processing packages, personnel at Bradley University took four samples (actually, the number of samples was much greater) of 50 pages each typed by WordPerfect and found

10 pages with a total of 12 errors.
12 pages with a total of 18 errors.
8 pages with a total of 15 errors.
17 pages with a total of 13 errors.

Four samples of 50 pages each typed by Professional Write revealed

2 pages with a total of 2 errors.
0 pages with errors.
1 page with a total of 1 error.
3 pages with a total of 3 errors.

Prepare a p-chart and a c-chart for these data.

35. *Up Your Cash Flow* (Granville Publications), by Harvey Goldstein, CPA, discusses various computer spreadsheets and the speed with which they can forecast budgets. Lilly Paper Products applied some of the principles found in the book. They discovered that 10 samples of size 15 of the number of days it took local offices to prepare their quarterly budgets yielded means and ranges of

Sample	Mean	Range
1	32.4	23.4
2	68.7	45.3
3	45.6	18.6
4	67.6	45.6
5	23.8	18.3
6	45.7	34.6
7	56.7	17.5
8	13.2	12.2
9	34.5	29.8
10	76.7	67.9

Construct $\overline{X}$- and R-charts. What can you conclude?

36. *Nation's Business* reported that Harvey Mackay's book, *Beware the Naked Man Who Offers You His Shirt* (Morrow), tells business executives, among other things, how to select a lawyer. A large law firm chooses one sample of size 30 each month over the last 15 months of the number of legal cases it handled. Recorded are the numbers of those cases that the firm lost: 5, 4, 12, 0, 19, 21, 4, 23, 8, 12, 19, 12, 23, 6, and 10. Construct a p-chart to determine whether the process is in control.

37. Kador, the world's most evil scientist, makes amulets to cast evil spells. To control quality, Kador's assistant, Meldok, selects 30 amulets and inspects each for defects. The purpose of the inspection is to determine whether a given amulet contains too many defects to use. The number of defects in each amulet is shown here. Construct the proper quality control tool, and determine whether the process is out of control.

Amulet	Number of Defects	Amulet	Number of Defects	Amulet	Number of Defects
1	3	11	4	21	8
2	2	12	2	22	2
3	4	13	0	23	7
4	1	14	0	24	3
5	0	15	5	25	1
6	1	16	2	26	9
7	3	17	3	27	7
8	4	18	4	28	0
9	0	19	5	29	0
10	3	20	7	30	1

38. A firm that prepares tax returns tries to double-check all forms it completes. However, from January to April 15, this is often impossible. The firm's policy is to allow a maximum of 1 percent of the returns to contain errors. If more errors are suspected, the entire batch must be redone. However, the firm does not want to redo a batch of returns if fewer than 1 percent contain errors, if this can be avoided. It decides to set a limit on recalculating a good batch to only 5 percent of the time. A sample of 20 taken from a large batch reveals five returns have mistakes. Should the entire batch be reworked?

39. Mother's Best sells doughnut holes retail. From a truckload, a sample of 100 is selected, and 8 holes are found to be defective. If Mother's Best is willing to accept a maximum of 10 percent defects, and its suppliers want to restrict their risk to 20 percent, should this shipment be sent back?

40. Yakov Smirnoff, a Russian-American comedian, advertises that Best Western has economical rooms for travelers. The cost of a night's lodging for 15 nights ($n = 15$) was averaged 20 times ($k = 20$ samples). The mean of those 20 sample means proved to be \$45.12, with a mean range of \$12.34. What are the values for $\bar{X}$- and R-charts?

41. Budget Rental, a nationwide car rental firm, practices a policy in which each car is put through a checklist before it is given to a customer. A recent assessment of 20 cars found the following number of checkpoints had been neglected: 3, 5, 7, 2, 6, 8, 10, 4, 9, 12, 7, 3, 6, 13, 12, 4, 15, 4, 5, and 9. Does it appear the checklist system is in control?

42. Bids by a construction firm for a job are monitored to determine whether it might increase the number of bids the firm wins over its competitors. Samples of size 40 bids are taken, yielding means and ranges shown here in thousands of dollars. Is the bidding process out of control?

Sample	Mean	Range
1	7.5	5.4
2	8.6	4.5
3	4.5	3.4
4	5.6	2.5
5	8.9	3.2

43. Suspicious that My Mother's Catch, a fishing boat in the Bering Sea, is using illegal means to augment its daily catch, the U.S. Coast Guard takes samples of five boats' hauls for six days over the past month. Could unlawful tactics be a possible assignable cause?

Boat	Mean Haul (tons)	Range
My Mother's Catch	39.4	12.2
Neptune's Spear	18.6	18.2
Salty Dog	19.6	21.2
Wind Ablow	38.8	22.5
Deep 6	21.2	19.2

44. Fox Pictures distributes many films to its movie theaters throughout the country. It decides to sample batches of a particular film to determine whether copies were reproduced without flaws. If the sampling process suggests that no more than 5 percent of the copies have a flaw, the entire lot will be distributed to the movie houses. Officials wish to reject good lots no more than 10 percent of the time. If they screen 20 copies of a film and find 7 with flaws, should the entire lot be destroyed?

45. In the 20 films Fox screened in Exercise 44, they find the following number of flaws in the films: 6, 7, 2, 12, 19, 10, 2, 2, 22, 21, 0, 1, 19, 0, 15, 3, 12, 21, 2, and 5. Does it appear that the reproduction process is out of control?

46. Labor, Inc., selects several samples of size 50 employees for whom it has recently found jobs, and finds that the number in each sample who still have the same job one year later is 10, 12, 4, 17, 2, 21, 34, 32, 43, 12, 5, and 5. Is the placement system out of control?

47. Calculate the final control limits in Exercise 46.

48. The IBM 4019 laser printer produces almost 10 pages per minute, on the average. Of 1,200 pages printed, 100 are selected at random and examined for errors. Twelve pages are found to have an average of 2.3 errors. Should the entire 1,200 pages be reprinted if AQL = 5 percent and producer risk is set at 15 percent?

49. Determine the control limits for a *c*-chart in Exercise 48.

50. Temperatures in refrigeration boxes are monitored over a 10-day period, during which the temperature is registered every hour for eight hours. The resulting means and ranges are shown. Does it appear that something should be done about the refrigeration process?

Sample	Mean (°F)	Range	Sample	Mean (°F)	Range
1	32	29	6	23	21
2	45	21	7	57	34
3	12	45	8	13	45
4	54	34	9	31	12
5	17	24	10	47	2

51. Federal Express takes eight samples of size 25 for the number of hours it took to deliver packages. The results of that survey are shown here. Need corrective action be taken?

Sample	Mean	Range	Sample	Mean	Range
1	22.2	3.2	5	24.6	3.3
2	17.5	3.4	6	23.3	2.4
3	18.0	2.9	7	21.5	2.4
4	23.4	2.5	8	19.8	3.1

CURTAIN CALL

Ray Murdock, the new CEO for Minot Industries, as mentioned in Setting the Stage at the beginning of this chapter, has pledged to improve the production standards at Minot. For many years the company has produced glassware of various types. Due to the introduction of more modern production techniques, Minot has suffered certain "growing pains" that have resulted in an unacceptable reduction in the quality of its product.

To combat this trend, analysts at Minot collected 5 samples of the weights measured in grams of the lead that is used to produce large crystal stemware. The data are recorded here.

Sample				
1	2	3	4	5
5.2	5.8	10.3	4.9	8.9
6.3	6.8	13.5	9.5	5.8
7.5	4.5	12.5	6.8	4.7
7.9	6.8	14.9	8.9	2.9
8.2	9.5	9.2	2.8	4.5
3.2	4.5	8.9	4.5	6.2
8.9	6.5	6.2	6.5	3.5

In addition, 10 samples of sizes 50 each are examined and the number of defective units in each sample is found to be 5, 6, 10, 15, 2, 5, 19, 3, 0, and 15. Finally, 20 individual glass canisters are randomly chosen. Each is inspected and defects for all 20 are recorded:

Canister	Number of Defects	Canister	Number of Defects
1	3	11	5
2	5	12	6
3	0	13	3
4	8	14	2
5	10	15	8
6	5	16	8
7	2	17	7
8	8	18	5
9	1	19	2
10	5	20	8

As the director of product quality, it is your job to construct the appropriate control charts and report your findings in the form of a statistical report as described in Appendix I.

From the Stage to Real Life

As the director of product quality at Minot Industries, from the Curtain Call exercise, you are likely to be a member of the American Productivity and Quality Center (APQC). If so, you are able to obtain a wide variety of support from this organization in the conduct of your job. A visit to the APQC web site (*http://www.apqc.org*) will acquaint you with the available training seminars and publications that relate to your goals at Minot.

At the home page, click on BENCHMARKING, a way to develop quality standards. At the next page, look at the list of training seminars. Examine several of the offerings and make a list of some that bear directly on the job ahead of you at Minot. Then go back to the Benchmarking page and scroll through their list of articles and publications. Make a list of some that bear directly on the situation at Minot.

Return to the APQC home page and click on the PRODUCTIVITY AND QUALITY area. Again, think about APQC resources that will help you to succeed in your job at Minot Industries.

APPENDIX I

Business Report Writing

A.1 Introduction

As the business environment grows in its complexity, the importance of skillful communication becomes essential in the pursuit of institutional goals. In addition to the need to develop adequate statistical skills, you will find it necessary to effectively communicate to others the results of your statistical studies. It is of little use to formulate solutions to business problems without transmitting this information to others involved in the problem-solving process. The importance of effectively communicating the results of your statistical study cannot be overemphasized.

Unfortunately, it seems that many business managers suffer from inadequate communication skills. The December 1990 issue of the *Training and Development Journal* reports that "Executives polled in a recent survey decry the lack of writing skills among job candidates." A report in a 1993 issue of *Management Review* notes the "liability imposed on businesses by poor writing skills." The report states that employers are beginning to place greater emphasis on communication in hiring practices. Many employers have adopted policies requiring job candidates to submit a brief written report as part of the screening process. An August 1992 issue of *Marketing News* reveals that "Employers seek motivated communicators for entry-level marketing positions." Obviously, the pressing lack of adequate writing and communications skills in American businesses is well documented.

Therefore, the purpose of this appendix is to illustrate some of the major principles of business communication and the preparation of business reports. We examine the general purpose and essential features of a report and stress the benefits of effective report writing. Emphasis is placed on the customary form a business report should take and the format, content, and purpose of its component parts. We will study illustrations of practical reports and the problems will provide the opportunity for students to develop and sharpen their communication skills.

A.2 The Need to Communicate

Most business decisions involve the cooperation and interaction of several individuals. Sometimes dozens of colleagues and co-workers strive in unison to realize mutual goals. Lines of communication must therefore be maintained to facilitate these joint efforts. Without communicating ideas and thoughts it would be impossible to identify common objectives and purposes necessary for successful operations. Without communication and the team effort it permits, the successful completion of any important project can be jeopardized. Some aspects of the project would be unnecessarily replicated while other tasks would be left unattended. Further, in the absence of adequate communication, colleagues would find themselves working at cross-purposes and perhaps pursuing opposing goals. What one team member may have worked to assemble one day, a second team member may dismantle the next. Without communication the chances for a successful outcome of any business endeavor are significantly reduced.

A.3 The Characteristics of the Reader

Business reports are quite often intended for a wide variety of different audiences. It is critical that you carefully identify the intended audience for your report, otherwise it is likely that your report will be misdirected and less effective. You should consider exactly what the readers of your report already know and what they need to know to make informed decisions.

You should also consider the attitude the audience will adopt toward your report. If you fear that the readers may be somewhat hostile toward your report, you may want to offer more supporting evidence and documentation than you would if their reception was thought to be more favorable. The educational background and work experience of the audience is also a key factor in the formulation of your report. A report written for top executives will differ considerably from that prepared for line supervisors in terms of style, word usage, and complexity. Even age, gender, and other demographic characteristics might serve to shape the report.

One thing is certain. Whether you earn your livelihood as an accountant, a marketing manager, a production supervisor, or a sales representative, you will not work in a vacuum. You will find it necessary to constantly communicate with others in order to successfully complete your job. Generally speaking, the larger the institution in which you work, the greater will be the need to prepare written reports. As the organization grows in complexity, so does the required degree of formal communication.

A.4 The Purpose of Statistical Reports

Given the importance of communication, it should come as no surprise that the primary purpose of a report is to convey information. In this effort, statistical reports are fairly concise and follow a rather predetermined pattern. This familiar pattern permits easy recognition of the essential features and allows the reader to quickly comprehend the study. To complete a statistical report you must isolate the problem and collect the necessary data. The population must be clearly identified and a sample carefully chosen. The researcher then conducts the study and prepares to report the results.

As noted above, the procedure to be followed in compiling a statistical report consists of rather precise and well-defined steps that may be modified only slightly. Immediately following the title page (which is illustrated in the example provided later), the statistical report provides an account of its conclusions and recommendations. In a business setting this opening statement is usually referred to as an **executive summary.** The executive summary, along with the other parts of a statistical report, are discussed in turn.

A. The Executive Summary

The intent of the executive summary is to immediately provide the time-constrained reader with the important facts and findings derived from the study. It summarizes these findings and conclusions, along with any recommendations, and places them at the beginning of the study. This placement provides easy access to the more important information relevant to any decision that a manager must make. If the manager is interested in any further details, he or she may consult the main body of the report.

The executive summary should be written in a nontechnical manner. It is intended for upper-level managers whose expertise often lies in business management and not in technical fields such as chemistry, physics, or even, in many cases, statistics. They generally have little concern for the technical aspect of the report. They only want to be assured that your have considered all relevant business factors and followed proper scientific procedures in the formulation of the report. If the reader then desires a more complete technical explanation, he or she can read any additional portion of the report. The executive summary seldom exceeds one or two pages.

Executive Summary A statement of conclusions and recommendations that is placed at the beginning of a report

Although the executive summary precedes the main report when it is submitted in final form, the summary is written only after the study has been conducted and the rest of the report has been completed. The summary should include no new information not presented in the report, and should not offer conclusions based on data or information not contained in the report.

B. Introduction

The second step is a brief introduction describing the nature and scope of the problem. Any relevant history or background of the problem that is essential to a thorough understanding and provides clarification for the rest of the study should also be included. A statement is made explaining why the resolution of this issue is important and the critical need to formulate a course of action.

C. Methodology

The third section of a statistical report is more technical than the rest of the study, as it explains the exact nature of the statistical tests that you intend to conduct. It describes in detail the precise quantitative tools and techniques to be used, and reveals the manner in which they will lead to the desired results. It is also customary to briefly characterize the data set and the manner in which the sample was taken. This will become familiar to you as you gain an increased understanding of statistical analysis and its many applications.

The methodology that you use will depend largely on what you want to accomplish. This fact too will become more evident as you gain more insight into the process of statistical analysis as described in this text.

D. Findings

It is here that the true statistical analysis is performed. The findings consist of the actual statistical computations that provide the information required to make decisions and recommendations. These calculations may vary from simple descriptive techniques to the more advanced inferential analysis. The computations are shown in sufficient detail to reveal and validate the statistical test without providing needless information or becoming overly cumbersome.

In addition, comments regarding the computations are provided to note the results and draw attention to their significance. That is, the results of the computations are merely cited or quoted. No effort is made to discuss or interpret these computations. This is left for the next segment.

E. Discussion and Interpretation

Based on the findings from the previous section, the researcher now offers a discussion and interpretation of the report's major implications. The researcher should provide an interpretation of the findings in a meaningful and yet nontechnical sense. This section has a considerable impact on the formulation of the solution to the problem described in the introduction, which motivated the report.

F. Conclusions and Recommendations

This final segment often repeats some of the information found in the executive summary, yet allows the researcher to explain in greater detail how and why the conclusions were reached. A more complete discussion of the recommendations may also be included. It is important that this section be based on the results of the findings and not offer conclusions or recommendations not supported by the analysis.

If reports are prepared in this organized form, they are inherently more useful and lend the researcher a sense of credibility and authority. The report will command respect from those who rely on it to make important decisions.

A.5 Illustrations and Examples

We can form a more complete picture of reports and abstracts by using examples from specific case problems. We will look first at a full statistical report designed to assist in the consequential decision regarding location for plant expansion. Such a decision would likely prompt an entire report, as opposed to an abstract, due to the cost involved and the long-term effect of plant location.

Realistically, such a decision would require statistical analysis beyond the mere descriptive tools presented here. However, we will approach the issue of plant expansion only with the simple descriptive analyses covered in the first two chapters of this text. With this limitation in mind, let us begin our examination of the report we would submit in our decision regarding plant site.

You have just been hired as a management analyst by Global Motors, Inc., in Detroit, Michigan. Mr. Sumner, CEO for GM, has requested that your management division prepare a statistical report on the feasibility of constructing a new assembly plant. Under consideration for the site are four cities: Houston, Detroit, Pittsburgh, and Boston. How would you respond?

After the title page, the report would present the executive summary. (Remember, the executive summary, summarizing all the main findings, conclusions, and recommendations, is drawn up only after the study has been completed.) The title page might appear as:

ALTERNATIVE PLANT SITES

FOR THE 1998 EXPANSION PLAN OF GLOBAL MOTORS

Submitted to
Samuel Sumner
Chief Executive Officer
Global Motors International
Executive Headquarters
Detroit, MI

Prepared by
Jarrod Hirsch, Chief
Managerial Analysis Division
Divisional Branch Headquarters
Global Motors International
Chicago, IL

August 10, 1998

A. The Executive Summary

The executive summary could appear as:

> Upon careful consideration of all relevant issues, the Managerial Analysis Division recommends that Houston be chosen for the new plant expansion site for Global Motors. After thorough review, the Division has found that Houston offers more of the requisite facilities and amenities for successful completion of the expansion project.
>
> The Division considered factors such as an available labor supply with the necessary training or potential for training, as well as the prevailing wage rates. We analyzed geographical access to raw materials. We concluded that local transportation facilities were adequate to accommodate the shipping volume required by the assembly operations.
>
> Cooperation with local and state governments in the Houston area seems assured. The state attorney general's office has offered certain tax incentives that exceed those forthcoming from the other potential sites. Further, the city of Houston has agreed to delay Global Motors' payment of property and city sales taxes for a period of two years. In addition, Texas is a right-to-work state. This is not the case in those states in which the other proposed sites are located.

The Division made a thorough comparison of housing facilities for both managerial and hourly workers. Our findings clearly indicate that the Houston market offers superior opportunities with reasonable mortgage rates. We also concluded after a complete comparative evaluation that the schools in Houston were at least comparable to those in the other potential sites.

It is hereby recommended that a transition team be selected to assist in the relocation of some of our key personnel who will temporarily staff the new facilities. An advance team may also be formed to maintain contact with the proper officials in both public and private organizations to facilitate in the completion of the expansion project.

Notice how the executive summary offers a set of conclusions based on the findings, and recommendations that logically follow from the information contained in the study. Furthermore, effort is taken to ensure that all critical concerns have been addressed. Attention was given to factors ranging from business taxes to schooling for the employees' children.

B. Introduction

The introduction is the next component of the statistical business report form. Recall that it addresses any relevant history and offers clarification as to why the issue needs resolution.

Since 1990, the production facilities for Global Motors have been inadequate to maintain pace with the required level of output. Demand is anticipated to increase in the near future. Based on these historic and projected events, it is essential that a viable plant site be identified for the purpose of expanding Global Motors' production capability.

Unless production facilities can be adequately enhanced, it is likely that Global Motors' market share will erode and the firm will be placed at a competitive disadvantage. Industry studies have shown that GM's competitors have already expanded production capabilities or plan to do so in the near future.

C. Methodology

The methodology section specifies the tools that will be used to complete the study. As noted above, since we have examined only basic descriptive tools, we will restrict our analysis of plant site selection to only these tools. In reality, of course, many other types of tools would be used. This section also includes a brief description of the data set.

METHODOLOGY:

Various descriptive tools will be applied to the data collected for the purpose of conducting this study. Distribution tables, contingency tables, and numerous pictorial displays will be used to analytically determine the optimum site for Global Motors' plant expansion. Each of these tools will be applied to the data obtained for all four cities. The intent will be to provide a basis of comparison sufficient to permit a conclusive argument as to which site is preferable.

Data for several relevant variables have been obtained directly from local governments in proposed site areas as well as from published sources. These sources include *Survey of Current Business* and *Urban Economics*. These data will be used in a comparative analysis of the proposed sites.

Notice how this section enumerates and explains the methodology and how each tool will be employed to derive a conclusion.

D. Findings

This section contains the actual statistical calculations. It consists of a presentation comparing all four sites using the various descriptive tools. The bar chart will show the tax incentives in each city, the frequency tables depict the costs of houses in each local market, and the contingency tables reflect the transportation facilities.

The relevant statistics displayed by the descriptive analysis are communicated in this section in a formal manner. Presume, for example, that the data analysis discloses the following:

Table A, which is a frequency table of housing costs for 1,000 homes surveyed in Houston, reveals that average housing costs are lowest in that city. As shown in the table, 56 percent of all houses are in the $100,000 to $120,000 range. Pittsburgh offers an average of $120,000.

Table A
Frequency Table for Housing Costs in Houston (in $000's)

Housing Costs	Frequency
$60 \leq 80$	92
$80 \leq 100$	115
$100 \leq 120$	560
$120 \leq 140$	135
$140 \leq 160$	98
	1,000

Chart 1 discloses that Houston offers access to 56 percent of all needed raw materials within 24 hours, while the other potential sites threaten delays of 72 hours.

Chart 2 for transportation costs in all cities shows that costs range from an average of $320 per month to $512 per month. The lowest is in Detroit.

Chart 3 for tax incentives shows that total tax savings in Houston should reach $2,000,000. In Detroit, however, the savings were projected to be as low as $500,000.

Chart 1
Pie Chart for Access to Raw Materials in Houston

Number of Hours Required to Receive Raw Materials	Percentage of Raw Materials	Degrees in Pie Chart
24	56	360 × .56 = 201.6
36	24	360 × .24 = 86.4
48	11	360 × .11 = 39.6
60	9	360 × .09 = 32.4
		360.0

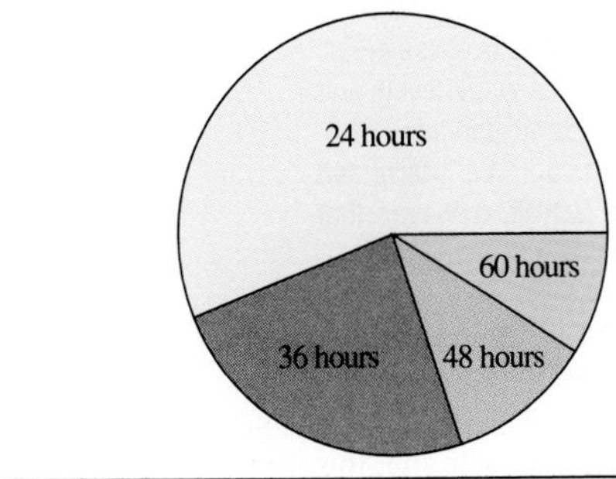

Chart 2
Average Monthly Transportation Costs for All Cities

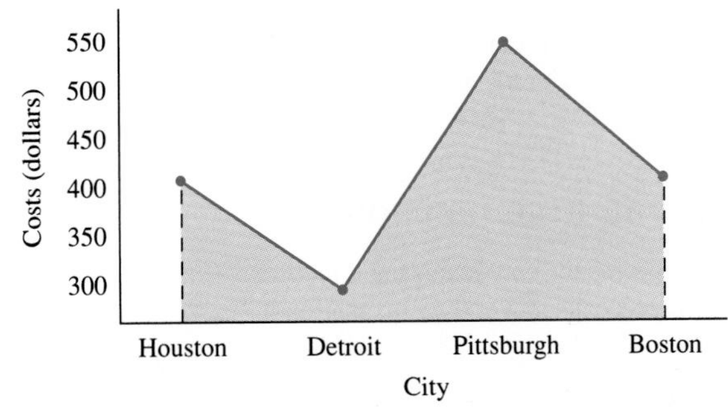

Chart 3
Tax Saving during First Year of Operations (in millions of dollars)

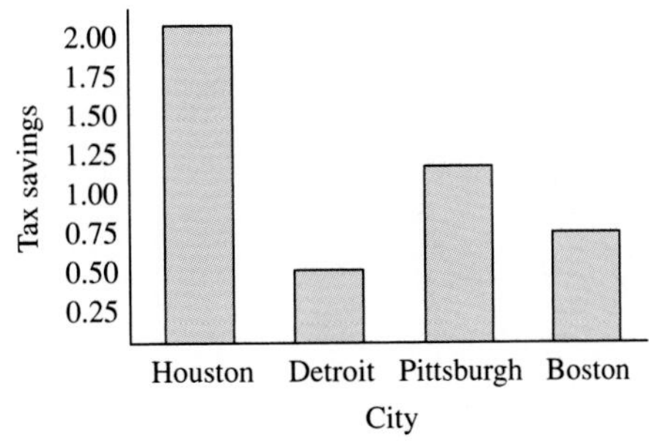

Notice that in this section no interpretation or significance is attached to the findings. That is left for the next section. In this section the numbers are quoted or cited; there is only a description or accounting of the data.

E. Discussion and Interpretation

The discussion and interpretation section highlights the relevant findings and offers an explanation. Presume that from the findings the following discussion and interpretation is possible:

> The findings provided by the pie chart for access to markets for raw materials reveals that Houston offers the greatest accessibility to all necessary materials within 24 hours. The other proposed sites average a much longer delay. This suggests that costs of transportation would be higher. Further, production planning would be more difficult. As shown in the frequency tables, the lower

> housing costs in the Houston area mean that wages could be kept at a lower level, minimizing labor costs.
>
> Although Pittsburgh reports lower overall housing costs, the real estate market in Pittsburgh has suffered a downturn recently. If this continues, it may be evidence that the homes purchased by our employees might prove to be an unfortunate investment.
>
> The stacked bar charts reflect considerable instability in city governments in several of the suggested sites. This suggests that serious political uncertainties may face any who choose to locate business operations in these areas.
>
> The contingency table reveals that wage levels and unemployment rates seem favorable for expansion activities in both Houston and Detroit. It could be interpreted on the basis of projected rates in Detroit, however, that this trend will not continue.

Given the numerous descriptive tools examined in this text, and the number of variables cited in the GM study, additional discussion and interpretation would be possible. However, this should be sufficient to illustrate that this section brings the most revealing findings to the attention of the reader and offers some meaningful interpretation. The numbers have already been cited in the previous section on findings. Now it is essential to offer meaning and significance to these numbers.

F. Conclusions and Recommendations

The final section of the report is the conclusions and recommendations section. It may repeat some of the information in the executive summary

> After careful review of numerous measures of business indexes and quality of life, the Managerial Analysis Division recommends that Houston be selected for the expansion site. Houston displayed more of the desirable traits of site selection than any other possible location.
>
> The findings strongly suggest that Houston alone promises at least potential success in all characteristics examined in the study. Furthermore, Houston posted a higher average success factor when every variable was considered.
>
> In the studied opinion of the Division, Houston is the premier site for expansion purposes. This conclusion is based on an objective and professional study, which considered all pertinent factors.

Although this example of a statistical business report contains all the essential elements and demonstrates the basic principles inherent in report writing, it should not be taken as a specific blueprint for all such reports. Each report must be custom tailored to the nature of the problem under study, data availability, and the general character and personality of those preparing the report. A series of other factors that influence its character and fine-tune its disposition will alter the report's final form. You should make every effort to bring your own style and manner into the creation of the final product.

APPENDIX II

Answers to Selected Even-Numbered Problems

Chapter 2

2. *a.* 9
b. 0.84; round to $1,000.
c. Answers will vary.

4.

Management Level	Education 1 (10–12)	2 (13–15)	3(16+)	Total
1	7	4	0	11
2	5	8	1	14
3	1	3	5	9
4	0	2	9	11
Total	13	17	15	45

A higher level of education seems associated with a higher management level.

6.

Stem	Leaf
3	2, 6, 7
4	2, 6, 7, 7, 8
5	4, 5, 5
6	2, 7, 8, 9

10. CI = 120,000

Class Interval
0 < 120,000
120,000 < 240,000
240,000 < 360,000
Etc.

16. *a.*

Stem	Leaf
5	1, 5, 9
6	5, 8
7	0, 2, 3
8	3, 4, 5, 5, 7, 8
9	1, 1, 3, 8, 9
10	0, 2, 3
11	0, 5, 7
12	3, 7
13	2, 4, 7
14	2, 3
15	0, 2, 3
16	0, 3, 3, 7
17	0, 3, 5

Class	Frequency	M	Relative Frequency
5 and under 7	5	6	5/42 = 0.119
7 and under 9	9	8	9/42 = 0.214
9 and under 11	8	10	8/42 = 0.190
11 and under 13	5	12	5/42 = 0.119
13 and under 15	5	14	5/42 = 0.119
15 and under 17	7	16	7/42 = 0.167
17 and under 19	3	18	3/42 = 0.071
	42		1.00

c. $2^c > 42; c \approx 6$

$$CI = \frac{17.5 - 5.1}{6} = 2.06 \approx 2.00$$

More Than Cumulative Frequency Distribution

Class	Cumulative Frequency
5 or more	42
7 or more	37
9 or more	28
11 or more	20
13 or more	15
15 or more	10
17 or more	3
19 or more	0

18.

Status	Range: $0 to 4,999	$5,000 to 9,999	$10,000 to 14,999	$15,000 and up	Total
Due	10 (0.083)	15 (0.125)	11 (0.092)	5 (0.042)	41 (0.342)
Overdue	5 (0.042)	10 (0.083)	10 (0.083)	7 (0.058)	32 (0.267)
Delinquent	10 (0.083)	12 (0.10)	18 (0.15)	7 (0.058)	47 (0.392)
Totals	25 (0.208)	37 (0.308)	39 (0.325)	19 (0.158)	120 (1.00)

Chapter 3

2. $\overline{X} = 15.24$
Median = 19.8
Mode = 21.6 and 22.3

4. Plan 1: 27.5%
Plan 2: 5.7%

8. Curly $\bar{X} = 2383$
$S = 1775$
Moe $\bar{X} = 638.4$
$S = 217.7$
Larry $\bar{X} = 534$
$S = D$
Curly has the highest mean, but Larry is most consistent.

10. Current data yield:
$\bar{X} = 10.41$
Median = 10.17
Mode = 10

12. *a.* $P_{75} - P_{25} = 62.25 - 20.75 = 41.5$
b./c. p_{50} = Median = 38
d. $P_{70} = 56$
e. $P_{30} = 27$

14. *a.* 68.3%
b. 95.5%
c. 99.7%
d. 0.15%
e. 15.85%

16. $CV_{age} = 22.6$
$CV_{income} = 18$

18. *a.* $\bar{X} = 45.304$
Median = 39.5
Mode = 69.875
b. $S^2 = 312.02$; $S = 17.664$
c. IQR = 40.625
d. $P_{40} = 38.8$

20. *a.* $\bar{X} = 6.939$
b. 0.424
c. $s = 0.276$

22. $1.90

24. $3.07 per foot

26. *a.* $6,925
b. $28.265 per share

28. *a.* $\bar{X} = 1077$
Median = 965
Mode = 673.33
b. $CV_{age} = 9.98$
$CV_{salary} = 61.04$

32. $s = \$1.78$; IQR = 3.62

34. *a.* 42
b. 267.43
c. 16.35
d. 20.5
e. 20.5
f. 30.5

36. $\bar{X}_g = 14$
Median = 13.882
Mode = 13.8

38. $p = 0$

40. *a.* $\bar{X}_A = 82.14$ $\quad \bar{X}_B = 71.5$
Median of A = 82 $\quad$ Median of B = 71.5
Mode of A = 75 $\quad$ Mode of B = none
b. $s_A = 12.034$ $\quad s_B = 15.35$

42. *a.* $\bar{X}_A = 7.3367$
$s = 1.5464$
b. 22.5
c. 29 i.e. *wl:* 2*s*

44. *a.* $P_{60} = 23$
$P_{25} = 14.29$
$P_{50} = 20.5$
$P_{75} = 26.25$
b. $P_{10} = 10$
$P_{90} = 31.67$

Chapter 4

4. Wrong. Flips are independent.

6. *a.* 27/52
b. 16/52
c. 9/52
d. 36/52

10. $(B \cup D)$ All females regardless of education or all nongraduates regardless of gender.

$(B \cap D)$ All females without an education.

14. *a.* 0.332
b. 0.083
c. 0.083
d. 0.167

16. *a.* 0.385
b. $P(S \mid A) = 0.385$
$P(S \mid G) = 0.385$
c. $P(C \mid P) = 0.227$
$P(C \mid A) = 0.308$
d. $P(S \mid G) = 0.385$
$P(E \mid G) = 0.615$
$P(C \mid G) = 0$

18. *a.* 0.80
b. 0.42
c. 0.40
d. 0.40
e. 0.78

20. *a.* 0.50
b. 0.10
c. 0.90
d. 0.70

22. *a.* 0.2275
b. No

24. $P(S \mid M) = 0.10 < 0.30$; yes

26. 720

28. 24

30. *a.* 37/75
b. 2/75
c. 21/75
d. 18/75
e. 56/75
f. 61/75

32. *a.* 3/120
b. 18/120
c. 65/120
d. 34/120
e. 37/120
f. 102/120

34. $0.15 \neq 0$

36. 0.0417

38. 17,576,000

40. 56.25%

42. 68.94%

Chapter 5

4. $\mu = 2.82$
$\sigma^2 = 3.76$
$\sigma = 1.95$

8. 1.8

10. *a.* 0.1209
b. 0.1115
c. 0.9452
d. 0.6331
e. 0.7779

12. 0.2403

14. 0.1231

16. 0.1833

18. *a.* 0.1363
b. 0.8647
c. 0.3067

20. $0.9896 > 0.30$; stock T-shirts

22. 0.8647

24. 0.9975

26. 0.9907

28. *a.* 13.9 and 18.1
b. 0.167

30. 61.7%

32. *a.* 0.2643
b. 0.7357
c. 0.7503
d. 0.0292

34. *a.* 50%
b. 16.11%
c. 98.75%
d. 38.50%

36. *a.* \$27.80
b. \$19.82
c. \$27.80
d. \$22.87

38. 0.0002

40. *a.* 0.2270
b. 0.1582
c. 0.0834
d. 0.9972

42. 0.0895

44. 0.9958

46. \$920.50

50. *a.* 33.3 to 36.7
b. 0.2941

52. 0.2138

58. 0.7764

60. 340.4 units

62. 99.18 days

64. $933.8 > 900$; no

66. 0.8438

68. 0.9222

Chapter 6

2. $\bar{\bar{X}} = 220$
$\sigma_{\bar{x}} = 31.22$

4. 3.95

10. *a.* 0.9772
b. 0.9772
c. 0.9818

12. 0.1646

14. 0.0668

16. 0.1251

24. 0.0375

26. 0.0082

28. 0.0901

32. 87.28 units

34. *a.* 0.1587
b. 0.0548

36. 0.3544

38. 0.7704

40. 0.3936

42. There is only a 7.64% chance that if your computer had 9% downtime the last 90 hours would be down 12 hours.

44. *a.* $\sigma_p = 0.044$
b. $\overline{P} = 0.45$
c. 0.2483

Chapter 7

4. $15.01 \leq \mu \leq 15.38$

6. $6.00 \leq \mu \leq 6.40$

8. $52.32 \leq \mu \leq 57.64$

10. $15.95 \leq \mu \leq 17.25$

12. $n \leq 30$; σ unknown: population is assumed to be normal.

14. $14.82 \leq \mu \leq 15.58$

16. $58{,}760 \leq \mu \leq 73, 020$

18. $1736 \leq \mu \leq 2994$

20. $0.62 \leq \pi \leq 0.70$; yes, 68% is in the interval.

22. $0.27 \leq \pi \leq 0.31$

24. $0.79 \leq \pi \leq 0.85$

26. 73

28. 51

30. 167

32. 1359

36. $0.4799 \leq \mu \leq 0.560$

38. *a.* $693.8 \leq \mu \leq 696.2$
b. GP can be 90% confident that the stand will yield an average between these two values.
c. No

40. $1.73 \leq \mu \leq 1.85$

42. $13.274 \leq \mu \leq 14.926$

44. $14.9 \leq \mu \leq 15.7$

46. 95%

48. $11.53 \leq \mu \leq 14.31$

50. $44.05 \leq \mu \leq 50.55$

52. $78.56 \leq \mu \leq 87.84$

54. $0.823 \leq \pi \leq 0.937$
Although FOA has a higher interval, the overlap suggests that there may be no difference in the proportion of satisfied customers.

56. $6.95 \leq \mu \leq 7.65$

58. $12.25 \leq \mu \leq 12.75$; do not raise price.

60. *a.* $0.623 \leq \pi \leq 0.757$
b. $0.647 \leq \pi \leq 0.733$
c. The smaller interval results in a lower level of confidence. No, because you must accept a lower level of confidence.

62. 112

64. 777

66. $0.5339 \leq \pi \leq 0.7661$

68. $0.235 \leq \pi \leq 0.285$
No; 30% is not in the interval.

70. 154

72. 757

Chapter 8

10. H_0: $\mu = 2{,}100$; $Z_{test} = 1.49$ is between ± 1.96; do not reject.

12. H_0: $\mu = 58$; $Z_{test} = -1.24$ is between ± 2.58; do not reject.

14. H_0: $\mu = 12$; $Z_{test} = -3.18 < -1.65$; reject.

16. H_0: $\mu = 32{,}533$; $Z_{test} = 0.77$ is between ± 2.58; do not reject.

18. The "equals" sign must appear in the null to provide some specific value to test at some specific alpha value.

20. H_0: $\mu \leq 7{,}880$; $Z_{test} = 0.50 < 2.33$; do not reject.

22. H_0: $\mu \geq 34.4$; $Z_{test} = -4.04 < -1.75$; reject.

24. H_0: $\mu \geq 10{,}000$; $Z_{test} = -5.84 < -2.33$; reject; yes.

26. H_0: $\mu \geq 325{,}500$; $Z_{test} = 0.25 > -1.65$; do not reject; yes.

28. H_0: $\mu = 800$; $Z_{test} = -1.20$ is between ± 1.96; do not reject. p-value $= 0.5000 - 0.3849 = 0.1151(^2) = 0.2302$

30. H_0: $\mu \leq 283$; $Z_{test} = 0.91 < 2.33$; do not reject. p-value $= 0.1814$

32. H_0: $\mu \leq 27{,}400$; $Z_{test} = 2.60 > 1.65$; reject. p-value $= 0.5000 - 0.4953 = 0.0047$.

34. H_0: $\mu \leq 5{,}775$; $t_{test} = 0.9395 < 2.624$; do not reject; discontinue the program.

36. H_0: $\mu \leq 5000$; $t_{test} = 0.31 < 1.711$; do not reject.

38. H_0: $\mu = 25$; $t_{test} = -0.91$ is between ± 2.797; do not reject.

40. H_0: $\mu = 500$; $t_{test} = 1.054$ is between ± 1.761; do not reject.

42. H_0: $\pi \leq 0.35$; $Z_{test} = 0.51 < 1.65$; do not reject; no. p-value $= 0.5000 - 0.1950 = 0.3050$

44. H_0: $\pi = 0.21$; $Z_{test} = -2.60 < -1.96$; reject. p-value $= 0.5000 - 0.4953 = 0.0047(2) = 0.0094$.

46. H_0: $\pi \geq 0.70$; $Z_{\text{test}} = -1.69 > -2.05$; do not reject; yes, implement the program.

54. H_0: $\mu = 18$; $Z_{\text{test}} = 1.35$ is between ± 1.96; do not reject. Do not adjust.
p-value $= 0.1819$

56. H_0: $\mu = 115{,}000$; $Z_{\text{test}} = 0.272$ is between ± 1.81; do not reject.
p-value $= 0.7868$

58. H_0: $\mu = 3.1$; $t_{\text{test}} = -0.63$ is between ± 3.106; do not reject.

60. H_0: $\pi = 0.25$; $Z_{\text{test}} = -2.64 < -1.65$; reject; p-value $= 0.0041$.

62. H_0: $\mu = 0.30$; $t_{\text{test}} = -1.06$ is between ± 3.707; do not reject; yes, Dean is happy.

64. H_0: $\pi = 0.50$; $Z_{\text{test}} = 1.41$ is between ± 1.96; do not reject.

66. H_0: $\mu \geq 0.25$; $Z_{\text{test}} = -3.25$; reject.

68. H_0: $\mu \leq 52{,}500$; $Z_{\text{test}} = 1.58$ between ± 1.65; do not reject; the new time is not better.

70. *a.* H_0: $\mu \leq 57$; $Z_{\text{test}} = 2.34 > 2.33$; reject; alter length.
b. p-value $= 0.0096$

72. H_0: $\pi \leq .53$; $Z_{\text{test}} = 1.45 < 1.75$; do not reject; money not spent well.

Chapter 9

2. $-5.77 \leq (\mu_1 - \mu_2) \leq 0.177$

4. $-0.037 \leq (\mu_1 - \mu_2) \leq 0.417$

6. Populations are normal or near normal; small sample; σ^2 unknown.

8. $-17.65 \leq (\mu_1 - \mu_2) \leq 8.05$; no, interval contains zero, suggesting no difference.

10. $-27.39 \leq (\mu_1 - \mu_2) \leq 330.62$

12. $0.99 \leq (\mu_1 - \mu_2) \leq 4.44$

14. $0.072 \leq (\mu_F - \mu_N) \leq 5.27$; play at Nugget.

16. $-2.94 \leq (\mu_1 - \mu_2) \leq 0.59$; since interval contains zero, makes no difference which investment is chosen.

18. $1.425 \leq (\mu_S - \mu_T) \leq 5.058$; since you get positive values by $\mu_S - \mu_T$, $\mu_S > \mu_T$.

20. $-0.114 \leq (\pi_{\text{out}} - \pi_{\text{in}}) \leq -0.026$; $\mu_{\text{in}} > \mu_{\text{out}}$

22. H_0: $\mu_1 - \mu_2$; $Z_{\text{test}} = -2.91 < -2.33$; reject.

24. H_0: $\mu_1 - \mu_2$; $t_{\text{test}} = -1.836$ is between ± 2.921; do not reject.

26. H_0: $\mu_1 \leq \mu_2$; $Z_{\text{test}} = 1.71 > 1.65$; reject.

28. H_0: $\mu_1 - \mu_2$; $t_{\text{test}} = 10.46 > 2.064$; reject.

30. H_0: $\pi_1 \leq \pi_2$; $Z_{\text{test}} = 1.43 > 1.28$; reject.

32. $-0.048 \leq (\mu_1 - \mu_2) \leq 0.408$

34. $1.343 \leq (\mu_1 - \mu_2) \leq 3.657$

36. $-9.474 \leq (\mu_1 - \mu_2) \leq -2.526$

38. $-22 \leq (\mu_1 - \mu_2) \leq 38.4$

40. $4268 \leq (\mu_1 - \mu_2) \leq 12{,}932$

42. $-3.78 \leq (\mu_1 - \mu_2) \leq 16.383$

44. *a.* $86 \leq (\mu_1 - \mu_2) \leq 136$
b. $n = 182$

46. $-15.366 \leq (\mu_1 - \mu_2) \leq -7.634$; you can be 95% confident that the mean life expectancy of alcoholics is between 7.634 years and 15.366 years shorter.

48. $0.6122 \leq (\mu_1 - \mu_2) \leq 0.6378$; you can be 99% confident that the mean price change is between 61¢ and 64¢ more on Fridays.

50. $-9.343 \leq (\mu_1 - \mu_2) \leq 51.143$

52. $-1.026 \leq (\mu_1 - \mu_2) \leq 0.134$

54. $0.1841 \leq (\mu_1 - \mu_2) \leq 0.2759$

56. $0.796 \leq (\mu_1 - \mu_2) \leq 6.204$; keep the old machine.

58. H_0:$(\mu_F = \mu_C)$; $t_{\text{test}} = 2.65 > 2.711$; reject; conclude $\mu_F - \mu_C$ since $\overline{X}_F > \overline{X}_C$.

60. *a.* $-0.0074 \leq (\mu_1 - \mu_2) \leq 1.4074$; since the interval contains zero, it appears there is no difference; Skinner is not supported.
b. $n = 20$

62. $12.31 \leq (\mu_1 - \mu_2) \leq 14.69$; μ_1 is larger.

64. H_0: $\pi_1 = \pi_2$; $Z_{\text{test}} = 0.423$ is between ± 1.96; do not reject.

66. $-0.199 \leq (\pi_1 - \pi_2) \leq 0.099$

68. *a.* $-0.215 \leq (\pi_1 - \pi_2) \leq 0.315$
b. $n = 1165$

70. H_0: $\pi_w \leq \pi_m$; $Z_{\text{test}} = -0.908$ is between $+1.65$; do not reject.

72. H_0: $\pi_c \leq \pi_l$; $Z_{\text{test}} = 3.37 > 1.28$; reject.

74. H_0: $\sigma_1^2 = \sigma_2^2$
$F = 1.46 < F_{0.005,7,9} = 6.88$; do not reject.

Chapter 10

2. $F = 20.69 > F_{0.05,3,24} = 3.01$; reject.

4. $F = 0.30 < 2.54$; do not reject.

6. $F = 22.315 > 4.02$; reject.
$T = 5.53$; $\underline{W\ \ Th\ \ T}$ $\underline{M\ \ F}$

8. $F = 4.84 > F_{0.05,5,10} = 3.33$; reject block.
$F = 9.37 > F_{0.05,2,10} = 4.10$; reject samples.
$T = 1.33$; only 2 and 3 do not differ significantly.

10. $F = 10.10 > 9.78$; reject block.
$F = 28.99 > 10.92$; reject samples.
Only 2 and 3 do not differ significantly.

12. $F = 17.906 > 10.92$; reject blocks.
$F = 0.17 < 9.78$; do not reject samples.

14. $F = 11 > 3.49$; reject samples.

16. $F = 0.200 < 99$; do not reject.

24. $F = 5.52 < 3.55$; reject.

26. $F = 1.26 < 2.70$; do not reject.

28. $F = 3.83 < 3.89$; do not reject.

30. $F = 184.71 > 6.93$; reject.

32. $F = 5.886 > 3.89$; reject.

34. $F = 199.85 > 5.29$; reject.

36. $F = 1.537 < 2.70$; do not reject.

38. $F = 3.94$; $T = 2.35$; LSD = 1.75

40. LSD = 1.98; $T = 2.41$

42. $F = 4.75 > 3.26$; reject blocks.
$F = 0.19 < 3.49$; do not reject samples.

44. $F = 71.616 > 7.01$; reject blocks.
$F = 1.025 < 8.65$; do not reject samples.

46. $F = 38.56 > 18$; reject blocks.
$F = 0.52 < 18$; do not reject samples.

Chapter 11

10. *b.* $\hat{C} = 1.777 + 0.558I$
c. \$15,346.77

12. *b.* $\hat{C} = 3.72 + 0.1259U$
c. \$4,664

14. $\hat{R} = 0.138 + 0.598S$; 4.324

20. $S_e = 2.251$

22. $S_e = 0.617$

30. $H_0\colon \beta_1 = 0$
$t_{\text{test}} = 7.376 > t_{0.01,10} = 3.169$; reject null; yes, is significant.

32. $H_0\colon \beta_1 = 0$
$t_{\text{test}} = 0.767 < t_{0.05,9} = 2.262$; do not reject; not significant.

38. $0.666 \le Y_X \le 5.67$

40. *a.* \$8,095.68
b. $\$584 \le Y_X \le \$15{,}606$

42. $r^2 = .916$

44. $5.32 \le \beta_1 \le 8.82$

46. $-30.81 \le \beta_1 \le -19.89$

48. $b_1 = 1.6687$; yes, $b_1 > 0$.

50. $H_0\colon \beta_1 = 0$; $t = -1.461$ between ± 3.169; do not reject.
$H_0\colon \rho = 0$; $t = 1.461$ between $\pm$ 3.169; do not reject.

52. *a.* $\hat{B} = 68.114 - 0.532TR$; no, there is a negative relationship between B and TR.
b. $r^2 = 0.8167$
c. $S_e = 0.4825$

54. $b_1 = 3.39 > 0$
$r = 0.896 > 0$

56. *a.* $H_0\colon \beta_1 = 0$; $t = 21.15 > Z = 1.65$; reject H_0.
b. $H_0\colon \rho = 0$; same results.

58. $29.10 \le \mu_{Y|X=10} \le 30.57$

Chapter 12

2. X_1 has a low t-value; it is not significant; consider removing it from the model.

4. It shows as P increases, people buy more. This is unlikely.

6. With a critical t of ± 1.96, I is significant but w is not.

8. *a.* 0:1 = 20.706 − 0.853T + 0.11287P + 0.001929PR
b. Temp and Price are not
c. The p-values
d. Remove Price.
e. $R^2 = 95.8\%$

10. The independent variable is not related to the dependent variable.

12. $H_0\colon \beta_i = 0$; DR; do not reject if t is between ± 2.052. Both are significant.

14. $H_0\colon \beta_i = 0$; do not reject if t is between ± 3.25; I is significant, r is not.

22. If $X_2 = 1$ when a strike occurred, $b_2 < 0$.

24. Two dummy variables are needed since there are three categories.

28. $\hat{Y} = 78.12 + 1.01(17) - 17.2(0) = 95.29$ in a district with an office.

$\hat{Y} = 78.12 + 1.01(17) - 17.2(1) = 78.09$ in a district without an office.

32. *b.* $\hat{T} = -31276206 + 874097NB$ (for linear model)
$r^2 = 78.9\%$
$\hat{T} = -9069460 + 172498NB + 5297NB^2$
$R^2 = 79.3\%$

34. $\hat{Y} = -39.6 + 0.144X_1 + 1.25X_2 + 0.683X_3$
(0.72) (2.53) (1.55)
[0.487] [0.028] [0.149]
t-values are in ( ) and p-values are in [ ].

36. $VIF_1 = 1.1$; $VIF_2 = 2.7$; $VIF_3 = 2.6$

38. $\hat{R} = 89 + 0.289$ SQFT $- 57.2$ DIST
(1.86) (−1.87)
[0.096] [0.094]
t-values are in ( ) and p-values are in [ ].

40.

	Rent	Square Feet
Rent	1.000	0.885
SQRT	0.885	1.050

VIF = 3.7

42. $114.40 more

44. $\hat{Y} = -111 + 0.193$ SQFT $+ 6.69$ LUX
This model is superior to the first based on $\bar{R}^2$, S_e; and both variables are significant.

46. *a.* $\hat{S} = -22.3 + 7.31E + 0.81S$
b. $t = 0.26 < 2.447$; do not reject $\beta_S = 0$.
c. $t = 16.32 > 2.447$; reject $\beta_E = 0$.
d. Test for AC is inconclusive.
No evidence of heteroscadasticity.

Chapter 13

4.

Day	3	4	5	6	7	8	9	10
Absences	49.875	46.625	41.875	41.875	46.5	49.875	49.625	48.5

6. $F_{10} = 214.152$; $MSE = 124.57$ (with $\alpha = 0.1$)
$F_{10} = 205.061$; $MSE = 171.16$ (with $\alpha = 0.8$)

8. $\hat{O} = 88.714 - 4.131t$; $\hat{O}_{Nov} = 43.27$; $\hat{O}_{Dec} = 39.14$

10. I = 0.7203; II = 0.8344; III = 0.9443; IV = 1.5010

12. I = 0.9045; II = 0.9334; III = 1.3881; IV = 0.7740

14.

	March	April	May	June	July
Sugar	83.66	96.24	100	98.53	102.78
Gum base	56.65	59.11	100	96.55	90.64
Corn 0:1	88.99	95.41	100	105.50	114.68

16. $L_{96} = 73.3$ $P_{96} = 74.03$
$L_{97} = 100$ $P_{97} = 100$
$L_{98} = 108.10$ $P_{98} = 103.42$

18. Jan = 0.8176 Jul = 1.1383
Feb = 0.8694 Aug = 1.2313
Mar = 0.9244 Sep = 1.0278
Apr = 0.9977 Oct = 0.8878
May = 1.0299 Nov = 1.0090
Jun = 1.1926 Dec = 0.8702

20. Jul 19.94 Oct 19.49
Aug 20.30 Nov 21.01
Sep 21.31 Dec 18.62

22. *a.*

	Inventories	Centered MA
1995 Jan	87.00	
Feb	93.00	
Mar	102.00	
Apr	112.00	
May	93.00	
Jun	82.00	
Jul	80.00	95.67
Aug	73.00	96.38
Sep	93.00	97.17
Oct	102.00	97.71
Nov	115.00	98.08
Dec	112.00	98.67
1996 Jan	95.00	99.13
Feb	102.00	99.50
Mar	112.00	99.38
Apr	115.00	98.46
May	99.00	96.96
Jun	90.00	95.13
Jul	83.00	
Aug	79.00	
Sep	84.00	
Oct	89.00	
Nov	92.00	
Dec	91.00	

b.

	Inventories	Centered MA
Jan	0.9467	
Feb	1.0126	
Mar	1.1133	
Apr	1.1538	
May	1.0086	
Jun	0.9346	
Jul	0.8260	
Aug	0.7482	
Sep	0.9455	
Oct	1.0312	
Nov	1.1582	
Dec	1.1213	

c.

	Inventories	Centered MA
1995 Jan	91.90	
Feb	91.84	

(*Continued*)

	Inventories	Centered MA
Mar	91.62	
Apr	97.07	
May	92.21	
Jun	87.74	
Jul	96.85	
Aug	97.56	
Sep	98.37	
Oct	98.91	
Nov	99.29	
Dec	99.88	
1996 Jan	100.35	
Feb	100.73	
Mar	100.60	
Apr	99.67	
May	98.15	
Jun	96.30	
Jul	100.48	
Aug	105.58	
Sep	88.85	
Oct	86.31	
Nov	79.43	
Dec	81.16	

24.

Jan	1.06	Jul	0.99
Feb	1.02	Aug	0.97
Mar	1.02	Sep	0.96
Apr	1.01	Oct	1.02
May	0.98	Nov	1.01
Jun	1.00	Dec	0.98

26. A decrease of $320 each month

28. *a.* The data show seasonal variations.

b.

	Debt	MA
1	14.1	
2	13.7	
3	12.1	
4	13.1	
5	13.5	
6	9.1	
7	7.2	11.0208
8	6.1	11.0833
9	8.7	11.1458
10	10.1	11.2250
11	11.8	11.2792
12	12.2	11.3167
13	15.2	11.3333
14	14.1	11.3500
15	13.2	11.3833
16	13.9	11.4583
17	14.0	11.5333
18	9.5	11.6000
19	7.2	11.5875
20	6.5	11.4583
21	9.1	11.3333
22	11.5	11.1958
23	12.2	11.0750
24	13.4	11.0000
25	13.7	10.9292
26	12.5	10.8708
27	11.8	10.8125
28	12.0	10.7042
29	13.0	10.5792
30	8.7	10.4583
31	6.3	
32	6.0	
33	8.2	
34	9.8	
35	10.9	
36	11.8	

c.

	Seasonal Index
Jan	1.2967
Feb	1.1955
Mar	1.1249
Apr	1.1665
May	1.2207
Jun	0.8250
Jul	0.6370
Aug	0.5585
Sep	0.7913
Oct	0.9630
Nov	1.0733
Dec	1.1475

d.

1995 Jan	10.8738
Feb	11.4599
Mar	10.7566
Apr	11.2304
May	11.0590
Jun	11.0303
Jul	11.3028
Aug	10.9213
Sep	10.9939
Oct	10.4883
Nov	10.9938
Dec	10.6315
1996 Jan	11.7221
Feb	11.7945
Mar	11.7345

(continued)

	Apr	11.9162
	May	11.4686
	Jun	11.5152
	Jul	11.3028
	Aug	11.6375
	Sep	11.4994
	Oct	11.9421
	Nov	11.3665
	Dec	11.6772
1997	Jan	10.5654
	Feb	10.4561
	Mar	10.4899
	Apr	10.2874
	May	10.6494
	Jun	10.5455
	Jul	9.8900
	Aug	10.7423
	Sep	10.3621
	Oct	10.1767
	Nov	10.1553
	Dec	10.2829

30. *b.* $\log \hat{Y} = 1.29 + 0.0956t$

c. $\log \hat{Y} = 1.29 + 0.0956\,(13) = 2.5328$

$\hat{Y} = \$341.04$ thousands

32.

	1996	1997	1998
Beef	100	124.68	125.64
Milk	100	115.24	119.52
Chicken	100	107.69	108.72
Bread	100	89.9	113.13

34. $PI_{90} = 60.44$ $PI_{93} = 100$

$PI_{91} = 69.27$ $PI_{94} = 111.38$

$PI_{92} = 86.93$ $PI_{95} = 116.98$

36.

	PI_{94}	PI_{95}	PI_{96}
Killer	90.86	109.14	126.90
Pyro	75	125	149.75
Maniac	95.24	104.76	114.29

38. $F = 151.19$

42. The increase from January to February is 2.6%. The increase from February to March is 2.9%. The increase from March to April is 3.6%.

Chapter 14

2. $\chi^2 = 0.72 < \chi^2_{05.2} = 5.991$; do not reject.

4. $\chi^2 = 5.98 < 11.348$; do not reject.

6. H_0: $m = P$; $P(x \leq 3) = 0.0287 < 0.05$; reject.

8. H_0: $m = P$; $P(x \geq =5 | n = 8, \pi = 0.5) = 0.3639 > 0.05$; do not reject.

10. H_0: $\mu_F \geq \mu_m$; $Z = -2.91 < -1.28$; reject.

12. H_0: $\mu_T = \mu_E$; $Z = -2.43 < -1.96$; reject.

14. H_0: $\rho_S = 0$; $r_S = 0.809 > 0.6091$; reject.

16. H_0: $\rho_S = 0$; $Z = 0.475 < -1.96$; reject.

18. $K = 4.24 < 5.991$; do not reject.

20. $K = 9.455 > 5.991$; reject; $C_K = 6.92$; 2 and 3 are not significantly different.

32. H_0: the specific pattern exists; $\chi^2 = 6.5 < 13.277$; do not reject.

34. H_0: distribution is normal; $\chi^2 = 8.33 < 9.488$; do not reject.

36. H_0: distribution is uniform; $\chi^2 = 35.677 > 13.277$; reject.

38. H_0: distribution is uniform; $\chi^2 = 3.77 < 15.086$; do not reject.

40. $\chi^2 = 86.661 > 16.919$; reject.

42. $\chi^2 = 1.602 < 9.488$; do not reject.

44. H_0: distance and preference are independent; $\chi^2 = 32.87 > 20.09$; reject.

46. H_0: size and importance are independent; $\chi^2 = 29.61 > 7.779$; reject.

48. H_0: $P \leq m$; $P(P \geq 7 | n = 8, \pi = .5) = 0.0351 < 0.05$; reject.

50. H_0: use occurs randomly; $r = 8$ runs is between 4 and 14; do not reject.

52. H_0: sales are random; 10 runs is not between 13 and 26; reject null and increase advertising.

54. H_0: sales are random; $z = -5.04 < -1.96$; reject null and move to 200.

56. H_0: $\mu_1 = \mu_2$; $Z = 1.01$ is between ± 2.58; do not reject.

58. H_0: $\mu_1 \leq \mu_2$; $Z = 2.40 > 1.65$; reject null.

60. H_0: $\mu_D \leq \mu_m$; $Z = 2.76 > 1.28$; reject.

62. H_0: failures are uniform; $\chi^2 = 1.17 < 11.345$; do not reject.

64. H_0: uniform distribution is preference; $\chi^2 = 4.40 < 6.251$; do not reject.

66. $\chi^2 = 1.71 < 7.815$; do not reject.

68. H_0: $\rho_S = 0$; $r_S = 0.25 < 0.6786$; do not reject.

70. H_0: rankings are independent; $z = 5.9 > 1.65$; reject.

72. H_0: rankings are independent; $z = -1.83 > -2.58$; do not reject.

Chapter 15

2. $UCL_{\bar{X}} = 19.567$
$LCL_{\bar{X}} = 10.533$
$UCL_R = 14.148$
$LCL_R = 0$

4. $UCL_{\bar{X}} = 12.11$
$LCL_{\bar{X}} = 5.082$
$UCL_R = 20.26$
$LCL_R = 2.54$

6. UCL = 0.2278
LCL = 0.0756

8. UCL = 12.57
LCL = −1.53 or 0

10. UCL = 10.58
LCL = − 1.911 or 0

14. $UCL_R = 58.31$
$LCL_R = 0$

16. $UCL_R = 12.056$
$LCL_R = 0$

18. $UCL_R = 29.46$
$LCL_R = 0$

20. $UCL_R = 9.99$
$LCL_R = 2.61$
$UCL_{\bar{X}} = 29.58$
$LCL_{\bar{X}} = 27.32$

22. $UCL_{\bar{X}} = \$386.74$
$LCL_{\bar{X}} = \$370.46$
$UCL_R = \$52.52$
$LCL_R = \$8.69$

24. π = AQL = 0.05
Producer risk = 0.20
$n = 50$
$c = 4$

26. The shipment will be accepted if the number of defects does not exceed 4.

28. π = AQL = 0.05
Producer risk = 0.10
$n = 50$
$c = 5$

30. $UCL_{\bar{X}} = 48.341$
$LCL_{\bar{X}} = 35.66$
$UCL_R = 31.69$
$LCL_R = 2.31$

32. $UCL_p = 0.524$
$LCL_p = 0$

34. For Word Perfect:
$UCL_p = 0.48$; $LCL_P = 0.098$
$UCL_c = 25.9$; $LCL_c = 3.07$
For Professional Write:
$UCL_p = 0.10$
$LCL_p = 0$
$UCL_c = 0.55$
$LCL_c = 0$

36. $UCL_p = 0.66$
$LCL_p = 0.12$

38. $\pi = 0.01$; producer risk = 0.05;
$n = 20$; $c = 1 < 5$; yes, must rework entire batch

40. $UCL_{\bar{X}} = \$47.87$
$LCL_{\bar{X}} = \$42.37$
$UCL_R = \$20.39$
$LCL_R = \$4.29$

42. $UCL_{\bar{X}} = 7.6$
$LCL_{\bar{X}} = 6.4$
$UCL_R = 5.9$
$LCL_R = 1.7$

44. AQL = 0.05; $\alpha = 0.1$; $n = 20$
$c = 7 > 2$; destroy the batch.

46. $UCL_p = 0.53$
$LCL_p = 0.13$

48. $\pi = 0.05$; producer risk = 0.15;
$n = 100$; $C = 7 < 12$; reprint the lot.

50. $UCL_{\bar{X}} = 43.1$
$LCL_{\bar{X}} = 23.1$
$UCL_R = 28.6$
$LCL_R = 3.63$

APPENDIX III

Statistical Tables

List of Statistical Tables

A. Random Numbers 553

B. Binomial Distribution 554

C. Cumulative Binomial Distribution 559

D. Poisson Distribution 569

E. The Normal Distribution 575

F. The t-Distribution 576

G. The F-Distribution 577

H. Chi-Square Distribution 586

I. Common Logarithms 587

J. The Greek Alphabet 589

K. Durbin-Watson Statistic 590

L. Critical Values of the Studentized Range Distribution 592

M. Critical Values of r in the Runs Test 594

N. Spearman's Rank Correlation, Combined Areas in Both Tails 595

O. Critical Factors for Control Charts 596

P. Combinatorials 597

Table A Random Numbers

	00–04	05–09	10–14	15–19	20–24	25–29	30–34	35–39	40–44	45–49
00	49317	61129	89131	29072	80328	28430	78219	60095	04875	30641
01	07046	86793	60292	56275	32920	27352	55677	34884	87794	22116
02	56428	89199	96669	95523	00874	01737	08316	00882	56108	34900
03	68900	32909	98886	85352	20112	46277	62505	69155	07346	92641
04	65662	92876	33167	85630	60153	25658	04163	81487	59085	33576
05	30626	89793	89030	39186	62672	34096	79259	15484	82961	86128
06	08944	92260	71141	63269	05390	42740	02812	98612	58029	78535
07	53490	30321	64325	57140	95602	92005	05120	24503	74878	21816
08	33484	23794	22548	16752	78833	64716	14800	69177	26377	02784
09	16467	95532	29912	12393	74101	24446	45482	55675	59413	91906
10	35648	85681	27823	00756	75951	51803	04182	35073	89864	78820
11	73724	25186	66154	26528	02112	53109	15320	44726	02152	14321
12	61085	53289	05080	77312	79142	58556	45233	37393	60769	37304
13	23284	89012	94167	81623	59675	85151	78454	84486	31295	94858
14	81334	97145	27866	93469	02050	99518	30914	79136	89952	51563
15	70229	95039	36517	04863	14328	71347	16221	92383	90054	08118
16	84379	45707	36649	43629	61046	93738	36678	57640	90478	50696
17	91202	42142	73277	70202	61335	18636	27563	02650	45680	24077
18	69071	10757	67521	59631	22410	24987	37794	12790	97416	19615
19	42822	63339	34940	43796	83207	39270	98714	70333	82408	52589
20	86633	11146	47855	13344	43564	53166	42681	00803	37026	44351
21	61596	11753	08231	18109	94006	35433	01043	39224	38726	13111
22	86215	20972	18304	21153	17059	12093	69457	56257	84432	05259
23	98688	73108	70887	75456	83201	93243	38804	66203	59053	90063
24	32796	91274	53344	24202	18083	07536	04096	55453	15316	11471
25	15977	05506	18654	22614	91478	64332	51332	63110	76297	19613
26	17925	59081	74018	14369	24886	19808	61363	19310	58818	99851
27	67049	15491	35555	35341	35698	97895	39569	07110	49428	50891
28	75900	74079	27038	77422	29686	24769	88667	16058	21021	04819
29	48659	92532	93316	11508	82066	12347	35076	23829	11305	48093
30	23159	60432	40676	89822	36698	69157	38945	01148	44429	78018
31	37587	46602	28947	12981	14217	76012	04095	04679	23535	31867
32	09754	64860	72470	18049	67372	37792	85406	05552	06024	27259
33	89173	97364	23088	43273	31372	23748	50282	89728	03484	80002
34	34997	55750	50195	60033	87970	94694	98383	47484	77607	53880
35	68498	33841	10761	73957	29175	19068	76619	60242	12495	44883
36	99127	03990	54471	01563	50411	63460	85032	53959	74689	78264
37	44161	42863	30138	21892	91664	93233	07974	44475	52732	21112
38	15269	95676	29448	72868	62829	44748	67316	21874	31629	92205
39	98973	40380	26128	53541	02008	12446	44222	22946	05278	12020

Table A Random Numbers (*continued*)

	50–54	55–59	60–64	65–69	70–74	75–79	80–84	85–89	90–94	95–99
00	03424	74864	11746	77342	24970	15430	76369	08232	05402	66087
01	01677	84988	35246	15095	08838	31175	20982	30309	18096	84899
02	57939	08859	48441	57896	84319	83283	14811	97076	89291	35910
03	27552	57307	58843	38377	02136	59389	82338	26309	28637	68452
04	97565	86873	98942	00360	64645	46932	71799	09485	09314	51819
05	84800	50323	33396	46177	09149	02865	00588	46994	99550	40506
06	52914	13681	23381	38797	28428	48170	03086	32809	75236	00058
07	54951	66790	09596	29427	05105	92584	45968	12386	07806	40655
08	80362	43955	61191	47628	11426	99325	69607	28305	73922	89271
09	62421	70476	37258	31697	61109	18333	91701	95563	46201	12514
10	33012	34971	29595	09899	95259	51098	16799	89517	09909	48352
11	93937	10140	85341	57364	65055	85239	68144	72578	85758	20926
12	47343	53008	64554	77142	54813	94272	13220	93276	12028	05842
13	36728	89534	32162	58174	07438	49352	68648	65773	47769	73026
14	54192	52552	94695	93188	69058	53322	86416	18973	95293	10967
15	73243	63347	17348	17122	59731	57994	34753	97620	20537	42766
16	38748	95561	20099	98539	36899	30760	28145	60312	83863	96312
17	95047	14426	44302	54731	18933	19080	72952	57627	56855	34859
18	77174	73993	06339	33863	27247	70802	72386	35801	43204	07923
19	75687	63671	09641	21688	19629	77186	34847	76911	77754	74082
20	65318	93663	57336	82518	72106	38375	45361	17294	32214	77321
21	39689	65062	26294	06957	28051	32978	04044	19522	00154	07399
22	86917	30252	02536	28503	08677	89051	37121	30540	24812	33251
23	87081	02290	11567	64665	52242	44974	06450	82159	86458	35857
24	20029	12125	22239	70058	66242	78416	53416	76656	37235	37497
25	41343	01619	68185	65843	30455	16122	43529	99837	08684	56947
26	48802	86690	70360	61800	96292	54364	27178	39817	58175	64075
27	00201	53674	62822	14069	80581	45643	92836	46278	82670	37519
28	96157	13631	45042	85158	13973	67170	14192	72897	13882	68487
29	66903	83523	64279	09547	78335	40315	74289	05578	98707	68894
30	77037	12096	69134	13504	00181	31991	79227	67942	70880	37872
31	07666	49845	86053	94798	83079	50421	68467	76689	02028	55555
32	60628	11373	54477	41349	96997	02999	16166	57749	13288	05359
33	08193	10440	76553	44186	83076	05119	31491	82985	61346	08473
34	64368	14947	82460	06619	79026	51058	65457	59765	09322	71875
35	17654	34052	30839	63725	84414	76157	74516	53829	88846	77860
36	73333	12388	33682	35931	08861	84952	54744	06407	28523	22183
37	71375	07499	20422	92949	04918	90317	23064	83117	82547	17584
38	46163	11272	64918	50711	54539	23970	17133	55776	16550	91313
39	49910	95947	81477	20980	47258	33546	64109	68526	73100	49610

Table B Binomial Distribution

		π									
n	*X*	0.05	0.10	0.15	0.20	0.25	0.30	0.35	0.40	0.45	0.50
1	0	0.9500	0.9000	0.8500	0.8000	0.7500	0.7000	0.6500	0.6000	0.5500	0.5000
	1	0.0500	0.1000	0.1500	0.2000	0.2500	0.3000	0.3500	0.4000	0.4500	0.5000
2	0	0.9025	0.8100	0.7225	0.6400	0.5625	0.4900	0.4225	0.3600	0.3025	0.2500
	1	0.0950	0.1800	0.2550	0.3200	0.3750	0.4200	0.4550	0.4800	0.4950	0.5000
	2	0.0025	0.0100	0.0225	0.0400	0.0625	0.0900	0.1225	0.1600	0.2025	0.2500
3	0	0.8574	0.7290	0.6141	0.5120	0.4219	0.3430	0.2746	0.2160	0.1664	0.1250
	1	0.1354	0.2430	0.3251	0.3840	0.4219	0.4410	0.4436	0.4320	0.4084	0.3750
	2	0.0071	0.0270	0.0574	0.0960	0.1406	0.1890	0.2389	0.2880	0.3341	0.3750
	3	0.0001	0.0010	0.0034	0.0080	0.0156	0.0270	0.0429	0.0640	0.0911	0.1250
4	0	0.8145	0.6561	0.5220	0.4096	0.3164	0.2401	0.1785	0.1296	0.0915	0.0625
	1	0.1715	0.2916	0.3685	0.4096	0.4219	0.4116	0.3845	0.3456	0.2995	0.2500
	2	0.0135	0.0486	0.0975	0.1536	0.2109	0.2646	0.3105	0.3456	0.3675	0.3750
	3	0.0005	0.0036	0.0115	0.0256	0.0469	0.0756	0.1115	0.1536	0.2005	0.2500
	4	0.0000	0.0001	0.0005	0.0016	0.0039	0.0081	0.0150	0.0256	0.0410	0.0625
5	0	0.7738	0.5905	0.4437	0.3277	0.2373	0.1681	0.1160	0.0778	0.0503	0.0313
	1	0.2036	0.3281	0.3915	0.4096	0.3955	0.3602	0.3124	0.2592	0.2059	0.1563
	2	0.0214	0.0729	0.1382	0.2048	0.2637	0.3087	0.3364	0.3456	0.3369	0.3125
	3	0.0011	0.0081	0.0244	0.0512	0.0879	0.1323	0.1811	0.2304	0.2757	0.3125
	4	0.0000	0.0005	0.0022	0.0064	0.0146	0.0284	0.0488	0.0768	0.1128	0.1563
	5	0.0000	0.0000	0.0001	0.0003	0.0010	0.0024	0.0053	0.0102	0.0185	0.0313
6	0	0.7351	0.5314	0.3771	0.2621	0.1780	0.1176	0.0754	0.0467	0.0277	0.0156
	1	0.2321	0.3543	0.3993	0.3932	0.3560	0.3025	0.2437	0.1866	0.1359	0.0938
	2	0.0305	0.0984	0.1762	0.2458	0.2966	0.3241	0.3280	0.3110	0.2780	0.2344
	3	0.0021	0.0146	0.0415	0.0819	0.1318	0.1852	0.2355	0.2765	0.3032	0.3125
	4	0.0001	0.0012	0.0055	0.0154	0.0330	0.0595	0.0951	0.1382	0.1861	0.2344
	5	0.0000	0.0001	0.0004	0.0015	0.0044	0.0102	0.0205	0.0369	0.0609	0.0938
	6	0.0000	0.0000	0.0000	0.0001	0.0002	0.0007	0.0018	0.0041	0.0083	0.0156
7	0	0.6983	0.4783	0.3206	0.2097	0.1335	0.0824	0.0490	0.0280	0.0152	0.0078
	1	0.2573	0.3720	0.3960	0.3670	0.3115	0.2471	0.1848	0.1306	0.0872	0.0547
	2	0.0406	0.1240	0.2097	0.2753	0.3115	0.3177	0.2985	0.2613	0.2140	0.1641
	3	0.0036	0.0230	0.0617	0.1147	0.1730	0.2269	0.2679	0.2903	0.2918	0.2734
	4	0.0002	0.0026	0.0109	0.0287	0.0577	0.0972	0.1442	0.1935	0.2388	0.2734
	5	0.0000	0.0002	0.0012	0.0043	0.0115	0.0250	0.0466	0.0774	0.1172	0.1641
	6	0.0000	0.0000	0.0001	0.0004	0.0013	0.0036	0.0084	0.0172	0.0320	0.0547
	7	0.0000	0.0000	0.0000	0.0000	0.0001	0.0002	0.0006	0.0016	0.0037	0.0078
8	0	0.6634	0.4305	0.2725	0.1678	0.1001	0.0576	0.0319	0.0168	0.0084	0.0039
	1	0.2793	0.3826	0.3847	0.3355	0.2670	0.1977	0.1373	0.0896	0.0548	0.0313
	2	0.0515	0.1488	0.2376	0.2936	0.3115	0.2965	0.2587	0.2090	0.1569	0.1094
	3	0.0054	0.0331	0.0839	0.1468	0.2076	0.2541	0.2786	0.2787	0.2568	0.2188
	4	0.0004	0.0046	0.0185	0.0459	0.0865	0.1361	0.1875	0.2322	0.2627	0.2734
	5	0.0000	0.0004	0.0026	0.0092	0.0231	0.0467	0.0808	0.1239	0.1719	0.2188
	6	0.0000	0.0000	0.0002	0.0011	0.0038	0.0100	0.0217	0.0413	0.0703	0.1094
	7	0.0000	0.0000	0.0000	0.0001	0.0004	0.0012	0.0033	0.0079	0.0164	0.0313
	8	0.0000	0.0000	0.0000	0.0000	0.0000	0.0001	0.0002	0.0007	0.0017	0.0039
9	0	0.6302	0.3874	0.2316	0.1342	0.0751	0.0404	0.0207	0.0101	0.0046	0.0020
	1	0.2985	0.3874	0.3679	0.3020	0.2253	0.1556	0.1004	0.0605	0.0339	0.0176

Table B Binomial Distribution (*continued*)

		π									
n	*X*	0.05	0.10	0.15	0.20	0.25	0.30	0.35	0.40	0.45	0.50
	2	0.0629	0.1722	0.2597	0.3020	0.3003	0.2668	0.2162	0.1612	0.1110	0.0703
	3	0.0077	0.0446	0.1069	0.1762	0.2336	0.2668	0.2716	0.2508	0.2119	0.1641
	4	0.0006	0.0074	0.0283	0.0661	0.1168	0.1715	0.2194	0.2508	0.2600	0.2461
	5	0.0000	0.0008	0.0050	0.0165	0.0389	0.0735	0.1181	0.1672	0.2128	0.2461
	6	0.0000	0.0001	0.0006	0.0028	0.0087	0.0210	0.0424	0.0743	0.1160	0.1641
	7	0.0000	0.0000	0.0000	0.0003	0.0012	0.0039	0.0098	0.0212	0.0407	0.0703
	8	0.0000	0.0000	0.0000	0.0000	0.0001	0.0004	0.0013	0.0035	0.0083	0.0176
	9	0.0000	0.0000	0.0000	0.0000	0.0000	0.0000	0.0001	0.0003	0.0008	0.0020
10	0	0.5987	0.3487	0.1969	0.1074	0.0563	0.0282	0.0135	0.0060	0.0025	0.0010
	1	0.3151	0.3874	0.3474	0.2684	0.1877	0.1211	0.0725	0.0403	0.0207	0.0098
	2	0.0746	0.1937	0.2759	0.3020	0.2816	0.2335	0.1757	0.1209	0.0763	0.0439
	3	0.0105	0.0574	0.1298	0.2013	0.2503	0.2668	0.2522	0.2150	0.1665	0.1172
	4	0.0010	0.0112	0.0401	0.0881	0.1460	0.2001	0.2377	0.2508	0.2384	0.2051
	5	0.0001	0.0015	0.0085	0.0264	0.0584	0.1029	0.1536	0.2007	0.2340	0.2461
	6	0.0000	0.0001	0.0012	0.0055	0.0162	0.0368	0.0689	0.1115	0.1596	0.2051
	7	0.0000	0.0000	0.0001	0.0008	0.0031	0.0090	0.0212	0.0425	0.0746	0.1172
	8	0.0000	0.0000	0.0000	0.0001	0.0004	0.0014	0.0043	0.0106	0.0229	0.0439
	9	0.0000	0.0000	0.0000	0.0000	0.0000	0.0001	0.0005	0.0016	0.0042	0.0098
	10	0.0000	0.0000	0.0000	0.0000	0.0000	0.0000	0.0000	0.0001	0.0003	0.0010
11	0	0.5688	0.3138	0.1673	0.0859	0.0422	0.0198	0.0088	0.0036	0.0014	0.0005
	1	0.3293	0.3835	0.3248	0.2362	0.1549	0.0932	0.0518	0.0266	0.0125	0.0054
	2	0.0867	0.2131	0.2866	0.2953	0.2581	0.1998	0.1395	0.0887	0.0513	0.0269
	3	0.0137	0.0710	0.1517	0.2215	0.2581	0.2568	0.2254	0.1774	0.1259	0.0806
	4	0.0014	0.0158	0.0536	0.1107	0.1721	0.2201	0.2428	0.2365	0.2060	0.1611
	5	0.0001	0.0025	0.0132	0.0388	0.0803	0.1321	0.1830	0.2207	0.2360	0.2256
	6	0.0000	0.0003	0.0023	0.0097	0.0268	0.0566	0.0985	0.1471	0.1931	0.2256
	7	0.0000	0.0000	0.0003	0.0017	0.0064	0.0173	0.0379	0.0701	0.1128	0.1611
	8	0.0000	0.0000	0.0000	0.0002	0.0011	0.0037	0.0102	0.0234	0.0462	0.0806
	9	0.0000	0.0000	0.0000	0.0000	0.0001	0.0005	0.0018	0.0052	0.0126	0.0269
	10	0.0000	0.0000	0.0000	0.0000	0.0000	0.0000	0.0002	0.0007	0.0021	0.0054
	11	0.0000	0.0000	0.0000	0.0000	0.0000	0.0000	0.0000	0.0000	0.0002	0.0005
12	0	0.5404	0.2824	0.1422	0.0687	0.0317	0.0138	0.0057	0.0022	0.0008	0.0002
	1	0.3413	0.3766	0.3012	0.2062	0.1267	0.0712	0.0368	0.0174	0.0075	0.0029
	2	0.0988	0.2301	0.2924	0.2835	0.2323	0.1678	0.1088	0.0639	0.0339	0.0161
	3	0.0173	0.0852	0.1720	0.2362	0.2581	0.2397	0.1954	0.1419	0.0923	0.0537
	4	0.0021	0.0213	0.0683	0.1329	0.1936	0.2311	0.2367	0.2128	0.1700	0.1208
	5	0.0002	0.0038	0.0193	0.0532	0.1032	0.1585	0.2039	0.2270	0.2225	0.1934
	6	0.0000	0.0005	0.0040	0.0155	0.0401	0.0792	0.1281	0.1766	0.2124	0.2256
	7	0.0000	0.0000	0.0006	0.0033	0.0115	0.0291	0.0591	0.1009	0.1489	0.1934
	8	0.0000	0.0000	0.0001	0.0005	0.0024	0.0078	0.0199	0.0420	0.0762	0.1208
	9	0.0000	0.0000	0.0000	0.0001	0.0004	0.0015	0.0048	0.0125	0.0277	0.0537
	10	0.0000	0.0000	0.0000	0.0000	0.0000	0.0002	0.0008	0.0025	0.0068	0.0161
	11	0.0000	0.0000	0.0000	0.0000	0.0000	0.0000	0.0001	0.0003	0.0010	0.0029
	12	0.0000	0.0000	0.0000	0.0000	0.0000	0.0000	0.0000	0.0000	0.0001	0.0002
13	0	0.5133	0.2542	0.1209	0.0550	0.0238	0.0097	0.0037	0.0013	0.0004	0.0001
	1	0.3512	0.3672	0.2774	0.1787	0.1029	0.0540	0.0259	0.0113	0.0045	0.0016

Table B Binomial Distribution (*continued*)

		π									
n	*X*	0.05	0.10	0.15	0.20	0.25	0.30	0.35	0.40	0.45	0.50
	2	0.1109	0.2448	0.2937	0.2680	0.2059	0.1388	0.0836	0.0453	0.0220	0.0095
	3	0.0214	0.0997	0.1900	0.2457	0.2517	0.2181	0.1651	0.1107	0.0660	0.0349
	4	0.0028	0.0277	0.0838	0.1535	0.2097	0.2337	0.2222	0.1845	0.1350	0.0873
	5	0.0003	0.0055	0.0266	0.0691	0.1258	0.1803	0.2154	0.2214	0.1989	0.1571
	6	0.0000	0.0008	0.0063	0.0230	0.0559	0.1030	0.1546	0.1968	0.2169	0.2095
	7	0.0000	0.0001	0.0011	0.0058	0.0186	0.0442	0.0833	0.1312	0.1775	0.2095
	8	0.0000	0.0000	0.0001	0.0011	0.0047	0.0142	0.0336	0.0656	0.1089	0.1571
	9	0.0000	0.0000	0.0000	0.0001	0.0009	0.0034	0.0101	0.0243	0.0495	0.0873
	10	0.0000	0.0000	0.0000	0.0000	0.0001	0.0006	0.0022	0.0065	0.0162	0.0349
	11	0.0000	0.0000	0.0000	0.0000	0.0000	0.0001	0.0003	0.0012	0.0036	0.0095
	12	0.0000	0.0000	0.0000	0.0000	0.0000	0.0000	0.0000	0.0001	0.0005	0.0016
	13	0.0000	0.0000	0.0000	0.0000	0.0000	0.0000	0.0000	0.0000	0.0000	0.0001
14	0	0.4877	0.2288	0.1028	0.0440	0.0178	0.0068	0.0024	0.0008	0.0002	0.0001
	1	0.3593	0.3559	0.2539	0.1539	0.0832	0.0407	0.0181	0.0073	0.0027	0.0009
	2	0.1229	0.2570	0.2912	0.2501	0.1802	0.1134	0.0634	0.0317	0.0141	0.0056
	3	0.0259	0.1142	0.2056	0.2501	0.2402	0.1943	0.1366	0.0845	0.0462	0.0222
	4	0.0037	0.0349	0.0998	0.1720	0.2202	0.2290	0.2022	0.1549	0.1040	0.0611
	5	0.0004	0.0078	0.0352	0.0860	0.1468	0.1963	0.2178	0.2066	0.1701	0.1222
	6	0.0000	0.0013	0.0093	0.0322	0.0734	0.1262	0.1759	0.2066	0.2088	0.1833
	7	0.0000	0.0002	0.0019	0.0092	0.0280	0.0618	0.1082	0.1574	0.1952	0.2095
	8	0.0000	0.0000	0.0003	0.0020	0.0082	0.0232	0.0510	0.0918	0.1398	0.1833
	9	0.0000	0.0000	0.0000	0.0003	0.0018	0.0066	0.0183	0.0408	0.0762	0.1222
	10	0.0000	0.0000	0.0000	0.0000	0.0003	0.0014	0.0049	0.0136	0.0312	0.0611
	11	0.0000	0.0000	0.0000	0.0000	0.0000	0.0002	0.0010	0.0033	0.0093	0.0222
	12	0.0000	0.0000	0.0000	0.0000	0.0000	0.0000	0.0001	0.0005	0.0019	0.0056
	13	0.0000	0.0000	0.0000	0.0000	0.0000	0.0000	0.0000	0.0001	0.0002	0.0009
	14	0.0000	0.0000	0.0000	0.0000	0.0000	0.0000	0.0000	0.0000	0.0000	0.0001
15	0	0.4633	0.2059	0.0874	0.0352	0.0134	0.0047	0.0016	0.0005	0.0001	0.0000
	1	0.3658	0.3432	0.2312	0.1319	0.0668	0.0305	0.0126	0.0047	0.0016	0.0005
	2	0.1348	0.2669	0.2856	0.2309	0.1559	0.0916	0.0476	0.0219	0.0090	0.0032
	3	0.0307	0.1285	0.2184	0.2501	0.2252	0.1700	0.1110	0.0634	0.0318	0.0139
	4	0.0049	0.0428	0.1156	0.1876	0.2252	0.2186	0.1792	0.1268	0.0780	0.0417
	5	0.0006	0.0105	0.0449	0.1032	0.1651	0.2061	0.2123	0.1859	0.1404	0.0916
	6	0.0000	0.0019	0.0132	0.0430	0.0917	0.1472	0.1906	0.2066	0.1914	0.1527
	7	0.0000	0.0003	0.0030	0.0138	0.0393	0.0811	0.1319	0.1771	0.2013	0.1964
	8	0.0000	0.0000	0.0005	0.0035	0.0131	0.0348	0.0710	0.1181	0.1647	0.1964
	9	0.0000	0.0000	0.0001	0.0007	0.0034	0.0116	0.0298	0.0612	0.1048	0.1527
	10	0.0000	0.0000	0.0000	0.0001	0.0007	0.0030	0.0096	0.0245	0.0515	0.0916
	11	0.0000	0.0000	0.0000	0.0000	0.0001	0.0006	0.0024	0.0074	0.0191	0.0417
	12	0.0000	0.0000	0.0000	0.0000	0.0000	0.0001	0.0004	0.0016	0.0052	0.0139
	13	0.0000	0.0000	0.0000	0.0000	0.0000	0.0000	0.0001	0.0003	0.0010	0.0032
	14	0.0000	0.0000	0.0000	0.0000	0.0000	0.0000	0.0000	0.0000	0.0001	0.0005
	15	0.0000	0.0000	0.0000	0.0000	0.0000	0.0000	0.0000	0.0000	0.0000	0.0000
16	0	0.4401	0.1853	0.0743	0.0281	0.0100	0.0033	0.0010	0.0003	0.0001	0.0000
	1	0.3706	0.3294	0.2097	0.1126	0.0535	0.0228	0.0087	0.0030	0.0009	0.0002
	2	0.1463	0.2745	0.2775	0.2111	0.1336	0.0732	0.0353	0.0150	0.0056	0.0018

Table B Binomial Distribution (*continued*)

n	X	π 0.05	0.10	0.15	0.20	0.25	0.30	0.35	0.40	0.45	0.50
	3	0.0359	0.1423	0.2285	0.2463	0.2079	0.1465	0.0888	0.0468	0.0215	0.0085
	4	0.0061	0.0514	0.1311	0.2001	0.2252	0.2040	0.1553	0.1014	0.0572	0.0278
	5	0.0008	0.0137	0.0555	0.1201	0.1802	0.2099	0.2008	0.1623	0.1123	0.0667
	6	0.0001	0.0028	0.0180	0.0550	0.1101	0.1649	0.1982	0.1983	0.1684	0.1222
	7	0.0000	0.0004	0.0045	0.0197	0.0524	0.1010	0.1524	0.1889	0.1969	0.1746
	8	0.0000	0.0001	0.0009	0.0055	0.0197	0.0487	0.0923	0.1417	0.1812	0.1964
	9	0.0000	0.0000	0.0001	0.0012	0.0058	0.0185	0.0442	0.0840	0.1318	0.1746
	10	0.0000	0.0000	0.0000	0.0002	0.0014	0.0056	0.0167	0.0392	0.0755	0.1222
	11	0.0000	0.0000	0.0000	0.0000	0.0002	0.0013	0.0049	0.0142	0.0337	0.0667
	12	0.0000	0.0000	0.0000	0.0000	0.0000	0.0002	0.0011	0.0040	0.0115	0.0278
	13	0.0000	0.0000	0.0000	0.0000	0.0000	0.0000	0.0002	0.0008	0.0029	0.0085
	14	0.0000	0.0000	0.0000	0.0000	0.0000	0.0000	0.0000	0.0001	0.0005	0.0018
	15	0.0000	0.0000	0.0000	0.0000	0.0000	0.0000	0.0000	0.0000	0.0001	0.0002
	16	0.0000	0.0000	0.0000	0.0000	0.0000	0.0000	0.0000	0.0000	0.0000	0.0000
17	0	0.4181	0.1668	0.0631	0.0225	0.0075	0.0023	0.0007	0.0002	0.0000	0.0000
	1	0.3741	0.3150	0.1893	0.0957	0.0426	0.0169	0.0060	0.0019	0.0005	0.0001
	2	0.1575	0.2800	0.2673	0.1914	0.1136	0.0581	0.0260	0.0102	0.0035	0.0010
	3	0.0415	0.1556	0.2359	0.2393	0.1893	0.1245	0.0701	0.0341	0.0144	0.0052
	4	0.0076	0.0605	0.1457	0.2093	0.2209	0.1868	0.1320	0.0796	0.0411	0.0182
	5	0.0010	0.0175	0.0668	0.1361	0.1914	0.2081	0.1849	0.1379	0.0875	0.0472
	6	0.0001	0.0039	0.0236	0.0680	0.1276	0.1784	0.1991	0.1839	0.1432	0.0944
	7	0.0000	0.0007	0.0065	0.0267	0.0668	0.1201	0.1685	0.1927	0.1841	0.1484
	8	0.0000	0.0001	0.0014	0.0084	0.0279	0.0644	0.1134	0.1606	0.1883	0.1855
	9	0.0000	0.0000	0.0003	0.0021	0.0093	0.0276	0.0611	0.1070	0.1540	0.1855
	10	0.0000	0.0000	0.0000	0.0004	0.0025	0.0095	0.0263	0.0571	0.1008	0.1484
	11	0.0000	0.0000	0.0000	0.0001	0.0005	0.0026	0.0090	0.0242	0.0525	0.0944
	12	0.0000	0.0000	0.0000	0.0000	0.0001	0.0006	0.0024	0.0081	0.0215	0.0472
	13	0.0000	0.0000	0.0000	0.0000	0.0000	0.0001	0.0005	0.0021	0.0068	0.0182
	14	0.0000	0.0000	0.0000	0.0000	0.0000	0.0000	0.0001	0.0004	0.0016	0.0052
	15	0.0000	0.0000	0.0000	0.0000	0.0000	0.0000	0.0000	0.0001	0.0003	0.0010
	16	0.0000	0.0000	0.0000	0.0000	0.0000	0.0000	0.0000	0.0000	0.0000	0.0001
	17	0.0000	0.0000	0.0000	0.0000	0.0000	0.0000	0.0000	0.0000	0.0000	0.0000
18	0	0.3972	0.1501	0.0536	0.0180	0.0056	0.0016	0.0004	0.0001	0.0000	0.0000
	1	0.3763	0.3002	0.1704	0.0811	0.0338	0.0126	0.0042	0.0012	0.0003	0.0001
	2	0.1683	0.2835	0.2556	0.1723	0.0958	0.0458	0.0190	0.0069	0.0022	0.0006
	3	0.0473	0.1680	0.2406	0.2297	0.1704	0.1046	0.0547	0.0246	0.0095	0.0031
	4	0.0093	0.0700	0.1592	0.2153	0.2130	0.1681	0.1104	0.0614	0.0291	0.0117
	5	0.0014	0.0218	0.0787	0.1507	0.1988	0.2017	0.1664	0.1146	0.0666	0.0327
	6	0.0002	0.0052	0.0301	0.0816	0.1436	0.1873	0.1941	0.1655	0.1181	0.0708
	7	0.0000	0.0010	0.0091	0.0350	0.0820	0.1376	0.1792	0.1892	0.1657	0.1214
	8	0.0000	0.0002	0.0022	0.0120	0.0376	0.0811	0.1327	0.1734	0.1864	0.1669
	9	0.0000	0.0000	0.0004	0.0033	0.0139	0.0386	0.0794	0.1284	0.1694	0.1855
	10	0.0000	0.0000	0.0001	0.0008	0.0042	0.0149	0.0385	0.0771	0.1248	0.1669
	11	0.0000	0.0000	0.0000	0.0001	0.0010	0.0046	0.0151	0.0374	0.0742	0.1214
	12	0.0000	0.0000	0.0000	0.0000	0.0002	0.0012	0.0047	0.0145	0.0354	0.0708
	13	0.0000	0.0000	0.0000	0.0000	0.0000	0.0002	0.0012	0.0045	0.0134	0.0327

Table B Binomial Distribution (*continued*)

		π									
n	*X*	0.05	0.10	0.15	0.20	0.25	0.30	0.35	0.40	0.45	0.50
	14	0.0000	0.0000	0.0000	0.0000	0.0000	0.0000	0.0002	0.0011	0.0039	0.0117
	15	0.0000	0.0000	0.0000	0.0000	0.0000	0.0000	0.0000	0.0002	0.0009	0.0031
	16	0.0000	0.0000	0.0000	0.0000	0.0000	0.0000	0.0000	0.0000	0.0001	0.0006
	17	0.0000	0.0000	0.0000	0.0000	0.0000	0.0000	0.0000	0.0000	0.0000	0.0001
	18	0.0000	0.0000	0.0000	0.0000	0.0000	0.0000	0.0000	0.0000	0.0000	0.0000
19	0	0.3774	0.1351	0.0456	0.0144	0.0042	0.0011	0.0003	0.0001	0.0000	0.0000
	1	0.3774	0.2852	0.1529	0.0685	0.0268	0.0093	0.0029	0.0008	0.0002	0.0000
	2	0.1787	0.2852	0.2428	0.1540	0.0803	0.0358	0.0138	0.0046	0.0013	0.0003
	3	0.0533	0.1796	0.2428	0.2182	0.1517	0.0869	0.0422	0.0175	0.0062	0.0018
	4	0.0112	0.0798	0.1714	0.2182	0.2023	0.1491	0.0909	0.0467	0.0203	0.0074
	5	0.0018	0.0266	0.0907	0.1636	0.2023	0.1916	0.1468	0.0933	0.0497	0.0222
	6	0.0002	0.0069	0.0374	0.0955	0.1574	0.1916	0.1844	0.1451	0.0949	0.0518
	7	0.0000	0.0014	0.0122	0.0443	0.0974	0.1525	0.1844	0.1797	0.1443	0.0961
	8	0.0000	0.0002	0.0032	0.0166	0.0487	0.0981	0.1489	0.1797	0.1771	0.1442
	9	0.0000	0.0000	0.0007	0.0051	0.0198	0.0514	0.0980	0.1464	0.1771	0.1762
	10	0.0000	0.0000	0.0001	0.0013	0.0066	0.0220	0.0528	0.0976	0.1449	0.1762
	11	0.0000	0.0000	0.0000	0.0003	0.0018	0.0077	0.0233	0.0532	0.0970	0.1442
	12	0.0000	0.0000	0.0000	0.0000	0.0004	0.0022	0.0083	0.0237	0.0529	0.0961
	13	0.0000	0.0000	0.0000	0.0000	0.0001	0.0005	0.0024	0.0085	0.0233	0.0518
	14	0.0000	0.0000	0.0000	0.0000	0.0000	0.0001	0.0006	0.0024	0.0082	0.0222
	15	0.0000	0.0000	0.0000	0.0000	0.0000	0.0000	0.0001	0.0005	0.0022	0.0074
	16	0.0000	0.0000	0.0000	0.0000	0.0000	0.0000	0.0000	0.0001	0.0005	0.0018
	17	0.0000	0.0000	0.0000	0.0000	0.0000	0.0000	0.0000	0.0000	0.0001	0.0003
	18	0.0000	0.0000	0.0000	0.0000	0.0000	0.0000	0.0000	0.0000	0.0000	0.0000
	19	0.0000	0.0000	0.0000	0.0000	0.0000	0.0000	0.0000	0.0000	0.0000	0.0000
20	0	0.3585	0.1216	0.0388	0.0115	0.0032	0.0008	0.0002	0.0000	0.0000	0.0000
	1	0.3774	0.2702	0.1368	0.0576	0.0211	0.0068	0.0020	0.0005	0.0001	0.0000
	2	0.1887	0.2852	0.2293	0.1369	0.0669	0.0278	0.0100	0.0031	0.0008	0.0002
	3	0.0596	0.1901	0.2428	0.2054	0.1339	0.0716	0.0323	0.0123	0.0040	0.0011
	4	0.0133	0.0898	0.1821	0.2182	0.1897	0.1304	0.0738	0.0350	0.0139	0.0046
	5	0.0022	0.0319	0.1028	0.1746	0.2023	0.1789	0.1272	0.0746	0.0365	0.0148
	6	0.0003	0.0089	0.0454	0.1091	0.1686	0.1916	0.1712	0.1244	0.0746	0.0370
	7	0.0000	0.0020	0.0160	0.0545	0.1124	0.1643	0.1844	0.1659	0.1221	0.0739
	8	0.0000	0.0004	0.0046	0.0222	0.0609	0.1144	0.1614	0.1797	0.1623	0.1201
	9	0.0000	0.0001	0.0011	0.0074	0.0271	0.0654	0.1158	0.1597	0.1771	0.1602
	10	0.0000	0.0000	0.0002	0.0020	0.0099	0.0308	0.0686	0.1171	0.1593	0.1762
	11	0.0000	0.0000	0.0000	0.0005	0.0030	0.0120	0.0336	0.0710	0.1185	0.1602
	12	0.0000	0.0000	0.0000	0.0001	0.0008	0.0039	0.0136	0.0355	0.0727	0.1201
	13	0.0000	0.0000	0.0000	0.0000	0.0002	0.0010	0.0045	0.0146	0.0366	0.0739
	14	0.0000	0.0000	0.0000	0.0000	0.0000	0.0002	0.0012	0.0049	0.0150	0.0370
	15	0.0000	0.0000	0.0000	0.0000	0.0000	0.0000	0.0003	0.0013	0.0049	0.0148
	16	0.0000	0.0000	0.0000	0.0000	0.0000	0.0000	0.0000	0.0003	0.0013	0.0046
	17	0.0000	0.0000	0.0000	0.0000	0.0000	0.0000	0.0000	0.0000	0.0002	0.0011
	18	0.0000	0.0000	0.0000	0.0000	0.0000	0.0000	0.0000	0.0000	0.0000	0.0002
	19	0.0000	0.0000	0.0000	0.0000	0.0000	0.0000	0.0000	0.0000	0.0000	0.0000

Table C Cumulative Binomial Distribution

		π										
n	*X*	0.01	0.05	0.10	0.15	0.20	0.25	0.30	0.35	0.40	0.45	0.50
2	0	0.9801	0.9025	0.8100	0.7225	0.6400	0.5625	0.4900	0.4225	0.3600	0.3025	0.2500
	1	0.9999	0.9975	0.9900	0.9775	0.9600	0.9375	0.9100	0.8775	0.8400	0.7975	0.7500
3	0	0.9703	0.8574	0.7290	0.6141	0.5120	0.4219	0.3430	0.2746	0.2160	0.1664	0.1250
	1	0.9997	0.9928	0.9720	0.9393	0.8960	0.8438	0.7840	0.7183	0.6480	0.5748	0.5000
	2	1.0000	0.9999	0.9990	0.9966	0.9920	0.9844	0.9730	0.9571	0.9360	0.9089	0.8750
4	0	0.9606	0.8145	0.6561	0.5220	0.4096	0.3164	0.2401	0.1785	0.1296	0.0915	0.0625
	1	0.9994	0.9860	0.9477	0.8905	0.8192	0.7383	0.6517	0.5630	0.4752	0.3910	0.3125
	2	1.0000	0.9995	0.9963	0.9880	0.9728	0.9492	0.9163	0.8735	0.8208	0.7585	0.6875
	3	1.0000	1.0000	0.9999	0.9995	0.9984	0.9961	0.9919	0.9850	0.9744	0.9590	0.9375
5	0	0.9510	0.7738	0.5905	0.4437	0.3277	0.2373	0.1681	0.1160	0.0778	0.0503	0.0313
	1	0.9990	0.9774	0.9185	0.8352	0.7373	0.6328	0.5282	0.4284	0.3370	0.2562	0.1875
	2	1.0000	0.9988	0.9914	0.9734	0.9421	0.8965	0.8369	0.7648	0.6826	0.5931	0.5000
	3	1.0000	1.0000	0.9995	0.9978	0.9933	0.9844	0.9692	0.9460	0.9130	0.8688	0.8125
	4	1.0000	1.0000	1.0000	0.9999	0.9997	0.9990	0.9976	0.9947	0.9898	0.9815	0.9688
6	0	0.9415	0.7351	0.5314	0.3771	0.2621	0.1780	0.1176	0.0754	0.0467	0.0277	0.0156
	1	0.9985	0.9672	0.8857	0.7765	0.6554	0.5339	0.4202	0.3191	0.2333	0.1636	0.1094
	2	1.0000	0.9978	0.9842	0.9527	0.9011	0.8306	0.7443	0.6471	0.5443	0.4415	0.3438
	3	1.0000	0.9999	0.9987	0.9941	0.9830	0.9624	0.9295	0.8826	0.8208	0.7447	0.6563
	4	1.0000	1.0000	0.9999	0.9996	0.9984	0.9954	0.9891	0.9777	0.9590	0.9308	0.8906
	5	1.0000	1.0000	1.0000	1.0000	0.9999	0.9998	0.9993	0.9982	0.9959	0.9917	0.9844
7	0	0.9321	0.6983	0.4783	0.3206	0.2097	0.1335	0.0824	0.0490	0.0280	0.0152	0.0078
	1	0.9980	0.9556	0.8503	0.7166	0.5767	0.4449	0.3294	0.2338	0.1586	0.1024	0.0625
	2	1.0000	0.9962	0.9743	0.9262	0.8520	0.7564	0.6471	0.5323	0.4199	0.3164	0.2266
	3	1.0000	0.9998	0.9973	0.9879	0.9667	0.9294	0.8740	0.8002	0.7102	0.6083	0.5000
	4	1.0000	1.0000	0.9998	0.9988	0.9953	0.9871	0.9712	0.9444	0.9037	0.8471	0.7734
	5	1.0000	1.0000	1.0000	0.9999	0.9996	0.9987	0.9962	0.9910	0.9812	0.9643	0.9375
	6	1.0000	1.0000	1.0000	1.0000	1.0000	0.9999	0.9998	0.9994	0.9984	0.9963	0.9922
8	0	0.9227	0.6634	0.4305	0.2725	0.1678	0.1001	0.0576	0.0319	0.0168	0.0084	0.0039
	1	0.9973	0.9428	0.8131	0.6572	0.5033	0.3671	0.2553	0.1691	0.1064	0.0632	0.0352
	2	0.9999	0.9942	0.9619	0.8948	0.7969	0.6785	0.5518	0.4278	0.3154	0.2201	0.1445
	3	1.0000	0.9996	0.9950	0.9786	0.9437	0.8862	0.8059	0.7064	0.5941	0.4770	0.3633
	4	1.0000	1.0000	0.9996	0.9971	0.9896	0.9727	0.9420	0.8939	0.8263	0.7396	0.6367
	5	1.0000	1.0000	1.0000	0.9998	0.9988	0.9958	0.9887	0.9747	0.9502	0.9115	0.8555
	6	1.0000	1.0000	1.0000	1.0000	0.9999	0.9996	0.9987	0.9964	0.9915	0.9819	0.9648
	7	1.0000	1.0000	1.0000	1.0000	1.0000	1.0000	0.9999	0.9998	0.9993	0.9983	0.9961
9	0	0.9135	0.6302	0.3874	0.2316	0.1342	0.0751	0.0404	0.0207	0.0101	0.0046	0.0020
	1	0.9966	0.9288	0.7748	0.5995	0.4362	0.3003	0.1960	0.1211	0.0705	0.0385	0.0195
	2	0.9999	0.9916	0.9470	0.8591	0.7382	0.6007	0.4628	0.3373	0.2318	0.1495	0.0898
	3	1.0000	0.9944	0.9917	0.9661	0.9144	0.8343	0.7297	0.6089	0.4826	0.3614	0.2539
	4	1.0000	1.0000	0.9991	0.9944	0.9804	0.9511	0.9012	0.8283	0.7334	0.6214	0.5000
	5	1.0000	1.0000	0.9999	0.9994	0.9969	0.9900	0.9747	0.9464	0.9006	0.8342	0.7461
	6	1.0000	1.0000	1.0000	1.0000	0.9997	0.9987	0.9957	0.9888	0.9750	0.9502	0.9102
	7	1.0000	1.0000	1.0000	1.0000	1.0000	0.9999	0.9996	0.9986	0.9962	0.9909	0.9805
	8	1.0000	1.0000	1.0000	1.0000	1.0000	1.0000	1.0000	0.9999	0.9997	0.9992	0.9980
10	0	0.9044	0.5987	0.3487	0.1969	0.1074	0.0563	0.0282	0.0135	0.0060	0.0025	0.0010

Table C Cumulative Binomial Distribution (*continued*)

		π										
n	*X*	0.01	0.05	0.10	0.15	0.20	0.25	0.30	0.35	0.40	0.45	0.50
10	1	0.9957	0.9139	0.7361	0.5443	0.3758	0.2440	0.1493	0.0860	0.0464	0.0233	0.0107
	2	0.9999	0.9885	0.9298	0.8202	0.6778	0.5256	0.3828	0.2616	0.1673	0.0996	0.0547
	3	1.0000	0.9990	0.9872	0.9500	0.8791	0.7759	0.6496	0.5138	0.3823	0.2660	0.1719
	4	1.0000	0.9999	0.9984	0.9901	0.9672	0.9219	0.8497	0.7515	0.6331	0.5044	0.3770
	5	1.0000	1.0000	0.9999	0.9986	0.9936	0.9803	0.9527	0.9051	0.8338	0.7384	0.6230
	6	1.0000	1.0000	1.0000	0.9999	0.9991	0.9965	0.9894	0.9740	0.9452	0.8980	0.8281
	7	1.0000	1.0000	1.0000	1.0000	0.9999	0.9996	0.9984	0.9952	0.9877	0.9726	0.9453
	8	1.0000	1.0000	1.0000	1.0000	1.0000	1.0000	0.9999	0.9995	0.9983	0.9955	0.9893
	9	1.0000	1.0000	1.0000	1.0000	1.0000	1.0000	1.0000	1.0000	0.9999	0.9997	0.9990
11	0	0.8953	0.5688	0.3138	0.1673	0.0859	0.0422	0.0198	0.0088	0.0036	0.0014	0.0005
	1	0.9948	0.8981	0.6974	0.4922	0.3221	0.1971	0.1130	0.0606	0.0302	0.0139	0.0059
	2	0.9998	0.9848	0.9104	0.7788	0.6174	0.4552	0.3127	0.2001	0.1189	0.0652	0.0327
	3	1.0000	0.9984	0.9815	0.9306	0.8389	0.7133	0.5696	0.4256	0.2963	0.1911	0.1133
	4	1.0000	0.9999	0.9972	0.9841	0.9496	0.8854	0.7897	0.6683	0.5328	0.3971	0.2744
	5	1.0000	1.0000	0.9997	0.9973	0.9883	0.9657	0.9218	0.8513	0.7535	0.6331	0.5000
	6	1.0000	1.0000	1.0000	0.9997	0.9980	0.9924	0.9784	0.9499	0.9006	0.8262	0.7256
	7	1.0000	1.0000	1.0000	1.0000	0.9998	0.9988	0.9957	0.9878	0.9707	0.9390	0.8867
	8	1.0000	1.0000	1.0000	1.0000	1.0000	0.9999	0.9994	0.9980	0.9941	0.9852	0.9673
	9	1.0000	1.0000	1.0000	1.0000	1.0000	1.0000	1.0000	0.9998	0.9993	0.9978	0.9941
	10	1.0000	1.0000	1.0000	1.0000	1.0000	1.0000	1.0000	1.0000	1.0000	0.9998	0.9995
12	0	0.8864	0.5404	0.2824	0.1422	0.0687	0.0317	0.0138	0.0057	0.0022	0.0008	0.0002
	1	0.9938	0.8816	0.6590	0.4435	0.2749	0.1584	0.0850	0.0424	0.0196	0.0083	0.0032
	2	0.9998	0.9804	0.8891	0.7358	0.5583	0.3907	0.2528	0.1513	0.0834	0.0421	0.0193
	3	1.0000	0.9978	0.9744	0.9078	0.7946	0.6488	0.4925	0.3467	0.2253	0.1345	0.0730
	4	1.0000	0.9998	0.9957	0.9761	0.9274	0.8424	0.7237	0.5833	0.4382	0.3044	0.1938
	5	1.0000	1.0000	0.9995	0.9954	0.9806	0.9456	0.8822	0.7873	0.6652	0.5269	0.3872
	6	1.0000	1.0000	0.9999	0.9993	0.9961	0.9857	0.9614	0.9154	0.8418	0.7393	0.6128
	7	1.0000	1.0000	1.0000	0.9999	0.9994	0.9972	0.9905	0.9745	0.9427	0.8883	0.8062
	8	1.0000	1.0000	1.0000	1.0000	0.9999	0.9996	0.9983	0.9944	0.9847	0.9644	0.9270
	9	1.0000	1.0000	1.0000	1.0000	1.0000	1.0000	0.9998	0.9992	0.9972	0.9921	0.9807
	10	1.0000	1.0000	1.0000	1.0000	1.0000	1.0000	1.0000	0.9999	0.9997	0.9989	0.9968
	11	1.0000	1.0000	1.0000	1.0000	1.0000	1.0000	1.0000	1.0000	1.0000	0.9999	0.9998
13	0	0.8775	0.5133	0.2542	0.1209	0.0550	0.0238	0.0097	0.0037	0.0013	0.0004	0.0001
	1	0.9928	0.8646	0.6213	0.3983	0.2336	0.1267	0.0637	0.0296	0.0126	0.0049	0.0017
	2	0.9997	0.9755	0.8661	0.6920	0.5017	0.3326	0.2025	0.1132	0.0579	0.0269	0.0112
	3	1.0000	0.9969	0.9658	0.8820	0.7473	0.5843	0.4206	0.2783	0.1686	0.0929	0.0461
	4	1.0000	0.9997	0.9935	0.9658	0.9009	0.7940	0.6543	0.5005	0.3530	0.2279	0.1334
	5	1.0000	1.0000	0.9991	0.9925	0.9700	0.9198	0.8346	0.7159	0.5744	0.4268	0.2905
	6	1.0000	1.0000	0.9999	0.9987	0.9930	0.9757	0.9376	0.8705	0.7712	0.6437	0.5000
	7	1.0000	1.0000	1.0000	0.9998	0.9988	0.9944	0.9818	0.9538	0.9023	0.8212	0.7095
	8	1.0000	1.0000	1.0000	1.0000	0.9998	0.9990	0.9960	0.9874	0.9679	0.9302	0.8666
	9	1.0000	1.0000	1.0000	1.0000	1.0000	0.9999	0.9993	0.9975	0.9922	0.9797	0.9539
	10	1.0000	1.0000	1.0000	1.0000	1.0000	1.0000	0.9999	0.9997	0.9987	0.9959	0.9888
	11	1.0000	1.0000	1.0000	1.0000	1.0000	1.0000	1.0000	1.0000	0.9999	0.9995	0.9983
	12	1.0000	1.0000	1.0000	1.0000	1.0000	1.0000	1.0000	1.0000	1.0000	1.0000	0.9999

Table C Cumulative Binomial Distribution (*continued*)

n	X	π 0.01	0.05	0.10	0.15	0.20	0.25	0.30	0.35	0.40	0.45	0.50
14	0	0.8687	0.4877	0.2288	0.1028	0.0440	0.0178	0.0068	0.0024	0.0008	0.0002	0.0001
	1	0.9916	0.8470	0.5846	0.3567	0.1979	0.1010	0.0475	0.0205	0.0081	0.0029	0.0009
	2	0.9997	0.9699	0.8416	0.6479	0.4481	0.2811	0.1608	0.0839	0.0398	0.0170	0.0065
	3	1.0000	0.9958	0.9559	0.8535	0.6982	0.5213	0.3552	0.2205	0.1243	0.0632	0.0287
	4	1.0000	0.9996	0.9908	0.9533	0.8702	0.7415	0.5842	0.4227	0.2793	0.1672	0.0898
	5	1.0000	1.0000	0.9985	0.9885	0.9561	0.8883	0.7805	0.6405	0.4859	0.3373	0.2120
	6	1.0000	1.0000	0.9998	0.9978	0.9884	0.9617	0.9067	0.8164	0.6925	0.5461	0.3953
	7	1.0000	1.0000	1.0000	0.9997	0.9976	0.9897	0.9685	0.9247	0.8499	0.7414	0.6047
	8	1.0000	1.0000	1.0000	1.0000	0.9996	0.9978	0.9917	0.9757	0.9417	0.8811	0.7880
	9	1.0000	1.0000	1.0000	1.0000	1.0000	0.9997	0.9983	0.9940	0.9825	0.9574	0.9102
	10	1.0000	1.0000	1.0000	1.0000	1.0000	1.0000	0.9998	0.9989	0.9961	0.9886	0.9713
	11	1.0000	1.0000	1.0000	1.0000	1.0000	1.0000	1.0000	0.9999	0.9994	0.9978	0.9935
	12	1.0000	1.0000	1.0000	1.0000	1.0000	1.0000	1.0000	1.0000	0.9999	0.9997	0.9991
	13	1.0000	1.0000	1.0000	1.0000	1.0000	1.0000	1.0000	1.0000	1.0000	1.0000	0.9999
15	0	0.8601	0.4633	0.2059	0.0874	0.0352	0.0134	0.0047	0.0016	0.0005	0.0001	0.0000
	1	0.9904	0.8290	0.5490	0.3186	0.1671	0.0802	0.0353	0.0142	0.0052	0.0017	0.0005
	2	0.9996	0.9638	0.8159	0.6042	0.3980	0.2361	0.1268	0.0617	0.0271	0.0107	0.0037
	3	1.0000	0.9945	0.9444	0.8227	0.6482	0.4613	0.2969	0.1727	0.0905	0.0424	0.0176
	4	1.0000	0.9994	0.9873	0.9383	0.8358	0.6865	0.5155	0.3519	0.2173	0.1204	0.0592
	5	1.0000	0.9999	0.9978	0.9832	0.9389	0.8516	0.7216	0.5643	0.4032	0.2608	0.1509
	6	1.0000	1.0000	0.9997	0.9964	0.9819	0.9434	0.8689	0.7548	0.6098	0.4522	0.3036
	7	1.0000	1.0000	1.0000	0.9994	0.9958	0.9827	0.9500	0.8868	0.7869	0.6535	0.5000
	8	1.0000	1.0000	1.0000	0.9999	0.9992	0.9958	0.9848	0.9578	0.9050	0.8182	0.6964
	9	1.0000	1.0000	1.0000	1.0000	0.9999	0.9992	0.9963	0.9876	0.9662	0.9231	0.8491
	10	1.0000	1.0000	1.0000	1.0000	1.0000	0.9999	0.9993	0.9972	0.9907	0.9745	0.9408
	11	1.0000	1.0000	1.0000	1.0000	1.0000	1.0000	0.9999	0.9995	0.9981	0.9937	0.9824
	12	1.0000	1.0000	1.0000	1.0000	1.0000	1.0000	1.0000	0.9999	0.9997	0.9989	0.9963
	13	1.0000	1.0000	1.0000	1.0000	1.0000	1.0000	1.0000	1.0000	1.0000	0.9999	0.9995
	14	1.0000	1.0000	1.0000	1.0000	1.0000	1.0000	1.0000	1.0000	1.0000	1.0000	1.0000
16	0	0.8515	0.4401	0.1853	0.0743	0.0281	0.0100	0.0033	0.0010	0.0003	0.0001	0.0000
	1	0.9891	0.8108	0.5147	0.2839	0.1407	0.0635	0.0261	0.0098	0.0033	0.0010	0.0003
	2	0.9995	0.9571	0.7892	0.5614	0.3518	0.1971	0.0994	0.0451	0.0183	0.0066	0.0021
	3	1.0000	0.9930	0.9316	0.7899	0.5981	0.4050	0.2459	0.1339	0.0651	0.0281	0.0106
	4	1.0000	0.9991	0.9830	0.9209	0.7982	0.6302	0.4499	0.2892	0.1666	0.0853	0.0384
	5	1.0000	0.9999	0.9967	0.9765	0.9183	0.8103	0.6598	0.4900	0.3288	0.1976	0.1051
	6	1.0000	1.0000	0.9995	0.9944	0.9733	0.9204	0.8247	0.6881	0.5272	0.3660	0.2272
	7	1.0000	1.0000	0.9999	0.9989	0.9930	0.9729	0.9256	0.8406	0.7161	0.5629	0.4018
	8	1.0000	1.0000	1.0000	0.9998	0.9985	0.9925	0.9743	0.9329	0.8577	0.7441	0.5982
	9	1.0000	1.0000	1.0000	1.0000	0.9998	0.9984	0.9929	0.9771	0.9417	0.8759	0.7728
	10	1.0000	1.0000	1.0000	1.0000	1.0000	0.9997	0.9984	0.9938	0.9809	0.9514	0.8949
	11	1.0000	1.0000	1.0000	1.0000	1.0000	1.0000	0.9997	0.9987	0.9951	0.9851	09616
	12	1.0000	1.0000	1.0000	1.0000	1.0000	1.0000	1.0000	0.9998	0.9991	0.9965	0.9894
	13	1.0000	1.0000	1.0000	1.0000	1.0000	1.0000	1.0000	1.0000	0.9999	0.9994	0.9979
	14	1.0000	1.0000	1.0000	1.0000	1.0000	1.0000	1.0000	1.0000	1.0000	0.9999	0.9997
	15	1.0000	1.0000	1.0000	1.0000	1.0000	1.0000	1.0000	1.0000	1.0000	1.0000	1.0000

Table C Cumulative Binomial Distribution (*continued*)

		π										
n	*X*	0.01	0.05	0.10	0.15	0.20	0.25	0.30	0.35	0.40	0.45	0.50
17	0	0.8429	0.4181	0.1668	0.0631	0.0225	0.0075	0.0023	0.0007	0.0002	0.0000	0.0000
	1	0.9877	0.7922	0.4818	0.2525	0.1182	0.0501	0.0193	0.0067	0.0021	0.0006	0.0001
	2	0.9994	0.9497	0.7618	0.5198	0.3096	0.1637	0.0774	0.0327	0.0123	0.0041	0.0012
	3	1.0000	0.9912	0.9174	0.7556	0.5489	0.3530	0.2019	0.1028	0.0464	0.0184	0.0064
	4	1.0000	0.9988	0.9779	0.9013	0.7582	0.5739	0.3887	0.2348	0.1260	0.0596	0.0245
	5	1.0000	0.9999	0.9953	0.9681	0.8943	0.7653	0.5968	0.4197	0.2639	0.1471	0.0717
	6	1.0000	1.0000	0.9992	0.9917	0.9623	0.8929	0.7752	0.6188	0.4478	0.2902	0.1662
	7	1.0000	1.0000	0.9999	0.9983	0.9891	0.9598	0.8954	0.7872	0.6405	0.4743	0.3145
	8	1.0000	1.0000	1.0000	0.9997	0.9974	0.9876	0.9597	0.9006	0.8011	0.6626	0.5000
	9	1.0000	1.0000	1.0000	1.0000	0.9995	0.9969	0.9873	0.9617	0.9081	0.8166	0.6855
	10	1.0000	1.0000	1.0000	1.0000	0.9999	0.9994	0.9968	0.9880	0.9652	0.9174	0.8338
	11	1.0000	1.0000	1.0000	1.0000	1.0000	0.9999	0.9993	0.9970	0.9894	0.9699	0.9283
	12	1.0000	1.0000	1.0000	1.0000	1.0000	1.0000	0.9999	0.9994	0.9975	0.9914	0.9755
	13	1.0000	1.0000	1.0000	1.0000	1.0000	1.0000	1.0000	0.9999	0.9995	0.9981	0.9936
	14	1.0000	1.0000	1.0000	1.0000	1.0000	1.0000	1.0000	1.0000	0.9999	0.9997	0.9988
	15	1.0000	1.0000	1.0000	1.0000	1.0000	1.0000	1.0000	1.0000	1.0000	1.0000	0.9999
	16	1.0000	1.0000	1.0000	1.0000	1.0000	1.0000	1.0000	1.0000	1.0000	1.0000	1.0000
18	0	0.8345	0.3972	0.1501	0.0536	0.0180	0.0056	0.0016	0.0004	0.0001	0.0000	0.0000
	1	0.9862	0.7735	0.4503	0.2241	0.0991	0.0395	0.0142	0.0046	0.0013	0.0003	0.0001
	2	0.9993	0.9419	0.7338	0.4797	0.2713	0.1353	0.0600	0.0236	0.0082	0.0025	0.0007
	3	1.0000	0.9891	0.9018	0.7202	0.5010	0.3057	0.1646	0.0783	0.0328	0.0120	0.0038
	4	1.0000	0.9985	0.9718	0.8794	0.7164	0.5187	0.3327	0.1886	0.0942	0.0411	0.0154
	5	1.0000	0.9998	0.9936	0.9581	0.8671	0.7175	0.5344	0.3550	0.2088	0.1077	0.0481
	6	1.0000	1.0000	0.9988	0.9882	0.9487	0.8610	0.7217	0.5491	0.3743	0.2258	0.1189
	7	1.0000	1.0000	0.9998	0.9973	0.9837	0.9431	0.8593	0.7283	0.5634	0.3915	0.2403
	8	1.0000	1.0000	1.0000	0.9995	0.9957	0.9807	0.9404	0.8609	0.7368	0.5778	0.4073
	9	1.0000	1.0000	1.0000	0.9999	0.9991	0.9946	0.9790	0.9403	0.8653	0.7473	0.5927
	10	1.0000	1.0000	1.0000	1.0000	0.9998	0.9988	0.9939	0.9788	0.9424	0.8720	0.7597
	11	1.0000	1.0000	1.0000	1.0000	1.0000	0.9998	0.9986	0.9938	0.9797	0.9463	0.8811
	12	1.0000	1.0000	1.0000	1.0000	1.0000	1.0000	0.9997	0.9986	0.9942	0.9817	0.9519
	13	1.0000	1.0000	1.0000	1.0000	1.0000	1.0000	1.0000	0.9997	0.9987	0.9951	0.9846
	14	1.0000	1.0000	1.0000	1.0000	1.0000	1.0000	1.0000	1.0000	0.9998	0.9990	0.9962
	15	1.0000	1.0000	1.0000	1.0000	1.0000	1.0000	1.0000	1.0000	1.0000	0.9999	0.9993
	16	1.0000	1.0000	1.0000	1.0000	1.0000	1.0000	1.0000	1.0000	1.0000	1.0000	0.9999
	17	1.0000	1.0000	1.0000	1.0000	1.0000	1.0000	1.0000	1.0000	1.0000	1.0000	1.0000
19	0	0.8262	0.3774	0.1351	0.0456	0.0144	0.0042	0.0011	0.0003	0.0001	0.0000	0.0000
	1	0.9847	0.7547	0.4203	0.1985	0.0829	0.0310	0.0104	0.0031	0.0008	0.0002	0.0000
	2	0.9991	0.9335	0.7054	0.4413	0.2369	0.1113	0.0462	0.0170	0.0055	0.0015	0.0004
	3	1.0000	0.9868	0.8850	0.6841	0.4551	0.2631	0.1332	0.0591	0.0230	0.0077	0.0022
	4	1.0000	0.9980	0.9648	0.8556	0.6733	0.4654	0.2822	0.1500	0.0696	0.0280	0.0096
	5	1.0000	0.9998	0.9914	0.9463	0.8369	0.6678	0.4739	0.2968	0.1629	0.0777	0.0318
	6	1.0000	1.0000	0.9983	0.9837	0.9324	0.8251	0.6655	0.4812	0.3081	0.1727	0.0835
	7	1.0000	1.0000	0.9997	0.9959	0.9767	0.9225	0.8180	0.6656	0.4878	0.3169	0.1796
	8	1.0000	1.0000	1.0000	0.9992	0.9933	0.9713	0.9161	0.8145	0.6675	0.4940	0.3238
	9	1.0000	1.0000	1.0000	0.9999	0.9984	0.9911	0.9674	0.9125	0.8139	0.6710	0.5000

Table C Cumulative Binomial Distribution (*continued*)

		π										
n	X	0.01	0.05	0.10	0.15	0.20	0.25	0.30	0.35	0.40	0.45	0.50
	10	1.0000	1.0000	1.0000	1.0000	0.9997	0.9977	0.9895	0.9653	0.9115	0.8159	0.6762
	11	1.0000	1.0000	1.0000	1.0000	1.0000	0.9995	0.9972	0.9886	0.9648	0.9129	0.8204
	12	1.0000	1.0000	1.0000	1.0000	1.0000	0.9999	0.9994	0.9969	0.9884	0.9658	0.9165
	13	1.0000	1.0000	1.0000	1.0000	1.0000	1.0000	0.9999	0.9993	0.9969	0.9891	0.9682
	14	1.0000	1.0000	1.0000	1.0000	1.0000	1.0000	1.0000	0.9999	0.9994	0.9972	0.9904
	15	1.0000	1.0000	1.0000	1.0000	1.0000	1.0000	1.0000	1.0000	0.9999	0.9995	0.9978
	16	1.0000	1.0000	1.0000	1.0000	1.0000	1.0000	1.0000	1.0000	1.0000	0.9999	0.9996
	17	1.0000	1.0000	1.0000	1.0000	1.0000	1.0000	1.0000	1.0000	1.0000	1.0000	1.0000
20	0	0.8179	0.3585	0.1216	0.0388	0.0115	0.0032	0.0008	0.0002	0.0000	0.0000	0.0000
	1	0.9831	0.7358	0.3917	0.1756	0.0692	0.0243	0.0076	0.0021	0.0005	0.0001	0.0000
	2	0.9990	0.9245	0.6769	0.4049	0.2061	0.0913	0.0355	0.0121	0.0036	0.0009	0.0002
	3	1.0000	0.9841	0.8670	0.6477	0.4114	0.2252	0.1071	0.0444	0.0160	0.0049	0.0013
	4	1.0000	0.9974	0.9568	0.8298	0.6296	0.4148	0.2375	0.1182	0.0510	0.0189	0.0059
	5	1.0000	0.9997	0.9887	0.9327	0.8042	0.6172	0.4164	0.2454	0.1256	0.0553	0.0207
	6	1.0000	1.0000	0.9976	0.9781	0.9133	0.7858	0.6080	0.4166	0.2500	0.1299	0.0577
	7	1.0000	1.0000	0.9996	0.9941	0.9679	0.8982	0.7723	0.6010	0.4159	0.2520	0.1316
	8	1.0000	1.0000	0.9999	0.9987	0.9900	0.9591	0.8867	0.7624	0.5956	0.4143	0.2517
	9	1.0000	1.0000	1.0000	0.9998	0.9974	0.9861	0.9520	0.8782	0.7553	0.5914	0.4119
	10	1.0000	1.0000	1.0000	1.0000	0.9994	0.9961	0.9829	0.9468	0.8725	0.7507	0.5881
	11	1.0000	1.0000	1.0000	1.0000	0.9999	0.9991	0.9949	0.9804	0.9435	0.8692	0.7483
	12	1.0000	1.0000	1.0000	1.0000	1.0000	0.9998	0.9987	0.9940	0.9790	0.9420	0.8684
	13	1.0000	1.0000	1.0000	1.0000	1.0000	1.0000	0.9997	0.9985	0.9935	0.9786	0.9423
	14	1.0000	1.0000	1.0000	1.0000	1.0000	1.0000	1.0000	0.9997	0.9984	0.9936	0.9793
	15	1.0000	1.0000	1.0000	1.0000	1.0000	1.0000	1.0000	1.0000	0.9997	0.9985	0.9941
	16	1.0000	1.0000	1.0000	1.0000	1.0000	1.0000	1.0000	1.0000	1.0000	0.9997	0.9987
	17	1.0000	1.0000	1.0000	1.0000	1.0000	1.0000	1.0000	1.0000	1.0000	1.0000	0.9998
	18	1.0000	1.0000	1.0000	1.0000	1.0000	1.0000	1.0000	1.0000	1.0000	1.0000	1.0000
21	0	0.8097	0.3406	0.1094	0.0329	0.0092	0.0024	0.0006	0.0001	0.0000	0.0000	0.0000
	1	0.9815	0.7170	0.3647	0.1550	0.0576	0.0190	0.0056	0.0014	0.0003	0.0001	0.0000
	2	0.9988	0.9151	0.6484	0.3705	0.1787	0.0745	0.0271	0.0086	0.0024	0.0006	0.0001
	3	0.9999	0.9811	0.8480	0.6113	0.3704	0.1917	0.0856	0.0331	0.0110	0.0031	0.0007
	4	1.0000	0.9968	0.9478	0.8025	0.5860	0.3674	0.1984	0.0924	0.0370	0.0126	0.0036
	5	1.0000	0.9996	0.9856	0.9173	0.7693	0.5666	0.3627	0.2009	0.0957	0.0389	0.0133
	6	1.0000	1.0000	0.9967	0.9713	0.8915	0.7436	0.5505	0.3567	0.2002	0.0964	0.0392
	7	1.0000	1.0000	0.9994	0.9917	0.9569	0.8701	0.7230	0.5365	0.3495	0.1971	0.0946
	8	1.0000	1.0000	0.9999	0.9980	0.9856	0.9439	0.8523	0.7059	0.5237	0.3413	0.1917
	9	1.0000	1.0000	1.0000	0.9996	0.9959	0.9794	0.9324	0.8377	0.6914	0.5117	0.3318
	10	1.0000	1.0000	1.0000	0.9999	0.9990	0.9936	0.9736	0.9228	0.8256	0.6790	0.5000
	11	1.0000	1.0000	1.0000	1.0000	0.9998	0.9983	0.9913	0.9687	0.9151	0.8159	0.6682
	12	1.0000	1.0000	1.0000	1.0000	1.0000	0.9996	0.9976	0.9892	0.9648	0.9092	0.8083
	13	1.0000	1.0000	1.0000	1.0000	1.0000	0.9999	0.9994	0.9969	0.9877	0.9621	0.9054
	14	1.0000	1.0000	1.0000	1.0000	1.0000	1.0000	0.9999	0.9993	0.9964	0.9868	0.9608
	15	1.0000	1.0000	1.0000	1.0000	1.0000	1.0000	1.0000	0.9999	0.9992	0.9963	0.9867
	16	1.0000	1.0000	1.0000	1.0000	1.0000	1.0000	1.0000	1.0000	0.9998	0.9992	0.9964
	17	1.0000	1.0000	1.0000	1.0000	1.0000	1.0000	1.0000	1.0000	1.0000	0.9999	0.9993

Table C Cumulative Binomial Distribution (*continued*)

		π										
n	*X*	0.01	0.05	0.10	0.15	0.20	0.25	0.30	0.35	0.40	0.45	0.50
	18	1.0000	1.0000	1.0000	1.0000	1.0000	1.0000	1.0000	1.0000	1.0000	1.0000	0.9999
	19	1.0000	1.0000	1.0000	1.0000	1.0000	1.0000	1.0000	1.0000	1.0000	1.0000	1.0000
22	0	0.8016	0.3235	0.0985	0.0280	0.0074	0.0018	0.0004	0.0001	0.0000	0.0000	0.0000
	1	0.9798	0.6982	0.3392	0.1367	0.0480	0.0149	0.0041	0.0010	0.0002	0.0000	0.0000
	2	0.9987	0.9052	0.6200	0.3382	0.1545	0.0606	0.0207	0.0061	0.0016	0.0003	0.0001
	3	0.9999	0.9778	0.8281	0.5752	0.3320	0.1624	0.0681	0.0245	0.0076	0.0020	0.0004
	4	1.0000	0.9960	0.9379	0.7738	0.5429	0.3235	0.1645	0.0716	0.0266	0.0083	0.0022
	5	1.0000	0.9994	0.9818	0.9001	0.7326	0.5168	0.3134	0.1629	0.0722	0.0271	0.0085
	6	1.0000	0.9999	0.9956	0.9632	0.8670	0.6994	0.4942	0.3022	0.1584	0.0705	0.0262
	7	1.0000	1.0000	0.9991	0.9886	0.9439	0.8385	0.6713	0.4736	0.2898	0.1518	0.0669
	8	1.0000	1.0000	0.9999	0.9970	0.9799	0.9254	0.8135	0.6466	0.4540	0.2764	0.1431
	9	1.0000	1.0000	1.0000	0.9993	0.9939	0.9705	0.9084	0.7916	0.6244	0.4350	0.2617
	10	1.0000	1.0000	1.0000	0.9999	0.9984	0.9900	0.9613	0.8930	0.7720	0.6037	0.4159
	11	1.0000	1.0000	1.0000	1.0000	0.9997	0.9971	0.9860	0.9526	0.8793	0.7543	0.5841
	12	1.0000	1.0000	1.0000	1.0000	0.9999	0.9993	0.9957	0.9820	0.9449	0.8672	0.7383
	13	1.0000	1.0000	1.0000	1.0000	1.0000	0.9999	0.9989	0.9942	0.9785	0.9383	0.8569
	14	1.0000	1.0000	1.0000	1.0000	1.0000	1.0000	0.9998	0.9984	0.9930	0.9757	0.9331
	15	1.0000	1.0000	1.0000	1.0000	1.0000	1.0000	1.0000	0.9997	0.9981	0.9920	0.9738
	16	1.0000	1.0000	1.0000	1.0000	1.0000	1.0000	1.0000	0.9999	0.9996	0.9979	0.9915
	17	1.0000	1.0000	1.0000	1.0000	1.0000	1.0000	1.0000	1.0000	0.9999	0.9995	0.9978
	18	1.0000	1.0000	1.0000	1.0000	1.0000	1.0000	1.0000	1.0000	1.0000	0.9999	0.9996
	19	1.0000	1.0000	1.0000	1.0000	1.0000	1.0000	1.0000	1.0000	1.0000	1.0000	0.9999
	20	1.0000	1.0000	1.0000	1.0000	1.0000	1.0000	1.0000	1.0000	1.0000	1.0000	1.0000
23	0	0.7936	0.3074	0.0886	0.0238	0.0059	0.0013	0.0003	0.0000	0.0000	0.0000	0.0000
	1	0.9780	0.6794	0.3151	0.1204	0.0398	0.0116	0.0030	0.0007	0.0001	0.0000	0.0000
	2	0.9985	0.8948	0.5920	0.3080	0.1332	0.0492	0.0157	0.0043	0.0010	0.0002	0.0000
	3	0.9999	0.9742	0.8073	0.5396	0.2965	0.1370	0.0538	0.0181	0.0052	0.0012	0.0002
	4	1.0000	0.9951	0.9269	0.7440	0.5007	0.2832	0.1356	0.0551	0.0190	0.0055	0.0013
	5	1.0000	0.9992	0.9774	0.8811	0.6947	0.4685	0.2688	0.1309	0.0540	0.0186	0.0053
	6	1.0000	0.9999	0.9942	0.9537	0.8402	0.6537	0.4399	0.2534	0.1240	0.0510	0.0173
	7	1.0000	1.0000	0.9988	0.9848	0.9285	0.8037	0.6181	0.4136	0.2373	0.1152	0.0466
	8	1.0000	1.0000	0.9998	0.9958	0.9727	0.9037	0.7709	0.5860	0.3884	0.2203	0.1050
	9	1.0000	1.0000	1.0000	0.9990	0.9911	0.9592	0.8799	0.7408	0.5562	0.3636	0.2024
	10	1.0000	1.0000	1.0000	0.9998	0.9975	0.9851	0.9454	0.8575	0.7129	0.5278	0.3388
	11	1.0000	1.0000	1.0000	1.0000	0.9994	0.9954	0.9786	0.9318	0.8364	0.6865	0.5000
	12	1.0000	1.0000	1.0000	1.0000	0.9999	0.9988	0.9928	0.9717	0.9187	0.8164	0.6612
	13	1.0000	1.0000	1.0000	1.0000	1.0000	0.9997	0.9979	0.9900	0.9651	0.9063	0.7976
	14	1.0000	1.0000	1.0000	1.0000	1.0000	0.9999	0.9995	0.9970	0.9872	0.9589	0.8950
	15	1.0000	1.0000	1.0000	1.0000	1.0000	1.0000	0.9999	0.9992	0.9960	0.9847	0.9534
	16	1.0000	1.0000	1.0000	1.0000	1.0000	1.0000	1.0000	0.9998	0.9990	0.9952	0.9827
	17	1.0000	1.0000	1.0000	1.0000	1.0000	1.0000	1.0000	1.0000	0.9998	0.9988	0.9947
	18	1.0000	1.0000	1.0000	1.0000	1.0000	1.0000	1.0000	1.0000	1.0000	0.9998	0.9987
	19	1.0000	1.0000	1.0000	1.0000	1.0000	1.0000	1.0000	1.0000	1.0000	1.0000	0.9998
	20	1.0000	1.0000	1.0000	1.0000	1.0000	1.0000	1.0000	1.0000	1.0000	1.0000	1.0000

Table C Cumulative Binomial Distribution (*continued*)

n	X	π 0.01	0.05	0.10	0.15	0.20	0.25	0.30	0.35	0.40	0.45	0.50
24	0	0.7857	0.2920	0.0798	0.0202	0.0047	0.0010	0.0002	0.0000	0.0000	0.0000	0.0000
	1	0.9761	0.6608	0.2925	0.1059	0.0331	0.0090	0.0022	0.0005	0.0001	0.0000	0.0000
	2	0.9983	0.8841	0.5643	0.2798	0.1145	0.0398	0.0119	0.0030	0.0007	0.0001	0.0000
	3	0.9999	0.9702	0.7857	0.5049	0.2639	0.1150	0.0424	0.0133	0.0035	0.0008	0.0001
	4	1.0000	0.9940	0.9149	0.7134	0.4599	0.2466	0.1111	0.0422	0.0134	0.0036	0.0008
	5	1.0000	0.9990	0.9723	0.8606	0.6559	0.4222	0.2288	0.1044	0.0400	0.0127	0.0033
	6	1.0000	0.9999	0.9925	0.9428	0.8111	0.6074	0.3886	0.2106	0.0960	0.0364	0.0113
	7	1.0000	1.0000	0.9983	0.9801	0.9108	0.7662	0.5647	0.3575	0.1919	0.0863	0.0320
	8	1.0000	1.0000	0.9997	0.9941	0.9638	0.8787	0.7250	0.5257	0.3279	0.1730	0.0758
	9	1.0000	1.0000	0.9999	0.9985	0.9874	0.9453	0.8472	0.6866	0.4891	0.2991	0.1537
	10	1.0000	1.0000	1.0000	0.9997	0.9962	0.9787	0.9258	0.8167	0.6502	0.4539	0.2706
	11	1.0000	1.0000	1.0000	0.9999	0.9990	0.9928	0.9686	0.9058	0.7870	0.6151	0.4194
	12	1.0000	1.0000	1.0000	1.0000	0.9998	0.9979	0.9885	0.9577	0.8857	0.7580	0.5806
	13	1.0000	1.0000	1.0000	1.0000	1.0000	0.9995	0.9964	0.9836	0.9465	0.8659	0.7294
	14	1.0000	1.0000	1.0000	1.0000	1.0000	0.9999	0.9990	0.9945	0.9783	0.9352	0.8463
	15	1.0000	1.0000	1.0000	1.0000	1.0000	1.0000	0.9998	0.9984	0.9925	0.9731	0.9242
	16	1.0000	1.0000	1.0000	1.0000	1.0000	1.0000	1.0000	0.9996	0.9978	0.9905	0.9680
	17	1.0000	1.0000	1.0000	1.0000	1.0000	1.0000	1.0000	0.9999	0.9995	0.9972	0.9887
	18	1.0000	1.0000	1.0000	1.0000	1.0000	1.0000	1.0000	1.0000	0.9999	0.9993	0.9967
	19	1.0000	1.0000	1.0000	1.0000	1.0000	1.0000	1.0000	1.0000	1.0000	0.9999	0.9992
	20	1.0000	1.0000	1.0000	1.0000	1.0000	1.0000	1.0000	1.0000	1.0000	1.0000	0.9999
	21	1.0000	1.0000	1.0000	1.0000	1.0000	1.0000	1.0000	1.0000	1.0000	1.0000	1.0000
25	0	0.7778	0.2774	0.0718	0.0172	0.0038	0.0008	0.0001	0.0000	0.0000	0.0000	0.0000
	1	0.9742	0.6424	0.2712	0.0931	0.0274	0.0070	0.0016	0.0003	0.0001	0.0000	0.0000
	2	0.9980	0.8729	0.5371	0.2537	0.0982	0.0321	0.0090	0.0021	0.0004	0.0001	0.0000
	3	0.9999	0.9659	0.7636	0.4711	0.2340	0.0962	0.0332	0.0097	0.0024	0.0005	0.0001
	4	1.0000	0.9928	0.9020	0.6821	0.4207	0.2137	0.0905	0.0320	0.0095	0.0023	0.0005
	5	1.0000	0.9988	0.9666	0.8385	0.6167	0.3783	0.1935	0.0826	0.0294	0.0086	0.0020
	6	1.0000	0.9998	0.9905	0.9305	0.7800	0.5611	0.3407	0.1734	0.0736	0.0258	0.0073
	7	1.0000	1.0000	0.9977	0.9745	0.8909	0.7265	0.5118	0.3061	0.1536	0.0639	0.0216
	8	1.0000	1.0000	0.9995	0.9920	0.9532	0.8506	0.6769	0.4668	0.2735	0.1340	0.0539
	9	1.0000	1.0000	0.9999	0.9979	0.9827	0.9287	0.8106	0.6303	0.4246	0.2424	0.1148
	10	1.0000	1.0000	1.0000	0.9995	0.9944	0.9703	0.9022	0.7712	0.5858	0.3843	0.2122
	11	1.0000	1.0000	1.0000	0.9999	0.9985	0.9893	0.9558	0.8746	0.7323	0.5426	0.3450
	12	1.0000	1.0000	1.0000	1.0000	0.9996	0.9966	0.9825	0.9396	0.8462	0.6937	0.5000
	13	1.0000	1.0000	1.0000	1.0000	0.9999	0.9991	0.9940	0.9745	0.9222	0.8173	0.6550
	14	1.0000	1.0000	1.0000	1.0000	1.0000	0.9998	0.9982	0.9907	0.9656	0.9040	0.7878
	15	1.0000	1.0000	1.0000	1.0000	1.0000	1.0000	0.9995	0.9971	0.9868	0.9560	0.8852
	16	1.0000	1.0000	1.0000	1.0000	1.0000	1.0000	0.9999	0.9992	0.9957	0.9826	0.9461
	17	1.0000	1.0000	1.0000	1.0000	1.0000	1.0000	1.0000	0.9998	0.9988	0.9942	0.9784
	18	1.0000	1.0000	1.0000	1.0000	1.0000	1.0000	1.0000	1.0000	0.9997	0.9984	0.9927
	19	1.0000	1.0000	1.0000	1.0000	1.0000	1.0000	1.0000	1.0000	0.9999	0.9996	0.9980
	20	1.0000	1.0000	1.0000	1.0000	1.0000	1.0000	1.0000	1.0000	1.0000	0.9999	0.9995
	21	1.0000	1.0000	1.0000	1.0000	1.0000	1.0000	1.0000	1.0000	1.0000	1.0000	0.9999
	22	1.0000	1.0000	1.0000	1.0000	1.0000	1.0000	1.0000	1.0000	1.0000	1.0000	1.0000

Table C Cumulative Binomial Distribution (*continued*)

							π					
n	*X*	0.01	0.05	0.10	0.15	0.20	0.25	0.30	0.35	0.40	0.45	0.50
50	0	0.6050	0.0769	0.0052	0.0003	0.0000	0.0000	0.0000	0.0000	0.0000	0.0000	0.0000
	1	0.9106	0.2794	0.0338	0.0029	0.0002	0.0000	0.0000	0.0000	0.0000	0.0000	0.0000
	2	0.9862	0.5405	0.1117	0.0142	0.0013	0.0001	0.0000	0.0000	0.0000	0.0000	0.0000
	3	0.9984	0.7604	0.2503	0.0460	0.0057	0.0005	0.0000	0.0000	0.0000	0.0000	0.0000
	4	0.9999	0.8964	0.4312	0.1121	0.0185	0.0021	0.0002	0.0000	0.0000	0.0000	0.0000
	5	1.0000	0.9622	0.6161	0.2194	0.0480	0.0070	0.0007	0.0001	0.0000	0.0000	0.0000
	6	1.0000	0.9882	0.7702	0.3613	0.1034	0.0194	0.0025	0.0002	0.0000	0.0000	0.0000
	7	1.0000	0.9968	0.8779	0.5188	0.1904	0.0453	0.0073	0.0008	0.0001	0.0000	0.0000
	8	1.0000	0.9992	0.9421	0.6681	0.3073	0.0916	0.0183	0.0025	0.0002	0.0000	0.0000
	9	1.0000	0.9998	0.9755	0.7911	0.4437	0.1637	0.0402	0.0067	0.0008	0.0001	0.0000
	10	1.0000	1.0000	0.9906	0.8801	0.5836	0.2622	0.0789	0.0160	0.0022	0.0002	0.0000
	11	1.0000	1.0000	0.9968	0.9372	0.7107	0.3816	0.1390	0.0342	0.0057	0.0006	0.0000
	12	1.0000	1.0000	0.9990	0.9699	0.8139	0.5110	0.2229	0.0661	0.0133	0.0018	0.0002
	13	1.0000	1.0000	0.9997	0.9868	0.8894	0.6370	0.3279	0.1163	0.0280	0.0045	0.0005
	14	1.0000	1.0000	0.9999	0.9947	0.9393	0.7481	0.4468	0.1878	0.0540	0.0104	0.0013
	15	1.0000	1.0000	1.0000	0.9981	0.9692	0.8369	0.5692	0.2801	0.0955	0.0220	0.0033
	16	1.0000	1.0000	1.0000	0.9993	0.9856	0.9017	0.6839	0.3889	0.1561	0.0427	0.0077
	17	1.0000	1.0000	1.0000	0.9998	0.9937	0.9449	0.7822	0.5060	0.2369	0.0765	0.0164
	18	1.0000	1.0000	1.0000	0.9999	0.9975	0.9713	0.8594	0.6216	0.3356	0.1273	0.0325
	19	1.0000	1.0000	1.0000	1.0000	0.9991	0.9861	0.9152	0.7264	0.4465	0.1974	0.0595
	20	1.0000	1.0000	1.0000	1.0000	0.9997	0.9937	0.9522	0.8139	0.5610	0.2862	0.1013
	21	1.0000	1.0000	1.0000	1.0000	0.9999	0.9974	0.9749	0.8813	0.6701	0.3900	0.1611
	22	1.0000	1.0000	1.0000	1.0000	1.0000	0.9990	0.9877	0.9290	0.7660	0.5019	0.2399
	23	1.0000	1.0000	1.0000	1.0000	1.0000	0.9996	0.9944	0.9604	0.8348	0.6134	0.3359
	24	1.0000	1.0000	1.0000	1.0000	1.0000	0.9999	0.9976	0.9793	0.9022	0.7160	0.4439
	25	1.0000	1.0000	1.0000	1.0000	1.0000	1.0000	0.9991	0.9900	0.9427	0.8034	0.5561
	26	1.0000	1.0000	1.0000	1.0000	1.0000	1.0000	0.9997	0.9955	0.9686	0.8721	0.6641
	27	1.0000	1.0000	1.0000	1.0000	1.0000	1.0000	0.9999	0.9981	0.9840	0.9220	0.7601
	28	1.0000	1.0000	1.0000	1.0000	1.0000	1.0000	1.0000	0.9993	0.9924	0.9556	0.8389
	29	1.0000	1.0000	1.0000	1.0000	1.0000	1.0000	1.0000	0.9997	0.9966	0.9765	0.8987
	30	1.0000	1.0000	1.0000	1.0000	1.0000	1.0000	1.0000	0.9999	0.9986	0.9884	0.9405
	31	1.0000	1.0000	1.0000	1.0000	1.0000	1.0000	1.0000	1.0000	0.9995	0.9947	0.9675
	32	1.0000	1.0000	1.0000	1.0000	1.0000	1.0000	1.0000	1.0000	0.9998	0.9978	0.9836
	33	1.0000	1.0000	1.0000	1.0000	1.0000	1.0000	1.0000	1.0000	0.9999	0.9991	0.9923
	34	1.0000	1.0000	1.0000	1.0000	1.0000	1.0000	1.0000	1.0000	1.0000	0.9997	0.9967
	35	1.0000	1.0000	1.0000	1.0000	1.0000	1.0000	1.0000	1.0000	1.0000	0.9999	0.9987
	36	1.0000	1.0000	1.0000	1.0000	1.0000	1.0000	1.0000	1.0000	1.0000	1.0000	0.9995
	37	1.0000	1.0000	1.0000	1.0000	1.0000	1.0000	1.0000	1.0000	1.0000	1.0000	0.9998
	38	1.0000	1.0000	1.0000	1.0000	1.0000	1.0000	1.0000	1.0000	1.0000	1.0000	1.0000
100	0	0.3660	0.0059	0.0000	0.0000	0.0000	0.0000	0.0000	0.0000	0.0000	0.0000	0.0000
	1	0.7358	0.0371	0.0003	0.0000	0.0000	0.0000	0.0000	0.0000	0.0000	0.0000	0.0000
	2	0.9206	0.1183	0.0019	0.0000	0.0000	0.0000	0.0000	0.0000	0.0000	0.0000	0.0000
	3	0.9816	0.2578	0.0078	0.0001	0.0000	0.0000	0.0000	0.0000	0.0000	0.0000	0.0000
	4	0.9966	0.4360	0.0237	0.0004	0.0000	0.0000	0.0000	0.0000	0.0000	0.0000	0.0000
	5	0.9995	0.6160	0.0576	0.0016	0.0000	0.0000	0.0000	0.0000	0.0000	0.0000	0.0000

Table C Cumulative Binomial Distribution (*continued*)

		π										
n	*X*	0.01	0.05	0.10	0.15	0.20	0.25	0.30	0.35	0.40	0.45	0.50
100	6	0.9999	0.7660	0.1172	0.0047	0.0001	0.0000	0.0000	0.0000	0.0000	0.0000	0.0000
	7	1.0000	0.8720	0.2061	0.0122	0.0003	0.0000	0.0000	0.0000	0.0000	0.0000	0.0000
	8	1.0000	0.9369	0.3209	0.0275	0.0009	0.0000	0.0000	0.0000	0.0000	0.0000	0.0000
	9	1.0000	0.9718	0.4513	0.0551	0.0023	0.0000	0.0000	0.0000	0.0000	0.0000	0.0000
	10	1.0000	0.9885	0.5832	0.0994	0.0057	0.0001	0.0000	0.0000	0.0000	0.0000	0.0000
	11	1.0000	0.9957	0.7030	0.1635	0.0126	0.0004	0.0000	0.0000	0.0000	0.0000	0.0000
	12	1.0000	0.9985	0.8018	0.2473	0.0253	0.0010	0.0000	0.0000	0.0000	0.0000	0.0000
	13	1.0000	0.9995	0.8761	0.3474	0.0469	0.0025	0.0001	0.0000	0.0000	0.0000	0.0000
	14	1.0000	0.9999	0.9274	0.4572	0.0804	0.0054	0.0002	0.0000	0.0000	0.0000	0.0000
	15	1.0000	1.0000	0.9601	0.5683	0.1285	0.0111	0.0004	0.0000	0.0000	0.0000	0.0000
	16	1.0000	1.0000	0.9794	0.6725	0.1923	0.0211	0.0010	0.0000	0.0000	0.0000	0.0000
	17	1.0000	1.0000	0.9900	0.7633	0.2712	0.0376	0.0022	0.0001	0.0000	0.0000	0.0000
	18	1.0000	1.0000	0.9954	0.8372	0.3621	0.0630	0.0045	0.0001	0.0000	0.0000	0.0000
	19	1.0000	1.0000	0.9980	0.8935	0.4602	0.0995	0.0089	0.0003	0.0000	0.0000	0.0000
	20	1.0000	1.0000	0.9992	0.9337	0.5595	0.1488	0.0165	0.0008	0.0000	0.0000	0.0000
	21	1.0000	1.0000	0.9997	0.9607	0.6540	0.2114	0.0288	0.0017	0.0000	0.0000	0.0000
	22	1.0000	1.0000	0.9999	0.9779	0.7389	0.2864	0.0479	0.0034	0.0001	0.0000	0.0000
	23	1.0000	1.0000	1.0000	0.9881	0.8109	0.3711	0.0755	0.0066	0.0003	0.0000	0.0000
	24	1.0000	1.0000	1.0000	0.9939	0.8686	0.4617	0.1136	0.0121	0.0006	0.0000	0.0000
	25	1.0000	1.0000	1.0000	0.9970	0.9125	0.5535	0.1631	0.0211	0.0012	0.0000	0.0000
	26	1.0000	1.0000	1.0000	0.9986	0.9442	0.6417	0.2244	0.0351	0.0024	0.0001	0.0000
	27	1.0000	1.0000	1.0000	0.9994	0.9658	0.7224	0.2964	0.0558	0.0046	0.0002	0.0000
	28	1.0000	1.0000	1.0000	0.9997	0.9800	0.7925	0.3768	0.0848	0.0084	0.0004	0.0000
	29	1.0000	1.0000	1.0000	0.9999	0.9888	0.8505	0.4623	0.1236	0.0148	0.0008	0.0000
	30	1.0000	1.0000	1.0000	1.0000	0.9939	0.8962	0.5491	0.1730	0.0248	0.0015	0.0000
	31	1.0000	1.0000	1.0000	1.0000	0.9969	0.9307	0.6331	0.2331	0.0398	0.0030	0.0001
	32	1.0000	1.0000	1.0000	1.0000	0.9984	0.9554	0.7107	0.3029	0.0615	0.0055	0.0002
	33	1.0000	1.0000	1.0000	1.0000	0.9993	0.9724	0.7793	0.3803	0.0913	0.0098	0.0004
	34	1.0000	1.0000	1.0000	1.0000	0.9997	0.9836	0.8371	0.4624	0.1303	0.0166	0.0009
	35	1.0000	1.0000	1.0000	1.0000	0.9999	0.9906	0.8839	0.5458	0.1795	0.0272	0.0018
	36	1.0000	1.0000	1.0000	1.0000	0.9999	0.9948	0.9201	0.6269	0.2386	0.0429	0.0033
	37	1.0000	1.0000	1.0000	1.0000	1.0000	0.9973	0.9470	0.7024	0.3068	0.0651	0.0060
	38	1.0000	1.0000	1.0000	1.0000	1.0000	0.9986	0.9660	0.7699	0.3822	0.0951	0.0105
	39	1.0000	1.0000	1.0000	1.0000	1.0000	0.9993	0.9790	0.8276	0.4621	0.1343	0.0176
	40	1.0000	1.0000	1.0000	1.0000	1.0000	0.9997	0.9875	0.8750	0.5433	0.1831	0.0284
	41	1.0000	1.0000	1.0000	1.0000	1.0000	0.9999	0.9928	0.9123	0.6225	0.2415	0.0443
	42	1.0000	1.0000	1.0000	1.0000	1.0000	0.9999	0.9960	0.9406	0.6967	0.3087	0.0666
	43	1.0000	1.0000	1.0000	1.0000	1.0000	1.0000	0.9979	0.9611	0.7635	0.3828	0.0967
	44	1.0000	1.0000	1.0000	1.0000	1.0000	1.0000	0.9989	0.9754	0.8211	0.4613	0.1356
	45	1.0000	1.0000	1.0000	1.0000	1.0000	1.0000	0.9995	0.9850	0.8689	0.5413	0.1841
	46	1.0000	1.0000	1.0000	1.0000	1.0000	1.0000	0.9997	0.9912	0.9070	0.6196	0.2421
	47	1.0000	1.0000	1.0000	1.0000	1.0000	1.0000	0.9999	0.9950	0.9362	0.6931	0.3086
	48	1.0000	1.0000	1.0000	1.0000	1.0000	1.0000	0.9999	0.9973	0.9577	0.7596	0.3822
	49	1.0000	1.0000	1.0000	1.0000	1.0000	1.0000	1.0000	0.9985	0.9729	0.8173	0.4602
	50	1.0000	1.0000	1.0000	1.0000	1.0000	1.0000	1.0000	0.9993	0.9832	0.8654	0.5398

Table C Cumulative Binomial Distribution (*continued*)

n	X	π 0.01	0.05	0.10	0.15	0.20	0.25	0.30	0.35	0.40	0.45	0.50
	51	1.0000	1.0000	1.0000	1.0000	1.0000	1.0000	1.0000	0.9996	0.9900	0.9040	0.6178
	52	1.0000	1.0000	1.0000	1.0000	1.0000	1.0000	1.0000	0.9998	0.9942	0.9338	0.6914
	53	1.0000	1.0000	1.0000	1.0000	1.0000	1.0000	1.0000	0.9999	0.9968	0.9559	0.7579
	54	1.0000	1.0000	1.0000	1.0000	1.0000	1.0000	1.0000	1.0000	0.9983	0.9716	0.8159
	55	1.0000	1.0000	1.0000	1.0000	1.0000	1.0000	1.0000	1.0000	0.9991	0.9824	0.8644
	56	1.0000	1.0000	1.0000	1.0000	1.0000	1.0000	1.0000	1.0000	0.9996	0.9894	0.9033
	57	1.0000	1.0000	1.0000	1.0000	1.0000	1.0000	1.0000	1.0000	0.9998	0.9939	0.9334
	58	1.0000	1.0000	1.0000	1.0000	1.0000	1.0000	1.0000	1.0000	0.9999	0.9966	0.9557
	59	1.0000	1.0000	1.0000	1.0000	1.0000	1.0000	1.0000	1.0000	1.0000	0.9982	0.9716
	60	1.0000	1.0000	1.0000	1.0000	1.0000	1.0000	1.0000	1.0000	1.0000	0.9991	0.9824
	61	1.0000	1.0000	1.0000	1.0000	1.0000	1.0000	1.0000	1.0000	1.0000	0.9995	0.9895
	62	1.0000	1.0000	1.0000	1.0000	1.0000	1.0000	1.0000	1.0000	1.0000	0.9998	0.9940
	63	1.0000	1.0000	1.0000	1.0000	1.0000	1.0000	1.0000	1.0000	1.0000	0.9999	0.9967
	64	1.0000	1.0000	1.0000	1.0000	1.0000	1.0000	1.0000	1.0000	1.0000	1.0000	0.9982
	65	1.0000	1.0000	1.0000	1.0000	1.0000	1.0000	1.0000	1.0000	1.0000	1.0000	0.9991
	66	1.0000	1.0000	1.0000	1.0000	1.0000	1.0000	1.0000	1.0000	1.0000	1.0000	0.9996
	67	1.0000	1.0000	1.0000	1.0000	1.0000	1.0000	1.0000	1.0000	1.0000	1.0000	0.9998
	68	1.0000	1.0000	1.0000	1.0000	1.0000	1.0000	1.0000	1.0000	1.0000	1.0000	0.9999
	69	1.0000	1.0000	1.0000	1.0000	1.0000	1.0000	1.0000	1.0000	1.0000	1.0000	1.0000

Table D Poisson Distribution

x	μ 0.1	0.2	0.3	0.4	0.5	0.6	0.7	0.8	0.9	1.0
0	0.9048	0.8187	0.7408	0.6703	0.6065	0.5488	0.4966	0.4493	0.4066	0.3679
1	0.0905	0.1637	0.2222	0.2681	0.3033	0.3293	0.3476	0.3595	0.3659	0.3679
2	0.0045	0.0164	0.0333	0.0536	0.0758	0.0988	0.1217	0.1438	0.1647	0.1839
3	0.0002	0.0011	0.0033	0.0072	0.0126	0.0198	0.0284	0.0383	0.0494	0.0613
4	0.0000	0.0001	0.0003	0.0007	0.0016	0.0030	0.0050	0.0077	0.0111	0.0153
5	0.0000	0.0000	0.0000	0.0001	0.0002	0.0004	0.0007	0.0012	0.0020	0.0031
6	0.0000	0.0000	0.0000	0.0000	0.0000	0.0000	0.0001	0.0002	0.0003	0.0005
7	0.0000	0.0000	0.0000	0.0000	0.0000	0.0000	0.0000	0.0000	0.0000	0.0001

x	μ 1.1	1.2	1.3	1.4	1.5	1.6	1.7	1.8	1.9	2.0
0	0.3329	0.3012	0.2725	0.2466	0.2231	0.2019	0.1827	0.1653	0.1496	0.1353
1	0.3662	0.3614	0.3543	0.3452	0.3347	0.3230	0.3106	0.2975	0.2842	0.2707
2	0.2014	0.2169	0.2303	0.2417	0.2510	0.2584	0.2640	0.2678	0.2700	0.2707
3	0.0738	0.0867	0.0998	0.1128	0.1255	0.1378	0.1496	0.1607	0.1710	0.1804
4	0.0203	0.0260	0.0324	0.0395	0.0471	0.0551	0.0636	0.0723	0.0812	0.0902
5	0.0045	0.0062	0.0084	0.0111	0.0141	0.0176	0.0216	0.0260	0.0309	0.0361
6	0.0008	0.0012	0.0018	0.0026	0.0035	0.0047	0.0061	0.0078	0.0098	0.0120
7	0.0001	0.0002	0.0003	0.0005	0.0008	0.0011	0.0015	0.0020	0.0027	0.0034
8	0.0000	0.0000	0.0001	0.0001	0.0001	0.0002	0.0003	0.0005	0.0006	0.0009

x	μ 2.1	2.2	2.3	2.4	2.5	2.6	2.7	2.8	2.9	3.0
0	0.1225	0.1108	0.1003	0.0907	0.0821	0.0743	0.0672	0.0608	0.0550	0.0498
1	0.2572	0.2438	0.2306	0.2177	0.2052	0.1931	0.1815	0.1703	0.1596	0.1494
2	0.2700	0.2681	0.2652	0.2613	0.2565	0.2510	0.2450	0.2384	0.2314	0.2240
3	0.1890	0.1966	0.2033	0.2090	0.2138	0.2176	0.2205	0.2225	0.2237	0.2240
4	0.0992	0.1082	0.1169	0.1254	0.1336	0.1414	0.1488	0.1557	0.1622	0.1680
5	0.0417	0.0476	0.0538	0.0602	0.0668	0.0735	0.0804	0.0872	0.0940	0.1008
6	0.0146	0.0174	0.0206	0.0241	0.0278	0.0319	0.0362	0.0407	0.0455	0.0504
7	0.0044	0.0055	0.0068	0.0083	0.0099	0.0118	0.0139	0.0163	0.0188	0.0216
8	0.0011	0.0015	0.0019	0.0025	0.0031	0.0038	0.0047	0.0057	0.0068	0.0081
9	0.0003	0.0004	0.0005	0.0007	0.0009	0.0011	0.0014	0.0018	0.0022	0.0027
10	0.0001	0.0001	0.0001	0.0002	0.0002	0.0003	0.0004	0.0005	0.0006	0.0008
11	0.0000	0.0000	0.0000	0.0000	0.0000	0.0001	0.0001	0.0001	0.0002	0.0002
12	0.0000	0.0000	0.0000	0.0000	0.0000	0.0000	0.0000	0.0000	0.0000	0.0001

x	μ 3.1	3.2	3.3	3.4	3.5	3.6	3.7	3.8	3.9	4.0
0	0.0450	0.0408	0.0369	0.0334	0.0302	0.0273	0.0247	0.0224	0.0202	0.0183
1	0.1397	0.1304	0.1217	0.1135	0.1057	0.0984	0.0915	0.0850	0.0789	0.0733
2	0.2165	0.2087	0.2008	0.1929	0.1850	0.1771	0.1692	0.1615	0.1539	0.1465
3	0.2237	0.2226	0.2209	0.2186	0.2158	0.2125	0.2087	0.2046	0.2001	0.1954
4	0.1733	0.1781	0.1823	0.1858	0.1888	0.1912	0.1931	0.1944	0.1951	0.1954
5	0.1075	0.1140	0.1203	0.1264	0.1322	0.1377	0.1429	0.1477	0.1522	0.1563

Table D Poisson Distribution (*continued*)

x	μ 3.1	3.2	3.3	3.4	3.5	3.6	3.7	3.8	3.9	4.0
6	0.0555	0.0608	0.0662	0.0716	0.0771	0.0826	0.0881	0.0936	0.0989	0.1042
7	0.0246	0.0278	0.0312	0.0348	0.0385	0.0425	0.0466	0.0508	0.0551	0.0595
8	0.0095	0.0111	0.0129	0.0148	0.0169	0.0191	0.0215	0.0241	0.0269	0.0298
9	0.0033	0.0040	0.0047	0.0056	0.0066	0.0076	0.0089	0.0102	0.0116	0.0132
10	0.0010	0.0013	0.0016	0.0019	0.0023	0.0028	0.0033	0.0039	0.0045	0.0053
11	0.0003	0.0004	0.0005	0.0006	0.0007	0.0009	0.0011	0.0013	0.0016	0.0019
12	0.0001	0.0001	0.0001	0.0002	0.0002	0.0003	0.0003	0.0004	0.0005	0.0006
13	0.0000	0.0000	0.0000	0.0000	0.0001	0.0001	0.0001	0.0001	0.0002	0.0002
14	0.0000	0.0000	0.0000	0.0000	0.0000	0.0000	0.0000	0.0000	0.0000	0.0001

x	μ 4.1	4.2	4.3	4.4	4.5	4.6	4.7	4.8	4.9	5.0
0	0.0166	0.0150	0.0136	0.0123	0.0111	0.0101	0.0091	0.0082	0.0074	0.0067
1	0.0679	0.0630	0.0583	0.0540	0.0500	0.0462	0.0427	0.0395	0.0365	0.0337
2	0.1393	0.1323	0.1254	0.1188	0.1125	0.1063	0.1005	0.0948	0.0894	0.0842
3	0.1904	0.1852	0.1798	0.1743	0.1687	0.1631	0.1574	0.1517	0.1460	0.1404
4	0.1951	0.1944	0.1933	0.1917	0.1898	0.1875	0.1849	0.1820	0.1789	0.1755
5	0.1600	0.1633	0.1662	0.1687	0.1708	0.1725	0.1738	0.1747	0.1753	0.1755
6	0.1093	0.1143	0.1191	0.1237	0.1281	0.1323	0.1362	0.1398	0.1432	0.1462
7	0.0640	0.0686	0.0732	0.0778	0.0824	0.0869	0.0914	0.0959	0.1002	0.1044
8	0.0328	0.0360	0.0393	0.0428	0.0463	0.0500	0.0537	0.0575	0.0614	0.0653
9	0.0150	0.0168	0.0188	0.0209	0.0232	0.0255	0.0281	0.0307	0.0334	0.0363
10	0.0061	0.0071	0.0081	0.0092	0.0104	0.0118	0.0132	0.0147	0.0164	0.0181
11	0.0023	0.0027	0.0032	0.0037	0.0043	0.0049	0.0056	0.0064	0.0073	0.0082
12	0.0008	0.0009	0.0011	0.0013	0.0016	0.0019	0.0022	0.0026	0.0030	0.0034
13	0.0002	0.0003	0.0004	0.0005	0.0006	0.0007	0.0008	0.0009	0.0011	0.0013
14	0.0001	0.0001	0.0001	0.0001	0.0002	0.0002	0.0003	0.0003	0.0004	0.0005
15	0.0000	0.0000	0.0000	0.0000	0.0001	0.0001	0.0001	0.0001	0.0001	0.0002

x	μ 5.1	5.2	5.3	5.4	5.5	5.6	5.7	5.8	5.9	6.0
0	0.0061	0.0055	0.0050	0.0045	0.0041	0.0037	0.0033	0.0030	0.0027	0.0025
1	0.0311	0.0287	0.0265	0.0244	0.0225	0.0207	0.0191	0.0176	0.0162	0.0149
2	0.0793	0.0746	0.0701	0.0659	0.0618	0.0580	0.0544	0.0509	0.0477	0.0446
3	0.1348	0.1293	0.1239	0.1185	0.1133	0.1082	0.1033	0.0985	0.0938	0.0892
4	0.1719	0.1681	0.1641	0.1600	0.1558	0.1515	0.1472	0.1428	0.1383	0.1339
5	0.1753	0.1748	0.1740	0.1728	0.1714	0.1697	0.1678	0.1656	0.1632	0.1606
6	0.1490	0.1515	0.1537	0.1555	0.1571	0.1584	0.1594	0.1601	0.1605	0.1606
7	0.1086	0.1125	0.1163	0.1200	0.1234	0.1267	0.1298	0.1326	0.1353	0.1377
8	0.0692	0.0731	0.0771	0.0810	0.0849	0.0887	0.0925	0.0962	0.0998	0.1033
9	0.0392	0.0423	0.0454	0.0486	0.0519	0.0552	0.0586	0.0620	0.0654	0.0688
10	0.0200	0.0220	0.0241	0.0262	0.0285	0.0309	0.0334	0.0359	0.0386	0.0413
11	0.0093	0.0104	0.0116	0.0129	0.0143	0.0157	0.0173	0.0190	0.0207	0.0225
12	0.0039	0.0045	0.0051	0.0058	0.0065	0.0073	0.0082	0.0092	0.0102	0.0113
13	0.0015	0.0018	0.0021	0.0024	0.0028	0.0032	0.0036	0.0041	0.0046	0.0052

Table D Poisson Distribution (*continued*)

x	μ 5.1	5.2	5.3	5.4	5.5	5.6	5.7	5.8	5.9	6.0
14	0.0006	0.0007	0.0008	0.0009	0.0011	0.0013	0.0015	0.0017	0.0019	0.0022
15	0.0002	0.0002	0.0003	0.0003	0.0004	0.0005	0.0006	0.0007	0.0008	0.0009
16	0.0001	0.0001	0.0001	0.0001	0.0001	0.0002	0.0002	0.0002	0.0003	0.0003
17	0.0000	0.0000	0.0000	0.0000	0.0000	0.0001	0.0001	0.0001	0.0001	0.0001

x	μ 6.1	6.2	6.3	6.4	6.5	6.6	6.7	6.8	6.9	7.0
0	0.0022	0.0020	0.0018	0.0017	0.0015	0.0014	0.0012	0.0011	0.0010	0.0009
1	0.0137	0.0126	0.0116	0.0106	0.0098	0.0090	0.0082	0.0076	0.0070	0.0064
2	0.0417	0.0390	0.0364	0.0340	0.0318	0.0296	0.0276	0.0258	0.0240	0.0223
3	0.0848	0.0806	0.0765	0.0726	0.0688	0.0652	0.0617	0.0584	0.0552	0.0521
4	0.1294	0.1249	0.1205	0.1162	0.1118	0.1076	0.1034	0.0992	0.0952	0.0912
5	0.1579	0.1549	0.1519	0.1487	0.1454	0.1420	0.1385	0.1349	0.1314	0.1277
6	0.1605	0.1601	0.1595	0.1586	0.1575	0.1562	0.1546	0.1529	0.1511	0.1490
7	0.1399	0.1418	0.1435	0.1450	0.1462	0.1472	0.1480	0.1486	0.1489	0.1490
8	0.1066	0.1099	0.1130	0.1160	0.1188	0.1215	0.1240	0.1263	0.1284	0.1304
9	0.0723	0.0757	0.0791	0.0825	0.0858	0.0891	0.0923	0.0954	0.0985	0.1014
10	0.0441	0.0469	0.0498	0.0528	0.0558	0.0588	0.0618	0.0649	0.0679	0.0710
11	0.0244	0.0265	0.0285	0.0307	0.0330	0.0353	0.0377	0.0401	0.0426	0.0452
12	0.0124	0.0137	0.0150	0.0164	0.0179	0.0194	0.0210	0.0227	0.0245	0.0263
13	0.0058	0.0065	0.0073	0.0081	0.0089	0.0099	0.0108	0.0119	0.0130	0.0142
14	0.0025	0.0029	0.0033	0.0037	0.0041	0.0046	0.0052	0.0058	0.0064	0.0071
15	0.0010	0.0012	0.0014	0.0016	0.0018	0.0020	0.0023	0.0026	0.0029	0.0033
16	0.0004	0.0005	0.0005	0.0006	0.0007	0.0008	0.0010	0.0011	0.0013	0.0014
17	0.0001	0.0002	0.0002	0.0002	0.0003	0.0003	0.0004	0.0004	0.0005	0.0006
18	0.0000	0.0001	0.0001	0.0001	0.0001	0.0001	0.0001	0.0002	0.0002	0.0002
19	0.0000	0.0000	0.0000	0.0000	0.0000	0.0000	0.0001	0.0001	0.0001	0.0001

x	μ 7.1	7.2	7.3	7.4	7.5	7.6	7.7	7.8	7.9	8.0
0	0.0008	0.0007	0.0007	0.0006	0.0006	0.0005	0.0005	0.0004	0.0004	0.0003
1	0.0059	0.0054	0.0049	0.0045	0.0041	0.0038	0.0035	0.0032	0.0029	0.0027
2	0.0208	0.0194	0.0180	0.0167	0.0156	0.0145	0.0134	0.0125	0.0116	0.0107
3	0.0492	0.0464	0.0438	0.0413	0.0389	0.0366	0.0345	0.0324	0.0305	0.0286
4	0.0874	0.0836	0.0799	0.0764	0.0729	0.0696	0.0663	0.0632	0.0602	0.0573
5	0.1241	0.1204	0.1167	0.1130	0.1094	0.1057	0.1021	0.0986	0.0951	0.0916
6	0.1468	0.1445	0.1420	0.1394	0.1367	0.1339	0.1311	0.1282	0.1252	0.1221
7	0.1489	0.1486	0.1481	0.1474	0.1465	0.1454	0.1442	0.1428	0.1413	0.1396
8	0.1321	0.1337	0.1351	0.1363	0.1373	0.1381	0.1388	0.1392	0.1395	0.1396
9	0.1042	0.1070	0.1096	0.1121	0.1144	0.1167	0.1187	0.1207	0.1224	0.1241
10	0.0740	0.0770	0.0800	0.0829	0.0858	0.0887	0.0914	0.0941	0.0967	0.0993
11	0.0478	0.0504	0.0531	0.0558	0.0585	0.0613	0.0640	0.0667	0.0695	0.0722
12	0.0283	0.0303	0.0323	0.0344	0.0366	0.0388	0.0411	0.0434	0.0457	0.0481
13	0.0154	0.0168	0.0181	0.0196	0.0211	0.0227	0.0243	0.0260	0.0278	0.0296
14	0.0078	0.0086	0.0095	0.0104	0.0113	0.0123	0.0134	0.0145	0.0157	0.0169

Table D Poisson Distribution (*continued*)

x	μ 7.1	7.2	7.3	7.4	7.5	7.6	7.7	7.8	7.9	8.0
15	0.0037	0.0041	0.0046	0.0051	0.0057	0.0062	0.0069	0.0075	0.0083	0.0090
16	0.0016	0.0019	0.0021	0.0024	0.0026	0.0030	0.0033	0.0037	0.0041	0.0045
17	0.0007	0.0008	0.0009	0.0010	0.0012	0.0013	0.0015	0.0017	0.0019	0.0021
18	0.0003	0.0003	0.0004	0.0004	0.0005	0.0006	0.0006	0.0007	0.0008	0.0009
19	0.0001	0.0001	0.0001	0.0002	0.0002	0.0002	0.0003	0.0003	0.0003	0.0004
20	0.0000	0.0000	0.0001	0.0001	0.0001	0.0001	0.0001	0.0001	0.0001	0.0002
21	0.0000	0.0000	0.0000	0.0000	0.0000	0.0000	0.0000	0.0000	0.0001	0.0001

x	μ 8.1	8.2	8.3	8.4	8.5	8.6	8.7	8.8	8.9	9.0
0	0.0003	0.0003	0.0002	0.0002	0.0002	0.0002	0.0002	0.0002	0.0001	0.0001
1	0.0025	0.0023	0.0021	0.0019	0.0017	0.0016	0.0014	0.0013	0.0012	0.0011
2	0.0100	0.0092	0.0086	0.0079	0.0074	0.0068	0.0063	0.0058	0.0054	0.0050
3	0.0269	0.0252	0.0237	0.0222	0.0208	0.0195	0.0183	0.0171	0.0160	0.0150
4	0.0544	0.0517	0.0491	0.0466	0.0443	0.0420	0.0398	0.0377	0.0357	0.0337
5	0.0882	0.0849	0.0816	0.0784	0.0752	0.0722	0.0692	0.0663	0.0635	0.0607
6	0.1191	0.1160	0.1128	0.1097	0.1066	0.1034	0.1003	0.0972	0.0941	0.0911
7	0.1378	0.1358	0.1338	0.1317	0.1294	0.1271	0.1247	0.1222	0.1197	0.1171
8	0.1395	0.1392	0.1388	0.1382	0.1375	0.1366	0.1356	0.1344	0.1332	0.1318
9	0.1256	0.1269	0.1280	0.1290	0.1299	0.1306	0.1311	0.1315	0.1317	0.1318
10	0.1017	0.1040	0.1063	0.1084	0.1104	0.1123	0.1140	0.1157	0.1172	0.1186
11	0.0749	0.0776	0.0802	0.0828	0.0853	0.0878	0.0902	0.0925	0.0948	0.0970
12	0.0505	0.0530	0.0555	0.0579	0.0604	0.0629	0.0654	0.0679	0.0703	0.0728
13	0.0315	0.0334	0.0354	0.0374	0.0395	0.0416	0.0438	0.0459	0.0481	0.0504
14	0.0182	0.0196	0.0210	0.0225	0.0240	0.0256	0.0272	0.0289	0.0306	0.0324
15	0.0098	0.0107	0.0116	0.0126	0.0136	0.0147	0.0158	0.0169	0.0182	0.0194
16	0.0050	0.0055	0.0060	0.0066	0.0072	0.0079	0.0086	0.0093	0.0101	0.0109
17	0.0024	0.0026	0.0029	0.0033	0.0036	0.0040	0.0044	0.0048	0.0053	0.0058
18	0.0011	0.0012	0.0014	0.0015	0.0017	0.0019	0.0021	0.0024	0.0026	0.0029
19	0.0005	0.0005	0.0006	0.0007	0.0008	0.0009	0.0010	0.0011	0.0012	0.0014
20	0.0002	0.0002	0.0002	0.0003	0.0003	0.0004	0.0004	0.0005	0.0005	0.0006
21	0.0001	0.0001	0.0001	0.0001	0.0001	0.0002	0.0002	0.0002	0.0002	0.0003
22	0.0000	0.0000	0.0000	0.0000	0.0001	0.0001	0.0001	0.0001	0.0001	0.0001

x	μ 9.1	9.2	9.3	9.4	9.5	9.6	9.7	9.8	9.9	10.0
0	0.0001	0.0001	0.0001	0.0001	0.0001	0.0001	0.0001	0.0001	0.0001	0.0000
1	0.0010	0.0009	0.0009	0.0008	0.0007	0.0007	0.0006	0.0005	0.0005	0.0005
2	0.0046	0.0043	0.0040	0.0037	0.0034	0.0031	0.0029	0.0027	0.0025	0.0023
3	0.0140	0.0131	0.0123	0.0115	0.0107	0.0100	0.0093	0.0087	0.0081	0.0076
4	0.0319	0.0302	0.0285	0.0269	0.0254	0.0240	0.0226	0.0213	0.0201	0.0189
5	0.0581	0.0555	0.0530	0.0506	0.0483	0.0460	0.0439	0.0418	0.0398	0.0378
6	0.0881	0.0851	0.0822	0.0793	0.0764	0.0736	0.0709	0.0682	0.0656	0.0631
7	0.1145	0.1118	0.1091	0.1064	0.1037	0.1010	0.0982	0.0955	0.0928	0.0901

Table D Poisson Distribution (*continued*)

	μ									
x	9.1	9.2	9.3	9.4	9.5	9.6	9.7	9.8	9.9	10.0
8	0.1302	0.1286	0.1269	0.1251	0.1232	0.1212	0.1191	0.1170	0.1148	0.1126
9	0.1317	0.1315	0.1311	0.1306	0.1300	0.1293	0.1284	0.1274	0.1263	0.1251
10	0.1198	0.1210	0.1219	0.1228	0.1235	0.1241	0.1245	0.1249	0.1250	0.1251
11	0.0991	0.1012	0.1031	0.1049	0.1067	0.1083	0.1098	0.1112	0.1125	0.1137
12	0.0752	0.0776	0.0799	0.0822	0.0844	0.0866	0.0888	0.0908	0.0928	0.0948
13	0.0526	0.0549	0.0572	0.0594	0.0617	0.0640	0.0662	0.0685	0.0707	0.0729
14	0.0342	0.0361	0.0380	0.0399	0.0419	0.0439	0.0459	0.0479	0.0500	0.0521
15	0.0208	0.0221	0.0235	0.0250	0.0265	0.0281	0.0297	0.0313	0.0330	0.0347
16	0.0118	0.0127	0.0137	0.0147	0.0157	0.0168	0.0180	0.0192	0.0204	0.0217
17	0.0063	0.0069	0.0075	0.0081	0.0088	0.0095	0.0103	0.0111	0.0119	0.0128
18	0.0032	0.0035	0.0039	0.0042	0.0046	0.0051	0.0055	0.0060	0.0065	0.0071
19	0.0015	0.0017	0.0019	0.0021	0.0023	0.0026	0.0028	0.0031	0.0034	0.0037
20	0.0007	0.0008	0.0009	0.0010	0.0011	0.0012	0.0014	0.0015	0.0017	0.0019
21	0.0003	0.0003	0.0004	0.0004	0.0005	0.0006	0.0006	0.0007	0.0008	0.0009
22	0.0001	0.0001	0.0002	0.0002	0.0002	0.0002	0.0003	0.0003	0.0004	0.0004
23	0.0000	0.0001	0.0001	0.0001	0.0001	0.0001	0.0001	0.0001	0.0002	0.0002
24	0.0000	0.0000	0.0000	0.0000	0.0000	0.0000	0.0000	0.0001	0.0001	0.0001

	μ									
x	11	12	13	14	15	16	17	18	19	20
0	0.0000	0.0000	0.0000	0.0000	0.0000	0.0000	0.0000	0.0000	0.0000	0.0000
1	0.0002	0.0001	0.0000	0.0000	0.0000	0.0000	0.0000	0.0000	0.0000	0.0000
2	0.0010	0.0004	0.0002	0.0001	0.0000	0.0000	0.0000	0.0000	0.0000	0.0000
3	0.0037	0.0018	0.0008	0.0004	0.0002	0.0001	0.0000	0.0000	0.0000	0.0000
4	0.0102	0.0053	0.0027	0.0013	0.0006	0.0003	0.0001	0.0001	0.0000	0.0000
5	0.0224	0.0127	0.0070	0.0037	0.0019	0.0010	0.0005	0.0002	0.0001	0.0001
6	0.0411	0.0255	0.0152	0.0087	0.0048	0.0026	0.0014	0.0007	0.0004	0.0002
7	0.0646	0.0437	0.0281	0.0174	0.0104	0.0060	0.0034	0.0019	0.0010	0.0005
8	0.0888	0.0655	0.0457	0.0304	0.0194	0.0120	0.0072	0.0042	0.0024	0.0013
9	0.1085	0.0874	0.0661	0.0473	0.0324	0.0213	0.0135	0.0083	0.0050	0.0029
10	0.1194	0.1048	0.0859	0.0663	0.0486	0.0341	0.0230	0.0150	0.0095	0.0058
11	0.1194	0.1144	0.1015	0.0844	0.0663	0.0496	0.0355	0.0245	0.0164	0.0106
12	0.1094	0.1144	0.1099	0.0984	0.0829	0.0661	0.0504	0.0368	0.0259	0.0176
13	0.0926	0.1056	0.1099	0.1060	0.0956	0.0814	0.0658	0.0509	0.0378	0.0271
14	0.0728	0.0905	0.1021	0.1060	0.1024	0.0930	0.0800	0.0655	0.0514	0.0387
15	0.0534	0.0724	0.0885	0.0989	0.1024	0.0992	0.0906	0.0786	0.0650	0.0516
16	0.0367	0.0543	0.0719	0.0866	0.0960	0.0992	0.0963	0.0884	0.0772	0.0646
17	0.0237	0.0383	0.0550	0.0713	0.0847	0.0934	0.0963	0.0936	0.0863	0.0760
18	0.0145	0.0255	0.0397	0.0554	0.0706	0.0830	0.0909	0.0936	0.0911	0.0844
19	0.0084	0.0161	0.0272	0.0409	0.0557	0.0699	0.0814	0.0887	0.0911	0.0888
20	0.0046	0.0097	0.0177	0.0286	0.0418	0.0559	0.0692	0.0798	0.0866	0.0888
21	0.0024	0.0055	0.0109	0.0191	0.0299	0.0426	0.0560	0.0684	0.0783	0.0846
22	0.0012	0.0030	0.0065	0.0121	0.0204	0.0310	0.0433	0.0560	0.0676	0.0769
23	0.0006	0.0016	0.0037	0.0074	0.0133	0.0216	0.0320	0.0438	0.0559	0.0669

Table D Poisson Distribution (*continued*)

	μ									
x	11	12	13	14	15	16	17	18	19	20
24	0.0003	0.0008	0.0020	0.0043	0.0083	0.0144	0.0226	0.0328	0.0442	0.0557
25	0.0001	0.0004	0.0010	0.0024	0.0050	0.0092	0.0154	0.0237	0.0336	0.0446
26	0.0000	0.0002	0.0005	0.0013	0.0029	0.0057	0.0101	0.0164	0.0246	0.0343
27	0.0000	0.0001	0.0002	0.0007	0.0016	0.0034	0.0063	0.0109	0.0173	0.0254
28	0.0000	0.0000	0.0001	0.0003	0.0009	0.0019	0.0038	0.0070	0.0117	0.0181
29	0.0000	0.0000	0.0001	0.0002	0.0004	0.0011	0.0023	0.0044	0.0077	0.0125
30	0.0000	0.0000	0.0000	0.0001	0.0002	0.0006	0.0013	0.0026	0.0049	0.0083
31	0.0000	0.0000	0.0000	0.0000	0.0001	0.0003	0.0007	0.0015	0.0030	0.0054
32	0.0000	0.0000	0.0000	0.0000	0.0001	0.0001	0.0004	0.0009	0.0018	0.0034
33	0.0000	0.0000	0.0000	0.0000	0.0000	0.0001	0.0002	0.0005	0.0010	0.0020
34	0.0000	0.0000	0.0000	0.0000	0.0000	0.0000	0.0001	0.0002	0.0006	0.0012
35	0.0000	0.0000	0.0000	0.0000	0.0000	0.0000	0.0000	0.0001	0.0003	0.0007
36	0.0000	0.0000	0.0000	0.0000	0.0000	0.0000	0.0000	0.0001	0.0002	0.0004
37	0.0000	0.0000	0.0000	0.0000	0.0000	0.0000	0.0000	0.0000	0.0001	0.0002
38	0.0000	0.0000	0.0000	0.0000	0.0000	0.0000	0.0000	0.0000	0.0000	0.0001
39	0.0000	0.0000	0.0000	0.0000	0.0000	0.0000	0.0000	0.0000	0.0000	0.0001

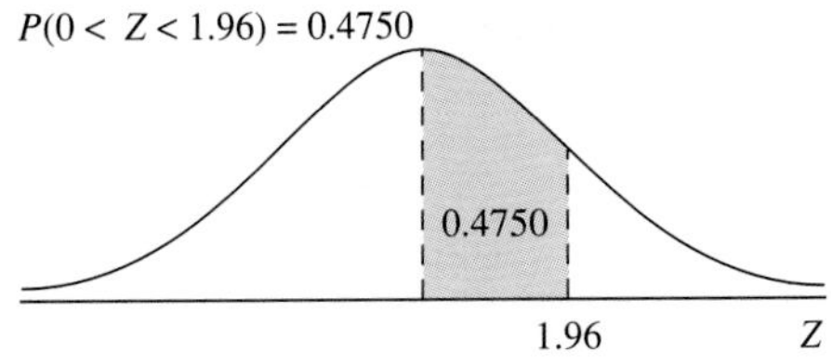

Table E The Normal Distribution

Z	0.00	0.01	0.02	0.03	0.04	0.05	0.06	0.07	0.08	0.09
0.0	0.0000	0.0040	0.0080	0.0120	0.0160	0.0199	0.0239	0.0279	0.0319	0.0359
0.1	0.0398	0.0438	0.0478	0.0517	0.0557	0.0596	0.0636	0.0675	0.0714	0.0753
0.2	0.0793	0.0832	0.0871	0.0910	0.0948	0.0987	0.1026	0.1064	0.1103	0.1141
0.3	0.1179	0.1217	0.1255	0.1293	0.1331	0.1368	0.1406	0.1443	0.1480	0.1517
0.4	0.1554	0.1591	0.1628	0.1664	0.1700	0.1736	0.1772	0.1808	0.1844	0.1879
0.5	0.1915	0.1950	0.1985	0.2019	0.2054	0.2088	0.2123	0.2157	0.2190	0.2224
0.6	0.2257	0.2291	0.2324	0.2357	0.2389	0.2422	0.2454	0.2486	0.2517	0.2549
0.7	0.2580	0.2611	0.2642	0.2673	0.2704	0.2734	0.2764	0.2794	0.2823	0.2852
0.8	0.2881	0.2910	0.2939	0.2967	0.2995	0.3023	0.3051	0.3078	0.3106	0.3133
0.9	0.3159	0.3186	0.3212	0.3238	0.3264	0.3289	0.3315	0.3340	0.3365	0.3389
1.0	0.3413	0.3438	0.3461	0.3485	0.3508	0.3531	0.3554	0.3577	0.3599	0.3621
1.1	0.3643	0.3665	0.3686	0.3708	0.3729	0.3749	0.3770	0.3790	0.3810	0.3830
1.2	0.3849	0.3869	0.3888	0.3907	0.3925	0.3944	0.3962	0.3980	0.3997	0.4015
1.3	0.4032	0.4049	0.4066	0.4082	0.4099	0.4115	0.4131	0.4147	0.4162	0.4177
1.4	0.4192	0.4207	0.4222	0.4236	0.4251	0.4265	0.4279	0.4292	0.4306	0.4319
1.5	0.4332	0.4345	0.4357	0.4370	0.4382	0.4394	0.4406	0.4418	0.4429	0.4441
1.6	0.4452	0.4463	0.4474	0.4484	0.4495	0.4505	0.4515	0.4525	0.4535	0.4545
1.7	0.4554	0.4564	0.4573	0.4582	0.4591	0.4599	0.4608	0.4616	0.4625	0.4633
1.8	0.4641	0.4649	0.4656	0.4664	0.4671	0.4678	0.4686	0.4693	0.4699	0.4706
1.9	0.4713	0.4719	0.4726	0.4732	0.4738	0.4744	**0.4750**	0.4756	0.4761	0.4767
2.0	0.4772	0.4778	0.4783	0.4788	0.4793	0.4798	0.4803	0.4808	0.4812	0.4817
2.1	0.4821	0.4826	0.4830	0.4834	0.4838	0.4842	0.4846	0.4850	0.4854	0.4857
2.2	0.4861	0.4864	0.4868	0.4871	0.4875	0.4878	0.4881	0.4884	0.4887	0.4890
2.3	0.4893	0.4896	0.4898	0.4901	0.4904	0.4906	0.4909	0.4911	0.4913	0.4916
2.4	0.4918	0.4920	0.4922	0.4925	0.4927	0.4929	0.4931	0.4932	0.4934	0.4936
2.5	0.4938	0.4940	0.4941	0.4943	0.4945	0.4946	0.4948	0.4949	0.4951	0.4952
2.6	0.4953	0.4955	0.4956	0.4957	0.4959	0.4960	0.4961	0.4962	0.4963	0.4964
2.7	0.4965	0.4966	0.4967	0.4968	0.4969	0.4970	0.4971	0.4972	0.4973	0.4974
2.8	0.4974	0.4975	0.4976	0.4977	0.4977	0.4978	0.4979	0.4979	0.4980	0.4981
2.9	0.4981	0.4982	0.4982	0.4983	0.4984	0.4984	0.4985	0.4985	0.4986	0.4986
3.0	0.4987	0.4987	0.4987	0.4988	0.4988	0.4989	0.4989	0.4989	0.4990	0.4990
3.1	0.4990	0.4991	0.4991	0.4991	0.4992	0.4992	0.4992	0.4992	0.4993	0.4993
3.2	0.4993	0.4993	0.4994	0.4994	0.4994	0.4994	0.4994	0.4995	0.4995	0.4995
3.3	0.4995	0.4995	0.4995	0.4996	0.4996	0.4996	0.4996	0.4996	0.4996	0.4997
3.4	0.4997	0.4997	0.4997	0.4997	0.4997	0.4997	0.4997	0.4997	0.4997	0.4998
3.5	0.4998	0.4998	0.4998	0.4998	0.4998	0.4998	0.4998	0.4998	0.4998	0.4498
3.6	0.4998	0.4998	0.4999	0.4999	0.4999	0.4999	0.4999	0.4999	0.4999	0.4999
3.7	0.4999	0.4999	0.4999	0.4999	0.4999	0.4999	0.4999	0.4999	0.4999	0.4999
3.8	0.4999	0.4999	0.4999	0.4999	0.4999	0.4999	0.4999	0.4999	0.4999	0.4999
3.9	0.5000	0.5000	0.5000	0.5000	0.5000	0.5000	0.5000	0.5000	0.5000	0.5000

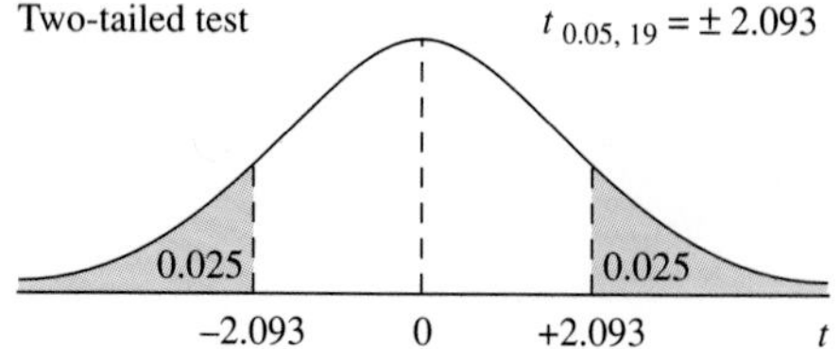

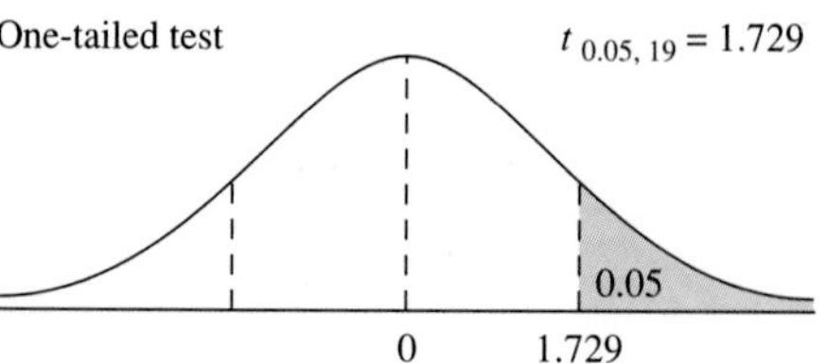

Table F The *t*-Distribution

	0.900	0.700	0.500	0.300	0.200	0.100	0.050	0.020	0.010	α value	Two-tailed test
	0.100	0.300	0.500	0.700	0.800	0.900	0.950	0.980	0.990	CL	
	0.450	0.350	0.250	0.150	0.100	0.050	0.025	0.010	0.005	α value	One-tailed test
	0.550	0.650	0.750	0.850	0.900	0.950	0.975	0.990	0.995	CL	
d.f.	**Values of *t***										
1	0.158	0.510	1.000	1.963	3.078	6.314	12.706	31.821	63.657		
2	0.142	0.445	0.816	1.386	1.886	2.920	4.303	6.965	9.925		
3	0.137	0.424	0.765	1.250	1.638	2.353	3.182	4.541	5.841		
4	0.134	0.414	0.741	1.190	1.533	2.132	2.776	3.747	4.604		
5	0.132	0.408	0.727	1.156	1.476	2.015	2.571	3.365	4.032		
6	0.131	0.404	0.718	1.134	1.440	1.943	2.447	3.143	3.707		
7	0.130	0.402	0.711	1.119	1.415	1.895	2.365	2.998	3.499		
8	0.130	0.399	0.706	1.108	1.397	1.860	2.306	2.896	3.355		
9	0.129	0.398	0.703	1.100	1.383	1.833	2.262	2.821	3.250		
10	0.129	0.397	0.700	1.093	1.372	1.812	2.228	2.764	3.169		
11	0.129	0.396	0.697	1.088	1.363	1.796	2.201	2.718	3.106		
12	0.128	0.395	0.695	1.083	1.356	1.782	2.179	2.681	3.055		
13	0.128	0.394	0.694	1.079	1.350	1.771	2.160	2.650	3.012		
14	0.128	0.393	0.692	1.076	1.345	1.761	2.145	2.624	2.977		
15	0.128	0.393	0.691	1.074	1.341	1.753	2.131	2.602	2.947		
16	0.128	0.392	0.690	1.071	1.337	1.746	2.120	2.583	2.921		
17	0.128	0.392	0.689	1.069	1.333	1.740	2.110	2.567	2.898		
18	0.127	0.392	0.688	1.067	1.330	1.734	2.101	2.552	2.878		
19	0.127	0.391	0.688	1.066	1.328	**1.729**	**2.093**	2.539	2.861		
20	0.127	0.391	0.687	1.064	1.325	1.725	2.086	2.528	2.845		
21	0.127	0.391	0.686	1.063	1.323	1.721	2.080	2.518	2.831		
22	0.127	0.390	0.686	1.061	1.321	1.717	2.074	2.508	2.819		
23	0.127	0.390	0.685	1.060	1.319	1.714	2.069	2.500	2.807		
24	0.127	0.390	0.685	1.059	1.318	1.711	2.064	2.492	2.797		
25	0.127	0.390	0.684	1.058	1.316	1.708	2.060	2.485	2.787		
26	0.127	0.390	0.684	1.058	1.315	1.706	2.056	2.479	2.779		
27	0.127	0.389	0.684	1.057	1.314	1.703	2.052	2.473	2.771		
28	0.127	0.389	0.683	1.056	1.313	1.701	2.048	2.467	2.763		
29	0.127	0.389	0.683	1.055	1.311	1.699	2.045	2.462	2.756		
30	0.127	0.389	0.683	1.055	1.310	1.697	2.042	2.457	2.750		
40	0.126	0.388	0.681	1.050	1.303	1.684	2.021	2.423	2.704		
60	0.126	0.387	0.679	1.045	1.296	1.671	2.000	2.390	2.660		
120	0.126	0.386	0.677	1.041	1.289	1.658	1.980	2.358	2.617		
∞	0.126	0.385	0.674	1.036	1.282	1.645	1.960	2.326	2.576		

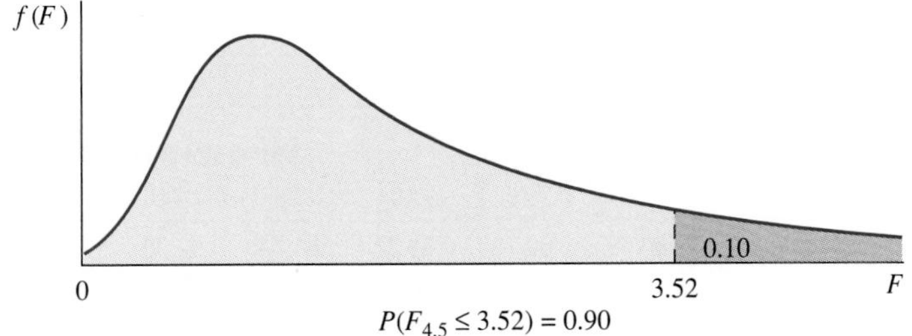

$P(F_{4,5} \le 3.52) = 0.90$

Table G The F-Distribution

$F_{0.90}$; $\alpha = 0.10$

Denominator Degrees of Freedom	Numerator Degrees of Freedom 1	2	3	4	5	6	7	8	9
1	39.86	49.50	53.59	55.83	57.24	58.20	58.91	59.44	59.86
2	8.53	9.00	9.16	9.24	9.29	9.33	9.35	9.37	9.38
3	5.54	5.46	5.39	5.34	5.31	5.28	5.27	5.25	5.24
4	4.54	4.32	4.19	4.11	4.05	4.01	3.98	3.95	3.94
5	4.06	3.78	3.62	3.52	3.45	3.40	3.37	3.34	3.32
6	3.78	3.46	3.29	3.18	3.11	3.05	3.01	2.98	2.96
7	3.59	3.26	3.07	2.96	2.88	2.83	2.78	2.75	2.72
8	3.46	3.11	2.92	2.81	2.73	2.67	2.62	2.59	2.56
9	3.36	3.01	2.81	2.69	2.61	2.55	2.51	2.47	2.44
10	3.29	2.92	2.13	2.61	2.52	2.46	2.41	2.38	2.35
11	3.23	2.86	2.66	2.54	2.45	2.39	2.34	2.30	2.27
12	3.18	2.81	2.61	2.48	2.39	2.33	2.28	2.24	2.21
13	3.14	2.76	2.56	2.43	2.35	2.28	2.23	2.20	2.16
14	3.10	2.73	2.52	2.39	2.31	2.24	2.19	2.15	2.12
15	3.07	2.70	2.49	2.36	2.27	2.21	2.16	2.12	2.09
16	3.05	2.67	2.46	2.33	2.24	2.18	2.13	2.09	2.06
17	3.03	2.64	2.44	2.31	2.22	2.15	2.10	2.06	2.03
18	3.01	2.62	2.42	2.29	2.20	2.13	2.08	2.04	2.00
19	2.99	2.61	2.40	2.27	2.18	2.11	2.06	2.02	1.98
20	2.97	2.59	2.38	2.25	2.16	2.09	2.04	2.00	1.96
21	2.96	2.57	2.36	2.23	2.14	2.08	2.02	1.98	1.95
22	2.95	2.56	2.35	2.22	2.13	2.06	2.01	1.97	1.93
23	2.94	2.55	2.34	2.21	2.11	2.05	1.99	1.95	1.92
24	2.93	2.54	2.33	2.19	2.10	2.04	1.98	1.94	1.91
25	2.92	2.53	2.32	2.18	2.09	2.02	1.97	1.93	1.89
26	2.91	2.52	2.31	2.17	2.08	2.01	1.96	1.92	1.88
27	2.90	2.51	2.30	2.17	2.07	2.00	1.95	1.91	1.87
28	2.89	2.50	2.29	2.16	2.06	2.00	1.94	1.90	1.87
29	2.89	2.50	2.28	2.15	2.06	1.99	1.93	1.89	1.86
30	2.88	2.49	2.28	2.14	2.05	1.98	1.93	1.88	1.85
40	2.84	2.44	2.23	2.09	2.00	1.93	1.87	1.83	1.79
60	2.79	2.39	2.18	2.04	1.95	1.87	1.82	1.77	1.74
120	2.75	2.35	2.13	1.99	1.90	1.82	1.77	1.72	1.68
∞	2.71	2.30	2.08	1.95	1.85	1.77	1.72	1.67	1.63

Table G The *F*-Distribution (*continued*)

	$F_{0.90}$; $\alpha = 0.10$									
Denominator Degrees of Freedom	Numerator Degrees of Freedom									
	10	12	15	20	24	30	40	60	120	∞
1	60.19	60.71	61.22	61.74	62.00	62.26	62.53	62.79	63.06	63.33
2	9.39	9.41	9.42	9.44	9.45	9.46	9.47	9.47	9.48	9.49
3	5.23	5.22	5.20	5.18	5.18	5.17	5.16	5.15	5.14	5.13
4	3.92	3.90	3.87	3.84	3.83	3.82	3.80	3.79	3.78	3.76
5	3.30	3.27	3.24	3.21	3.19	3.17	3.16	3.14	3.12	3.11
6	2.94	2.90	2.87	2.84	2.82	2.80	2.78	2.76	2.74	2.72
7	2.70	2.67	2.63	2.59	2.58	2.56	2.54	2.51	2.49	2.47
8	2.54	2.50	2.46	2.42	2.40	2.38	2.36	2.34	2.32	2.29
9	2.42	2.38	2.34	2.30	2.28	2.25	2.23	2.21	2.18	2.16
10	2.32	2.28	2.24	2.20	2.18	2.16	2.13	2.11	2.08	2.06
11	2.25	2.21	2.17	2.12	2.10	2.08	2.05	2.03	2.00	1.97
12	2.19	2.15	2.10	2.06	2.04	2.01	1.99	1.96	1.93	1.90
13	2.14	2.10	2.05	2.01	1.98	1.96	1.93	1.90	1.88	1.85
14	2.10	2.05	2.01	1.96	1.94	1.91	1.89	1.86	1.83	1.80
15	2.06	2.02	1.97	1.92	1.90	1.87	1.85	1.82	1.79	1.76
16	2.03	1.99	1.94	1.89	1.87	1.84	1.81	1.78	1.75	1.72
17	2.00	1.96	1.91	1.86	1.84	1.81	1.78	1.75	1.72	1.69
18	1.98	1.93	1.89	1.84	1.81	1.78	1.75	1.72	1.69	1.66
19	1.96	1.91	1.86	1.81	1.79	1.76	1.73	1.70	1.67	1.63
20	1.94	1.89	1.84	1.79	1.77	1.74	1.71	1.68	1.64	1.61
21	1.92	1.87	1.83	1.78	1.75	1.72	1.69	1.66	1.62	1.59
22	1.90	1.86	1.81	1.76	1.73	1.70	1.67	1.64	1.60	1.57
23	1.89	1.84	1.80	1.74	1.72	1.69	1.66	1.62	1.59	1.55
24	1.88	1.83	1.78	1.73	1.70	1.67	1.64	1.61	1.57	1.53
25	1.87	1.82	1.77	1.72	1.69	1.66	1.63	1.59	1.56	1.52
26	1.86	1.81	1.76	1.71	1.68	1.65	1.61	1.58	1.54	1..50
27	1.85	1.80	1.75	1.70	1.67	1.64	1.60	1.57	1.53	1.49
28	1.84	1.79	1.74	1.69	1.66	1.63	1.59	1.56	1.52	1.48
29	1.83	1.78	1.73	1.68	1.65	1.62	1.58	1.55	1.51	1.47
30	1.82	1.77	1.72	1.67	1.64	1.61	1.57	1.54	1.50	1.46
40	1.76	1.71	1.66	1.61	1.57	1.54	1.51	1.47	1.42	1.38
60	1.71	1.66	1.60	1.54	1.51	1.48	1.44	1.40	1.35	1.29
120	1.65	1.60	1.55	1.48	1.45	1.41	1.37	1.32	1.26	1.19
∞	1.60	1.55	1.49	1.42	1.38	1.34	1.30	1.24	1.17	1.00

	$F_{0.95}$; $\alpha = 0.05$								
Denominator Degrees of Freedom	Numerator Degrees of Freedom								
	1	2	3	4	5	6	7	8	9
1	161.45	199.50	215.71	224.58	230.16	233.99	236.77	238.88	240.54
2	18.51	19.00	19.16	19.25	19.30	19.33	19.35	19.37	19.38
3	10.13	9.55	9.28	9.12	9.01	8.94	8.89	8.85	8.81
4	7.71	6.94	6.59	6.39	6.26	6.16	6.09	6.04	6.00

Table G The *F*-Distribution (*continued*)

$F_{0.95}$; $\alpha = 0.05$

Denominator Degrees of Freedom	Numerator Degrees of Freedom 1	2	3	4	5	6	7	8	9
5	6.61	5.79	5.41	5.19	5.05	4.95	4.88	4.82	4.77
6	5.99	5.14	4.76	4.53	4.39	4.28	4.21	4.15	4.10
7	5.59	4.74	4.35	4.12	3.97	3.87	3.79	3.73	3.68
8	5.32	4.46	4.07	3.84	3.69	3.58	3.50	3.44	3.39
9	5.12	4.26	3.86	3.63	3.48	3.37	3.29	3.23	3.18
10	4.96	4.10	3.71	3.48	3.33	3.22	3.14	3.07	3.02
11	4.84	3.98	3.59	3.36	3.20	3.09	3.01	2.95	2.90
12	4.75	3.89	3.49	3.26	3.11	3.00	2.91	2.85	2.80
13	4.67	3.81	3.41	3.18	3.03	2.92	2.83	2.77	2.71
14	4.60	3.74	3.34	3.11	2.96	2.85	2.76	2.70	2.65
15	4.54	3.68	3.29	3.06	2.90	2.79	2.71	2.64	2.59
16	4.49	3.63	3.24	3.01	2.85	2.74	2.66	2.59	2.54
17	4.45	3.59	3.20	2.96	2.81	2.70	2.61	2.55	2.49
18	4.41	3.55	3.16	2.93	2.77	2.66	2.58	2.51	2.46
19	4.38	3.52	3.13	2.90	2.74	2.63	2.54	2.48	2.42
20	4.35	3.49	3.10	2.87	2.71	2.60	2.51	2.45	2.39
21	4.32	3.47	3.07	2.84	2.68	2.57	2.49	2.42	2.37
22	4.30	3.44	3.05	2.82	2.66	2.55	2.46	2.40	2.34
23	4.28	3.42	3.03	2.80	2.64	2.53	2.44	2.37	2.32
24	4.26	3.40	3.01	2.78	2.62	2.51	2.42	2.36	2.30
25	4.24	3.39	2.99	2.76	2.60	2.49	2.40	2.34	2.28
26	4.23	3.37	2.98	2.74	2.59	2.47	2.39	2.32	2.27
27	4.21	3.35	2.96	2.73	2.57	2.46	2.37	2.31	2.25
28	4.20	3.34	2.95	2.71	2.56	2.45	2.36	2.29	2.24
29	4.18	3.33	2.93	2.70	2.55	2.43	2.35	2.28	2.22
30	4.17	3.32	2.92	2.69	2.53	2.42	2.33	2.27	2.21
40	4.08	3.23	2.84	2.61	2.45	2.34	2.25	2.18	2.12
60	4.00	3.15	2.76	2.53	2.37	2.25	2.17	2.10	2.04
120	3.92	3.07	2.68	2.45	2.29	2.18	2.09	2.02	1.96
∞	3.84	3.00	2.61	2.37	2.21	2.10	2.01	1.94	1.88

$F_{0.95}$; $\alpha = 0.05$

Denominator Degrees of Freedom	Numerator Degrees of Freedom 10	12	15	20	24	30	40	60	120	∞
1	241.88	243.91	245.95	248.01	249.05	250.10	251.14	252.20	253.25	254.31
2	19.40	19.41	19.43	19.45	19.45	19.46	19.47	19.48	19.49	19.50
3	8.79	8.74	8.70	8.66	8.64	8.62	8.59	8.57	8.55	8..53
4	5.96	5.91	5.86	5.80	5.77	5.75	5.72	5.69	5.66	5.63
5	4.74	4.68	4.62	4.56	4.53	4.50	4.46	4.43	4.40	4.37
6	4.06	4.00	3.94	3.87	3.84	3.81	3.77	3.74	3.70	3.67
7	3.64	3.57	3.51	3.44	3.41	3.38	3.34	3.30	3.27	3.23
8	3.35	3.28	3.22	3.15	3.12	3.08	3.04	3.01	2.97	2.93
9	3.14	3.07	3.01	2.94	2.90	2.86	2.83	2.79	2.75	2.71

Table G The *F*-Distribution (*continued*)

$F_{0.95}$; $\alpha = 0.05$

Denominator Degrees of Freedom	Numerator Degrees of Freedom									
	10	12	15	20	24	30	40	60	120	∞
10	2.98	2.91	2.85	2.77	2.74	2.70	2.66	2.62	2.58	2.54
11	2.85	2.79	2.72	2.65	2.61	2.57	2.53	2.49	2.45	2.40
12	2.75	2.69	2.62	2.54	2.51	2.47	2.43	2.38	2.34	2.30
13	2.67	2.60	2.53	2.46	2.42	2.38	2.34	2.30	2.25	2.21
14	2.60	2.53	2.46	2.39	2.35	2.31	2.27	2.22	2.18	2.13
15	2.54	2.48	2.40	2.33	2.29	2.25	2.20	2.16	2.11	2.07
16	2.49	2.42	2.35	2.28	2.24	2.19	2.15	2.11	2.06	2.01
17	2.45	2.38	2.31	2.23	2.19	2.15	2.10	2.06	2.01	1.96
18	2.41	2.34	2.27	2.19	2.15	2.11	2.06	2.02	1.97	1.92
19	2.38	2.31	2.23	2.16	2.11	2.07	2.03	1.98	1.93	1.88
20	2.35	2.28	2.20	2.12	2.08	2.04	1.99	1.95	1.90	1.84
21	2.32	2.25	2.18	2.10	2.05	2.01	1.96	1.92	1.87	1.81
22	2.30	2.23	2.15	2.07	2.03	1.98	1.94	1.89	1.84	1.78
23	2.27	2.20	2.13	2.05	2.01	1.96	1.91	1.86	1.81	1.76
24	2.25	2.18	2.11	2.03	1.98	1.94	1.89	1.84	1.79	1.73
25	2.24	2.16	2.09	2.01	1.96	1.92	1.87	1.82	1.77	1.71
26	2.22	2.15	2.07	1.99	1.95	1.90	1.85	1.80	1.75	1.69
27	2.20	2.13	2.06	1.97	1.93	1.88	1.84	1.79	1.73	1.67
28	2.19	2.12	2.04	1.96	1.91	1.87	1.82	1.77	1.71	1.65
29	2.18	2.10	2.03	1.94	1.90	1.85	1.81	1.75	1.70	1.64
30	2.16	2.09	2.01	1.93	1.89	1.84	1.79	1.74	1.68	1.62
40	2.08	2.00	1.92	1.84	1.79	1.74	1.69	1.64	1.58	1.51
60	1.99	1.92	1.84	1.75	1.70	1.65	1.59	1.53	1.47	1.39
120	1.91	1.83	1.75	1.66	1.61	1.55	1.50	1.43	1.35	1.25
∞	1.83	1.75	1.67	1.57	1.52	1.46	1.39	1.32	1.22	1.00

$F_{0.975}$; $\alpha = 0.025$

Denominator Degrees of Freedom	Numerator Degrees of Freedom								
	1	2	3	4	5	6	7	8	9
1	647.8	799.5	864.2	899.6	921.8	937.1	948.2	956.7	963.3
2	38.51	39.00	39.17	39.25	39.30	39.33	39.36	39.37	39.39
3	17.44	16.04	15.44	15.10	14.88	14.73	14.62	14.54	14.47
4	12.22	10.65	9.98	9.60	9.36	9.20	9.07	8.98	8.90
5	10.01	8.43	7.76	7.39	7.15	6.98	6.85	6.76	6.68
6	8.81	7.26	6.60	6.23	5.99	5.82	5.70	5.60	5.52
7	8.07	6.54	5.89	5.52	5.29	5.12	4.99	4.90	4.82
8	7.57	6.06	5.42	5.05	4.82	4.65	4.53	4.43	4.36
9	7.21	5.71	5.08	4.72	4.48	4.32	4.20	4.10	4.03
10	6.94	5.46	4.83	4.47	4.24	4.07	3.95	3.85	3.78
11	6.72	5.26	4.63	4.28	4.04	3.88	3.76	3.66	3.59
12	6.55	5.10	4.47	4.12	3.89	3.73	3.61	3.51	3.44
13	6.41	4.97	4.35	4.00	3.77	3.60	3.48	3.39	3.31

Table G The *F*-Distribution (*continued*)

$F_{0.975}$; $\alpha = 0.025$

Denominator Degrees of Freedom	Numerator Degrees of Freedom 1	2	3	4	5	6	7	8	9
14	6.30	4.86	4.24	3.89	3.66	3.50	3.38	3.29	3.21
15	6.20	4.77	4.15	3.80	3.58	3.41	3.29	3.20	3.12
16	6.12	4.69	4.08	3.73	3.50	3.34	3.22	3.12	3.05
17	6.04	4.62	4.01	3.66	3.44	3.28	3.16	3.06	2.98
18	5.98	4.56	3.95	3.61	3.38	3.22	3.10	3.01	2.93
19	5.92	4.51	3.90	3.56	3.33	3.17	3.05	2.96	2.88
20	5.87	4.46	3.86	3.51	3.29	3.13	3.01	2.91	2.84
21	5.83	4.42	3.82	3.48	3.25	3.09	2.97	2.87	2.80
22	5.79	4.38	3.78	3.44	3.22	3.05	2.93	2.84	2.76
23	5.75	4.35	3.75	3.41	3.18	3.02	2.90	2.81	2.73
24	5.72	4.32	3.72	3.38	3.15	2.99	2.87	2.78	2.70
25	5.69	4.29	3.69	3.35	3.13	2.97	2.85	2.75	2.68
26	5.66	4.27	3.67	3.33	3.10	2.94	2.82	2.73	2.65
27	5.63	4.24	3.65	3.31	3.08	2.92	2.80	2.71	2.63
28	5.61	4.22	3.63	3.29	3.06	2.90	2.78	2.69	2.61
29	5.59	4.20	3.61	3.27	3.04	2.88	2.76	2.67	2.59
30	5.57	4.18	3.59	3.25	3.03	2.87	2.75	2.65	2.57
40	5.42	4.05	3.46	3.13	2.90	2.74	2.62	2.53	2.45
60	5.29	3.93	3.34	3.01	2.79	2.63	2.51	2.41	2.33
120	5.15	3.80	3.23	2.89	2.67	2.52	2.39	2.30	2.22
∞	5.02	3.69	3.12	2.79	2.57	2.41	2.29	2.19	2.11

$F_{0.975}$; $\alpha = 0.025$

Denominator Degrees of Freedom	Numerator Degrees of Freedom 10	12	15	20	24	30	40	60	120	∞
1	968.6	976.7	984.9	993.1	997.2	1001.4	1005.6	1009.8	1014.0	1018.2
2	39.40	39.41	39.43	39.45	39.46	39.46	39.47	39.48	39.49	39.50
3	14.42	14.34	14.25	14.17	14.12	14.08	14.04	13.99	13.95	13.90
4	8.84	8.75	8.66	8.56	8.51	8.46	8.41	8.36	8.31	8.26
5	6.62	6.52	6.43	6.33	6.28	6.23	6.18	6.12	6.07	6.02
6	5.46	5.37	5.27	5.17	5.12	5.07	5.01	4.96	4.90	4.85
7	4.76	4.67	4.57	4.47	4.41	4.36	4.31	4.25	4.20	4.14
8	4.30	4.20	4.10	4.00	3.95	3.89	3.84	3.78	3.73	3.67
9	3.96	3.87	3.77	3.67	3.61	3.56	3.51	3.45	3.39	3.33
10	3.72	3.62	3.52	3.42	3.37	3.31	3.26	3.20	3.14	3.08
11	3.53	3.43	3.33	3.23	3.17	3.12	3.06	3.00	2.94	2.88
12	3.37	3.28	3.18	3.07	3.02	2.96	2.91	2.85	2.79	2.73
13	3.25	3.15	3.05	2.95	2.89	2.84	2.78	2.72	2.66	2.60
14	3.15	3.05	2.95	2.84	2.79	2.73	2.67	2.61	2.55	2.49
15	3.06	2.96	2.86	2.76	2.70	2.64	2.59	2.52	2.46	2.40
16	2.99	2.89	2.79	2.68	2.63	2.57	2.51	2.45	2.38	2.32

Table G The *F*-Distribution (*continued*)

$F_{0.975}$; $\alpha = 0.025$

Denominator Degrees of Freedom	Numerator Degrees of Freedom 10	12	15	20	24	30	40	60	120	∞
17	2.92	2.82	2.72	2.62	2.56	2.50	2.44	2.38	2.32	2.25
18	2.87	2.77	2.67	2.56	2.50	2.44	2.38	2.32	2.26	2.19
19	2.82	2.72	2.62	2.51	2.45	2.39	2.33	2.27	2.20	2.13
20	2.77	2.68	2.57	2.46	2.41	2.35	2.29	2.22	2.16	2.09
21	2.73	2.64	2.53	2.42	2.37	2.31	2.25	2.18	2.11	2.04
22	2.70	2.60	2.50	2.39	2.33	2.27	2.21	2.14	2.08	2.00
23	2.67	2.57	2.47	2.36	2.30	2.24	2.18	2.11	2.04	1.97
24	2.64	2.54	2.44	2.33	2.27	2.21	2.15	2.08	2.01	1.94
25	2.61	2.51	2.41	2.30	2.24	2.18	2.12	2.05	1.98	1.91
26	2.59	2.49	2.39	2.28	2.22	2.16	2.09	2.03	1.95	1.88
27	2.57	2.47	2.36	2.25	2.19	2.13	2.07	2.00	1.93	1.85
28	2.55	2.45	2.34	2.23	2.17	2.11	2.05	1.98	1.91	1.83
29	2.53	2.43	2.32	2.21	2.15	2.09	2.03	1.96	1.89	1.81
30	2.51	2.41	2.31	2.20	2.14	2.07	2.01	1.94	1.87	1.79
40	2.39	2.29	2.18	2.07	2.01	1.94	1.88	1.80	1.72	1.64
60	2.27	2.17	2.06	1.94	1.88	1.82	1.74	1.67	1.58	1.48
120	2.16	2.05	1.94	1.82	1.76	1.69	1.61	1.53	1.43	1.31
∞	2.05	1.95	1.83	1.71	1.64	1.57	1.48	1.39	1.27	1.00

$F_{0.99}$; $\alpha = 0.01$

Denominator Degrees of Freedom	Numerator Degrees of Freedom 1	2	3	4	5	6	7	8	9
1	4052.2	4999.5	5403.4	5624.6	5763.6	5859.0	5928.4	5981.1	6022.5
2	98.50	99.00	99.17	99.25	99.30	99.33	99.36	99.37	99.39
3	34.12	30.82	29.46	28.71	28.24	27.91	27.67	27.49	27.35
4	21.20	18.00	16.69	15.98	15.52	15.21	14.98	14.80	14.66
5	16.26	13.27	12.06	11.39	10.97	10.67	10.46	10.29	10.16
6	13.75	10.92	9.78	9.15	8.75	8.47	8.26	8.10	7.98
7	12.25	9.55	8.45	7.85	7.46	7.19	6.99	6.84	6.72
8	11.26	8.65	7.59	7.01	6.63	6.37	6.18	6.03	5.91
9	10.56	8.02	6.99	6.42	6.06	5.80	5.61	5.47	5.35
10	10.04	7.56	6.55	5.99	5.64	5.39	5.20	5.06	4.94
11	9.65	7.21	6.22	5.67	5.32	5.07	4.89	4.74	4.63
12	9.33	6.93	5.95	5.41	5.06	4.82	4.64	4.50	4.39
13	9.07	6.70	5.74	5.21	4.86	4.62	4.44	4.30	4.19
14	8.86	6.51	5.56	5.04	4.69	4.46	4.28	4.14	4.03
15	8.68	6.36	5.42	4.89	4.56	4.32	4.14	4.00	3.89
16	8.53	6.23	5.29	4.77	4.44	4.20	4.03	3.89	3.78
17	8.40	6.11	5.18	4.67	4.34	4.10	3.93	3.79	3.68
18	8.29	6.01	5.09	4.58	4.25	4.01	3.84	3.71	3.60
19	8.18	5.93	5.01	4.50	4.17	3.94	3.77	3.63	3.52

Table G The *F*-Distribution (*continued*)

	$F_{0.99}$; $\alpha = 0.01$								
Denominator Degrees of Freedom	**Numerator Degrees of Freedom**								
	1	**2**	**3**	**4**	**5**	**6**	**7**	**8**	**9**
20	8.10	5.85	4.94	4.43	4.10	3.87	3.70	3.56	3.46
21	8.02	5.78	4.87	4.37	4.04	3.81	3.64	3.51	3.40
22	7.95	5.72	4.82	4.31	3.99	3.76	3.59	3.45	3.35
23	7.88	5.66	4.76	4.26	3.94	3.71	3.54	3.41	3.30
24	7.82	5.61	4.72	4.22	3.90	3.67	3.50	3.36	3.26
25	7.77	5.57	4.68	4.18	3.85	3.63	3.46	3.32	3.22
26	7.72	5.53	4.64	4.14	3.82	3.59	3.42	3.29	3.18
27	7.68	5.49	4.60	4.11	3.78	3.56	3.39	3.26	3.15
28	7.64	5.45	4.57	4.07	3.75	3.53	3.36	3.23	3.12
29	7.60	5.42	4.54	4.04	3.73	3.50	3.33	3.20	3.09
30	7.56	5.39	4.51	4.02	3.70	3.47	3.30	3.17	3.07
40	7.31	5.18	4.31	3.83	3.51	3.29	3.12	2.99	2.89
60	7.08	4.98	4.13	3.65	3.34	3.12	2.95	2.82	2.72
120	6.85	4.79	3.95	3.48	3.17	2.96	2.79	2.66	2.56
∞	6.64	4.61	3.78	3.32	3.02	2.80	2.64	2.51	2.41

	$F_{0.99}$; $\alpha = 0.01$									
Denominator Degrees of Freedom	**Numerator Degrees of Freedom**									
	10	**12**	**15**	**20**	**24**	**30**	**40**	**60**	**120**	**∞**
1	6055.8	6106.3	6157.3	6208.7	6234.6	6260.6	6286.8	6313.0	6339.4	6365.8
2	99.40	99.42	99.43	99.45	99.46	99.47	99.47	99.48	99.49	99.50
3	27.23	27.05	26.87	26.69	26.60	26.50	26.41	26.32	26.22	26.13
4	14.55	14.37	14.20	14.02	13.93	13.84	13.75	13.65	13.56	13.46
5	10.05	9.89	9.72	9.55	9.47	9.38	9.29	9.20	9.11	9.02
6	7.87	8.72	7.56	7.40	7.31	7.23	7.14	7.06	6.97	6.88
7	6.62	6.47	6.31	6.16	6.07	5.99	5.91	5.82	5.74	5.65
8	5.81	5.67	5.52	5.36	5.28	5.20	5.12	5.03	4.95	4.86
9	5.26	5.11	4.96	4.81	4.73	4.65	4.57	4.48	4.40	4.31
10	4.85	4.71	4.56	4.41	4.33	4.25	4.17	4.08	4.00	3.91
11	4.54	4.40	4.25	4.10	4.02	3.94	3.86	3.78	3.69	3.60
12	4.30	4.16	4.01	3.86	3.78	3.70	3.62	3.54	3.45	3.36
13	4.10	3.96	3.82	3.66	3.59	3.51	3.43	3.34	3.25	3.17
14	3.94	3.80	3.66	3.51	3.43	3.35	3.27	3.18	3.09	3.00
15	3.80	3.67	3.52	3.37	3.29	3.21	3.13	3.05	2.96	2.87
16	3.69	3.55	3.41	3.26	3.18	3.10	3.02	2.93	2.84	2.75
17	3.59	3.46	3.31	3.16	3.08	3.00	2.92	2.83	2.75	2.65
18	3.51	3.37	3.23	3.08	3.00	2.92	2.84	2.75	2.66	2.57
19	3.43	3.30	3.15	3.00	2.92	2.84	2.76	2.67	2.58	2.49
20	3.37	3.23	3.09	2.94	2.86	2.78	2.69	2.61	2.52	2.42
21	3.31	3.17	3.03	2.88	2.80	2.72	2.64	2.55	2.46	2.36
22	3.26	3.12	2.98	2.83	2.75	2.67	2.58	2.50	2.40	2.31
23	3.21	3.07	2.93	2.78	2.70	2.62	2.54	2.45	2.35	2.26
24	3.17	3.03	2.89	2.74	2.66	2.58	2.49	2.40	2.31	2.21

Table G The *F*-Distribution (*continued*)

	$F_{0.99}$; $\alpha = 0.01$									
Denominator Degrees of Freedom	Numerator Degrees of Freedom									
	10	12	15	20	24	30	40	60	120	∞
25	3.13	2.99	2.85	2.70	2.62	2.54	2.45	2.36	2.27	2.17
26	3.09	2.96	2.81	2.66	2.58	2.50	2.42	2.33	2.23	2.13
27	3.06	2.93	2.78	2.63	2.55	2.47	2.38	2.29	2.20	2.10
28	3.03	2.90	2.75	2.60	2.52	2.44	2.35	2.26	2.17	2.06
29	3.00	2.87	2.73	2.57	2.49	2.41	2.33	2.23	2.14	2.03
30	2.98	2.84	2.70	2.55	2.47	2.39	2.30	2.21	2.11	2.01
40	2.80	2.66	2.52	2.37	2.29	2.20	2.11	2.02	1.92	1.81
60	2.63	2.50	2.35	2.20	2.12	2.03	1.94	1.84	1.73	1.60
120	2.47	2.34	2.19	2.03	1.95	1.86	1.76	1.66	1.53	1.38
∞	2.32	2.19	2.04	1.88	1.79	1.70	1.59	1.47	1.33	1.00

	$F_{0.995}$; $\alpha = 0.005$								
Denominator Degrees of Freedom	Numerator Degrees of Freedom								
	1	2	3	4	5	6	7	8	9
1	16211	20000	21615	22500	23056	23437	23715	23925	24091
2	198.50	199.00	199.17	199.25	199.30	199.33	199.36	199.37	199.39
3	55.55	49.80	47.47	46.19	45.39	44.84	44.43	44.13	43.88
4	31.33	26.28	24.26	23.15	22.46	21.97	21.62	21.35	21.14
5	22.78	18.31	16.53	15.56	14.94	14.51	14.20	13.96	13.77
6	18.63	14.54	12.92	12.03	11.46	11.07	10.79	10.57	10.39
7	16.24	12.40	10.88	10.05	9.52	9.16	8.89	8.68	8.51
8	14.69	11.04	9.60	8.81	8.30	7.95	7.69	7.50	7.34
9	13.61	10.11	8.72	7.96	7.47	7.13	6.88	6.69	6.54
10	12.83	9.43	8.08	7.34	6.87	6.54	6.30	6.12	5.97
11	12.23	8.91	7.60	6.88	6.42	6.10	5.86	5.68	5.54
12	11.75	8.51	7.23	6.52	6.07	5.76	5.52	5.35	5.20
13	11.37	8.19	6.93	6.23	5.79	5.48	5.25	5.08	4.94
14	11.06	7.92	6.68	6.00	5.56	5.26	5.03	4.86	4.72
15	10.80	7.70	6.48	5.80	5.37	5.07	4.85	4.67	4.54
16	10.58	7.51	6.30	5.64	5.21	4.91	4.69	4.52	4.38
17	10.38	7.35	6.16	5.50	5.07	4.78	4.56	4.39	4.25
18	10.22	7.21	6.03	5.37	4.96	4.66	4.44	4.28	4.14
19	10.07	7.09	5.92	5.27	4.85	4.56	4.34	4.18	4.04
20	9.94	6.99	5.82	5.17	4.76	4.47	4.26	4.09	3.96
21	9.83	6.89	5.73	5.09	4.68	4.39	4.18	4.01	3.88
22	9.73	6.81	5.65	5.02	4.61	4.32	4.11	3.94	3.81
23	9.63	6.73	5.58	4.95	4.54	4.26	4.05	3.88	3.75
24	9.55	6.66	5.52	4.89	4.49	4.20	3.99	3.83	3.69
25	9.48	6.60	5.46	4.84	4.43	4.15	3.94	3.78	3.64
26	9.41	6.54	5.41	4.79	4.38	4.10	3.89	3.73	3.60
27	9.34	6.49	5.36	4.74	4.34	4.06	3.85	3.69	3.56
28	9.28	6.44	5.32	4.70	4.30	4.02	3.81	3.65	3.52
29	9.23	6.40	5.28	4.66	4.26	3.98	3.77	3.61	3.48

Table G The *F*-Distribution (*concluded*)

	$F_{0.995}$; $\alpha = 0.005$								
Denominator Degrees of Freedom	**Numerator Degrees of Freedom**								
	1	2	3	4	5	6	7	8	9
30	9.18	6.35	5.24	4.62	4.23	3.95	3.74	3.58	3.45
40	8.83	6.07	4.98	4.37	3.99	3.71	3.51	3.35	3.22
60	8.49	5.79	4.73	4.14	3.76	3.49	3.29	3.13	3.01
120	8.18	5.54	4.50	3.92	3.55	3.28	3.09	2.93	2.81
∞	7.88	5.30	4.28	3.72	3.35	3.09	2.90	2.75	2.62

	$F_{0.995}$; $\alpha = 0.005$									
Denominator Degrees of Freedom	**Numerator Degrees of Freedom**									
	10	12	15	20	24	30	40	60	120	∞
1	24224	24426	24630	24836	24940	25044	25148	25253	25359	25464
2	199.40	199.42	199.43	199.45	199.46	199.47	199.47	199.48	199.49	199.50
3	43.69	43.39	43.08	42.78	42.62	42.47	42.31	42.15	41.99	41.83
4	20.97	20.70	20.44	20.17	20.03	19.89	19.75	19.61	19.47	19.33
5	13.62	13.38	13.15	12.90	12.78	12.66	12.53	12.40	12.27	12.14
6	10.25	10.03	9.81	9.59	9.47	9.36	9.24	9.12	9.00	8.88
7	8.38	8.18	7.97	7.75	7.64	7.53	7.42	7.31	7.19	7.08
8	7.21	7.01	6.81	6.61	6.50	6.40	6.29	6.18	6.06	5.95
9	6.42	6.23	6.03	5.83	5.73	5.62	5.52	5.41	5.30	5.19
10	5.85	5.66	5.47	5.27	5.17	5.07	4.97	4.86	4.75	4.64
11	5.42	5.24	5.05	4.86	4.76	4.65	4.55	4.45	4.34	4.23
12	5.09	4.91	4.72	4.53	4.43	4.33	4.23	4.12	4.01	3.90
13	4.82	4.64	4.46	4.27	4.17	4.07	3.97	3.87	3.76	3.65
14	4.60	4.43	4.25	4.06	3.96	3.86	3.76	3.66	3.55	3.44
15	4.42	4.25	4.07	3.88	3.79	3.69	3.58	3.48	3.37	3.26
16	4.27	4.10	3.92	3.73	3.64	3.54	3.44	3.33	3.22	3.11
17	4.14	3.97	3.79	3.61	3.51	3.41	3.31	3.21	3.10	2.98
18	4.03	3.86	3.68	3.50	3.40	3.30	3.20	3.10	2.99	2.87
19	3.93	3.76	3.59	3.40	3.31	3.21	3.11	3.00	2.89	2.78
20	3.85	3.68	3.50	3.32	3.22	3.12	3.02	2.92	2.81	2.69
21	3.77	3.60	3.43	3.24	3.15	3.05	2.95	2.84	2.73	2.61
22	3.70	3.54	3.36	3.18	3.08	2.98	2.88	2.77	2.66	2.55
23	3.64	3.47	3.30	3.12	3.02	2.92	2.82	2.71	2.60	2.48
24	3.59	3.42	3.25	3.06	2.97	2.87	2.77	2.66	2.55	2.43
25	3.54	3.37	3.20	3.01	2.92	2.82	2.72	2.61	2.50	2.38
26	3.49	3.33	3.15	2.97	2.87	2.77	2.67	2.56	2.45	2.33
27	3.45	3.28	3.11	2.93	2.83	2.73	2.63	2.52	2.41	2.29
28	3.41	3.25	3.07	2.89	2.79	2.69	2.59	2.48	2.37	2.25
29	3.38	3.21	3.04	2.86	2.76	2.66	2.56	2.45	2.33	2.21
30	3.34	3.18	3.01	2.82	2.73	2.63	2.52	2.42	2.30	2.18
40	3.12	2.95	2.78	2.60	2.50	2.40	2.30	2.18	2.06	1.93
60	2.90	2.74	2.57	2.39	2.29	2.19	2.08	1.96	1.83	1.69
120	2.71	2.54	2.37	2.19	2.09	1.98	1.87	1.75	1.61	1.43
∞	2.52	2.36	2.19	2.00	1.90	1.79	1.67	1.53	1.36	1.00

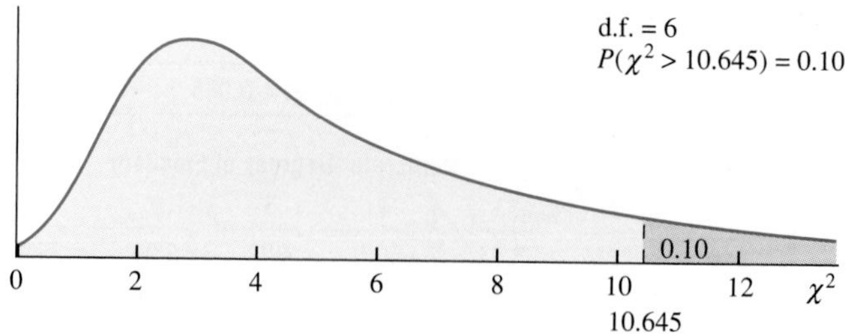

Table H Chi-Square Distribution

d.f.	$\chi^2_{0.995}$	$\chi^2_{0.990}$	$\chi^2_{0.975}$	$\chi^2_{0.950}$	$\chi^2_{0.900}$	$\chi^2_{0.700}$	$\chi^2_{0.500}$	$\chi^2_{0.300}$	$\chi^2_{0.200}$	$\chi^2_{0.100}$	$\chi^2_{0.050}$	$\chi^2_{0.025}$	$\chi^2_{0.020}$	$\chi^2_{0.010}$	$\chi^2_{0.005}$
1	0.000	0.000	0.001	0.004	0.016	0.148	0.455	1.074	1.642	2.706	3.841	5.024	5.412	6.635	7.879
2	0.010	0.020	0.051	0.103	0.211	0.713	1.386	2.408	3.219	4.605	5.991	7.378	7.824	9.210	10.597
3	0.072	0.115	0.216	0.352	0.584	1.424	2.366	3.665	4.642	6.251	7.815	9.348	9.837	11.345	12.838
4	0.207	0.297	0.484	0.711	1.064	2.195	3.357	4.878	5.989	7.779	9.488	11.143	11.668	13.277	14.860
5	0.412	0.554	0.831	1.145	1.610	3.000	4.351	6.064	7.289	9.236	11.070	12.833	13.388	15.086	16.750
6	0.676	0.872	1.237	1.635	2.204	3.828	5.348	7.231	8.558	10.645	12.592	14.449	15.033	16.812	18.548
7	0.989	1.239	1.690	2.167	2.833	4.671	6.346	8.383	9.803	12.017	14.067	16.013	16.622	18.475	20.278
8	1.344	1.646	2.180	2.733	3.490	5.527	7.344	9.524	11.030	13.362	15.507	17.535	18.168	20.090	21.955
9	1.735	2.088	2.700	3.325	4.168	6.393	8.343	10.656	12.242	14.684	16.919	19.023	19.679	21.666	23.589
10	2.156	2.558	3.247	3.940	4.865	7.267	9.342	11.781	13.442	15.987	18.307	20.483	21.161	23.209	25.188
11	2.603	3.053	3.816	4.575	5.578	8.148	10.341	12.899	14.631	17.275	19.675	21.920	22.618	24.725	26.757
12	3.074	3.571	4.404	5.226	6.304	9.034	11.340	14.011	15.812	18.549	21.026	23.337	24.054	26.217	28.299
13	3.565	4.107	5.009	5.892	7.042	9.926	12.340	15.119	16.985	19.812	22.362	24.736	25.472	27.688	29.819
14	4.075	4.660	5.629	6.571	7.790	10.821	13.339	16.222	18.151	21.064	23.685	26.119	26.873	29.141	31.319
15	4.601	5.229	6.262	7.261	8.547	11.721	14.339	17.322	19.311	22.307	24.996	27.488	28.259	30.578	32.801
16	5.142	5.812	6.908	7.962	9.312	12.624	15.338	18.418	20.465	23.542	26.296	28.845	29.633	32.000	34.267
17	5.697	6.408	7.564	8.672	10.085	13.531	16.338	19.511	21.615	24.769	27.587	30.191	30.995	33.409	35.718
18	6.265	7.015	8.231	9.390	10.865	14.440	17.338	20.601	22.760	25.989	28.869	31.526	32.346	34.805	37.156
19	6.844	7.633	8.907	10.117	11.651	15.352	18.338	21.689	23.900	27.204	30.144	32.852	33.687	36.191	38.582
20	7.434	8.260	9.591	10.851	12.443	16.266	19.337	22.775	25.038	28.412	31.410	34.170	35.020	37.566	39.997
21	8.034	8.897	10.283	11.591	13.240	17.182	20.337	23.858	26.171	29.615	32.671	35.479	36.343	38.932	41.401
22	8.643	9.542	10.982	12.338	14.041	18.101	21.337	24.939	27.301	30.813	33.924	36.781	37.659	40.289	42.796
23	9.260	10.196	11.689	13.091	14.848	19.021	22.337	26.018	28.429	32.007	35.172	38.076	38.968	41.638	44.181
24	9.886	10.856	12.401	13.848	15.659	19.943	23.337	27.096	29.553	33.196	36.415	39.364	40.270	42.980	45.559
25	10.520	11.524	13.120	14.611	16.473	20.867	24.337	28.172	30.675	34.382	37.652	40.646	41.566	44.314	46.928
26	11.160	12.198	13.844	15.379	17.292	21.792	25.336	29.246	31.795	35.563	38.885	41.923	42.856	45.642	48.290
27	11.808	12.879	14.573	16.151	18.114	22.719	26.336	30.319	32.912	36.741	40.113	43.194	44.140	46.963	49.645
28	12.461	13.565	15.308	16.928	18.939	23.647	27.336	31.391	34.027	37.916	41.337	44.461	45.419	48.278	50.993
29	13.121	14.256	16.047	17.708	19.768	24.577	28.336	32.461	35.139	39.087	42.557	45.722	46.693	49.588	52.336
30	13.787	14.953	16.791	18.493	20.599	25.508	29.336	33.530	36.250	40.256	43.773	46.979	47.962	50.892	53.672
40	20.707	22.164	24.433	26.509	29.051	34.872	39.335	44.165	47.269	51.805	55.758	59.342	60.436	63.691	66.766
50	27.991	29.707	32.357	34.764	37.689	44.313	49.335	54.723	58.164	63.167	67.505	71.420	72.613	76.154	79.490
60	35.534	37.485	40.482	43.188	46.459	53.809	59.335	65.227	68.972	74.397	79.082	83.298	84.580	88.379	91.952
70	43.275	45.442	48.758	51.739	55.329	63.346	69.334	75.689	79.715	85.527	90.531	95.023	96.388	100.425	104.215
80	51.172	53.540	57.153	60.391	64.278	72.915	79.334	86.120	90.405	96.578	101.879	106.629	108.069	112.329	116.321
90	59.196	61.754	65.647	69.126	73.291	82.511	89.334	96.524	101.054	107.565	113.145	118.136	119.648	124.116	128.299
100	67.328	70.065	74.222	77.929	82.358	92.129	99.334	106.906	111.667	118.498	124.342	129.561	131.142	135.807	140.169

Table 1 Common Logarithms

	0.0	0.1	0.2	0.3	0.4	0.5	0.6	0.7	0.8	0.9
1	0.0000	0.0414	0.0792	0.1139	0.1461	0.1761	0.2041	0.2304	0.2553	0.2788
2	0.3010	0.3222	0.3424	0.3617	0.3802	0.3979	0.4150	0.4314	0.4472	0.4624
3	0.4771	0.4914	0.5051	0.5185	0.5315	0.5441	0.5563	0.5682	0.5798	0.5911
4	0.6021	0.6128	0.6232	0.6335	0.6435	0.6532	0.6628	0.6721	0.6812	0.6902
5	0.6990	0.7076	0.7160	0.7243	0.7324	0.7404	0.7482	0.7559	0.7634	0.7709
6	0.7782	0.7853	0.7924	0.7993	0.8062	0.8129	0.8195	0.8261	0.8325	0.8388
7	0.8451	0.8513	0.8573	0.8633	0.8692	0.8751	0.8808	0.8865	0.8921	0.8976
8	0.9031	0.9085	0.9138	0.9191	0.9243	0.9294	0.9345	0.9395	0.9445	0.9494
9	0.9542	0.9590	0.9638	0.9685	0.9731	0.9777	0.9823	0.9868	0.9912	0.9956
10	1.0000	1.0043	1.0086	1.0128	1.0170	1.0212	1.0253	1.0294	1.0334	1.0374
11	1.0414	1.0453	1.0492	1.0531	1.0569	1.0607	1.0645	1.0682	1.0719	1.0755
12	1.0792	1.0828	1.0864	1.0899	1.0934	1.0969	1.1004	1.1038	1.1072	1.1106
13	1.1139	1.1173	1.1206	1.1239	1.1271	1.1303	1.1335	1.1367	1.1399	1.1430
14	1.1461	1.1492	1.1523	1.1553	1.1584	1.1614	1.1644	1.1673	1.1703	1.1732
15	1.1761	1.1790	1.1818	1.1847	1.1875	1.1903	1.1931	1.1959	1.1987	1.2014
16	1.2041	1.2068	1.2095	1.2122	1.2148	1.2175	1.2201	1.2227	1.2253	1.2279
17	1.2304	1.2330	1.2355	1.2380	1.2405	1.2430	1.2455	1.2480	1.2504	1.2529
18	1.2553	1.2577	1.2601	1.2625	1.2648	1.2672	1.2695	1.2718	1.2742	1.2765
19	1.2788	1.2810	1.2833	1.2856	1.2878	1.2900	1.2923	1.2945	1.2967	1.2989
20	1.3010	1.3032	1.3054	1.3075	1.3096	1.3118	1.3139	1.3160	1.3181	1.3201
21	1.3222	1.3243	1.3263	1.3284	1.3304	1.3324	1.3345	1.3365	1.3385	1.3404
22	1.3424	1.3444	1.3464	1.3483	1.3502	1.3522	1.3541	1.3560	1.3579	1.3598
23	1.3617	1.3636	1.3655	1.3674	1.3692	1.3711	1.3729	1.3747	1.3766	1.3784
24	1.3802	1.3820	1.3838	1.3856	1.3874	1.3892	1.3909	1.3927	1.3945	1.3962
25	1.3979	1.3997	1.4014	1.4031	1.4048	1.4065	1.4082	1.4099	1.4116	1.4133
26	1.4150	1.4166	1.4183	1.4200	1.4216	1.4232	1.4249	1.4265	1.4281	1.4298
27	1.4314	1.4330	1.4346	1.4362	1.4378	1.4393	1.4409	1.4425	1.4440	1.4456
28	1.4472	1.4487	1.4502	1.4518	1.4533	1.4548	1.4564	1.4579	1.4594	1.4609
29	1.4624	1.4639	1.4654	1.4669	1.4683	1.4698	1.4713	1.4728	1.4742	1.4757
30	1.4771	1.4786	1.4800	1.4814	1.4829	1.4843	1.4857	1.4871	1.4886	1.4900
31	1.4914	1.4928	1.4942	1.4955	1.4969	1.4983	1.4997	1.5011	1.5024	1.5038
32	1.5051	1.5065	1.5079	1.5092	1.5105	1.5119	1.5132	1.5145	1.5159	1.5172
33	1.5185	1.5198	1.5211	1.5224	1.5237	1.5250	1.5263	1.5276	1.5289	1.5302
34	1.5315	1.5328	1.5340	1.5353	1.5366	1.5378	1.5391	1.5403	1.5416	1.5428
35	1.5441	1.5453	1.5465	1.5478	1.5490	1.5502	1.5514	1.5527	1.5539	1.5551
36	1.5563	1.5575	1.5587	1.5599	1.5611	1.5623	1.5635	1.5647	1.5658	1.5670
37	1.5682	1.5694	1.5705	1.5717	1.5729	1.5740	1.5752	1.5763	1.5775	1.5786
38	1.5798	1.5809	1.5821	1.5832	1.5843	1.5855	1.5866	1.5877	1.5888	1.5899
39	1.5911	1.5922	1.5933	1.5944	1.5955	1.5966	1.5977	1.5988	1.5999	1.6010
40	1.6021	1.6031	1.6042	1.6053	1.6064	1.6075	1.6085	1.6096	1.6107	1.6117
41	1.6128	1.6138	1.6149	1.6160	1.6170	1.6180	1.6191	1.6201	1.6212	1.6222
42	1.6232	1.6243	1.6253	1.6263	1.6274	1.6284	1.6294	1.6304	1.6314	1.6325
43	1.6335	1.6345	1.6355	1.6365	1.6375	1.6385	1.6395	1.6405	1.6415	1.6425
44	1.6435	1.6444	1.6454	1.6464	1.6474	1.6484	1.6493	1.6503	1.6513	1.6522
45	1.6532	1.6542	1.6551	1.6561	1.6571	1.6580	1.6590	1.6599	1.6609	1.6618

Table 1 Common Logarithms (*continued*)

	0.0	0.1	0.2	0.3	0.4	0.5	0.6	0.7	0.8	0.9
46	1.6628	1.6637	1.6646	1.6656	1,6665	1.6675	1.6684	1.6693	1.6702	1.6712
47	1.6721	1.6730	1.6739	1.6749	1.6758	1.6767	1.6776	1.6785	1.6794	1.6803
48	1.6812	1.6821	1.6830	1.6839	1.6848	1.6857	1.6866	1.6875	1.6884	1.6893
49	1.6902	1.6911	1.6920	1.6928	1.6937	1.6946	1.6955	1.6964	1.6972	1.6981
50	1.6990	1.6998	1.7007	1.7016	1.7024	1.7033	1.7042	1.7050	1.7059	1.7067
51	1.7076	1.7084	1.7093	1.7101	1.7110	1.7118	1.7126	1.7135	1.7143	1.7152
52	1.7160	1.7168	1.7177	1.7185	1.7193	1.7202	1.7210	1.7218	1.7226	1.7235
53	1.7243	1.7251	1.7259	1.7267	1.7275	1.7284	1.7292	1.7300	1.7308	1.7316
54	1.7324	1.7332	1.7340	1.7348	1.7356	1.7364	1.7372	1.7380	1.7388	1.7396
55	1.7404	1.7412	1.7419	1.7427	1.7435	1.7443	1.7451	1.7459	1.7466	1.7474
56	1.7482	1.7490	1.7497	1.7505	1.7513	1.7520	1.7528	1.7536	1.7543	1.7551
57	1.7559	1.7566	1.7574	1.7582	1.7589	1.7597	1.7604	1.7612	1.7619	1.7627
58	1.7634	1.7642	1.7649	1.7657	1.7664	1.7672	1.7679	1.7686	1.7694	1.7701
59	1.7709	1.7716	1.7723	1.7731	1.7738	1.7745	1.7752	1.7760	1.7767	1.7774
60	1.7782	1.7789	1.7796	1.7803	1.7810	1.7818	1.7825	1.7832	1.7839	1.7846
61	1.7853	1.7860	1.7868	1.7875	1.7882	1.7889	1.7896	1.7903	1.7910	1.7917
62	1.7924	1.7931	1.7938	1.7945	1.7952	1.7959	1.7966	1.7973	1.7980	1.7987
63	1.7993	1.8000	1.8007	1.8014	1.8021	1.8028	1.8035	1.8041	1.8048	1.8055
64	1.8062	1.8069	1.8075	1.8082	1.8089	1.8096	1.8102	1.8109	1.8116	1.8122
65	1.8129	1.8136	1.8142	1.8149	1.8156	1.8162	1.8169	1.8176	1.8182	1.8189
66	1.8195	1.8202	1.8209	1.8215	1.8222	1.8228	1.8235	1.8241	1.8248	1.8254
67	1.8261	1.8267	1.8274	1.8280	1.8287	1.8293	1.8299	1.8306	1.8312	1.8319
68	1.8325	1.8331	1.8338	1.8344	1.8351	1.8357	1.8363	1.8370	1.8376	1.8382
69	1.8388	1.8395	1.8401	1.8407	1.8414	1.8420	1.8426	1.8432	1.8439	1.8445
70	1.8451	1.8457	1.8463	1.8470	1.8476	1.8482	1.8488	1.8494	1.8500	1.8506
71	1.8513	1.8519	1.8525	1.8531	1.8537	1.8543	1.8549	1.8555	1.8561	1.8567
72	1.8573	1.8579	1.8585	1.8591	1.8597	1.8603	1.8609	1.8615	1.8621	1.8627
73	1.8633	1.8639	1.8645	1.8651	1.8657	1.8663	1.8669	1.8675	1.8681	1.8686
74	1.8692	1.8698	1.8704	1.8710	1.8716	1.8722	1.8727	1.8733	1.8739	1.8745
75	1.8751	1.8756	1.8762	1.8768	1.8774	1.8779	1.8785	1.8791	1.8797	1.8802
76	1.8808	1.8814	1.8820	1.8825	1.8831	1.8837	1.8842	1.8848	1.8854	1.8859
77	1.8865	1.8871	1.8876	1.8882	1.8887	1.8893	1.8899	1.8904	1.8910	1.8915
78	1.8921	1.8927	1.8932	1.8938	1.8943	1.8949	1.8954	1.8960	1.8965	1.8971
79	1.8976	1.8982	1.8987	1.8993	1.8998	1.9004	1.9009	1.9015	1.9020	1.9025
80	1.9031	1,9036	1.9042	1.9047	1.9053	1.9058	1.9063	1.9069	1.9074	1.9079
81	1.9085	1.9090	1.9096	1.9101	1.9106	1.9112	1.9117	1.9122	1.9128	1.9133
82	1.9138	1.9143	1.9149	1.9154	1.9159	1.9165	1.9170	1.9175	1.9180	1.9186
83	1.9191	1.9196	1.9201	1.9206	1.9212	1.9217	1.9222	1.9227	1.9232	1.9238
84	1.9243	1.9248	1.9253	1.9258	1.9263	1.9269	1.9274	1.9279	1.9284	1.9289
85	1.9294	1.9299	1.9304	1.9309	1.9315	1.9320	1.9325	1.9330	1.9335	1.9340
86	1.9345	1.9350	1.9355	1.9360	1.9365	1.9370	1.9375	1.9380	1.9385	1.9390
87	1.9395	1.9400	1.9405	1.9410	1.9415	1.9420	1.9425	1.9430	1.9435	1.9440
88	1.9445	1.9450	1.9455	1.9460	1.9465	1.9469	1.9474	1.9479	1.9484	1.9489
89	1.9494	1.9499	1.9504	1.9509	1.9513	1.9518	1.9523	1.9528	1.9533	1.9538
90	1.9542	1.9547	1.9552	1.9557	1.9562	1.9566	1.9571	1.9576	1.9581	1.9586

Table I Common Logarithms (*concluded*)

	0.0	0.1	0.2	0.3	0.4	0.5	0.6	0.7	0.8	0.9
91	1.9590	1.9595	1.9600	1.9605	1.9609	1.9614	1.9619	1.9624	1.9628	1.9633
92	1.9638	1.9643	1.9647	1.9652	1.9657	1.9661	1.9666	1.9671	1.9675	1.9680
93	1.9685	1.9689	1.9694	1.9699	1.9703	1.9708	1.9713	1.9717	1.9722	1.9727
94	1.9731	1.9736	1.9741	1.9745	1.9750	1.9754	1.9759	1.9763	1.9768	1.9773
95	1.9777	1.9782	1.9786	1.9791	1.9795	1.9800	1.9805	1.9809	1.9814	1.9818
96	1.9823	1.9827	1.9832	1.9836	1.9841	1.9845	1.9850	1.9854	1.9859	1.9863
97	1.9868	1.9872	1.9877	1.9881	1.9886	1.9890	1.9894	1.9899	1.9903	1.9908
98	1.9912	1.9917	1.9921	1.9926	1.9930	1.9934	1.9939	1.9943	1.9948	1.9952
99	1.9956	1.9961	1.9965	1.9969	1.9974	1.9978	1.9983	1.9987	1.9991	1.9996

Table J The Greek Alphabet

Α	α	alpha	Ν	ν	nu
Β	β	beta	Ξ	ξ	xi
Γ	γ	gamma	Ο	o	omicron
Δ	δ	delta	Π	π	pi
Ε	ϵ	epsilon	Ρ	ρ	rho
Ζ	ζ	zeta	Σ	σ	sigma
Η	η	eta	Τ	τ	tau
Θ	θ	theta	Υ	υ	upsilon
Ι	ι	iota	Φ	ϕ	phi
Κ	κ	kappa	Χ	χ	chi
Λ	λ	lambda	Ψ	ψ	psi
Μ	μ	mu	Ω	ω	omega

Table K Durbin-Watson Statistic (d). Significance Points of d_L and d_U (1 percent)

	$k = 1$		$k = 2$		$k = 3$		$k = 4$		$k = 5$	
n	d_L	d_U	d_L	d_U	d_L	d_U	d_L	d_U	d_L	d_U
15	0.81	1.07	0.70	1.25	0.59	1.46	0.49	1.70	0.39	1.96
16	0.84	1.09	0.74	1.25	0.63	1.44	0.53	1.66	0.44	1.90
17	0.87	1.10	0.77	1.25	0.67	1.43	0.57	1.63	0.48	1.85
18	0.90	1.12	0.80	1.26	0.71	1.42	0.61	1.60	0.52	1.80
19	0.93	1.13	0.83	1.26	0.74	1.41	0.65	1.58	0.56	1.77
20	0.95	1.15	0.86	1.27	0.77	1.41	0.68	1.57	0.60	1.74
21	0.97	1.16	0.89	1.27	0.80	1.41	0.72	1.55	0.63	1.71
22	1.00	1.17	0.91	1.28	0.83	1.40	0.75	1.54	0.66	1.69
23	1.02	1.19	0.94	1.29	0.86	1.40	0.77	1.53	0.70	1.67
24	1.04	1.20	0.96	1.30	0.88	1.41	0.80	1.53	0.72	1.66
25	1.05	1.21	0.98	1.30	0.90	1.41	0.83	1.52	0.75	1.65
26	1.07	1.22	1.00	1.31	0.93	1.41	0.85	1.52	0.78	1.64
27	1.09	1.23	1.02	1.32	0.95	1.41	0.88	1.51	0.81	1.63
28	1.10	1.24	1.04	1.32	0.97	1.41	0.90	1.51	0.83	1.62
29	1.12	1.25	1.05	1.33	0.99	1.42	0.92	1.51	0.85	1.61
30	1.13	1.26	1.07	1.34	1.01	1.42	0.94	1.51	0.88	1.61
31	1.15	1.27	1.08	1.34	1.02	1.42	0.96	1.51	0.90	1.60
32	1.16	1.28	1.10	1.35	1.04	1.43	0.98	1.51	0.92	1.60
33	1.17	1.29	1.11	1.36	1.05	1.43	1.00	1.51	0.94	1.59
34	1.18	1.30	1.13	1.36	1.07	1.43	1.01	1.51	0.95	1.59
35	1.19	1.31	1.14	1.37	1.08	1.44	1.03	1.51	0.97	1.59
36	1.21	1.32	1.15	1.38	1.10	1.44	1.04	1.51	0.99	1.59
37	1.22	1.32	1.16	1.38	1.11	1.45	1.06	1.51	1.00	1.59
38	1.23	1.33	1.18	1.39	1.12	1.45	1.07	1.52	1.02	1.58
39	1.24	1.34	1.19	1.39	1.14	1.45	1.09	1.52	1.03	1.58
40	1.25	1.34	1.20	1.40	1.15	1.46	1.10	1.52	1.05	1.58
45	1.29	1.38	1.24	1.42	1.20	1.48	1.16	1.53	1.11	1.58
50	1.32	1.40	1.28	1.45	1.24	1.49	1.20	1.54	1.16	1.59
55	1.36	1.43	1.32	1.47	1.28	1.51	1.25	1.55	1.21	1.59
60	1.38	1.45	1.35	1.48	1.32	1.52	1.28	1.56	1.25	1.60
65	1.41	1.47	1.38	1.50	1.35	1.53	1.31	1.57	1.28	1.61
70	1.43	1.49	1.40	1.52	1.37	1.55	1.34	1.58	1.31	1.61
75	1.45	1.50	1.42	1.53	1.39	1.56	1.37	1.59	1.34	1.62
80	1.47	1.52	1.44	1.54	1.42	1.57	1.39	1.60	1.36	1.62
85	1.48	1.53	1.46	1.55	1.43	1.58	1.41	1.60	1.39	1.63
90	1.50	1.54	1.47	1.56	1.45	1.59	1.43	1.61	1.41	1.64
95	1.51	1.55	1.49	1.57	1.47	1.60	1.45	1.62	1.42	1.64
100	1.52	1.56	1.50	1.58	1.48	1.60	1.46	1.63	1.44	1.65

n = number of observations.

k = number of explanatory variables.

This table is reproduced from *Biometrika,* vol. 41, 1951, p. 175, with the permission of the trustees.

Table K Durbin-Watson Statistic (d) (*continued*). Significance Points of d_L and d_U (5 percent)

	$k = 1$		$k = 2$		$k = 3$		$k = 4$		$k = 5$	
n	d_L	d_U	d_L	d_U	d_L	d_U	d_L	d_U	d_L	d_U
15	1.08	1.36	0.95	1.54	0.82	1.75	0.69	1.97	0.56	2.21
16	1.10	1.37	0.98	1.54	0.86	1.73	0.74	1.93	0.62	2.15
17	1.13	1.38	1.02	1.54	0.90	1.71	0.78	1.90	0.67	2.10
18	1.16	1.39	1.05	1.53	0.93	1.69	0.82	1.87	0.71	2.06
19	1.18	1.40	1.08	1.53	0.97	1.68	0.86	1.85	0.75	2.02
20	1.20	1.41	1.10	1.54	1.00	1.68	0.90	1.83	0.79	1.99
21	1.22	1.42	1.13	1.54	1.03	1.67	0.93	1.81	0.83	1.96
22	1.24	1.43	1.15	1.54	1.05	1.66	0.96	1.80	0.86	1.94
23	1.26	1.44	1.17	1.54	1.08	1.66	0.99	1.79	0.90	1.92
24	1.27	1.45	1.19	1.55	1.10	1.66	1.01	1.78	0.93	1.90
25	1.29	1.45	1.21	1.55	1.12	1.66	1.04	1.77	0.95	1.89
26	1.30	1.46	1.22	1.55	1.14	1.65	1.06	1.76	0.98	1.88
27	1.32	1.47	1.24	1.56	1.16	1.65	1.08	1.76	1.01	1.86
28	1.33	1.48	1.26	1.56	1.18	1.65	1.10	1.75	1.03	1.85
29	1.34	1.48	1.27	1.56	1.20	1.65	1.12	1.74	1.05	1.84
30	1.35	1.49	1.28	1.57	1.21	1.65	1.14	1.74	1.07	1.83
31	1.36	1.50	1.30	1.57	1.23	1.65	1.16	1.74	1.09	1.83
32	1.37	1.50	1.31	1.57	1.24	1.65	1.18	1.73	1.11	1.82
33	1.38	1.51	1.32	1.58	1.26	1.65	1.19	1.73	1.13	1.81
34	1.39	1.51	1.33	1.58	1.27	1.65	1.21	1.73	1.15	1.81
35	1.40	1.52	1.34	1.58	1.28	1.65	1.22	1.73	1.16	1.80
36	1.41	1.52	1.35	1.59	1.29	1.65	1.24	1.73	1.18	1.80
37	1.42	1.53	1.36	1.59	1.31	1.66	1.25	1.72	1.19	1.80
38	1.43	1.54	1.37	1.59	1.32	1.66	1.26	1.72	1.21	1.79
39	1.43	1.54	1.38	1.60	1.33	1.66	1.27	1.72	1.22	1.79
40	1.44	1.54	1.39	1.60	1.34	1.66	1.29	1.72	1.23	1.79
45	1.48	1.57	1.43	1.62	1.38	1.67	1.34	1.72	1.29	1.78
50	1.50	1.59	1.46	1.63	1.42	1.67	1.38	1.72	1.34	1.77
55	1.53	1.60	1.49	1.64	1.45	1.68	1.41	1.72	1.38	1.77
60	1.55	1.62	1.51	1.65	1.48	1.69	1.44	1.73	1.41	1.77
65	1.57	1.63	1.54	1.66	1.50	1.70	1.47	1.73	1.44	1.77
70	1.58	1.64	1.55	1.67	1.52	1.70	1.49	1.74	1.46	1.77
75	1.60	1.65	1.57	1.68	1.54	1.71	1.51	1.74	1.49	1.77
80	1.61	1.66	1.59	1.69	1.56	1.72	1.53	1.74	1.51	1.77
85	1.62	1.67	1.60	1.70	1.57	1.72	1.55	1.75	1.52	1.77
90	1.63	1.68	1.61	1.70	1.59	1.73	1.57	1.75	1.54	1.78
95	1.64	1.69	1.62	1.71	1.60	1.73	1.58	1.75	1.56	1.78
100	1.65	1.69	1.63	1.72	1.61	1.74	1.59	1.76	1.57	1.78

n = number of observations.

k = number of explanatory variables.

This table is reproduced from *Biometrika,* vol. 41, 1951, p. 173, with the permission of the trustees.

Table L Critical Values of the Studentized Range Distribution for $\alpha = 0.05$

$n - c$	*c* 2	3	4	5	6	7	8	9	10	11	12	13	14	15	16	17	18	19	20
1	18.0	27.0	32.8	37.1	40.4	43.1	45.4	47.4	49.1	50.6	52.0	53.2	54.3	55.4	56.3	57.2	58.0	58.8	59.6
2	6.08	8.33	9.80	10.9	11.7	12.4	13.0	13.5	14.0	14.4	14.7	15.1	15.4	15.7	15.9	16.1	16.4	16.6	16.8
3	4.50	5.91	6.82	7.50	8.04	8.48	8.85	9.18	9.46	9.72	9.95	10.2	10.3	10.5	10.7	10.8	11.0	11.1	11.2
4	3.93	5.04	5.76	6.29	6.71	7.05	7.35	7.60	7.83	8.03	8.21	8.37	8.52	8.66	8.79	8.91	9.03	9.13	9.23
5	3.64	4.60	5.22	5.67	6.03	6.33	6.58	6.80	6.99	7.17	7.32	7.47	7.60	7.72	7.83	7.93	8.03	8.12	8.21
6	3.46	4.34	4.90	5.30	5.63	5.90	6.12	6.32	6.49	6.65	6.79	6.92	7.03	7.14	7.24	7.34	7.43	7.51	7.59
7	3.34	4.16	4.68	5.06	5.36	5.61	5.82	6.00	6.16	6.30	6.43	6.55	6.66	6.76	6.85	6.94	7.02	7.10	7.17
8	3.26	4.04	4.53	4.89	5.17	5.40	5.60	5.77	5.92	6.05	6.18	6.29	6.39	6.48	6.57	6.65	6.73	6.80	6.87
9	3.20	3.95	4.41	4.76	5.02	5.24	5.43	5.59	5.74	5.87	5.98	6.09	6.19	6.28	6.36	6.44	6.51	6.58	6.64
10	3.15	3.88	4.33	4.65	4.91	5.12	5.30	5.46	5.60	5.72	5.83	5.93	6.03	6.11	6.19	6.27	6.34	6.40	6.47
11	3.11	3.82	4.26	4.57	4.82	5.03	5.20	5.35	5.49	5.61	5.71	5.81	5.90	5.98	6.06	6.13	6.20	6.27	6.33
12	3.08	3.77	4.20	4.51	4.75	4.95	5.12	5.27	5.39	5.51	5.61	5.71	5.80	5.88	5.95	6.02	6.09	6.15	6.21
13	3.06	3.73	4.15	4.45	4.69	4.88	5.05	5.19	5.32	5.43	5.53	5.63	5.71	5.79	5.86	5.93	5.99	6.05	6.11
14	3.03	3.70	4.11	4.41	4.64	4.83	4.99	5.13	5.25	5.36	5.46	5.55	5.64	5.71	5.79	5.85	5.91	5.97	6.03
15	3.01	3.67	4.08	4.37	4.59	4.78	4.94	5.08	5.20	5.31	5.40	5.49	5.57	5.65	5.72	5.78	5.85	5.90	5.96
16	3.00	3.65	4.05	4.33	4.56	4.74	4.90	5.03	5.15	5.26	5.35	5.44	5.52	5.59	5.66	5.73	5.79	5.84	5.90
17	2.98	3.63	4.02	4.30	4.52	4.70	4.86	4.99	5.11	5.21	5.31	5.39	5.47	5.54	5.61	5.67	5.73	5.79	5.84
18	2.97	3.61	4.00	4.28	4.49	4.67	4.82	4.96	5.07	5.17	5.27	5.35	5.43	5.50	5.57	5.63	5.69	5.74	5.79
19	2.96	3.59	3.98	4.25	4.47	4.65	4.79	4.92	5.04	5.14	5.23	5.31	5.39	5.46	5.53	5.59	5.65	5.70	5.75
20	2.95	3.58	3.96	4.23	4.45	4.62	4.77	4.90	5.01	5.11	5.20	5.28	5.36	5.43	5.49	5.55	5.61	5.66	5.71
24	2.92	3.53	3.90	4.17	4.37	4.54	4.68	4.81	4.92	5.01	5.10	5.18	5.25	5.32	5.38	5.44	5.49	5.55	5.59
30	2.89	3.49	3.85	4.10	4.30	4.46	4.60	4.72	4.82	4.92	5.00	5.08	5.15	5.21	5.27	5.33	5.38	5.43	5.47
40	2.86	3.44	3.79	4.04	4.23	4.39	4.52	4.63	4.73	4.82	4.90	4.98	5.04	5.11	5.16	5.22	5.27	5.31	5.36
60	2.83	3.40	3.74	3.98	4.16	4.31	4.44	4.55	4.65	4.73	4.81	4.88	4.94	5.00	5.06	5.11	5.15	5.20	5.24
120	2.80	3.36	3.68	3.92	4.10	4.24	4.36	4.47	4.56	4.64	4.71	4.78	4.84	4.90	4.95	5.00	5.04	5.09	5.13
α	2.77	3.31	3.63	3.86	4.03	4.17	4.29	4.39	4.47	4.55	4.62	4.68	4.74	4.80	4.85	4.89	4.93	4.97	5.01

Source: Reprinted by permission of the *Biometrika* trustees from E. S. Pearson and H. O. Hartley, eds., *Biometrika Tables for Statisticians*, vol. 1, 3rd ed. (Cambridge University Press, 1966).

Table L Critical Values of the Studentized Range Distribution for $\alpha = 0.01$ (*concluded*)

	c																		
$n - c$	2	3	4	5	6	7	8	9	10	11	12	13	14	15	16	17	18	19	20
1	90.0	135	164	186	202	216	227	237	246	253	260	266	272	277	282	286	290	294	298
2	14.0	19.0	22.3	24.7	26.6	28.2	29.5	30.7	31.7	32.6	33.4	34.1	34.8	35.4	36.0	36.5	37.0	37.5	37.9
3	8.26	10.6	12.2	13.3	14.2	15.0	15.6	16.2	16.7	17.1	17.5	17.9	18.2	18.5	18.8	19.1	19.3	19.5	19.8
4	6.51	8.12	9.17	9.96	10.6	11.1	11.5	11.9	12.3	12.6	12.8	13.1	13.3	13.5	13.7	13.9	14.1	14.2	14.4
5	5.70	6.97	7.80	8.42	8.91	9.32	9.67	9.97	10.2	10.5	10.7	10.9	11.1	11.2	11.4	11.6	11.7	11.8	11.9
6	5.24	6.33	7.03	7.56	7.97	8.32	8.61	8.87	9.10	9.30	9.49	9.65	9.81	9.95	10.1	10.2	10.3	10.4	10.5
7	4.95	5.92	6.54	7.01	7.37	7.68	7.94	8.17	8.37	8.55	8.71	8.86	9.00	9.12	9.24	9.35	9.46	9.55	9.65
8	4.74	5.63	6.20	6.63	6.96	7.24	7.47	7.68	7.87	8.03	8.18	8.31	8.44	8.55	8.66	8.76	8.85	8.94	9.03
9	4.60	5.43	5.96	6.35	6.66	6.91	7.13	7.32	7.49	7.65	7.78	7.91	8.03	8.13	8.23	8.32	8.41	8.49	8.57
10	4.48	5.27	5.77	6.14	6.43	6.67	6.87	7.05	7.21	7.36	7.48	7.60	7.71	7.81	7.91	7.99	8.07	8.15	8.22
11	4.39	5.14	5.62	5.97	6.25	6.48	6.67	6.84	6.99	7.13	7.25	7.36	7.46	7.56	7.65	7.73	7.81	7.88	7.95
12	4.32	5.04	5.50	5.84	6.10	6.32	6.51	6.67	6.81	6.94	7.06	7.17	7.26	7.36	7.44	7.52	7.59	7.66	7.73
13	4.26	4.96	5.40	5.73	5.98	6.19	6.37	6.53	6.67	6.79	6.90	7.01	7.10	7.19	7.27	7.34	7.42	7.48	7.55
14	4.21	4.89	5.32	5.63	5.88	6.08	6.26	6.41	6.54	6.66	6.77	6.87	6.96	7.05	7.12	7.20	7.27	7.33	7.39
15	4.17	4.83	5.25	5.56	5.80	5.99	6.16	6.31	6.44	6.55	6.66	6.76	6.84	6.93	7.00	7.07	7.14	7.20	7.26
16	4.13	4.78	5.19	5.49	5.72	5.92	6.08	6.22	6.35	6.46	6.56	6.66	6.74	6.82	6.90	6.97	7.03	7.09	7.15
17	4.10	4.74	5.14	5.43	5.66	5.85	6.01	6.15	6.27	6.38	6.48	6.57	6.66	6.73	6.80	6.87	6.94	7.00	7.05
18	4.07	4.70	5.09	5.38	5.60	5.79	5.94	6.08	6.20	6.31	6.41	6.50	6.58	6.65	6.72	6.79	6.85	6.91	6.96
19	4.05	4.67	5.05	5.33	5.55	5.73	5.89	6.02	6.14	6.25	6.34	6.43	6.51	6.58	6.65	6.72	6.78	6.84	6.89
20	4.02	4.64	5.02	5.29	5.51	5.69	5.84	5.97	6.09	6.19	6.29	6.37	6.45	6.52	6.59	6.65	6.71	6.76	6.82
24	3.96	4.54	4.91	5.17	5.37	5.54	5.69	5.81	5.92	6.02	6.11	6.19	6.26	6.33	6.39	6.45	6.51	6.56	6.61
30	3.89	4.45	4.80	5.05	5.24	5.40	5.54	5.65	5.76	5.85	5.93	6.01	6.08	6.14	6.20	6.26	6.31	6.36	6.41
40	3.82	4.37	4.70	4.93	5.11	5.27	5.39	5.50	5.60	5.69	5.77	5.84	5.90	5.96	6.02	6.07	6.12	6.17	6.21
60	3.76	4.28	4.60	4.82	4.99	5.13	5.25	5.36	5.45	5.53	5.60	5.67	5.73	5.79	5.84	5.89	5.93	5.98	6.02
120	3.70	4.20	4.50	4.71	4.87	5.01	5.12	5.21	5.30	5.38	5.44	5.51	5.56	5.61	5.66	5.71	5.75	5.79	5.83
α	3.64	4.12	4.40	4.60	4.76	4.88	4.99	5.08	5.16	5.23	5.29	5.35	5.40	5.45	5.49	5.54	5.57	5.61	5.65

Source: Reprinted by permission of the *Biometrika* trustees from E. S. Pearson and H. O. Hartley, eds., *Biometrika Tables for Statisticians,* vol. 1, 3rd ed. (Cambridge University Press, 1966).

Table M Critical Values of r in the Runs Test

Table M1 and Table M2 contain various critical values of r for various values of n_1 and n_2. For the one-sample runs test, any value of r that is equal to or smaller than that shown in Table M1 or equal to or larger than that shown in Table M2 is significant at the 0.05 level.

Table M1

n_1 \ n_2	2	3	4	5	6	7	8	9	10	11	12	13	14	15	16	17	18	19	20
2											2	2	2	2	2	2	2	2	2
3					2	2	2	2	2	2	2	2	2	3	3	3	3	3	3
4				2	2	2	3	3	3	3	3	3	3	3	4	4	4	4	4
5			2	2	3	3	3	3	3	4	4	4	4	4	4	4	5	5	5
6		2	2	3	3	3	3	4	4	4	4	5	5	5	5	5	5	6	6
7		2	2	3	3	3	4	4	5	5	5	5	5	6	6	6	6	6	6
8		2	3	3	3	4	4	5	5	5	6	6	6	6	6	7	7	7	7
9		2	3	3	4	4	5	5	5	6	6	6	7	7	7	7	8	8	8
10		2	3	3	4	5	5	5	6	6	7	7	7	7	8	8	8	8	9
11		2	3	4	4	5	5	6	6	7	7	7	8	8	8	9	9	9	9
12	2	2	3	4	4	5	6	6	7	7	7	8	8	8	9	9	9	10	10
13	2	2	3	4	5	5	6	6	7	7	8	8	9	9	9	10	10	10	10
14	2	2	3	4	5	5	6	7	7	8	8	9	9	9	10	10	10	11	11
15	2	3	3	4	5	6	6	7	7	8	8	9	9	10	10	11	11	11	12
16	2	3	4	4	5	6	6	7	8	8	9	9	10	10	11	11	11	12	12
17	2	3	4	4	5	6	7	7	8	9	9	10	10	11	11	11	12	12	13
18	2	3	4	5	5	6	7	8	8	9	9	10	10	11	11	12	12	13	13
19	2	3	4	5	6	6	7	8	8	9	10	10	11	11	12	12	13	13	13
20	2	3	4	5	6	6	7	8	9	9	10	10	11	12	12	13	13	13	14

Table M2

n_1 \ n_2	2	3	4	5	6	7	8	9	10	11	12	13	14	15	16	17	18	19	20
2																			
3																			
4				9	9														
5			9	10	10	11	11												
6			9	10	11	12	12	13	13	13	13								
7				11	12	13	13	14	14	14	14	15	15	15					
8				11	12	13	14	14	15	15	16	16	16	16	17	17	17	17	17
9					13	14	14	15	16	16	16	17	17	18	18	18	18	18	18
10					13	14	15	16	16	17	17	18	18	18	19	19	19	20	20
11					13	14	15	16	17	17	18	19	19	19	20	20	20	21	21
12					13	14	16	16	17	18	19	19	20	20	21	21	21	22	22
13						15	16	17	18	19	19	20	20	21	21	22	22	23	23
14						15	16	17	18	19	20	20	21	22	22	23	23	23	24
15						15	16	18	18	19	20	21	22	22	23	23	24	24	25
16							17	18	19	20	21	21	22	23	23	24	25	25	25
17							17	18	19	20	21	22	23	23	24	25	25	26	26
18							17	18	19	20	21	22	23	24	25	25	26	26	27
19							17	18	20	21	22	23	23	24	25	26	26	27	27
20							17	18	20	21	22	23	24	25	25	26	27	27	28

Source: Adapted from Frieda S. Swed and C. Eisenhart, "Tables for Testing Randomness of Grouping in a Sequence of Alternatives," *Annals of Mathematical Statistics* 14, 1943, pp. 66–87. Used by permission.

Table N Spearman's Rank Correlation, Combined Areas in Both Tails

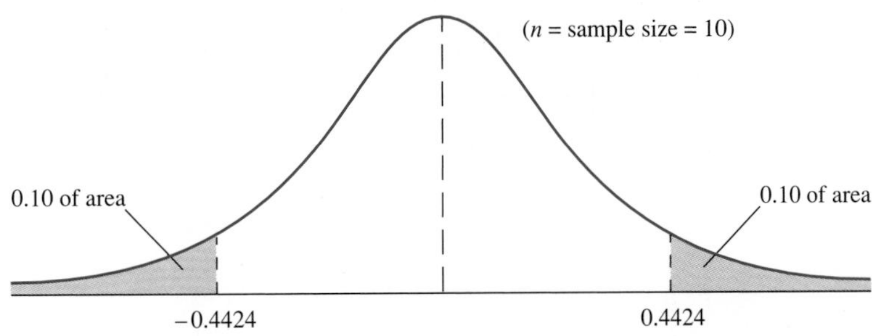

Example: For a two-tailed test of significance at the 0.20 level, with $n = 10$, the appropriate value for r can be found by looking under the 0.20 column and proceeding down to the 10; there we find the appropriate r_s value to be 0.4424.

n	0.20	0.10	0.05	0.02	0.01	0.002
4	0.8000	0.8000				
5	0.7000	0.8000	0.9000	0.9000		
6	0.6000	0.7714	0.8286	0.8857	0.9429	
7	0.5357	0.6786	0.7450	0.8571	0.8929	0.9643
8	0.5000	0.6190	0.7143	0.8095	0.8571	0.9286
9	0.4667	0.5833	0.6833	0.7667	0.8167	0.9000
10	**0.4424**	0.5515	0.6364	0.7333	0.7818	0.8667
11	0.4182	0.5273	0.6091	0.7000	0.7455	0.8364
12	0.3986	0.4965	0.5804	0.6713	0.7273	0.8182
13	0.3791	0.4780	0.5549	0.6429	0.6978	0.7912
14	0.3626	0.4593	0.5341	0.6220	0.6747	0.7670
15	0.3500	0.4429	0.5179	0.6000	0.6536	0.7464
16	0.3382	0.4265	0.5000	0.5824	0.6324	0.7265
17	0.3260	0.4118	0.4853	0.5637	0.6152	0.7083
18	0.3148	0.3994	0.4716	0.5480	0.5975	0.6904
19	0.3070	0.3895	0.4579	0.5333	0.5825	0.6737
20	0.2977	0.3789	0.4451	0.5203	0.5684	0.6586
21	0.2909	0.3688	0.4351	0.5078	0.5545	0.6455
22	0.2829	0.3597	0.4241	0.4963	0.5426	0.6318
23	0.2767	0.3518	0.4150	0.4852	0.5306	0.6186
24	0.2704	0.3435	0.4061	0.4748	0.5200	0.6070
25	0.2646	0.3362	0.3977	0.4654	0.5100	0.5962
26	0.2588	0.3299	0.3894	0.4564	0.5002	0.5856
27	0.2540	0.3236	0.3822	0.4481	0.4915	0.5757
28	0.2490	0.3175	0.3749	0.4401	0.4828	0.5660
29	0.2443	0.3113	0.3685	0.4320	0.4744	0.5567
30	0.2400	0.3059	0.3620	0.4251	0.4665	0.5479

Source: Adapted from Glasser and Winter, *Biometrika,* 1961, with the permission of the *Biometrika* trustees.

Table O Critical Factors for Control Charts

	Chart for Averages	Chart for Ranges			
	Factor for Control Limit	Factor for Central Line	Factors for Control Limits		
n	A_2	d_2	D_3	D_4	d_3
2	1.880	1.128	0	3.267	0.8525
3	1.023	1.693	0	2.575	0.8884
4	0.729	2.059	0	2.282	0.8798
5	0.577	2.326	0	2.115	0.8641
6	0.483	2.534	0	2.004	0.8480
7	0.419	2.704	0.076	1.924	0.833
8	0.373	2.847	0.136	1.864	0.820
9	0.337	2.970	0.184	1.816	0.808
10	0.308	3.078	0.223	1.777	0.797
11	0.285	3.173	0.256	1.744	0.787
12	0.266	3.258	0.284	1.716	0.778
13	0.249	3.336	0.308	1.692	0.770
14	0.235	3.407	0.329	1.671	0.762
15	0.223	3.472	0.348	1.652	0.755
16	0.212	3.532	0.364	1.636	0.749
17	0.203	3.588	0.379	1.621	0.743
18	0.194	3.640	0.392	1.608	0.738
19	0.187	3.689	0.404	1.596	0.733
20	0.180	3.735	0.414	1.586	0.729
21	0.173	3.778	0.425	1.575	0.724
22	0.167	3.819	0.434	1.566	0.720
23	0.162	3.858	0.443	1.557	0.716
24	0.157	3.895	0.452	1.548	0.712
25	0.153	3.931	0.459	1.541	0.709

Source: Values of d_2 and d_3 are from E. S. Pearson, "The Percentage Limits for the Distribution of Range in Samples from a Normal Population," *Biometrika 24,* 1932, p. 416. Used by permission of the *Biometrika* trustees.

$A_2 = 3/(d_2\sqrt{n})$, $D_3 = 1 - 3(d_3/d_2)$, $D_4 = 1 + 3(d_3/d_2)$.

Table P Combinatorials

n	${}_nC_0$	${}_nC_1$	${}_nC_2$	${}_nC_3$	${}_nC_4$	${}_nC_5$	${}_nC_6$	${}_nC_7$	${}_nC_8$	${}_nC_9$	${}_nC_{10}$
0	1										
1	1	1									
2	1	2	1								
3	1	3	3	1							
4	1	4	6	4	1						
5	1	5	10	10	5	1					
6	1	6	15	20	15	6	1				
7	1	7	21	35	35	21	7	1			
8	1	8	28	56	70	56	28	8	1		
9	1	9	36	84	126	126	84	36	9	1	
10	1	10	45	120	210	252	210	120	45	10	1
11	1	11	55	165	330	462	462	330	165	55	11
12	1	12	66	220	495	792	924	792	495	220	66
13	1	13	78	286	715	1287	1716	1716	1287	715	286
14	1	14	91	364	1001	2002	3003	3432	3003	2002	1001
15	1	15	105	455	1365	3003	5005	6435	6435	5005	3003
16	1	16	120	560	1820	4368	8008	11440	12870	11440	8008
17	1	17	136	680	2380	6188	12376	19448	24310	24310	19448
18	1	18	153	816	3060	8568	18564	31824	43758	48620	43758
19	1	19	171	969	3876	11628	27132	50388	75582	92378	92378
20	1	20	190	1140	4845	15504	38760	77520	125970	167960	184756

Index

A

Acceptance number, 521
Acceptance quality level (AQL), 8, 520
Acceptance sampling, 8, 520–523
Accuracy, 10–11
Addition rule of probability, 87–89
Adjusted coefficient of determination, 370
Alpha-value, 171–172, 196, 197, 249
Alternative hypothesis, 195; *see also* Null hypothesis
Analysis of variance (ANOVA), 266–268; *see also* One-way ANOVA; Two-way ANOVA
 F-ratio, 270
 multiple regression model, 371–372
 for regression model, 348–349
 table, 274–277
 test for balanced design, 277–280
 test for unbalanced design, 280–283
Arithmetic mean, 41; *see also* Mean
Assignable cause variation, 501
Attribute control charts
 c-charts, 515–518
 p-charts, 511–515
Autocorrelation, 330–331
Averages, 40–41

B

Balanced designs, tests for; *see also* Unbalanced designs
 least significant difference approach, 278–280
 Tukey's criterion, 278
Bayes, Rev. Thomas, 89
Bayes Theorem, 89–92
Bell-shaped symmetrical curve, 60
Bernoulli, Jacob, 106
Bernoulli process, 106
Beta coefficients; *see* Standardized regression coefficients
Between-sample variation, 269
Bias, sampling, 11, 158
Bimodal data set, 42
Binomial distributions, 132
 calculating, 107–108
 cumulative, 109–110
 defined, 106
 mean, 108
 normal approximation to, 130–131, 135
 properties of, 106
 using computer for, 110–111
 variance, 109
Bivariate regression; *see* Simple regression
Blocking, 283–286
Blocking design, 293
Business report writing, 535–540

C

C. I.; *see* Confidence interval (C. I.)
Causation, 339
C-charts, 515–518
Cells, 25
Central Limit Theorem, 148–149
Central tendency; *see* Measures of central tendency
Chance variation, 501
Chebyshev, P. L., 59
Chebyshev's Theorem, 59
Chi-square (X^2) distribution
 goodness-of-fit tests, 447–454
 tests for independence, 454–459
Class(es), *c*, 21–24
 boundaries, 22
 determining number of, 22
 interval, 22–23
 midpoint, *M*, 22
 rule for determining number of, 22
Classical approach to probability, 78
Cluster sampling, 160
Coefficient of determination, 338–339
Coefficient of multiple determination, 369–370
Coefficient of skewness, 62
Coefficient of variation (CV), 63
Collective exhaustive events, 81
Combinations, 92–93
Complementary events, 82
Completely randomized design, 293; *see also* One-way ANOVA
Composite price index, 423–424
Computers; *see* Excel; Minitab
Conditional mean, 343–345
Conditional probability, 84–85, 90–91
Confidence coefficient, 169, 170
Confidence interval (C. I.), 168–169
 of the conditional mean, 344
 controlling width of, 179–180
 for difference between two proportions, 238–240
 interpretation, 171–172
 of population mean
  large samples, 170–174
  small sample, 174–177
 for population proportions, 177–178
 for the predictive interval, 346
 principle of, 169–170
 when population standard deviation is known, 172–173
Consistent estimator, 185
Constraints, 51
Consumer Price Index (CPI), 429–432
Consumer risk, 521

Contingency tables, 24–25, 454–459
  for probability of events, 82–86
Continuity correction factor, 131
Continuous random variable, 103
Continuous variable, 10
Control charts, 499
  for attributes
    c-charts, 515–518
    p-charts, 511–515
  interpreting, 518–519
  for variables, 501–504
    $\underline{R}$-chart, 507–510
    $\overline{X}$-chart, 504–507
Conversion formula; *see* *Z* formula
Correlation, causation and, 339–340
Correlation analysis, 336–339
Correlation coefficient *(r)*, 336–338
Counting techniques, 92–94
Critical values, for *Z* and rejection regions, 196–197
Cumulative binomial distributions, 109–110
Curvilinear regression
  defined, 317–318
  logarithmic models, 389–391
  polynomial models, 388–389
Cyclical fluctuations, 401
Cyclical variation, 419–420

D
Data, methods of organizing, 20–21; *see also* Grouped data
Deasonalized values, 416
Deciles, 57–58
Decision rule, 197
Deflating, a time series, 431
Degrees of freedom, 51
  for unequal population variances, 232–233
Deming, W. Edward, 499–501
Dependent events, probability of, 86
Dependent variable, 316–317
Depths, 29
Descriptive statistics, 10
Deterministic relationships, 319
Deviation, measures of, 337–338
Discrete distributions, 104–106
Discrete random variable, 103
Discrete variable, 10
Dispersion; *see* Measures of dispersion
Distribution
  binomial, 106–111
  discrete, 104–106
  exponential, 116–118
  hypergeometric, 111–113
  normal, 121–131
  Poisson, 113–116
  sampling, 143–148
Distribution—*Cont.*
  uniform, 118–121
Distribution-free tests; *see* Nonparametric tests
Dow Jones industrial average, 430
Dummy variables, 383–387
Durbin-Watson test, 331

E
Economic analysts, 6
Education Industry Report, 4
Efficient estimator, 185
80/20 rule, 7
Empirical Rule, 60–62, 121–123, 169, 334
Error
  level of significance and, 197
  tolerable, 180
  Type I, 197
  Type II, 197
Error mean square (MSE), 273
Error sum of squares (SSE), 271–272
Estimates, 168–169
  defined, 183–184
Estimators
  defined, 183–184
  properties of good, 184–186
Events, 80–82
Excel
  for binomial distributions, 110–111
  exponential distribution, 117–118
  for hypergeometric distributions, 113
  Poisson distribution, 115–116
Executive summary, 536, 537–538
Expected frequencies, 450–451
Expected value *E*(*X*), for probability distribution, 104
Experiment, defined, 77
Experimental units, 267
Explained deviation, 337
Exponential distribution, 116–117, 133
  using the computer, 117–118
Exponential smoothing, 406–409

F
Factorial analysis, 292–296
Failure, probability of $(1 - \pi)$, 106
F-distribution, 248–250
Financial analysts, 6
Finite population correction factor (fpc), 147
Fisher, Sir Ronald A., 248
Fixed-effects model, 267
Fluctuations, 400–401
F-ratio, 249
  as used in ANOVA, 270
Frequency distribution, 21–24
  less-than cumulative, 23–24

Frequency distribution—*Cont.*
  more-than cumulative, 23
  relative, 23–24

G
Galton, Sir Francis, 317
Geometric mean, 44–46
Goodness-of-fit; *see also* Standard error of the estimate
  for chi-square (X^2), 447–454
  coefficient of multiple determination, 369–370
Grand mean, 144–145, 269
Gross national product (GNP), 431
Grouped data
  mean, 53–54
  median, 54
  mode, 54–55
  variance and standard deviation for, 55–56
Gusset, William S., 174

H
Heteroscedasticity, 329
High-low close chart, 28–29
Histogram, 27–28
Homoscedasticity, 328–329
Hypergeometric distribution, 111–113, 132
Hyperplane, 366
Hypothesis
  alternative, 195
  null, 195
Hypothesis testing
  principle of, 195–197
  probability of error in, 197
  rejection regions in, 196–197
  steps in, 198
Hypothesis tests
  for differences in proportions, 247–248
  with paired data, 245–246
  two means with independent sampling
    large samples, 241–244
    small sample estimation, 244–245

I
Independent events, 81–82
  joint probability of, 85–86
Independent samples, for two-population tests, 227
Independent sampling
  large sample estimation, 227–230
  small sample estimation, 230–234
Independent variable, 316–317
Index number
  composite price, 423–424
  simple price, 421–423
  weighted composite price
    Laspeyres, 424–429
    Paasche, 426–429
Industrial production index, 430
Inferential statistics, 10, 142–143
Interaction, 294–295
Internet, career information on, 16–17
Intersection, 80
Interval
  factors influencing width of, 347–348
  Interval estimation, 168–169
  confidence interval for differences between two proportions, 238–240
  independent sampling
    large sample, 227–230
    small sample, 230–234
  paired sampling, 234–238
  in regression analysis, 343–348
Interval measurements, 13, 14
Irregular fluctuations, 401
Irregular variation, 420–421

J
Joint events, 80
  determining probability of, 85–87
Joint probabilities, 83
Juran, Joseph, 501

K
Kruskal-Wallis test, 476–480

L
Laspeyres index, 424–429
Latin square design, 296–298
LCL; *see* Lower confidence limit (LCL)
Leaf unit, 29
Least significant difference (LSD)
  for balanced designs, 277–280
  for unbalanced designs, 280–283
Less-than cumulative frequency distribution, 23–24
Level of significance, 196
  probability error and, 197
Linear regression
  assumptions of, 328–332
  defined, 317–318
  determining model, 318–320
  ordinary least squares (OLS) model, 320–323
  standard error of the estimate, 332–336
Line of best fit, 322
Logarithmic models of curvilinear regression, 389–391
Lower confidence limit (LCL), 169

M
Main-effects test, 293
Malcolm Baldrige National Quality Award, 500–501

Mann-Whitney *U*-Test, 467–472, 480
Marginal probabilities, 83
Mean; *see also* Population mean; Sample mean
  binomial distributions, 108
  compared to median and mode, 46–47
  confidence interval of population, 170–173
  geometric, 44–46
  grouped, 53–54
  one-tailed test for, 201–203
  of probability distribution, 104
  of the sample means, 144–145
  sample size for, 181
  selecting proper test statistic for, 176
  small sample intervals for, 174–176
  small-sample tests for, 209–211
  two-tailed test for, 198–199
  weighted, 43–44
Mean ratio to moving average, 415
Mean square error (MSE), 273
Mean square treatment (MSTR), 273
Mean sums of squares, 272–274
Measurement, levels of
  interval, 13
  nominal, 12–13
  ordinal, 13
  ratio, 14
Measures of central tendency, 40–41
  comparing, 46–47
  geometric mean, 44–46
  for grouped data, 53–55
  mean, 41
  media, 42
  mode, 42–43
  weighted mean, 43
Measures of dispersion, 41, 47–48, 57–58
  defined, 46–47
  for grouped data, 55–57
  range, 48
  relative, 63
  standard deviation, 48–50
  variance, 48–50
Median, 42
  compared to mean and mode, 46–47
  for grouped data, 54
Minitab
  for binomial distributions, 110–111
  confidence intervals, 172–173
  Poisson distribution, 115–116
  p-value, 207
  two-tailed test for mu, 199
  uniform distribution, 120–121
Mode, 42–43
  compared to median and mean, 46–47
  for grouped data, 54–55
More-than cumulative frequency distribution, 23
Moving average (MA), 403–406
Multicollinearity, 365, 377–381
Multiple-choice counting method, 94
Multiple regression, 317
  adjusted coefficient of determination, 370
  coefficient of multiple determination, 369–370
  model, 365–366
  standard error of the estimate, 367–369
  tests of significance, 371–374
Multiple sampling plans, 522
Multiplication rule of probability, 85–87
Mutual Fund Investor's Center, 73
Mutually exclusive events, 81

N
Negative autocorrelation, 330–331
Net regression coefficients, 365
Nominal measurements, 12–13
Nonparametric tests, 446–447
  chi-square distribution, 447–459
  compared to parametric tests, 480
  Kruskal-Wallis test, 476–480
  Mann-Whitney *U* Test, 467–472
  runs test, 463–467
  sign test, 459–463
  Spearman rank correlation, 472–476
Normal approximation, to binomial distribution, 130–131, 135
Normal deviate, 123–124, 181
  calculating probabilities with, 124–128
  for sampling distribution for proportions, 156
Normal distribution, 59–62, 121–124, 133–134
Normalization ratio, 415–416
Normal populations
  comparing the variance of two, 248–250
Null hypothesis, 195

O
One-tailed test
  Mann-Whitney *U* Test, 470–471
  for mu (μ), 201–203
One-way ANOVA
  defined, 268–269
  principles, 269–270
Operating characteristic (OC) curves, 522–523
Ordered array, 21, 29
Ordinal measurements, 13
Ordinary least squares (OLS), 320–323
  runs test application, 465–467
Outcome, 77
Outliers, 46

P

Paasche index, 426–429
Pair comparison
 least significant difference (LSD), 277–280
 Tukey's criterion, 277–278
Paired samples, 234–238
 hypotheses tests with, 245–246
 for two-population tests, 227
Parameter, 9
Parametric tests, 446
 compared to nonparametric tests, 480
Pareto, Vilfrado, 7
Pareto chart, 7
Partial regression coefficients, 365
 testing individual, 372–374
Patterns, detection of, 464
P-charts, 511–515
Pearson, Karl, 336
Pearsonian coefficient of skewness, 62
Pearsonian product-moment correlation coefficient, 336
Percentage point increase, 422
Percentiles, 57–58
Permutations, 92–93
Pictorial displays; *see specific method*
Pie charts, 28
Point estimate, 168–169
Poisson, Simeon, 113
Poisson distribution, 113–116, 133
 using computer for, 115–116
Polynomial models of curvilinear regression, 388–389
Pooled estimate, 230
Population, 142; *see also* Mean
 defined, 8–9
 standard deviation, 48–50
 variance, 48–50
Population correlation coefficient, tests for, 342–343
Population mean, 41
Population parameters, tests for, 340–343
Population proportion, 177–178
 tests for, 212–214
Positional average; *see* Median
Positive autocorrelation, 330–331
Predictive interval, 343
 for a single value of *Y*, 345–348
Probability, 76–77
 addition rule for, 87–89
 classical approach, 78–79
 conditional, 84–85
 multiplication rule for, 85–87
 relative frequency approach, 77–78
 subjective approach, 78
Probability distribution, 103–104
 mean of, 104
Probability distribution—*Cont.*
 standard deviation of, 105
 variance of, 104–105
Probability of failure, 106
Probability of success, 106
Probability tables, for events, 82–83
Produce price index, 430
Producer risk, 520
Product improvement; *see* Quality control (QC)
p-value
 defined, 206–207
 two-tailed tests and, 207–208

Q

Qualitative variable, 10, 384
Quality control (QC), 7
 history of, 499–501
Quality control (QC) circles, 7
Quality function deployment (QFD), 7
Quantitative variable, 10
Quartiles, 57–58

R

Random-effects model, 267
Random fluctuation, 401
Randomized block design, 283–292
Randomness, 463–465
Random variable, 102–103
 continuous, 103
 discrete, 103
Random walk exhibits, 399
Range, 48
Ratio measurements, 14
Rational subgrouping, 502
Ratio to moving average, 415
R-chart, 507–510
Real gross national product (GNP), 432
Real income, 431
Regression analysis, 317–318; *see also* Multiple regression
 interval estimation in, 343–348
 limitations of, 339–350
 ordinary least squares (OLS), 320–323
 simple linear model, 318–320
 standard error of the estimate, 332–335
Regression coefficient, 322–323
 comparing, 381–382
Regression plane, 366
Relative frequency, 77–78
Relative frequency distribution, 23–24
Report writing, 535–540
Rules of probability
 addition, 87–89
 multiplication, 85–87
Run, 463
Runs test, 463–467, 480

S

Sample, 10, 142
  defined, 9
  standard deviation *s*, 50–52
  variance, 50–52
Sample mean (*X*-bar), 41
Sample size
  determining proper, 180–182
  increasing, 180
  for population estimate (π), 182
  selecting proper, 240–241
Sample space (SS), 77
Sample standard deviation, for grouped data, 55–56
Sample variance, 271
  for grouped data, 55–56
Sampling
  cluster, 160
  with replacement, 147
  simple random sample, 158–159
  stratified, 159
  systematic, 159
Sampling bias, 11, 158
Sampling distribution, 150–151, 169
  defined, 143–144
  for proportions, 155–158
    expect value, 155–156
    standard error, 156
  for sample means, 144–145
    applications, 150–154
    Central Limit Theorem, 148–149
    mean, 144–145
    standard error, 145–147
    variance, 145–147
Sampling error, 143
  causes of, 11
  defined, 11
  sources, 158
Sampling methods, 158–161
  cluster, 160
  simple random, 158–159
  stratified, 159
  systematic, 159
Sampling plans, 522
Scatter diagrams, 317–318
Seasonal fluctuations, 400
Seasonal variation, 413–419
Secular trend, 400
Sequential sampling plans, 522
Set, 80
Shewhart, Walter, 501
Sign test, 459–463, 480
Simple price index, 420–423
Simple random sample, 158–159
Simple regression, 317
Skewness, 62
Small-sample tests, mean and, 209–211
Smoothing techniques
  exponential, 406–409
  moving average, 403–406
Spearman rank correlation, 472–476, 480
Specification bias, 381
Spurious correlation, 340
Standard deviation
  common uses for, 59–64
  confidence intervals and, 172–173
  population, 48–50
  of probability distributions, 105
  sample *s*, 50–52
Standard error
  of the conditional mean, 344
  for difference in two sample proportions, 238–239
  of the forecast, 346
  impact of sample size on, 147
  for sample means, 145–147
  using finite population correction factor (fpc), 147
Standard error of the estimate (*Se*), 332–336
  for multiple regression, 367–369
Standardized regression coefficients, 382
Standard normal distribution, 123
Standard & Poor's composite index, 430
Statistical literacy, need for, 8
Statistically insignificant difference, 195–196
Statistical norm, in cyclical variation, 419–420
Statistical quality control (SQC), 7, 8
Statistics
  career opportunities in, 6–8
  defined, 9
  descriptive, 10
  function of, 11–12
  importance of, 4–5
  inferential, 10
  universal application of, 6
Stem-and-leaf design, 29
Stepwise regression, 383
Stochastic relationships, 319
Stratified sampling, 159
Student's *t* distribution, 174–176
Subgroup, 501–503
Subjective approach to probability, 78
Success, probability of (π), 106
Sufficient estimator, 185–186
Sum of squared errors, 321–322
Sum of the squares of the row block (SSRB), 297–298
Sums of squares, 270–272
Systematic sampling, 159

T

t-distribution, 230–234, 244–245; *see also* Student's *t*-distribution

Ticks and tabs, 29
Time series
 components, 399–401
 decomposition of
  irregular variation, 420–421
  isolating cyclical variation, 419–420
  isolating seasonal component, 413–419
 models, 402
 smoothing techniques, 402–409
 trend analysis, 410–413
Tolerable error, 180
Total deviation, 337
Total mean squares (MST), 272–273
Total quality management (TQM), 7–8
Total variation, 269, 270
Tradeline Mutual Fund Center, 73
Treatment, 266–267, 293
Treatment effect, 270
Treatment sum of squares, 271
Tree diagram, 90
Trend analysis, 410–413
Tukey, J., 29
Tukey's criterion (*T*), 277–278
Two populations, 226–227
Two-population tests
 independent samples, 227–233
 paired samples, 227, 234–238
Two-tailed tests, 198–199
 Mann-Whitney *U* Test, 470
 p-value for, 207–208
Two-way (ANOVA); *see also* Analysis of variance (ANOVA)
 randomized block design, 283–292
Type I error, 197
 acceptance sampling, 520
Type II error, 197
 acceptance sampling, 521

U
UCL; *see* Upper confidence limit (UCL)
Unbalanced designs; *see also* Balanced designs, tests for
 alternate LSD approach, 280–283
Unbiased estimator (theta), 184
Unequal population variances, degrees of freedom for, 232–233
Unexplained deviation, 337–338
Uniform distribution, 133
Uniform probability distribution, 118–121
 using computer for, 120–121
Union events, 80–81
Universe; *see* Population
Upper confidence limit (UCL), 169
U Test; *See* Mann-Whitney *U*-Test

V
Variable
 continuous, 10
 defined, 9–10
 discrete, 10
 interval, 13
 nominal, 12–13
 ordinal, 13
 qualitative, 10
 quantitative, 10
 random, 102–103
 ratio, 14
Variable control charts
 R-charts, 507–510
 $\bar{X}$, 504–507
Variance
 binomial distributions, 109
 comparing, of two normal populations, 248–250
 population, 48–50
 of probability distribution, 104–105
 problems, 49
 sample, 50–52
 for sample means, 145–147
Variance inflation factor (VIF), 379
Variation, 269
Venn, John, 80
Venn diagram, 80
VIF; *See* Variance inflation factor (VIF)

W
Walter Shewhart, 499
Weighted composite price index
 Laspeyres, 424–429
 Paasche, 426–429
Weighted mean, 43–44
Within-sample variation, 269

X
$\bar{X}$-chart, 504–507
X-values
 calculating, from a known probability, 128–130

Z
Z-distribution, 174
Z-formula, 123–124, 150
Z (test), 212–214
Z-test statistic
 for large samples, 241–242
Z-value, 123–124, 169, 196–197
 calculating X-values from known, 128–130

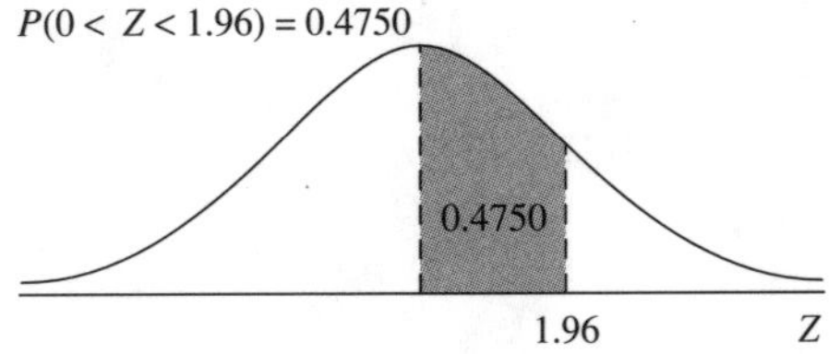

Table E The Normal Distribution

z	0.00	0.01	0.02	0.03	0.04	0.05	0.06	0.07	0.08	0.09
0.0	0.0000	0.0040	0.0080	0.0120	0.0160	0.0199	0.0239	0.0279	0.0319	0.0359
0.1	0.0398	0.0438	0.0478	0.0517	0.0557	0.0596	0.0636	0.0675	0.0714	0.0753
0.2	0.0793	0.0832	0.0871	0.0910	0.0948	0.0987	0.1026	0.1064	0.1103	0.1141
0.3	0.1179	0.1217	0.1255	0.1293	0.1331	0.1368	0.1406	0.1443	0.1480	0.1517
0.4	0.1554	0.1591	0.1628	0.1664	0.1700	0.1736	0.1772	0.1808	0.1844	0.1879
0.5	0.1915	0.1950	0.1985	0.2019	0.2054	0.2088	0.2123	0.2157	0.2190	0.2224
0.6	0.2257	0.2291	0.2324	0.2357	0.2389	0.2422	0.2454	0.2486	0.2517	0.2549
0.7	0.2580	0.2611	0.2642	0.2673	0.2704	0.2734	0.2764	0.2794	0.2823	0.2852
0.8	0.2881	0.2910	0.2939	0.2967	0.2995	0.3023	0.3051	0.3078	0.3106	0.3133
0.9	0.3159	0.3186	0.3212	0.3238	0.3264	0.3289	0.3315	0.3340	0.3365	0.3389
1.0	0.3413	0.3438	0.3461	0.3485	0.3508	0.3531	0.3554	0.3577	0.3599	0.3621
1.1	0.3643	0.3665	0.3686	0.3708	0.3729	0.3749	0.3770	0.3790	0.3810	0.3830
1.2	0.3849	0.3869	0.3888	0.3907	0.3925	0.3944	0.3962	0.3980	0.3997	0.4015
1.3	0.4032	0.4049	0.4066	0.4082	0.4099	0.4115	0.4131	0.4147	0.4162	0.4177
1.4	0.4192	0.4207	0.4222	0.4236	0.4251	0.4265	0.4279	0.4292	0.4306	0.4319
1.5	0.4332	0.4345	0.4357	0.4370	0.4382	0.4394	0.4406	0.4418	0.4429	0.4441
1.6	0.4452	0.4463	0.4474	0.4484	0.4495	0.4505	0.4515	0.4525	0.4535	0.4545
1.7	0.4554	0.4564	0.4573	0.4582	0.4591	0.4599	0.4608	0.4616	0.4625	0.4633
1.8	0.4641	0.4649	0.4656	0.4664	0.4671	0.4678	0.4686	0.4693	0.4699	0.4706
1.9	0.4713	0.4719	0.4726	0.4732	0.4738	0.4744	**0.4750**	0.4756	0.4761	0.4767
2.0	0.4772	0.4778	0.4783	0.4788	0.4793	0.4798	0.4803	0.4808	0.4812	0.4817
2.1	0.4821	0.4826	0.4830	0.4834	0.4838	0.4842	0.4846	0.4850	0.4854	0.4857
2.2	0.4861	0.4864	0.4868	0.4871	0.4875	0.4878	0.4881	0.4884	0.4887	0.4890
2.3	0.4893	0.4896	0.4898	0.4901	0.4904	0.4906	0.4909	0.4911	0.4913	0.4916
2.4	0.4918	0.4920	0.4922	0.4925	0.4927	0.4929	0.4931	0.4932	0.4934	0.4936
2.5	0.4938	0.4940	0.4941	0.4943	0.4945	0.4946	0.4948	0.4949	0.4951	0.4952
2.6	0.4953	0.4955	0.4956	0.4957	0.4959	0.4960	0.4961	0.4962	0.4963	0.4964
2.7	0.4965	0.4966	0.4967	0.4968	0.4969	0.4970	0.4971	0.4972	0.4973	0.4974
2.8	0.4974	0.4975	0.4976	0.4977	0.4977	0.4978	0.4979	0.4979	0.4980	0.4981
2.9	0.4981	0.4982	0.4982	0.4983	0.4984	0.4984	0.4985	0.4985	0.4986	0.4986
3.0	0.4987	0.4987	0.4987	0.4988	0.4988	0.4989	0.4989	0.4989	0.4990	0.4990
3.1	0.4990	0.4991	0.4991	0.4991	0.4992	0.4992	0.4992	0.4992	0.4993	0.4993
3.2	0.4993	0.4993	0.4994	0.4994	0.4994	0.4994	0.4994	0.4995	0.4995	0.4995
3.3	0.4995	0.4995	0.4995	0.4996	0.4996	0.4996	0.4996	0.4996	0.4996	0.4997
3.4	0.4997	0.4997	0.4997	0.4997	0.4997	0.4997	0.4997	0.4997	0.4997	0.4998
3.5	0.4998	0.4998	0.4998	0.4998	0.4998	0.4998	0.4998	0.4998	0.4998	0.4498
3.6	0.4998	0.4998	0.4999	0.4999	0.4999	0.4999	0.4999	0.4999	0.4999	0.4999
3.7	0.4999	0.4999	0.4999	0.4999	0.4999	0.4999	0.4999	0.4999	0.4999	0.4999
3.8	0.4999	0.4999	0.4999	0.4999	0.4999	0.4999	0.4999	0.4999	0.4999	0.4999
3.9	0.5000	0.5000	0.5000	0.5000	0.5000	0.5000	0.5000	0.5000	0.5000	0.5000

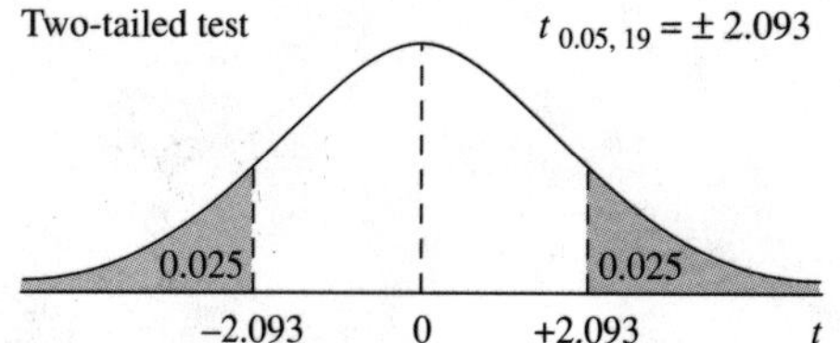

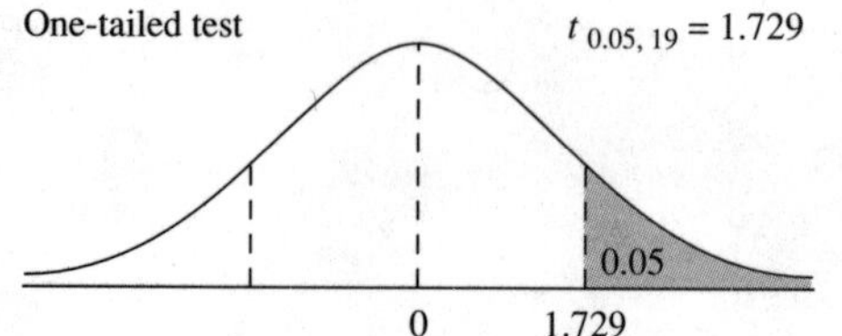

Table F The *t*-Distribution

	0.900	0.700	0.500	0.300	0.200	0.100	0.050	0.020	0.010	α value	taile
	0.100	0.300	0.500	0.700	0.800	0.900	0.950	0.980	0.990	CL	
	0.450	0.350	0.250	0.150	0.100	0.050	0.025	0.010	0.005	α value	taile
	0.550	0.650	0.750	0.850	0.900	0.950	0.975	0.990	0.995	CL	
d.f.	**Values of *t***										
1	0.158	0.510	1.000	1.963	3.078	6.314	12.706	31.821	63.657		
2	0.142	0.445	0.816	1.386	1.886	2.920	4.303	6.965	9.925		
3	0.137	0.424	0.765	1.250	1.638	2.353	3.182	4.541	5.841		
4	0.134	0.414	0.741	1.190	1.533	2.132	2.776	3.747	4.604		
5	0.132	0.408	0.727	1.156	1.476	2.015	2.571	3.365	4.032		
6	0.131	0.404	0.718	1.134	1.440	1.943	2.447	3.143	3.707		
7	0.130	0.402	0.711	1.119	1.415	1.895	2.365	2.998	3.499		
8	0.130	0.399	0.706	1.108	1.397	1.860	2.306	2.896	3.355		
9	0.129	0.398	0.703	1.100	1.383	1.833	2.262	2.821	3.250		
10	0.129	0.397	0.700	1.093	1.372	1.812	2.228	2.764	3.169		
11	0.129	0.396	0.697	1.088	1.363	1.796	2.201	2.718	3.106		
12	0.128	0.395	0.695	1.083	1.356	1.782	2.179	2.681	3.055		
13	0.128	0.394	0.694	1.079	1.350	1.771	2.160	2.650	3.012		
14	0.128	0.393	0.692	1.076	1.345	1.761	2.145	2.624	2.977		
15	0.128	0.393	0.691	1.074	1.341	1.753	2.131	2.602	2.947		
16	0.128	0.392	0.690	1.071	1.337	1.746	2.120	2.583	2.921		
17	0.128	0.392	0.689	1.069	1.333	1.740	2.110	2.567	2.898		
18	0.127	0.392	0.688	1.067	1.330	1.734	2.101	2.552	2.878		
19	0.127	0.391	0.688	1.066	1.328	**1.729**	**2.093**	2.539	2.861		
20	0.127	0.391	0.687	1.064	1.325	1.725	2.086	2.528	2.845		
21	0.127	0.391	0.686	1.063	1.323	1.721	2.080	2.518	2.831		
22	0.127	0.390	0.686	1.061	1.321	1.717	2.074	2.508	2.819		
23	0.127	0.390	0.685	1.060	1.319	1.714	2.069	2.500	2.807		
24	0.127	0.390	0.685	1.059	1.318	1.711	2.064	2.492	2.797		
25	0.127	0.390	0.684	1.058	1.316	1.708	2.060	2.485	2.787		
26	0.127	0.390	0.684	1.058	1.315	1.706	2.056	2.479	2.779		
27	0.127	0.389	0.684	1.057	1.314	1.703	2.052	2.473	2.771		
28	0.127	0.389	0.683	1.056	1.313	1.701	2.048	2.467	2.763		
29	0.127	0.389	0.683	1.055	1.311	1.699	2.045	2.462	2.756		
30	0.127	0.389	0.683	1.055	1.310	1.697	2.042	2.457	2.750		
40	0.126	0.388	0.681	1.050	1.303	1.684	2.021	2.423	2.704		
60	0.126	0.387	0.679	1.045	1.296	1.671	2.000	2.390	2.660		
120	0.126	0.386	0.677	1.041	1.289	1.658	1.980	2.358	2.617		
∞	0.126	0.385	0.674	1.036	1.282	1.645	1.960	2.326	2.576		